A Companion to Victorian Literature and Culture

Blackwell Companions to Literature and Culture

This series offers comprehensive, newly written surveys of key periods and movements and certain major authors, in English literary culture and history. Extensive volumes provide new perspectives and positions on contexts and on canonical and post-canonical texts, orientating the beginning student in new fields of study and providing the experienced undergraduate and new graduate with current and new directions, as pioneered and developed by leading scholars in the field.

Published

A Companion to Chaucer	*Edited by Peter Brown*
A Feminist Companion to Shakespeare	*Edited by Dympna Callaghan*
A Companion to Milton	*Edited by Thomas N. Corns*
A Companion to Victorian Poetry	*Edited by Richard Cronin, Anthony Harrison and Alison Chapman*
A Companion to English Renaissance Literature and Culture	*Edited by Michael Hattaway*
A Companion to Shakespeare	*Edited by David Scott Kastan*
The Blackwell Companion to Renaissance Drama	*Edited by Arthur F. Kinney*
The Blackwell Companion to Modern Irish Culture	*Edited by William J. McCormack*
A Companion to Restoration Drama	*Edited by Susan J. Owen*
A Companion to Anglo-Saxon Literature	*Edited by Phillip Pulsiano and Elaine Treharne*
A Companion to the Gothic	*Edited by David Punter*
A Companion to Twentieth-Century Poetry	*Edited by Neil Roberts*
A Companion to Art Theory	*Edited by Paul Smith and Carolyn Wilde*
A Companion to Victorian Literature and Culture	*Edited by Herbert F. Tucker*
A Companion to Literature from Milton to Blake	*Edited by David Womersley*
A Companion to Romanticism	*Edited by Duncan Wu*

Forthcoming

A Companion to Modernist Literature and Culture	*Edited by David Bradshaw*
The Blackwell Companion to the Victorian Novel	*Edited by Patrick Brantlinger and William Thesing*
A Companion to Medieval English Literature and Culture	*Edited by Peter Brown*
A Companion to American Regional Literature	*Edited by Charles Crow*
A Companion to Science Fiction	*Edited by Thomas Foster*
The Blackwell Companion to American Poetry	*Edited by Albert Gelpi and Gareth Reeves*
A Companion to the Literature and Culture of the American South	*Edited by Richard Grey*
A Companion to Children's Literature and Culture	*Edited by Peter Hunt*
A Companion to American Literature and Culture	*Edited by Paul Lauter*
A Companion to Old Norse-Icelandic Literature	*Edited by Rory McTurk*
The Blackwell Companion to Early Modern Women's Writing	*Edited by Anita Pacheco*
A Companion to Postcolonial Studies	*Edited by Henry Schwartz and Sangeeta Ray*
The Blackwell Companion to the Enlightenment	*Edited by John Yolton, Barbara Stafford, Pat Rogers and Roy Porter*

A COMPANION TO

VICTORIAN LITERATURE & CULTURE

EDITED BY **HERBERT F. TUCKER**

BLACKWELL
Publishers

First published 1999
First published in paperback 1999
Reprinted 2002

Blackwell Publishers Inc.
350 Main Street
Malden, Massachusetts 02148
USA

Blackwell Publishers Ltd
108 Cowley Road
Oxford OX4 1JF
UK

Library of Congress Cataloging-in-Publication Data
A companion to Victorian literature and culture / edited by Herbert F. Tucker.
p. cm. – (Blackwell companions to literature and culture: 2)
Includes bibliographical references and index.
ISBN 0–631–20463–6 (hbk: acid-free paper)   ISBN 0–631–21876–9 (pbk: acid-free paper)
1. English literature – 19th century –History and criticism.
2. Literature and society – Great Britiain– History– 19th century.
3. Great Britain – History – Victoria, 1837–1901. 4. Great Britain –
Civilization – 19th century. I. Tucker, Herbert F. II. Series.
PR461.C597 1999 820.9 ' 008 –dc21
98-19517 CIP

British Library Cataloguing in Publication Data

A CIP catalogue record for this book is available from the British Library.

Typeset in 11 on 13 pt Garamond 3.
by Best-set Typesetter Ltd, Hong Kong
Printed in Great Britain by T. J. International Ltd, Padstow, Cornwall.

This book is printed on acid-free paper.

For Scott, brother builder, who knows about work

Contents

PART THREE Walks of Life

PART FOUR Kinds of Writing

Introduction

This book has been planned to meet both short-term and long-range needs. To begin with, it is a reference work for consultation. The reader with a question about, say, the provisions or effects of the Forster Education Act of 1870 will be guided by the index to a number of places where these matters are discussed; then, as the need for punctual answers ripens into ampler curiosity, the context provided by our historical chapter 3 on "1870" or our chapter 14 on "Educational" careers will offer an expanded prospect. To take another example, the student of nineteenth-century poetry who has started to wonder what ideas about literature were in circulation during the Victorian era, and in which venues they ordinarily appeared, will find a conspective discussion in our chapter 26, "Literary Criticism." At every chapter's end, a list of capitalized CROSS-REFERENCES indicates where else to turn in the book for an additional viewpoint or elaboration. Finally, the bibliographies that round off each chapter gesture beyond the covers of this book to hundreds of others recommended for further reading. Here then, in the first instance, is a *Companion* of somewhat the pocket-tool sort: several devices in one, designed for convenient multiple use.

Still, a companion is more than a consultant; and our book aims to do more than provide quick reference help. The *Victorian Literature and Culture* embraced by its title identifies a subject of vista so immense, and of crannies so multitudinous, that the student who means to confront that subject whole is likely to want, beyond mere information, the presence of an experienced guide. This long-range need has been anticipated in an overall plan linking the book's chapters into discrete parts, which the student may read in order to grasp, respectively, the history of Victorian Britain (part one), the phases in a Victorian life (part two), the leading professions and careers that filled out the phase of mature adulthood (part three), the major Victorian literary genres (part four), and the limits Victorians recognized as defining their persons, their homes, and their national identities (part five). Within parts one, two, and five the editor has embraced as the organizing principle a linear narrative of development and expansion that is itself unabashedly Victorian; and the discerning reader will see how a like principle sustains the march of parts three and four, as they move from traditional cultural formations toward emergent ones. Furthermore, because the individual chapters more often than not organize their information along historical narrative lines, our book gives considerable internal reinforcement to patterns of origin and development, progress and decline, that themselves became intellectual second-nature during the period under study. This past-and-present congruence between nineteenth-century and contemporary structures of understanding has obvious advantages but certain drawbacks too. So the reader is hereby reminded that other, less aggressively linear modes of putting Victorian literature and culture into each other are also desirable, and that they are indeed made possible by our schemes of index and cross-reference. Advice on this score admittedly seems less urgent in view of the decentering effect that arises when a book mirrors, as this one does, thirty different minds freshly at work on topics in which they take strong interest. Stylistic, procedural, and theoretical variety among our contributors will give the *Companion* an agreeably protean character, it is hoped, for that inner circle of readers who accompany us all the way from start to finish, in quest of a comprehensive yet complex perspective on the Victorian age.

Given this prefatory reassurance about our plan for uniting comprehensiveness with convenience, the reader may want to proceed to the chapters right away. For those disposed to linger here, though, the editor offers this introductory perch as a viewing point from which to remark some unplanned benefits that have accrued en route. While contributors have heeded the editor's warning against lengthy assessment of the state and trend of scholarship – matters of compelling interest within the guild, but not companionable in the sense that matters here – the chapters below do in effect constitute a veritable cross-section of scholarly Victorianism at the close of the twentieth century. A familiar canon of authors is alive and well, to judge from both the quantitative frequency and qualitative respectfulness of their citation here. Dickens and Eliot retain preeminence among the novelists, with strong support from Thackeray and even stronger from Trollope. Carlyle, Mill, and Arnold still lead the way as Victorian sages. Tennyson remains in a poetic class by himself, Robert Browning being a doughty second (unless Elizabeth Barrett Browning now shares that honor), with the Rossettis, Swinburne, and Hopkins receiving honorable if infrequent mention.

It is generally in the middle distance of renown that notable shifts occur. Collins and Gaskell are more often cited as cultural exponents and major fiction artists than they would have been a generation ago, at the expense perhaps of the now less-cited Brontës and Meredith, while in nonfiction prose such paraliterary figures as Bentham and Mayhew, Darwin and Marx have come to adjoin the aesthetic and social witness long since canonized in Ruskin and Morris, Pater and Wilde. For *Middlemarch* and *In Memoriam* as many uses have been found in our time as half a century ago, although the distinct novelty of some of these uses lets one affirm that stability in the canon has no automatic correlation, and by no means a simply inverse correlation, with diversification of critical approaches and findings. At all events the value that literary and cultural theory have recently accorded to difference, heterogeneity, and contestation brings *Vanity Fair* and *The Ring and the Book* to the fore in more than one of the following chapters, among other works sharing their dispersive qualities of irony and masquerade. To some extent these patterns of spontaneous preference may result from our joint mission to coordinate the events of literary history with the prevailing conditions and decisive changes that defined Victorian culture at large. When seeking to demonstrate the reciprocal influence of text and context, it makes sense to turn on one hand to writings that enjoyed wide circulation, and on the other hand to writings that expressly reflected a broad spectrum of contemporary concerns. Writings that did both, like the great social-issue novels of Dickens, accordingly loom large in our *Companion*.

Something of the same kind may be observed about another of the book's collective determinations, that of periodization. Our annualist historical chapters in part one set the framing limits of the period deliberately far apart. Chapter 1 ("1832") finds its center half a decade before the young queen's ascension to the throne and glances back beyond that date into the late 1820s; chapter 4 ("1897"), from its vantage half a decade before the old queen's death, opens out into numerous issues pertinent to the Edwardian moment that was to follow. Our chronological frame thus claims as "Victorian" roughly the period 1830–1900 – threescore years and ten, and then some – and several contributors offer energetic, fertile speculation about its outer reaches; about the 1830s and 1880s, for example, two turbulent decades whose literary and cultural history is even now far from settled. Within this expanded framework, however, contributors with few exceptions (and with the editor's blessing) have made centripetal choices about what texts, authors, and movements to discuss: none of us implies that Wordsworth or Mary Shelley, Conrad or H. G. Wells should be enlisted on strictly calendrical grounds as a Victorian. Moreover, by the collective choices of its contributors this book unmistakably confirms as High Victorian the core years 1850–75, a quarter-century which repeatedly focuses our chapters and from whose literary, legislative, and social achievements our chief examples are repeatedly drawn. From causes that exceed the capacity of an editor to declare – and that have called for *tours de force* in the composition of chapters 2 and 3 – these were the years when the interactivity between British literature and its ambient culture was most radiantly strong, year after year and right across the genres, from *In Memoriam* and Macaulay's *History of England* to "The Wreck of the *Deutschland*" and *The Way We Live Now*. No wonder our *Companion* gives special privilege to writings from this core period: they ring still with that textual–contextual synergy which made literature and culture such boon companions for one another at the Victorian noontide.

While certain topics traditionally prominent or recently urgent in Victorian studies do not receive frontal treatment here, their omission is in most cases merely apparent. Neither utilitarianism nor socialism gets a chapter to itself; the evangelical and the aesthete are alike passed over; for essays dedicated to the contest of science with religion, or to the dilemma of the woman writer, the reader will scan our table of contents in vain. But that is because these topics are the very reverse of negligible: so insistently do they require our notice that they appear (witness the index) as ingredient themes throughout the book, which is where at our *fin de siècle* the editor thinks they belong, rather than in isolation as token or special interests. The reason the *Companion* lacks a chapter on the working class is that the contributors have been urged to build a working-class perspective into each account. On the record, the literary documentation of Victorian experience remains overwhelmingly middle-class; but Victorian writers would never have left the record they did had the middle classes been less acutely aware of the political insistence of those whose social and economic "inferiority" defined, and indeed enabled, what ranked as a comfortable bourgeois "norm." This feature of cultural history — like others respecting sexuality, ethnicity, denominational faith — is best conveyed by means of saturation. Our reader will therefore find, say, the 1864 Contagious Diseases Act discussed not in quarantine but all over the book, because the institutional and ideological bearings that regulated Victorian sexuality were all over the culture that the book is about.

It is a scholarly generation now, and a conspicuously changeful one at that, since three independently yet similarly organized *Guides to Research* took survey of the environs and prospects for Victorianist study of fiction (ed. Lionel Stevenson 1964, revised 1980), of poetry (ed. Frederic Faverty 1956, revised 1968), and of prose (ed. David De Laura 1973). Those authoritative volumes address a more advanced scholarly audience than ours does, an audience for that matter that has included most of our contributors at different stages of their professional development. While this *Companion* has never been intended to supersede the *Guides*, the bibliographies it contains acknowledge enough new scholarship — sufficiently various in kind, diversified in scope and innovative in method — to warrant their revision and probably reconception, along fresh lines that depart from the author-centered programs of study that held sway a quarter-century ago. Until the *Guides* are superseded, though, it is to them that readers of this book who go on to independent research should turn in the pursuit of detailed information about the principal nineteenth- and twentieth-century repositories of information and channels for intellectual exchange. Also recommended here is a much more recent literary study, Robin Gilmour's excellent *The Victorian Period* (1993), to whose steady single-point perspective on intellectual and cultural contexts our omnibus *Companion* offers a more kaleidoscopic complement. Decades hence the late-century efforts of every one of us are likely to be noticed, if at all, for their quaint adherence to narrative explanation, to the expository paragraph, and above all to the medium of print. But it is a safe bet that the hunger to understand our antecedents will survive us, together with the desire to appreciate those literary achievements which remain the Victorians' most subtly demanding legacy to a posterity no less vexed and inquisitive than they.

The editor thanks Andrew McNeillie for initiative and support, and Rob Pursley, Maury Shepherd, Jack Messenger, and Marie Lorimer for discerning technical assistance.

Contributors

James Eli Adams teaches at Indiana University, where he co-edits *Victorian Studies*. He is the author of *Dandies and Desert Saints: Styles of Victorian Masculinity* (1995) and the editor, with Andrew H. Miller, of *Sexualities in Victorian Britain* (1996).

Richard D. Altick is Regents' Professor of English, Emeritus, at Ohio State University. His most recent book is *"Punch": The Lively Youth of a British Institution, 1841– 1851* (1997). The 1998 edition of his *The English Common Reader* contains an extensive supplementary bibliography.

Stephen Arata is Associate Professor of English at the University of Virginia and the author of *Fictions of Loss in the Victorian Fin de Siècle* (1996).

James Buzard is Associate Professor of Literature at MIT and the author of *The Beaten Track: European Tourism, Literature, and the Ways to "Culture," 1800–1918* (1993). His current project is "Anywhere's Nowhere: Fictions of Autoethnography in the United Kingdom."

Karen Chase is Professor of English at the University of Virginia and the author of *Eros and Psyche: The Representation of Personality in Charlotte Brontë, Charles Dickens, George Eliot* (1984) and *George Eliot: Middlemarch* (1991). With Michael Levenson, she has recently completed *The Spectacle of Intimacy: Victorian Family Life on the Public Stage*.

Christina Crosby, Professor of English and Women's Studies at Wesleyan University, is the author of *The Ends of History: Victorians and "The Woman Question"* (1991) and essays on other Victorian and feminist topics. She is currently working on a book titled "Money Changes Everything: Victorian Literary Economies."

Alan Fischler is Professor of English at Le Moyne College. He is the author of *Modified Rapture: Comedy in W. S. Gilbert's Savoy Operas* (1991) and has published articles on Gilbert, Douglas Jerrold, Madame Vestris, and J. R. Planché. He is currently at work on a book about the favorite theme of Victorian drama, tentatively titled "The Rise of the Fallen Woman."

Antony H. Harrison is Professor of English at North Carolina State University. He is editor of the four-volume *Letters of Christina Rossetti* (1997–2001), *Refiguring Christina Rossetti* (1999), and *Gender and Discourse in Victorian Literature and Art* (1992). He has authored *Victorian Poets and the Politics of Culture: Discourse and Ideology* (1998); *Victorian Poets and Romantic Poems: Intertextuality and Ideology* (1990); *Christina Rossetti in Context* (1988); and *Swinburne's Medievalism: A Study in Victorian Love Poetry* (1988).

Thomas William Heyck teaches modern British and Irish history at Northwestern University, where he is Charles Deering McCormick Professor. He has published books on late-Victorian Anglo-Irish relations, Victorian intellectual life, and the general history of the peoples of the British Isles since 1688. Currently, he is writing a book on intellectuals and intellectual life in twentieth-century Britain.

Linda K. Hughes, Professor of English at Texas Christian University, is author of a book on Tennyson's dramatic monologues (1987), guest editor of a special issue on women poets in *Victorian Poetry* (1995), and co-author, with Michael Lund, of *The Victorian Serial* (1991) and a forthcoming book on Elizabeth Gaskell. More recently her work has focused on women poets of the 1890s, especially Graham R. Tomson.

Gerhard Joseph, Professor of English at Lehman College and the Graduate Center, City University of New York, is the author of *Tennyson and the Text: The Weaver's Shuttle* (1992), along with numerous articles on nineteenth-century subjects. His current project is a book-length study of legitimate and illegitimate "copying" in nineteenth-century English and American literature.

Christine L. Krueger, Associate Professor of English at Marquette University, is the author of *The Reader's Repentance: Women Preachers, Women Writers, and Nineteenth-Century Social Discourse* (1992) and articles on Elizabeth Gaskell, George Eliot, and Victorian literature and law.

David E. Latané, Jr, teaches British literature, with a particular interest in poetry and poetics in the early nineteenth and late twentieth centuries, at Virginia Commonwealth University. In addition to essays and reviews on such figures as Blake, Susan Ferrier, Maginn, Larkin, and Hughes, he is the author of *Browning's "Sordello" and the Aesthetics of Difficulty* (1987). He currently serves as US Editor for *Stand Magazine* (UK).

Michael Levenson, Professor of English at the University of Virginia, has written *A Genealogy of Modernism: English Literary Doctrine 1908–1922* (1984) and *Modernism and the Fate of Individuality* (1991). He is the editor of the forthcoming *Cambridge Companion to Modernism* and co-author (with Karen Chase) of *The Spectacle of Intimacy: Victorian Family Life on the Public Stage*.

Teresa Mangum is an Associate Professor of English at the University of Iowa. In addition to essays on aging, detection, and sensation fiction, she has also published a book, *Middle-Class, Middle-Brow, and Millitant: Sarah Grand and the New Woman Novel* (1998). Currently, she is working on a book titled "The Victorian Invention of Old Age."

Joss Marsh is an Associate Professor of English at Indiana University. Her book *Word Crimes: Blasphemy, Culture, and Literature in Nineteenth-Century England* appeared in 1998; she owes her interest in visual culture, on which she has published articles in media as diverse as the *Times Literary Supplement* and *Select* rock magazine, in part to membership in a three-generation filmmaking family.

Helena Michie is a Professor of English at Rice University. The author of *The Flesh Made Word: Female Figures, Women's Bodies* (1987), *Sororophobia: Differences Among Women in Literature and Culture* (1991), and, with Naomi R. Cahn, of *Confinements: Fertility and Infertility in Contemporary U.S. Culture* (1997), she specializes in Victorian literature and culture and in feminist studies. She is currently at work on a book on Victorian honeymoons.

Claudia Nelson teaches children's literature and Victorian literature at Southwest Texas State University. Her books include *Boys Will Be Girls: The Feminine Ethic and British Children's Fiction, 1857–1917* (1991); *The Girl's Own: Cultural Histories of the Anglo-American Girl, 1830–1915* (co-edited 1994 with Lynne Vallone); *Invisible Men: Fatherhood in Victorian Periodicals, 1850–1910* (1995); and *Maternal Instincts: Visions of Motherhood and Sexuality in Britain, 1875–1925* (co-edited 1997 with Ann Sumner Holmes).

Robert Newsom is Professor of English at the University of California, Irvine. Author of *Dickens on the Romantic Side of Familiar Things: Bleak House and the Novel Tradition* (1977) and of *A Likely Story: Probability and Play in Fiction* (1988), he is currently working on a new volume on Dickens for the Twayne's English Authors Series and a book with the working title "Just Pleasure: Dickens in the Bentham World."

Timothy Peltason teaches at Wellesley College, and his publications include a book on Tennyson's *In Memoriam* (1985) and an edition of Arnold's poetry (1994). He has written essays on Tennyson, Dickens, Arnold, Eliot, Ruskin, and other Victorians – and also on the contemporary state of literary education and academic literary criticism.

Simon Petch is Senior Lecturer in the Department of English, University of Sydney. His main research interest is the legal culture of Victorian England, in its relationship to the literature of the period.

Linda H. Peterson is Professor of English at Yale University. Her publications include *Victorian Autobiography: The Tradition of Self-Interpretation* (1986), *Victorian*

Women Artists and Authors (1994, with Susan Casteras), and a forthcoming book on Victorian women's autobiography, *The Poetics and Politics of Women's Life Writing in 19th-Century Britain*. She is also general editor of *The Norton Reader* (5th edn, 1996).

Lawrence Poston is Professor of English and Associate Dean, College of Liberal Arts and Sciences, at the University of Illinois at Chicago. He has published numerous journal articles as part of an ongoing study of the transition between the Romantic and Victorian eras in poetry and fiction.

John R. Reed is a Distinguished Professor of English at Wayne State University. He has published widely in nineteenth- and twentieth-century British literature and culture. His most recent book was *Dickens and Thackeray: Punishment and Forgiveness* (1995). He is now at work on a book-length literary and cultural study of the military in nineteenth-century Britain.

Lawrence Rothfield is Associate Professor of English and Comparative Literature at the University of Chicago. He is the author of *Vital Signs: Medical Realism in Nineteenth-Century Fiction* (1992), as well as numerous articles on the interrelations of literature and the human sciences.

Hilary Schor is Associate Professor of English at the University of Southern California. She is the author of *Scheherezade in the Marketplace: Elizabeth Gaskell and the Victorian Novel* (1992) and of articles on Victorian women writers and contemporary fiction. Her forthcoming book concerns Charles Dickens and narratives of female property.

E. Warwick Slinn is Associate Professor of English at Massey University in New Zealand. He has been a Fulbright Scholar at the University of Virginia and Duke University and is the author of *Browning and the Fictions of Identity* (1982) and *The Discourse of Self in Victorian Poetry* (1991).

Herbert Sussman, Professor of English at Northeastern University, is the author of *Victorian Masculinities: Manhood and Masculine Poetics in Early Victorian Literature and Art* (1995); *Fact into Figure: Typology in Carlyle, Ruskin, and the Pre-Raphaelite Brotherhood* (1979); *and Victorians and the Machine: The Literary Response to Technology* (1968).

Herbert F. Tucker, Professor of English at the University of Virginia, has written books on Browning (1980) and Tennyson (1988). His editorial undertakings include an anthology of Tennyson scholarship (1993), a book on critical pedagogy, theory, and practice (*Under Criticism*, 1998, with David Sofield), and a forthcoming anthology of Victorian literature (with Dorothy Mermin). He is also associate editor of *New Literary History*.

Chris R. Vanden Bossche, Professor of English at the University of Notre Dame, is the author of several studies of Victorian literature and culture, among them essays on Dickens, Tennyson, Scott, and Ruskin, and a book entitled *Carlyle and the Search for Authority* (1991). He is also editor of Carlyle's *Historical Essays* (1999).

Jennifer Wicke is Professor of English at the University of Virginia, having taught also at Yale and at New York Universities, in the field of English and comparative literature. She has written widely on the intersections between nineteenth- and twentieth-century Anglo-American literature and its cultural forms, in works such as *Advertising Fictions: Literature, Advertisement, and Social Reading* (1988), and her forthcoming *Born to Shop: Modernity and the Work of Consumption.*

PART ONE
History in Focus

1

1832

Lawrence Poston

Finding the Beginning

When did the Victorian age begin? While the senescence of Victorian England has been located anywhere from the Queen's Golden Jubilee in 1887 to the Battle of the Somme in 1916, its beginning – the "Victorian prelude" – has been placed as far back as the 1780s, which saw the moral reaction in English manners portended by the Wesleyans and the Evangelical revival. Here "Victorianism" is simplistically equated with a social conservatism that both antedates and postdates the queen herself; Mrs Grundy, it seems, was on the throne longer still. A literal reading of the term implies that the Victorian era begins with the accession of Victoria to the throne in 1837 and ends with her own demise in 1901. Yet the first generation of authors we now know as "Victorian" was born at the end of the eighteenth century and in the first two decades of the nineteenth. Carlyle, Mill, Macaulay, Newman were all publishing in the 1820s; Tennyson and Browning in the early 1830s. Strict adherence to the dates of reign ignores these larger continuities.

The *Wellesley Index to Victorian Periodicals* has canonized another date: 1824, the year of Byron's death and of the founding of the *Westminster Review* as a party organ for the Benthamites, designed to add a Radical voice to the select upper-middle-class reading scene dominated by the Tory *Quarterly Review* and the Whig *Edinburgh Review*. Byron's own contemporaries saw his death in symbolically charged terms. As Edward Bulwer (later the much-maligned Bulwer-Lytton) put it in his study of English society, politics, arts, and manners, *England and the English* (1833), "When Byron passed away, the feeling he had represented craved utterance no more. With a sigh we turned to the actual and practical career of life; we awoke from the morbid, the passionate, the dreaming" (p. 286). For Bulwer, the utilitarian Bentham had succeeded the romantic egoist Byron as the cultural symbol of his day. The very strength of the recoil from Byron was a tribute to the sway his passionate and sometimes morbid nature had exercised over the reading public. Yet even Byron had prepared the way for Bentham, to the extent that the poet's own assaults on national prejudices had engendered a more skeptical climate receptive to Bentham's querying of national institutions.

Byron and Bentham as twin cultural symbols have a powerful resonance for the student of the period. But between them they do not begin to account either for the multitude of voices counseling different things in the years immediately preceding Victoria, or for a rapidly changing political climate. While it may be more suspicious than auspicious to proclaim the emergence of a distinctive self-awareness at a particular moment in history, most of us do so at the beginning of a new decade; we use the terms "Sixties," "Seventies," "Eighties" as code words for a cluster of political and cultural assumptions; and if we keep diaries and watch our own biological clock the onset of a new decade is likely to breed still more self-examination than a new year. One can make a case for 1830 as one of those possible Victorian beginnings. Two diarists in January 1830 saw that something was afoot, and they did not like what they saw. One of them was Charles Greville, the diarist of the reigns of George IV, William IV, and Victoria, whose sheltered position as clerk to the Privy Council gave him unparalleled access to politicians of all factions. On January 7 he wrote, "The revenue has fallen off one million and more. The accounts of distress from the country grow worse and more desponding" (Greville 1875: I, 224). Ten days later finds him in a more perturbed vein: "The country gentlemen are beginning to arrive, and they all tell the same story as to the universally prevailing distress and the certainty of things becoming much worse; of the failure of rents all over England, and the necessity of some decisive measures or the prospect of general ruin" (ibid., p. 226). The other is one of those country gentlemen, General William Dyott, a Staffordshire magnate then 68 years old, writing on New Year's Day 1830: "I believe a year never opened with less cheering prospects to a country than the present for old England; distress attending all classes of the community. . . . Meetings held in various parts of the kingdom to represent the distress of the country" (Darwin 1951: I, 248). For such disturbed but insular observers, the question was whether the Duke of Wellington and Robert Peel between them could produce any program capable of alleviating the widespread economic distress of the countryside, and thus a threat to the old order.

More shocks, some of them not altogether unwelcome, like the death of the widely discredited old rake George IV on June 26, followed throughout the year. At home, talk of reform, the antislavery agitation which Greville attributed to the bothersome Methodists, and a new Parliament in his words "full of boys and all sorts of strange men" all seemed to herald transition. So, abroad, did the overthrow of the French monarchy, in the three days of July, which in England revived radical hopes and fears; for the first time since the 1790s, the tricolor was hoisted in several English cities, and even the cautious Whigs were viewed by some of their more conservative colleagues as contemplating a doctrinaire reform in the French style. It was, again, Bulwer who sensed the impending change and embraced it openly:

> Just at the time when with George the Fourth an *old* era expired, the excitement of a
> popular election concurred with the three days of July in France, to give a decisive tone

to the *new*. The question of Reform came on, and, to the astonishment of the nation itself, it was hailed at once by the national heart. From that moment, the intellectual spirit hitherto partially directed to, became *wholly* absorbed in, politics; and whatever lighter works have since obtained a warm and general hearing, have either developed the errors of the social system, or the vices of the legislative. (Bulwer-Lytton 1833: 288–9)

The Reform currents given new life in England by events on the Continent had, by the time *England and the English* was published, found expression in the First Reform Act of 1832. That date itself is indeed the most convenient point around which to gather the various reforming clusters of the decade preceding Victoria's accession, and to mark an evolution from older paternalist to newer entrepreneurial ideas of the social order. Yet the latter part of Bulwer's statement suggests another aspect of the 1830s which is particularly striking to the student of literature: the displacement of works of the imagination by the all-consuming task of Reform, or their subordination to the political agendas which so preoccupied the larger public.

The paradox of the 1830s has often been described in terms of the striking contrast between the richness of their political history – Reform, the growth of political and labor unions and at the end of the decade the movement for the redress of working-class grievances, Chartism, the first stirrings of the Anti-Corn Law League, the beginning of systematic government intervention in prison conditions, education, welfare, working hours, and public order – and the apparent barrenness of the cultural scene. That prodigiously diligent later Victorian woman of letters, Margaret Oliphant, trying to account for the strange hiatus in poetry and fiction between about 1825 and 1840, wrote that "the period which witnessed Her Majesty's happy accession was not in itself a very glorious one, at least as far as literature is concerned. It was a season of lull, of silence and emptiness, such as must naturally come after the exhausting brilliance of the days just gone by" (Oliphant and Oliphant 1892: I, 1). But Bulwer's post-Byronic characterization of a shift in sensibility from the dreaming to the practical suggests a more productive approach. It echoes in the attempt of more recent scholars to isolate a distinctive "public voice" in English literature of the 1830s and 1840s, a voice intended to "transcend the doubt which by 1830 had fatally touched the fundamental Romantic faith, while the self-consciousness of this effort found expression in the 'private' voice which qualified the work of the best writers" (Madden 1963: 97). But those writers must first of all be seen in the context of an age which itself was coming to greater self-consciousness about its aims and purposes.

Georgian or Victorian? The Political Scene

The man who succeeded George IV as king in 1830 was hardly of the stuff to give his name to an age. The kindly, choleric, well-intentioned, essentially honest Duke of Clarence had earlier discarded a mistress in the interests of respectability and in the hope that one of his legitimate children might inherit his throne. Known as Sailor Bill because of his navy career, he was also, on account of his fondness for making intemperate and embarrassing public utterances, referred to by the even less dignified sobriquet of Silly Billy. Harriet Martineau described him as "a sovereign who could not help agreeing with the last speaker, and who was always impetuous on behalf of his latest impression." Or, as one of Greville's colleagues observed, "What can you expect of a man with a head shaped like a pineapple?" Yet William IV, irresolute and capricious though he sometimes was, warrants some credit for restoring an aura of respectability to the monarchy after the reign of his dissolute brother. He was not, however, the best-equipped of men to preside over an age of Reform.

Reform has its origin in the 1820s, with the repeal of Test and Corporation Acts in 1828 and Catholic Emancipation in 1829, both of them measures aimed at easing the political disabilities that had hemmed in the rights of Protestant dissenters on the one hand and Roman Catholics on the other. These measures deeply divided the governing Tory party, factions of which participated in the overthrow of Wellington's Tory government in 1830. Tories were disgusted by the duke's willingness to move in the direction of free trade and by his about-face on Catholic Emancipation, and they paved the way for the Whig government of Earl Grey, whom the king summoned to office at the end of 1830 following Wellington's refusal to countenance any further change in the British constitution.

The calls for Reform were spurred on by those riots among farm laborers and that manufacturing unrest which echo in the diaries of Dyott and Greville. In March 1831 Lord John Russell introduced a bill in the House of Commons that removed Parliamentary representation from many small electoral boroughs and gave such representation to the nation's growing industrial centers. The bill also attempted to regularize inconsistencies in the relationship between property-holding and the right to the franchise. It passed by a majority of only one at 3:00 a.m. on March 22, but still required a clause-by-clause reading and the approval of a hostile House of Lords. The defeat of one of the clauses led Grey to advise the king to dissolve Parliament and ask for new elections. The result was a referendum on a single issue: "the bill, the whole bill, and nothing but the bill" (Arnstein 1996: 12). Many elections in England at this time were uncontested, but in those boroughs where there was a contest, it was the reformers who were returned to power. Russell's second version of the bill commanded a substantial majority on its second reading in Commons, but ran aground in the House of Lords, where it was defeated after a five-day debate.

The opposition of the Lords seemed to call into question the very viability of the constitution. The cities were outraged; arsonists destroyed Nottingham Castle; Bristol succumbed for a few days to mob rule. That December Grey's government went back to work and produced a third reform bill much like the second. With the bill threatened once again by a hostile House of Lords, Grey called on the king to create 50 new peers to override the opposition. William IV thought 50 a bit much; Grey found the counter-offer of 20 too few, and resigned. The Duke of Wellington, however, whom the king called back to power, was incapable of meeting the rising storm of discontent. At that juncture the king turned to Grey and reluctantly acceded to the demand to create new peers, but the House of Lords, reading the tea leaves, acquiesced in the bill rather than permit itself to be swamped with new appointees. The bill became law on June 7, 1832.

The first Reform Act is itself a transition piece, much like William's reign; it looks different from different angles. Along with the Municipal Corporations Act of 1835, the 1832 bill may well have saved England from revolution, and it certainly moved the country peacefully and without Continental-style convulsions toward democracy. Those Whigs who orchestrated Reform in the difficult first months of the decade saw the bill quite differently, as an end rather than a beginning. As one historian puts it, "the Bill had been like the legitimate heir of a loveless marriage, the child rather of necessity than of desire" (Kitson Clark 1964: 64). Though prodded by Radical colleagues on their left, with whom the Whigs had an uneasy relationship, the drafters of the bill viewed traditional social groups as providing the essential frame of reference. Grey's charge to the Committee of Four which he appointed to draft the bill is revealing. The legislation, he wrote, should be "of such a scope and description as to satisfy all reasonable demands, and remove at once, and for ever, all rational grounds for complaint from the minds of the intelligent and independent portion of the community." This in essence was Macaulay's famous advice to Parliament in his speech of 1831: "Reform, that you may preserve." Though Peel had opposed Reform, after its passage he accepted it in his Tamworth manifesto to the electors as "a final and irrevocable settlement of a great constitutional question," and his Whig opponent Lord John Russell earned the nickname "Finality Jack" for the emphasis with which he insisted, both on the floor of the House and in writing, that the authors of the bill were "peculiarly committed to finality" and that to tolerate further Reform measures "would be to confess that [the reformers] had deceived the people or themselves" (Southgate 1962: 99).

Viewed in this way, the bill looks more like Georgian farewell than Victorian halloo, just as the England of that year to many of its citizens probably seemed not so very different from the latter years of the eighteenth century. In 1833, writes a leading administrative historian, England "was not orderly, it was not planned, it was not centralized, it was not efficient, and it did little for the well-being of the citizens." Education, health, and poor relief lay beyond the purview of the national government, and the last was administered erratically by 15,000 parishes also in charge of public order (Roberts 1959: 195). Hindsight makes clearer the beginnings of slow, almost glacial changes beneath the surface of daily events. Contemporaries feel the shocks but not the trends; the earthquakes, not the subtle erosions or the drawn-out process of sedimentation. The England that James Fenimore Cooper visited in the late winter and early spring of 1828 was still the England of the great Whig houses and the breakfasts of the poet Samuel Rogers, one of the last of the Augustans, where Cooper met Coleridge, Sir Walter Scott, Thomas Campbell, John Gibson Lockhart, Thomas Moore, Earl Grey, and Lord John Russell. Cows still grazed in the heart of London. Green Park and St James Park were "one open space" separated only by a fence, the first in Cooper's words "nothing but a large field, cropped down like velvet, irregularly dotted with trees, and without any carriage way" (Cooper 1837: 28). This England survived well into the 1830s. Jeremy Bentham died in 1832 at the age of 84; as an undergraduate he had attended Blackstone's lectures on law at Oxford in the 1760s. Charles Grey, who shepherded through the first Reform Bill in 1832, was nearly 70 and, like his party, had spent almost half a century in the political wilderness; in the 1790s he had joined the Society of Friends of the People and introduced his first motion on Parliamentary reform. John Scott, Lord Chancellor and first Earl Eldon, was 81 when, to his disgust, the Reform Bill became law; as Attorney General he had been identified with various of the repressive acts of the 1790s and at the turn of the century was opposing the abolition of the slave trade. But power was passing to Palmerston, Russell, and Peel, while at the further end of the age spectrum the young Gladstone at 22, listening to the Reform debates in the galleries, was still a few months from his first seat; Disraeli, six years and four defeats from his.

One striking symbol of transition is Grey's successor as the leader of the Whigs. William Lamb, second Viscount Melbourne, was the last prime minister ever to be dismissed unilaterally by a reigning monarch and the first to become prime minister as the result of a general election, against that monarch's will. Melbourne was in his mid-fifties upon his appointment as prime minister in 1834 and therefore presumably at the height of his powers if he chose to use them. It was an open question whether or not he would. Elegant, languid, debonair, with a political record at best equivocal on the major issues of the day, the jotter of numerous cynical reflections on society in his commonplace book, Melbourne told his secretary, upon being offered the reins of government, that it was "a damned bore" to decide whether or not to accept. It is one of the finer ironies of the decade that this Whig aristocrat, twice cited as an adulterous co-respondent in the Brandon and Norton divorce cases (the second of these during his prime ministership), should be found in 1837 at the ear of the impressionable, rather conventional young queen as avuncular counselor and friend. Perhaps, with the changed moral atmosphere that journalists of the day were already commenting on, the transition from Regency gentleman to Victorian paterfamilias was not so difficult or arduous after all, but then Melbourne was nothing if not flexible. Much of the foregoing description is, of course, caricature; Melbourne's dilettantism was to a large extent a pose, and he was capable of decisive action, but what is interesting is that he apparently abandoned the dilettante's pose for the firm kindliness to which the 18-year-old queen responded with tremulous gratitude.

Meanwhile, the Whig assumption of "finality" in political arrangements was already being battered by changes which the Reform Bill could hardly have been drafted to prevent and which made it clear that 1832 was an opening salvo, not a concluding salute. The creation of inspectors of factories (1833) and prisons (1835), the New Poor Law (1834), the new Education Committee of the Privy Council, represented stages toward the centralization which Dickens's Mr Podsnap, a quarter of a century later, was to decry as "not English." Government was becoming increasingly conscious of its own powers. It is no accident that the 1830s saw the rise of statistics-gathering, of select Parliamentary commissions on matters requiring reform, of "blue books" that constituted the gathering of evidence for the purpose, and in general an almost obsessive documentation of "the condition of England question," which resonates in the novels of Disraeli, Gaskell, Charlotte Brontë, and Kingsley in the next decade. Perhaps the very *ad hoc* nature of much of this activity was responsible for what looked to foreign observers like a remarkably resilient political system. The spirit of English legislation, Alexis de Tocqueville thought when he visited the country in 1835, was "an incomprehensible mixture of the spirits of innovation and routine, which perfects the details of law without noticing their principles" (Tocqueville 1835: 82). He saw stability in the openness of the aristocratic class to newcomers and the absence of class hatred, the presence of a relatively democratic group of reformers who respected religion and property, and the spirit of individualism that flourished under the government, along with a fair amount of administrative muddle. "In France," marveled another French visitor, the Baron d'Haussez, "a revolution is accomplished in three days. In England, the country deliberates many years before the work of reform is entered on and, once commenced, the results are without danger, for the passions . . . are already cooled" (d'Haussez 1833: I, 154–5).

Such assessments may have been both accurate and premonitory. Some worried Englishmen of the day would have seen them as premature. The six points of the People's Charter (1837) called for universal manhood suffrage, annual Parliaments, voting by secret ballot, equal electoral districts, the abolition of property qualifications for members of Parliament, and pay for members of Parliament. The passing of the Factory Act of 1833, limiting the working hours of children in factories, and the agitation against the seeming inhumanities of the New Poor Law (which readers now know chiefly through Dickens's vivid portrayal of the workhouse in *Oliver Twist*) are both symptoms of a broader and less focused discontent than that which clustered around the Reform Act. Reform, after all, did not bring about economic change, though it generated some utopian hopes.

Historians continue to divide on the extent to which the Act of 1832 was a genuine step forward, and if so what step it took. Influential studies by Norman Gash and D. C. Moore have suggested the danger of using the Reform Act to underplay trends and events long antedating and postdating it. A more traditional view, recently reargued, has been that the Act made possible the steps toward "an essentially modern electoral system based on rigid partisanship and clearly articulated political principle" (Phillips and Wetherell 1995: 412). For most of the reforming Whigs, the bill was intended to seal the past by increasing the total British electorate from 435,000 to 813,000 out of an adult male population of some six million, and it was drafted to guarantee that the counties would not be overbalanced by the new towns. In five general elections between 1832 and 1847 only just over half of the constituencies were contested. But it was also true that "the general election of 1841 was the first in which the government of the day, previously holding a majority in the lower House, was defeated by a disciplined opposition for electoral purposes" (Gash 1953: xii–xiii).

Nonetheless, what was not fully understood at the time turned out in the event to be a harbinger of significant if deferred change. The significance of the Reform Act was less in the measurable difference it made in the atmosphere than in the precedent it set for the Acts of 1867 and 1884: something sacred, in this case the constitution itself, had been proven nonetheless to be alterable.

The Missing Generation

On the night of October 16, 1834, the skies over London were irradiated with a glow that could be seen miles away. The Palace of Westminster had caught fire, and while the next morning's light showed that Westminster Hall had survived, the old Parliament House of St Stephen and the surrounding lawcourts were destroyed. In 1835 a Parliamentary Commission set up to consider the rebuilding of Parliament decided to hold a competition that was to require the submission of architectural designs in either the Gothic or Elizabethan modes. The winning design, submitted by a young architect named Charles Barry, constituted a clearcut identification of England's political glories with the Gothic.

In part, this has been seen as a moral revulsion against the age of the Georges, for whom the classic had been the dominant style. In part it anticipates the concurrent movement toward the Gothic as an attempt to evoke the piety as well as the pride of the medieval past, a movement which finds its distinctive moment in the publication in 1836 of Augustus Welby Pugin's *Contrasts*, which polemically juxtaposed pictures of fourteenth- and fifteenth-century buildings with the ugly creations of his own day. For a more recent writer, the building of the Houses of Parliament in 1834–7 marks "a cultural monument of a time neither Georgian nor Victorian," but rather "a tribute to the power of creativity between orthodoxies" (Rorabaugh 1973: 174–5). But the initial decision to exclude classical models is perhaps the most striking attribute of the competition itself. What was at stake was both a return to real or imagined national origins, and a rejection of what the immediately preceding era had come to symbolize.

The shift from "Georgian" to "Victorian" in the broader political and cultural context is almost as delusively tidy and elusively traceable as the shift from "Romantic" to "Victorian" is for the literary historian. In the visual arts, the deaths of the brilliant young painter and watercolorist Richard Parkes Bonington in 1828 and the fashionable portraitist Thomas Lawrence in 1830 can be set against the continuance of the work of Constable, Haydon, Turner, and Martin throughout the decade (Constable dying first of these, in 1837). But in poetry Keats died in 1821, Shelley in 1822, Byron in 1824. Sir Walter Scott, his life shortened by his gallant efforts to pay off creditors, died in 1832. Coleridge lingered on until 1834 and Wordsworth until 1850, but only the most ardent revisionists now contest the fact that their best creative work lay behind them. Scholars have made the most of such symbolically charged moments as Wordsworth's toast to the young Robert Browning upon the publication of *Paracelsus* in 1835, or Tennyson's highly unsatisfactory interview with the sage of Rydal Mount in 1845, during which the younger poet sought, unsuccessfully by his own account, to rouse the flagging interest of Wordsworth in natural beauty. But the fact is that there is very little to be made of such occasions as these; they heighten, rather than minimize, the effect of disjuncture. It is startling to recall that Wordsworth's successor as national literary sage, Thomas Carlyle, was only a few weeks younger than Keats, but that at the time Keats died Carlyle had barely embarked on a career as a hack writer for the encyclopedias.

The 1830s do indeed see the beginnings of several brilliant, though sometimes slow-starting, careers. But they provide little evidence of an 1830s equivalent for what has been called the Auden generation of the 1930s. In both decades an atmosphere of impending crisis pervades the scene, but the emerging writers of the 1830s were too young, their lines of activity too disparate, and Carlyle too idiosyncratic to serve as a consistent mentor. If to be, to act, and to conceive oneself as part of a literary generation requires a developed self-consciousness as well as a defined corporate identity, the emerging writers of the thirties do not qualify. Yet in measurable ways all of them were products of a common historical milieu and all of them are barometers of what we can now define as a post-Romantic ethos. A number of these lines of development have been traced by scholars: the dwindling cult of Byron, the exhaustion of the Wordsworthian paradigm of the unity between man and nature, a growing uncertainty as to the nature of the audience for high literature, and a concern with political themes drawn from the past, often in a context – as in Browning's *Sordello* (1840) or Henry Taylor's once-popular verse drama *Philip van Artevelde* (1834) – which suggests the limits of the individual hero in an unheroic age. Even in their collectivity, however, these themes stop short of providing us with a genuinely synoptic view of the decade.

Another way to assess that decade is less thematic than generic. One of the most interesting phenomena of the 1830s is the blurring of conventional generic distinctions: Tennyson's inward-turning lyrics which chart new journeys of the mind, Browning's disruption of the conventions of historical narrative in *Sordello*, Dickens's imposition of a reformist vision on the eighteenth-century picaresque novel, or Carlyle's *Sartor Resartus* (1834), by turns autobiographical fragment, philosophical treatise, novel, and editorial doodling – possibly the biggest put-on in English literature since *Tristram Shandy*. It is tempting to make Carlyle the generic center of the decade, beginning with his splendid review-essay "Characteristics" in 1831, continuing through such works as *The French Revolution* (1837) in which history fades into a drama of lived memory, reawakened by the more recent three days of July 1830, and culminating in *Heroes and Hero-Worship*, the lectures of 1840 in which Carlyle attempts to proclaim a new ethic of leadership.

Yet a work like *Sartor* requires also to be read in the context of its original place of publication, *Fraser's Magazine*, whose brilliant and eccentric editor William Maginn collected a veritable rogue's gallery of wits and satirists who left subscribers reeling. Similarly, Dickens in the latter 1830s was a young journalist whose *Sketches by Boz* (1836) can now be seen, more clearly than by Boz's first readers, as a trial run for *Pickwick Papers* (1837). The generic issue here is linked to a larger one: the need to go beyond masterpieces to explain the wonderfully diverse achievements of the 1830s. As scholars of Victorian popular culture like Patrick Brantlinger have shown us, the decade offers a remarkably pristine case for testing the familiar, recurrent process whereby literature is refreshed from below; de Tocqueville's comments on the openness of the English upper class to new influences from the emerging middle class can be replicated in the context of "high" and "low" art. Thus, behind the careers of the two major novelists of the forties and fifties, Dickens and Thackeray, lies the *Punch* circle of the late thirties – Mark Lemon, the Mayhews, Tom Hood, Douglas Jerrold and others, nearly all of whom had experienced bankruptcy and debt, who wrote reformist melodramas (Jerrold) or poetry enlivened by popular idioms (Hood), some of which is visible in the early dramatic lyrics of Browning. This middle world which at intervals feeds the high literature of the time should be expanded to include the larger world of popular tracts and stories for working-class audiences: not only the collection of Cobbett's *Rural Rides* in book form at the beginning of the decade, but Harriet Martineau's *Illustrations of Political Economy* in the form of didactic stories (1832–4), the commencement of Charles Knight's *Penny Magazine* in 1832, or the numerous pamphlets issued beginning in 1825 by the Society for the Diffusion of Useful Knowledge. And in turn beneath that world, much of which admittedly smacks of keeping a lid on working-class discontent, lie such attempts to give voice to the inchoate class consciousness as are represented by *The Poor Man's Guardian* or the Chartist *Northern Star*.

The novel of the 1830s has often been viewed as a barren stretch, enlivened perhaps only by the sea stories of Captain Marryat, and certainly it is difficult to see much that is redeeming in a time when the prolix and sometimes embarrassing Bulwer has come to stand as the chief figure, chronologically speaking, between Scott and Dickens. For nearly half a century, the rest has been relegated to the classification – a form of dismissal – of large numbers of works into "silver fork" novels (of high society) and "Newgate" novels (drawing on popular literature of crime and punishment). But in fact such fictional subgenres are much more permeable than the classifications admit. A single novel may draw on both Newgate and silver fork elements, because writers of the 1830s, as well as their audiences, were aware of increasingly fluid class boundaries: wild speculation in the early years of uncontrolled entrepreneurship, with the enhanced possibilities of making and losing entire fortunes, and the breakdown of older Tory theories of class obligation. We cannot hold fiction such as this to the test of mid-Victorian realism of George Eliot or Anthony Trollope, with its emphasis on compromise, the repatterning rather than the jettisoning of the social order, the process by which an individual consciousness comes to maturity in the context of a larger and organically evolving community. Harriet Martineau's fine (and still too seldom read) *Deerbrook* (1839) is perhaps the earliest novel in which we can even glimpse such Middlemarchian possibilities.

The thirties also offer an almost unexampled opportunity to explore public rhetoric along a political continuum ranging from post-Tory prophetic radicalism à la Carlyle to the leftist philosophical radicalism of James and John Stuart Mill, as well as of language of working-class radicalism, the centrist language of compromise being represented by Macaulay, Russell, and Peel's Tamworth Manifesto. Brantlinger (1977) sees in the literature of the 1830s a movement from utopian, Shelleyan politics on the liberal side, or from the corporatist Tory thinking of Southey and Coleridge on the conservative side, toward gradual social improvement. For this purpose he suggests as a fitting epigraph Macaulay's famous aphorism, "an acre of Middlesex is better than a principality in Utopia," an early intimation of the mid-Victorian gospel of progress. But Macaulay is as dangerous an example as Carlyle (whose atypicality is widely proclaimed by many of his contemporaries and present-day historians alike), perhaps all the more so because the neatly balanced antitheses of Macaulay's rhetoric, with its Augustan appeal to reason and restraint in speeches that seem to have been designed more for posterity than for the passage of legislation, suggest all the rationalities of that compromise with which the liberal imagination is comfortable. Psychic as well as political terrors lurk close to the surface in this decade, and Macaulay himself is no exception: the public man gives little hint of the lonely, passionate bachelor whose letters to his sisters breathe what has struck many readers as more than fraternal devotion. Since liberty and order are issues of the self as well as of politics, the history of public and private languages of the 1830s may indeed affirm both the emergence of a centrist rhetoric and the disruptive potential which it keeps at bay. Beneath these contestations, a common ground can be found for understanding the aspirations of sages, politicians, maybe even gentleman-diarists, and almost certainly the yet-nameless writers struggling to come to terms not only with the first industrial revolution but with the very meaning of reform itself.

How It Struck Some Contemporaries

For some Victorians at mid-century, the 1830s were an originary decade which was already assuming the status of myth. In *Middlemarch* (1872), but even more lovingly in the opening pages of *Felix Holt* (1867), George Eliot revisited a pastoral time in which "the glory had not yet departed from the old coach-roads" and the railroads were only barely thought of, while as late as 1911 Frederic Harrison's *Autobiographic Memoirs* evoked a green and pleasant space on Muswell Hill subsequently blanketed with suburban sprawl in his own lifetime. For John Henry Newman, this narrative of origins even had a date: July 14, 1833, when John Keble preached the Assize Sermon in the University Pulpit at Oxford on the subject of "National Apostasy," "the start," Newman put it in his *Apologia pro Vita Sua* (1864–5), "of the religious movement of 1833." The ensuing Tractarian Movement was itself a myth of origins, an attempt to lead the Church of England back to its own Catholicity and thus to offer a *via media* between Rome and Protestantism. On the eve of Keble's sermon, Newman's emotionally charged homecoming from his mysterious illness in Sicily to England takes on the character of a pilgrimage providentially guided by his rediscovery of the early Church Fathers and culminating more than a decade later at the hands of the Passionist priest who received him into the Roman Catholic flock.

But for those writing as the decade was unfolding, particularly those for whom the rediscovery of Catholic orthodoxy was no solution, there were no origins, only an end not yet discernible in the events of the day. For perhaps more than in any preceding decade in England, writers of the 1830s were conscious of theirs as a time of transition. The popularity of such terms as "the spirit of the age," the title of an essay by William Hazlitt in 1825, was seized upon by John Stuart Mill with the remark that he did not believe it was "to be met with in any work exceeding fifty years in antiquity." Carlyle's "Signs of the Times" (1829) and "Characteristics" (1831), both published in the *Edinburgh Review*, Mill's own "The Spirit of the Age" published in the weekly *Examiner* from January through May of 1831, and Bulwer's already-mentioned *England and the English* (1833) are all evidences of the fascination – if not, indeed, the obsession – with that process by which one becomes aware of something different and as yet not fully formed in one's own times. Carlyle the transcendentalist skeptical of transitory political nostrums, Mill the rationalist, Bulwer the dandy-reformer who asked Mill to write an appendix on Bentham for *England and the English* but later turned Conservative, make uneasy company; yet enough of a common temper enters these works to explain Carlyle's first hope that Mill was a "new Mystic" and Mill's exhortation to Carlyle to read Bulwer. Though Carlyle had earlier expressed the belief that Bulwer was a "poor fribble," he concluded his reading of *England and the English* with an expression of astonishment at "the contrast of the man and his enterprise."

What were the common elements of these disparate works? Even Carlyle, who in such catch-phrases as "spirit of the age" and "progress of the species" professed to find symptoms of that disease of self-consciousness which he felt had paralyzed the times, was forced to the task of anatomist he deplored. Like Carlyle, whose "Characteristics" began with the words, "The healthy know not of their health, but only the sick," Mill resorted to a medical metaphor when he attempted to describe the inconstancy of opinion in an unsettled time: "The men of the present day rather incline to an opinion than embrace it; few, except the very penetrating, or the very presumptuous, have full confidence in their own convictions. This is not a state of health, but, at the best, of convalescence." Mill's desire for greater social confidence resembles what Carlyle called "spontaneity" and "unconsciousness," the signs of a healthy organism, individual or social, working harmoniously: "Had Adam remained in Paradise," the sage of Chelsea succinctly observed, "there had been no Anatomy and no Metaphysics."

Of the three, Bulwer was perhaps unexpectedly the most eloquent. Like Carlyle he saw the uncertainties of an era marked by the eclipse if not extinction of earlier verities as a necessary if painful preface to reconstruction. "We live," Bulwer wrote,

> in an age of visible transition – an age of disquietude and doubt – of the removal of time-worn landmarks, and the breaking up of the hereditary elements of society – old opinions, feelings – ancestral customs and institutions are crumbling away, and both the spiritual and temporal worlds are darkened by the shadows of change. The commencement of one of these epochs – periodical in the history of mankind – is hailed by the sanguine as the coming of a new Millennium – a great iconoclastic reformation, by which

all false gods shall be overthrown. To me such epochs appear but as the dark passages in the appointed progress of mankind – the times of greatest unhappiness to our species – passages into which we have no reason to rejoice at our entrance, save from the hope of being sooner landed on the opposite side. (Bulwer-Lytton 1833: 318–19)

While Bulwer here refers to the millennialism of the latter-day *philosophes*, James Mill and Bentham, and thus exhibits one of those curious and characteristic recoils from those he professes to admire, Mill and Carlyle read disquieting signs of the thirties in the prophecies of Edward Irving and other preachers predicting the approaching Second Coming. In "Signs of the Times," Carlyle had distanced himself from Millites and Millenarians alike as false prophets, and in "The Spirit of the Age" Mill comments with subdued amazement on how "even the religious world teems with new interpretations of the prophecies." Though Mill and Carlyle differ on the role of a new religion, they are not far apart in seeing the crisis as, finally, one of faith. For Carlyle, the "noblest class" of would-be believers are neither those who "take up with worn-out Symbols of the Godlike" nor those who, denying all forms of faith, seek only pleasure, but rather those who "have dared to say No, and cannot yet say Yea." This is not so far from Mill's pronouncement that "at present, we are in a mixed state; some fight fiercely under their several banners, and these chiefly the least instructed; while the others (those few excepted who have strength to stand by themselves) are blown about by every breath, having no steady opinion – or at least no deep-rooted conviction that their opinion is true."

More wedded to a specific political program than Carlyle, Bulwer and Mill stood together in seeing the displacement of an aristocratic class from political power as a necessary step toward the restoration of stability; their concern was that the transition be peaceful, and that power be relocated in the hands of the most competent, which the upper class, what Mill called the "stationary part of mankind," manifestly was not. Carlyle, though he did not tackle this issue in "Characteristics," would have agreed to the extent that in his view outward trappings in church, state or society were merely a hollow shell of pretense, the "old clothes" he denounced in *Sartor*. Bulwer's denunciation of the materialist tenor of English philosophy, which he regarded as having been essentially at a standstill since Locke, is likewise not far from Carlyle's lament at the ascendancy of "mechanism" over "organism" in English society.

Finally, all three men were concerned with an issue of fundamental importance in the politics of the decade: how stability and change might be mutually accommodated. In particular, Carlyle and Mill took full account of, and gave due credit to, those with whom they might have been expected to have little in common. Surveying an apparently widening gap between rich and poor, Carlyle confessed that "the ancient methods of administration will no longer suffice," that in change there was "nothing terrible, nothing supernatural," and that "if Memory have its force and worth, so also has hope." On the other hand, it is not a little curious to see the son of James Mill affirming that old prejudices were preferable to new impressions, that free discussion might weaken error without insuring its replacement by informed opinion, that wise men and not merely an enlarged electorate were demanded by the times, and that the object of an age of transition, rightly guided, was to call forth a new "natural state" in which "worldly power, and moral influence, are habitually and indisputably exercised by the fittest persons." When John Stuart Mill declares that "every age contains in itself the germ of all future ages as surely as the acorn contains the future forest," utilitarian rhetoric has at least been brushed by Romantic organicism.

A curiously paradoxical decade, then, in that while in politics and social life the sense of division must have seemed deeper than ever, this was also arguably the last decade in which such fundamentally different persons as Bulwer, Mill, and Carlyle could agree on something resembling a common diagnosis of social ills and their remedies. Conversely, as England experienced the crises of the Hungry Forties that followed, they took diverse paths. Carlyle's earlier generosity of spirit seems to evaporate in the increasingly shrill harangues that culminate years later in *Latter-Day Pamphlets* (1850) and "Shooting Niagara" (1867), while for his part, Mill spent much of the remainder of the decade as a publicist for the increasingly chimerical goal of forming an effective Radical party in Parliament, an object for which Carlyle had no sympathy and for which Mill's own hopes were to be finally and effectively dashed by the election of 1841. Bulwer, longing for the life and status of a landed gentleman and never fundamentally at ease with many of his Radical colleagues, ended his political journey by making his peace with the Conservatives and briefly holding a cabinet post under Derby at mid-century, while energetically pursuing his own career as a popular novelist.

Literature courses that focus on such mid-Victorian sages as Carlyle, Mill, Arnold, Newman, and Ruskin tend to overemphasize their representativeness. Most of these prophets reposed on the far side of a gulf which was widening between them and the larger public, and as is all too often apparent from the reviews, they tended to be regarded as at best idiosyncratic and at worst irrelevant. One may view the 1830s either with regret as marking the recession of hopes for a shared cultural consensus or with interested curiosity as inaugurating an invigorating interchange between "high" and "low" forms of art. The first is perhaps an especially dangerous oversimplification because it represents a particularly egregious form of cultural elitism; by any reasonable modern standard, there was nothing resembling a mass audience for their diagnoses. Yet in their own ways Carlyle, Mill, and Bulwer all read the signs of the times with considerable accuracy. Through their voices resonate those larger symptoms of cultural uncertainty that give the 1830s their peculiar character. They knew more clearly than the generation of political leaders reaching the end of their careers that the thirties were not Georgian aftermath but the seedtime of a new era.

I am grateful to Walter L. Arnstein and James J. Sack for their readings of an earlier version of this article.

See also ADMINISTRATIVE; FICTION, SAGE WRITING; SHORE

REFERENCES

Arnstein, Walter (1996) *Britain Yesterday and To-day: 1830 to the Present*, 7th edn. Lexington, MA: D. C. Heath.

Brantlinger, Patrick (1977) *The Spirit of Reform: British Literature and Politics, 1832–1867*. Cambridge, MA and London: Harvard University Press.

Bulwer-Lytton, Edward (1833) *England and the English*, ed. Standish Meacham. Chicago: University of Chicago Press, 1970.

Carlyle, Thomas (1829) "Signs of the Times." First published in the *Edinburgh Review*, and widely reprinted.

——(1831) "Characteristics." First published in the *Edinburgh Review*, and widely reprinted.

Cooper, James Fenimore (1837) *Gleanings in Europe: England*, ed. Donald A. Ringe and Kenneth W. Staggs. Albany: State University Press of New York, 1982.

Darwin, Bernard (1951) "Country Life and Sport." In G. M. Young (ed.) *Early Victorian England, 1830–1865*, 2 vols. Oxford: Oxford University Press.

Gash, Norman (1953) *Politics in the Age of Peel: A Study in the Technique of Parliamentary Representation, 1830–1850*. New York: W. W. Norton.

Greville, Charles C. F. (1875) *A Journal of the Reigns of King George IV and King William IV*, ed. Henry Reeve. New York: Appleton.

d'Haussez, Charles le Mercher de Longpré, Baron (1833) *Great Britain in 1833*, 2 vols. London: Richard Bentley.

Kitson Clark, George (1964) *Peel and the Conservative Party: A Study in Party Politics, 1832–1841*, 2nd edn. London: Cass.

Madden, William (1963) "The Victorian Sensibility." *Victorian Studies*, 7, 67–97.

Martineau, Harriet (1877) *A History of the Thirty Years' Peace*, A.D. *1816–1846*, 4 vols. London: George Bell.

Mill, John Stuart (1831) "The Spirit of the Age." First published in *The Examiner* at intervals 9 January–29 May. In *Collected Edition of the Works of John Stuart Mill*, ed. Ann P. Robson and John M. Robson, vol. 22. Toronto: University of Toronto Press; London: Routledge and Kegan Paul, 1986.

Oliphant, Margaret and Oliphant, F. R. (1892) *The Victorian Age of English Literature*, 2 vols. London: Perceval.

Phillips, John A. and Wetherell, Charles (1995) "The Great Reform Act of 1832 and the Political Modernization of England." *American Historical Review*, 100, 411–36.

Roberts, David (1959) "Jeremy Bentham and the Victorian Administrative State," *Victorian Studies*, 2, 193–210.

Rorabaugh, W. J. (1973) "Politics and the Architectural Competition for the Houses of Parliament, 1834–1837." *Victorian Studies*, 17, 155–75.

Southgate, Donald (1962) *The Passing of the Whigs, 1832–1886*. London: Macmillan; New York: St Martin's.

Tocqueville, Alexis de (1835) *Journeys to England and Ireland*, tr. George Lawrence and K. P. Mayer, ed. J. P. Mayer. London: Faber and Faber, 1958.

FURTHER READING

Aldburgham, Alison (1983) *Silver Fork Society: Fashionable Life and Literature, 1814–1840*. London: Constable.

Altick, Richard D. (1957) *The English Common Reader: A Social History of the Mass Reading Public, 1800–1900*. Chicago: University of Chicago Press.

Armstrong, Isobel (1993) *Victorian Poetry: Poetry, Poetics, and Politics*. London and New York: Routledge.

Harrison, J. F. C. (1971) *The Early Victorians, 1832–1851.* London: Weidenfeld & Nicolson.

Hollingsworth, Keith (1963) *The Newgate Novel, 1830–1847: Bulwer, Ainsworth, Dickens, and Thackeray.* Detroit: Wayne State University Press.

Jordan, Robert Furneaux (1966) *Victorian Architecture.* Harmondsworth and Baltimore: Penguin Books.

Steegman, John (1950) *Victorian Taste: A Study of the Arts and Architecture from 1830 to 1870.* Originally published as *Consort of Taste.* Cambridge, MA: MIT Press, 1971.

Stein, Richard (1987) *Victoria's Year: English Literature and Culture, 1837–1838.* New York and Oxford: Oxford University Press.

Vicinus, Martha (1974) *The Industrial Muse: A Study of Nineteenth Century British Working-Class Literature.* New York: Barnes and Noble.

Webb, Robert K. (1955) *The English Working Class Reader, 1790–1848: Literacy and Social Tension.* London: Allen and Unwin.

2
1848
Antony H. Harrison

Revolution and Reform

Matthew Arnold's "Dover Beach" (ca. 1851) concludes with his speaker looking away from the chalk cliffs of England toward continental Europe and lamenting that

> . . . the world, which seems
> To lie before us like a land of dreams,
> So various, so beautiful, so new,
> Hath really neither joy, nor love, nor light,
> Nor certitude, nor peace, nor help for pain;
> And we are here as on a darkling plain
> Swept with confused alarms of struggle and flight,
> Where ignorant armies clash by night. (ll. 30–7)

The disturbing worldview presented here originated with tumultuous historical events that shattered the relative calm of Europe at mid-century. In the autumn of 1848 (some eight months after Marx's *Communist Manifesto* was issued in England), Arnold traveled to the Continent and witnessed the aftershocks of unprecedented political chaos. Revolutionary activity had rocked Sicily in January, Paris in late February, Germany and Italy in March. The fall of Austria's once powerful chancellor, Clemens Metternich, on March 13 had signalled political disintegration. In April hostilities had erupted between Germany and Poland. At the same time, Russia had prepared for war to preserve its hold on Poland.

By the spring of the following year, when Arnold once again traveled to Europe, matters had not improved. In March of 1849 Sardinia renewed its war against Austria, begun the previous year. On April 30, French forces clashed with Garibaldi's republican troops in Italy. In April, as well, Austrian and Hungarian forces became embattled, and in July Russian troops quashed revolutionary stirrings in Moldavia and

Wallachia (Taylor 4–34). During the years immediately after the European countries shaken by revolutionary turmoil became stabilized, the standoff between major powers, all eager to usurp territory or protect what they already possessed, dominated political discourse in Europe. The German provinces were at issue between Austria and Prussia; France desired more land along the Rhine; Italy rankled under the protection of Austria; and a conflict between Russia and Turkey in the Near East seemed inevitable. Eventually, after a series of stopgap treaties and protocols had failed, Britain and France declared war on Russia in February of 1854 and inaugurated the Crimean debacle (Taylor 24–70; McCord 1991: 244–9). These events are the political subtexts of "Dover Beach."

In England, too, throughout the 1840s (but especially during the early, economically depressed years known as the Hungry Forties), insurrection was feared by the middle and upper classes, and writers often expressed their apprehensions iconoclastically. The "condition of England" question, responses to which normally focused on the social effects of laissez-faire capitalism and on class conflict, dominated novels of the period such as Benjamin Disraeli's *Sybil; or The Two Nations* (1845), Charles Kingsley's *Yeast* (1848) and *Alton Locke* (1850), and Elizabeth Gaskell's *Mary Barton* (1848), as well as the work of popular poets and essayists. In "The Cry of the Human" (1842) Elizabeth Barrett decried "the plague of gold" that "strikes far and near" and its effects upon the human heart:

> Our thoughts grow blank, our words grow strange,
>   We cheer the pale gold-diggers,
> Each soul is worth so much on Change,
>   And marked, like sheep, with figures.

Thomas Carlyle was also concerned with the dehumanizing effects of industrial capitalism. Anticipating Arnold's strategy in "Dover Beach," in *Past and Present* (1843) he compared the Middle Ages, idealized as a period of political, social, and religious stability, to industrialized England and prophetically concluded:

> I well venture to believe that in no time, since the beginnings of Society, was the lot of [the] dumb millions of toilers so entirely unbearable as it is even in the days now passing over us. It is not to die, or even to die of hunger, that makes a man wretched; many men have died, all men must die. . . . But it is to live miserable we know not why; to work sore and yet gain nothing; to be heartworn, weary, yet isolated, unrelated, girt-in with a cold universal Laissez-faire: it is to die slowly all our life long, imprisoned in a deaf, dead, Infinite Injustice. . . . This is and remains for ever intolerable to all men whom God has made. Do we wonder at French Revolutions, Chartisms, Revolts of Three Days? The times, if we will consider them, are really unexampled. (Book 3, ch. 8)

Carlyle collapsed the manifold threats to the survival of the English nation into two essential and momentous problems: a lack of spiritual unity or brotherhood among men, and the invisibility of great leaders who were desperately needed to reform British society.

In her preface to *Mary Barton* (dated October, 1848) Mrs Gaskell expressed the conflicted feelings of sympathy and fear that often characterized the middle-class response to the condition of the working classes:

> If it be an error, that the woes, which come with ever-returning tide-like flood to overwhelm the workmen in our manufacturing towns, pass unregarded by all but the sufferers, it is at any rate an error so bitter in its consequences to all parties, that whatever public effort can do in the way of legislation, or private effort in the way of merciful deeds, or helpless love in the way of widow's mites, should be done, and that speedily, to disabuse the work-people of so miserable a misapprehension. At present they seem to me to be left in a state, wherein lamentations and tears are thrown aside as useless, but in which the lips are compressed for curses, and the hands clenched and ready to smite.

The general subject of Gaskell's novel is the rift between rich and poor, perhaps nowhere in England more apparent during the 1840s than in Manchester, where *Mary Barton* is set. Like many other social novels of the forties, this one attempts to raise middle-class consciousness that political insurrection resulting from social and economic conditions was a very real danger in England. To her publisher Gaskell acknowledged that her book was "such as to excite attention at the present time of the struggle on the part of work people to obtain what they esteem their rights" (March 21, 1848).

The living and working conditions of the lower classes, who at mid-century constituted some 70 percent of the British population (McCord 1991: 214–19), were examined not only by novelists and poets, but also in parliamentary blue books and by numerous essayists. Perhaps the most excruciating chronicles of working-class life emerged in Friedrich Engels's *The Condition of the Working Classes in England* (first published in Germany in 1845) and Henry Mayhew's *London Labour and the London Poor* (issued serially in 1851–2). Engels presents the first major study of the effects of industrialization on workers: the occupational diseases that afflicted them, the inadequacy of their diets, clothing, medical care and education, the dangers of their work in mines, mills, and factories, their victimization by the cycles of the marketplace, and the horrors of their living conditions. Typical are his descriptions of the working-class districts of north-eastern Manchester, an area where the "coal-black, stagnant, stinking" Medlock river divided two "disgusting" neighborhoods of 4,000 people inhabiting 400 dilapidated one-room cottages, these surrounded by "heaps of refuse, offal and sickening filth." Engels describes a neighborhood polluted by stench and thick factory smoke, an area where hordes of "ragged women and children swarm about the streets . . . just as dirty as the pigs which wallow" nearby. He concludes that this population has "sunk to the lowest level of humanity" imaginable and suggests that its members would have little to lose in an uprising against their oppressors (Engels

1958: 71). Mayhew's survey is less polemical and more systematic than Engels's. He lays "before the reader a catalogue of such occupations in London as yield a bare subsistence to the parties engaged in them," along with descriptions of "the dwellings of the unrelieved poor." In the process he exposes "not only on how little they subsist, but [also] . . . the rent they are charged for their waterless, drainless, floorless, and almost roofless tenements" and "calculate[s] the interest that the petty capitalist reaps from their necessities" (Mayhew 1985: xix). Despite his awareness that his subjects are victimized by the hegemony of laissez-faire economic values, Mayhew, unlike Engels, prescribes no course of political action for this "proletariat."

The condition of the working classes in England did result in numerous incidents of localized violence during the 1840s, but the extraordinary historical fact is that no large-scale revolutionary movement emerged. Indeed, despite the apprehensions of many in the middle and upper classes, others expressed confidence that all would be well. About the time of his second novel, *The Kellys and the O'Kellys*, published in 1848, Anthony Trollope insisted "that there is no ground to fear any general rising. . . . I think there is too much intelligence in England for any large body of men to look for any sudden improvement" (Trollope 1983 1: 17). Historians have offered various explanations for England's relative quiescence. G. M. Young's landmark conclusion is typical:

> The storm which swept away half the Governments of Europe passed harmlessly over the islands, and the words which Macaulay wrote at the beginning of his [*History of England from the Accession of James II* (vols. 1 and 2, 1848)], that his checkered narrative would excite thankfulness in all religious minds and hope in the breast of all patriots, had a deep significance for his first readers, watching the nations of Europe sink one by one from convulsive anarchy back into despotism, and seeing, in the recovered unity, as much as in the prosperity of England, a triumphant vindication of the historic English way. (Young 1936: 78)

"The historic English way" was, at the private level, the way of the stiff upper lip and muddling through; at the public level it was the way of constitutional monarchy. Well before 1848 clear evidence of legislative progress toward the amelioration of political, social, and economic ills afflicting "the lower orders" was visible. Moreover, attempts to organize workers and their supporters into a force that would have proved threatening to England's political and social stability had, by the close of 1848, proven ineffectual. The most prominent among these were the Chartist movement and the efforts of the Anti-Corn Law League.

In 1836 the radical William Lovett founded the London Working Men's Association, made up largely of self-educated artisans. Two years later he and the reformer Francis Place drew up a program for massive political reform detailed in the "People's Charter," a document ultimately submitted as a petition for Parliamentary action three times: in 1839, 1842, and 1848. Based in many respects on Benthamite reformist ideals, it supported "Six Points" of radical change: universal male suffrage, equal electoral districts, removal of property qualifications for members of Parliament, payment for MPs, a secret ballot, and annual general elections. The Chartists in 1838 established bases of operation in three major industrial cities (London, Birmingham, and Leeds) and organized large meetings of working people who were addressed by zealous speakers. The movement grew with impressive speed, and by the spring of 1839 at their National Convention the Chartists presented to Parliament a great petition with hundreds of thousands of signatures. The convention moved to Birmingham in May, but in July the House of Commons, despite localized strikes and riots, rejected the petition now boasting well over a million signatures. It did so for a second time in 1842 when the Charter was taken to Westminster from a preliminary mass meeting in Lincoln's Inn Fields. By the time of the Chartists' third (and final) attempt to move Parliament to action in April of 1848, tensions surrounding England's deep class divisions had reached an extraordinary pitch, especially in light of events on the Continent. Although the Whig government under the leadership of Lord John Russell was prepared for widespread insurrection and had banned mass demonstrations, some 50,000 Chartist supporters and observers gathered on Kensington Common. But 8,000 troops had been ordered up, in addition to more than 4,000 London policemen and a massive reserve force of special constables (which some commentators estimate at over 100,000). Thirty guns were held ready at the Tower of London, with steamers prepared to transport them to Parliament. The Chartists clearly faced overwhelming opposition, and once again Parliament could afford to be unresponsive. This was the case, however, in part because widespread support for the movement surfaced typically in times of economic hardship, and by 1848 England's economy was expanding toward prosperity.

In addition, many of the issues Chartists wanted addressed through direct and dramatic political change had already been dealt with through legislation enacted after the First Reform Act of 1832 had expanded the franchise. The list of subsequent measures designed to improve the working and living conditions of the "lower orders" is extensive. It includes the Poor Law Amendment Act of 1834 and later revisions of it; the reduction of tariffs on imported items (1842); Factory Acts of 1844 and 1848 that limited the number of hours women and children could work; the Town Improvement Clauses Act of 1847, which expedited implementation of measures for paving, draining, and lighting streets in British cities; the Public Health Act of 1848; and, as important as any of these pieces of legislation, the repeal of the Corn Laws in 1846.

Four years earlier, Elizabeth Barrett had lamented "The curse of gold upon the land" which "The lack of bread enforces." The people of England had suffered for decades from artifically high prices induced by laws which limited the quantities of grain that could be imported and which imposed high tariffs on such imports. No longer an agrarian green and pleasant land, England was a nation, according to Barrett, in which

> The rail-cars snort from strand to strand,
>   Like more of Death's White Horses.
> The rich preach "rights" and "future days,"
>   And hear no angel scoffing;
> The poor die mute, with starving gaze
>   On corn-ships in the offing. ("The Cry of the Human," 1842)

In the same year that Chartism emerged, the Anti-Corn Law League was formed. A wide and varied, politically savvy and well-funded constituency was soon brought together in a crusade against the protection of agricultural interests, most of them wealthy landowners. Despite the power of this landed opposition, the League was able to rout it within eight years.

Thus, by the time of the last Chartist demonstrations in 1848, bread was relatively cheap in England, working and living conditions for the poor were improving measurably, demand for English goods in foreign markets and at home was high, and wages were increasing accordingly. Britain was producing more than half the world's pig iron (and would treble her output during the next 30 years); her commercial steamships (and her navy) dominated the world's seas; within 20 years her foreign trade would be more than that of France, Germany, and Italy combined, and nearly four times that of the United States. England was heading toward a period of prosperity that was sustained for two decades and that was signaled by the opening on 1 May 1851 of the famous Crystal Palace international exhibition of new consumer goods and cutting-edge technologies, hailed by *The Times* as "a sight the like of which has never happened before, and which, in the nature of things, can never be repeated. . . . Some were most reminded of that day when all ages and climes shall be gathered round the throne of their Maker."

Unlike the rest of Europe, during the 1840s England had undergone no cataclysmic revolution but rather experienced a gradual movement toward higher standards of living sustained in subsequent decades and impelled by the ineluctable forces of industrial capitalism and legislative reform. "Progress" became the byword of the day (though the fact of it was often unperceived by many of the still-impoverished lower classes). Between 1851 and 1883 the national income was to double; real income per head to rise nearly 30 percent; and exports to increase 229 percent (Burn 1964: 16). Mid-century was a period of phenomenal growth based on technological advances and greater industrial efficiency. The pace of building – railroads, canals, bridges, factories, centers of government administration, warehouses, churches, and middle-class suburbs – was frenetic. Across the seas, Britain found ready markets for its goods, some of them in the expanding Empire. The policy of liberal imperialism established by Lord Durham's "Report on Canada" in 1839 was extended, as emigrants were directed to the most fertile of England's colonies. With the annexation of the Punjab in 1849, the dominion of the British over the vast riches and population of India was completed. In 1851, the discovery of gold at Ballarat in Australia resulted in large-scale immigration. And in 1854 New Zealand was granted self-government based on the

Canadian model; its population grew to a quarter of a million by 1870 (Thompson 1950: 168). These outposts of the Empire were unified by the inheritance of British political traditions and capitalist values.

Such values were registered in the predominantly realistic fiction produced by High Victorian novelists like Thackeray, Trollope, George Eliot, Hardy, and George Meredith, where money and financial problems are dominant issues that often provide the basis for plots. The work of these writers was readily embraced by bourgeois audiences, whose interest in their own progress toward financial prosperity and enhanced social status was boundless. The approach of such readers to getting on in the world emerges toward the end of *David Copperfield* (1850). Dickens's hero attributes his successes to a set of "golden rules" that Oscar Wilde at the close of the century would lampoon as quintessentially Victorian. David explains that "whatever I have tried to do in life, I have tried with all my heart to do well . . . whatever I have devoted myself to, I have devoted myself to completely. . . . [T]here is no substitute for thorough-going, ardent, and sincere earnestness" (chapter 42).

Matthew Arnold, an indisputably earnest Victorian, writing to his close friend Arthur Hugh Clough in September of 1849, showed less concern with the situation of the working classes in England than with the plight of middle-class men like himself, living in a "modern" society defined by ambition, greed, "sick hurry," and "divided aims." "These are damned times," he sputtered,

> everything is against one – the height to which knowledge is come, the spread of luxury, our physical enervation, the absence of great *natures*, the unavoidable contact with millions of small ones, newspapers, cities, light profligate friends, moral desperadoes like Carlyle, our own selves, and the sickening consciousness of our difficulties. (September 23, 1849)

The destabilizing "difficulties" that afflicted middle-class consciousness at mid-century were not exclusively social and political: they involved moral, religious, aesthetic and gender issues as well. In public fora and in their own hearts, mid-Victorians were often preoccupied with questions surrounding religious faith, men's and women's roles in and outside of the home, and the moral and social ramifications of aesthetic values.

Religion

Although what may have been the most important book of the century, Darwin's *The Origin of Species*, did not appear until 1859, the unparalleled controversy that its publication provoked was merely an extension of heated public and private debates about religious values and practices that had preoccupied Victorians since the 1830s. Charles Lyell's 1,600-page tome *The Principles of Geology* (1833) anticipated the theories of Darwin and inspired many thinking men and women, including Alfred

Tennyson, to examine evolution as a serious challenge to the biblical story of creation and therefore as a threat to religious orthodoxies grounded in a literal acceptance of the Bible. New scientific theories and discoveries, along with the breathtaking velocity of technological advance, appeared to many observers evidence of an increasing cultural emphasis on secular matters that threatened traditional religious belief. The expanding dominion of scientific inquiry was demonstrated by the opening of honours schools in natural science at Cambridge in 1848 and at Oxford four years later, while the marvels of new technology were both exhibited and embodied in the "Great Exhibition of the Works of Industry of All Nations." The Crystal Palace, Joseph Paxton's architectural masterpiece of prefabricated iron and glass, remained open for six months in 1851. Britain and its colonies dominated the 13,000 exhibits of raw materials, machinery, fine arts, and manufactures which included huge marine engines, locomotives, hydraulic presses, newly designed reapers, and a telegraph connected with Edinburgh and Manchester.

Some felt that religious faith was endangered not just by such developments in science and in the world of getting and spending. Eighteen years before the Great Exhibition, a group of conservative Oxford clerics and teachers identified fundamental threats to religious orthodoxy that had emerged within the Anglican Church itself, which they believed had strayed from firm belief, adherence to traditional rituals, and its true origins in Catholicism. In 1833 John Henry Newman joined forces with Richard Hurrell Froude and John Keble in a profoundly controversial attempt to reform the Church that soon came to be known as the Oxford Movement. Later joined by Edward Pusey, these educators over the course of eight years published a series of *Tracts for the Times* that attacked rationalism and liberal theology, asserted the necessity of the visible Church as the vehicle of invisible grace, and reemphasized the importance of the sacraments and Church ritual. According to the liberal-minded Thomas Arnold (the poet's father), these men's "intense love for the forms of the Church . . . absolutely engrossed their whole nature" (Arnold 1833: 82). When Newman converted to Catholicism in 1845, the public debate spawned by Tractarian teachings and writings intensified in some quarters, and it remained widespread and enduring. But by the 1840s "what was at issue was no longer the validity of Anglican orders, but for an increasing number of thinking people the validity of Christianity itself" (Gilmour 1993: 86). Discussion of religious issues continued in a variety of fora, including the novel. Newman's own *Loss and Gain* appeared in 1848, while James Anthony Froude's *The Nemesis of Faith*, in which his religious uncertainties and anti-Tractarian bias surfaced, was published the following year. Even during the 1850s controversy over vitriolic sermons delivered by conservative clergymen who were scions of the Oxford Movement caused riots outside London churches. At the other end of the spectrum, the publication in 1860 of *Essays and Reviews*, written by six Broad Church clergymen and one layman on a variety of sensitive religious topics, ignited a furor nearly as explosive as that caused by the Tractarians. (Two of the contributors were prosecuted for heresy.) The volume attacked biblical literalism in light of recent scientific discoveries, while it questioned the divine inspiration of the scriptures and the validity of events described as miracles in the New Testament. Its authors also insisted that the true bond among members of the Church as a national institution was morality rather than dogma. They demanded that scripture and dogma both be understood relativistically, in terms of the historical contexts out of which they emerged.

The controversies surrounding Tractarianism and the publication of *Essays and Reviews*, like the debate over evolution, were explosive because the questions they raised left little cover for an uneasiness about religious faith already deeply felt by many educated people groping for direction in a world destabilized by the vertiginous effects of industrialism and the new science on social and moral values. The poet Arthur Hugh Clough situates himself at the skeptical end of the spectrum in works like "The New Sinai" (1844):

> Lo, here is God, and there is God!
>   Believe it not, O Man;
> In such vain sort to this and that
>   The ancient heathen ran:
> Though Old Religion shake her head,
>   And say in bitter grief,
> The day behold, at first foretold,
>   Of atheist unbelief:
> Take better part, with manly heart,
>   Thine adult spirit can;
> Receive it not, believe it not,
>   Believe it not, O Man!

Clough's attacks on orthodoxy were relentless. In "Easter Day: Naples, 1849," he attempts once more to expose the hollowness of faith on the most sacred of Christian holidays:

> My heart was hot within me; till at last
>   My brain was lightened when my tongue had said
>   Christ is not risen!
>   Christ is not risen, no —
>   He lies and moulders low.

(Presumably, the pun on "lies" is deliberate.) Clough's friend Matthew Arnold appears equally unorthodox. Though not an atheist, in poems like "To Marguerite: Continued" written around 1848, Arnold scoffs at the Christian illusion of a benevolent deity. In his view, a contrast to John Donne's, all individuals are, metaphorically, islands afflicted by a futile craving for reunion with their fellows in a continental humanity.

> Who order'd that their longing's fire
> Should be, as soon as kindled, cool'd?
> Who renders vain their deep desire? –
>   A God, a God their severance rul'd;
> And bade betwixt their shores to be
> The unplumb'd, salt, estranging sea.

This malevolent God designed human life as an exercise in sadism:

>   For, alas! he left us each retaining
> Shreds of gifts which he refus'd in full.
> Still these waste us with their hopeless straining –
> Still the attempt to use them proves them null. ("Self-Deception," 1852)

The profoundly frustrating result, for Arnold, is that "on earth we wander, groping, reeling."

Alfred Tennyson appears similarly disoriented in his search for a solid ground of faith in the early stanzas of his great poem *In Memoriam* (1850), a spiritual autobiography occasioned by the death of his intimate friend, Arthur Henry Hallam. This extraordinary elegy is composed of 131 lyrics of varying lengths written between 1833 and 1849. After enduring a period of virtual nihilism chronicled in the first quarter of the work, Tennyson describes his attempts to embrace traditional, consolatory Christian notions of resurrection and the afterlife, but these repeatedly fail him. Acknowledging the evidence of what Darwin was later to term natural selection ("finding that of fifty seeds," nature "often brings but one to bear"), Tennyson laments in poem 55,

> I falter where I firmly trod,
>   And falling with my weight of cares
>   Upon the great world's altar-stairs
> That slope thro' darkness up to God,
>
> I stretch lame hands of faith, and grope,
>   And gather dust and chaff.

Allusions to pre-Darwinian theories of evolution derived from geological treatises (Lyell's in particular) constitute the metaphorical strata of this poem. By its conclusion, however, a unique variety of faith has indeed evolved from the extensive process of epistemological and teleological interrogation enacted in the work. In poem 124, Tennyson can confidently announce his discovery of the *telos*,

> That which we dare invoke to bless;
>   Our dearest faith, our ghastliest doubt;
>   He, They, One, All, within, without;
> The Power in darkness whom we guess.

And with this discovery emerges a perfectibilian view of the future of mankind grounded in his agonized spiritual experience, the dark night of the soul which his friend Hallam's death has precipitated: "I dream a dream of good, / And mingle all the world with thee" (poem 128). The final lines of *In Memoriam* direct readers, with assured, apocalyptic optimism, to

> That God, which ever lives and loves,
>   One God, one law, one element,
>   And one far-off divine event,
> To which the whole creation moves.

Balanced against the outright skepticism of the Cloughs and Arnolds of mid-Victorian England, and the waverings of the Froudes and Tennysons, is the fervor of religious conviction in works written by the literary heirs of the Oxford Movement. In 1847 Charlotte Mary Yonge, who was tutored in Anglican history and theology by John Keble, published *Scenes and Characters*, an early novel that depicts life in a scrupulously Anglican household. In the same year Christina Rossetti, "the true inheritor of the Tractarian devotional mode in poetry" (Tennyson 198), began her career with the (private) printing of her first volume, simply entitled *Verses*. The intense piety of Rossetti's five subsequent books of poetry and five volumes of devotional prose typifies one important stance in the religious debates of the day. Her embrace of orthodoxy in "Sweet Death" (written in 1849) counters the *agon* of uncertainty that dominates the first half of *In Memoriam* (completed the same year). Repudiation of this world's vanities and resignation to the will of the Almighty are recurrent themes of Rossetti's work, as they are in this brief lyric, which concludes,

> . . . youth and beauty die.
>   So be it, O my God, thou God of truth:
>   Better than beauty and than youth
> Are Saints and Angels, a glad company;
>   And Thou, O Lord, our Rest and Ease,
>   Are better far than these.

Despite the apparent simplicity, in such verses, of Rossetti's ostensibly unobjectionable religious faith, her awareness of its controversial political ramifications emerges in an elegiac sonnet on John Henry Newman (who died in 1890). There she describes the leader of the Oxford Movement as a "Champion of the Cross" whose "tides were springtides, set against the neap / Of calmer souls." Unflinchingly, she asserts that his "flood rebuked their rill."

The Woman Question

Many of Christina Rossetti's nondevotional poems appear to modern readers distinctly less conservative than her religious works, intervening as they do in the mid-century controversy over women's social roles. Though she would, in the 1870s, decline an invitation from Augusta Webster to sign a petition for women's suffrage, much of Rossetti's work of the fifties and sixties in fact presents a critique of amatory relationships, the institution of marriage, or Victorian domestic values and practices and thus aligns itself with liberal and even radical commentaries on "The Woman Question" which began to emerge in the 1840s.

The Women of England: Their Social Duties and Domestic Habits, a best-seller by Sarah Stickney Ellis published in 1839, defines what is now known as the "domestic ideology," a widely accepted conservative theory of social roles and "separate spheres" of activity for Victorian middle-class men and women. According to this ideology as Ellis formulates it, "to men belongs the potent . . . consideration of worldly aggrandizement." They operate in the professions, governmental services, and the world of business and industry to acquire property, advance themselves, and improve the material condition of their wives and families. The world in which they move is seen to be dominated by "inborn selfishness," temptation, and vice. Women, by contrast ensconced in the domestic sphere, are understood to be "clothed in moral beauty" – selfless, disinterested, and spiritually pure by "nature." They are protected against worldly evils and possess a "secret [moral] influence" that can correct men's missteps. Ellis and like-minded thinkers (including the writers of ubiquitous conduct and childrearing manuals during the 1840s) assumed that a woman's goal in life was marriage and her vocation to bear and raise children. Coventry Patmore presents an idolatrous version of this cultural myth in his famous poem *The Angel in the House* (1854–62). The education of girls (satirized by Elizabeth Barrett Browning in the second book of her 1856 epic novel/poem *Aurora Leigh*) was therefore focused on "the minutiae of domestic comfort" (Ellis's phrase). In their capacity as domestic saints, English women could claim an "importance in society far beyond what their unobtrusive virtues would appear to claim." Ellis goes so far as to attribute the greatest accomplishments of the men of her nation to the "moral greatness" of its women (Ellis 1839: 70–3).

In the 1840s and 1850s this view of gender roles began to come under fire by liberal thinkers, in part because demographic realities prevented many women from living out a myth which by mid-century had ideologically subjugated the middle classes and in part because the widespread acceptance of that myth continued to deprive women of legal, economic, and political rights. Middle-class women had little choice but to aspire to marry, since work outside the domestic arena was generally considered unrespectable. The 1851 census lists only 7 percent of middle-class women as working, most of these as governesses, writers, or artists, and only 3 percent owning businesses or managing farms (Helsinger et al. 1989 2: 134). But because women outnumbered men in the population at large and because older men tended to marry younger women, in that same census only 57 percent of women over 20 are listed as married. Thus, nearly half had no spouse to support them and were considered "redundant," a term first used in this context by John Ruskin (ibid. 2: 135).

We see early reaction against the limited rights, social roles, and education of women in works from the 1840s such as Tennyson's long poem *The Princess* and Charlotte Brontë's *Jane Eyre*, both published in 1847. While Jane Eyre rankles against the limitations of female education and constrained roles for women, Princess Ida, the central character in Tennyson's poem, formulates these problems in more abstract terms, insisting that "The woman's cause is man's; they rise or sink / Together": "If she be small, slight-natured, miserable, / How shall men grow?" Ida insists that if "the parasitic forms / That seem to keep [woman] up but drag her down" are cleared away, "Then comes the statelier Eden back" (Part 7: 243–77).

Until this period, married women of the middle and upper classes had been defined legally (by the doctrine of coverture) as objects rather than subjects with rights; a husband was responsible for his wife's actions, and he controlled her property. By mid-century, however, a number of Victorian men and women had begun the effort to remove obstacles to women's equality and advancement. Unmarried women of these classes were traditionally dependents (of their fathers or brothers). Caroline Norton, whose husband had unreasonably deprived her of access to her children, was instrumental in the passage of the Infants and Child Custody Bill of 1839. Writers like Norton, Harriet Martineau, Barbara Leigh Smith Bodichon, and Bessie Rayner Parkes influenced parliamentary debates throughout the 1850s. Norton and Bodichon played special roles in promoting the Matrimonial Causes Act of 1857, which empowered the courts to order payment of a maintenance to a wife separated from her husband and recovered a married woman's "rights to inherit or bequeath her own property, to enter into contracts, and to sue or be sued as if she were single." The petition to Parliament sponsored by Bodichon after her pamphlet *The Most Important Laws Concerning Women* appeared in 1854 garnered 26,000 signatures, including those of Jane Carlyle, Elizabeth Gaskell, Geraldine Jewsbury, Harriet Martineau, and Bessie Rayner Parkes (Helsinger et al. 1989 2: 14–17). Male writers also played an important role in raising the Woman Question and bringing to the attention of middle-class readers oppressive inequities in the legal and social treatment of women. In 1849 the *Morning Chronicle* published William Acton's interviews with London seamstresses turned-prostitutes, in an effort to dispel common stereotypes of the prostitute as an evil temptress rather than a social victim. Five years later George Drysdale countered studies of female sexuality that reinforced popular stereotypes of the "sexless" Angel in the House. In *The Elements of Social Science* he presented a thorough and systematic defense of women's sexual equality. And Acton's 1857 book on prostitution attempted to "convince doctors and administrators of the need for a more rational, 'humane' attitude" toward prostitutes (Helsinger et al. 1989 2: 57, 152–6), much like that espoused by the speaker in Dante Rossetti's poem "Jenny" (first drafted in 1848), which concludes with a commitment to "strive to clear" the "dark path" of middle-class misconceptions about these social outcasts.

Revolutionary Art

Though not truly a social revolutionary, Rossetti, a painter as well as a poet, was nonetheless instrumental in forwarding what by the end of the century could be seen as a virtual revolution in Victorian taste and aesthetic values. In 1848 he along with his brother William Michael Rossetti and fellow artists William Holman Hunt, John Everett Millais, Thomas Woolner, James Collinson, and Frederick George Stephens established the Pre-Raphaelite Brotherhood. The goal of these young men was to challenge the stodgy (that is, neoclassical and Platonic) tenets of Royal Academy painting. John Ruskin approvingly ascribed the "schism" they caused in the art world to their "assertion that the principles on which art has been taught for these three hundred years back are essentially wrong" (Sambrook 1974: 92).

The work of the Pre-Raphaelite painters can be seen as quintessentially, and some might say paradoxically, mid-Victorian. They looked to the medieval era and early Renaissance for models of artistic "sincerity" and "naturalism" (fidelity to the details of the real world) as means to avoid the formalism and artificiality of contemporary painting. Their emphasis on the expressive value of art, on technical accuracy and on coloring inaugurated the values of aestheticism and the avant-garde that came to dominate pictorial art as well as literature by the end of the century. Their goal was not only "*épater le bourgeois*," but also ultimately to reform tastes. Thus, like Carlyle, Ruskin, and Arnold, along with members of the Oxford Movement and many novelists of the period, they sought out models of value and behavior from the past (especially the medieval past) that might serve the future. And, like the work of such commentators, their critique of the status quo helped to bring about change. In 1854, the year after the Brotherhood disbanded, Ruskin could observe that the Pre-Raphaelites had been "opposed with all the influence and all the bitterness of art and criticism." Yet their "heresy" had "gained ground, and the pictures painted on these new principles [had] obtained a most extensive popularity" (ibid.). The Brothers even founded a journal to propound their new dogma, *The Germ: Thoughts Toward Nature in Poetry, Literature and Art*. It survived for only four issues, all published in 1850, but is the forerunner of the many avant-garde magazines that began to proliferate in the 1890s. By the 1860s and 1870s Millais, Hunt, and Rossetti were three of the most admired and sought after painters in England, and their works fetched huge sums. The weapons they employed in the gradual "revolution" they accomplished, with a good deal of help from prominent cultural critics like Ruskin, were ideological. This fact is underscored by the raging controversies generated by the work of poets writing during the second phase of Pre-Raphaelite activity, Rossetti, William Morris, A. C. Swinburne, and Christina Rossetti. Rossetti's *Poems* (1870) and Swinburne's *Poems and Ballads, First Series* (1866) especially were viewed by puritanical reviewers as disturbingly "fleshly" and subversive. The later socialist writings of William Morris were similarly worrisome to many commentators. But by the eighties and nineties these men were often idolized, and their style, aesthetic values, and liberalism (both moral and political) were widely emulated.

The success of Pre-Raphaelitism, a movement for reform that at first met with intense opposition but whose values and principles eventually became appropriated by the culture it challenged, might be seen as a paradigm of ideological change in mid-Victorian England. While Chartism, the Anti-Corn Law League, and legislation to improve the working and living conditions of England's poor were all hotly opposed when they emerged in the political arena, by the 1860s Britain was moving inexorably toward expansion of the franchise, toward increased intervention by government in the lives of its people, and eventually toward a welfare state. Similarly, the controversial challenges posed by the Oxford Movement thinkers on the right and proponents of extended rights for women on the left brought about greater tolerance, cultural diversity, and freedom of action for all people. The mid-century years of revolution in Europe, though not a period of widespread violent insurrection in Britain, were thus pivotal in the political and social transformation of this first industrial nation, as the chronicle of change during the second half of the century demonstrates.

See also SEXUALITIES; CLERICAL, INDUSTRIAL, COMMERCIAL; FICTION; SHORE

REFERENCES

Arnold, Thomas (1833) *Principles of Church Reform*. London: B. Fellowes.

Burn, W. L. (1964) *The Age of Equipoise: A Study of the Mid-Victorian Generation*. London: George Allen and Unwin.

Ellis, Sarah Stickney (1839) *The Women of England: Their Social Duties and Domestic Habits*. London: Fisher and Son.

Engels, Friedrich (1958) *The Condition of the Working Classes in England*. Oxford: Basil Blackwell.

Gaskell, Elizabeth Cleghorn (1967) *The Letters of Mrs Gaskell*, ed. J. A. V. Chapple and Arthur Pollard. Cambridge, MA: Harvard University Press.

Gilmour, Robin (1993) *The Victorian Period: The Intellectual and Cultural Context of English Literature, 1830–1890*. Harlow: Longman.

Helsinger, Elizabeth K., Sheets, Robin Lauterbach, and Veeder, William (eds) (1989) *The Woman Question: Society and Literature in Britain and America, 1837–1883*. Chicago: University of Chicago Press.

Mayhew, Henry (1985) *London Labour and the London Poor*. Harmondsworth: Penguin Books.

McCord, Norman (1991) *British History: 1815–1906*. Oxford: Oxford University Press.

Sambrook, James (ed.) (1974) *Pre-Raphaelitism: A Collection of Critical Essays*, Chicago: University of Chicago Press.

Tennyson, G. B. (1981) *Victorian Devotional Poetry: The Tractarian Mode*. Cambridge, MA: Harvard University Press.

Thompson, David (1950) *England in the Nineteenth Century (1815–1914)*. Harmondsworth: Penguin Books.

Trollope, Anthony (1983) *The Letters of Anthony Trollope*, 2 vols, ed. N. John Hall. Stanford: Stanford University Press.

Young, G. M. (1936) *Victorian England: Portrait of an Age*. Oxford: Oxford University Press.

FURTHER READING

Armstrong, Isobel (1993) *Victorian Poetry: Poetry, Poetics and Politics*. London: Routledge.

Baker, Joseph Ellis (1932) *The Novel and the Oxford Movement*. Princeton: Princeton University Press.

Bodenheimer, Rosemarie (1988) *The Politics of Story in Victorian Social Fiction*. Ithaca, NY: Cornell University Press.

Cockshutt, A. O. J. (ed.) (1966) *Religious Controversies of the Nineteenth Century: Selected Documents*. Lincoln: University of Nebraska Press.

Dawson, Carl (1979) *Victorian Noon: English Literature in 1850*. Baltimore: Johns Hopkins University Press.

Erickson, Lee (1996) *The Economy of Literary Form: English Literature and the Industrialization of Publishing, 1800–1850*. Baltimore: Johns Hopkins University Press.

Ford, Boris (1989) *Victorian Britain* (The Cambridge Cultural History of Britain, vol. 7). Cambridge: Cambridge University Press.

Gallagher, Catherine (1985) *The Industrial Reformation of English Fiction, 1832–1867*. Chicago: University of Chicago Press.

Houghton, Walter E. (1957) *The Victorian Frame of Mind*. New Haven, CT: Yale University Press.

Mason, Michael (1995) *The Making of Victorian Sexuality*. Oxford: Oxford University Press.

Morse, David (1993) *High Victorian Culture*. New York: New York University Press.

Paz, D. G. (ed.) (1995) *Nineteenth-Century Religious Traditions: Retrospect and Prospect*. Westport, CT: Greenwood.

Reardon, Bernard M. G. (1995) *Religious Thought in the Victorian Age: A Survey from Coleridge to Gore*. London: Longman.

Richards, Bernard (1988) *English Poetry of the Victorian Period, 1830–1890*. Harlow: Longman.

Schroeder, Paul W. (1994) *The Transformation of European Politics, 1763–1848*. Oxford: Clarendon Press.

Tillotson, Kathleen (1953) *Novels of the Eighteen-Forties*. Oxford: Oxford University Press.

Vicinus, Martha (1974) *The Industrial Muse: A Study of Nineteenth Century British Working-Class Literature*. New York: Barnes and Noble.

Williams, Raymond (1958) *Culture and Society*. London: Chatto and Windus.

3

1870

Linda K. Hughes

"Our age, by virtue of its very artificiality and scientific culture," the *British Quarterly Review* pronounced in 1870, "is so far unfitted to catch the significance of life in its broadest and most individual aspects. Its self-consciousness makes it as unable to receive and accept [the] highest and most unconscious art as it is to produce it" (51 [1870]: 203). The pronouncement is less compelling as criticism than as evidence of mid-Victorian legacies coexisting with an underlying shift toward modernity in 1870. If the review echoed Carlyle's attack on self-consciousness dating back to 1831 (in "Characteristics"), it also attested to the new preeminence of science and to the writer's anxiety that culture was being constructed on such new lines that its general outlines could no longer be surveyed.

Social historian Jose Harris in fact argues that the 1870s and 1880s, more than World War I, mark the crucial turning point between one era and another. The 1870 Forster Education Act, for example, established elementary education for the masses, helping usher in an era of mass (print) media and mass leisure, both of which had profound implications for British literary production. The point is clear in George Gissing's *New Grub Street* (1891) when Whelpdale, a failed author but aspiring literary entrepreneur of the 1880s, creates a mass-circulation paper addressed to "the quarter-educated, that is to say, the great new generation that is being turned out by the Board schools" (ch. 33). Though it seems no more possible now than in 1870 to articulate a model of unified culture in that year, this chapter looks in turn at a number of cultural formations that derived from early- and mid-Victorian assumptions but paradoxically helped precipitate a society that differed from earlier eras in fundamental ways.

Legislation of Social Change: 1867 and 1870

Passage of the Forster Education Act, which mandated schooling for all children five to twelve years old within their districts under the oversight of Inspectors and School

Boards, was inseparable from the Second Reform Bill of 1867; MPs voting on the Education Act in 1870 were elected by those enfranchised in 1867. A reform bill had been introduced by William Gladstone, Chancellor of the Exchequer in the Liberal cabinet of Lord John Russell, in March 1866 but never won passage because the Liberal government first fell over a technicality (its proposal that the borough franchise be based on rents, not rates). The Conservative government headed by the Earl of Derby and relying on Benjamin Disraeli to orchestrate legislation in the Commons passed the 1867 bill, which admitted more than three times as many voters to the franchise as that proposed by Gladstone in 1866 (see Cowling 1967).

As in 1832 and 1848, political debate over reform aroused conflicting voices and public agitations. Committed to leadership by divinely inspired men, Thomas Carlyle thundered against the reform measure, which he termed "The calling in of new supplies of blockheadism, gullibility, bribeability, amenability to beer and balder-dash," in the August 1867 *Macmillan's Magazine*. Carlyle's fears of catastrophe were implicit in his title: "Shooting Niagara – And After?" In contrast, the *Annual Register* recorded demonstrations in support of the bill in Trafalgar Square (attended by 10,000), Guildhall, Manchester, Leeds, Glasgow, Edinburgh, and London. But support became notorious in the Hyde Park Riot on July 23, 1866, when demonstrators thwarted by police from entering the park tore down the railings. This incident became the referent for "anarchy" in Matthew Arnold's *Culture and Anarchy* (1869), which also played a crucial role in the education debates leading to the Forster Act. Arnold's title was a kind of rhetorical agitation (Dowling 1996: 1), considering that the Hyde Park Riot inspired less fear of anarchy than had the Chartist demonstrations of 1848. By mid-August 1867 the Second Reform Bill was law, Carlyle ceased to comment on English politics, and Arnold lectured on their implications for culture.

The bill enfranchised male heads of households who paid rates (taxes) directly, thus including some lodgers as well. The bill effectively doubled the number of voters in England and, when Reform Bills were enacted for Ireland and Scotland in 1868, extended the voting rolls there, if less dramatically. But legislators were not legislating democracy so much as extending prior law. As Harris remarks, "The admission to the constitution of urban male householders who paid their own rates was very deliberately designed to maintain that ancient tradition of a limited polity of independent freemen, and to exclude those deemed incapable of political and economic independence (women, lunatics, agricultural labourers, and the 'residuum' of the casual poor)" (Harris 1994: 14). But when an 1873 Act provided for "compounding," allocating the vote to those who paid rates indirectly in the form of rents owed to absentee landlords, even slum residents acquired the vote; and the traditional link between property and political power was broken, with permanent and pervasive results.

Though most English-language readers were unaware of the fact, Karl Marx's *Das Kapital* was published the same year the Second Reform Bill was adopted, Marx himself having moved to London in 1849 after being tried for treason, acquitted, then expelled from Prussia following the 1848 revolution. At the time of the Reform Bill he was living in Soho, serving as unofficial leader of the International Workingmen's Association (1864–72) (Hobsbawm 1975: 110–11). His works began to be published in English in the later 1870s and 1880s, and his daughter Eleanor contributed to the pages of *Commonweal* edited by William Morris (1886–90), who with Ernest Belfort Bax also summarized Marx's doctrine in a *Commonweal* series entitled *Socialism from the Roots Up* (1886–8). In 1867 socialist organizations such as the Social Democratic Federation and the Fabian Society, both founded in 1884, were almost two decades away, but the last quarter of the century is generally identified as an era of increasing class consciousness. In 1867 and after, moreover, male workers had access (not always exercised) to direct political participation, with universal male suffrage legislated in 1918.

Workers also soon had wider access to education. In the first election held after passage of the Second Reform Bill, in late 1868, voters returned the Liberal Party to power, and Gladstone became prime minister for the first time. This Parliament ratified the Education Act named after W. E. Forster, Vice-President of the Committee of Council on Education (who then became a member of Gladstone's cabinet), in August 1870. Though the effects of this legislation would not be felt until additional schools were built and a bureaucracy established, henceforth Great Britain had in place one of the givens of late capitalist culture, a literate and universally educated populace with the requisite skills to sustain mass production, innovation, and consumption. Still, the major thrust of this reform was to educate the masses for democratic responsibility as informed citizens, an ideal based more on classical Republicanism familiar to Oxbridge-educated MPs than on systematic socioeconomic planning. And, as Harris (1994) suggests, because study of the Bible was admitted while specifically sectarian teaching was excluded from schools, one effect of the Education Act may have been to promote vaguely defined religious sensibility just when traditional Christian belief was under siege from the Higher Criticism and alternative cosmologies provided by science (ibid.: 191, 178). The legislation had literary implications as well: henceforth stories such as those of David Copperfield exiled from learning while working at the blacking factory, or of Jo the crossing sweeper in *Bleak House* (1853), would be less imaginable than in mid-Victorian England. In effect the Education Act lengthened working-class childhoods by postponing employment – though the possibility of cruelty and humiliation at school, as in *Nicholas Nickleby* (1839), continued. In a one-room schoolhouse in the Fens, Kate Mary Edwards was forced in the 1880s to perform the work of a maid for the teachers and commented later, "Teachers in them days . . . must have despised us all as poor, ignorant creatures of a different sort from theirselves, and treated us more like animals than child'en" (Murray 1982: 250–1).

Women, Reform, and Sexuality

In the midst of debate over the Second Reform Bill, J. S. Mill, then an MP for Westminster, proposed an amendment that gave women the vote: it was quickly rejected, though Mill's public interventions on behalf of women's rights continued with *The Subjection of Women*, published in 1869. Legislation in 1870 was more favorable to women's interests, though leaving intact fundamental gender inequities. At the time of Victoria's ascension married women had no legal rights regarding their offspring. When writer Caroline Norton left her husband on the grounds of cruelty, she lost legal access to her children, and in consequence campaigned for legislation that resulted in the Infants Custody Act of 1839. Nor did married women have rights to their own property under the principle of coverture – the absorption of the wife's identity into her husband's subsequent to marriage – unless separate property was settled on the woman at the time of marriage, a practice confined to the wealthy because of legal fees. Even in a happy marriage like that of Elizabeth and William Gaskell the novelist records in one of her letters her husband pocketing the cheque paid out for "Lizzie Leigh." For a woman like Norton the implications were severe: her public letter to the queen in 1855 revealed that the husband from whom she was alienated subpoenaed her publishers to claim her royalties and was legally entitled to her copyrights (Helsinger et al. 1983 2: 15–16). The 1857 Divorce Bill remedied this situation, giving women legally separated from their husbands sole right to subsequent earnings (though under the same bill women had to prove adultery plus desertion, cruelty, or bigamy to obtain a divorce, men merely a single act of a wife's adultery). A bill giving all married women these property rights failed in 1857.

The Married Women's Property Act of 1870 grew out of efforts by a group of Manchester feminists aided by the Social Science Association (founded in 1857) and their allies in Parliament. Though feminists hoped for legislation that gave women the same property rights enjoyed by men, the 1870 Act granted only that all wives (the poor as well as the wealthy) had rights to "separate property" comprised of their earnings, investments, and some legacies acquired after marriage. Even this bill might not have passed without the new legislative body returned after the 1867 Reform Bill. Not until the Married Women's Property Act of 1882, which Mary Shanley terms "arguably the single most important change in the legal status of women in the nineteenth century" (Shanley 1989: 103), did wives have rights to their property acquired before *and* during marriage, as well as rights and liabilities related to suits and torts. Even in 1882, however, legislation refrained from acknowledging wives' equal identity before the law.

If women's property rights were inseparable from the 1867 Reform Bill, women's social position was intimately connected to educational reform. After losing the battle for property rights in 1857, Barbara Leigh Smith Bodichon and other members of the Langham Place Circle in London focused on education and employment opportunities; Elizabeth Wolstenholme and Josephine Butler, crucial organizers for legislation affecting women in the 1870s and 1880s, helped form the North of England Council for Promoting the Higher Education of Women in 1867. Girton College was founded in 1869 by Bodichon and Emily Davies, Newnham College in 1871 by Henry Sidgwick and Anna Jemima Clough (sister to poet Arthur Hugh Clough). Though women could not take degrees at Cambridge, those at Girton took the same examinations as male students; both Girton and Newnham, moreover, provided a site for women's community and independent living (Vicinus 1985: 121–62). The colleges also produced such alumnae as poet Amy Levy (1861–89), the first Jewish student to attend Newnham.

Burgeoning openings for elementary schoolteachers following the 1870 Education Act provided new employment opportunities for women; women could also vote and run for membership on the school boards established by the 1870 Act, children's education being considered part of women's assigned sphere (Harris 1994: 25, 191). In 1870 Lydia Becker, who founded the *Women's Suffrage Journal* the same year, was elected to the Manchester School Board, while Emily Davies and Elizabeth Garrett Anderson were elected to school boards in London (Young 1953: 179). Augusta Webster, whose important collection of dramatic monologues *Portraits* was published in 1870, was elected a member of the London School Board from Chelsea in 1879 (Boos 1985: 283). As mention of Becker's journal indicates, suffrage was by no means a moribund issue in the 1870s even though it failed to secure parliamentary ratification. The 1869 Municipal Corporations Act restored to single rate-paying women the right they had had until 1835 to vote in local government elections (Harris 1994: 190). And an 1870 suffrage bill actually carried a majority in the House on its second reading – until Gladstone announced his opposition and the bill died (Shanley 1989: 109–10).

A last crucial focus of feminist activism in 1870 concerned the Contagious Diseases Acts (see Walkowitz 1980). Acts passed in 1864, 1866, and 1869 mandated compulsory genital inspection for venereal disease in suspected prostitutes and detention in lock hospitals for infected women. The legislation originated in concerns with sanitation (the focus of Florence Nightingale's reforms during the Crimean War) and the spread of venereal disease among enlisted men in military garrisons and ports. But men were neither inspected nor penalized, in part because, as military leaders insisted, enforced genital inspection of men was humiliating and lowered morale. Since fallen women were already shamed, it was reasoned, no harm was done to them. An 1867 proposal to extend the CD Acts from military garrisons to civilian precincts ignited repeal efforts, first among male political liberals (who initially excluded women from the National Association for the Repeal of the Contagious Diseases Acts) and then among the Ladies' National Association (formed December 1869) under the leadership of Josephine Butler.

"The Ladies' Appeal and Protest Against the Contagious Diseases Acts" was published in the March 14, 1870 *Shield* (reprinted in Murray 1982: 428–32), the official journal of the National Association. This declaration opposed the CD Acts on grounds that they violated women's civil rights, intruded monstrously on privacy (Butler spoke in public about "instrumental rape"), ratified the sexual double standard, and failed to eradicate venereal disease; it was signed not only by Butler but also by Harriet Martineau, Florence Nightingale, and some 250 other women (ibid.: 432). Not until 1886 were the Acts repealed, but the feminist activism of the 1870s and 1880s provided models of women's political organization, leadership, and militant activism; and later suffragists looked back to Butler "as a great founding mother of modern feminism" (Walkowitz 1980: 255). In literature the CD controversy forms the context for poems on prostitutes by D. G. Rossetti ("Jenny") and Augusta Webster ("A Castaway"), published in the same year as the "Ladies' Appeal and Protest" (see Brown 1991). The eruption of sexually transgressive subject matter within respectable bourgeois circles represented by Butler's campaign also had its counterpart in the rise of sensation fiction in the 1860s. Novels like *Lady Audley's Secret* (1862) cracked open seemingly smooth domestic surfaces to reveal criminal intent and potential violence within – though this genre also owed its formation to the increasing role of police and divorce court proceedings in Victorian newspapers.

Sexual surveillance to control "deviancy" was not restricted to prostitutes in 1870. The same year transvestites Ernest Boulton and Frederick William Park were arrested for indecent behavior and tried in 1871 for conspiracy to commit sodomite acts. Their arrest and trial, widely reported in the press, revealed significant legal confusion over the boundaries and signs of homosexuality (Weeks 1981). The death penalty for sodomy had been lifted in 1861, replaced by lengthy imprisonment, but the category of "homosexual" had not yet clearly emerged in Britain – though Foucault (1980) dates the birth of homosexuality to 1870 because of an article published that year by Carl Westphal. Only in the Labouchere Amendment to the Criminal Law Amendment Act of 1885 were British "acts of gross indecency between men" stipulated as misdemeanors carrying the penalty of two years' hard labor. Lesbian women were exempted from prosecution both because they were not deemed as socially dangerous as male homosexuals and because of their relative invisibility – though poems such as Swinburne's "Anactoria" in *Poems and Ballads* (1866) functioned along with Baudelaire's *Fleurs du Mal* (1857) to circulate the discourse of lesbianism.

The 1885 Criminal Amendment Act was another point of convergence between the CD Acts and the formation of homosexual identities. The Act, raising the age of sexual consent from 13 to 16, was prompted not only by general anxieties about child prostitution but also by W. T. Stead's sensational "Maiden Tribute to Modern Babylon" in the 1885 *Pall Mall Gazette*. Both the Act and its anti-sodomy amendment reflected antagonism toward aristocratic profligacy deemed responsible for an array of corrupt practices. As well, the 1885 legislation signaled the displacement of feminist politics of the early CD repeal movement onto social purity campaigns designed to control male vice.

Reform and Religion

The Disestablishment of the Irish Church in 1869, earlier Fenian campaigns (Hobsbawm 1975: 92–3), and of course England's rule of Ireland dating back to Elizabeth I led in 1870 to the Irish Land Act, which "imposed statutory rent control and compelled landlords to compensate tenants for improvements" (Harris 1994:

121). The Irish legislation thus points at once to issues of order, religion (itself inseparable from Victorian science), and colonialism.

Because the period 1848–70 is often characterized as one of peace and prosperity (see, for example, Young 1953: 71; Hobsbawm 1975: 4–5), it is useful to be reminded that in Britain, as in other postindustrial societies not officially at war, acts of violence and disruption nonetheless occurred. In 1866–8 a series of Fenian terrorist acts in England pressured Parliament to enact reform. In December 1867, for example, Fenians attempted to blow up the House of Detention at Clerkenwell, which housed Irish prisoners; the explosion injured 40 people and killed 8. In May 1868 in Australia, the visiting Duke of Edinburgh, Victoria's son Alfred, was shot in the back by a Fenian (Alfred recovered; his assailant was executed). These events make especially notable Trollope's choice of an Irishman as hero of his parliamentary novel *Phineas Finn*, subtitled *The Irish Member*, serialized from October 1867 to May 1869. Meanwhile, violence was occurring in Ireland itself, which the government in London met by suspending habeas corpus in Ireland between 1866 and 1868.

Such violence took place amidst debate over the second Reform Bill, which underlay the disestablishment of the Irish Church, that is, the Anglican Church in Ireland, a country principally Roman Catholic. During the 1868 session Gladstone, an opposition MP, introduced a bill for disestablishment, which carried. Disraeli then called for a new election in November – the same that brought in the Liberal majority so decisive in the Forster Education and Married Women's Property Acts of 1870. But the principal issue in the election campaign was disestablishment of the Irish Church, which became law in July 1869. The dilemma of Ireland – predicated on English rule and principal ownership of land – was far from over; but at least faithful Catholics would no longer be forced to tithe to the Anglican Church.

In the wake of the first Reform Bill (1832), Parliament's proposal to eliminate ten Irish bishoprics had elicited John Keble's July 14, 1833 sermon on "National Apostasy" (so called because a secular body presumed to intervene in church governance), inaugurating the Oxford Movement. But now in 1869 the entire Irish Church was dismantled at a single blow with remarkably little protest, an indication of increasing secularism. This secularism did not necessarily indicate religious apathy. Intense interest in religious doctrine caused a splintering of believers into diverse denominations (Primitive Methodists, Wesleyans, Presbyterians, Baptists, Roman Catholics, etc.). Hence, governmental institutions increasingly adopted stances of neutrality, and religion became an increasingly private matter (Harris 1994: 166–8, 171). This cultural formation is mirrored by Tennyson's 1869 "Holy Grail," which amasses five different views of the grail quest ranging from fervent belief to skepticism without having King Arthur privilege a single faith.

Religious pluralism is also evident in the 1869 founding of the Metaphysical Society, devoted to discussion of philosophical and theological issues among clergymen, scientists, and men of letters whose beliefs ranged from orthodox Anglicanism and Roman Catholicism to Unitarianism and agnosticism; members included Tennyson, Thomas Henry Huxley, Leslie Stephen, Gladstone, and Cardinal Manning.

Attempting to retain the paramount importance of spirituality in the face of divergent technologies of knowledge, the society failed after a decade, suggesting yet again the same pressure of secularization which had wrested elementary education away from churches and shifted it to the state in 1870 (Gilmour 1993: 102–3). Indeed, Gladstone's government opened teaching fellowships at Oxford and Cambridge to non-Anglicans in 1871 (Dissenters having gained admission to BA studies in 1858). As of 1870 the head of Balliol College, Oxford was Benjamin Jowett, the distinguished Greek scholar whose influence on Swinburne and a host of other undergraduates was immense; earlier Jowett had been attacked for his prominent role in *Essays and Reviews* (1860), which approached the Bible as an historical rather than divinely inspired text. Secularism also had implications for literary production, since the suspension of religious justification for art made "art for art's sake" more credible (Chadwick 1970: 463).

Reforming and Constructing Orders of Knowledge: Victorian Science

Another factor in the retreat of religion from the public sphere was the expanding role of science. By mid-century geology's formulation of deep time and the evidence of the fossil record were exerting pressure on traditional faith, as in Tennyson's *In Memoriam* (1850). Though ideas of evolution had been circulating since the end of the prior century, Charles Darwin's *Origin of Species* (1859) gave compelling form to the argument through the mechanism of natural selection and Darwin's massive accumulation of instances, which put to scientific use the same piling of detail on detail that gave massive mid-Victorian novels like Thackeray's *The Newcomes* (1853–5) their effect of realism (see Beer 1983). In the *Origin* Darwin did not shrink from opposing his evolutionary model to biblical creationism, but he drew most of his evidence on evolution from animal and plant life, leaving the more controversial issue of human evolution to a later date. If the 1859 work evoked heated controversy and resistance, however, the real surprise was "the readiness of the evolutionists publicly to challenge the forces of tradition – and their comparatively rapid triumph" (Hobsbawm 1975: 260), an acceptance evident in Elizabeth Gaskell's modeling the hero of her final novel, *Wives and Daughters* (1864–6), after Darwin, her distant kinsman.

In 1870 Darwin was completing *The Descent of Man, and Selection in Relation to Sex*, published in February 1871. Here Darwin carefully laid out evidence for the descent of humankind from "lower forms" and the importance of sexual selection for producing distinctive human and secondary sex characteristics not immediately connected to survival. These latter principles played an important role in subsequent naturalist fiction and works exploring the relation of the sexes (e.g. Thomas Hardy's *The Woodlanders*, 1886–7), and in feminist debate as well. If, for example, conservatives pointed to evolutionary theory to refute Mill's *Subjection* by arguing that women's subordinate position was the fit outcome of natural selection, evolution could also suggest to feminists that women were evolving into a new and higher form, as Olive Schreiner suggested in *Story of an African Farm* (1883).

Indeed, Darwinian theory was accepted in part because it could readily be appropriated not only by radical thinkers opposed to orthodoxy and the social stratification it helped support, but also by conservatives. Darwin, for example, was deeply admired by Karl Marx (Beer 1983: 57), whose request to dedicate the 1867 *Kapital* to him Darwin politely refused (Hobsbawm 1975: 260). Yet Darwinian evolution could also be construed as reinforcing bourgeois commitments to competition, "progress," and uniform laws that promised continuity rather than radical dislocation. Herbert Spencer's "Social Darwinism" emphasized competition and survival, and *First Principles of a New System of Philosophy* (1862) applied evolution not only to social development (which moved invariably from simple to complex) but also to racial difference: "civilised [i.e. European] men depart more widely from the general type of the placental mammalia, than do the lowest men" (ch. 15). Such thinking also supported class difference, since Darwinian failure offered a more comforting explanation of poverty than did a hard look at social inequities.

In *Descent* Darwin's chapter on "The Races of Man" repudiated the notion that differing races comprised separate species and acknowledged "that it is hardly possible to discover clear distinctive characters between them." But uncritical assumptions about the inherent superiority of "civilized" Europeans erupt in his text nevertheless; he expresses surprise that Fuegians and a "full-blooded negro" on board the *Beagle* shared his own mental traits and argues that "With civilised nations, the reduced size of the jaws from lessened use, the habitual play of different muscles serving to express different emotions, and the increased size of the brain from greater intellectual activity, have together produced a considerable effect on their general appearance in comparison with savages."

Victorian science, then, both reflected and helped construct in vital ways assumptions about race that also underlay the expansion of the British Empire in the last third of the century. Indeed, another principal development of Victorian science is anthropology, the interdisciplinary field that emerged from philology, travel writing, folklore, law, philosophy, and immediately out of physical anthropology and ethnology (Hobsbawm 1975: 261, 266). E. B. Tylor, preeminent among the group George Stocking terms "sociocultural evolutionists," published *Researches into the Early History of Mankind* in 1865, John Lubbock *The Origin of Civilisation* in 1870 – both cited by Darwin in *Descent*. In 1871, the Royal Anthropological Institute was founded, and Tylor published his landmark *Primitive Culture: Researches into the Development of Mythology, Philosophy, Religion, Language, Art, and Custom*. Like nineteenth-century science as a whole, comprised in earlier decades of loosely coordinated efforts among diverse practitioners, including amateurs like Revd Farebrother in *Middlemarch* (1871–2) or artisan naturalist Job Legh in Gaskell's *Mary Barton* (1848), anthropology was being transformed into an organized body of professionals committed to shared methodologies and sanctioned credentialing. Anthropology and other sciences were also deeply pervaded by and embedded in other social discourses. Sociocultural evolutionists argued that human spirituality and religious belief were subject to the same forces of evolution as physiological development, and that in some cases "survivals" from earlier phases of primitive development underlay advanced stages of civilization (Stocking 1987: 161–3). In this respect anthropologists blurred distinctions between British and other peoples and gestured toward shared cultural processes. But the application of such knowledge often resorted to the racial hierarchy evident in Spencer and Darwin and likewise served to validate bourgeois norms. Thus for Tylor, Lubbock, and other colleagues, religion and marriage were the two central institutions by which the rise from primitivism to higher civilization was gauged, with Victorian bourgeois marriage the hallmark of higher civilization (ibid.: 197, 204). The overlap of literature and anthropology was to be clearer one to two decades later in the work of Andrew Lang or James Frazer, but Tennyson's "Lucretius," first published in *Macmillan's Magazine* in May 1868, already shows the impress of modern anthropology as well as Darwinian evolution in the scientist–philosopher's susceptibility to "the brute brain within the man's," when his physiological and moral balance is destroyed by an aphrodisiac.

Education, Imperialism, and Culture

In February of 1870 Ruskin presented his inaugural address as the first Slade Professor of Fine Art to a crowd of one thousand in the Sheldonian Theatre at Oxford. Not surprisingly, Ruskin affirmed that "The art of any country is the exponent of its social and political virtues" (214) and urged the necessity of protecting English skies from pollution and English lives from the ills of poverty and vice. But the man whose essay "The Nature of Gothic" (1853) influenced the socialism of William Morris then veered in another direction:

> There is a destiny now possible to us – the highest ever set before a nation to be accepted or refused. We are still undegenerate in race; a race mingled of the best northern blood. . . . Within the last few years we have had the laws of natural science opened to us with a rapidity which has been blinding by its brightness; and means of transit and communication given to us, which have made but one kingdom of the habitable globe. . . . And this is what [England] must either do, or perish: she must found colonies as fast and as far as she is able, formed of her most energetic and worthiest men; – seizing every piece of fruitful waste ground she can set her foot on, and there teaching these her colonists that their first aim is to be to advance the power of England by land and sea.

Art and Oxford are here indissolubly joined to British Empire. Indeed, there is a direct link between Ruskinian art criticism and the scramble for Africa, since a copy of the Inaugural Address was one of the prized possessions of Cecil Rhodes, who entered Oxford from South Africa in 1873 (Symonds 1986: 25–6, 161). Ruskin's debut as Slade Professor of Fine Art usefully inscribes the degree to which empire permeated every facet of Victorian England, structuring subjectivities. As Harris (1994) observes, "at a more day-to-day level, imperial visions injected a powerful stain of hierarchy, militarism, 'frontier mentality', administrative rationality, and masculine civic virtue into British political culture, at a time when domestic political forces were running in quite the opposite direction, towards egalitarianism, 'progressivism', consumerism, popular democracy, feminism and women's rights" (ibid.: 6). Empire was thus a means by which Britain consolidated power but also a source of struggle, conflict, and negotiation (both political and cultural) at the imperial center and in far-flung colonies.

In the same year the Second Reform Bill was ratified, for example, British consul C. D. Cameron and other British subjects were detained by King Theodore II in Abyssinia (as Ethiopia was then called) after two prior emissaries sent by Great Britain had been murdered by rebel troops opposed to Theodore's rule. General Robert Napier, commander of forces at Bombay, was sent to Africa and handily defeated Theodore's forces in early 1868, though the campaign was formidably expensive. (In fact, Davis and Huttenback (1986) conclude that the empire cost Britain more than it earned, though enriching individual investors.)

That available military forces in Bombay could serve at need as roving imperial troops underlines the importance of India. Yet even here, a decade earlier, British dominance had suffered a major challenge with lasting political results in the Indian Mutiny (1857–8). This armed opposition to British rule (then under the aegis of the East India Company) erupted because of resentment over annexation of Indian territories, growing concerns about the westernizing of Indian culture, and British insensitivities to religious practices: indigenous soldiers came to believe that the cartridges they were ordered to handle were greased with either cow or pig fat, in violation of Hindu or Muslim observance. The rebellion began on May 10, 1857 among Bengal troops and spread throughout the northern plains, with rebels soon capturing Delhi. The single most devastating event in British eyes, however, was the massacre at Cawnpore (Brantlinger 1988: 199–224). After negotiating the removal of the British from Cawnpore, Indian troops under the leadership of Nana Sahib opened fire when the British embarked on boats for safe passage to Allahabad, and a massacre ensued. Women and children who survived the massacre were imprisoned, hacked to death, and their bodies thrown down a well on July 17. The horror such events inspired can be inferred from the poem that follows *Goblin Market* in Christina Rossetti's debut volume (1862). "In the Round Tower at Jhansi, June 8, 1857," composed September 1857, recounts how the Englishman Skene and "his pale young wife" determine on murder-suicide rather than put themselves at the mercy of attacking Indians ("The swarming howling wretches below"), and focuses on the moment of their farewells before Skene puts a gun to his wife's forehead and fires. Rossetti's note to the poem acknowledged its historical inaccuracy but defended the poem as an indication of reaction in England to news of the mutiny. The rebellion was soon subdued and governance of India transferred from the East India Company to the British Crown in August 1858, thus inaugurating British imperial rule.

The Caribbean branch of empire commanded attention in March 1867, when legal proceedings began against Governor Edward John Eyre for his role in the October 1865 Jamaican uprising. After black Jamaicans had attempted to rescue a black prisoner from the court house, encounters between rebels and the white minority escalated until white magistrates and volunteer soldiers were killed and plantation owners fled in terror. Some 20 Europeans were killed; Eyre retaliated by killing 600 black Jamaicans. Those who put a premium on maintaining order defended Eyre, including Tennyson, Carlyle, Dickens, Ruskin, and Arnold. J. S. Mill, Thomas Henry Huxley, and Lord Chief Justice Cockburn were incensed by Eyre's brutality and worked to ensure that he faced prosecution, though their attempts ultimately failed: Eyre was stripped of the governorship but allowed to retire on a pension.

In the wake of such events ideals of racial harmony were themselves under siege, and Harris (1994) argues that from "the 1860s onwards, . . . the concept of race as a medium of common cultural inheritance was gradually rivalled by and intermingled with a sense of race as a deterministic biological force" (ibid.: 234). Constrained notions of brotherhood inhabit Tennyson's "The Coming of Arthur" (1869), which opposes petty kings to encroaching heathens and finds resolution in an Arthur who arrives, expels heathen hordes from England, and unifies the realm. The shock of the opening installment of *The Mystery of Edwin Drood* in April 1870 – a novel left unfinished when Dickens died on June 9, 1870 – was precisely that a Chinaman, a Lascar, and an English Choir Master lie entwined on the same dirty bed in opium-induced stupor, and that the white female proprietor of the opium den resembles a Chinaman through long practice at her trade. Dickens mocks and subverts racial purity in this lurid opening scene but depends on audience assumptions of racial demarcation to create his sensation.

Succeeding years ushered in the defining events of imperialism, including the rapid annexation of 4,750,000 square miles of land from 1874 until 1902 (Girouard 1981: 224), Disraeli's exaltation of empire during his second ministry (1874–80), the crowning of Victoria as Empress of India in 1876, and the emergence of imperial rule as cult and pseudo-philosophy. Just as in Tennyson's 1869 *Idylls*, however, the impetus to imperialism was due as much to external threats as to actions at the imperial center.

Prussia, the United States, and the Decentering of British Hegemony

During the 1860s the modern state of Germany had begun to form under the leadership of Otto von Bismarck, leaving France under Napoleon III wary of the new power along its border. In 1870 the offer of a vacant Spanish throne to the cousin of the Prussian king prompted French protest, and war between Prussia and France was declared on July 19, 1870, precipitating the downfall of Napoleon III, the birth of the Third French Republic, the Paris Commune of 1871, and the emergence of Prussia as a dominant world power.

Ruskin responded to the outbreak of war in his first lecture on sculpture at Oxford in November 1870 (included in *Aratra Pentelici*, 1872). In pacific mood now, he illustrated points of sculpture by means of the plowshare deposited on his lecture table. A much wider audience was reached by another response to the Franco-Prussian war, George Tompkins Chesney's "The Battle of Dorking," first published in the May 1871 issue of *Blackwood's Edinburgh Magazine*, then in pamphlet form bought by thousands more readers. As David Finkelstein observes, this story representing the invasion of England by Prussia stirred so much anxiety that Gladstone was obliged to dispel the fears it generated. Though ephemeral in literary impact, the story illustrates the looming threat a newly unified Germany posed to British minds, especially since Germany was also fully industrialized, technologically advanced, and increasingly formidable as a commercial competitor of Britain (see Hobsbawm 1975: 40–1, 256).

A significant poem was also to be inspired by events of 1870–1, though not for another 15 years. This was William Morris's *The Pilgrims of Hope*, a poem about the Paris Commune of 1871 that was serialized in the socialist paper *Commonweal* from March 1885 to July 1886. Fueled by communist resentment over French losses ratified by the February 1871 Franco-Prussian peace treaty and by the policies of the Third Republic, armed conflict erupted on March 18, 1871 and the Commune was declared on March 28 following election of a Communal Assembly in Paris. This early communist government lasted only two months, but Morris's poem suggests its importance in providing hope that socialist revolution was possible.

The United States was also making its impact on British life felt in 1870 as it had during the Civil War (1861–5), when the blockade of ports in the South prevented cotton from reaching textile centers in Lancashire, causing the "Cotton Famine" of 1862. In Manchester Elizabeth Gaskell and her daughters worked to the point of exhaustion to alleviate suffering. Not surprisingly, most British newspapers and journals supported the South against the North, which was seen as the aggressor. After the Civil War ended, the American conflict still drained British coffers, for in 1868 the United States claimed compensation from the British government for commercial maritime losses due to depredations by the Confederate ship *Alabama*. In the end Britain was forced to pay more than three million pounds in damages.

The economic impact on Great Britain of events in the US continued with the rapid postwar development of the US railroad, much of it financed by British capital. The sometime frenzy of the situation is reflected in Trollope's *The Way We Live Now* (1874–5) when an American touting a scheme for the South Central Pacific and Mexican railway, running from Salt Lake City to Vera Cruz, comes to England to bilk British capitalists. If America represented a prime investment opportunity, however, the completion of its railway network soon made the US a powerful industrial nation that challenged British dominance (see Clapham 1952: 212–13, 239).

Though many financiers fleeing Paris during the Franco-Prussian war went to London, helping transform London into the world's major center of finance (Harris 1994: 19–20), the Prussian victory was also the signal that Britain's status as unrivaled naval and commercial power was ending. Forced to compete with Prussia and the US, which looked to world markets and territorial expansion of their own, Britain under Disraeli's second ministry launched its policy of imperialism, and British territory grew year by year. This growth, however, was more vexed than the seemingly unlimited opportunity for progress that characterized mid-Victorian writings by Macaulay or Spencer. In this context Eliot's *Daniel Deronda* (1876) is not only a novel of empire but also one that, in having Deronda look to Jerusalem rather than London for his political career, acknowledges multiple centers of rule rather than unitary British predominance. After 1870 confident assumptions about Britain's steady "progress" and its potential for unchecked prosperity were more tenuous, more laboriously maintained. Doubt as to the desirability of the status quo became an increasingly credible position for middle-class intellectuals as well as reformers and working-class organizers.

Emergent Futures, Contingent Pasts

A number of events just prior to 1870 disclosed shifting intellectual as well as social formations in England, particularly the professionalizing of knowledge, which in turn depended on Victorian capital, Adam Smith's principle of the division of labor, and the immense prestige of scientific method (see Heyck 1982). The *Academy*, founded by Dr Charles Appleton, and *Nature*, founded by astronomer Norman Lockyer (still an important scientific publication today), debuted in 1869. Appleton had studied Hegelian philosophy in Germany after earning his BA at Oxford and founded the *Academy* to provide an outlet for scholarly publication, promote German-style research universities in England, and feature writing that attained cultural authority through "disinterested" inquiry (see also Brake 1994: 36–50). In the 1870s Appleton also contributed to *Nature* six articles promoting "The Endowment of Research" at universities, indicating the degree to which specialist knowledge depended on association with scientific method and standards of reliability.

This emergent professionalizing of knowledge also played a role in Browning's displacing Tennyson as preeminent poet among intellectuals. By 1870 Tennyson's very popularity rendered his accessibility suspect; Browning's formerly notorious obscurity became in contrast a badge of depth and cerebration for those identified with cultural elites. Browning himself engaged epistemological impasses, and his recondite allusions and intricate syntax also called for (and thus validated) expert commentators steeped in contemporary theory and committed to rigorous exegesis. The language of expertise and scientific method, in contrast to that of amateur appreciation (associated with feminine – or effeminate – producers and consumers), is evident in the March 1869 review by John Morley of Browning's newly completed *The Ring and the Book*

(November 1868–February 1869) in the *Fortnightly Review*. Morley sneered at Tennyson's "graceful presentation of the Arthurian legend for drawing-rooms, by idylls, not robust and Theocritean, but such little pictures as might adorn a ladies' school" (p. 331), and praised in contrast the intellectual vigor of Browning's poem, the ending of which might serve as "no unfit epilogue to a scientific essay on history" (p. 338). The reference to "scientific . . . history" also chimes with the replacement of Charles Kingsley by John Robert Seeley as Regius Chair of Modern History at Cambridge. Reflecting the influence of German universities yet again, history was increasingly displaced from the hands of generalists such as Kingsley or Carlyle to scholars trained in rigorous research of original documents and approved protocols for presenting evidence. Such historians elevated the practice of biography, which they associated with disinterested "fact," over history conceived as literary narrative, which could be informed by a rhetoricity less amenable to scientific verification or consensus. "Scientific" history also promoted study free from contemporary political conflict (see Amigoni 1993).

Gender and class were additional factors in the rise of professions. Just as women were gaining a footing in Oxbridge, the institutionalization of professions raised more barriers in their way. "Professions" were also carefully distinguished from trade unions – though concepts of expertise might be appropriated by feminist and working-class groups to validate their distinctive voices and social roles.

In 1870, then, even the disciplines through which we approach the study of Victorian literature today (with their unsettling historicity) were in the process of formation. Yet to those living at that moment, such developments might have been invisible. A bourgeois youth who had come of age during the Great Exhibition (1851) would have looked upon a Great Britain still prosperous, since the great agricultural depression that would deplete rural estates in the late 1870s was offstage. Matters in Ireland had quieted down, at least relative to 1866–8, and no other immediate threat challenged British sovereignty. Positions in Parliament and the ministry were overwhelmingly in the hands of the aristocracy, whose social prestige and collective wealth were undiminished. Married women could hold some property and work in the interests of elementary school children on school boards but could neither vote in parliamentary elections nor earn Oxbridge degrees. If labor strikes were a regular feature of British life, no socialist organization had yet been founded. Dickens had recently died, and before him Charlotte Brontë, Thackeray, and Gaskell, but Tennyson was squarely in place as poet laureate and would serve as an icon of British cultural life until his death in 1892. Nevertheless, as we have seen here, this apparent stability overlay profound social change, which moved inexorably toward a modernity that would have astonished that mid-Victorian youth and his contemporaries, and which ushered in the world that continues to perplex their modern and postmodern heirs.

See also SEXUALITIES; EDUCATIONAL, COMMERCIAL; PARAPETS, SHORE

REFERENCES

Amigoni, David (1993) *Victorian Biography: Intellectuals and the Ordering of Discourse*. New York: St Martin's Press.

Beer, Gillian (1983) *Darwin's Plots: Evolutionary Narrative in Darwin, George Eliot and Nineteenth-Century Fiction*. London: Routledge & Kegan Paul.

Boos, Florence (1985) "Augusta Webster." *Dictionary of Literary Biography*, vol. 35: *Victorian Poets after 1850*. Detroit: Gale Research, 280–4.

Brake, Laurel (1994) *Subjugated Knowledges: Journalism, Gender & Literature in the Nineteenth Century*. Washington Square, NY: New York University Press.

Brantlinger, Patrick (1988) *Rule of Darkness: British Literature and Imperialism, 1830–1914*. Ithaca, NY and London: Cornell University Press.

Brown, Susan (1991) "Economical Representations: Dante Gabriel Rossetti's 'Jenny,' Augusta Webster's 'A Castaway,' and the Campaign Against the Contagious Diseases Acts." *Victorian Review* 17.1 (summer), 78–95.

Chadwick, Owen (1970) *The Victorian Church. Part II: 1860–1901*. London: Adam & Charles Black.

Clapham, Sir John (1952) *An Economic History of Modern Britain: Free Trade and Steel 1850–1886*. Cambridge: Cambridge University Press.

Cowling, Maurice (1967) *1867: Disraeli, Gladstone and Revolution: The Passing of the Second Reform Bill*. Cambridge: Cambridge University Press.

Davis, Lance E. and Huttenback, Robert A., assisted by Susan Gray Davis (1986) *Mammon and the Pursuit of Empire: The Political Economy of British Imperialism, 1860–1912*. Cambridge: Cambridge University Press.

Dowling, Linda (1996) *The Vulgarization of Art: The Victorians and Aesthetic Democracy*. Charlottesville and London: University Press of Virginia.

Finkelstein, David (forthcoming) *The House of Blackwood: A Study of Authorship and Publishing*. University Park: Pennsylvania State University Press.

Foucault, Michel (1980) *The History of Sexuality*, vol. 1: *An Introduction*. New York: Random House.

Gilmour, Robin (1993) *The Victorian Period: The Intellectual and Cultural Context of English Literature 1830–1890*. London and New York: Longman.

Girouard, Mark (1981) *The Return to Camelot: Chivalry and the English Gentleman*. New Haven, CT and London: Yale University Press.

Harris, Jose (1994) *Private Lives, Public Spirit: Britain 1870–1914*. Penguin Social History of Britain series. Harmondsworth: Penguin Books.

Helsinger, Elizabeth K., Sheets, Robin Lauterbach, and Veeder, William (eds) (1983) *The Woman Question: Society and Literature in Britain and America 1837–1883*, 3 vols. Chicago and London: University of Chicago Press.

Heyck, T. W. (1982) *The Transformation of Intellectual Life in Victorian England*. New York: St Martin's Press.

Hobsbawm, E. J. (1975) *The Age of Capital 1848–1875*. New York: Charles Scribner's Sons.

Murray, Janet Horowitz (ed.) (1982) *Strong Minded Women and Other Lost Vices from Nineteenth-Century England*. New York: Pantheon Books.

Shanley, Mary Lyndon (1989) *Feminism, Marriage, and the Law in Victorian England, 1850–1895*. Princeton: Princeton University Press.

Stocking, George (1987) *Victorian Anthropology*. New York: Free Press.

Symonds, Richard (1986) *Oxford and Empire: The Last Lost Cause?* New York: St Martin's Press.

Vicinus, Martha (1985) *Independent Women: Work and Community for Single Women 1850–1920*. Chicago and London: University of Chicago Press.

Walkowitz, Judith R. (1980) *Prostitution and Victorian Society: Women, Class, and the State*. Cambridge: Cambridge University Press.

Weeks, Jeffrey (1981) *Sex, Politics and Society: The Regulation of Sexuality since 1800*. London and New York: Longman.

Young, G. M. (1953) *Victorian England: Portrait of an Age*, 2nd edn. Oxford: Oxford University Press.

4

1897

Stephen Arata

I

Of all the verses written during the summer of 1897 to commemorate Queen Victoria's Diamond Jubilee – and there were a great many – the only ones delivered personally into sovereign hands were those of Alfred Austin, Britain's poet laureate. On a fine June morning, Austin arrived at Windsor Castle with a specially printed copy of "Victoria" for Victoria, along with some roses from his garden. There (as he wrote some years later in his *Autobiography*) he was gratified to learn "how delighted the Queen was with the Poem, which she had already seen" in her daily newspaper. Victoria received the "proffered gift," Austin recalled, with "that mixture of gracious-ness and dignity observed by all who approached her" (ii, 261). So pleased was Her Majesty that she later asked Sir Arthur Sullivan to set "Victoria" to music so that it could be sung "in every church throughout the Empire" (Crowell 1953: 208). Out-wardly gracious and inwardly appalled, Sullivan declined.

Indeed, though Victoria liked her poem, she was just about the only one who did. Austin's "Jubilee effusion" – Sullivan's private description – was greeted with derision by reviewers, as were most of the laureate's poetic productions. Few laureates have been held in lower esteem (though fewer still have thought more highly of themselves) than Alfred Austin. More to the point, however, was the widespread belief that his very mediocrity fitted him for the office. Shortly after Austin assumed his post, the London *Literary Digest* (February 8, 1896) quoted William Dean Howells's response to the news: "The notion of any great man seriously performing [the laureate's] duties is inextinguishably comic; and the selection of a man who is not great and never can be great has the highest propriety and fitness imaginable, as far as these duties are concerned" (p. 10). Never mind that Alfred Tennyson, Austin's predecessor and Britain's longest-serving laureate, was regarded as a great man, one who had discharged his official duties for 42 years without comicality. By the 1890s the idea of a poet laureate had come to seem faintly ludicrous. When Tennyson died in

1892, many felt that the office ought to die with him. For three years the post was left vacant, as if to acknowledge that, as William Butler Yeats put it, only "an unreadable mediocrity or fluent monger of platitudes" was likely to want the job (Beckson 1992: 99). If a poet of Tennyson's public stature were suddenly to appear on the scene, one sign of his artistic integrity would be his scorn for the very idea of the laureateship, a scorn one could not imagine Tennyson himself having felt in 1850. The only contemporary poet who came close to enjoying such stature, William Morris, un-equivocally declined to be considered for the position. Austin was finally chosen, it was said, at the insistence of the prime minister, Lord Salisbury, as a reward for unflinching support of Tory causes as long-time editor of the fanatically conservative *National Review*. He remained a favorite of Victoria (though not of her successor, Edward VII), continuing to turn out volumes of verse with regularity right up until the year of his death, 1913.

II

As George Eliot wrote in another context, these things are a parable. When Victorian thinkers wanted to work through difficult intellectual problems – such as, say, how to articulate the relation of history to literature, Jubilee to Ode – they often turned to parables. The 1880s and 1890s marked the culmination of a century-long resur-gence of interest in parabolic forms of narrative: folktales, fairy tales, myths, romances, ballads, sagas, allegories. The central monument in this tradition is J. G. Frazer's *The Golden Bough*, the first volume of which appeared in 1890, but many other examples could be gathered, from Andrew Lang's collections of fairy tales to Morris's translations of Norse epics to Yeats's compilations of Celtic myth and folklore. Not just the recovery of old but the creation of new forms of parabolic narrative was common practice among *fin-de-siècle* writers. The utopian fictions of Morris and Richard Jeffries, the allegories of Oscar Wilde, the Gothic tales of Robert Louis Stevenson and Bram Stoker, and the science fiction of H. G. Wells all fall into this category. Even narratives conceived in more traditionally realistic modes – such as Arthur Conan Doyle's Sherlock Holmes stories, Rudyard Kipling's Anglo-Indian stories, and Joseph Conrad's sea tales – often possess the feel of modern parables or myths.

Though true, the story of Alfred Austin presenting his Ode to Queen Victoria has to my mind the properties of a parable. It synthesizes a complex set of social, historical, and ideological issues into a narrative that invites, indeed requires, multiple exegesis. On the one side there is History writ large in the form of the Jubilee, a grandiose spectacle designed to underscore Great Britain's preeminence on the world stage, its status, in *The Times'* immodest phrasing, as the "mightiest and most beneficial Empire ever known in the annals of mankind" (Morris 1968: 31). In the last two decades of the century, the empire became, as never before, a central component of Britain's collec-tive self-definition. (We need only compare the 1897 Jubilee to the 1851 Exhibition, a comparable spectacle of national definition and self-assertion, to see the changes in the way Britain represented itself to itself.) Imperialism and its ideological offshoots saturated nearly every aspect of *fin-de-siècle* cultural life (see Hobsbawm 1989; Mackenzie 1984; Bristow 1991; Brantlinger 1988). In 1897 the British Empire was, indeed, the largest in the history of the world. Victoria ruled one-quarter of the world's population, a fact the newspapers never tired of repeating.

Yet to many the Jubilee celebrations seemed finally to exude an autumnal chill. The event served inadvertently to underscore the frailty of the 78-year-old monarch, whose increasing debility could be taken to stand for that of the empire as a whole. Austin's first publication as laureate had been a spirited defense in verse of Leander Starr Jameson's ill-fated and unauthorized attempt to seize the Transvaal from the Boers in January 1896. The poem had pleased the queen but embarrassed the government; in the summer of 1897 a parliamentary investigation into Jameson's Raid became the occasion for some anguished and angry debate over the future of the empire. As many noted, too, the emergence of Germany and the United States as industrial and imperial powers seemed to presage Britain's imminent eclipse. The Berlin Conference of 1884 had divided Africa among the European powers, though in Britain the comfort of clear colonial borders was partially offset by the realization that asserting the nation's imperial will was now a trickier matter. Two years after the Jubilee, as British losses mounted in the Boer War, the crisis of public confidence in the imperial idea would deepen, but even in 1897 there were many who saw in jingoistic extravaganzas like the Jubilee a sign of worry, not security. In this atmosphere, it is not surprising that the one Jubilee poem to win wide acclaim was Kipling's "Recessional," which, as its title suggests, is more concerned with endings than beginnings. The poem's austerely elegiac tone captured Kipling's firm commitment to the ideology of empire, but also his deep sense of historical belatedness.

And here we turn to the other half of our parable and the figure of the laureate. For many late-Victorian observers, the most obvious lesson to be drawn from what *Punch*, with its customary sneer, referred to as the Tale of Alfred the Great (Tennyson) and Alfred the Little (Austin) was that the heirs of the century's great writers were themselves far from great. Throughout the 1880s and 1890s, the passings of the Victorian literary giants – George Eliot (1880), Thomas Carlyle (1881), Dante Gabriel Rossetti (1882), Anthony Trollope (1882), Matthew Arnold (1888), Wilkie Collins (1889), Robert Browning (1889), Christina Rossetti (1894), Walter Pater (1894) – were seen as Historical Events of great import, markers of an uneasy transition in the life of the nation. Speaking at a Royal Literary Fund dinner in 1893, Arthur Balfour despairingly noted that "the great names which rendered illustrious the early years of the great Victorian epoch are, one by one, dropping away" and that there was now no one fit "to occupy the thrones thus left vacant" (Cross 1985: 214). The deaths of iconic figures like Carlyle, Eliot, and Browning were greeted with prolonged and sincere lamentation. Tennyson's funeral prompted public mourning on a scale not seen since the deaths of Wellington and Prince Albert in mid-century, and not to be seen again until Victoria herself died in January 1901.

Yet the jeers that greeted Austin were not simply the result of his poetic shortcomings. In a sense, those jeers were directed as much at the office as at the poet. Austin, as laureate, stood for a kind of writer whose cultural capital had long since been spent. The laureateship in the 1890s was a bankrupt position from which to speak; no one took you seriously. This fact in turn gestures toward a complex set of historical developments that changed the ways in which writers and readers thought of themselves and of their mutual relations. Had "Victoria" been a good poem, and it was not, it would still not have been received in the way that "Recessional" was. Kipling, like Austin, was a "public poet," though of a quite different kind. Indeed, to compare Kipling to earlier figures like Tennyson or Arnold is to begin to see how, during the last quarter of the nineteenth century, the notion of a public writer had changed. Or rather, notions: at no point earlier in the century were there so many different *ways* to be a writer. Indeed, one was no longer simply a writer, but a particular kind of writer: decadent, aesthetic, naturalist, socialist, radical, feminist, journalistic, romantic. This proliferation of modifying adjectives not only indicates the range of professional personae now available to authors, but also indirectly points towards some fundamental changes in publishing and reading practices. The last decades of the century saw wide-ranging alterations in the methods by which literature was produced, distributed, and consumed, and it was these changes that laid the ground for transformations in how writers and audiences imagined themselves and their shared relation to the history through which they were living.

III

"Recessional" first appeared in a newspaper. So did many of Kipling's poems and stories. This fact was both a defining feature of Kipling's artistic persona and an indication of the centrality of the popular press in late-Victorian culture. In 1860 there had been 31 daily papers in the whole of Britain; in 1890 there were 150, with London alone claiming more than a dozen. A number of material changes had led to this expansion, most notably the repeal of tax and paper duties in the 1850s, the steady fall of newsprint prices (itself resulting largely from the change from cotton rags to esparto and then to wood pulp in the making of paper), and the invention of the web rotary press and of mechanical typesetting machines. These changes, coupled with improvements in communication and transportation and the development of centralized news-gathering associations like Reuters, helped make late-Victorian periodicals cheaper to produce, more diverse in content, and significantly more influential than their mid-century counterparts had been.

"The newspaper is the plague, or black death of the modern world": this from Arthur Symons in 1903 (Stokes 1989: 29). He could have been writing at any time during the preceding 20 years; vitriolic denunciations of the press were a staple of *fin-de-siècle* literary discourse. In Symons's view, popular journalists had usurped the position once occupied by artists and intellectuals. Newspapers had become the primary conduit through which the majority of readers transacted with "the world." The result, many claimed, was a vulgarization of public discourse. Or perhaps "democratization" is the better word: in a May 1887 essay published in *The Nineteenth Century*, Matthew Arnold argued that what he termed the "new journalism" (the tag stuck) was the voice of "the new voters, the *democracy*, as people are fond of calling them," who had been enfranchised by the Reform Bills of 1867 and 1884. It was in the nature of a democracy to be full of "life, movement, sympathy, good instincts" but to be unable, collectively, to "think fairly and seriously" about serious issues. In a word, wrote Arnold, a democracy was *"feather-brained,"* as were the journalists who spoke to and for it (p. 638).

Arnold singled out W. T. Stead, the editor of the *Pall Mall Gazette*, as the epitome of the New Journalist. Stead was indeed unapologetic when it came to discussing the power, actual and potential, of the press. "In a democratic age, in the midst of a population which is able to read, no position is comparable for permanent influence and far-reaching power to that of an editor who understands his vocation," Stead wrote in an 1886 *Contemporary Review* essay titled "Government by Journalism." "In him are vested almost all the attributes of real sovereignty" (p. 661). Stead believed that legislative bodies like Parliament were fast becoming irrelevant to the conduct of public business. In fact as well as in name, legislators were now the servants of a populace whose will was being expressed through the medium of the press. "The telegraph and the printing-press have converted Great Britain into a vast agora, or assembly of the whole community, in which the discussion of the affairs of State is carried on from day to day in the hearing of the whole people" (p. 654). At the same time, an enterprising editor could shape and direct such discussion to an unprecedented extent. "The editorial pen is a sceptre of power, compared with which the sceptre of many a monarch is but a gilded lath" (p. 661).

Hyperbole, yes, but there is no doubting the influence Stead wielded in the 1880s and 1890s. The investigative journalism he practiced under the banner of social reform was often sensationalist, underinformed, and dangerously misleading, but it also helped focus public attention on a wide variety of pressing problems. His reports on East End slum conditions were important precursors (though of course not the only ones) to the scientific studies of urban poverty compiled by Charles Booth in *Life and Labour of the People in London* (1892–7) and Seebohm Rowntree in *Poverty: A Study of Town Life* (1901). And in one instance at least Stead's ideal of "government by journalism" seemed close to realization. "The Maiden Tribute of Modern Babylon," Stead's exposé of a "white slavery" trade in underaged London girls, spurred a public outcry that led directly to the passing of the Criminal Law Amendment Act of 1885; it also inspired an enormous variety of grassroots political activities (Walkowitz 1992: 81–120). From our perspective, the 1885 Act looks, to be sure, both well-intentioned and feather-brained. Designed to advance the cause of "social purity" by raising the age of consent for girls and regulating a range of nonmarital sexual relations, in practice the Act was used primarily to harass, and sometimes to prosecute, working-class women and homosexual men. The most famous victim was Oscar Wilde, convicted in

1895 of "acts of gross indecency" with other men and sentenced to two years in prison. The conviction not only destroyed Wilde's career (he died in 1900, aged only 46) but also drove underground for at least two more generations a burgeoning gay culture in London.

Whatever its long-term effects, Stead's exposé demonstrated the newfound power of the periodical press. No high-culture writer of the late-Victorian period was able to shape public discourse in the way Stead and other New Journalists like T. P. O'Connor and H. W. Massingham did. The problem, as press accounts of the "Maiden Tribute" affair and, three years later, the Jack the Ripper murders amply showed, was the ease with which social activism slid into sensationalism when its investigative journalism turned yellow. Critics claimed that the popular press did little more than pander to, and ultimately exacerbate, the lurid tastes of its readership, and that in doing so it irreparably coarsened discussion of vital political and cultural issues. "They aim to be as vulgar as the average reader," complained *The Literary Digest* in an April 1896 essay whose title — "New Journalism versus Civilization" — indicates the form such discussions usually took. By the mid-1890s even Stead's journalism seemed restrained in comparison to that found in the papers of Alfred Harmsworth, whose *Daily Mail* was the most sensational and — with a circulation of 543,000 in 1898, twice that of its nearest competitor — the most widely read periodical in England.

Motivating much of the criticism directed at the New Journalists was the fear many felt at the expansion of the reading public. The Education Act of 1870 had made elementary education compulsory in England and Wales (Scotland had long had it). Literacy rates rose steadily as a result, though at nowhere near the rate imagined by alarmed observers, who feared the prospect of a half-educated public engaged, as Frederic Harrison put it, in "aimless, promiscuous, vapid reading" or, worse, "the poisonous inhalation of mere literary garbage and bad men's worst thoughts" (Cross 1985: 205). Coincidentally, 1870 was also the year the birth rate peaked in nineteenth-century Britain at 36 per 1,000. The generation that came of age in the 1890s was thus more numerous than any of its predecessors. Throughout the period there was a push to make education more widely available. Acts of 1892 and 1894 helped fund public libraries throughout the country; in 1895 a Royal Commission recommended a system of compulsory secondary education as well as the establishment of a national Board of Education, both of which were in place by 1902.

Yet these advances stirred anxiety at their possible consequences. Attending Tennyson's funeral in 1892, Edmund Gosse was made uneasy by the spectacle of the "unparalleled masses of the curious" crowding around Westminster Abbey. These masses, Gosse wrote later in the *New Review* (November 1892), had turned out not to honor Tennyson the poet but to ogle what remained of Tennyson the celebrity. Thanks to the vulgarizing influences of the mass media, the ancient "prestige of verse" had given way to a modern cult of personality (p. 516). Few in the crowd had either the taste or the training necessary for a true appreciation of poetry, Gosse surmised, and he worried that public opinion would pressure the government to choose a new laureate based on "mere commercial success" rather than "literary merit" (p. 516). Seeing in the old laureate's funeral "a parable of the condition of poetry in England" (p. 514), Gosse ominously warned of "the eruption of a sort of Commune in literature," an "outbreak of rebellion against tradition" that would finally overwhelm "whatever is rare, or delicate, or abstruse" (pp. 520–1).

Gosse's choice of analogies is telling. His own candidate for laureate was Algernon Swinburne, whose ardent support for the real Commune – the one briefly established in Paris in 1871 – was of a piece with his life-long republicanism. Gosse's worries concerning a "Commune in literature," then, had little to do with political ideology or literary convention. By either criterion Swinburne was an extremist, but he nevertheless retained what Gosse considered the aura of a poet. In slightly less mystified terms, this meant that his work had not been swept up into the machinery of mass culture. (At Tennyson's funeral Gosse had been distressed by the sight of street vendors hawking broadsheets of "Crossing the Bar.") The penny-paper, the mass-market periodical, the music-hall, popular theater like the variety and burlesque, and, beginning in 1896 at the Empire Theatre, the cinema – for Gosse as for many others these were signs that a radical split had opened up between genteel and popular culture. The masses, enfranchised and educated and largely uninterested in the rare or delicate or abstruse, were seeking their own forms of cultural expression. When, in George Gissing's *New Grub Street* (1891), the writer Whelpdale at last abandons his high literary aspirations, it is so that he can make his fortune by publishing a magazine aimed at "the quarter-educated, that is to say, the great new generation that is being turned out by the Board Schools" (ch. 33). Gissing's response to mass culture was invariably sour, and in this he had much company. Thanks to the Reform Bills and the Education Act, wrote an apoplectic Robert Buchanan in *A Look Round Literature* (1887), the "great waters of Democracy" were "arising to swallow up and cover the last landmarks" of high Victorian culture. "After the School Board has come the Deluge" (pp. 359–60).

IV

In his still helpful study, *The Eighteen Nineties* (1913), Holbrook Jackson points out that the period was "to no small extent the battleground of . . . two types of culture – the one represented by *The Yellow Book*, the other by the Yellow Press" (p. 61). Jackson is right to insist on the connection of these two phenomena. If the *fin-de-siècle* saw the apotheosis of the mass-market periodical, it also witnessed the emergence of that characteristically Modernist venue, the little magazine. If papers like the *Daily Mail* and the *Pall Mall Gazette* spoke to and for the average middle-class reader, short-lived publications like *The Century Guild Hobby Horse, The Dial, The Butterfly, The Dome, The Equinox, The Pagan Review,* and *The Savoy* were self-consciously avant-garde in their orientation. As Ian Fletcher notes, the little magazine was one sign of collapse in the Victorian cultural synthesis that had been embodied in the quarterly reviews, and of a corresponding "shift toward the coterie, the movement, . . . the privilegedly unprivileged circle" (Fletcher 1979: 173). Yet, as *The Yellow Book* briefly proved, a coterie publication properly marketed could also be a commercial success. Published between 1894 and 1897 by Elkin Matthews and John Lane, the *fin-de-siècle*'s most visible purveyors of limited edition and "fine" books, *The Yellow Book* frankly presented itself as a high-culture periodical, one whose ethos was diametrically opposed to that of the vulgar masses. Its contributors were aggressively elitist in their self-representations, and so too was *The Yellow Book* as a whole. Yet, perversely, the magazine was popular, if by popular we mean that it sold well. Matthews and Lane were among the savviest marketers of their era, and *The Yellow Book* was among the most financially successful of their publications. Its readership, moreover, was almost exclusively middle class – the very class that *The Yellow Book* professed to despise.

These facts suggest that the relation between mainstream culture and the avant-garde in the *fin-de-siècle* was considerably more tangled than is usually thought. Jackson indicates one aspect of this entanglement when he writes that *The Yellow Book* and the *Daily Mail* each exemplified "the characteristic excitability and hunger for sensation" of the period. Post-Paterian aestheticism, in other words, was simply sensationalism "seen from the cultured side" (Jackson 1913: 61–2). Indeed, the commercial success of *The Yellow Book* resulted largely from Lane's ability to market "culture" to the many. Like other Lane publications, *The Yellow Book* was relatively inexpensive to produce, but it did not *look* inexpensive. "Beautiful to see and convenient to handle," as its Prospectus put it, *The Yellow Book* appeared anything but mass-produced, which it was. The elegantly distinctive look of its pages – generous leading, wide margins, clean lines, slightly larger than usual typeface, ample white space – positively oozed culture, as did the sinuously sinister lines of Aubrey Beardsley's drawings. Yet this layout also called to mind the design features of such lowbrow periodicals as George Newnes's *Tit-Bits*, which relied on large type and wide margins to draw in readers who might feel daunted by the densely packed pages characteristic of Victorian journals. Like *Tit-Bits*, too, *The Yellow Book* trafficked in short, easily digestible essays, tales, and verse, pieces that could be consumed several at a sitting. And the line block technology that Beardsley favored to reproduce his drawings had originally been developed in order to print simple illustrations quickly and cheaply in popular magazines like the *Illustrated London News* or the *Graphic*. There were of course differences in artistic quality, but the underlying aesthetic was the same. *The Yellow Book* sold culture to the middle classes in the same way that *Tit-Bits* and the *Graphic* sold entertainment.

Lane's mass-market elitism opened up new opportunities for certain classes of *fin-de-siècle* writer. *The Yellow Book* marketed itself as England's definitive avant-garde periodical, and it quickly became associated in the public mind with broader literary movements, especially poetic movements like aestheticism, symbolism, and decadence. (Indeed, contemporary poetry was one of Lane's sincerest passions, and most English poets of the 1890s eventually published in *The Yellow Book*.) What these movements shared was a pronounced distaste for bourgeois aesthetics, a distaste that manifested itself most conspicuously in a loud disregard for the common reader. Lane's triumph was to recognize and exploit the public's desire to hear itself abused. It was thus no accident that Henry Harland, *The Yellow Book*'s literary editor, asked Henry James to contribute the opening story to the first volume. As England's best-known unpopular writer, James occupied the precise market niche *The Yellow Book* aspired to. By the 1890s, James had recognized that unpopularity possessed a certain cachet, that some kinds of failure meant success – not just aesthetic success, but financial as well. Like the more flamboyant Wilde, James knew the value of a sharply conceived and shrewdly disseminated public persona. The tale he offered to Harland, "The Death of the Lion," reads like a proleptic parody (the hero is a writer named Paraday) of *The Yellow Book* itself. In telling the story of Paraday's fatal encounter with the forces of mass culture, James stages a familiar confrontation between art and commerce, but he does so in such a way that the distinction between the two terms finally makes no sense. At the heart of the tale is a "sacred" text, Paraday's manuscript notes for an as yet unwritten novel. No one can adequately appreciate its artistry, yet – or perhaps we should say, and so – it becomes the basis of his celebrity. Precisely because the book is too beautiful to read, it acquires the aura that makes for commercial success.

V

Paraday becomes a public figure by shunning publicity; his financial success stems from a sincere disregard for money. His is a characteristically *fin-de-siècle* persona, one that would be adopted and further refined by the rising generation of Modernists. In practice, though, disdain for the marketplace could be indulged only by writers like James whose commercial sense was sufficiently shrewd. For the less shrewd, help was available after 1884 in the form of the Society of Authors. In the words of its founder and driving engine, Walter Besant, the Society's primary goal was "to spread abroad and to cultivate" among writers "the knowledge of the reality of literary property" by throwing "a flood of light upon all those matters connected with the literary trade which have hitherto been kept mysteriously dark and secret," namely, matters of economics and trade (Besant 1970: 306). Besant was tireless in his efforts to convince writers to consider their works first and foremost as property and themselves as businessmen. Through the Society and its journal, *The Author*, Besant was instrumental in furthering what Arnold Bennett later called "the economic education of the creative artist" (Keating 1989: 66). The Society worked to standardize book contracts, to make royalty agreements more equitable, to weaken the influence of lending libraries, to promote the use of literary agents, and to strengthen international copyright laws. Besant insured the legitimacy of the Society by persuading Tennyson to be its first president; he was followed in this largely ceremonial role by George Meredith and Thomas Hardy. Despite the initial mistrust of some writers who disliked Besant's mercantile bent, Society membership grew rapidly, from 68 in 1884, to 870 in 1892, to over 2,000 after the turn of the century. Thanks in part to its efforts, international copyright laws were strengthened among European nations through the Berne Treaty of 1886 (revised in 1896 and 1910), while in the United States the Chace Act of 1891 at last made it difficult for American publishers to pirate English literary works without paying royalties, a practice that had exasperated English writers throughout the century. Perhaps the clearest sign of the Society's success, however, was the decision of 58 publishers to band together to form their own professional organization, the Publishers' Association, in 1896.

Besant's ultimate goal was twofold. Not only should writers be fairly paid, he argued, they should also be accorded the respect they deserved. The "contempt of letters" existing "deep down in the national heart" would only be erased when writers began to comport themselves as "professionals" (Besant 1970: 314–15). He hoped that the Society of Authors would "ultimately do for literature what the Inns of Court do for law and the Medical Corporations do for the medical profession" and so ensure that "literature in every branch . . . takes its place as a recognized and honourable profession" (ibid.: 313). In Besant's view, the writer provided a service to society as valuable and useful as that provided by the solicitor, the doctor, the clergyman, or the soldier. One sign that writers had achieved their rightful stature, he argued, would be when they, like other professionals, began to be awarded knighthoods and peerages. The notion that authors could be considered professionals does not originate in the *fin-de-siècle*, though it does then gain a certain clarity, and not only because Besant was himself made a knight in 1895 for his "services to the dignity of letters." The new professional author arose in reaction to and defined himself against a diverse array of other possible personae – the Grub Street hack, the court poet, the New Journalist, the dilettante, the high priest of art, and, yes, the poet laureate – in order to assume his rightful place in the social hierarchy.

VI

I use "him" and "his" advisedly here, since what is likely to strike us is how the professionalizing of authorship worked, in Gaye Tuchman's (1989) phrase, to "edge women out" of the field. To call authors professionals – or alternatively priests, as many aesthetes did – is subtly to define writing as a masculine activity, since the professions were primarily, and the clergy exclusively, male enclaves in this period. While the existence of organizations like the Society of Women Journalists, founded in 1894, indicates that women writers were beginning actively to appropriate the status of professionals, the last quarter of the century also saw a backlash against what many male writers considered as the feminizing of British letters. The backlash took a variety of forms (see Miller 1994: 10–38; Showalter 1990: 59–104; Keating 1989: 241–84). Legitimate complaints about censorship and Grundyism, for instance, were often couched in terms that laid blame solely at the door of an unduly moralistic female public. Membership in the infamous National Vigilance Association, organized in 1885 to root out public vice in every form, was largely male, though from reading some contemporary accounts one might think the reverse was true. One might also think, upon reading George Moore's influential 1885 polemic, "Literature at Nurse," that all the three-deckers purchased by circulating libraries were written by and for timid women. Thanks to Mudie's and their ilk, Moore lamented, "men have ceased to read novels" (Moore 1976: 22). The dramatic collapse in the 1890s of those two bulwarks of Victorian publishing – the circulating library and the three-volume novel – was due not simply to changes in the economics of the book trade but also to a concerted effort on the part of "serious" writers, mostly male, to redefine what counted as real literature.

And what did not. During this period words like "literature" and "literary" fully take on their modern connotations. They become primarily terms of exclusion, ways to make sharp demarcations between different forms of writing and thus to delegitimate certain kinds of texts. The furor over the "New Woman" novel is a case in point. The New Woman herself – typically portrayed as self-reliant, adventuresome, outspoken, and intelligent – clearly affronted conventional notions of femininity. By contrast, the novels in which she appeared tended, formally speaking, to be quite conventional. As developed by writers like Sarah Grand, Mona Caird, Ella Hepworth Dixon, Olive Schreiner, Emma Brooke, and Gertrude Dix, the New Woman novel represents a late flowering of two highly respectable Victorian forms, the social problem novel and the novel of domestic realism. Yet these heirs to the tradition of Gaskell and Dickens were dismissed by hostile critics who labeled their works "polemical," "pedantic," and thus "unartistic." Writing in the *Westminster Review* on "The Tyranny of the Modern Novel" (April 1895), D. F. Hannigan deplored "that tendency toward pedantry which appears to beset all women of profound learning and fixed intellectual habits" (p. 304). The novels such women produced, he suggested, were not works of art but screeds. As if in response, the artist–heroine of Grand's *The Beth Book* (1897) defiantly asserts that "manner has always been less to me than matter. When I think of all the preventable sin and misery there is in the world, I pray God give us books of good intention – never mind the style!" (ch. 47). Such a sentiment, which Dickens would undoubtedly have applauded, was now more often greeted with sneers.

To equate artistry with formal or stylistic innovation, as critics first began to do at this time, is among other things to devalue certain kinds of politically charged writing. Writers like Grand, Caird, and Schreiner consciously presented themselves as public intellectuals in the tradition of Carlyle and Arnold, though they received nothing resembling the respect their predecessors enjoyed. More generally, Judith Walkowitz has noted how "middle-class women's forceful entry into the world of publicity and politics" in the 1880s and 1890s fundamentally changed the terms of public discourse (Walkowitz 1992: 7). Women were "visible" as never before, a situation that caused no end of uneasiness in some quarters. Activists like Josephine Butler, Florence Fenwick Miller, Frances Power Cobbe, Clementina Black, and Annie Besant were instrumental in shaping public discussion and political policy on a wide range of issues. Women's rights advanced on a number of fronts in this period, though the pace of reform remained glacial. The generations-long push to secure women's property rights culminated in the Married Women's Property Act of 1882. The iniquitous Contagious Diseases Acts of the 1860s were at last repealed in 1886. The move towards suffrage gained ground as well. Under the 1870 Education Act women could stand for election to the newly created school boards; in 1888 they gained the vote in municipal and county elections; and in 1894 the Local Government Act decreed that "no person shall be disqualified by sex or marriage from being elected" to district or parish councils. (Women continued to be barred from voting in national elections, however, despite the introduction of several full suffrage bills into Parliament during the 1890s.) Educational opportunities also widened, though women did not receive fully accredited degrees from either Cambridge or Oxford until well into the twentieth century.

For many feminists, efforts to advance women's rights inevitably formed part of a larger political struggle to reform, enlighten, and humanize the social realm as a whole. Annie Besant, for instance, was active across a range of causes whose interconnections she continually stressed. One-time spouse of an Anglican minister, she renounced both marriage and faith in 1873; over the next 20 years she became known as a leading figure in the National Secular Society, the Malthusian Society (which advocated birth control), and the socialist Fabian Society; a frequent contributor to the radical *National Reformer*, and a co-founder of the Freethought Publishing Company; and a charismatic public speaker. In the 1880s she turned more firmly toward socialist and labor causes, earning her greatest notoriety from the role she played in the Bryant and May match-girl strike in 1888. A decisive event in the history of labor unions, the strike not only focused public attention on the industry's deplorable working conditions and unfair wages but also – thanks largely to Besant's keen instincts in manipulating the press – demonstrated how public opinion could be effectively mobilized to gain political advantage.

VII

For students of the period, Annie Besant's career illuminates two facts about the *fin-de-siècle* worth keeping in mind. The first is that the 1880s and 1890s were a time of extraordinarily rich political ferment. At no time since the 1840s had the political landscape in Britain been quite so unsettled. If to our eyes a writer like Besant seems to have been bewilderingly active in causes, that is in part because there were so many causes to be active in. The match-girls' strike, for instance, was only one of the culture-altering labor actions of the period. In 1889 gas workers in Beckton successfully struck for higher wages and an eight-hour day; within a year 30,000 additional laborers had joined the newly formed Gas Workers' and General Labourers' Union. That same year 10,000 London dock workers struck for four weeks, eventually winning wage increases, overtime pay, and the end of piece work. The success of these and other strikes (most notably by miners) accelerated the nascent labor movement – in all, over

200,000 workers joined unions between 1888 and 1890 – and heightened the visibility of the burgeoning socialist movement in Britain. Some key dates in what has been called the late-Victorian socialist revival are 1884, which saw the founding of both H. M. Hyndman's moderately radical Socialist Democratic Federation and the more mainstream Fabian Society; 1892, when James Keir Hardie became the first labor candidate to win a seat in Parliament; and 1893, when the Independent Labour Party was formed under Hardie's leadership.

For many, of course, agitation on behalf of workers' rights gave cause for much wringing of hands. Tensions were especially high in London, where attempts on the part of the government to suppress or at least control an increasingly radicalized proletariat led to a number of dramatic confrontations. The "Black Sunday" riots in Trafalgar Square in February 1886 led to a ban on public meetings in the square, which in turned provoked socialist and radical groups (with the backing of Stead's *Pall Mall Gazette*) to plan an even larger demonstration for November 1887. Some 20,000 marchers – whose numbers included Stead, Hyndman, Annie Besant, William Morris, Bernard Shaw, the Scots radical R. B. Cunninghame Graham, and Karl Marx's daughter Eleanor Aveling – were met by 2,400 soldiers and policemen deployed by the chief commissioner of police. The resulting clash, memorialized as "Bloody Sunday," while not in fact very bloody, passed quickly into public mythology and inspired several subsequent generations of British radicals.

To read the letters, diaries, and memoirs of many of the period's leading literary figures – and this is the second lesson to be learned from contemplating Annie Besant's career – is to see how deeply involved they were in the political and social struggles of the day. It is also to confirm how thoroughly enwoven, for them, were aesthetics and politics. This kind of awareness was especially notable in British drama, which awoke from its long Victorian slumber to become once again a socially engaged art form. D. T. Grein's notorious 1891 production of Ibsen's *Ghosts* for the Independent Theatre of London was for many spectators the defining theatrical event of the age. Ibsen's plays, ably translated throughout the 1880s and 1890s by William Archer, in turn provided a model of socially efficacious drama that British playwrights such as Shaw, Arthur Wing Pinero, and Henry Arthur Jones sought to emulate.

At the same time, the Victorian *fin-de-siècle* is unquestionably the moment when the impulse to disentangle the public from the private begins to gather strength. To their Modernist successors and critics that inward turn away from political commitment seemed, for good or ill, the definitive gesture of the late-Victorian artist. To read the *fin-de-siècle* exclusively in this way, however, is seriously to distort and diminish its accomplishments. It is to undervalue the achievements – and they continue to be consistently undervalued – of writers like Shaw and Morris. It is also entirely to erase the work of someone like Besant, who over the course of her long career published so much writing on such diverse topics: marriage, private property, population control, land reform, socialism, prostitution, art, imperialism, labor, religion, political equality. Much of her writing is superb: rhetorically sophisticated, intellectually challenging, aesthetically engaging. None of it is much read now, at least by students of literature. That it is not is one among many indications of our continued enthrallment to Modernist critical standards.

VIII

During the summer of 1897 Thomas Hardy traveled to Switzerland, partly to escape the Jubilee. Toward midnight on June 27 he found himself, by coincidence, staying at the very hotel in Lausanne where, precisely 110 years earlier and virtually on the eve of the French Revolution, Edward Gibbon had written the final words of his *Decline and Fall of the Roman Empire*. The poem Hardy wrote to commemorate this moment, "Lausanne," conspicuously avoids the temptation to use Gibbon as an occasion to comment directly on the Jubilee celebrations or the fate of empires or even on the question of history itself. Instead, he conjures up the shade of the historian in order to cast him as the prototype of the Modern writer, one who knows that to tell the truth one must tell it slant. "How fares the Truth now?" Gibbon inquires of the poet. "Do pens but slily further her advance? / May one not speed her but in phrase askance?" For Hardy in 1897, still smarting from the critical abuse heaped on *Tess of the D'Urbervilles* and *Jude the Obscure*, the askant phrase now seemed the one remaining avenue open to the writer. Any more direct speech brought only censure. In the trajectory of Hardy's career, from Victorian novelist to Modernist lyricist, we can trace the more general turn from public to private utterance characteristic of twentieth-century literature. In Hardy's hands even poems on public figures, such as his poem on Gibbon or, four years later, his strikingly cold and distanced elegy for Queen Victoria ("V.R. 1819–1901"), do not pretend to speak to or for a wider audience, nor do they offer poetic speech as a way to make sense of the flux of history or of the individual life. Indeed, "V.R." seems in part an elegy for elegy, a lament for a kind of utterance that, like Victoria herself, was now dead and laid to rest beside the century's corpse outlent.

See also PUBLISHING; POETRY; SHORE

REFERENCES

Beckson, Karl (1992) *London in the 1890s: A Cultural History*. New York: W. W. Norton.

Besant, Walter (1970) *Essays and Historiettes*. Port Washington, NY: Kennikat Press.

Brantlinger, Patrick (1988) *Rule of Darkness: British Literature and Imperialism, 1830–1914*. Ithaca, NY: Cornell University Press.

Bristow, Joseph (1991) *Empire Boys: Adventures in a Man's World*. London: HarperCollins.

Cross, Nigel (1985) *The Common Writer: Life in Nineteenth-Century Grub Street*. Cambridge: Cambridge University Press.

Crowell, Norton B. (1953) *Alfred Austin: Victorian*. Albuquerque: University of New Mexico Press.

Fletcher, Ian (ed.) (1979) *Decadence and the 1890s*. London: Edward Arnold.

Freedman, Jonathan (1990) *Professions of Taste: Henry James, British Aestheticism, and Commodity Culture*. Stanford: Stanford University Press.

Hobsbawm, Eric (1989) *The Age of Empire 1875–1914*. New York: Vintage.

Jackson, Holbrook (1913) *The Eighteen Nineties: A Review of Art and Ideas at the Close of the Nineteenth Century*. London: Grant Richards.

Keating, Peter (1989) *The Haunted Study: A Social History of the English Novel 1875–1914*. London: Secker & Warburg.

Mackenzie, John (1984) *Propaganda and Empire: The Manipulation of British Public Opinion, 1880–1960*. Manchester: Manchester University Press.

Miller, Jane Eldridge (1994) *Rebel Women: Feminism, Modernism and the Edwardian Novel*. London: Virago.

Moore, George (1976) *Literature at Nurse*. Atlantic Highlands, NJ: Humanities Press.

Morris, James (1968) *Pax Britannica: The Climax of an Empire*. San Diego: Harvest/HBJ.

Showalter, Elaine (1990) *Sexual Anarchy: Gender and Culture at the Fin de Siècle*. Harmondsworth: Penguin Books.

Stokes, John (1989) *In the Nineties*. Hemel Hempstead: Harvester Wheatsheaf.

Tuchman, Gaye (1989) *Edging Women Out: Victorian Novelists, Publishers, and Social Change*. New Haven, CT: Yale University Press.

Walkowitz, Judith (1992) *City of Dreadful Delight: Narratives of Sexual Danger in Victorian London*. Chicago: University of Chicago Press.

FURTHER READING

Arata, Stephen (1996) *Fictions of Loss in the Victorian Fin de Siècle*. Cambridge: Cambridge University Press.

Ardis, Ann L. (1990) *New Women, New Novels: Feminism and Early Modernism*. New Brunswick: Rutgers University Press.

Brown, Lucy (1985) *Victorian News and Newspapers*. Oxford: Clarendon Press.

Dowling, Linda (1986) "Letterpress and Picture in the Victorian Periodicals." *Yearbook of English Studies* 16, 117–31.

Ensor, R. C. K. (1936) *England 1870–1914*. Oxford: Clarendon Press.

Gagnier, Regenia (1986) *Idylls of the Marketplace. Oscar Wilde and the Victorian Public*. Stanford: Stanford University Press.

Keating, Peter (ed.) (1976) *Into Unknown England 1866–1913: Selections from the Social Explorers*. Manchester: Manchester University Press.

Ledger, Sally and McCracken, Scott (eds) (1995) *Cultural Politics at the Fin de Siècle*. Cambridge: Cambridge University Press.

Pittock, Murray G. H. (1993) *Spectrum of Decadence: The Literature of the 1890s*. London: Routledge.

Richards, Thomas (1990) *The Commodity Culture of Victorian England: Advertising and Spectacle 1851–1914*. Stanford: Stanford University Press.

Trotter, David (1993) *The English Novel in History 1895–1920*. London: Routledge.

Vicinus, Martha (1985) *Independent Women: Work and Community for Single Women 1850–1920*. London: Virago.

Wiener, Joel H. (ed.) (1988) *Papers for the Millions: The New Journalism in Britain, 1850s to 1914*. New York: Greenwood Press.

PART TWO
Passages of Life

5

Growing Up: Childhood

Claudia Nelson

Historical stereotypes notwithstanding, the Victorian era did not "discover" child-hood. The tendency to define childhood as intrinsically different from adulthood had been growing over many decades before the teenage queen ascended the throne, as evinced by the attention given to child psychology and the training of the young by such figures as John Locke (1632–1704), Jean-Jacques Rousseau (1712–78), and Irish educationists Richard Lovell Edgeworth (1744–1817) and his daughter Maria (1768–1849). These theorists' ideas about the developmental significance of environment and empirical experience shaped Victorian views, and indeed still resonate today. Nor can the Victorians be credited with having invented children's literature. What is often termed the first picture book for children, Johannes Amos Comenius's *Orbis Sensualium Pictus*, appeared in 1658, while the eighteenth century produced much fiction and poetry aimed at the young, and today's scholars continue to argue the place of children's reading in earlier cultures: medieval Europe, classical Rome, even ancient Sumer.

But even while we concede that the Victorians inherited from older generations their interest in childhood, and some of their ideas about it, we may legitimately contend that Victorian conceptions of childrearing, of the state of being a child, and of the emotional importance of children to a society dominated by adults took on such weight as to represent something new in Western history. Never before had childhood become an obsession within the culture at large – yet in this case "obsession" is not too strong a word. Sociologist Charles Booth concluded from census data in 1886 that in every decade from 1851 to 1881 children under 15 made up slightly over 35 percent of the population of England and Wales, outnumbering both adult males and adult females (see Jordan 1987). In Carolyn Steedman's phrase, "Mid-Victorian society was a society of the young," and their elders knew it.

Childhood, then, was omnipresent, especially since compulsory schooling only gradually removed children from adult notice during the day; the 1851 education census suggests that about 55 percent of boys and 62 percent of girls aged 3 to 15 were not in school, and Henry Mayhew estimated in the same year that some 10,000 children were scratching a living on the streets of London, very much in the public eye. But adult attitudes toward childhood varied. For some Victorians, it was a threat, a stage during which desire outstripped self-control and animal nature proved the ineffectuality of civilization. For many others, it was the arena within which a better society might be engineered, whether through adept molding of the malleable young or through the reform of men and women whose hearts were to be softened by contact with childish innocence. For a third group, it was a reminder of personal and social injustices endured in youth that continued to shape their adult lives, as Charles Dickens's enforced sojourn in a blacking warehouse at age 12 resurfaces throughout his fiction. And for still others, childhood was a commodity to be marketed, in forms ranging from child labor to the sentimental greeting card, giving rise to both profit and protest. In short, the range of Victorian responses to childhood is far too wide to be covered adequately here; this chapter can only summarize, emphasize, and suggest the development, boundaries, and repercussions of nineteenth-century Britain's fascination with childhood real and imagined.

Real Children I: The Privileged

While Victorian writers on domesticity stressed the wonders of the parent–child bond within the privileged classes, in practice children belonging to those classes often had minimal contact with their parents. Small children were cared for by nursemaids, older ones taught by governesses, who had some 50,000 children in their charge in 1851 (see Jordan 1987); boys aged seven and older were increasingly likely to be boarders at preparatory or public schools. Many Victorians, then, saw childrearing as a matter for specialists – not necessarily trained professionals, as teachers and childcare workers retained a certain amateur quality until comparatively late in the century, but certainly individuals who devoted all their time to the effort. Perhaps as a result, a major genre during the period consisted of works relating to raising the young. Housekeeping manuals offered advice for supervising nursemaids, outfitting nurseries, ensuring children's health; domestic writers exalted the gentle influence of the middle-class mother, which was to permeate the schoolroom and impart morals to her offspring; scientists and philosophers, from Charles Darwin to Herbert Spencer, theorized about the mind of the infant and the training of the growing child.

Much of this outpouring of articles and treatises concerned education, especially that of boys. Beginning in 1828, when Thomas Arnold became headmaster of Rugby, the British public schools underwent substantial reorganization and reconceptualization, and the century also witnessed the founding of many new schools after the Arnoldian reforms gained a foothold. Whereas eighteenth-century public schools had pursued a policy of purposeful neglect, leaving pupils outside the classroom to their own, often anarchic, devices, Arnold sought to institute a tighter discipline and a nobler outlook among his boys, turning Rugby into an establishment where the godly middle classes would be happy to send their sons. Moving on to govern other schools in their turn, Arnold's disciples expanded on his principles, especially by using athleticism as a pivotal force in the attempt to breed manly Britons. Curricular reforms – the introduction of subjects other than mathematics and the classics as important to boys' education – were secondary to the reform of identity, which became so central to the public schools' project that many educators claimed that even wealthy, leisured parents were incapable of raising sons well. To be sure, the schools themselves were not beyond reproach; the findings of Parliament's Public Schools Commission in 1864 were largely uncomplimentary, and commentators throughout the century continued to note educational failings, although headmasters gained significantly in the public esteem over the century. Nevertheless, attendance at a public school was increasingly an unwritten requirement for admission into England's ruling elite.

This linkage of formal education and public power helped to motivate the changes that took place in the way middle-class girls were educated during this period. The mid-century agitation for higher education for women encompassed also a drive for better secondary schooling for girls. Reformers launched a major effort to found girls' schools that would function as equivalents to the great boys' public schools and raise the status of women associated with these institutions as teachers or as graduates. The campaign was highly successful. By the time of the Bryce Commission on Secondary Education in 1894 there were at least 218 endowed and proprietary schools for girls, most of them founded since 1870 (see Pedersen 1987). More numerous still were private schools, which differed from "public" endowed and proprietary (joint-stock) institutions in that they were the property of an individual or a family. Through them passed an estimated 70 percent of those girls enjoying a secondary education at the end of the century. Like Victorian headmasters, female educators saw themselves as training character as well as intellect; they also often congratulated themselves on enabling the continued reshaping of gender relations and of women's role in the England of the future.

Real Children II: The Poor

Working-class childhood presented a darker picture. Although modern research suggests that working-class households usually accepted middle-class morality and ideas about marriage and parenthood (see Gillis 1985), many nineteenth-century commentators painted family life among the lower working classes as damaged and damaging, dominated not by loving domesticity but by brutishness or ignorance. Working-class mothers were criticized as unversed in housekeeping and child nurturance, so that their offspring grew up puny and unfit; working-class fathers were characterized as abusive drunkards incapable of normal husbandhood and fatherhood. Such views increasingly led to a sense that the nation should step in to care for the "children of the state." Over the course of Victoria's reign, more and more legislation was aimed at the children of the poor, especially the urban poor; these laws were designed both to protect and to control.

Thus, from the 1830s onward, especially in London, we notice new and vocal anxiety about "street children" – a category that might include children with homes and parents as well as waifs, children who earned money by boot-blacking or flower-selling or tumbling as well as children who seemed to be running wild. Just as some writers considered even middle-class boys a more "primitive" species than adult men (the dichotomy did not typically apply to females), the children of the urban poor were often described as "savages," implicitly establishing the responsibility of the ostensibly more highly evolved to bring these children to civilization, by force if necessary. Because they were often associated not merely with poverty and ignorance but also with criminality, with their own offenses present and future and with those of their parents, creating new laws to affect them seemed a logical response.

These laws typically sought to remove children from the power of individual adults, who were presumed likely to misuse their authority, and to place them under the control of the state. Over a lifetime of philanthropic effort, Anthony Ashley Cooper, seventh Earl of Shaftesbury, paid particular attention to the young; causes to which he lent his name included legislation for the protection of the "climbing boys" apprenticed to chimney sweeps and of child acrobats, the London Society for the Prevention of Cruelty to Children (founded in 1884, the year before his death), and Thomas Barnardo's work with homeless children, in addition to an assortment of building and sanitary reforms designed to promote the well-being of the working-class family as a unit. The scope of Shaftesbury's concern mirrors the range of issues with which Parliament occupied itself over the period. Children in mines, in factories, in theaters, on farms, even in their own homes gradually came under the eye of what its opponents dubbed "grandmotherly government," just as children from wealthier families involved in custody disputes were increasingly seen as belonging not to their fathers (who would once have gained custody almost automatically) but rather, in a sense, to the judicial system, which had new power to determine their disposition.

Since Parliament was reluctant to intrude into the internal affairs of the home, legislation affecting the relationship between employer and employee was easier to enact than that affecting the relationship between parent and child. Nevertheless, child labor did not disappear during Victoria's reign. The working classes could not afford that middle-class luxury, an extended childhood; their offspring entered domestic service, agricultural labor, apprenticeships, and other employment at ages when their richer peers were deemed incapable of supporting themselves or of contributing to the family exchequer. If the regulation or the economic decline of a particular industry lessened the chance of a child's employment in it, the presence of the young in other jobs might swell. Thus, for instance, only about half as many children worked in the mines in England and Wales in 1881 as had done so in 1841, before the enactment of various pieces of legislation – but during the same period, the number of children working as servants nearly doubled (see Jordan 1987). Numerous commentators welcomed the idea that working-class girls, in particular, would be exposed to middle-class housekeeping practices and removed from the potentially noxious influence of their own parents; domestic service could be seen, conveniently, as a missionary endeavor in which the "converts" did all the work.

In this regard certain forms of child labor might serve the same functions as more official means of separating endangered children from their parents. Consider the Victorian interest in reformatories for young delinquents, "Ragged Schools" for waifs, and group homes for children whose parents had died or proved unworthy; all these institutions were intended to redress the faults of domestic life among the lower orders by substituting a loving and responsible discipline for the chaotic and probably criminal parenthood that the children in question had presumably experienced. Accustomed to the idea that their own boys might be best raised in boarding schools, the privileged classes had no qualms about making this decision for their social inferiors as well. Sending a delinquent boy to a reformatory, wrote W. R. Greg in the influential *Edinburgh Review* in April 1855, shortly after the passage of the Reformatory Schools Act, "is the greatest kindness you can render him," because the reformatory is "more healthy, more kindly" than the boy's family is likely to be, "softening and training, not crushing or terrifying." Similar theories were applied to destitute children who had committed no crime; whereas until 1853 such children were usually remanded to workhouses, along with destitute adults, after 1853 they might go to "barrack schools" or "industrial schools," there to be taught the life skills and mores approved by middle-class reformers. In addition to getting intellectual and moral instruction, girls would learn to perform housewifely tasks, while boys would receive manual training. By such means, the children of the lower working classes could be used to inject bourgeois ideals into the proletariat, and (so ran the theory) future crime would diminish accordingly.

In this formula, children are both the object and the vehicle for social reform. And although most Victorians saw a wide gulf between the undeserving poor – criminals, vagrants, drunkards – and the respectably employed deserving poor, whose children were unlikely to require institutional care, we may nonetheless discern in the push for compulsory schooling a desire to colonize or convert even the latter group. At the beginning of the century, voluntary or charity schools played the leading role in the effort to educate the working-class child; especially important was the eighteenth-century institution of the Sunday school, which instilled in children sufficient literacy to permit Bible reading and emphasized character training through religion. Sunday schools expanded dramatically in the first three-quarters of the nineteenth century, at their height enrolling nearly six million, but reformers deemed their efforts inadequate. As Charles Booth argued in an unpublished article of 1873, state-supported education could exert a much-needed "humanizing influence" upon the working classes (see Himmelfarb 1991). Parliamentary inquiries indicated that working-class children were profoundly ignorant. In slow response, a series of Education Acts from 1802 onward extended the categories of children required to attend school and the number of hours each day to be spent in the classroom, while the average number of years of schooling rose correspondingly. Until it was superseded in 1902, the Act of

1870 was the most influential. Upon its passage, 26 percent of school-age children were attending classes; ten years later that number stood at 46 percent, while the number of elementary teachers went from 13,729 in 1870 to 94,943 in 1896 (see Bergen 1982). The point of instituting these changes was not merely to provide England with a more literate workforce, but also, as many commentators pointed out in the pages of prestigious periodicals, to redress the inadequacies of the working-class family, even among the respectable poor. Again, children were the key to social reform.

Imagined Children I: Literature for Children

One result of increasing literacy – and also of improvements in printing technologies and transportation networks for the distribution of commercial products, to name only two other factors – was to expand the market for children's reading over the course of the nineteenth century: more potential readers existed, and books and magazines might be produced and shipped more efficiently, than ever before. The boom in Victorian periodical publishing, for instance, was as evident in the nursery as in the smoking-room or boudoir; by Diana Dixon's (1986) count, the five children's magazines extant in England in 1824 had ballooned to 160 by 1900. By the end of the century, children's periodicals could afford to specialize, aiming at the urban working-class boy or girl as well as at middle-class consumers such as the public-school boy, the Tractarian young lady, even the young vegetarian or Theosophist or anti-smoking enthusiast. Other forms of children's literature proliferated as well, perhaps most notably the illustrated book. Under the stimulus of newly inexpensive and effective color printing techniques and the new right of illustrators to copyright their work, scores of elaborately bound gift books destined for the middle class appeared on the Christmas market, adorned with glowing pictures by such artists as Randolph Caldecott and Walter Crane – and later by Kate Greenaway, Arthur Rackham, Edmund Dulac, and other luminaries of this "Golden Age of Book Illustration."

If the quantity of books available and the quality of their design changed dramatically over Victoria's reign, so too did their content. Early nineteenth-century children's literature typically emphasizes either Evangelical religion or secular rationalism. Often described as the first work of Victorian children's literature, Catherine Sinclair's *Holiday House* (1838) offers a new priority, fun. To be sure, religious sentiment is not lacking, in that the virtuous older brother of feckless Harry and Laura dies a saintly death for the joint edification of his siblings and the reader, but the primary focus lies on the entertainment rather than on the serious messages hidden beneath it. As Laura cuts off her hair and Harry sets fire to the nursery, the reader is more likely to enjoy the children's attack on domestic order than to worry about whether they are doomed to perdition.

In this sense, Sinclair bridges two apparently unrelated forms, the Evangelical moral tale and Victorian nonsense writing, since the great exemplar of the latter, Lewis Carroll, likewise based *Alice's Adventures in Wonderland* (1865) and *Through the Looking-Glass* (1871) on an undermining of the nursery regimen. The antididacticism of the *Alice* books, suggested a contemporary reviewer, was the secret of their popularity. And the idea that there is pleasure to be found in identifying with the child who subverts conventional domesticity – usually characterized in these texts as rigid or otherwise inadequate – continues through a host of mischievous literary "pickles" to the end of the century, with Rudyard Kipling's wolf-boy Mowgli and E. Nesbit's energetic Bastables.

But we cannot well argue that the difference between Victorian children's literature and what preceded it is the difference between the amoral and the moral. After all, a major function of children's literature is to explain to the young the principles, ethical as well as practical, by which the society that has produced it works or should work. We might rather postulate (although such judgments are necessarily subjective) that much – not all – Victorian writing for children attacks what the author perceives to be the established order, emphasizing the ideal over the status quo. Working-class children were not the only objects of social engineering during this period; through their pleasure reading, middle-class children too could be indoctrinated with ethical and political views of which their parents might not always approve. Beneath the apparently innocent surface of many stories and poems for the young, critics have discerned radical statements on three overlapping principles in particular: religion, social class, and gender and sexuality.

Pre-Victorian religious tracts for children focus largely on what the child must do to achieve salvation. Examples of error abound – the eponymous Sluggard of Isaac Watts's verse, too lazy to read his Bible; Mary Martha Sherwood's Augusta Noble, interested only in the trappings of privilege, who burns to death when her frock catches fire, unprepared as she is for God's judgment. In contrast, Victorian religious works for children often locate error not in the protagonist but in the surrounding adult population. Take the best-selling novel *Jessica's First Prayer*, written in 1867 by "Hesba Stretton" (Sarah Smith). Jessica is a street child, the daughter of an alcoholic actress; her religious education and her general well being have been utterly neglected. Yet it is she who brings the main adult character to salvation, not vice versa. Her innocent trust in God both indicts middle-class society, which is more interested in respectability and in avoiding unpleasantness than in fulfilling the divine will, and establishes the waif as an object of emotional interest: Stretton's short work touched off a boom in waif fiction, some religious, some secular, all sentimental in tone and activist in implication.

Religious fiction for the young might also concern itself with the educated classes, as the work of the prolific Tractarian writer Charlotte Mary Yonge shows. A protégée of noted Anglican divine John Keble, Yonge specialized in family sagas and historical novels that brought moral and doctrinal questions into daily life. The answers to these questions, as so often in Victorian women's fiction, involve self-sacrifice and not "putting oneself forward"; at the same time, the novels insist upon the importance of the flawed individual, who plays a central role in the story. Similarly, Yonge's adored father sanctioned her writing only if it was intended as an offering to God and not as self-aggrandizement – yet this dutiful daughter wrote herself into the position of best-selling author, magazine editor, and role model for untold middle-class girls with High Church leanings.

The paradox of Charlotte Yonge, an antifeminist whose works teem with strong-minded and interesting women, informs many Victorian children's novels by female authors. On the one hand, the nineteenth century saw childrearing as a primarily female duty. Since entertaining children, understanding them, and training them through gentle moral suasion were considered well suited to women's capabilities, few people would complain that a woman who wrote children's books was improper and unfeminine, which helps to explain why so many female writers talented and untalented entered this field. On the other hand, as today's feminist critics have noted, children's fiction by women often quietly subverts established gender mores. Dinah Mulock Craik's *The Little Lame Prince* (1875) is a good example, in which the feminized title character is barred by his physique from the world of male prerogative yet derives moral strength from his physical weakness. Male authors, too, might employ children's literature to suggest female superiority, as in the case of the important Scottish novelist George MacDonald, a supporter of women's higher education whose fantasies feature goddess figures astonishing for their wisdom, virtue, and power.

Predictably, boys' literature also has much to say about gender, and as various critics have argued, it offers an excellent way to chart changes in ideals of manliness over the Victorian period. The two major genres within Victorian boys' fiction are the public school story and the adventure tale; the one reached its peak after the Arnoldian reforms established moral training as a goal of the middle- and upper-class educational system, the other after Britain became accustomed to thinking of itself as an imperial power. The school story, whose popularity was set in 1857 with the publication of Thomas Hughes's *Tom Brown's Schooldays*, a story of Arnold's Rugby, tends to describe self-mastering within a system in which one begins as an inferior (a new boy, a younger child, and so on). In contrast, the adventure tale often focuses on reaching some exterior goal – discovering pirate treasure in Robert Louis Stevenson's *Treasure Island* (1883), slaughtering three dozen gorillas in R. M. Ballantyne's *The Gorilla Hunters* (1861), triumphing over a foe in countless military or naval dramas. Even so, this outward object typically confers upon its possessor new maturity and manhood; readers understand that an inner victory has been gained as well.

Boys' stories suggest a redefinition of manliness over the second half of the nineteenth century, a movement away from emotionalism and androgynous virtue and toward a more hard-bitten, stoic, and physical ideal. Children's magazines and textbooks sought to shape young empire-builders, particularly boys, by instilling a set of attitudes toward the inhabitants of India, Africa, and China that would prepare readers for their colonial responsibilities and privileges (see Castle 1996). Adventure serial after adventure serial in the late-Victorian years minimized introspection in favor of action and unquestioning belief in British superiority. Writers such as G. A. Henty chronicled dozens of military campaigns without wasting ink on character development, signaling to readers that history is about derring-do, not feelings. Yet even while this form dominated boys' fiction, other writers upheld an older version of manliness involving passionate same-sex friendship, doubts, tenderness, and soul-searching. If girl's stories often covertly asserted the superiority of the feminine over the masculine, directly or indirectly supporting the feminist cause, boys' stories often suggested that manliness, too, could benefit from embracing womanly ideals.

The strategy of two magazines published by the Religious Tract Society, the *Boy's Own Paper* (founded 1879) and the *Girl's Own Paper* (founded 1880), mirrored that of Victorian children's literature overall. First, both titles stressed audience appeal, quickly becoming the most popular adolescent periodicals of the late-Victorian age, with weekly sales of around 200,000 copies each; since children typically shared copies, actual readership was considerably higher (see Drotner 1988). Second, their primary goal was neither entertainment nor profit – indeed, the more high-minded members of the Society found the magazines' financial health dismaying – but social engineering. The founders' object was to offer young readers an appealing but clean alternative to sensational literature, then as now often considered socially destructive, in order to improve the moral tone of the rising generation in the upper working class and above. But in order to sustain the entertainment value necessary to keep the attention of the desired audience, both magazines had to submerge their didactic intent. Overt religious messages are often lacking, while messages about the nature of manliness or womanliness, appropriate gender roles, imperial responsibilities, and the like derive much of their interest from their ambiguity. In this regard these periodicals serve as a synecdoche for the children's literature of their era, which combines instruction and delight – but often in such a way as to turn the instruction into something surprising, even potentially radical.

Imagined Children II: Children for Adult Consumption

Arguably, nineteenth-century adult literature is as morally and politically didactic as its counterpart for children. Indeed, it is sometimes hard to assign a particular work to one category or the other, especially since much fiction and poetry was intended for, and enjoyed by, a multigenerational audience. Take Christina Rossetti's "Goblin Market" (1862), a poem about adolescents that was aimed at an adult audience but that found its way into school anthologies by the end of the century; by the 1970s, it was simultaneously available in the United States in picture-book format and in *Playboy* (see Kooistra 1997). This crossover appeal characterizes other Victorian poems of faëry for adults, such as William Allingham's "The Fairies" (1850) and Matthew Arnold's "The Forsaken Merman" (1849), and indeed the scholarly, artistic, and popular fascination with "the Little People" after the middle of the century bears a strong kinship to the simultaneous scholarly, artistic, and popular fascination with those other "little people," children. Similarly, Victorian poetry for children such as Stevenson's *A Child's Garden of Verses* (1885) has always given considerable nostalgic delight to adults, and the parodies and nonsense verse of, say, Edward Lear and Hilaire Belloc defy classification along generational lines.

Such "cross-writing" is facilitated in Victorian fiction by nineteenth-century adult authors' fondness for using child characters. Jacqueline Banerjee (1996) observes that such child figures serve a variety of purposes: to exorcise their own childish unhappiness, to escape to a golden past, to mourn dead offspring, to improve the lot of living children, to experiment with new ways of depicting human consciousness. We may even see a correlation between an author's interest in childhood and his or her status in our own day, since the novelists most likely to appear on a late twentieth-century university syllabus – Dickens, the Brontës, George Eliot – are also those fascinated by childhood and by the detailed description of children's thought processes.

The *Bildungsroman*, or novel about maturation, was a popular form among Victorian authors following upon Thomas Carlyle's 1824 translation of Goethe's *Wilhelm Meister's Apprenticeship* (1795–6), a novel that Steedman (1995) identifies as seminal to nineteenth-century conceptions of the child. Thus, there are many Victorian protagonists whose recorded histories end in adulthood but begin in childhood or even at birth: David Copperfield and Pip, Jane Eyre, Heathcliff, Maggie Tulliver, Henry Esmond, Ernest Pontifex, Molly Gibson of *Wives and Daughters*, Lyndall of *The Story of an African Farm* – the distinguished list continues. For many of these fictional characters, and perhaps for their creators as well, childhood is an intensely frustrating time, shaped by loneliness, boredom, abuse or neglect, and shame at their own inadequacies or misdeeds. Adulthood has its miseries, but insofar as it brings some authority over the self, it usually seems preferable to youth.

The cumulative effect of such narratives, especially when taken in tandem with such major exercises in the writing of real lives as Elizabeth Gaskell's *The Life of Charlotte Brontë* (1857) and John Stuart Mill's *Autobiography* (1873), is to produce an indictment of adult attitudes toward childhood much more scathing than is to be found in most children's literature. Victorian children's fiction about social injustice typically suggests that children can soften the hard hearts of their seniors, as Jessica does for Daniel Standring and as little Lord Fauntleroy does for his curmudgeonly grandfather; indeed, this trope seems to have had still more appeal for adults than for child readers. Victorian adult fiction may use the same plot trajectory, often in strikingly similar ways, when the protagonist is the adult and the child exists primarily as a device to explain radical character change: witness *Silas Marner* (1861), the story of a misanthropic linen-weaver redeemed by adopting a foundling girl. But adult fiction about injustice or the abuse of authority offers a bleaker picture when the narrative focuses closely on the feelings of the child, instead of treating that child iconically. Jane Eyre fails to stir the affections of her Aunt Reed or of Mr Brocklehurst, although both love their own children. Florence Dombey wins the hearts of all the good people she encounters, but cannot gain her father's love until she is an adult and he a broken man; Oliver Twist makes a lengthy odyssey from workhouse to undertaker's establishment to thieves' den before finally achieving the middle-class security and affection that are his birthright. Maggie Tulliver, daughter of a fond father, nonetheless never manages to conform to the rules laid down for girls within her rural society. The happy endings that mark Victorian children's fiction are, at best, harder to achieve within novels for adults.

In an era fascinated by education and child development, the misery-filled lives of these fictional children suggest that the most serious charge leveled against the adult world is not outright sadism, which is comparatively rare, but rather neglect and an inability to fathom childish needs. Appropriately, one popular sentimental novel of 1869, by Florence Montgomery, takes as its title the single word *Misunderstood*: adult incomprehension, Montgomery charges, may prove lethal even to the children of wealthy, aristocratic, and normally conscientious adults. Given the frequency with which such literary accusations were made, it is not surprising that the later decades of the century saw a backlash in the form of sugary magazine fiction about intensely loving relationships between golden-haired moppets and older men who, like Silas Marners flattened to unidimensionality, devote their lives to surrogate fatherhood.

Such stories indicate that although the Victorians were taking steps to curtail child labor, children were still often contemplated in light of what they could do for the adult world, and not merely what the adult world could or should do for them. A major function of childhood in the mid- to late-nineteenth century was to serve, in rhetoric if not always in fact, as a kind of spiritual palate cleanser – a dose of innocence and purity protecting adult men, in particular, from the moral dubiousness of the public sphere. In earlier centuries, children's major value was often economic: they performed work of real monetary value to their parents or other employers, or they were used to cement alliances between two powerful families, for instance through betrothal. In the nineteenth century, raising a child within the middle or upper classes meant considerable expense, not profit. Nevertheless, children could be seen as assets not only in terms of conspicuous consumption (the parent who can afford many costly sons and daughters must be wealthy) but also because of their emotional and iconic value. So, at any rate, went the rhetoric that was current in Victorian society, which worked hard to turn children into panaceas for adult malaise.

Recent scholars, notably James Kincaid (1992), are eloquent on what they see as the pedophilic tendencies of Victorian society, with its emphasis on the beauty and desirability of young girls and boys. To a great extent, however, this now-disturbing imagery was intended not to open childhood to adult contamination, but to open adulthood to childish purity. In a culture greatly concerned by sexuality and its repercussions, middle-class children – often presumed to be nonsexual – were seen as pointing to a solution, not as part of the problem. Late-Victorian sex-education manuals, for instance, typically assume that the careful parent can both enlighten children's ignorance and preserve their virtue, helping to create a culture of social purity; similarly, the man who forms loving bonds with children is establishing for himself an emotional life centered on innocence, purifying his own existence retroactively. And in a culture distressed by the undesirable side effects of money-making, middle-class children, who operated outside the economy, suggested that life has other purposes than financial profit. That working-class children appeared to be implicated to a greater extent than their more affluent peers in issues relating to sexuality, money, and the public sphere in general helps to explain the anxieties they aroused in reformers, and why those reformers should so often have concluded that it was vital to import such children into the bourgeois sphere of influence.

In an era of rapid change, social instability, and religious doubt, adults felt the need for faith. One kind of faith was furnished by the wave of sentimentality that washed across the century, emphasizing the healing power of emotion and promising ready access to human virtue, since to feel one's heart touched is to confirm that one still has a heart, that the harshness of the modern world has not destroyed one's finer self. And to a great extent, sentimentality invoked the image of the child. Illustrations and greeting cards, paintings and photographs, verses and novels and advertisements, offered up children for adult consumption. Such fictional – or fictionalized – children share certain important characteristics: they are depicted as infantile, with large heads or rosebud mouths or lisps, and thus as innocent; as vulnerable, in need of adult protection; as trusting, perceiving only the good in the world.

The tendency to use children as instruments for social engineering, then, worked in two ways. On the one hand, we see behind the reformist rhetoric of the era a conviction that children could be acted upon. *Tabulae rasae*, they might be shaped and molded to middle-class adult specifications to create a new society. The eugenists of the end of the century sought to approach perfection in future generations by cleansing the gene pool, encouraging the fit to breed and the unfit to remain childless; the moral reformers who busied themselves with reclaiming delinquents or with instilling ethical concepts through children's fiction sought to accomplish this utopian end by psychological rather than biological means. On the other hand, we see simultaneously a conviction that children could themselves accomplish the reformation of their elders, serving as the instrument rather than as the object of character change. If many works of art achieve their emotional power by portraying the child as unable to elicit sympathy from the surrounding adults, this power depends on the assumption that the work's adult *audience* can and will feel the understanding and concern that the adult characters do not provide; the real world is to profit morally from the flaws of the fictional one. The Victorian obsession with childhood becomes the more explicable when we consider the importance of the tasks that many in the nineteenth century hoped to use children to accomplish.

See also EDUCATIONAL, PUBLISHING; LIFE WRITING; SKINS

REFERENCES

Banerjee, J. (1996) *Through the Northern Gate: Childhood and Growing Up in British Fiction, 1719–1901*. New York: Peter Lang.

Bergen, B. H. (1982) "Only a Schoolmaster: Gender, Class, and the Effort to Professionalize Elementary Teaching in England, 1870–1910." *History of Education Quarterly*, 22, 1–21.

Castle, K. (1996) *Britannia's Children: Reading Colonialism through Children's Books and Magazines*. Manchester: Manchester University Press.

Dixon, D. (1986) "From Instruction to Amusement: Attitudes of Authority in Children's Periodicals before 1914." *Victorian Periodicals Review*, 19, 63–7.

Drotner, K. (1988) *English Children and Their Magazines, 1751–1945*. New Haven, CT: Yale University Press.

Gillis, J. R. (1985) *For Better, for Worse: British Marriages, 1600 to the Present*. New York: Oxford University Press.

Greg, W. R. (1855) "The Correction of Juvenile Offenders." *Edinburgh Review*, 101, American edition 197–213.

Himmelfarb, G. (1991) *Poverty and Compassion: The Moral Imagination of the Late Victorians*. New York: Vintage.

Jordan, T. E. (1987) *Victorian Childhood: Themes and Variations*. Albany: State University of New York Press.

Kincaid, J. R. (1992) *Child-Loving: The Erotic Child and Victorian Culture*. New York: Routledge.

Kooistra, L. J. (1997) "*Goblin Market* as a Cross-Audienced Poem: Children's Fairy Tale, Adult Erotic Fantasy." *Children's Literature*, 25, 181–204.

Nelson, C. (1991) *Boys Will Be Girls: The Feminine Ethic and British Children's Fiction, 1857–1917*. New Brunswick: Rutgers University Press.

——(1997). " 'Under the Guidance of a Wise Mother': British Sex Education at the Fin de Siècle." In C. Nelson and A. S. Holmes (eds) *Maternal Instincts: Visions of Motherhood and Sexuality in Britain, 1875–1925*. Houndmills, Basingstoke: Macmillan.

Pedersen, J. S. (1987) *The Reform of Girls' Secondary and Higher Education in Victorian England: A Study of Elites and Social Change*. New York: Garland.

Steedman, C. (1995) *Strange Dislocations: Childhood and the Idea of Human Interiority, 1780–1930*. Cambridge, MA: Harvard University Press.

FURTHER READING

Bratton, J. S. (1981) *The Impact of Victorian Children's Fiction*. London: Croom Helm.

Cunningham, H. (1991) *The Children of the Poor: Representations of Childhood since the Seventeenth Century*. Oxford: Blackwell Publishers.

Dyhouse, C. (1981) *Girls Growing Up in Late Victorian and Edwardian England*. London: Routledge and Kegan Paul.

Green, M. (1980) *Dreams of Adventure, Deeds of Empire*. New York: Basic Books.

Mangan, J. A. and Walvin J. (eds) (1987) *Manliness and Morality: Middle-Class Masculinity in Britain and America, 1800–1940*. Manchester: Manchester University Press.

Mitchell, S. (1995) *The New Girl: Girls' Culture in England, 1880–1915*. New York: Columbia University Press.

Nelson, C. (1991) *Invisible Men: Fatherhood in Victorian Periodicals, 1850–1910*. Athens, GA: University of Georgia Press.

Reynolds, K. (1990) *Girls Only? Gender and Popular Children's Fiction in Britain, 1880–1910*. New York: Harvester Wheatsheaf.

Spencer, H. (1896, orig. 1861) *Education, Intellectual, Moral and Physical*. New York: Appleton.

Spender, D. (ed.) (1987) *The Education Papers: Women's Quest for Equality in Britain, 1850–1912*. London: Routledge and Kegan Paul.

6

Moving Out: Adolescence
Chris R. Vanden Bossche

The Victorians were very much concerned with the question when one stopped being a child and became an adult. It was during the Victorian era that the years from age 13 to 24 came to be regarded as a distinct epoch in individual development: adolescence. The word "adolescence" came into vogue in the late nineteenth century, and the first major sociological study of it, G. Stanley Hall's *Adolescence*, appeared in 1905. While adolescents came to be regarded as distinctly different from children or adults, the concept of adolescence (the word is derived from the Latin *adolescere*, "to grow up") was implicitly tied to Victorian notions of what it meant to be an adult. Consequently, it was regarded as a complex social, psychological, and moral process that was intimately linked to the Victorian ideal of the independent, mature, and cultivated adult self. Arriving at adulthood meant not just coming of age, but developing a particular kind of self. If these concerns seem familiar, it is probably because in the twentieth century the new fields of psychology and sociology were built up from a foundation in the Victorian conception of adolescence and the process of human development. Indeed, Hall's *Adolescence* both looked back at the Victorian era and pointed forward to modern concerns. The Victorian formulation of adolescence is, in fact, just one part of a larger set of concepts related to the process of coming of age that arose as the Victorians sought to come to terms with changes in the social structure and the institutions, such as marriage, through which that structure manifested itself.

The Victorians employed various rituals to mark one's symbolic entry into adulthood. In elite society, a young woman would be presented to the queen soon after her eighteenth birthday, in a ritual known as "coming out" (a term that had quite another meaning for the Victorians than for us). Further down the social ladder, a family might indicate a woman's coming out by participation in a private dance or hunt ball. Outside the upper classes, a woman might indicate she had come of age by putting up her hair, wearing long skirts, joining the adults for dinner, or calling on friends with her mother. Most importantly, coming out meant that a woman was available for courtship and marriage. It is perhaps indicative of the Victorian tendency to situate men and women in separate spheres of activity that, whereas the emphasis for women was on "coming out," the important moment for men was "coming of age," reaching their majority. At age 21, heirs would take possession of their property and guardianship would end. "Coming out" and "coming of age" were rituals intended to indicate that an individual had crossed the threshold into adulthood. The change from cloistered adolescent to debutante was often compared to the butterfly's emerging from its chrysalis, and the corresponding notion of a metamorphosis from dependency to autonomy was at the heart of the Victorian idea of adolescence.

Yet merely being presented to society or passing one's twenty-first birthday did not ensure that one had reached mature adulthood. Such events were symbolic markers of what was understood to be a long and complex process that began in adolescence and in most cases was not to be concluded until about age 30. These events stood for, but did not cause, the transition. The arbitrariness of birthdays as markers of coming of age is pointed up by the paradoxical situation of Frederick in Gilbert's *The Pirates of Penzance* (1879). This virtuous young hero discovers that, although he has lived for 21 years, he has reached only his fifth birthday because he was born on February 29; technically, he has not come of age and must remain indentured to a band of pirates. Like other Victorian heroes and heroines, Frederick must undergo a series of trials before earning adult status.

The Victorians did not explicitly divide the process of maturation into specific stages, but one can recognize in social and literary history an implicit set of conditions for achieving the culminating condition of adulthood. The transformation began with the stage at which the child began to be differentiated from parents and family and ended with the achievement of a fully realized and autonomous self. Important milestones included leaving school, choice of vocation, marriage, and setting up a household. The relationship to one's family was at the heart of this process, for each stage was a point at which one achieved a degree of independence from one's family of origin and moved towards self-definition in relation to a new family of one's own. Of course, it was possible to achieve adult status without going through all of these stages, and, by the same token, passage through these stages, like passage through the rituals of coming out and coming of age, did not necessarily mean that one had become an adult. Rather, adulthood was understood as a psychological state defined by how successfully one negotiated each of these life stages.

At the core of the idea that successful achievement of adulthood meant the fulfillment of one's capacity for intellectual, emotional, and moral development was the idea of culture. In the eighteenth century, educational reformers had depicted education as the cultivation of a plant, and the term *culture* had been transferred from agri*culture* to the nurture of human beings. In the nineteenth century, the idea of culture broadened to comprehend the general process of individual development. The metaphor underlying the concept of culture suggested that this development was a gradual, "natural" process. This idea was most eloquently expressed in Matthew Arnold's *Culture and Anarchy* (1869), where he contended that human perfection consists in constant "growing and becoming." The ideal adult remained open and capable of responding positively to new experiences that would further develop his or her intellectual, emotional, and moral capacities. This concept of the continuous unfolding of the self meant that achievement of adulthood could be regarded as always tentative, for one could always move on to a higher stage of development from the perspective of which one's former self appeared immature. Thus, in his *Autobiography* (1873) John Stuart Mill depicted his life as a series of crises, each of which enabled him to move closer to self-completion and self-understanding. Correspondingly, Victorian literature often depicts heroes or heroines who have achieved a high level of self-culture by comparison with which other characters appear to remain perennially adolescent.

Closely linked to this concept of self-culture was the belief that the ideal adult ought to be independent and autonomous. This status was achieved only in part by financial independence from one's parents. Just as important was the achievement of emotional and psychological autonomy. At the heart of Mill's endless quest for more complete knowledge was his belief that one cannot depend on the thinking of others, that one must master knowledge for oneself; indeed, Mill was the era's most eloquent defender of individual liberty. The idea that each individual should seek to make his way in the world without the aid of others also provided the title and basic argument for Samuel Smiles's highly popular *Self-Help* (1859), as well as for innumerable narratives depicting the self-made man. Yet many Victorians were concerned that the desire for individual autonomy was at odds with the achievement of social harmony; if all individuals sought only to promote their own personal gain, they would inevitably come into conflict with one another. The role of culture was to enable one to achieve a perspective from which to understand one's individual needs in terms of the needs of society as a whole.

The beginning of adolescence was marked by puberty, which popular medical manuals described as a transformative moment. Because sexual difference became obvious at this stage, parents were encouraged to treat boys and girls differently. Puberty thus marked the point at which one assumed one's sexual and gender identity, and signaled the beginning of the transformation into adult men and women. But the idea of adolescence also meant that puberty did not have to be regarded as completely transforming the child into the adult; rather, the period of transformation was understood to extend beyond puberty and into the early twenties. Indeed, historians ascribe the "invention" of adolescence to the sharp increase in the practice, among the middle and upper classes, of sending children of this age to boarding schools where they led a life quite separate both from that of younger "children" and from the world of "adults." The effect of such schooling was to delay the transition to adulthood, both by keeping young people out of the work force and by keeping a rein on their development. It has even been argued that the public schools became widely favored in the later nineteenth century precisely because they could be trusted to impede the student's progress towards maturity more successfully than could parents. As one schoolmaster put it, their goal was to "keep boys boys – children children – young men young men" (Musgrove 1965: 55). Like the ideal of culture, the concept of adolescence meant that the process of growing up could be regarded as never-ending, with adulthood remaining always just beyond the horizon.

While the situation was different among the working classes, where children often went to work at the beginning of the adolescent years, working-class adolescents remained, in many ways, dependent children. In fact, the age at which young people left home rose steadily during the Victorian era because working-class adolescents could not afford to set up a household of their own. Universal schooling, instituted in 1870, also encouraged the tendency to remain at home, and the age of school-leaving rose throughout the century. The education movement in turn was prompted in part by the desire to keep adolescents off the streets and out of the work force. So while adolescence tended to be more abbreviated in the working classes, it was increasingly recognized as a transitional stage between childhood and adulthood there as well as among the middle and upper classes.

If self-culture was a continuous process, then one's education could not be confined to formal schooling, and must continue beyond the school years into early adulthood. John Henry Newman argued in *The Idea of a University* (1873) that forcing "a mass of undigested knowledge" on students will only distract and "enfeeble" them (section 8). The aim of the teacher, he went on to say, should be to inculcate a "habit of mind," rather than rote learning (section 1). Like Arnold, he contended that knowledge should be pursued for its own sake, not for practical ends; specific knowledge, techniques, and information are always finite, he concluded, while life's possibilities are infinite. The ideal of education was to develop a habit of mind that would enable one to deal wisely with any situation. Although Samuel Smiles approached the question of education quite differently – like much of the middle class he was suspicious of the classical curriculum of the ancient schools and universities – his *Self-Help* promoted an ideal of "self-culture," as opposed to formal education, that had much in common with the ideal advocated by Newman and Arnold. For Smiles, formal education could be expected to provide only the "beginnings" of an education that must be completed by experiencing "actual life" (ch. 11). In this regard, achieving adulthood meant completion of the process of self cultivation, the attainment of complete womanhood or manhood. While these writers disagreed about which curriculum best realized the goal of self-culture, they shared the assumption that education should not be about acquiring a specific body of knowledge but about developing "character" – the cultivated self – and that, therefore, education was a process that inevitably continued long after leaving school.

This concept of culture can be seen at work in the treatment of education in Victorian narratives of self-development. Educational reformers were worried that too many schools resembled greenhouses in which teachers were attempting to force children to develop at a faster rate than they would in nature. Following their lead, Dickens describes Blimber's Academy as "a great hot-house in which there was a forcing apparatus incessantly at work" and "Nature [was] of no consequence at all"

(*Dombey and Son* [1848], ch. 11). Driven to maturity too quickly, the young scholars never really blossom but proceed into premature decline: Mr Toots's brains are addled and young Paul Dombey, whose father is trying to hurry him into adulthood, wastes away and dies. What concerns Dickens is not the school subjects themselves, but rather the fact that they are pursued single-mindedly with no attention to the children's moral and psychological development.

Not surprisingly, when literary works depict more positive school experiences, the focus is not on formal learning, but on development of character through personal relationships and extra-curricular experiences. Thus, Esther Summerson and Jane Eyre emphasize the importance of their relationships with fellow students and teachers; deprived of formal education, Maggie Tulliver and Aurora Leigh pursue intellectual development on their own, supported only by a supply of books. Thomas Hughes's fictional account of Rugby School focuses on the development of a code of honor among the boys, and treats participation in sports – Tom's first major experience at the school is playing in a football match – as an important learning experience. Completing one's formal education, even at a good school like Dr Strong's in *David Copperfield* (1850), is no guarantee that one is ready for adult life. Dickens demonstrates that David still has everything to learn about life by having him develop an absurd infatuation with the elder Miss Larkins – she shortly thereafter marries a well-to-do hop-grower – during his last weeks at school. As with many of his fictional counterparts, David's education must continue during his first years as a working man and into his married life as well.

For boys, leaving school almost inevitably meant entering on a career. Most were likely to follow in their parents' footsteps. Members of the genteel professions – the law, the Church, and medicine – almost always sought to have their sons follow their profession. The sons of manufacturers, tradesmen, or bankers were likely to obtain employment in the family business or through a family connection. In the early Victorian period this tendency was reinforced by the fact that (owing to the absence of limited liability) most firms were owned by contractual partnerships rather than stockholders; the result was that most businesses were run by a group of partners who were related to and could trust one another. For the majority of the working poor, a future of manual labor was almost certain, and opportunity for advancement limited, even after the institution of universal education in 1870. Of course there were numerous exceptions. An intelligent working-class boy might become a schoolmaster, or a couple might save enough to open a public house or shop. Among the more prosperous classes, there were sons who rebelled against their middle-class parents and refused to enter the family firm, while there were others who succeeded in rising above the fortunes of their parents. The prevalence of stories about individuals rising from a humble station to wealth and eminence – however exceptional such ascents were in actual fact – supported the ideal of self-culture, and encouraged belief in the possibility of social mobility, while also reinforcing the idea that one's character was more important than one's career.

In the middle and upper classes, the situation for girls and for boys was entirely different, since their families invariably strove to avoid circumstances that would require girls to earn an income. Most middle-class women performed a great deal of labor in the home, but they were also counseled by authors of domestic manuals to keep their labor out of the public eye. While the daughter who remained at home would help with running the household, she would not seek paid employment unless left without resources. In the latter circumstances – as when a father died without leaving a sufficient inheritance and his daughter remained unmarried – teaching was the sole respectable option. Whereas the number of employed women among the middle and upper classes was minuscule, nearly all working-class women did indeed "work" for wages at one time or another, as domestic servants, agricultural laborers, or factory laborers, and young women entered the work force at about the same time as their brothers. Indeed, about a third of manual laborers were women, including the vast majority of domestic servants. Nonetheless, the ideal of keeping wives and daughters at home appears to have been adopted increasingly by the working classes, and working-class women often gave up paid labor after marrying and bearing children.

Working-class women had little choice in the matter, but many women in the upper classes, recognizing that the ideal of the cultivated self was at odds with the ideal of the nonworking woman, were not content with confining themselves to running a household. One of the most famous instances was Florence Nightingale, who, having lamented in *Cassandra* (1852) that women had nothing meaningful to do, set out to make nursing a respectable career. Middle-class moral concern with idleness made the social ideal of the nonworking wife and daughters an uncomfortably conflicted one. Nightingale's choice of nursing was a partial resolution to the conflict, as this profession could be pursued for other than monetary rewards. Nightingale's solution suggests that for women the kind of work mattered more than for men. The attention that Nightingale and others focused on the need for a greater variety of respectable employment for women led, in the last decades of the century, to new careers for women – as clerical workers, shop assistants, and so on.

In any case, going to work or choosing a career seems to have had only an indirect relationship to the transition to autonomous cultivated adulthood. To be sure, some professions did confer more status than others. But by focusing on work itself, rather than the particular profession, Victorian literature was in tune with the reality that the majority of individuals chose the career dictated by their family background. More important than the career itself was the work ethic one exhibited in pursuing that career. Thus, the ideal Victorian entrepreneur was the active manager, not the passive investor. Thomas Carlyle, who preached a gospel of "work" in *Past and Present* (1843), praised energetic entrepreneurs, designating them the "working aristocracy" in marked contrast with the "unworking aristocracy," who merely collected their rents and sat idly by while the poor starved (book 3, chs 8–11). The virtue of persistent effort was also at the core of Smiles's philosophy in *Self-Help*, which describes case after case of men who rose to prominence through their own hard work. Even Sarah

Stickney Ellis's manuals on feminine behavior, which reinforced the commonplace that women should not work, insisted that it was shameful for women to avoid work when circumstances required it. Paradigmatic of the Victorian belief in the virtue of work is Mr Thornton in Gaskell's *North and South* (1855), who works tirelessly to pay off his father's debts and to raise his family back to their former status and affluence. It was not just hard work that mattered, but the moral character affiliated with it, as evinced by Thornton's perseverance, honesty, and self-sacrifice. In literature, the results of such labor were not measured by the income they produced; rather, they were regarded as moral training that prepared one both for the responsibility of supporting a family and for one's social responsibilities in the public sphere. The adult self was thus capable of comprehending the needs of others as well as harmonizing the interests of others with individual desires.

As with education, the goal of work was development of the autonomous moral self. Walter Gay, David Copperfield, Aurora Leigh, Lucy Snowe, and many others find the route to happiness through dedication to their professions, rather than in the professions themselves. Work can provide the education that school has failed to complete. Tom Tulliver's father errs in choosing a teacher who will give him the education of a gentleman rather than the practical education appropriate for his class, and Tom achieves manhood by working to pay off his father's debts. Some literary characters abandon an initial career that hampers their individual progress and adopt a new career that allows them to develop independence and moral character. Thus, Walter Hartright, in Wilkie Collins's *The Woman in White* (1860), begins as a drawing master, a career that limits him because it makes him subordinate to the families that employ him to teach their daughters. His subsequent career as an illustrator for a London newspaper might appear to be a step down the social ladder, but it makes him a free agent and requires energetic exertion, as opposed to his servantlike existence in a genteel country house. Or consider David Copperfield, who begins to take charge of his life only when he is forced to abandon the situation that has been purchased for him in a law office and begins rigorous training for becoming a court reporter, a change that leads to his eventual success as a novelist. By contrast, Richard Carstone in *Bleak House* (1853) cannot settle down to any profession because he has adopted the genteel view that he need not work at all; *his* coming of age leads not to the achievement of manhood but decline and death. If finding one's work enabled one to come of age, it seems, the failure to find it meant one would never mature at all.

If work bore a somewhat indirect relationship to coming of age, marriage was absolutely central to it. As W. G. Hamley put it, in an essay entitled "Old Maids" (1872), "to be married is, with perhaps the majority of women, the entrance into life" (p. 126). Marriage marked the point at which young adults began to define themselves primarily in relation to each other rather than to their birth families. Marriage also coincided with two other key markers of coming of age: embarking on a career and setting up a household. Because a man could not think of marrying unless he could support a family, marriage often went hand in hand with obtaining a job, becoming a partner in a firm, or inheriting property. Among the working classes, the combined incomes of husband and wife would determine whether they could afford to marry. In the middle classes, the husband's opportunities would be decisive, but his wife's family might contribute by making him a partner in the family firm. At the same time, marriage did not necessarily mean immediate independence, for couples in all classes often lived with one of their families until such time as they had the financial resources to establish a separate household. The need to provide for the expenses of setting up house is considered the principal reason that, on average, most individuals did not marry until about age 25.

The role of marriage as a rite of coming of age was complicated by the fact that the institution had changed considerably over the previous three centuries. In the sixteenth century, when the primary consideration had been economic or social advantage, parents chose their children's spouses. By the nineteenth century, when prior personal affection, physical attraction, and romantic affinity had come to be considered legitimate grounds for marriage, it was taken for granted that children would choose their own spouses. Influences ranging from puritanism to the rise of individualism gave increasing weight to the principle that husband and wife were equals, as opposed to the earlier patriarchal ideal in which the husband was regarded as ruler of wife and children alike. These new assumptions in turn led to higher expectations of emotional compatibility in marriage. Browning could not have created the complex ironies of "My Last Duchess" (1842) – in which the Duke complains about the inadequacy of his first wife while negotiating the dowry for his second – if he had not been able to set the Victorian reader's expectations about marital relations against the duke's renaissance views. For Browning's audience, this effect was undoubtedly reinforced by the fact that expectations about marriage were still too much in flux to be taken for granted and remained subject to discussion throughout the century.

For the most part, the newly emergent conception of companionate marriage was widely shared across all of the classes. In spite of its disadvantages, most women preferred marriage to spinsterhood, for both emotional and more pragmatic reasons. The issues of property that concerned the upper and middle classes were not at stake for the working classes, but working-class men and women seem to have felt that their economic condition would be better if they married than if they remained single. While various folk customs such as the practice of marriage by "jumping over the broomstick" lingered into the early Victorian era, modern middle-class assumptions about marriage were widely accepted among the working classes. Variations in marriage practices and married life in the different classes ultimately had more to do with variations in their living conditions than with differences in their attitudes about marriage.

Yet while ideas about marriage had been changing, equality between husband and wife was still a new idea accepted only by a few, and the laws of England concerning marriage remained in several important respects what they had been three centuries earlier. One of the main problems was how to reconcile the ideal of equality between spouses with the assumption that men and women were fundamentally different. In the late eighteenth century, just as the principle of married equality was coming to be widely accepted, the principle of separate spheres began to emerge. The doctrine of separate male and female spheres, which was set forth in innumerable etiquette books and manuals for domestic management, dictated that men should struggle in the competitive wilderness of commerce in order to provide for their families, while women should provide a peaceful refuge in which to apply balm to the wounds men received while engaged in business. Because both spouses possessed authority in their respective spheres, the idea of separate spheres was compatible with the notion of relative equality between wife and husband. But it also implicitly supported the older assumption that women's sphere was relative and subordinate to men's. Because the husband generated the income that supported the domestic establishment, his wife was financially dependent on him. Although the work of supervising servants, raising children, and, in many cases, cooking and cleaning made an important contribution to the household economy, the authors of domestic manuals nonetheless insisted that women should not appear to work (signs of labor would ruin the peaceful aspect of the domestic sphere) and so perpetuated the myth that women were not involved in the economy proper. Like the principle that women should not work, the principle of separate spheres suggested that women should remain, in this crucial regard, adolescent. The ideal of the cultured self was at odds with both of these principles. Thus, while the idea of separate spheres was so widespread that its influence can be detected everywhere in Victorian literature, it seldom appears there as a rigid doctrine. Rather, the ambiguities built into the idea enabled writers to produce endless variations on the marriage plot, and so to reimagine marriage and the social relationships it symbolized.

Prior to the last two decades of the century, the Victorians were content to reimagine marriage rather than to question its viability. When in 1851 John Stuart Mill and Harriet Taylor, two of the era's most eloquent advocates for the rights of women, contemplated marriage, they set out to reinvent the marriage contract so that they could obtain the emotional benefits of marriage without its psychological and economic constraints. Two months before their wedding, Mill put in writing a "solemn promise" never to use the powers conferred on him by British law and pledging that Harriet Taylor should "retain in all respects whatever the same absolute freedom of action and freedom of disposal of herself . . . as if no such marriage had taken place" (Mill and Taylor 1970: 45–6). The problem of how to reconcile marriage with individual autonomy was, as Mill and Taylor recognized, related to the idea of separate masculine and feminine spheres, which, in its doctrinaire form, was at odds with the cultivation of the self and achievement of mature adulthood. As Taylor argued in "The Enfranchisement of Women" (1851), the "proper sphere for all human beings is the largest and highest they are able to attain to." In other words, reform of the institution of marriage could not be limited to the legal and financial realm, but must apply to the moral and psychological domains as well.

Mill's and Taylor's attempt to create their own marriage outside of the legal institution was akin to the use of the marriage plot in Victorian literature to imagine new forms of relationship. The marriage plot is a literary device with a long history and so is not unique to the Victorian era. What distinguishes the Victorian marriage plot from the marriage plot in the comedies of Shakespeare is the kinds of questions it raises about marriage. Just to cite one instance, whereas a comedy such as *A Midsummer Night's Dream* does not concern itself with the question of what makes the lovers suitable to one another, the question of suitability is pursued almost obsessively in Victorian literature. In order to reconcile the principle of equality and mutual respect with legal institutions and the idea of sexual difference, Victorian authors sought to imagine ways to equalize the economic and psychological power equation. Even a conservative like Sarah Stickney Ellis advised her female readers to judge carefully the character of their prospective mates, precisely because they would be in their power. Novelists like Charlotte Brontë went further, attempting to imagine circumstances that would equalize the power relations between husband and wife. While individuals were now free to choose their own marriage partner, they were expected to choose someone of the same socioeconomic status, and financial or status considerations were considered just as important as romantic attraction. Nonetheless, novels like *Jane Eyre* (1847) take as a given the principle that a marriage based solely on financial or class considerations cannot be happy. The basic problem in *Jane Eyre* is that, while Jane has declared that in "spirit" she and Rochester are "equal," marriage – as a social, not merely spiritual, institution – favors Rochester, who is older, wealthier, and better connected. Brontë attempts to solve this dilemma by changing the social relations between the two: Jane inherits a fortune that gives her economic autonomy; Rochester, maimed in a fire that destroys his country house, thus loses his physical and psychological advantages. Brontë has shaped social circumstances so as to reshape the marriage relation in a new form, albeit a form that does not solve all of the problems the novel raises. But the ideal aimed at is one in which husband and wife each are able to move out together, to develop into fully mature and independent adults.

While in its more doctrinaire forms the principle of separate spheres drew a sharp line between male and female, Victorian literature frequently depicted the ideal of self-culture as involving a convergence of the two spheres. This possibility was opened up by a central tenet of the separate-spheres doctrine, namely that the male commercial sphere was amoral, if not actually immoral, and that women should therefore serve as moral guides. While in its more conventional form this tenet reinforced gender difference, it also led many Victorian authors to conclude that the ideals of the domestic sphere should be injected into the commercial realm. Thus, the problem with Mr Dombey in Dickens's *Dombey and Son* (1848) is that he does not recognize the value of his daughter, Florence, and cares only about his business; girls, he declares, "have nothing to do with Dombey and Son" (ch. 10). By contrast, Thornton, the hero of Gaskell's *North and South*, combines the male virtues of energy and industry with a feminine cultivation that sets him apart from his fellow mill-owners. Under the feminine moral influence of Margaret Hale, Thornton joins his employees in establishing a cooperative dining room, thus supplementing what had formerly been a purely commercial relationship with a domestic one. Dombey and Thornton are representative of many Victorian heroes whose ability to recognize the virtues of the novel's heroine entails the recognition of the value of the feminine and even the acquisition of feminine characteristics. In this regard, self-culture involves recognition and acceptance of feminine aspects of oneself as a means of achieving a balance between individual desire and social responsibility.

Corresponding to these heroes, Victorian literature depicts as strong-minded, intelligent, and active women such heroines as Jane Eyre, Shirley Keeldar, Margaret Hale, Maggie Tulliver, Dorothea Brooke, Esther Summerson, and Aurora Leigh. Typically, the heroine chooses between two suitors, one who fails to recognize her intelligence and autonomy and another who, although perhaps less attractive in other ways, not only appreciates her intellect and respects her independent spirit but also acknowledges her superiority. These heroines moreover take a leading role in courtship and in running the ménage once they marry. Margaret Hale's capital enables Thornton to re-establish himself in business, and, after the failure of his utopian project, Romney Leigh submits to Aurora Leigh's moral and domestic authority. Of course, acknowledging a woman's moral superiority could simply reinforce the idea that men and women are fundamentally different and therefore in certain respects not equal. Indeed, the device of demonstrating a woman's worth and superiority by suggesting that she deserves an equally superior husband tends to turn back against itself. For by providing a husband who matches his wife in intellect and moral character, the author assures us that the heroine will not threaten the dignity of the hero by presuming to dominate their relationship. Thus, while Dickens implies that Dombey must learn the value of the feminine and that the feeble-minded Mr Toots does well to marry the strong-minded Susan Nipper, in the same novel he depicts Captain Bunby's marriage to the domineering Mrs MacStinger as a scene of comic horror. Nonetheless, like Victorian heroes, Victorian heroines tend to achieve self-completion by combining within themselves aspects of the masculine and feminine domain and so reconciling the needs of self and other. As the Prince concludes in Tennyson's *The Princess* (1847):

> For woman is not undevelopt man,
> But diverse: could we make her as the man,
> Sweet love were slain: his dearest bond is this,
> Not like to like, but like in difference.
> Yet in the long years liker must they grow;
> The man be more of woman, she of man . . . (VII. 259–64)

Underlying these plots is the principle, enunciated by Harriet Taylor, that marriage should enable, rather than preclude, individual self-development. As Frances Power Cobbe argued in "Criminals, Idiots, Women, and Minors" (1868), the laws that denied women property and legal rights implied that all women, even those who had legally come of age, were "minors." Brontë's Shirley Keeldar and Gaskell's

Margaret Thornton initially resist marriage because it would restrict their independence and the possibility of self-development, a concern justified by the experiences of married women in their social circles. Margaret's cousin Edith is not unhappy in marriage, but she fails to mature into a maternal woman; both she and her husband, who resigns his army commission shortly after they marry, lead socially useless lives that provide no opportunity for self-development. The appeal of childlike women is a recurrent theme in Dickens, yet he also recognized, as does David Copperfield, that a "child-wife" like his Dora, who never reaches adulthood, will always leave "something wanting" (ch. 48). Furthermore, David's recognition that his choice of Dora as wife was the result of an "undisciplined heart" suggests that he too has not reached maturity and that his marriage has inhibited his growth (ch. 45). Only when Dora dies and he marries the ideal domestic woman, Agnes Wickfield, is he able to complete himself.

The heroine's marriage to a man who can appreciate her unique character enables the literary work to imagine a marriage in which a woman can do what Victorian law and separate-spheres doctrine seem to have decreed impossible: come of age and reach her full potential as an autonomous individual. While it has sometimes been suggested that in their fondness for the marriage plot the Victorians assumed that women could not achieve fulfillment without marriage, the model of self-culture can enable us to see the marriage plot in a different light. Victorian literature tends to ask instead how, given that marriage was assumed to be likely for most individuals, individual development could proceed to completion within marriage. The goal of the marriage plot thus amounted to something of a paradox. What undoubtedly scandalized many of the first readers of *Jane Eyre* was that Jane sees in marriage not a social institution – she cares nothing for gaining status or money for their own sake – so much as a means of achieving individual fulfillment.

As the laws regarding marriage were debated and changed from the 1850s forward, Victorian literature began to explore possibilities outside the traditional marriage plot. In "Rebecca and Rowena" (1850) Thackeray had complained that too many novels end "prematurely" with the marriage of the hero and heroine; he concluded that we need more "middle age" novels that record the vagaries of their married lives. In *Vanity Fair* (1848) he did just that, depicting a marriage in which the hero and heroine do not live happily ever after. However, the plot of *Vanity Fair* is finally not unlike that of contemporary novels, such as *Wuthering Heights* (1847) or *Middlemarch* (1872), in which the unhappy marriage depicted in the first part of the novel is used to raise problems that are solved by the marriage with which it concludes. The sensation novels of the 1860s – such as Collins's *The Woman in White* (1860) and Braddon's *Lady Audley's Secret* (1862) – brought the darker side of marriage more to the foreground, but they too worked within a comic framework in which a romantic marriage succeeds a disastrous one. What set sensation novels apart from earlier examples of the marriage plot was that, while the marriages with which they concluded brought together the hero and heroine, this marriage did not depict romantic self-completion. Increasingly, then, individual development was imagined separately from marriage. The "New Woman" novels of the 1890s – such as Hardy's *Tess of the D'Urbervilles* (1891) and *Jude the Obscure* (1896), and Sarah Grand's *Heavenly Twins* (1893) and *The Beth Book* (1897) – were unrelenting in their portrayal of mismatched couples whose marriages have disastrous consequences for both parties. But although these novels sometimes explored the possibilities of self-development and romantic attachment outside marriage, they were equally skeptical about the idea of self-culture itself. Hardy's protracted adolescent Jude, adopting Smiles's ideal of self-culture, attempts to teach himself Latin so that he can study at the university, only to discover that he is shut out from advancement by fate and social prejudice. Thus, the decline of the marriage plot coincided with the rise of skepticism about the very possibility of achieving autonomy and self-completion.

What should be clear from the way coming of age is represented in Victorian literature is that it involved the acquisition of certain mental or psychological qualities in addition to physical development and changes in one's material circumstances. Florence Nightingale never married and remained financially dependent on her family, but no one would doubt that she had become fully adult, not only because she set up her own household, but because of the qualities she exhibited in the Crimea and during her subsequent career. Nightingale could break with Victorian expectations about women's roles in part because she shared with her fellow Victorians another set of expectations about self-culture and in part because she had the financial resources to do so.

The latter circumstance should help us keep in mind that, although the idea of self-culture explicitly depicted maturation as a natural process that all individuals undergo, it was to a certain degree class-bound. Several of the principal moral and psychological qualities that signaled arrival at maturity – energetic industry, selflessness, and self-discipline – were particularly valued by the middle class. Furthermore, adult laborers faced, along with women, the contradiction between the idea of coming of age and the idea that they were perennial "minors." The relationship between factory owners and workers was often described as a relationship between parent and child, and workers' inability to save money as a reserve to fall back on during hard times was regarded by some as a sign of their childish tendency to think only about the present. Other, less sympathetic, observers regarded them simply as unreasoning "brutes." Victorian literature frequently criticizes this tendency to dehumanize the laborer, but it nonetheless holds up as a standard of adult maturity the acquisition of qualities more suited to the middle class than to laborers.

At the same time, the ideal of coming of age, like the ideal of culture to which it was linked, reflected the Victorian desire to imagine the resolution of class conflict. One of the few novels to take as its hero a working-class character, Charles Kingsley's *Alton Locke, Tailor and Poet* (1850), depicts Locke achieving maturity when he leaves behind his belief in the use of "brute" force that would, the novel suggests, achieve only narrow political aims and commits himself to peaceful social reform based on broadly conceived religious principles. The fact that coming of age means Locke must abandon his political cause manifests Kingsley's middle-class bias. Yet recognition of this bias should not prevent us from understanding that, as in novels depicting the coming of age of middle-class males, the novelist is here seeking to imagine a transformation not only of the individual but also of society as a whole. At the climax of Kingsley's novel, Locke falls ill and has a long hallucinatory dream in which he recapitulates animal evolution, from madrepore (coral) to human being, followed by the evolution of human society as it moves toward utopian mutual cooperation. Kingsley is drawing on popular ideas about evolution – Darwin's *Origin of Species* would appear in 1859 – that influenced social scientists such as Herbert Spencer, whose *Principles of Sociology* (1876–96) linked the maturation of the individual and of human society. In this context, it should come as no surprise that Hall's *Adolescence* would explain the existence of an adolescent phase of human development by suggesting that each individual recapitulates the history of the human race. Perhaps the best example of this utopian impulse to link the evolution of self and society is Tennyson's *In Memoriam* (1850), which culminates with the celebration of a marriage that the poet hopes will produce a "crowning race" (Epilogue, 1. 128).

In this context, we should keep in mind that "culture" referred not only to the development of the individual, but also to the complex of beliefs and institutions that made up a social group. As the examples just cited indicate, growth and maturation were key metaphors underlying not only ideas of self-development, but also ideas of social progress. While these metaphors tended to privilege members of those groups that were regarded as more "adult" – men, the middle class, the English – those that had been traditionally regarded as "minors" – women, the working class, non-Europeans – could use the metaphor of maturation to insist on their ability, and right, to enter the adult world. Thus, while narratives of coming of age reflected class assumptions about individual development, they were also a means of imagining the coming of age of British society as a process that had always arrived yet was always, also, about to happen.

See also EDUCATIONAL, INDUSTRIAL; FICTION, LIFE WRITING; SKINS, PARAPETS

REFERENCES

Hall, G. Stanley (1905) *Adolescence; Its Psychology and its Relations to Physiology, Anthropology, Sociology, Sex, Crime, Religion and Education*. New York: Appleton.

Hamley, William G. (1872) *Blackwood's Magazine* 112, 94–108. In Patricia Jalland and John Hooper (eds) *Women from Birth to Death: The Female Life Cycle in Britain 1830–1914*. Atlantic Highlands, NJ: Humanities Press International, 1986.

Mill, John Stuart and Taylor Mill, Harriet (1970) *Essays on Sex Equality*, ed. Alice S. Rossi. Chicago: University of Chicago Press.

Musgrove, Frank (1965) *Youth and the Social Order*. Bloomington: Indiana University Press.

FURTHER READING

Armstrong, Nancy (1987) *Desire and Domestic Fiction: A Political History of the Novel*. New York: Oxford University Press.

Boone, Joseph Allen (1987) *Tradition Counter Tradition: Love and the Form of Fiction*. Chicago: University of Chicago Press.

Davidoff, Leonore (1973) *The Best Circles: Society, Etiquette and the Season*. London: Croom Helm.

—— (1987) *Family Fortunes: Men and Women of the English Middle Class, 1780–1850*. Chicago: University of Chicago Press.

Ellis, Sarah Stickney (1839) *The Women of England*. London.

Frost, Ginger Suzanne (1995) *Promises Broken: Courtship, Class, and Gender in Victorian England*. Charlottesville: University Press of Virginia.

Gallagher, Catherine (1985) *The Industrial Reformation of English Fiction: Social Discourse and Narrative Form, 1832–1867*. Chicago: University of Chicago Press.

Gillis, John R. (1974) *Youth and History: Tradition and Change in European Age Relations, 1770–Present*. New York: Academic Press.

—— (1985) *For Better, For Worse: British Marriages, 1600 to the Present*. New York: Oxford University Press.

Langland, Elizabeth (1995) *Nobody's Angels: Middle-Class Women and Domestic Ideology in Victorian Culture*. Ithaca, NY: Cornell University Press.

Perkin, Harold James (1969) *The Origins of Modern English Society 1780–1880*. London: Routledge; Toronto: University of Toronto Press.

Perkin, Joan (1989) *Women and Marriage in Nineteenth-Century England*. Chicago: Lyceum.

Poovey, Mary (1988) *Uneven Developments: The Ideological Work of Gender in Mid-Victorian England*. Chicago: University of Chicago Press.

Springhall, John (1986) *Coming of Age: Adolescence in Britain, 1860–1960*. Dublin: Gill and Macmillan.

Stone, Lawrence (1977) *The Family, Sex and Marriage in England, 1500–1800*. New York: Harper & Row.

Vicinus, Martha (1985) *Independent Women: Work and Community for Single Women, 1850–1920*. Chicago: University of Chicago Press.

Williams, Raymond (1958) *Culture and Society, 1780–1950*. New York: Columbia University Press.

7

Growing Old: Age

Teresa Mangum

"'Old Age,'" muses the anonymous author of "The Art of Growing Old" in *The Argosy* for 1866, "in theory, demands respect, veneration, and even admiration. 'Old Age,' in reality, suffers contempt, ridicule, and neglect" (p. 39). Pulled between these extremes of expected veneration and practical neglect, Victorian writers and artists responded with diverse and often contradictory representations of old age. Even a quick survey of popular poetry provides evidence of the many ways of experiencing old age and of varied attitudes toward aging during the period. Thus, we find William Barnes's colloquial celebration of late love in "Uncle an' Aunt" (1840) and the speaker's booming invitation, "Grow old along with me! / The best is yet to be," in Robert Browning's dramatic monologue "Rabbi Ben Ezra" (1864). Matthew Arnold's "Growing Old" (1867) mourns emotional paralysis caused by old age, a stark contrast with the speaker's gathering wisdom in Alfred Tennyson's "Locksley Hall Sixty Years After" (1886) or Dollie Radford's witty portrait of healthy elderly egotism in "Soliloquy of a Maiden Aunt" (1891). The visual artists of the period were also inspired by the faces, relationships, and social circumstances particular to the elderly. Larits Tuxen's famous family portrait of "Europe's Grandmama" (otherwise known as Queen Victoria), *The Royal Family at the Time of the Jubilee* (1887), places the aging queen squarely at the center of an enormous family gathering, while other family paintings push elderly figures to the margins, as does George Elgar Hicks's sweeping canvas of a bridal party, *Changing Homes* (1863). The consequences of being at once elderly, female, and poor are rendered with special poignancy in George Clausen's *Schoolgirls* (1880), where elegant young ladies in the foreground disdainfully turn their backs on an elderly worker struggling with heavy buckets. Even common speech reveals a fascination with old people and the experience of aging. Victorian synonyms and adjectives used to describe elderly people tended to attribute particular traits and habits to aging, as suggested by phrases like "old bird," "old trout," "old crow," "tabby," "old maid," or "gay old dog" (Covey 1988).

Of the many literary works that contemplate old age, one is particularly attentive to Victorian debates about the place of the elderly in society. At 67 and approaching his death, Anthony Trollope drew upon popular conceptions of aging in *The Fixed Period* (1882), a futurist novel set in 1979–80 on the island of Britannula, settled 40 years earlier by English colonists. In the early days of the colony when most settlers were in their thirties, they agreed to a policy called the Fixed Period. To abolish "the miseries, weakness, and *fainéant* imbecility of old age," their Parliament, having established 67 as the average age at which reason, labor, and independence fail, decreed that on that birthday men and women would voluntarily withdraw for a year of meditation, followed by euthanasia and cremation. The middle-aged narrator disingenuously acknowledges that the policy will liberate young men from the encumbering authority of powerful older men and absolve society of caring for the elderly. The novel mocks fears of overpopulation sparked by Thomas Malthus's *An Essay on the Principle of Population* (1798) and fanned by popularizations of Charles Darwin's studies in evolutionary biology which reduced Darwin's complex ideas into the simplistic aphorism "Only the strong survive." A witty satire, *The Fixed Period* succinctly summarizes growing Victorian concern over what was falsely perceived to be an increasing "aged" population in an era obsessed with youth, energy, activity, and progress.

The Science of Defining Old Age

One of the most important changes in the nineteenth-century understanding of old age is that intuitive folk ways of defining old age, which took little note of actual birthdates, gradually gave way to quantitative systems of definition that possessed the advantage of uniformity but the disadvantage of over-generality. Accordingly, a chief difficulty in studying an issue like aging – which compounds genuine physiological changes with socially constructed beliefs and practices – is that while popular opinions have the least direct connection to scientific developments or government reports, they may have great bearing on an individual's experience of growing old and on a society's treatment of its older citizens. First of all, Victorians were far less committed to chronology when they defined aging than we are today. Before the British Pension Plan of 1908 dictated the need for a specific age at which individuals were eligible for state support, old age had been a floating, flexible identity. As sociologist Janet Roebuck explains (Roebuck 1979), before the nineteenth century a person was considered old only when two things happened simultaneously: first, a person must exhibit behavior betraying physical and mental failure; and, second, the person must look old. Authorities like Poor Law Guardians who decided when to give aid to the elderly did not label anyone old based on chronological age alone. Instead, a person was assumed to be aging but not actually old until he or she manifested these two conditions – behavioral infirmity and physical deterioration.

Nineteenth-century popular standards for deciding when old age began seem even more arbitrary if we consider Victorian arguments that women grow old before men. While government programs and medical prescriptions often treated all old people as if they were the same, and most Victorians routinely used gender-neutral terms like "the aged" or "the elderly" to refer to old people, men and women were deemed old based on very different criteria. For men, age was largely determined by their ability to work. Before 1908 most English men (that is working-class and working middle-class men) labored until they died. Women, however, were labeled old with reference to their reproductive rather than productive capacity. Thus, most popular medical advice texts subscribed to the traditional belief that menopause signaled the onset of old age. We see in literature as well as in popular lore evidence of an underlying assumption that men and women are fundamentally dissimilar and therefore will experience old age differently. Because of its attention to details of character, fiction in particular often accentuated discrepancies between men's and women's experiences in later life. For instance, Elizabeth Gaskell's domestic novel *Cranford* (1853) elaborates the stratagems by which lower middle- and middle-class elderly widows and spinsters with little income piece together self-respect and a meager independence in their provincial village. The social roles available to older women – grandmother, widow, old maid – also inspired such poems as Frances Browne's "Recollections of a Faded Beauty" (1830), Tennyson's dramatic monologue "The Grandmother" (1859), and Alice Meynell's poignant "A Letter from a Girl to Her Own Old Age" (1875).

Furthermore, literature wrestled with a subtler connection between gender and old age. Often, after a male character has accepted the status of being old, he finds that status involves if not an outright loss of sexual identity then a lapse into a state akin to helpless femininity. In *Vanity Fair* (1848), Thackeray portrays the fall of Amelia Sedley's elderly father from businessman to bankrupt. Humbled, feeble, and friendless, Mr Sedley lives in seclusion with his wife, daughter, and grandson. Bowing to his sad fate, he serves as a pathetic version of the feminizing effects of old age. However, this feminization, while representing a fall from one kind of idealized man – the youthful, virile, assertive man of action – sometimes signals moral, spiritual, and domestic fulfillment. The tolerance for a gentler, more maternal masculinity in old age helps to explain the appeal of characters like Dickens's reformed Scrooge in *A Christmas Carol* (1843), Job Legh (who is single-handedly raising his granddaughter) in Gaskell's *Mary Barton* (1848), Eliot's ineffectual but beloved elderly protagonist in *Silas Marner* (1861), or the Tibetan lama with his winning blend of wisdom and innocence in Rudyard Kipling's *Kim* (1901). As all of these examples suggest, clarifying when old age began was complicated by the inconsistency of the criteria – labor here, biology there – that Victorians used to determine age and by the way each individual's experience of old age was affected by being male or female, poor or prosperous, British or foreign-born.

Other popular conceptions of aging or old age were shaped by changing understandings of life stages. "Ages of Man" paintings, which depicted life as a journey marked by childhood, maturity, parenthood, and so forth, have existed for centuries and remained popular in the first half of the Victorian period, but early versions of these paintings tied life stages to seasonal changes and functioned allegorically to represent the life span as natural and universal. By mid-century, life stages were represented as distinct, incremental, and measurable by doctors and social scientists. It hardly seems an accident that the same American psychologist, G. Stanley Hall, who formulated the concept of adolescence in the 1880s, later staked out *Senescence* (1920) as a particular life stage. Such changes in definition justified imaginatively and literally relocating older people to workhouses, hospitals, and even chimney corners. They also encouraged middle-aged Victorians to pigeonhole old people and children as the two age groups most in need of care (Hareven 1986). The cultural consequences of using the metaphor "second childhood" for old age abound in Victorian children's literature. Dozens of Edward Lear's *Nonsense* limericks (1846, 1872) begin, "There was an old person of . . ."; the old person then behaves like a naughty child. John Tenniel's drawings of Lewis Carroll's Queen and Duchess in *Alice's Adventures in Wonderland* (1864) render Alice a dull adult by comparison with her rowdy, puerile elders, and many of the fairies and godmothers that people the Victorian fairy tales of writers like Charles Dickens, Anne Isabella Ritchie, Mary De Morgan, and Frances Browne are, like their child readers, diminutive, squeaky, and sentimentalized, even when they share irritation at adult authority. While quaint and amusing, these fictional embodiments of second childhood (like the metaphor itself) reinforce the view that older people are inept, unreasonable, and helpless; however, the old suffer doubly from the comparison because, unlike children, they are past the age when society accepts dependency as an appropriate or endearing quality.

One of the most enduring fantasies about old age focused on the social roles of elderly people in an imagined past and is therefore referred to in current studies of aging as the Golden Age fantasy. The belief in a past when the old were revered led to two common assumptions that have survived into the present. First, it was assumed that at some earlier time in history older people were venerated for their wisdom; and, second, it was believed that in this imagined past the elderly were lovingly cared for by families. The first fantasy arises from several misconceptions: that before 1800 few people survived into old age; that before widespread literacy older people's knowledge was crucial to a group's survival; that in the past extended families were common, and that adult children once felt more compelled to care for aging parents. Proponents of the Golden Age theory argued that the rise of industrialism disrupted traditional support systems for elders. This view of old age tended to romanticize earlier attitudes toward aging, to obscure historical continuities with the past, and to discount cultural and psychological aspects of aging by focusing exclusively on the very real impact of broad economic changes.

Twentieth-century family history and demographic studies offer statistical evidence to counter the Golden Age claim that fewer elderly people existed before 1800 and that elders were more valued by earlier societies. Demographic historians explain that although the mean age for life expectancy during the nineteenth century may have been 40.9 in 1838 and only 46 by 1900, these figures taken alone are misleading. Death rates were extremely high for children under five; those who survived infancy, however, could expect to reach adulthood, and those who reached 40 were likely to live into their sixties, even seventies. The mean life expectancy, then, reflected a high infant mortality rate rather than a scarcity of old people. There is also a difference between actual *numbers* of the elderly and the *proportion* of any age group in the total population. The number of old people actually fell slightly in the nineteenth century. Nevertheless, even though the predicted life span did not increase during the Victorian period, as the birth rate began to drop the proportion of the population over 40 rose significantly in England and Wales and more slowly in Scotland (Laslett 1977; Tranter 1973). In other words, although great numbers of people did not start living longer until the 1930s, the increasing proportion of elderly attracted attention in the news, the government, the medical profession, and literature long before, creating a general but false impression in the second half of the century that England was growing old.

Another reason that the Golden Age fantasy persisted was that as village gossip, newspapers, periodicals, and novels circulated stories about the harsh conditions of workhouses at mid-century and as government reports disclosed the sufferings of the elderly poor late in the century, upper- and middle-class Victorians grappled with the embarrassing revelation that one of the wealthiest countries in the world was allowing its old people to starve. These perceived inhumanities to the elderly heightened the nostalgic appeal of the second Golden Age fantasy: that in the past families had customarily cared for their own. Twentieth-century scholars, drawing on parish, poorhouse, and census records, have refuted this second supposition (Laslett 1977; Wall 1995). Such records indicate that throughout recorded history elderly people have preferred to live on their own. Even an imperfect demographic record suffices to unsettle images either of families as all-embracing, intergenerational assemblies or of old people as helpless dependents.

As these examples suggest, the Golden Age idealization of the past cast elderly Victorians as victims. While scholars use empirical data to combat the excesses of Golden Age fantasies, literature offers a different kind of corrective. As an avocation, literature offered a few privileged poets and philosophers perhaps the most distinguished social role available to an elderly Victorian man, that of the sage. But literary texts themselves were heavily populated with more common figures who offered alternatives to being a mere victim. Though novels are hardly repositories of fact, the genre's attention to relations among characters does suggest that, faced with the trials of aging, many Victorians showed both agency and initiative. Indeed, one recurring character type hints that older people who held on too tightly to property or to power were more unnerving than those who became burdens. In contrast to the quiet lives of accommodation or yearning that mark realist fiction like Trollope's Barchester and Palliser novels or his posthumous *An Old Man's Love* (1884), popular narrative genres that permitted extravagant exaggeration of fears and social tensions – sensation fiction, Gothic fiction, fantasy, adventure, science fiction – often treated older characters who eluded death as evil predators. Many sensation novels wove plots around wealthy old men and the writing, hiding, and challenging of wills. Sheridan Le Fanu's sensation villain in *Uncle Silas* (1864) schemes to murder his niece in order to keep the family fortune, while even in the less hyperbolic sensation-style subplot George Eliot included in *Middlemarch* (1872), Mr Featherstone maliciously toys with potential inheritors and then leaves his estate to his illegitimate son Joshua Rigg. Dickens carries the image of the rapacious old person to grotesque extremes in the Smallweed subplot of *Bleak House* (1853), where even grandchildren are described as being prematurely aged by their obsession with family money. In H. Rider Haggard's adventure novel *King Solomon's Mines* (1885) an African witch who has lived for centuries holds the destiny of her people hostage, while the heroine of *She* (1887), uncomfortably similar to Victoria, is a tyrannical queen who has prolonged life for thousands of years to grieve for a dead lover. Traveling to the future, the protagonist of H. G. Wells's science fiction novel *The Time Machine* (1895) encounters gray-haired, wizened, subterranean Morlocks, who cannibalize childlike surface dwellers. Contrary to the images of helpless and uncared-for elderly implicit in Golden Age fantasies, the rapacity of so many fictional elders bespeaks increasing anxiety among middle-class, middle-aged readers that old people might abuse rather than lose authority over time.

One final public spectacle that drew attention to old age in the nineteenth century was the queen herself: her reign from 1837 to 1901 spanned three generations of Victorians. Her subjects must have been uniquely aware of the particulars of aging as they watched their queen's protracted widowhood and determined refusal to turn the reins of government over to her son, the Prince Regent, who was himself an elderly man by 1900. In effect, she became England's most prominent and most costly elderly dependent. The aging of Queen Victoria also suggests how coincidental connections lead to sometimes intractable associations, in this case among old age, an aged queen, and an old order. By the end of the century, the term "Victorian" itself had assumed the nastier characteristics stereotypical of old age: creaky, antiquated, prudish, burdensome, and antithetical to youth, a newborn century, and modernity.

Despite assumptions to the contrary, empirical evidence indicates that "the aged" did not emerge as a class of record-breaking numbers during the nineteenth century. What, then, prompted such a commonly expressed view and its Victorian consequences? One answer lies in the sheer proliferation of information possible in an age of mass-market publishing. Throughout the century, books and articles touted diets for prolonged life, debated the length of the human life span, offered evidence of alleged centenarians, and wrangled over society's responsibilities to these long-lived Victorians. Whatever the facts and figures, from as early as mid-century the aged were a Victorian media event.

Consequences for Elderly Care

Perhaps the longest running story of old age can be traced in print through periodical, newspaper, parliamentary, and parish discussions of how to provide for old people, and in practice through the consequences that ensured. Financial security and care obviously varied across class and economic lines. Wealthy Victorians could afford to pay nurses, servants, and family members for whatever assistance they required; but for the vast majority of the people, surviving into old age meant facing financial hardship. A very small number of working-class people derived retirement income by participating in occupation-based Friendly Societies or trade union subscriptions, and many elderly women received small government pensions, but most people saved only enough for emergencies or burials. The English Poor Law Reform Act of 1834 promoted Victorian values of work and self-help, curbing so-called "outdoor relief" by giving local authorities the power to administer aid only to the "deserving poor" and by forcing beneficiaries to enter sex-segregated workhouses where they were forced to work in order to qualify for aid. While earlier versions of this institution had existed and later versions would persist until 1948, Victorian workhouses inspired particular abhorrence. Occupants over 50 were granted a few privileges due to age: they were exempt from restrictions on diet, alcohol, tobacco, wearing uniforms, and even sex-segregated living arrangements, since they were sometimes allowed to share quarters with married partners. Nevertheless, few chose this option. Workhouse rosters suggest that in 1851 fewer than one in eight workhouse inmates were 65; by 1891 the ratio increased to one-third in most regions; however, the increase was partially brought about when younger mentally or physically ill workhouse inmates were hospitalized, so that the proportion of the elderly increased more than actual numbers (Thomson 1983). Institutions in industrial centers, especially London, on the other hand, housed far greater numbers of poor elderly people. Also, by the end of the century far more women than men were living in these institutions.

Again, reality seldom impeded fantasy. The large population of elderly poor in the cities created an indelible impression in the public imagination that workhouses largely served (and abused) older people. Public perceptions were grim, as suggested by the drunken, exploitative harridans who steal personal belongings from the dying in Dickens's *Oliver Twist* (1838) or the mournful old women in Hubert Von Herkomer's painting *Eventide. Scene in the Westminster Union* (1878). At the same time, the warm relations between the parish-housed old men and the title character of Anthony Trollope's novel *The Warden* (1855) offer a uniquely congenial depiction of assistance to the elderly poor.

In the 1870s, changes in the law harshly cut back pensions, coerced families to care for older members, and pressured old people to support themselves. As social support ebbed, labor unions and employees of the Civil Service, major banks, the mining and railroad industries, and other businesses lobbied for work-related subsidies, and Parliament deliberated on the merits of a national pension plan and mandatory retirement. Factories required workers capable of speed, adroitness, and tolerance for repetitive tasks under sometimes brutal working conditions; since older workers were stigmatized as slow, inept, and prone to accidents, retirement seemed to serve the interests of industry and individuals. Though economic changes alone did not prompt associations between the term "old" and images of inadequacy, Golden Age proponents were certainly right to claim that the drive toward speed and mass production contributed to these stereotypes. Even so, through the end of the century "old age" resisted definition. While the Friendly Societies Act of 1875 established 50 as the age at which people could receive charitable gifts, the government waffled on pension eligibility. The Old Age Pensions Committee of 1898 first named 65 the retirement age for men. However, after considering the cost to the nation of paying from age 65, members of Parliament pushed old age up to 70 before passing the Old Age Pensions Act of 1908. This Act finally established a clear onset of "old age": a generic, quantified life span now superseded Victorian measures of age-identity.

While the workhouse and the pension plan dictated how Victorian society would care for "the aged" collectively, the aging body also attracted the attention of social scientists. In the last decades of the nineteenth century, Charles Booth (the founder of the Salvation Army) conducted Royal Commission research on poverty and then on pensions. Available to the larger reading audience as *Pauperism, a Picture; and The Endowment of Old Age, an Argument* (1892), *The Aged Poor in England and Wales* (1894), and *Old Age Pensions and the Aged Poor* (1899), Booth's research revealed that poor people were often old people. Parliamentary discussion of the reports was regularly covered in newspapers and periodicals, heightening contemporary belief that the aged were proliferating, in need of care, and threatening to become a national burden.

The Pathologizing of Old Age

The desire to document, quantify, and classify old age swept the physical sciences as well. Prior to the nineteenth century, no clear distinction separates what we would now call medical information from philosophical speculation, as suggested by what may be the first survey in English of literature on aging, Sir John Sinclair's four-volume *Code of Longevity* (1807). An eclectic collection of letters, classical quotations, and scientific explanations for aging, Sinclair's nearly 2,000 references document theories, treatments, and consolations offered by past authorities. Since old age was, inevitably, a prelude to the end of life, most of these earlier studies urged readers to accept death with stoicism once symptoms of illness or frailty appeared. We can see evidence of medical practitioners' acquiescence to the long-held belief that the elderly could not expect to be given the same treatments as younger people in doctors' willingness to pronounce the verdict "death of old age" when they filled out death certificates. An impressive medical statistical study appeared in 1889 when Sir George Humphrey published *Old Age*, a survey of nearly 900 people who had reached 80, including 74 centenarians.

Whereas many practicing Victorian doctors clung to past beliefs about old age, traditional wisdom faltered before modern science in laboratories across Europe where medical researchers, using greatly improved microscopes, launched sophisticated clinical examinations of the tissues and organs that comprised the aging body. The rise of large hospitals magnified attention to aging because charity hospitals housed so many elderly poor people. In France, the Saltpetrière, a hospital for women that at times slept 5,000, provided a grim wealth of illnesses and cadavers, leading researchers like Jean-Martin Charcot to seek in aging tissue and later in cells an explanation for physical decline and decrepitude. Charcot's *Clinical Lectures on the Diseases of Old Age* (1867), translated into English in 1881, dramatically affected how European scientists studied aging because Charcot emphasized clinical investigation of the body rather than caring for old people. England lagged behind Germany, Russia, and France in clinical medicine, and the English public were deeply suspicious of European practices. Only late in the century did the Chelsea Royal Hospital, home to invalid elderly soldiers, become an important English site for research under the direction of Daniel MacLachlan.

Examining the impact of medical studies on perceptions of old age, Stephen Katz (1996) traces an emerging "discourse of senescence" in the competing Victorian medical explanations for old age. Katz argues that one effect of nineteenth-century medical researchers' careful classification of the workings of the human body was that the body became fixed in description as a set of signs. Because these signs were interpreted as indicators of health or infirmity and of normality or deviance, researchers laying the groundwork for the disciplines of gerontology and geriatrics were also imposing discipline upon the body. The old body was treated as a sign system which signaled deterioration and degeneration, and these signs could be interpreted only by scientists. While sociological and political surveys of old people encouraged the Victorians to conceptualize a faceless impersonal mass of the aged, clinical studies threatened to reduce the complex psychological and social experience of aging to a study of tissue and organ damage. These clinical studies provided valuable information about the diseases and changes endemic to the aging body, but years would pass before the discoveries prompted practical medical treatments that actually improved old people's health or longevity.

The greatest achievement of nineteenth-century researchers may have been paving the way for the formal establishment of geriatrics and gerontology in the early twentieth century. Over the course of a century, medical studies of aging had moved from characterizing old age as a distinct and special time of life when an individual was best served by a bland diet, an end to illicit pleasures, and moderation in all things to viewing old age as the last of a systematically classified series of life stages in which aging was notable for distinct biological signs of deterioration. As medicine gained cultural as well as scientific authority, these medical opinions had far-reaching pragmatic consequences. One of the most immediate was that the testimony of medical experts was regularly used in courtrooms to determine when elderly people should be denied their rights to run family businesses, to write wills, to command resources, or to live independently.

For the most part, clinical medicine had a far less immediate effect upon the reading public than popular advice literature, readily available in books, periodical essays, and even in the testimonials that accompanied advertisements for tonics or medicines. Two long-held, contradictory conceptions of old age were argued with tenacity by popular medical authors. The first, the vitality model, defined old age as the gradual oozing away of limited energy and ability. This theory participated in a general fear that contrary to optimists' insistence that England was the world's center of industry and activity, England might just as easily be sliding into entropic and degenerate decline. Utterly contrary to this view, the second theory contended that a "grand climacteric" marked the change of life. Proponents argued that old age emerged suddenly, causing pronounced physical collapse, a loss of sexual identity and desire, and often abrupt mental deterioration (Haber 1983). For women the climacteric was believed to occur between 45 and 55 with the advent of menopause, while men could expect the sudden change between 50 and 75. Because women were thought to have less authority and social status to lose in the first place, they supposedly weathered the dramatic change more easily than men. The climacteric was also linked to senility, a word that accrued ominous associations in the Victorian age in both clinical and popular medical contexts. Formerly, "senile" had simply meant belonging to or characteristic of old age. During the nineteenth century, however, to be senile was to be not only old but also mentally or morally incompetent; alleged symptoms of nineteenth-century senility sounded more like moral judgments than evaluations of health. Thus, diagnoses might comment on selfishness, querulousness, miserliness, or lasciviousness as though they were on a par with lung congestion or rheumatism.

Just as a gap yawned between the demographer's numbers and the Victorian perception that more people were living into deep old age, for lay people medical lore had greater appeal than medical sciences. Like readers today who furtively peruse magazine headlines that promise eternal youth, Victorians read both advice literature for prolonging life and published accounts that claimed to document lives of 105, 120, even 150 years. Christopher Hufeland's book *The Art of Prolonging the Life of Man* (1797) remained popular in translation in England throughout the century. Thomas Bailey's *Records of Longevity: With an Introductory Discourse on Vital Statistics* (1857) included an alphabetical list of centenarians along with their places and dates of birth and death. Like its classical antecedents, Aristotle's comments on youth and aging, Galen's *De Sanitate Tuenda*, and Cicero's *De Senectute*, Bailey's volume and those of many fellow Victorian writers continued the tradition of entangling medical nostrums for the preservation of the body's energy with philosophical arguments for resignation to the loss of that energy. Victorian writers tailored even contrary classical arguments to fit contemporary bourgeois values such as thrift, independence, and self-denial. Thus, Bailey's prescription for long life restates ancient philosophy as moral economy: a person could "profanely consume life, by a profligate expenditure of its unappreciable powers, in riotous excess; or let its energies run to waste by a listless disregard to the performance of its important and responsible duties" or, instead, could prolong life on the "due preservation and right employment of which our creatural responsibility mainly depends".

Few Victorians seem to have heeded the dangers of prolonging life without prolonging youth, even though literature of the period often warns of the potentially dire consequences. Jonathan Swift's peevish, decrepit *struldbruggs* are memorable among the foreign civilizations encountered in *Gulliver's Travels* (1726), a novel that was still popular in the nineteenth century. Tennyson's mournful poem "Tithonus" (1860) retells the classical myth in which Tithonus's immortal lover secures Zeus's promise that Tithonus will live forever but neglects to request eternal youth, leaving him to excruciating, interminable aging. The moral dangers of prolonged aging suffuse Oscar Wilde's *The Picture of Dorian Gray* (1891). When the seductively decadent Lord Henry laments the miseries of growing old and the fleeting pleasures of youth, Dorian barters his soul for perpetual youth, but his portrait records the horrors of lascivious old age. The sunny periodical essays that continued to advise moderation of diet, pleasures, and sex form a curious foil for what is perhaps the most famous of all prolongation narratives, Bram Stoker's *Dracula* (1897). Dracula's erotic appetite for life-sustaining young blood was a motif in vampire-manqué tales as well. The title character of Mary Elizabeth Braddon's "Good Lady Ducayne" (*The Strand*, 1896) hires a doctor to use the new and dangerous technology of blood transfusion to milk the veins of young women. These writers, it should be noted, were merely exaggerating experimental medical practices of the day, such as injections of crushed animal testicles, which promised to rejuvenate youth, vitality, and sexual performance, or the still extremely dangerous transfusion of blood.

The first serious challenge to claims of extraordinary life spans was William Thoms's *Human Longevity: Its Facts and Its Fictions* (1873). The Deputy Librarian to the House of Lords, Thoms set out to apply what he called scientific standards to the investigation of alleged centenarians. Noting that in the 1851 census some 111 men and 208 women were listed as being from 100 to 119 years old, Thoms painstakingly proved that lost or inaccurate records made most cases impossible to verify; he also quickly realized that many poor and illiterate claimants had no real idea of their true birthdates.

Though studies of aging like Thoms's took formal shape in the world of medicine, the social "disease" of ageism mutated into ever more resistant strains there as elsewhere. When the famous Canadian physician William Osler left his position as head of Johns Hopkins Medical School to accept a named chair at Oxford University, his 1905 farewell speech "The Fixed Period" (a direct allusion to Trollope's novel) bemoaned the uselessness of men over 40 and jokingly advocated chloroforming men over 60. Osler's speech fomented outraged attacks from American and British doctors and newspapers alike in a contretemps that provides a snapshot of attitudes toward old age at the end of the century. Then, as now, the public imagination was capable of supporting deeply contradictory images. On one hand, the elderly were cast as children or old dears who deserved loving care and state support. On the other, older people were represented as an emerging, recalcitrant class of dependents who refused to contribute their fair share to the nation. This second view was heavily influenced by the more pessimistic among the Social Darwinists and eugenists, who believed that weaker members of society, including the infirm, the poor, and the old, were threatening the health of the nation.

Once again Victorian culture capaciously incorporated both extremes in varying gradations. As figures of popular culture, older characters appeared in the guise of comical spinsters in children's fiction like *Dame Wiggins of Lee and Her Seven Wonderful Cats* (1823); the gentle, loving grandmotherly character of Juliana Ewing's *Mrs Overtheway's Remembrances* (1894); or the wise supernatural ancestor of George MacDonald's many children's novels, including *The Princess and the Goblin* (1872). And yet old age could also be cast in malevolent forms such as the demonic, ill-spirited witches or fairies or goblins or ogres of countless Victorian fairy tales. Older figures represented in high culture also indicate contrasting opinions about old age: compare Tennyson's morose narrator of "Ulysses" (1842), champing against the constraints of an "aged wife" and the disappearance of his own youth, with the ennobled elders (Tennyson among them) in the tableaux of Julia Margaret Cameron. The mass market was saturated with replicas of the elderly queen stamped on commemoration curios and splashed across newspaper and magazine pages. And, of course, then as now, old people were many things: mothers or gentle and hard-working "grans" or helpful aging neighbors or bountiful great aunts and uncles – or they were the lined faces in sepia snapshots. Resisting attempts (like Osler's) to summarize old age or old people in a phrase, these fleeting images and details challenge any simplistic account of what it meant to anticipate old age, to grow old, or to be old a century ago.

See also MEDICAL; FICTION, SAGE WRITING; SKINS

REFERENCES

Covey, H. C. (1988) "Historical Terminology Used to Represent Older People." *Gerontologist*, 28, 291–7.

Haber, C. (1983) *Beyond Sixty-Five: The Dilemma of Old Age in America's Past.* Cambridge: Cambridge University Press.

Hareven, T. K. (1986) "Historical Changes in the Social Construction of the Life Course." *Human Development* 29, 171–80.

Katz, S. (1996) *Disciplining Old Age: The Formation of Gerontological Knowledge.* Charlottesville: University Press of Virginia.

Laslett, P. (1977) *Family Life and Illicit Love in Earlier Generations.* Cambridge: Cambridge University Press.

Roebuck, J. (1979) "When Does 'Old Age' Begin? The Evolution of the English Definition." *Journal of Social History* 12, 416–28.

Thane, P. (1993) "Old Age in English History." In C. Conrad and H. Kondratowitz (eds) *Zur Kulturgeschichte des Alterns: Towards a Cultural History of Aging.* Berlin: Deutsche Centrum fur Altersfrage.

Thomson, D. (1983) "Workhouse to Nursing Home: Residential Care of Elderly People in England Since 1840." *Ageing and Society* 3, 43–69.

Tranter, N. L. (1973) *Population Since the Industrial Revolution: The Case of England and Wales.* London: Croom Helm.

Wall, R. (1995) "Elderly Persons and Members of Their Households in England and Wales from Preindustrial Times to the Present." In D. I. Kertzer and P. Laslett (eds) *Aging in the Past: Demography, Society, and Old Age.* Berkeley: University of California Press.

FURTHER READING

Casteras, S. (1987) *Images of Victorian Womanhood in English Art*. London: Associated University Presses.

Covey, H. C. (1991) *Images of Older People in Western Art and Society*. New York: Praeger.

Featherstone, M. and Wernick A. (eds) (1995) *Images of Aging: Cultural Representations of Later Life*. London: Routledge.

Gullette, M. M. (1994) "Male Midlife Sexuality in a Gerontocratic Economy: The Privileged Stage of the Long Midlife in Nineteenth-Century Age-Ideology." *Journal of the History of Sexuality*, 5, 58–89.

Hannah, L. (1986) *Inventing Retirement: The Development of Occupational Pensions in Britain*. Cambridge: Cambridge University Press.

Kohli, Martin (1986) "The World We Forgot: A Historical Review of the Life Course." In V. W. Marshall and B. Hills (eds) *Later Life: The Social Psychology of Aging*. Beverly Hills: Sage.

Pelling, M. and Smith, R. M. (eds) (1991) *Life, Death and the Elderly: Historical Perspectives*. London: Routledge.

Quadagno, J. (1982) *Aging in Early Industrial Society: Work, Family and Social Policy in Nineteenth Century England*. New York: Academic Press.

Roebuck, J. and Slaughter, J. (1979) "Ladies and Pensioners: Stereotypes and Public Policy Affecting Old Women in England, 1880–1940." *Journal of Social History* 13, 105–14.

Tamke, S. (1978) "Human Values and Aging: The Perspective of the Victorian Nursery." In S. F. Spicker, K. M. Woodward, and D. D. Van Tassel (eds) *Aging and the Elderly: Humanistic Perspectives in Gerontology*. New Jersey: Humanities Press.

Thane, P. (1993) "Geriatrics." In W. F. Bynum and R. Porter (eds) *Companion Encyclopedia of the History of Medicine*. London: Routledge.

Woodward, K. and Schwartz, M. M. (eds) (1985) *Memory and Desire: Aging – Literature – Psychoanalysis*. Bloomington: Indiana University Press.

8

Passing On: Death

Gerhard Joseph and Herbert F. Tucker

A religion in a state of transition from supernatural belief to humanism is very poorly equipped to face death, and must dwell on it for that very reason.

Humphry House, The Dickens World

Death is the catastrophic knowledge, the truly forbidden thing, that everyone has to be protected from because no one can be.

Adam Phillips, On Flirtation

I

The Victorians wrote about death because they couldn't help it. They didn't know any better. Like us, and like every generation since self-consciousness dawned on mortality, Victorian people could not know death at first hand. Yet they could not but know, and talk, *about* it. The one experience inescapably entailed by life, death nevertheless remains by definition empirically inaccessible to the living: a cognitive zero, it gives rise to an unending discursive speculation that exhausts whatever imaginative options culture and history make available to the speculator. Each society, each epoch fills in the blank of mortality with what lies to hand, and what lies to hand is its own clutch of preoccupations. So what the Victorians themselves never tired of invoking as death's mystery makes our topic in this chapter an ideal register for understanding them and the cultural forms they produced. Death the Penalty, Death the Prize, Death the Wall, Death the Threshold, Death the Abyss: for the historian of literature these and other common Victorian tropes all present aspects of a cultural complex. Call it Death the Portrait – if not, indeed, with the period's most celebrated framer of mortal speculations, Death the Mirror: "And on the depths of death there swims / The reflex of a human face" (Tennyson, *In Memoriam* [1850], section 108). When the Victorians coped with their unbearable yet inevitable ignorance of the topic, they were depicting themselves (Goodwin and Bronfen 1993; Stewart 1984; Wheeler 1990).

Victorian speculation on death tended, as did nineteenth-century thought generally, to assume a narrative shape. What Victorians knew about nature or culture (or thought they knew) they habitually cast in the form of a story of development; so, understandably, it was story that furnished the forms in which they reassured themselves about what they did not know. What they believed about death produced two master narratives with which we shall be principally concerned here. The first has to do with the act and fact of dying itself: its scene of choice is that favorite Victorian topos the gently lighted and lovingly attended deathbed; its conventions include the deliberate taking of leave, the face turned to the wall or else the gaze cast upward beyond this world, the passage through pain into illumination, the word or gesture expressive of a life's concentrated essence. Our second master narrative concerns not the hour of death but the days and months afterward, as experienced by the survivor in mourning. Mourning, unlike dying, is a lived and to that extent a communicable experience; still, it was a notorious peculiarity of Victorian culture to shroud its mourning in as richly mystified, even eroticized, a ritual narrative as that which it accorded to dying. Within this narrative the mourner underwent a process that led, by halting steps, from the prostrating disintegrations of a wildly private grief, through beneficent touches of recognition and commemoration, to the reconstruction of a changed yet strengthened self, healed within and also embraced anew as a wiser if sadder member of the Victorian social body.

Each of these shapely narratives was in effect a manual for safe conduct along the darkest of itineraries. Small wonder, given this prescriptive function, if in their cultural dissemination Victorian death stories sometimes stiffened into maudlin sentiment, saccharine hypocrisy, compulsory gloom or cheer. While we latter-day moderns can scarcely avoid deflating their pomp and deriding their circumstance, we should first acknowledge the height of agonized terror, the depth of numb despair, through which the Victorian master narratives offered passage. We mock these stories of passing-on at our cost; they were, after all, equipment for living, which Victorian people valued for their practical therapeutic force and to which they clung the more fervently the less they could credit the age-old Christian *ars moriendi* or could depend on traditional networks of support among an extended family and community. Still, stories are what they were, and we cannot appreciate their fictive ideality without also coming to terms with the subversions that took place every time Victorian reality came in the unlovely form of a grotesque or pointless death, of a mourning brutally foreclosed or else drawn out into addictive grieving. Such inevitable failure to conform to the "stock story" thrust on the Victorian mind what we shall call, borrowing from another context, a "counterstory" (Harris 1996). This counterstory about death and grief foregrounded elements of absurdity and irresolution that Victorians could hardly welcome yet must have found uncannily familiar, for these elements attested the cultural underside or repressed bad faith of the era's official confidence that the last word on last things should be good. That cultural master narratives thus secrete their own opposites is not only a sociological key to the understanding of complex modernity; it is also, we suggest, a core insight of the most highly imaginative literature about death. Great fiction and poetry that combine stock story with counterstory most accurately represent their age, and for the same reason that keeps such works most compelling for posterity: it is there that visions of death and dying find their most dialectically complete form.

II

What then are the qualities of the conventional or stock story, our reigning cultural narrative concerning Victorian death? "As everyone allows," says Garrett Stewart, "characters die more often, more slowly, and more vocally in the Victorian age than ever before or since" (Stewart 1984: 8); and the novels and poems John Reed itemizes in his section on death in *Victorian Conventions* (1975) display that period's "system of death" (Vovelle 1990) with compelling evidentiary force. In illustration here of what "everyone allows," we might look at a specific pathos-filled death scene originating not in Victorian fiction or poetry but in that fiction by another name, biographical anecdote. For several days before his decease in 1892, and well aware of its imminence, Alfred Tennyson took to summoning his most illustrious predecessor in the English literary pantheon. "Where is my Shakespeare? I must have my Shakespeare," his son Hallam remembers him repeatedly calling out — so that the poet could touch the volume even when he could not read it. On the evening of his death, his last meal taken, he found all reading impossible. In the moon-drenched room he opened the volume instead, to the lines from late in *Cymbeline* where Posthumus and Imogen are reconciled amid the play of a joyous wit that announces the restoration of their marriage after five long acts of division and delay. Shortly thereafter Tennyson spoke his last words of blessing to the assembled family and advanced to meet his Pilot face to face, one finger inserted into his Shakespeare at the *Cymbeline* passage, a laurel wreath from Virgil's tomb placed at his side by his wife and son (Tennyson 1897 2: 25–9).

The salient characteristics of a Victorian death are impossible to miss in this famous, final rite of passage, lovingly recorded yet artfully wrought too, in fitting tribute to one of the most representative of Victorian men. The composed, elaborated quality is what most strikes us: the stately pace, the allusive and premeditated weave. It is diverting but finally not surprising to know that the laurel wreath from Virgil's tomb was a gift from Alfred Austin, who had gathered its leaves abroad 11 years earlier in express anticipation of Tennyson's passing, and whose ambition to succeed to the laureateship was to be duly realized within a few years of Tennyson's decease (Martin 1980: 582). The entire cultural text is an aestheticized "good death," and a spiritualized one too, an ideal valediction with or without the validation of such orthodox ministries as the priestly performance of last rites. This death that is patently designed to take national center-stage also takes place — so the cultural script ordains it — within the warmth of home, in the company of family and of the dying man's personal physician and friend, one Dr Dabbs.

Last but not least, here as so often in the stock story of Victorian death, famous last words put a culminating full stop to the life they epitomize (Guthke 1992). Whatever one thinks of the enigmatic leave taken by the dying Kurtz in *Heart of Darkness* (1899), when Marlow unswervingly receives "The horror!" as a mad sage's summary judgment on the human condition, the message could hardly be more starkly, existentially modern; and yet, in the very confidence of his construal, Marlow displays impeccably Victorian credentials. In Tennyson's case, family tradition took down from dying lips the words "I opened it." Opened his Shakespeare, one literal-mindedly supposes, though the phrase properly nurtured opens an eye on eternity in as Tennysonian a fashion as might be hoped for. Not so witty as "That wallpaper has to go or I do" (irresistibly if apocryphally attributed to Oscar Wilde), but withal deeply appropriate to the poet's life-long susceptibility both to Shakespeare and to diaphanously adumbrated eternal longings.

And longings they had to be, not certitudes. The final clause in the stock-story script of death would be less than fully Victorian were there not something inconclusive about it. As the protagonist of a death good enough for his own (Morte d') Arthur, Tennyson virtually had to go on record saying it was finished by saying it was opened. For the Victorian good death was not to be cloistered by the confines of holy writ or ecclesiastical dogma. In chapter 9 of the third book of *A Tale of Two Cities* (1859) Sidney Carton's incantation of "I am the Resurrection and the Life" (John 11: 25) constitutes a social and secular liturgy that reflects Dickens's vigilance to canonize a modern urban martyr on the novel's terms, not the Bible's. Scripture is included, but only on condition that it be circumscribed by fiction; that Carton die for, and into, literature. That same Bible phrase from the gospel of John galvanizes the moribund St John himself, the speaker of Robert Browning's 1864 monologue "A Death in the Desert," into dictating from his deathbed hideout a postscript that is, in effect, a latter-day hermeneut's prescription for faith. The Victorian resurrection of Christianity, its rescue from the fundamentalism of the dead letter, would entail betting the true Church on the figurality of scripture, its capacity to be "opened" like poetry (or Tennyson's fingered Shakespeare) to contemporary uses. Thus, when Browning's saintly Pompilia expires a few years later in *The Ring and the Book* (1868–9), it is only after explicitly giving scripture her seal of approval, not vice versa. Within the Tennysonian idealization of death, the casement always "grows a glimmering square" ("Tears, Idle Tears" [1847]), an aperture that outlines an otherworldly opportunity at the same time that it invites perennial lingering, Enoch Arden-like, at the sill. Where the mere intimation of immortality meant so much, there arose a distinctive tendency to immortalize the intimation, to read death's text by the glimmering twilight of a faith in doubt. Not for nothing did the Victorian spiritualist medium drive a brisk trade, or the Metaphysical Society (1869) and the Society for Psychical Research (1882) attract eminent membership rosters (Oppenheim 1985).

In order to explain something as overdetermined as a period's attitude towards death, historians evoke a plurality of causes. The "beautiful death" that Philippe Ariès sees as a Victorian cultural style results, he argues in his influential *The Hour of Our Death* (1981), from a Romantic transformation of eighteenth-century terrors into something beautiful, something to be eagerly awaited and orchestrated into the sort of deathbed finale we have just been considering. Pat Jalland (1997), on the other hand, cautions against applying to Britain what is limited and eccentric in the work done on death by Ariès and his *Annales* school. Ariès's analysis is largely based upon the records left behind by a Brontë family ravaged by tuberculosis – he elaborates as his prime example the episode of Helen Burns's death in *Jane Eyre* (1847) – and his view is furthermore Catholic rather than Protestant in emphasis. By contrast Jalland, having studied in manuscript a collection of private diaries, extensive correspondence, wills, and memorials of death covering over 50 families and almost 100 years, suggests that "if death in nineteenth-century Britain is to be characterized in terms of a single model or an ideal, then it should be the Evangelical 'good death' and not Ariès's 'beautiful death'" (Jalland 1997: 8). In aid of such a death there were not only numberless evangelical tracts, but also such older works as Bishop Jeremy Taylor's *The Rule and Exercises of Holy Dying* (1651), which George Eliot's novel *Adam Bede* (1859, ch. 19) names as the standard Victorian reference guide to the good death in an Anglican home.

In death as in philosophy, of course, the romantically beautiful and the evangelically good might prove compatible. Much Victorian devotional verse (especially women's) was devoted to illustrating just this compatibility. So was much Victorian fashion (especially men's). Men in black sustained for decades variations on a masculine aesthetic that united severe elegance with sober power, casting its shadow across a national "cult of death" that was "funereal even when feasting" (Harvey 1995: 177). Not only in *Little Dorrit* (1855) and *Great Expectations* (1861) and *Middlemarch* (1873) was there something coffinlike about domestic interiors, where recreational or study space denoted masculine was especially liable to be somber-wooded and plumb-boxed. On the street and square as well, the sarcophagus bulk of state architecture and imperial monument recorded in bronze and stone the Victorian habit of sacrificing at death's cryptic altar, engarlanding public honor with the crape of commemoration. The same Tennyson who reverently hoped to see his Pilot face to face when he had crossed the bar of an evangelical transformation had, just a few lines before, booked passage on a flood of sensuous and hypnotic beauty, "such a tide as moving seems asleep, / Too full for sound and foam" ("Crossing the Bar" [1889]). Both moments in the poem flow with the Victorian mainstream, which might indeed be worse conceived than as an habitually rehearsed passage from the one moment to the other, a current from sense to soul connecting – or hoping to connect – the fleshly with the metaphysical. It was at the ideal hour of death, or at the frequent but no less ideal anticipations of death with which Victorians punctuated their lives, that beauty could be truth, truth beauty. And such beauty frequently took the form of the dying maiden, the elegiac female object enshrouded in dreamlike haze who haunts Pre-Raphaelite stanzas and canvases, especially, but is seldom far to seek in Victorian poetry and painting at large.

III

Whether Romantic or Evangelical influence furnishes the best explanation for the obsession with death in the Victorian period, material factors also have to be taken into account. For one thing, there was so much more early death – especially among the very young – than at present, when most people in the industrialized West die at a relatively mature age. Anthony Wohl (1983) calls it a "massacre of the innocents": in any given year during the High Victorian period something like 100,000 children died before their first birthday. The death rate in England and Wales for infant mortality per thousand was 154 in 1840, 148 in 1860, 154 in 1890. A persistent if slow decline thereafter brought the rate to 100 in 1916 and below 16 in 1983. In appreciating the Victorian encounter with death, then, we must multiply tenfold our own apprehensiveness over a baby's survival, compounded by a comparable if less statistically daunting risk to the life of the baby's mother. Among us the advance of age has supplanted the fact of birth as the most probable cause for death; to reverse these proportions is to conceive what stern necessities underlay the omnipresence of death to the Victorian mind as it tried to keep in bearable view a reality that could never be kept at bay, in any family, for long.

Two turning points may be mentioned in the history of these accommodations to necessity (Jalland 1997). The first centers roughly on 1870, when, in a textbook Victorian shift of priorities, an advancing science supervened on a religion in retreat. As sanitary reforms took hold, and as antiseptic and obstetric medicine progressed with the century, life and death expectancy came more predictably under human control; this matter of fact soon became (what is not the same thing) a matter of faith, and it did so the more readily with the recession of orthodox belief that marked the last quarter of the century. As moral psychology uncoupled convictions about sin from certainties of penal torment in Hell (in which fewer and fewer Victorians put real faith), the physical pain of dying came into focus as a *summum malum*. In this connection Dr William Munk's 1887 textbook *Euthanasia; or Medical Treatment in Aid of an Easy Death*, while its title denotes not mercy killing but the tranquil passing-on spelled out in its subtitle, nevertheless marks a modern corner turned.

A second and more acute turning point confronts us in World War I, which effected a traumatically abrupt change in the national imagination of death. The horror of mass extinction in the trenches, decimating a generation of young Britons, was if anything made more horrible by contrast to the "good" and "beautiful" ideals of dying that their forebears had cherished (Cannadine 1981; Fussell 1975). That this decisive historical watershed was post-Victorian is precisely our point, for in no respect did the Great War cashier Victorian conventions more dramatically than in this. What

the nineteenth century had constructed as a tranquil and carefully attended rapprochement with a foreknown end yielded overnight to staccato cataclysm. Suddenly death
betokened cruel caprice, absurdity, a moral anomie that was ironically embittered by
the Victorians' recently won conviction that dying might become a medically manage-
able, secular process.

In another sense, though, the pointless violence which overtook the Western
imagination of death with the Great War merely brought to public consciousness an
extensive knowledge that Victorian culture had extensively suppressed. War stories
had the effect of promoting into a new stock story for the twentieth century what had
been the old counterstory of the nineteenth. Which energetically neglected considerations, then, had informed that counterstory all along? For one thing, the issue of class:
the story on which we have thus far dwelt is on the whole an upper-middle-class story,
and while it has frequently been assumed that the attitudes of the upper classes filtered
down to the working classes, such an assumption, Ruth Richardson (1989) affirms, is
quite mistaken. Death for the working class, especially the indigent whose number
was legion during the Victorian period, was a decidedly grimmer matter than for their
social betters.

One horror in particular attached to the approach of poor people's death that was
unknown among the well-to-do, who were nevertheless its chief if chiefly unknowing
beneficiaries. This was the possibility of what the celebrated final sentence of Emily
Brontë's *Wuthering Heights* (1847) calls, albeit preventively, "unquiet slumbers, for the
sleepers in that quiet earth." The supply of cadavers for medical research and teaching
was legally limited at the turn of the nineteenth century to the census of hanged
murderers transferred into medical hands by the arm of the law, and these were
relatively few. As a result, the sale of bodies illegally snatched from cemeteries, in
which paupers' graves enjoyed least protection, became a lucrative business during the
eighteenth century. Still, a persistent shortage of corpses led anatomists, surgeons, and
others to press for an expansion and legitimation of the supply, which were eventually
granted in the Anatomy Act of 1832. Intended to preempt the most ghoulish of black
markets, the Act stipulated that government should surrender for medical dissection
the bodies not merely of hanged felons, but now too of paupers dying in workhouses
and hospitals who lacked the funds to defray their own funerals. What generations of
the poor since 1750 had feared and hated as a penalty for murder thus became in 1832
a statutory penalty for poverty itself. Thereafter body-snatching did largely disappear,
enough so to dwindle into macabre comic relief in the Cruncher subplot from *A Tale
of Two Cities*. But the terror of a pauper's death remained; and the Anatomy Act goes
a long way towards explaining the growing prestige of the respectable funeral among
Victorian poor people, and of the death-insurance and undertaking businesses that
guaranteed and carried it out (Richardson 1989).

That not all Victorian deaths were the stately and ritualized affairs of stock story
was in fact evident to members of all classes and not merely to the poor: the egalitarian
democracy of death made persons up and down the social ladder liable to violent or
hideous ends. For a demonstrative supplement to the idealized death of Tennyson, we

turn again to biography, this time to Tennyson's only contemporary rival in literary eminence, Charles Dickens. If one accepts the retrospective approximations of his biographers, Dickens's life did not come to a graceful close: his end broke suddenly and unexpectedly and awkwardly, as many Victorian deaths surely did, *in medias res*. To be sure, he had been unwell during his last years, too exhausted to write much: Wilkie Collins petulantly assures us that the late *Mystery of Edwin Drood* was "Dickens's last laboured effort, the melancholy work of a worn-out brain," George Bernard Shaw that it was "the gesture by a man already threequarters dead" (Fielding 1958: 246, 242). On June 8, 1870, nevertheless, Dickens spent all day working alone at Gad's Hill on *Drood*. At dinner he confessed that he had been feeling ill. Then, abruptly, he rose and fell to the floor. Georgina Hogarth, his sister-in-law and the only family member present, sent away for the children and (apparently) for his mistress Ellen Ternan. While Dickens lived through the night and all the next day, he never regained consciousness and died on the evening of June 9.

No preparation, no final *mot*, no bracing valedictory with which the family (already skewed from the norm) could console itself during the mourning period; just an anti-climactic dying fall without meaning, an apoplectic bang and then hours of whimper petering out into insignificance – such are the mortal certainties of the case, although biographers wrapping things up with the stately funeral at Westminster Abbey dispose us to think otherwise. We concentrate here upon the bleak death of Dickens the man precisely because of its incongruity with the drawn-out, emotionally upholstered and fully articulated deaths of so many of his characters, among them Jo in *Bleak House* (1853), Nell and her grandfather in *The Old Curiosity Shop* (1841), Paul in *Dombey and Son* (1848), each presumably transported into that second of Dickens's "two cities," the "far, far better place" towards which Sidney Carton also exits. Not all deaths in Dickens wear this aura of aestheticized solemnity and sentimental spirituality, of course. There are also the violent, unredeemed drownings of Eugene Wrayburn and Gaffer Hexam in *Our Mutual Friend* (1865) and of Quilp in *The Old Curiosity Shop*, the morcellation of Carker's body by the railway locomotive that disfigures a "he" into an "it," the Byronic whelming of Steerforth in *David Copperfield* (1850).

Like the definitive extreme case from *Bleak House*, Krook's notoriously spontaneous combustion, these fast and dirty deaths were spectacular but were also exceptional. Such blunt ends got comparatively short shrift in Dickens's book – the great mid-century genre of the novel, that is – and one reason was that they made for scant copy. (In our book too: note above how few words Dickens's death takes next to Tennyson's.) It was pre-pondered death that preponderated: the long deaths of Kingsley's Alton Locke (1850), Thackeray's Colonel Newcome (1855), Trollope's Septimus Harding (*The Last Chronicle of Barset*, 1867), Eliot's Mordecai Cohen (*Daniel Deronda*, 1876) all represent different values; but across a quarter-century they represent in common an established mode of making values tell.

The High Victorian narrative advantage went to plots of passing-on that were laid thick with foreshadowing, were prolonged with care, and above all were sequel-friendly. Styles of dying thus entrained other aspects of style that prepared or attended the Victorian mortal climax. Indeed, the end of the line for serial three-decker novels came into view when 1860s sensation fiction started weaning readers from the long fadeout and habituating them instead to the stab in the back and the shot in the dark. Even so severe a High-Church apostate from secular fashion as Gerard Manley Hopkins was spurred into sacred song, not by extreme unction, but by the quick ecstasy of an accidental disaster written up in the news ("The Wreck of the *Deutschland*" [1876]). This vogue for death by surprise heralded a late-century taste for racier closures, more of them and at a swifter clip, and thus cooperated with the morbid thematics of the Decadent movement to usher in the abbreviated literary forms that typified literary production by the 1890s. In a longer work like *Jude the Obscure* (1895), one way Hardy put paid to High Victorian fiction was with the grim zest of an indecorum that dotted the novel with signally graceless deaths. Dickens had led a life of literary innovation; even the unDickensian manner of his demise seems, in retrospect, to have portended emerging lines of change within the genre over which he had presided while alive.

IV

Sigmund Freud became the twentieth century's psychic mythmaker because he had been the nineteenth century's psychic mapmaker first; and it is to his "Mourning and Melancholia" that we turn for the stock story on Victorian bereavement (Sacks 1985; Ramazani 1994). The death of a loved one brings on the painful affect of grief, which mourning works through in a gradual process divisible into "stages" on the way to recovery (Kübler-Ross 1970). For all its attendant anguish, mourning is consolatory and restorative: once the mourner has passed through its stages he or she can proceed, if not to new objects of desire, then at least to a life relatively free of incapacitating pain. Still, mourning is made exquisitely difficult by the ferocity with which the grieving self can resist its own cure:

> People never willingly abandon a libidinal position, not even, indeed, when a substitute is already beckoning to them. This opposition can be so intense that a turning away from reality takes place and a clinging to the object through the medium of hallucinatory wishful psychosis. Normally, respect for reality gains the day. Nevertheless its orders cannot be obeyed at once. They are carried out bit by bit, at great expense of time and cathectic energy, and in the meantime the existence of the lost object is psychically prolonged. Each single one of the memories and expectations in which the libido is bound to the object is brought up and hypercathected, and detachment of the libido is accomplished in respect of it. (Freud 1915 14: 244–5)

Freud emphasizes the "expense of time and cathectic energy" that is required of individual consciousness. But that psychic economy must be further understood in its interdependent relation with the larger cultural economy. As Esther Schor has recently maintained (Schor 1994), to focus exclusively on the isolated act of mourning may well be wrongheaded, since acts of mourning are diffusively conditioned by larger epistemic considerations.

Every society develops rules and rituals by and against which individuals define themselves, so that public acts of mourning – for the Duke of Wellington once upon a time, for Princess Diana yesterday – both shape and are shaped by the responses to death in one's immediate ken. This dialectic, which Victorian writers grasped very well, made it possible for a literature of private grief to enjoy a mass circulation, not only in the several splendid elegies produced by the era's poets but also in the pronouncedly elegiac strain that suffuses much of its classic autobiographical and fictional prose. At the official level, mourning rituals were marked by extraordinary ostentation, the sumptuous obsequies of Wellington in 1852 elaborating a High Victorian ideal for state funeral pomp: a million and a half mourners along the parade route, a coffin of quadruple ply, a hearse costing £11,000, and £80,000 expended on funeral seating alone. By 1880, less showy funerals were coming to be preferred, thanks partly to efforts by the National Funeral and Mourning Reform Association (founded 1875), partly to the medical–religious authority transfer we glanced at earlier: witness the widespread condemnation of lavish display at the 1865 funerals of the Duke of Northumberland and Cardinal Wiseman, or the relative simplicity of Gladstone's in 1898. Clearly, however, for a long time sheer aggrandizement was reckoned desirable in both highlighting a national grief and facilitating a national therapy. The more extravagant the display, the more expeditious might be the public catharsis.

At the level of private grief we find a similar extravagance, manifest in elaborate memorial rites (fixed periods of mourning, with special mourning stationery, jewelry, attire, and so on), as well as the establishment in suburban London of eight new cemeteries permitting the observance of those rites in monumental splendor within a garden setting. Thus, private family burials, at least among the more prosperous members of the middle class, as a rule took their cue from the funerals of state. What these private acts of mourning might lack in ostentation, they could make up for in temporal extension. This was especially the case for women, for while bourgeois men did also mourn, their need to go to work in a man's world encouraged a discourse of Victorian mourning that remained gender-marked: etiquette books, for example, tended to enunciate rules for mourning on the part of widows and mothers. During the first year of mourning over a parent, spouse, or child, women clad in jet black were expected to behave as veritable social outcasts and refuse all invitations to leave the home. But once the specified period of mourning was past, there set in a no less binding expectation that the mourner speedily reactivate her discarded social identity.

The compromise that society thus struck between an intensely elaborated commemoration, and a consolation distant yet secure, achieved its classic literary treatment with *In Memoriam A. H. H.* This is so, not in spite of what can seem duplicitous about the rhythm of remembering and forgetting in Tennyson's elegy, but because of it. Duplicitous, or else profoundly paradoxical: according to Freud the ego, in its desire for self-preservation, remembers *in order* to forget, prolongs the attachment *in order* to effect a detachment on terms the ego can accept. "The lost object," says Christopher Craft about the homoerotics of *In Memoriam*, "thus suffers a thousand posthumous deaths at the now murderous hands of the mourner" who, however stealthily, prepares to bind himself to a new object in the chain of recuperative substitutions we call life (Craft 1993: 166). No wonder the mourning speaker, shot through with shame at abandoning his loved object, wants at times to write himself off as a creeping "guilty thing" (*In Memoriam*, section 7). Still, the iron law demarcating mourning from melancholia – and governing the Victorian persistence of the classical elegiac genre – is that the object shall at last be put aside. Eventually even *In Memoriam* becomes street-legal, subsiding unspecifiably yet undeniably into a consolation that is crowned by the celebration of a marriage. But the reluctance of Tennyson's compliance with the law manifestly strains the limits it confirms. The most Victorian quality about this elegy, its inordinate length, repeatedly raises the possibility that, if a pageant of grief can last for 131 meandering lyrics and for at least three Christmases, it just might last forever.

V

This possibility did not go unrealized in fact or fiction. Exceptions were abundant to the Victorian mourner's narrative of progress through intense bereavement to muted recovery; the recent widow whose "hair has turned quite gold from grief" would not have raised the laugh she still gets in act one of Wilde's *The Importance of Being Earnest* (1895) had real-life exemplars been wanting. Then as now some spouses, heirs, and other skeptics were quite capable of accepting the loss of intimates with quiet relief or frank indifference. Because the stock story made no place for such reactions, however, and also because such reactions were by nature not very news- or plot-worthy, they remain matter largely for inference, e.g. as sources of the mourner's diffuse guilt in *In Memoriam*, or of the gentle comic thread that stitches Trollope's Barsetshire novels. More conspicuous in the Victorian newspapers, and in novels of sensation such as M. E. Braddon's *Lady Audley's Secret* (1862), were splashier cases in which the survivor was believed to have taken an active role in helping the death along. Such cases, as well as the many instances of Victorian suicide (Gates 1989), bore out the logic generally operative in scandal: they owed their notoriety to the norms which they scandalized – and thus served to reinforce – norms sufficiently stringent that few Victorian dissidents against compulsory mourning withheld the tribute of lip service. (Witness, again, Wilde's *Earnest*, with Jack's deadpan dumbshow of grief over the non-person Bunbury in act two.)

The most remarkable cultural opposition to the regime of Victorian mourning was the one that emerged from within it, born of its very triumph: melancholia, the stock story of mourning minus the scripted denouement; mourning that ceased to be mourning precisely because it would not cease. Letters, diaries and journals of the period provide ample evidence of chronic grief, wherein mourning no longer *worked* but went instead on permanent detour into the wilds of sorrow. Imaginative enlargements of this cultural disorder appear as the Victorian undead, caricatures of survivorship who command attention in Tennyson's "Tithonus" (1860), Haggard's *She* (1887), and Stoker's *Dracula* (1897). Trollope created in Lily Dale a character who, for all the social realism of *The Small House at Allington* (1864), stands comparison with these fantasy survivals in her steadfastness to a love that is stillborn because unrequited, absurdly disproportionate to its undeserving object – yet that her stunned heart will not surrender. As may be seen from the extraordinary record of multiple bereavement that charges Margaret Oliphant's unpublished autobiography, some Victorians never did recover from the death of a beloved spouse or child. Refusing the final therapeutic turn toward integration, they incurred the additional pain of censure at the hands of a society whose highly visible mourning customs made instances of nonconforming refusal impossible to miss and easy to interpret as antisocial vanity.

So, while as a matter of literary history the mourning of a Victorian elegist like Swinburne may have had more in common with Spenser's three centuries before him than with Wilfred Owen's atavistic, violent, and untranscendable modernist melancholia three decades after, as a cultural phenomenon full-blown "'melancholic' mourning" (Ramazani 1994) did not have to wait for the twentieth century. The Victorian period, Jalland (1997) shows in detail, had its share of inconsolables already; and none more amply represented the disposition of the nation and age toward extravagance in bereavement than that foremost of cultural icons, Queen Victoria herself. Victoria's elaborate mourning for Prince Albert after his death by typhus made her an archetype whose influence upon subsequent custom was crucial and pervasive. Quintessential ideal of middle-class Christian wifehood, she became in 1861 the instigator and impeccable exemplar of a cult of flamboyant widowhood, whose adherents took the staying power of grief to be the surest authentication of the marital sanctities it ratified. But then the queen's stipulated period of formal mourning doubled from two years to four, and then quadrupled to eight, swelling exponentially into a twenty-year retreat from public life into sovereign sequestration at Balmoral and Windsor Castles. Victoria's subjects became at first increasingly suspicious, and at last inevitably convinced, that there was something wrong about their monarch's prostration, something downright pathological – and a combined journalistic and parliamentary campaign said so in strong terms.

But even an empress may claim her counterstory, and even melancholia may have its uses. Victoria's response to the death of Albert surely was – or it became – more complex with the years than the well advertised, duly received story of unrelievable suffering would suggest. While Victoria's mourning for her husband (and for other close relatives as well) was indeed extravagant, she did without question, and in well under two decades, recover mental equipoise and self-command. So it is sensible to suppose that the officially circulated tale served other purposes; that the queen, in keeping to herself, kept the trappings of stricken privacy in full public view with a conscious theatrical flair and evident political results (Munich 1996). Had the "Widow at Windsor" – Kipling's 1890 poem caught a slogan that was already in the air – gotten over her sorrow in too public a fashion, it might have brought pressure on her to marry again, or might have sponsored even more fancifully intimate tales than made the rounds anyhow concerning her friendship with the devoted and beloved servant John Brown. The decorously flirtatious homage that Disraeli paid the queen during his years of parliamentary ascendancy highlights from a different side the relation Victoria's aggressively defended widowhood bore to questions of political advantage.

To these personal motives we add here a cultural one: Victorian society needed a scapegoat on which to fix the burden of its own self-delightingly morbid excess. On one hand the conventions of mourning were too prescriptively rigid to fit the varieties of emotional aftermath actually experienced by survivors guilty, complacent, or otherwise. On the other hand those conventions were pathetically inadequate to the towering passions that bereavement could release, passions whose capacity to become habit-forming many Victorians must have glimpsed in themselves as possibilities and observed more or less actualized in others. On either hand the Victorian system of mourning thus generated a surplus; and whether this surplus was apprehended as hypocrisy or as addiction, the already idealized figurehead of the queen attracted it with all the occult force that the nascent mass culture of the nineteenth century vested in celebrity. The realm at large thus converged on Victoria's endlessly grieving widowhood as both a congratulatory and a cautionary tale, fashioned by her even as she was fashioned by it, for the sake of a common welfare more felt after than planned or understood.

If we would seek the dead – and what else is this scholarly seance of ours with Victorian cultural ancestors? – we have no choice but to inquire among the living. This is so in several senses. One is that in which the literature of death perforce concerns survivors rather than predecessors. The subtle evangelical Browning knew as much when he put at the focus of "An Epistle . . . of Karshish" (1855) not the perished and resurrected Lazarus but the medical student who, having examined Lazarus as a patient, can neither understand what he has met nor stop trying. Likewise the unsubtle evangelical Edward Bickersteth, who, having put the protagonist of *Yesterday, To-Day, and For Ever* (1867) to good death in an opening episode, made him his own survivor for 11 more books of epically detailed witness from the afterlife. The needs of life directed Victorian death in another sense, too: the phenomena of necroculture that this chapter has considered were stabilizing devices, which the Victorians installed to counteract what they saw, with real cause, as the unprecedented chase they were leading each other. If the whole society appeared funereal, that is because it was in mourning for lost fixtures, in the world and of the spirit, which the acceleration of a coveted yet feared modernity had swept away. It was toward us, of course, and through us, that the force of that acceleration swept, and sweeps. Our house of mourning today is by Victorian standards spare and drafty and cold. We now treat with hasty neglect the great last fact of life that once obsessed our forebears, and part of the price we pay is that our observance of death defaults to a threadbare, hollow repetition of theirs. Among many human necessities for which the anglophone West still calls on Victorian help, the needs of dying and mourning may be foremost.

See also CLERICAL, MEDICAL; POETRY; PARAPETS

REFERENCES

Ariès, Philippe (1981) *The Hour of Our Death*, trans. Helen Weaver. New York: Knopf.

Cannadine, David (1981) "War and Death, Grief and Mourning in Modern Britain." In *Mirrors of Mortality*, ed. Joachim Whaley. New York: St Martin's Press.

Craft, Christopher (1993) "'Descend and Touch and Enter': Tennyson's Strange Manner of Address." In *Critical Essays on Alfred Tennyson*, ed. Herbert F. Tucker. New York: G. K. Hall.

Fielding, K. J. (1958) *Charles Dickens: A Critical Introduction*. Boston: Houghton Mifflin.

Freud, Sigmund [1915] (1953–74) "Mourning and Melancholia." In *The Standard Edition of the Complete Works of Sigmund Freud*, trans. James Strachey. London: Hogarth Press.

Fussell, Paul (1975) *The Great War and Modern Memory*. London: Oxford University Press.

Gates, Barbara (1989) *Victorian Suicide: Mad Crimes and Sad Histories*. Princeton: Princeton University Press.

Goodwin, Sarah Webster and Bronfen, Elizabeth (1993) *Death and Representation*. Baltimore: Johns Hopkins University Press.

Guthke, Karl (1992) *Last Words: Variations on a Theme in Cultural History*. Princeton: Princeton Princeton University Press.

Harris, Janice Hubbard (1996) *Edwardian Stories of Divorce*. New Brunswick: Rutgers University Press.

Harvey, John (1995) *Men in Black*. Chicago: University of Chicago Press.

House, Humphry (1941) *The Dickens World*. London: Oxford University Press.

Jalland, Pat (1997) *Death in the Victorian Family*. London: Oxford University Press.

Kübler-Ross, Elisabeth (1970) *On Death and Dying*. London: Routledge.

Martin, Robert Bernard (1980) *Tennyson: The Unquiet Heart*. Oxford: Clarendon Press.

Munich, Adrienne (1996) *Queen Victoria's Secrets*. New York: Columbia University Press.

Munk, William (1887) *Euthanasia: or Medical Treatment in Aid of an Easy Death*. London: Longmans, Green, and Co.

Oppenheim, Janet (1985) *The Other World: Spiritualism and Psychical Research in England 1850–1914*. Cambridge: Cambridge University Press.

Phillips, Adam (1994) *On Flirtation: Psychoanalytic Essays on the Uncommitted Life*. Cambridge, MA: Harvard University Press.

Ramazani, Jahan (1994) *The Poetry of Mourning: The Modern Elegy from Hardy to Yeats*. Chicago: University of Chicago Press.

Reed, John R. (1975) *Victorian Conventions*. Athens, OH: Ohio University Press.

Richardson, Ruth (1989) *Death, Dissection, and the Destitute*. London: Penguin Books.

Sacks, Peter (1985) *The English Elegy: Studies in the Genre from Spenser to Yeats*. Baltimore: Johns Hopkins University Press.

Schor, Esther (1994) *Bearing the Dead: The British Culture of Mourning from the Enlightenment to Victoria*. Princeton: Princeton University Press.

Stewart, Garrett (1984) *Death Sentences: Styles of Dying in British Fiction*. Cambridge, MA: Harvard University Press.

Tennyson, Hallam (1897) *Alfred Lord Tennyson: A Memoir*, 2 vols. London: Macmillan.

Vovelle, Michel (1990) *Ideologies and Mentalities*, trans. Eamon O'Flaherty. Chicago: University of Chicago Press.

Wheeler, Michael (1990) *Death and the Future Life in Victorian Literature and Theology*. Cambridge: Cambridge University Press.

Wohl, Anthony (1983) *Endangered Lives: Public Health in Victorian Britain*. Cambridge, MA: Harvard University Press.

FURTHER READING

Bronfen, Elizabeth (1992) *Over Her Dead Body: Death, Femininity, and the Aesthetic*. New York: Routledge.

Curl, James Stephen (1972) *The Western Celebration of Death*. Newton Abbot: David and Charles.

McManners, John (1981) *Death and the Enlightenment*. Oxford: Oxford University Press.

Morley, John (1971) *Death, Heaven, and the Victorians*. Pittsburgh: University of Pittsburgh Press.

Rowell, Geoffrey (1974) *Hell and the Victorians: A Study of the Nineteenth-Century Theological Controversies Concerning Eternal Punishment and the Future Life*. Oxford: Oxford University Press.

Shaw, W. David (1994) *Elegy and Paradox: Testing the Conventions*. Baltimore: Johns Hopkins University Press.

9
Victorian Sexualities
James Eli Adams

For the young Virginia Woolf, the world changed one spring evening in 1908, when her friend Lytton Strachey pointed at a stain on her sister's dress and inquired, "Semen?" "With that one word," she recalled,

> all barriers of reticence and reserve went down. . . . Sex permeated our conversation. The word bugger was never far from our lips. We discussed copulation with the same excitement and openness that we had discussed the nature of good. . . . So there was now nothing that one could not say, nothing that one could not do, at 46 Gordon Square. It was, I think, a great advance in civilisation. (*Moments of Being*, ch. 3)

This galvanizing moment in the formation of "Bloomsbury" may suggest how powerfully the Victorians, those unmentioned parents against whom Woolf and her friends were rebelling, have shaped twentieth-century understandings of sexuality – never more powerfully, perhaps, than in such moments of self-conscious rebellion.

Almost from its first wide currency in the late nineteenth century, "Victorian" has been a byword for a rigorous moralism centered on sexual repression. Long after Strachey challenged Victorian "reticence and reserve," however, its effects continued to be felt in the assumption that the most private and intimate facts about human beings have to do with sex. In the work of Sigmund Freud, himself an eminent late Victorian, sexuality became the paradigm of "deep" truth about human identity. Moreover, sexual repression as Freud described it could be both the foundation of human discipline and the archetype of human oppression. To speak the truth about sex – merely to speak *of* sex – was therefore to address the most basic structures of knowledge and power. To pronounce the word "semen" in mixed company was not merely a breach of etiquette; it amounted to a revolution. The exhilaration Woolf recalls thus helps to explain why we have been so long entertained by anecdotes about anxious or anesthetic Victorians draping piano legs, concocting euphemistic names for chicken parts, and being told on their wedding nights to "close your eyes and think of

England." We have enjoyed this image of Victorian sexuality – or rather, of the Victorian avoidance of sexuality – because it provided us with a basis for proclaiming our own liberation and enlightenment. But this self-congratulation required averting our own gaze from more complicated realities.

Received wisdom about the Victorians and sex has recently been challenged on two broad fronts. First, archival research has led to more thorough knowledge of Victorian private lives and public commentary on them. This research has uncovered much more variety of sexual experience – including erotic fulfillment – and much less unanimity in official stories about that experience. What has been called "the most notorious of Victorian statements about sex," for example, the remark of the physician William Acton that "the majority of women . . . are not very much troubled with sexual feeling of any kind," seems to have been a relatively eccentric medical opinion (Mason 1994: 195). Yet the remark continues to be cited as a representative Victorian view, 30 years after it was given prominence in Steven Marcus's pioneering study *The Other Victorians* (1966) – a persistence which suggests the strength of our curiously wishful thinking about the Victorians.

Such wishful thinking has been most trenchantly criticized by the French historian Michel Foucault, who is the main voice of a second, more radical questioning of received views about Victorian sexuality. The Victorians, Foucault urges in his Introduction to *The History of Sexuality* (1978), far from being silent about sex, were caught up in manifold and urgent imperatives to talk about it, and to translate it into "discourses" of knowledge and power. The very concept of "sexuality," we are reminded, is a nineteenth-century invention, which took shape when the traditional moral agency of the priest was subsumed and transformed by developing discourses of (among other things) medicine, biology, psychology, political economy, sanitation, criminology, and law. "The reticences of 'Victorian puritanism,'" in this view, were "a digression, a refinement, a tactical diversion in the great process of transforming sex into discourse" (ibid.: 22), a process vigorously forwarded in Woolf's Gordon Square flat. And as this transformation turned sexuality into an object of knowledge and regulation, Foucault contends, it also constructed multiple, heterogeneous forms of sexual identity, in which norms were reinforced by hosts of perversions: sexuality gave way to sexualities, most notably that enduringly tendentious binary, "homosexual" and "heterosexual."

History is of course less neat than this schematic overview implies. But Foucault's suggestions have been provocative in several respects. First, they urge us to see ostensibly marginal or "deviant" forms of sexuality as central to understandings of human identity generally. The very concept of "the heterosexual," for example, is a nineteenth-century invention that follows closely – both logically and chronologically – the construction of "the homosexual." Moreover, by approaching sexuality as a discursive configuration, Foucault's views have encouraged a fuller awareness of sexuality – the way in which we organize our understanding and experience of erotic life – as a profoundly historical phenomenon, which is responsive to social and political forces that may seem far removed from the world of instinctual drives. In provoking such reflection, finally, Foucault carries on one of the great skeptical commitments of Victorian ethics – one nobly urged by John Stuart Mill, among others: an alertness to the moral obfuscations often wrought by invocations of "nature" and "the natural."

Efforts to comprehend distinctively "Victorian" attitudes to sexuality typically begin well before the birth of the monarch herself, in the late eighteenth-century religious revival loosely known as the "Evangelical" movement. Under the leadership of William Wilberforce, the Evangelicals from roughly the 1780s sought to transform both British politics and everyday conduct by reinvigorating Christian piety, and approaching human life as an arena of constant moral struggle, of resistance to temptation and mastery of desire. For the most vigorous of Evangelicals, pleasure itself was memorably suspect: as Leslie Stephen (Virginia Woolf's father) recalled of his father, "He once smoked a cigar, and found it so delicious that he never smoked again" (Houghton 1957: 236).

Of course, the body and its pleasures had always held an uneasy place in Christian ethics, and the Church had long been the dominant sexual authority in the Christian West. In the nineteenth century, however, sex was subjected to a broader array of disciplines; its traditional place in concerns of individual and familial welfare – whether physical, emotional, or spiritual – was subsumed in large economic and political questions. We glimpse this reconfiguration in the economic tropes widely associated with Victorian attitudes to sexuality: sex is a vital force to be carefully regulated and conserved, with potentially dire consequences awaiting those who "spend" too much. There was nothing novel in the mere idea of a sexual economy, which responds to the commonplace experience of sex as a loss of self-possession, the lapse of (traditionally masculine) mastery over oneself and the world (Gay 1984: 317). What was distinctive was the vigor and pervasiveness with which Victorians elaborated the congruence of *homo sexualis* and *homo economicus*. That elaboration reflected the remarkable Victorian faith in the power of will. The Industrial Revolution represented a massive and breathtakingly successful investment in disciplining the earth and its inhabitants to human control. The emergent discourse of political economy accordingly pointed the way to success through self-mastery, the power to defer present gratification for later, greater rewards. So, for example, the capitalist's profit was understood as reward for his "abstinence," while the working man was exhorted to emulate that self-discipline as the keystone of what Samuel Smiles called, in one of the best-selling books of the period, "Self-Help" (1859).

Economic thought thus turned the energies of evangelicalism to powerful secular use in pointing a markedly ascetic path to fulfillment: the young Karl Marx wryly called political economy "the science of renunciation." This asceticism was also reinforced by emergent sciences of population, most notably the work of Thomas Malthus, who influentially placed sexuality at the very center of socioeconomic thought. In his *Essay on the Principle of Population* (1798) Malthus famously proposed that human reproduction has an inherent tendency to outstrip advances in food supply. On this view, the very future of mankind depended on a proper regulation of human sexuality – a challenge that led to economics being dubbed "the dismal science." Conservative as it might sound, Malthus's work in fact shocked many conservative commentators. The very framing of the problem insisted that sex was a central feature of healthy human life, even as it confounded the biblical exhortation to be fruitful and multiply. At the same time, Malthus (who was an Anglican clergyman) believed that sex was intended solely for reproduction, which led him to refuse one obvious solution to the ostensible problem, contraception. The leading response to the challenge, Malthus urged, would be "moral restraint" – an emphasis echoed throughout the writings of early political economists, who nowhere allow for the possibility that population dynamics might be shaped by other kinds of human intervention (Folbre 1992).

Well before Victoria came to the throne, then, self-discipline was a pervasive theme in British culture, whose prominence confounds any simple understanding of sexual politics. Malthus, for example, intended his *Essay* principally as a rebuke to the utopianism of the French Revolution and its sympathizers – most notably, the British philosophical radical William Godwin. And yet Godwin's own vision of an ideal society, set forth in *Political Justice* (1793), was itself powerfully antisensual: the progress of civilization, it held, would be marked by the withering away of sexual desire, to the point where reproduction would be a social duty wholly susceptible to rational control. This unexpected congruence points to a further strand in the genealogy of Victorian sexualities, which emerges most clearly in avowedly radical or dissident stances: post-Enlightenment schemes of progress often disdain sex as an "animal" function at odds with a distinctively human rationality. Thus, the early feminist Mary Wollstonecraft complained in *A Vindication of the Rights of Woman* (1792) that the education of women solely for marriage made "mere animals of them," turning them into "weak beings fit only for a seraglio." More than half a century later, John Stuart Mill – the leading mid-Victorian male advocate of women's rights – confided to his diary that "any great improvement in human life is not to be looked for so long as the animal instinct of sex occupies the absurdly disproportionate place it does therein."

As it makes for such unlikely bedfellows – conservative and radical, atheist and pious – the pervasiveness of Victorian asceticism suggests the political leverage inherent in the ideal of sexual discipline. In authorizing attacks on an allegedly dissolute, profligate aristocracy for failing to live up to its inherited authority, self-restraint became a highly effective basis for claiming moral authority for the middle classes. Despite the persistent assumption that Victorian public and private realms were "separate spheres" divided along rigidly gendered lines, Victorian domestic virtues were charged with public significance (anticipating in this regard their late twentieth-century recrudescence as "family values"). This significance, arising out of Evangelical celebrations of the family, gained wide currency with George IV's divorce proceedings against his wife, Caroline, in 1820. That the notoriously dissolute, adulterous king should publicly accuse his wife of infidelity aroused widespread revulsion, and prompted a host of tributes to an imagined "quiet domestic nest" set against George's public debauchery (Davidoff and Hall 1987: 153). The ascension of a female monarch in 1837 provided occasion for locating such a refuge at the very heart of the British state.

Over much of Victoria's reign the quiet domestic nest was elaborated into a conception of "home" as an ideal repository of sympathy and tranquillity centered around the middle-class wife and mother, who was apotheosized in John Ruskin's *Sesame and Lilies* (1865). In what became the most enduring icon of Victorian antisensualism, the domestic woman was "the angel in the house" (Coventry Patmore's phrase), a quasi-spiritual being selflessly dispensing love and moral guidance to her family, largely untroubled by wayward personal desires – including erotic longing. What we now know about the rich sensuality of many Victorian marriages makes this peculiar ideal seem all the stranger. The most familiar explanation – that it made the home a haven from the cutthroat world of Victorian economic struggle – focuses on its appeal to men, and does not account for its antieroticism. But the angelic ideal did offer women a dignity absent in traditional notions of the woman as temptress, that image of unregulated sensuality against which Wollstonecraft and others had rebelled. "Passionlessness," as Nancy Cott (1978) has argued, might seem a norm worth embracing in return for this moral elevation. Nonetheless, the persistent dichotomy between dignity and desire – the absence of a middle ground between erotic enthrall-ment and a perfectly disinterested "influence" – tellingly reflects the enduring force of antisensualism in all its forms.

The angel's appeal to men seems easier to grasp: not only did she offer an image of complete subservience, but she enforced a disjunction between female morality and female power. The very unworldliness of woman's love, it was claimed, made it important that she be insulated from the coarsening influences of public life – such as the right to vote. Still, for all but the closest readers of *Paradise Lost*, sex with an angel might seem a daunting prospect. Yet many men seem to have thought angelic womanhood crucial to ensuring the continued subordination of women: as Krafft-Ebing remarked in his *Psychopathia Sexualis* (9th edn, 1894), "Were it not so, the whole world be a bordello, and marriage and the family unthinkable" (Gay 1984: 154). Even in Krafft-Ebing's cynicism, however, we glimpse a further, more subtle impulse animating the angelic ideal: an unease with male sexual aggression that is widespread in Victorian culture. In political economy, evangelical religion, and radical politics over the first half of the century, the aristocratic manhood that stressed social graces and sexual prowess was challenged by a norm of "character" understood as inward fortitude, self-regulation, and a sense of duty. The ascendancy of this new ideal can be measured by the force of sexual scandals in Victorian politics. Whereas the widely known sexual adventures of Melbourne and Palmerston, two of Victoria's early prime ministers, were politely overlooked, the careers of two important late-century MPs, Charles Parnell and Sir Charles Dilke, were destroyed by extramarital affairs. In the interval, Tennyson's vastly popular *Idylls of the King* (1859–85), with its markedly passive, feminized king likening his unfaithful queen to a virulent "disease," suggested that the angel in the house could appeal to men as an emblem of freedom from – or at least the mastery of – desires that they themselves found discomforting. A similar point might be drawn from the many ritual humiliations of male characters in Victorian fiction – Charlotte Brontë's Rochester, Dickens's Eugene Wrayburn, and Thackeray's Henry Esmond, among others – who enjoy moral redemption, and the love of the heroine, only after their aggression has been thoroughly disarmed, even to the extent of physical incapacitation. While these scenarios typically conjure up the redemptive agency of a woman in gratification of a man's desires, they also place the heroes in conditions of traditionally feminine passivity – and at times evoke the less orthodox pleasures of masochism.

As they set morality in collision with sexuality, the idealizing impulses of Victorian domesticity point to the culmination of Victorian asceticism in Freud's pronouncement that "It is not possible for the claims of the sexual instinct to be reconciled with the demands of culture" (Marcus 1966: vii). Ironically, however, by the time of Freud's assessment, culture had come to seem in many respects more sexually hospitable. Although British writers rarely displayed the sexual license invariably associated with all things French, popular novelists addressing a largely working-class audience, such as G. W. M. Reynolds, had long presented female characters in highly sensual prose that sometimes borders on soft-core pornography. And even domestic novelists aiming at a more decorous readership developed rich strategies of indirection and obliquity for representing sexuality, not only by projecting it onto stigmatized bodies – fallen women and predatory men – but also through more subtle embodiments of desire in morally compelling characters. The sheer power of repression displayed by George Eliot's heroines, for example, works as much to evoke as to regulate a richly sensual inner life, reminding us that the very austerities of "character" could be sexy. Indeed, repression itself is frequently eroticized in Victorian novels, where it is presented as a seductive index of libidinal depth, as in the contrast between Jane Eyre and her overtly sensual rivals, Blanche Ingram and Bertha Rochester (aristocracy and madness both signifying a failure of erotic discipline). The sensuality repudiated in *Jane Eyre* became a more central and overtly disruptive presence in the "sensation" novels of the 1860s, in the wake of national debate over women's rights to property ownership and divorce: heroines like Mary Braddon's Lady Audley, who resisted or cunningly manipulated norms of domestic femininity, invariably conjured up a troubling yet seductive sexual autonomy. Meanwhile, adventure narratives animated by an expanding consciousness of imperial rule became a popular vehicle for renewed celebration of physically aggressive masculinity. In his sermons and novels like *Westward Ho!* (1855) Charles Kingsley became the leading voice of "muscular Christianity," which repudiated the early-Victorian austerity of the Oxford Movement within the Anglican Church. In the works of "the apostle of the flesh," as Kingsley was dubbed, sexual desire was ostensibly sublimated in athletic prowess, but critics recognized in Kingsley's glorification of the body and its instincts a recrudescence of traditional marital norms that (they objected) could be taken to license profligacy.

Kingsley's career opens a surprising link between the Victorian cult of athleticism and the rise of aestheticism, another cultural development centrally concerned with rescuing the body from ascetic morality. As "morality" in popular usage became increasingly identified with purity, conflicts over the moral dimensions of art were typically fought out in terms of its sexual content. Swinburne, at the forefront of the cultural avant-garde in the 1860s, claimed moral autonomy for his poetry through the sexual audacity of its subject matter, which included incest, necrophilia, homoerotic desire, and a consistently sado-masochistic rendering of pleasure in terms of domination and pain. The 1850s and 1860s also saw a revival of interest in the sexual content of painting and sculpture, whether in debate over the morality of the nude as artistic subject or (more subtly) in speculation over the erotics of creativity and collecting, a recurrent preoccupation of Robert Browning's monologues. Criticism of erotic content in art predictably took a highly sexualized bent as well – although of a divided character that would prove increasingly central to late-century understandings of culture. The representation of women in avant-garde painting and poetry was frequently attacked as a form of traditional male promiscuity: "the fleshly school of poetry" was one critic's phrase for the work of Swinburne and D. G. Rossetti. Yet avant-garde celebrations of ancient Greece as a culture unburdened by "conscience" – and thus a model for contemporary artists – aroused another, more nervous suspicion in conservative commentators: that the forms of Greek art might cater to powerful homoerotic desires.

Mid-Victorian culture was thus marked by a newly emphatic, broad-based concern with the uses of pleasure (an emphasis congruent with the shifting focus of economic theory from production to consumption). In medicine, this concern was most pointedly registered in the issue of contraception: although still opposed by the medical establishment, it was evidently widely used by the 1860s, to gauge by the marked decline in middle-class family size from that decade. Indeed, one of the best-selling medical works of the period, *The Elements of Social Science* (1855), was an "underground" treatise by the elusive George Drysdale, which offered an account of reproductive health united with an apology for free love (and the use of contraceptives) as a remedy to both personal and social problems. The extraordinary popularity of Drysdale's book suggests that antisensual medical authority was often of limited influence. The well-known Victorian obsession with masturbation is the leading exception, representing as it does a remarkably widespread and psychologically traumatic fantasy. "Masturbation mania" remains a perplexing phenomenon, but as it focuses suspicion and discipline on the most antisocial of sexual practices, the one least amenable to regulation, it perfectly exemplifies Foucauldian dicta regarding the far-reaching authority of "medico-juridical" discourse. Nonetheless, Victorian medical literature on the whole displays a more diverse and, from a modern vantage, much healthier array of attitudes than most Foucauldian accounts allow. Female orgasm, for example, is ubiquitous in medical literature, not least because of widespread belief that women must experience orgasm to conceive (Mason 1994: 201ff.). Thus, the familiar image of a Victorian married woman's "joyless inhibition and ignorance," Mason suggests, may conceal another somber reality, "of women fearing and regretting sexual pleasure because they above all wished to avoid having another child." Despite all the reserve surrounding female sexuality, however, for Victorian medical writers marriage in large part *is* sex, the one arena in which sexual activity is not merely licensed but encouraged – a fact stressed more obliquely in the large families that populate so much Victorian fiction.

Reproduction became a more problematic issue in relation to what Engels famously called "the condition of the working class." For almost all commentators (few of whom were themselves working class) the problems of the urban poor were centrally bound up with sexuality, which was typically understood as a challenge of sanitation. Victorian urban surveyors such as James Kay-Shuttleworth, Henry Mayhew, and William Booth were invariably agitated by a "promiscuous mixture of the sexes" within the crowded spaces inhabited by the urban poor. "How they lay down to rest, how they sleep, how they can preserve common decency, how unutterable horrors are avoided, is beyond all conception," one observer wrote (Mort 1987: 38). As Frank Mort points out, this discourse offered no positive representations of sexuality: it was a form of "licentiousness" quite explicitly likened to disease or contagion. It is against this backdrop of foreboding and danger that the middle-class characters of Dickens, for example, venture into the hovel of the nameless brickmaker's family in *Bleak House* (1853). Such visits, which frequently suggest a proto-anthropological contact with alien cultures, might have many different motivations; even the more disinterested accounts, however, tend to have a profound aura of fantasy, depicting as they do either exaggerated submission or complete obliviousness on the part of the poor to the strangers who have been ushered into their homes. In the mesmerized preoccupation of urban chroniclers, the sexual anxieties of Malthus, under which the reproductive body is a constant threat to social well-being, were reinforced by what seemed a demonic subversion of Victorian domesticity, in which the threat of incest is unmistakable.

The condition of the urban poor was a standing embarrassment to Victorian schemes of progress, a reminder of how many seemed to have been left behind. In this regard, as George Stocking (1987) has pointed out, Victorians confronted a "savageness" at home as well as abroad, which in both locales was associated with a dangerously unregulated sexuality. That very association provided one answer to the social problem, the loosely Malthusian view that the poor were largely responsible for their own predicament, owing to their lack of self-discipline. "Done because we are too many," the grotesque suicide note left by "Father Time" in Hardy's *Jude the Obscure* (1895), offers a mordant comment on this logic. In middle-class representations of working-class men, this failure was typically figured as a tendency to drunkenness and violence. Among the female poor, the failure of self-control was more often identified with promiscuous sexuality. But the sympathy frequently accorded the "fallen woman" in contemporary novels and melodrama – in Gaskell's *Ruth* (1853) and Dickens's *Oliver Twist* (1838), to name just two – not only acknowledges the social pressures besetting working-class women; it also evokes a distinctly Victorian pathos, which tacitly sets a sexualized degradation against the lost redemptive possibility of female domesticity. A less sentimental view is offered by widespread accounts of female workers sexually exploited by their employers, or by affluent strangers such as the pseudonymous Walter in *My Secret Life* (ca. 1890), for whom working-class women were virtually indistinguishable from prostitutes.

Prostitution has long seemed the most glaring example of the Victorian double standard. While commentators of every stripe celebrated the virtues of self-control and marital fidelity, prostitution became an ever more visible feature of life in the burgeoning towns and cities. In large part this prominence seems to have been a by-product of social mobility and economic insecurity. Middle-class men – and those with ambitions to be such – increasingly postponed marriage until they achieved a modicum of economic security requisite to "respectability," and in the interval – licensed by traditional norms of masculinity – seem to have found sexual gratification in prostitutes. On the other hand, for many women, predominantly but not exclusively working class, prostitution was a means of supplementing or replacing the notoriously dismal wages and working conditions of domestic service or piece work. Yet the demographics of prostitution remain elusive, not only because of the circumspection inherent in the activity, but because contemporary surveys were typically responsive to spasmodic outbreaks of something akin to moral panic in the popular press. In such panic, one glimpses a further reason for the prominence of prostitution in the Victorian imagination: the uneasy recognition later codified by Freud, that when "culture" is identified with sexual purity, many erotic drives can be satisfied only outside the bounds of respectability.

Prostitution would occasion the single most controversial state intervention into Victorian sexuality, the series of Contagious Diseases Acts passed during the 1860s. Here public anxiety was aroused by the effects of prostitution, not on respectable domesticity or urban life, but on the health of the military, where it was feared that sexually transmitted diseases would undermine Britain's imperial vigor. Under the Acts, which applied to an increasing number of naval ports and army garrison towns, women suspected of prostitution were subject to forced medical examination and detention without trial for up to three (subsequently six) months. The legislation quickly prompted what would become one of the galvanizing episodes in an emergent feminist movement, as many women protested that these regulations only reaffirmed the traditional sexual double standard, failing to require any self-restraint on the part of men while depriving women of basic civil liberties. The familiar rhetorics of early Victorian sexual discipline were thus harnessed to new political concerns: in Josephine Butler's words, the outcry was that of "women crushed under the yoke of legalized vice" (Mort 1987: 93).

But these protests had reverberations beyond feminist politics. The Acts represented a newly specific intervention of state authority in sexual conduct, which entailed not only intensified forms of police surveillance, but also increasingly precise typologies of sexual deviance (which, ironically, often proved unable to distinguish prostitutes from "respectable" women). Although the Acts were repealed in 1886, opposition to them had been subsumed in a nationwide purity campaign that in turn generated new targets of sexual regulation (and new sexual norms). In 1885, the editor of the *Pall Mall Gazette*, W. T. Stead, published a series of articles entitled "The Maiden Tribute of Modern Babylon," luridly exposing child prostitution in England. The resultant storm of protest goaded Parliament to pass the Criminal Law Amendment, "An Act to make further provision for the Protection of Women and Girls, the suppression of brothels, and other purposes." While the Act was principally concerned to formalize ages of consent and dictate harsher punishment for owners of brothels, it has since become best known for a last-minute addition, the so-called Labouchere amendment (section 11), which introduced into law a new statutory category. Any man convicted of "any act of gross indecency with another male person," it stipulated, might be punished by up to two years at hard labor – the very sentence that ten years later would be passed on Oscar Wilde. The concern with regulation of male lust thus converged with a new conception of sexual identity anticipated in the rise of aestheticism: the homosexual.

This new category is the best-known outgrowth of the far-reaching "normalizing" of sexuality over the course of the nineteenth century. Sex between men has been around from time immemorial, but there is little evidence that men who enjoyed such activity therefore thought of themselves as different *in kind* from other men. At some point, however, in Foucault's influential rendering, what had been an activity was reconceived as a form of identity: "The sodomite had been a temporary aberration; the homosexual was now a species" (Foucault 1978: 43). British law included long-standing prohibitions against sodomy, but this crime traditionally had been understood as any sexual act "against nature," not just between men. What was new in the Labouchere amendment was the inclusiveness of the term "acts of gross indecency" and its specific application to relations between men as a separate category of offense – a category further solidified by the concept of the "homosexual," a term that gained currency in Britain in the 1890s following the translation of Krafft-Ebing's *Psychopathia Sexualis*. Labouchere's statute, moreover, firmly rebuked the secularizing tolerance of utilitarian reform through much of the century: Bentham himself had drafted various arguments for decriminalizing sexual relations between men, although it was a measure of the force of traditional morality that even this intrepid dissident refrained from publication.

More difficult to gauge are understandings of transgressive sexual desire outside "official" discourse. This has proved a special challenge with regard to lesbian relationships, which were more readily confined within traditionally feminine privacies, and thus amenable to greater circumspection under the guise of "romantic friendship" or spinsterhood. Among men, what Eve Kosofsky Sedgwick (1992) has called "the homosocial continuum" of male–male relations is not only more visible, but far more central to social power: traditionally almost every social structure – including marriage – locates power in some form of bond between men. Much recent work on Victorian sexualities has explored the erotic investments of those bonds – such as the friendship between Tennyson and A. H. Hallam, commemorated in *In Memoriam* – particularly as they were affected by what Sedgwick calls "male homosexual panic," the fear of being perceived to be "interested in men." In this context, the figure of "the homosexual" codifies a homophobia that imposes on the homosocial continuum (and, more broadly, the field of gendered identity) a single, momentous binary of sexual object choice. Like the work of Foucault, Sedgwick's speculations thus offer an influential account of the social and political dimensions of ostensibly private desires.

More elusive than homophobia, unsurprisingly, are sympathetic constructions of unorthodox sexualities, which would attempt to transform stigma into affirmation. Half a century after Bentham's plea for tolerance, as Linda Dowling (1995) has shown, a more concerted, although still guarded, apology for male–male desire developed out of the Victorian interest in classical Greece. As the rise of aestheticism drew new attention to the place of sexuality in art, a group of writers associated with Oxford liberalism subtly emphasized the pronounced homoeroticism informing Greek art and culture. The writings of Plato and the relics of Greek sculpture, in particular, thus provided occasion to celebrate not only individual liberty, but a distinctly homoerotic cultural tradition, and with it a sense of historical and ethical community – an achievement most evocatively realized in Walter Pater's 1867 essay "Winckelmann." By the 1890s, this project had branched into a host of offshoots, including a "Uranian" poetry of pederastic desire, a "new chivalry" of male comradeship that looked to the model of Sparta, and Wilde's arch punning on "Dorian" beauty. Through such apologies, a proscribed sexual identity became associated not only with a particular historical epoch, but with rhetorical strategies that would become hallmarks of literary modernism. As homoerotic writers tacitly addressed an informed, sympathetic elite within a larger audience, they invited a form of "double reading," thereby developing strategies of obliquity and reserve that would be central to the emergence of modernist writing in the works of Henry James and others.

Such rich strategies of obliquity and indirection depended on a body of sexual knowledge that was unsettled, multiple, and often indeterminate. Writers like Pater and Wilde daringly exploited points of contact and disjunction between the often radically different modes of awareness that distinguished initiates from the culture at large. The newspaper-reading public certainly would have had glimpses of homo-sexual subcultures from at least 1870, which saw the widely reported prosecution of two male transvestites, Boulton and Park; in 1889, the exposure of a male brothel in Cleveland Street caused a much greater sensation, which included the rumored in-volvement of Prince Albert Victor. But even in such widely publicized cases, discretion typically veiled the most telling details, both sexual and social. This reticence allowed the scandals to be submerged in vaguer and more familiar tales of aristocratic profligacy or working-class corruption, which evoked in turn a public response recall-ing early Victorian attacks on debauchery. Only with the trials of Oscar Wilde in 1895 was a clear image of "the homosexual" firmly fixed in the public mind, along with a vivid association of literary and sexual "decadence."

In the Wilde trials, oblique and idealizing literary constructions of a new masculin-ity collided with the demotic world of sexual trade. For middle- and upper-class men, male–male sexuality was largely governed by the cash nexus: it was most readily available through prostitutes. This was a predicament rife with potential for extortion

– the Labouchere amendment quickly was dubbed "the blackmailer's charter" – and thus for scandal, on which the popular press increasingly seized. Wilde, however, offered prosecutors and journalists a uniquely resonant possibility for denouncing both the cultural avant-garde and sexual deviancy as facets of a more inclusive "degeneration" (the title of Max Nordau's 1895 best-seller). The result was an enduring popular image of both homosexual and artist. The middle-class Wilde, as Alan Sinfield (1994) points out, had appropriated a traditionally aristocratic "effeminacy" of demeanor as a means of underscoring his cultural pretensions: with his arrest and conviction, that attribute became the distinguishing mark of the homosexual. The vagaries surrounding "gross indecency" were dispelled by a damningly unequivocal image, conjured up by the anguished confession of the title character in E. M. Forster's 1912 novel *Maurice*: "I'm an unspeakable of the Oscar Wilde sort" (ch. 31).

Wilde thus became the prototype of the "homosexual role," which, as Mary McIntosh has argued (1968), serves to carefully delimit a disturbing presence, to keep the rest of society pure, much as the labeling of delinquency helps to keep the rest of society law-abiding. The stigmatizing force of the Wilde trials helped to freeze what had been a decade of tremendous upheaval in sex and gender roles. During this tumult, which George Gissing summed up as "sexual anarchy," new possibilities and confusions were debated and enacted in virtually every realm of British life. In the midst of the purity campaigns of the 1880s, a literary avant-garde welcomed a wealth of sexually daring foreign works, most notably Zola's novels and Ibsen's dramas, both of which launched frontal assaults on conventional morality, not least through associating its effects with inherited syphilis. A more subtle but wide-ranging scrutiny of domesticity was sparked in 1888 by Mona Caird's series of columns in the *Daily Telegraph*, "Is Marriage a Failure?", which elicited a staggering 27,000 replies. As the controversy aired visions of alternatives to domesticity, it helped shape an image of the "New Woman," who refused the consolations of marriage to pursue new forms of independence and fulfillment, sometimes alone, sometimes with men outside of marriage, sometimes with other women, and sometimes in agonized indecision – the last memorably embodied in the character of Sue Bridehead in Hardy's *Jude the Obscure*. In the so-called "New Woman" fiction of Sarah Grand, George Egerton and others, writers discarded the familiar marriage plot to evoke female autonomy through narrative innovation and indeterminacy. As in most forms of Victorian reticence, however, the refusal of normative sexuality tends to be much clearer than the affirmation of an alternative. A similar indeterminacy attends the male "decadent," who is a counterpart of the New Woman in his refusal of familiar norms of gendered destiny. Although most often associated with homosexuality, the decadent as embodied in such figures as Wilde's Dorian Gray is a manifoldly "perverse" character, estranged from not only conventional sexual relations but social life generally, along with most traditional moral imperatives.

This seeming explosion of new sexual possibilities – at once exhilarating, threatening, and bewildering – confounds the familiar associations of "Victorian" with repression; indeed, it has struck many as an uncanny foreshadowing of our own *fin-de-siècle*.

But the congruence between late Victorian sexualities and our own goes beyond the well-publicized and fiercely debated proliferation of sexual alternatives. The very notion of sexuality as a subject of critical study is itself an outgrowth of the "sexual anarchy" that prompted the pioneering "sexology" undertaken by Havelock Ellis and others in the 1890s. And this genealogy may confirm the larger relevance of Victorian attitudes to our own time, not as a benightedness over which we have triumphed, but as the prototype of our own powerfully divided understandings of sexuality: as both bestial and angelic, utterly banal and profoundly mysterious, a "natural" instinct and a cultural imperative, merely "animal" yet a crux of human identity, "unspeakable" and yet our enduring obsession.

See also MEDICAL, INDUSTRIAL; FICTION; SKINS, PARAPETS, SHORE

REFERENCES

Cott, Nancy (1978) "Passionlessness: An Interpretation of Victorian Sexual Ideology, 1790–1850." *Signs* 4, 219–36.

Davidoff, Leonore and Hall, Catherine (1987) *Family Fortunes: Men and Women of the English Middle Class, 1780–1850.* Chicago: University of Chicago Press.

Folbre, Nancy (1992) "'The Improper Arts': Sex in Classical Political Economy." *Population and Development Review* 18, 105–21.

Foucault, Michel (1978) *The History of Sexuality*, vol. 1: *An Introduction*, trans. Robert Hurley. New York: Random House.

Gay, Peter (1984) *The Bourgeois Experience: Victoria to Freud*, vol. 1: *Education of the Senses*. New York: Oxford University Press.

Houghton, Walter (1957) *The Victorian Frame of Mind*. New Haven, CT: Yale University Press.

McIntosh, Mary (1968) "The Homosexual Role." *Social Problems* 16, 182–92.

Marcus, Stephen (1966) *The Other Victorians: A Study of Sexuality and Pornography in Mid-Nineteenth-Century England.* New York: Basic Books.

Mason, Michael (1994) *The Making of Victorian Sexuality*. Oxford and New York: Oxford University Press.

Mort, Frank (1987) *Dangerous Sexualities: Medico-Moral Politics in England since 1830.* London and New York: Routledge and Kegan Paul.

Sedgwick, Eve Kosofsky (1985) *Between Men: English Literature and Male Homosocial Desire.* New York: Columbia University Press.

Sinfield, Alan (1994) *The Wilde Century: Effeminacy, Oscar Wilde, and the Queer Moment.* New York: Columbia University Press.

FURTHER READING

Adams, James Eli (1995) *Dandies and Desert Saints: Styles of Victorian Masculinity.* Ithaca, NY and London: Cornell University Press.

Cohen, William A. (1996) *Sex Scandal: The Private Parts of Victorian Fiction.* Durham, NC: Duke University Press.

Craft, Christopher (1994) *Another Kind of Love.* Berkeley: University of California Press.

Dellamora, Richard (1990) *Masculine Desire: The Sexual Politics of Victorian Aestheticism.* Chapel Hill: University of North Carolina Press.

Dowling, Linda (1995) *Hellenism and Homosexuality in Victorian Oxford.* Ithaca, NY: Cornell University Press.

Gallagher, Catherine (1986) "The Body versus the Social Body in the Works of Thomas Malthus

and Henry Mayhew." *Representations* 14, 83–
106.

Gay, Peter (1986) *The Bourgeois Experience: Victoria
to Freud*, vol. 2: *The Tender Passion*. New York:
Oxford University Press.

Kucich, John (1987) *Repression in Victorian Fiction:
Charlotte Brontë, George Eliot, and Charles Dickens*.
Berkeley: University of California Press.

Mason, Michael (1994) *The Making of Victorian
Sexual Attitudes*. Oxford and New York: Oxford
University Press.

Maynard, John (1993) *Victorian Discourses of Sexuality and Religion*. Cambridge: Cambridge University Press.

Miller, Andrew H. and Adams, James Eli
(eds) (1996) *Sexualities in Victorian Britain*.
Bloomington: Indiana University Press.

Nead, Lynda (1988) *Myths of Sexuality: Representations of Women in Victorian Britain*. Oxford:
Blackwell Publishers.

Sedgwick, Eve Kosofsky (1992) *Epistemology
of the Closet*. Berkeley: University of California
Press.

Showalter, Elaine (1990) *Sexual Anarchy: Gender
and Culture at the Fin de Siècle*. New York:
Penguin Books.

Stocking, George W., Jr (1987) *Victorian
Anthropology*. New York: Free Press.

Vicinus, Martha (1992) "'They Wonder to What
Sex I Belong': The Historical Roots of the Modern Lesbian Identity." *Feminist Studies* 18, 467–
97.

Walkowitz, Judith (1980) *Prostitution in Victorian
Society*. Cambridge: Cambridge University
Press.

Weeks, Jeffrey (1977) *Coming Out: Homosexual Politics in Britain, from the Nineteenth Century to the
Present*. London: Quartet.

PART THREE
Walks of Life

10

Clerical

Christine L. Krueger

Victorian varieties of religious vocation defy strict definitions of "clergy," ranging instead from priests to lay preachers to believers who experienced a calling to repent and share the gospel, a calling which could come to anyone, including uneducated workers and women. The term "clergy" may refer exclusively to ordained ministers – bishops, priests, and deacons – who enjoyed their institutional and spiritual status by virtue of the sacrament of holy orders, first conferred on the Apostles. Most denominations, particularly the Anglican and Roman Catholic Churches, restricted certain sacramental and pastoral duties to ordained clergymen: they alone performed baptisms, marriages, funerals, and conferred holy orders. Along with law, medicine, and the military, entering the Church was one of the four traditional vocations for gentlemen. Victorians worried about the contradiction between Christian humility and an elite clergy even as they were conferring celebrity status on such ministers as Cardinal Manning, who was to receive the dubious distinction of a chapter in Lytton Strachey's *Eminent Victorians* (1918), or Dr John Cumming, the evangelical preacher attacked by George Eliot for ignorance and bigotry who attracted huge crowds to his London sermons. In the lives of many clergymen, however, elite professional status and humble service were reconciled. For example, the Revd John Keble, founder of the Oxford Movement and author of *The Christian Year* (1827), one of the century's most popular poems, was known to his country parishioners not as a celebrity with an international reputation but as the parson who lived among them, conducted their services, and taught daily in the village school (Colloms 1977: 24).

In St Peter's use of the term, "*kleros*" (1 Peter 5: 3) comprised the entire priesthood of believers. In many nonconforming Protestant sects, such as the Quakers and Primitive Baptists, lay persons preached, taught scripture, and led prayer. During the Victorian period, laity in the established Church also came to share more pastoral duties with clergy. Conversely, the ordained clergy participated in secular activities as scientists, philologists, historians, and literary authors. It must be remembered that since only Roman Catholic priests vowed celibacy, most clergy, like most Victorians in other walks of life, functioned in a network of domestic relationships, and that members of their families – especially parsons' wives – were expected to share parish duties, though they had no formal status. In significant respects, the boundaries between clergy and laity were permeable, and many Victorians understood themselves to have a religious vocation whether they enjoyed institutional recognition or not, while others held a clerical title but felt no sense of vocation whatsoever.

In predominantly Christian Britain, people with a sense of spiritual vocation, ordained or lay, regardless of denomination, shared one common ground: the Bible. The Bible, therefore, is an appropriate starting point for a discussion of clerical life in Victorian Britain. An appreciation of the extent of lay people's Bible literacy is key to understanding Victorian culture. The Bible was preached from pulpits, read daily by heads of households to family members and servants and by Bible readers in the homes of the poor, dispensed through domestic and foreign mission societies, studied in Church-sponsored and nonconforming study groups, as well as by clerical biblical scholars. Victorian printing technologies enabled the realization of evangelical dreams of mass Bible distribution: for example, John Cassell's *Illustrated Family Bible* (1836–8) sold 300,000 copies a week in one-penny numbers. The Bible provided a common cultural currency for clergy and laity – what Elizabeth Gaskell in *Mary Barton* (1848) called "Bible language" – and, as George Landow has shown, a widely shared typology by which to interpret history, politics, art, and individual experience. In 1828 Macaulay declared of the English Bible that, "if everything else in our language should perish, [it] would alone suffice to show the whole extent of its beauty and power."

Controversies centered on the Bible demonstrate its importance as a cohesive force in Victorian culture. Victorian biblical scholars upset both fellow clerics and the laity when, in 1870, they appeared ready to sacrifice the beauty and power of the King James Version to historical and linguistic accuracy with a new translation. Scholarly expertise and Church authority could not subdue personal devotion, however, and the KJV continued to sell briskly after the English Revised Version was published in 1881 (New Testament) and 1885 (Old Testament). The Revised Version was only one consequence of the principal religious controversy of the Victorian period, which pitted a majority of clerics and lay people, committed to a belief in scripture as the word of God, against historical biblical scholars and their followers, who brought scientific and linguistic tools to bear on the sacred text. Geology and biology may have threatened biblical literalism from without, but clerics engaged in textual and philological criticism – such as B. F. Westcott, Cambridge Divinity Professor and Bishop of Durham, and his colleague the Revd Fenton J. A. Hort, who together produced a major critical text of the Greek New Testament (1881) – opened a gap between naive and critical belief within both the clergy and the laity. Faced with these challenges to belief, the best Alfred Tennyson could offer in *In Memoriam* (1850) was "faith that comes from self-control" (CXXXI. 9). And Matthew Arnold, son of the Broad Church leader Dr Thomas Arnold, in "Stanzas from the Grande Chartreuse" (1861) described himself as "Wandering between two worlds, one dead, / The other powerless to be born" (85–6). Yet Thomas Carlyle could assert an "Everlasting Yea" against skepticism in his spiritual autobiography *Sartor Resartus* (1838), and in the same year as *In Memoriam* Robert Browning's poem *Christmas-Eve and Easter-Day* would review the options of German Higher Criticism and Roman Catholicism only to reassert the vitality of Nonconformist Protestantism. From one point of view, then, the clash between literalists and critics produced a "crisis of faith," and ultimately led to a decline in religious belief. But from another point of view, both of these movements contributed to a consequence fully consistent with the logic of Protestantism: the empowerment of individual conscience as the final authority in religious questions, realizing a "priesthood of the people."

Against this backdrop of a pervasive Bible Christianity, we can turn to the diversity of clerical experience in the Victorian period. A man entering the Anglican priesthood at the opening of Victoria's reign was entering a powerful but troubled institution, while the ministers of the nonconforming denominations and, eventually, Roman Catholic priests, were gaining in prestige and influence. Throughout the period, Britain was a predominantly Protestant country, with a Roman Catholic majority in Ireland and growing minority in England, and a small Jewish population centered in London. Its established Church was actually two: the Church of England, which was episcopal (bishop-governed), and the Church of Scotland, which was presbyterian (elder-governed). This bit of illogic predicated on Scottish nationalism and English political compromise was not lost on Victorian supporters of disestablishment, nor was the condition of an established Church rejected by seven-eighths of the Irish population. Numerous nonconforming or dissenting sects existed alongside the established Church, with their own ministers and governing organizations. Most prominent among these groups were the Methodists, Quakers, Presbyterians, Congregationalists, Unitarians, and Baptists. The repeal of the Test Act in 1828, and Catholic Emancipation in 1829, removed the most serious handicaps against people who were not communicants of the established Church, allowing them to sit in Parliament and obtain university degrees. In 1850, the Roman Catholic hierarchy was restored by Pope Pius IX. Though threatened, the established Church remained politically dominant, not only through such means as mandatory tithes, control of the schools and universities, and blasphemy and heresy prosecutions, but also because of the gentlemanly status of the majority of Anglican clergy and their followers. The Anglican Church was jokingly known as the Tory party at prayer. Much of the impetus for disestablishment stemmed from Dissenters, Irish Catholics, and Radicals, who for diverse reasons resented supporting a clergy that neither represented nor served them.

The elaborate hierarchy of the established Church suggests why Victorian detractors characterized the clergy as preoccupied with professional status and governance rather than pastoral duties. The established Church was headed by Queen Victoria, who inherited from Henry VIII the title "Defender of the Faith." The government appointed the clerical leaders of the Church, the Archbishops of Canterbury, York, Durham, and Dublin. At the next level of hierarchy were bishops, also appointed by the government, who presided over dioceses administered from cathedral towns.

Bishops also sat in the House of Lords, and they, or their agents, sat as judges in the Ecclesiastical Courts, which heard cases ranging from heresy to (until 1857) inheritance. The dioceses, in turn, were made up of parishes organized into deaneries and archdeaneries. Only ordained priests appointed by the bishops served in all of these roles, as deans and archdeacons, and, at the parish level, as rectors, vicars, and curates. Bishops made up the first order of the ministry, priests the second; a third order, deacons, were ordained to assist the clergy, but were not empowered to perform the sacraments themselves. The terms "rector," "vicar," and "parson" all referred to a priest who held the benefice or living of a parish, an income derived from fees on Church lands and parish tithes and who, theoretically, performed sacramental and pastoral duties for his parishioners. Too often, in practice, curates hired by incumbents did the lion's share of the labor for little pay.

The complex hierarchy suggested by even this rudimentary taxonomy of Anglican clerical roles explains why sociologists point to clerical organization as the paradigm for status mechanisms in professions at large. Anthony Trollope rose to prominence chronicling clerical politics in his six Barsetshire novels (1855–67). Another literary example helps to illustrate what these gradations of clerical prestige and authority may have meant to a parishioner in the 1830s. In George Eliot's *Middlemarch* (1872) the status-conscious Peter Featherstone contemplates his funeral:

> Having a contempt for curates, whom he always called understrappers, he was resolved to be buried by a beneficed clergyman. Mr Casaubon was out of the question, not merely because he declined duty of this sort, but because Featherstone had an especial dislike to him as the rector of his own parish, who had a lien on the land in the shape of a tithe, also as the deliverer of morning sermons, which the old man, being in his pew and not at all sleepy, had been obliged to sit through with an inward snarl. He had an objection to a parson stuck up above his head preaching to him. (Ch. 34)

Featherstone resolves this status conflict in favor of the rector of a neighboring parish, Revd Cadwallader, because this priest has been obliged to seek his permission to fish his stream.

Featherstone's attitude towards the clergy, like all his values, is decidedly worldly. And though it may be exaggerated, it is one indication that reform-minded Victorians would count the Anglican Church amongst the institutions targeted for change in the 1830s. To obtain holy orders, the vast majority of candidates completed a university degree or, in smaller but increasing numbers, attended a theological college. A tiny number without formal training, referred to as "literates," were ordained, generally in remote areas. A candidate presented himself, with references, to a bishop for an interview. But there were no strict requirements as to his spiritual credentials (except, perhaps, for the literates, who distinguished themselves in no other way). Too many benefices were held by the younger sons of aristocratic families, "squarsons" as they were derisively called, for whom the clerical life was little more than a means of supporting their hounds and horses. While such abuses were notorious, it was also the inadequacy of many livings that restricted clerical appointments to men who could supplement their pay with private income. For example, after the Napoleonic Wars, when about 80 percent of livings produced less than £400 annually, many former officers entered the Church, bringing their half-pay army and navy pensions with them (Colloms 1977: 18–19). The failure of these funding systems in the late eighteenth century had demoralized the lowest ranks of clergy and left many parishes without a priest in residence. The diocesan reports of 1827 and 1829 indicated that fewer than 42 percent of Anglican incumbents resided in their parishes. Pluralities, or the holding of multiple benefices (out of greed or necessity), accounted for much of the nonresidence. The curates who filled these absences frequently received a stipend so paltry as to give the term "perpetual curate" the ring of a life sentence rather than a permanent appointment. With very few exceptions, all British subjects, whether they were Church members or not, had no choice but to pay for the clergy and its services. It is certainly true that many devout parsons soldiered on, ministering to their congregations under difficult conditions. But the success of dissenting sects in areas of rural poverty and in the growing industrial cities testified to the failure of the established Church to demand vocational zeal from its clergy, to support them in their duties, and send clergy where they were needed.

These problems made the established Church vulnerable to critics within Parliament and its own ranks. The secular zeal that had produced the Reform Bill of 1832 could be turned, as well as religious fervor could, on traditional Church authority in the spirit of reform. The celebrated Anglican clergyman and wit Sydney Smith wrote in the early 1830s, "No man could tell to what excesses the new power conferred on the multitude would carry them. It was not safe for a clergyman to appear in the streets. I bought a blue coat, and did not despair in time of looking like a layman" (Chadwick 1966 I: 129). The first crisis came in Ireland, where Dr Richard Whately, appointed Archbishop of Dublin in 1831, complained loudly of the injustice of a bloated Protestant hierarchy ruling over a Roman Catholic majority, and talk of disestablishment was heard in Parliament. In the end, to the bitter regret of Irish members, the Church of Ireland was not disestablished, but was sufficiently reduced in size to horrify staunch supporters of the established Church. Another crisis came in the Church of Scotland. In 1834 the General Assembly of the Church of Scotland, under the influence of evangelicals who objected to Peel's reforms, especially Catholic Emancipation, sought to expand their independence from the government by ruling, in direct opposition to the law, that congregations could not be forced to accept pastors appointed against their will. The upshot of the ensuing contest between the Church of Scotland and Westminster was the Scottish Disruption of 1843. Over 200 representatives to the 1843 General Assembly, including the charismatic clergyman and reformer Dr Thomas Chalmers, withdrew in protest to form the Free Church of Scotland, taking 474 of the 1,200 ministers of the Church of Scotland with them and leaving the Church of Scotland with little support outside the aristocracy.

The predominantly Tory Anglican bishops dug in their heels against the Whig reforms of the 1830s, but soon they would be overtaken by reform movements from within the Church itself: Evangelicalism, Tractarianism (or the Oxford Movement), and the Broad Church movement. Though these groups sparred over the particulars of clerical reform, they shared a conviction that the national Church must defend itself against unsympathetic government reformers, and together they effected a revival of the Anglican clergy.

Evangelical Christianity was a potent religious force in a culture keen on promoting Lockean and capitalistic individualism and expanding a global empire. The eighteenth-century evangelical revival from which Methodism arose had synthesized teachings that can be traced to pre-Reformation Christianity, and, with such charismatic preachers as the Anglican ministers John Wesley and George Whitefield, spearheaded a substantial reformation of late eighteenth- and nineteenth-century Christian practice. Evangelicalism emphasized a personal relationship between the believer and God, marked by a profound and intimate conversion experience in which God called the believer to a life of Bible reading, prayer, reformed habits, and, perhaps most importantly, spreading the gospel to others – both at home and abroad. By the late eighteenth century, prominent Anglicans were adopting evangelical teachings and practices. The Clapham Sect, a group of Anglican laymen founded by William Wilberforce, undertook various projects, including Sunday schools for the poor, agitation for the abolition of slavery, publication of religious tracts, and the dissemination of Bibles. This was only the most celebrated of Anglican laymen's groups joining with dissenting clergy and lay people in such evangelistic and philanthropic activities.

To the founders of the Oxford Movement, evangelicalism represented a threat to clerical authority, but not so great a threat as that offered by the government. In a series of Tracts beginning in 1833, three Oxford clergymen, John Keble, John Henry Newman, and Edward Pusey, denounced the government's actions against the Irish Church and called for a renewed commitment to the established Church – its doctrines, services, clergy, and hierarchy. A declaration of the clergy, signed by 7,000 clergymen, and an address of the laity, with 230,000 signatures, were presented to Archbishop Howley of Canterbury in 1834, acknowledging the need for reform but insisting that it come from within, that the power of the bishops as the heirs of Apostolic Succession not be used by the government to undermine Church authority. Although the direct result of these actions was minimal – as Owen Chadwick notes, the declaration was a web of compromises satisfying no one and playing into the hands of Tory conservatives (Chadwick 1966 I: 75–8) – the diffusive effects of the Oxford movement were considerable, renewing devotion among clergy and laity.

The Broad Church movement or latitudinarians argued, as did Dr Thomas Arnold in *The Principles of Church Reform* (1833), that tolerance rather than sacerdotal vigilance would attract the largest number of followers to the Church of England. Samuel Taylor Coleridge maintained in his *Constitution of Church and State* (1829) that a national Church must be central to Britain's spiritual and cultural life. Only a tolerant and inclusive Church could command such loyalty. Religious reformers may have split over Liberal vs. Tory politics, pacifism, the empire, and whether to identify themselves with evangelicalism or against it, yet the effects of reform were generally evangelical in nature, permeating the Church as they had the chapels and the culture at large.

The charges Wesley had leveled against the Anglican priesthood – neglect of the faithful and lack of evangelical fervor – were addressed in the Victorian period by efforts to increase the number of men ordained and, more importantly, to enhance their training, sense of mission, and pastoral duties. Preaching at Sunday morning and evening services was supplemented by mid-week services, as well as by prayer meetings, Bible studies and house-visitations, in imitation of such activities carried on by dissenting sects. An aggressive church building campaign was initiated as well, constructing almost 3,000 churches between 1840 and 1870. To increase the supply of clergy for the north of England, Wales, and urban parishes, the Church expanded the theological colleges and ordained more men who were not Oxbridge graduates. At the same time, the ordination of literates was limited to rare exceptions. Despite growing numbers of ordinands from the 1840s to the end of the century, however, it proved impossible to keep pace with the rapidly expanding population. In 1841 there was one clergyman for each 1,098 people in England and Wales; in 1901, the ratio was 1 : 1,288. Still, the clergy became a more energetic presence in the culture, in part simply because the influx of new ordinands at mid-century meant that over half of the Anglican clergy were under 45 years of age, and only one-fifth older than 55 (Haig 1984: 4). Infused with evangelical fervor or Tractarian devotion, these young clergymen sought to set an example by their own manner of living. Although the fox-hunting parson did not disappear – the Revd John "Jack" Russell, the sportsman whose name is carried on by the terriers he bred, served as Perpetual Curate of Swymbridge from 1832–80 – many clergy lived abstemiously, forgoing drink, sports, and dancing. Undeniably, there were sanctimonious hypocrites, such as Trollope satirized in the character of the evangelical clergyman Mr Slope in the Barsetshire novels. But there were also men whose example and service, like that of Mr Tryan in George Eliot's *Scenes of Clerical Life* (1858), effected a humanitarian reform of manners in their congregations.

Members of the Broad Church movement, notably the Revd F. D. Maurice and the Revd Charles Kingsley, promoted a social consciousness amongst the clergy, urging them to support the working poor. Kingsley's novel *Alton Locke* (1850) spread his view of Christian Socialism, dramatized through the trials of its working-class hero. Many clergymen did labor quietly to alleviate the suffering of the sick and unemployed, to educate, and to persuade wealthy landowners to charity. A very few lent public support to workers' organizations. Though vastly outnumbered in urban areas by the rapidly expanding population, clergymen nevertheless made their presence felt thanks to the cooperation of lay ministers and charity workers, who helped to extend their influence and spread God's word in such organizations as the London City Mission (1835) and Evangelical Alliance (1845). The Church Pastoral Aid Society (1836) sent staff to assist clergy in needy parishes. The London City Mission, a joint effort of Anglicans and Nonconformists, employed 375 laymen in 1860, whose schedules of home Bible reading reached an estimated 375,000 Londoners, more than 10 percent of the city's population. Ellen Ranyard's Bible Society, founded in 1857, sent out 137 women as visitors and 119 scripture readers.

Imperial ambitions also boosted government and popular support for the Church. Foreign mission activity of the established Church and dissenting sects had waned by mid-century when high taxation, skepticism regarding imperial expansion, and the Crimean War discouraged contributions. David Livingstone's return in 1856 from Africa and the Indian Mutiny of 1857 lent new urgency to the missionary effort. Bishop Samuel Wilberforce took up Livingstone's cry of "Commerce and Christianity," declaring at a meeting of the Oxford and Cambridge Mission to Central Africa in 1859 that "Commerce is a mighty machinery laid down in the wants of man by the Almighty Creator of all things, to promote the intercourse and communion of one race with another, and especially of the more civilized races of the earth with the less civilized" (Stanley 1983: 75). Expanded missionary activity, particularly in India, Africa, and China, transformed the Anglican Church into a global organization, and at ten-year intervals beginning in 1867, Anglican bishops from around the world gathered in London for the Lambeth Conference. But the more missionaries went abroad, the more clergy were exposed to non-Christian religions. Among the most famous instances of this cross-fertilization was that exerted by the Zulus on Bishop Colenso of Natal. Assisting in his translation of the Bible into the Zulu language, they led him to question a literal reading of scripture. Colenso's bizarre work on the Pentateuch (1862–3), attacking literalism through arithmetic calculations, resulted in his being deposed from the see of Natal, though he continued to fight for Zulus' rights in the courts. Biblical scholars in England were embarrassed by Colenso's methods; however, more sophisticated scholarship would complicate domestic evangelism as the century wore on.

David Bebbington argues that, despite the notorious difficulty of interpreting the 1851 Census of Religious Worship (a count of attendance at churches and chapels in England and Wales on Sunday, March 30, 1851), it demonstrates the success of domestic evangelistic efforts within and outside the established church (Bebbington 1989: 107–11). Methodism, Congregationalism, and Presbyterianism had all grown in comparison to the total population, and while the Church of England as a whole had gained members, its evangelical parishes had done much better in recruitment. Different denominations thrived in various areas of the country and with various classes of people: thus, the north of England was predominantly Methodist and Evangelical Anglican. Generally, rates of churchgoing were highest among the middle and upper classes. Skilled labor gravitated towards nonconforming sects, making up a majority of the Primitive Methodists, to cite one example. Although skilled and even nonskilled laborers played an active role in nonconforming sects, the widespread alienation of workers from organized religion remained a scandal in Victorian Britain, and a focus of evangelical activity. Yet it should be noted that organized secularism, such as the National Secular Society (1870), fared no better with this group. Instead, as Victorian folklorists demonstrated, folk religions remained vital among the poor, especially in remote rural areas.

In sum, despite a significant revival in the Victorian Anglican Church, and the efforts of its reformed clergy, it failed to displace nonconforming sects or stem the growth of Roman Catholicism and win over a majority of Britons. Though the ordination of nongraduate clergy both increased and diversified the clergy's ranks, these parsons were denied the influence in local affairs that their gentlemanly predecessors had enjoyed. What is more, the solicitation of lay people to assist clergy in pastoral duties and philanthropic projects institutionalized a priesthood of the people and helped pave the way for the secular welfare state, which eventually moved the clergy out of their traditional roles in the community.

Certain famous Victorian attacks on dissenting clergy make it difficult to appreciate their appeal. Valentine Cunningham, who titled his study of dissent in the Victorian novel *Everywhere Spoken Against* (1975), catalogues the popular Victorian stereotypes of Dissenters as vulgar, hypocritical, social-climbing, ignorant, etc. Dickens's Mr Chadband in *Bleak House* (1853), forever raising his hand before intoning some platitude, indelibly etches smug inhumanity on the imagination. Matthew Arnold in *Culture and Anarchy* (1869) rather snidely referred to the enthusiasm for division amongst dissenting sects as "the protest of Protestantism," identifying disputation as the essential activity of a religion founded on the principle of dissent. Still, it is worth noting that many divisions stemmed from the earnest convictions of small groups of people that their interpretations of scripture were true, while their leaders' preachings were prevarications or corruptions of God's word. Alongside the lengthy list of dissenting sects named by Cunningham were many informal groups without institutional identities. Cunningham quotes from Brooke Herford's 1867 biography of Travers Madge, a friend of Elizabeth Gaskell who gave up his Unitarian ministry in 1859 to hold meetings in a room in Hulme:

> Religious life in our great cities takes more varied forms than most people are aware of. Not even the divergent types of the Anglican church, with the varieties of Baptist and Independent Nonconformity, and the multiform sections of the great Methodist family, can satisfy the restless individuality of the human soul. . . . Probably there is no large town but has, here and there in its great wilderness of absorbed busy life, some half dozen of these little sporadic churches, that, mostly in little upper rooms in back streets, are carrying on their humble work and worship, and aiming at something nearer to their ideal of what a church of Christ should be, than their members have been able to find in the larger ecclesiasticism of the religious world. (Cunningham 1975: 31)

This is not to say that clerical hierarchy was absent in dissenting sects. The Methodist Connexion, Baptist Union, and Congregational Union evidence the growing institutionalization of Victorian dissent. Nor were dissenting ministers mainly untrained amateurs. The Congregationalist divine Samuel Davidson, professor of biblical literature at the Lancashire Independent College, cited German biblical criticism in his scholarship as early as 1856. Elizabeth Gaskell's husband William, a Unitarian minister, was a noted linguist, and her friend, the Unitarian minister Revd William Turner, helped to found the Newcastle Literary and Philosophical Society. But the traditions of old dissent, notably the unprogrammed worship among Quakers and the evangelical teachings of the Methodists, Baptists, and their offshoots, encouraged lay ministries that were difficult to supervise or contain, especially in remote rural areas and cities that had been neglected by the Anglican Church.

The Anglican effort to ordain more nongraduates (Hardy's Jude pursues ordination by license) reflects the impossibility of supplying sufficient clergy from the ranks of university men, even if none of these men had been reluctant to accept appointments in unpopular places like Wales or the north of England. But that effort also suggests that the homogeneous product turned out by Oxbridge could not meet the needs of a socially diverse population. Thomas Wright defended his fellow working men against the perception that absence from church meant irreligion, writing in 1868,

> the Dissenting sects have the greatest attractions [for working men]. Their services and ministers are considered simpler and more practical than those of the Church; the ministers are paid with a nearer approach to equality, and have, to a far greater extent than those of the Church, entered into their profession from personal predilection, or as they put it, from having "experienced a call." (Moore 1995 III: 325)

What is more, dissenting sects allowed ministries to women, who were the group most grotesquely unrepresented by the Anglican clergy, in that they made up a majority of churchgoers.

Dinah Morris, a character in George Eliot's *Adam Bede* (1859), was once the best-known example of a female preacher, and one who submitted to the Methodist Connexion's injunction against women's preaching at that. But scholarship has restored the significance of the scores of female preachers who flourished in the nineteenth century. The census of 1901 indicates that there were 4,803 women serving as local preachers (Chadwick 1970 II: 244). Among the most notable of the nineteenth-century women preachers was Elizabeth Fry, a Quaker who began a ministry to female prisoners and founded the Ladies' British Society for Promoting Reformation of Female Prisoners (1821). She testified before a Select Committee of Parliament on prison reform, influencing legislation enacted later in the century. Fry inspired Sarah Martin, a woman from a humble background, to preach and conduct services at the Yarmouth Prison, for which she received favorable notice in a parliamentary report of 1835. Florence Nightingale embarked on her mission to train female nurses after visiting a German institution for the training of deaconesses in 1851. Having articulated her belief in women's religious vocation in her prophetic work *Cassandra* (1860), she went on to become immortalized as "the Lady with the Lamp" for her pioneering nursing services to British soldiers in the Crimean War. Similarly, Catherine Booth, a founder of the Salvation Army, urged an evangelical mission on all women in her "Female Ministry; or, a Woman's Right to Preach the Gospel" in *Papers on Practical Religion* (1878). Women served as officers in the Salvation Army.

Harriet Taylor Mill sneered at such female philanthropists in *The Emancipation of Women* (1851), labeling them a "sentimental priesthood." Still, Victorian feminism drew effectively on the Evangelical notion of a calling to ministry. Frances Power Cobbe was born into an Evangelical family in Dublin, and, though she rejected orthodox Christianity, based her *Duties of Women* (1881) on a religious conception of duty. Likewise, Josephine Butler, the key campaigner against the Contagious Diseases Acts, claimed that women were "redeemed" by philanthropic work.

Women's religious ministries encouraged the founding of Anglican sisterhoods in the nineteenth century. The Sisters of Mercy, for example, were founded in 1848 by Lydia Sellon in Devonport in response to Bishop Phillpott's appeal for help in ministering to seacoast towns. Maria Rossetti, sister of Christina and Dante Gabriel, entered the Sisters of Mercy. By the end of the century there were 80 communities of Anglican sisters with a membership of 2,000–3,000. From 1862 women served as deaconesses in the Church of England, and by 1897 limited permission was granted to elect them as churchwardens, legitimating the practice of a few parishes that had previously gone unnoticed. In these ways, Anglicans followed the lead of the Quakers and other dissenting sects.

Whereas women's ministries continued to flourish throughout the nineteenth century, the influence of the Anglican clergy eventually declined. Several factors contributed to this decline. For one, clerical reform had produced a paradoxical result. By emphasizing a vocational calling, reformers had encouraged potential clergymen to scrutinize their beliefs more closely. Since other professions, such as the civil service, were opening up to young gentlemen, they were free to chose careers that made fewer demands on their souls. Still, ordinations peaked in the 1880s and did not fall off seriously until the nineties (Haig 1984: 4–5). Many potential clergymen and those already ordained were troubled by historical and scientific critiques of the Bible and religious belief. *Essays and Reviews*, published in 1860 by Benjamin Jowett, along with other clergy and one layman, encouraged open discussion of challenges to biblical literalism and other matters, which they believed would contribute to the intellectual well-being of the Church. They ignited a tinderbox. Evangelical and Tractarian bishops alike condemned the volume and several of the authors were prosecuted for heresy, but a judicial committee of the privy council overturned judgments against them. Indeed, one of the authors, Frederick Temple, went on to become Archbishop of Canterbury. These events alone would have sorely tested the simple faith of earnest clergymen, but the increasing controversies over geological discoveries, Darwin's evolutionary theory – staged most famously in Bishop Samuel Wilberforce's debate with T. H. Huxley – along with historical biblical criticism, left many reeling. Clergymen's spiritual crises retained their cultural significance through the final decades of the century, as is evidenced by William Hale White's novel *The Autobiography of Mark Rutherford* (1881), Mary Ward's best-seller *Robert Elsmere* (1888), and Thomas Hardy's *Jude the Obscure* (1895). The authority of dissenting clergy suffered too, as Edmund Gosse recorded in *Father and Son* (1907), an account of his disillusionment with the biblical literalism of his father, a Plymouth Brethren clergyman.

What is more, the Oxford Movement, which had sought to strengthen the established Church by emphasizing Apostolic Succession, ritual, and doctrine, unintentionally strengthened the appeal of Roman Catholicism. When the Tractarian leader John Henry Newman converted to Roman Catholicism in 1845, many of his disciples faced the dilemma: Rome or doubt? Gerard Manley Hopkins, for one, chose Rome in 1866 and entered the Society of Jesus in 1868. The poetry he wrote privately was deeply influenced by scholasticism. J. A. Froude, at one time a great admirer of Newman, was among those who could not embrace Rome. His novel *The Nemesis of Faith* (1849) chronicled the doubts that led its hero to resign his living and its author to resign his fellowship. He became a prominent historian whose *History of England* (1856–70) would occasion the controversy between one of its reviewers, Charles Kingsley, and Newman that prompted the latter to write *Apologia pro Vita Sua* (1864). The sensational conversion of Newman, who would become the Roman Catholic Bishop of Birmingham, alarmed devout Protestants who feared the evangelistic power of so prominent a witness. Indeed, Dr Nicholas Wiseman sought Tractarian support in his efforts to restore the Roman Catholic hierarchy in Britain. Old Catholic families in England and Irish Catholics had been served by vicars since the Reformation; the influx of Irish immigrants, however, called for a more elaborate Church organization in England. In 1850 Pope Pius IX approved Wiseman's request and established 13 sees in England and named Wiseman Archbishop of Westminster. Wiseman's flamboyant announcement of the Pope's decision further alarmed British Protestants. Anglican clergy protested "papal aggression," yet more conversions followed. Among them was the prominent Anglican churchman Henry Manning, who would succeed Wiseman as Archbishop of Westminster in 1865. Manning, with his less confrontational style, did much to involve Roman Catholics in the life of the nation, supporting Irish causes, national education, and workers' rights. Newman's *Apologia* likewise encouraged rapprochement between Protestants and Catholics. Though anti-Catholic prejudice persisted, it became less vitriolic. The Irish Church was disestablished in 1871. Victoria, Defender of the Faith, welcomed a papal envoy to her jubilee in 1887.

In his novel *The Way of All Flesh* (1901) Samuel Butler, who was the son of a rector and grandson of a bishop, offers an especially savage account of the decline of the Anglican clergy. Despite his religious doubts, Ernest Pontifex takes holy orders at the insistence of his father, a tyrannical evangelical clergyman who was himself forced to enter the Church by his father. Warped by his repressive religious upbringing, Ernest sexually assaults a woman. After serving a prison sentence and enduring other misadventures, he retires to a contented existence as a secular man of letters. Butler's novel depicts the growing secularism in the final decades of the Victorian period, but it is hardly representative of Victorian religious attitudes. Even the movements for disestablishment, as Owen Chadwick argues, were signs less of secularization than of a desire on the part of fervent Christians to worship as they liked (Chadwick 1970 II: 427). Although the University Tests Act of 1871 opened all degrees and offices to non-Anglicans, in the 1880s undergraduate religious societies flourished, university religious services increased in number, and students were active in evangelical and relief missions to London's poor. Of particular importance to students of literature is what Joel Christenson calls "the theologization of literary studies" by the clergymen who guided the introduction of English into university curricula. Even in the non-sectarian University of London, the first two appointments as professor of poetry were held by Anglican clergymen: Thomas Dale and F. D. Maurice. The belief that resulted in their appointments – that literature was a source of inspiration and moral guidance – profoundly influenced academic literary study in Britain and America well into the twentieth century. With scholars continuing to complicate the biblical text, earnest devotion could be transferred to literature, and professors – clerical and lay – became priests of poetry. As Matthew Arnold, son of the famous Victorian clergyman, wrote in "The Study of Poetry" (1880):

> The future of poetry is immense, because in poetry, where it is worthy of its high destinies, our race, as time goes on, will find an ever surer and surer stay. There is not a creed which is not shaken, not an accredited dogma which is not shown to be questionable, not a received tradition which does not threaten to dissolve. . . . The strongest part of our religion today is its unconscious poetry.

See also 1832, 1848; PASSING ON, SEXUALITIES; LEGAL, EDUCATIONAL; SAGE WRITING

REFERENCES

Bebbington, David (1989) *Evangelicalism in Modern Britain: A History from the 1730s to the 1980s.* Grand Rapids: Baker Book House.

Chadwick, Owen (1966, 1970) *The Victorian Church*, 2 vols. New York: Oxford University Press.

Christenson, Joel (1997) *The Theologization of English Studies.* Unpublished dissertation. Milwaukee: Marquette University.

Colloms, Brenda (1977) *Victorian Country Parsons.* Lincoln, NB and London: University of Nebraska Press.

Cunningham, Valentine (1975) *Everywhere Spoken Against: Dissent in the Victorian Novel.* Oxford: Clarendon Press.

Haig, Alan (1984) *The Victorian Clergy.* London and Sydney: Croom Helm.

Landow, George (1980) *Victorian Types, Victorian Shadows: Biblical Typology in Victorian Literature, Art, and Thought.* Boston and London: Routledge and Kegan Paul.

Moore, James R. (ed.) (1995) *Religion in Victorian Britain*, vol. 3. Manchester: Manchester University Press.

Stanley, Brian (1983) " 'Commerce and Christianity': Providence Theory, the Missionary Movement, and the Imperialism of Free Trade, 1842–1860." *The Historical Journal* 26.1, 71–94.

FURTHER READING

Davie, Donald (1978) *A Gathered Church: The Literature of the English Dissenting Interest, 1770–1930.* New York: Oxford University Press.

Davies, Horton (1961) *Worship and Theology in England: From Watts and Wesley to Maurice,* 1690–1850. Princeton: Princeton University Press.

——(1962) *Worship and Theology in England: From Newman to Martineau, 1850–1900.* Princeton: Princeton University Press.

Halévy, Elie (1924–34) *A History of the English People in the Nineteenth Century*, 5 vols, trans. by E. I. Watkin and D. A. Burker. London: T. Fisher Unwin and Ernest Benn.

——(1971) *The Birth of Methodism in England*, trans. and ed. by Bernard Semmel. Chicago: University of Chicago Press.

Jay, Elizabeth (1979) *The Religion of the Heart: Anglican Evangelicalism and the Nineteenth-Century Novel*. Oxford: Clarendon Press.

Johnson, Dale A. (1983) *Women in English Religion, 1700–1925*. New York and Toronto: Edwin Mellen Press.

Knoepflmacher, U. C. (1965) *Religious Humanism and the Victorian Novel: George Eliot, Walter Pater and Samuel Butler*. Princeton: Princeton University Press.

Krueger, Christine L. (1992) *The Reader's Repentance: Women Preachers, Women Writers, and Nineteenth-Century Social Discourse*. Chicago: University of Chicago Press.

Machin, G. I. T. (1977) *Politics and the Churches in Great Britain, 1832–1868*. Oxford: Clarendon Press.

Norman, E. R. (1976) *Church and Society in England, 1770–1970: A Historical Study*. Oxford: Clarendon Press.

Owen, Alex (1990) *The Darkened Room: Women, Power and Spiritualism in Late Victorian England*. Philadelphia: University of Pennsylvania Press.

Semmel, Bernard (1973) *The Methodist Revolution*. New York: Basic Books.

Valenze, Deborah M. (1985) *Prophetic Sons and Daughters: Female Preaching and Popular Religion in Industrial England*. Princeton: Princeton University Press.

Wheeler, Michael (1994) *Heaven, Hell, and the Victorians*. Cambridge: Cambridge University Press.

Wolffe, John (1994) *God and Greater Britain: Religion and National Life in Britain and Ireland, 1843–1945*. London: Routledge.

11
Legal
Simon Petch

Theory

The theory and philosophy of law in Victorian England were shaped by seven English-men: Jeremy Bentham (1748–1832), John Austin (1790–1859), Henry Sumner Maine (1822–88), James Fitzjames Stephen (1829–94), Albert Venn Dicey (1835–1922), Frederick Pollock (1845–1937) and Frederic William Maitland (1850–1906). Although they all practised to some degree, only Stephen enjoyed a full professional career in the law, and with the exception of Bentham they were all primarily involved in legal education. They discovered precedents and suggestions for their own theories and methods in Roman law and in the writings of German jurists (especially Karl von Savigny [1779–1861]), and their recurrent resource for contrast and comparison with English law was the Code Napoléon of France. Their methods were analytical, histori-cal, and comparative, and it was their common aspiration to establish law as a science. The Official Law Reports, instituted in the 1860s and edited by Pollock, in which judicial precedents were systematically recorded, acquired an important place in the establishment of legal science. Pollock was also the founding editor of the first academic law journal in English, the *Law Quarterly Review*, the first issue of which appeared in 1885 – two years before the *Harvard Law Review*. The next year Maitland helped found the Selden Society (named after the sixteenth-century jurist John Selden) to advance the knowledge of the history of English law, primarily through the publication of manuscript sources. In turning to the textual sources of English law, Maitland brought the scientific methods of late nineteenth-century historiography to bear upon the law. All these jurists explore English law as a set of cultural and linguistic practices that are the expression of the community they affect – "It is we who are guilty of our own law," as Maitland put it (*Westminster Review*, 1879) – and their writings focus, from varying legal perspectives, the tension between authority and individualism that pervades Victorian thought.

Bentham believed that the replacement of case-law (on which the common law was based) by a code would necessarily establish a science of legislation. "Codification" is

Bentham's neologism (*OED*, 1817), and it became a catch-phrase for law-reformers throughout the nineteenth century. It had no greater devotee than Fitzjames Stephen, who spent three years in India codifying Indian law (1869–72), and who believed that codification would have brought to English law the certainty of Bradshaw's *Railway Guide* (Stephen 1895: 347). Suggesting predictability as well as certainty, the comparison reveals the extent to which a legal code might curb judicial discretion. This was crucial to Bentham's intention to thwart the power of the conservative combination of "Judge and Co.," and was anathema to the opponents of codification, who believed in the authority of the individual judgment. Unlike Bentham, Austin did not oppose judge-made law, but made it the basis of his call to codification, which he advocated as a rationalization of the existing system. Austin's theory that the principles on which cases are decided could themselves be codified and turned into statute-law was based on the inductive model of scientific method: "For what is that process of induction by which the principle is gathered before it is applied, but this very process of codifying such principles, performed on a particular occasion, and performed on a small scale?" (Austin 1885 II: 666). The analytical method demonstrated by this argument (i.e. that the principles of English law were elicited from precedents by comparison and induction) reached its apotheosis in the work of Pollock. There natural science, civil law, case-law, even ethics, are conditioned by precedent, habituated by custom, and aligned in a system of analogical relationship whose principle of uniformity is reached through the inductive method.

A foundational principle of Bentham's attempt to establish a science of legislation had been his repudiation of legal fictions, procedural pretenses the purpose of which is to give jurisdiction. Stone (1985: 127) cites a dictionary definition of 1854: "A 'Fiction in Law' is an assumption of a thing made for the purposes of justice, though the same thing could not be proved and may be literally untrue." Bentham hated such pretenses: to him they were manifestations of language in its least controllable form. But Maine, relishing any opportunity to define his ideas against those of Bentham, claimed that Bentham was ignorant of the role of legal fiction as a way of making law, one of the three "agencies by which Law is brought into harmony with society," the other two being equity and legislation (Maine 1986: 20). Maine extended the meaning of the term from its sense as false averment, "to signify any assumption which conceals, or affects to conceal, the fact that a rule of law has undergone alteration, its letter remaining unchanged, its operation being modified" (ibid.: 21–2). The semantic leverage afforded by this daring redefinition liberates the spirit from the letter of the law. To Maine, fictions are creative instruments of change, a species of virtual legislation which transforms a system of laws while concealing that transformation. Maine appeals to the double-language of case-law, in which each decision adds to the precedents while purporting to be merely a continuation of already established precedents. Fictions are a way of doing things both with and without words, for while the language of the law does not change, its meaning is on the move. Dicey's analysis of the reform of the law concerning the property of married women might be offered as an example of Maine's evolutionary pattern of law reform in Fiction, Equity, and Legislation (Dicey 1905: 369–96). The reform culminated in legislation, it began in equity, and it turned on fiction. Under the equitable jurisdiction of the Court of Chancery, which had originally been a court of conscience designed to mitigate the harshness of the common law according to the discretionary principles of justice, fairness, and good conscience, it was possible for a married woman to "possess separate property over which her husband had no control whatever" (ibid.: 377). But marriage settlements in equity (as such arrangements were called) were for the rich; the poor were vulnerable to common-law rights of the husband. (Dicey adduces Thackeray's *Barry Lyndon* to exemplify the husband who abuses his common-law rights.) The Married Women's Property Act of 1870, thanks to a legal fiction, secured for all married women "the rights which the Court of Chancery had secured for those women who enjoyed the advantage of a marriage settlement." In Dicey's memorable words: "The rules of equity, framed for the daughters of the rich, have at last been extended to the daughters of the poor" (ibid.: 386, 393). Fiction and Equity had contended with the might of the Common Law to produce progressive Legislation.

Thus law, in Victorian theory, was not natural, but made – by codes, judges, or fiction. Carlyle was the strident if lonely voice of the law of nature, but he was marginalized by a culture of increasing legal positivism that had no place for a law of nature – an idea which, in Austin's formulation, confounds law "with all those wants and necessities of mankind which are causes of its institution" (Austin 1954: 376). Darwin's rewriting of the laws of nature further compromised the meaning of natural law, the subsequent complications of which pervade Hardy's writing, caught between Romantic and Darwinian conceptions of nature.

To Fitzjames Stephen the procedures by which the law was applied constituted the strength of the English common law, as represented by its system of criminal justice. These procedures, which Stephen characterizes as "litigious," are initiated by private litigation, rather than by the public inquiry of the French inquisitorial system with which he contrasts it (Stephen 1863: ch. 5). The adversarial practices of English law are continuous with the individualism of Victorian culture, and indeed the canonical texts of Victorian individualism are frequently cast as adversarial discourse, and are thus in some measure modeled on the law. Mill's *On Liberty* (1859) depends on images of conflict and adversarial process. Law supplied Mill with a language for his discussion of individual judgment, in which all opinions must be given a "hearing." In Mill's *Westminster Review* essays on Bentham and Coleridge (1838–40), progressive and conservative modes of thought clash in Bentham v Coleridge, and his *Autobiography* (1872) brings opposed philosophical schools into the relationship of Intuition v Experience. Newman's *Apologia pro Vita Sua* (1864) is the case for the defense in Kingsley v Newman, and also an advocate's case for the Roman Church and its clergy. Wilde's exercise in self-justification, *De Profundis* (1905), written in jail during 1896–7, recasts Wilde v Queensberry as Wilde v Lord Alfred Douglas. And in Hopkins's response, in "The Wreck of the *Deutschland*" (1876), to the Protestant culture of

Germany as represented by the Falck laws from which five Franciscan nuns were escaping, his poetic voice is cast in impassioned advocacy on behalf of Christ against Luther.

Stephen's argument for the superiority of the English system is based on his belief in cross-examination as the best instrument for the sifting and testing of evidence. Whereas the inquisitorial procedure, in which someone may be examined on the same matter on several occasions, results in evidence "like handwriting scratched out and altered so often as to become, at last, one unintelligible mass of blotches and scratches" (Stephen 1863: 459), the adversarial procedure brings the crucial evidence into immediate focus. Cross-examination is the key technique of the adversarial method, and Stephen's lucid account of the rules and conventions governing the examination and cross-examination of witnesses in English criminal procedure (ibid.: ch. 5) can stand as a defense of the English system against the case made by Trollope in *Orley Farm* (1862). Trollope criticizes cross-examination as the bullying of witnesses, and yet his novel is written by the practice against which it voices such anger. The most striking feature of its narrative manner is the use of many narrated monologues in which the characters subject themselves to rigorous cross-examination as they interrogate themselves about their own motives. Cross-examination is part of the grammar of their interior lives, and their various and conflicting loyalties are tested, with the help of the narrative voice, by the language of the law. Such intrasubjectivity is integral to the performative analysis of legal discourse in Browning's *The Ring and the Book* (1868–9): the monologic speakers incorporate other viewpoints than their own by "quoting" arguments and objections which they can then answer.

"Evidence is the basis of justice," Bentham had claimed in his *Rationale of Judicial Evidence* (1827). The many substantial Victorian reforms of the law of evidence in the nineteenth century culminated in the Criminal Evidence Act of 1898 (which gave the criminal accused the right to testify on oath at his own trial), and fascination with the epistemology of evidence increased as the century developed. Stephen's introductory remarks on "The Nature of Evidence" could have prefaced *Middlemarch*: "All the facts with which we are acquainted, visible or invisible, internal or external, are connected together in a vast series of sequences which we call cause and effect, and the constitution of things is such, that men are able to infer from one fact the existence, either past or future, of other facts" (Stephen 1863: 235–6). Inference, like induction, is a process of reasoning from effects to causes which underlies many forms of inquiry, but the mind may be baffled by the ambiguous epistemological spaces in which evidence is constituted. In Stevenson's *Strange Case of Dr Jekyll and Mr Hyde* (1886) the narrative is focalized through the lawyer Utterson, whose legal imagination is challenged by the unravelling of events which he tries to construe as evidence. The confidence with which he casts himself as Mr Seek is confounded by the mysteries of Jekyll's laboratory, which are beyond the reach of legal science (Jekyll is a Doctor of Civil Law as well as a Doctor of Medicine). Collins's *The Moonstone* (1868) anticipates Stevenson in its supersession of conventionally legal evidence, as Franklin Blake investigates a mystery to which the key is his own unconscious behavior, symbolized by opium and the shifting sands. In such strangely configured fictional worlds, Stephen's certainty dissolves.

In contrast to these anticipations of the modern fascination with the unconscious, Victorians generally stressed consciousness of responsibility, and throughout the period the language of legal identity informs the sense of moral responsibility. Gladstone (1864) thought the qualities necessary to the exercise of the franchise were "self-command, self-control, respect for order, patience under suffering, confidence in the law, regard for superiors" (Wiener 1990: 144). His phraseology echoes the advice of Pallas to Tennyson's Oenone: "Self-reverence, self-knowledge, self-control, / These three alone lead life to sovereign power" ("Oenone," ll. 142–3). As the subsequent lines of the poem reveal, "sovereign" here has legal force, as indeed it does for Mill in *On Liberty*: "Over himself, over his own body and mind, the individual is sovereign" (ch. 1). In both these cases the language of individualism is legally inflected, as it is in John Henry Newman's claim that "religious men would rather be in error with the sanction of their conscience, than be right with the mere judgment of their reason" (*Apologia*, Note G); his "sanction" draws its force from Austin's definition of a law as "the command of a sovereign enforced by a sanction" (Stephen 1900 III: 321). When Mr Harding in *The Warden* (1855) has finally resolved to resign his wardenship, he has "had his suit finally adjudicated upon in a court of conscience," a court that registers "a judgment without power of appeal" (ch. 19). To the religious imagination, the conscience is an intuitive faculty, whereas to the utilitarians the conscience was conditioned by reason into a habit – an idea resoundingly endorsed by Darwin's theory in *The Descent of Man* (1871) of a conscience habituated by social instincts. But the sovereign self, the self with a conscience, is assumed by both intuitionists and utilitarians, and is at the heart of Victorian legal thought.

The criminal law was a discourse of responsibility, part of a broader Victorian "discourse of character" (Wiener 1990: 38) built upon the individual sense of right and wrong. For Fitzjames Stephen it was "absolutely necessary that legal definitions of crimes should be based upon moral distinctions" (Stephen 1863: 82), and he uses the concept of "malice" because it is his criterion of legal responsibility for criminal intention. Victorian notions of criminal intention and responsibility were complicated, however, by M'Naghten's case (1843). Daniel M'Naghten, in attempting to assassinate the prime minister Sir Robert Peel, killed his private secretary, and was tried for murder. Because medical evidence suggested that M'Naghten was suffering severe delusions of persecution, the judge directed the jury to find him not guilty on the grounds of insanity. The M'Naghten Rules (as they are still known) evolved from subsequent debate among the judges, who, called before the House of Lords to answer general questions arising from this case, arrived at the following formula worded by Chief Justice Tindal: to establish an insanity defense, the accused had to be under such a defect of reason "as not to know the nature and quality of the act he was doing, or, if he did know it, that he did not know he was doing what was wrong." In his *General View* Stephen acknowledged that if the existence of "moral insanity" and "irresistible impulses" were proved, it "would disprove malice" (ibid.: 95); later he would argue that the law should acknowledge mental diseases – irresistible impulses, delusions, morbid excitements – which destroy the power of self-control. On these grounds, Porphyria's lover would not have been held legally responsible for his action. In contrast, in Hardy's *Far from the Madding Crowd* (1874) Boldwood's reprieve from the death penalty because of the general conviction that he "had not been morally responsible for his later acts" is complicated by the idea of the sovereign (responsible) self. Gabriel Oak, eager that Boldwood be saved "even though in his conscience he felt that he ought to die," is a barometer of the moral pressure, and Boldwood's reprieve leaves questions of responsibility and madness uncomfortably unsettled (chs 53–5).

Conceptions of sanity were implicated in the legal doctrine of the sanctity and liberty of contract. As George Jessel said (1875): "If there is one thing more than another that public policy requires it is that men of full age and competent under-standing shall have the utmost liberty of contracting, and that their contracts when entered into freely and voluntarily shall be held sacred" (Cornish and Clark 1989: 269). For Maine the condition of individualism is the power to contract, which is in turn the condition of social development. Contract is the jurisprudential principle of discipline in Maine's individualist vision, and the obligation of contract represents "the complete reciprocity and indissoluble connection of rights and duties," which Maine figures as a chain of law between the contracting parties. Bentham, in his reaction against the conservative ideology of Blackstone and Burke, had disavowed any form of social contract other than the greatest happiness of the greatest number, thereby referring the test of justice to a felicific calculus of pain and pleasure. Maine's stress on reciprocal obligation promoted a Benthamic individualism, but his terminol-ogy of rights and duties (the Roman *jus* had covered both) implied a social contract subtending agreements between individuals. The terminology runs through the social thought of the period: in Carlyle's *Chartism* (1839) it had been used to differentiate between the nexus of Cash Payment (individual contract) and the nexus according to the law of nature (comprehensive social contract); Mill tried to avoid it in *On Liberty*, but found himself compelled to consider the nature of social obligations; and in *Culture and Anarchy* (1869) Matthew Arnold, with both Carlyle and Mill in mind, tried to put the terms into relationship by subsuming them in the concept of "welfare."

Maine's language instantiates a web of social obligations, for chains are infinitely extendable, even into universal contracts: "For so the whole round earth is every way / Bound by gold chains about the feet of God" (Tennyson, "Morte d'Arthur" [1842], ll. 254–5). Once a chain has begun, where will it end? It was a real legal question, and it followed from the basic rhetorical model of contract law as formulated by William Anson, for whom contract is created by the acceptance of an offer: "Acceptance is to Offer what a lighted match is to a train of gunpowder" (*Principles of the English Law of Contract* [1879], 7th edn 1893). Anson's analogy exploded into the courts in the landmark case of Carlill v Carbolic Smoke Ball Co. (1892–3). The question here was whether the defendants' advertised offer of £100 to anyone who, after using their product in accordance with the printed directions, contracted influenza, constituted an intention to enter into legal relations. The defendants maintained that their offer was too vague to be taken seriously, and that a unilateral contract was not legally possible; but they had deposited £1,000 in a bank account "showing our sincerity in the matter," and when Mrs Carlill caught influenza and her husband brought an action, the judges took the advertisement at its word and found for the plaintiff. The judgment extended the range of social contracts by forging a chain of law between the rights of unspecified individuals and the "obligation" implied by companies' public offers.

Maine believed that contracts, together with wills, held modern society together (Maine 1986: 169). But in *Our Mutual Friend* (1865) the links in Maine's chain of law do not hold: Wrayburn complains of "people's breaking promises and contracts and bargains of all sorts" (book 2, ch. 2), and the will of Robert Baldwin is a *mise en abyme*, an internal symbol of misdirected will (book 3, ch. 6). *Our Mutual Friend* depicts Maine's world turned upside down, and indeed throughout Victorian literature contracts, wills, and settlements are the occasion of conflict. The settlement is best understood as an intergenerational family contract whereby inherited lands belong to the family rather than to the individuals who comprise the family at a particular time. Because of this institution's infinite capacity for focusing tension within families, settlements in fiction are invariably the site of the conflicting demands of social contract and individualism. In the compounding uncertainties of *Daniel Deronda* (1876), heralded by the gambling with which the novel so strikingly opens, and configured by wills, settlements, and threatened disinheritance, these conflicting demands are unresolved. In Trollope's *Cousin Henry* (1879) the missing will on which the story turns is a metonym for a broken entail, the restoration of which fulfills an "implied contract" in a family-based society (ch. 24). But a settlement could also be a catalyst for self-determination against family identity. Female independence in Victorian literature is frequently signified by a woman's rejection of what is legally hers to inherit: Dorothea Casaubon rejects the will of her husband in Eliot's *Middlemarch* (1872), and Esther Lyon turns from the Transome estate in *Felix Holt* (1866). Aurora Leigh's refusal of Romney's offer of marriage is a powerful assertion of gendered independence: by rejecting his reduction of love to a "simple law-clause" she liberates herself from the patriarchal system of settled estates (*Aurora Leigh* [1856] 2: 785).

In his claim that the movement of progressive societies "has hitherto been a movement *from Status to Contract*" (Maine 1986: 141), Maine's "hitherto" embodies a challenge which signifies a crisis: whither contract, and the individualism it expresses, in the increasingly regulated context of English society? In various ways, as the century developed, the law curbed and inhibited the Benthamite principle of laissez-faire. The growth of liability insurance, and of the limited liability company, meant that responsibility was focused less upon individuals, and distributed more generally throughout social mechanisms (Wiener 1990: 203); and a shift in emphasis in the criminal law, from moral condemnation to social regulation, enhanced its function as the instrument of public order (ibid.: 260). In Dicey's extreme view, the Factory Acts of the mid-century decisively signaled the defeat of individualism by collectivism: this legislation "introduced socialistic enactments into the laws of England" by recognizing "the principle that the regulation of public labour is the concern of the State" (Dicey 1905: 237–8). Trollope responded to such irritants in the legal culture by turning to the imaginary spaces of the new world. In *The Way We Live Now* (1875) Winifred Hurtle's courageous individualism is validated by the summary justice of Oregon and Kansas, which the novel offers as a refreshing contrast to the moribund practices of English law; and her story challenges the reader's imagination with the possibilities of a new legal frontier.

Practice

The range of aspirations to the legal profession in Victorian England is exemplified by the contrasting ambitions of two young men in Elizabeth Gaskell's *The Moorland Cottage* (1850). Frank Buxton, the son of a wealthy yeoman, who is poised to lift his family into the gentry by becoming a barrister, wants "to gain some idea of the code which makes and shows a nation's conscience" (ch. 5). Edward Browne, from a tenant family, decides to become an attorney because "there are hundreds and thousands a-year to be picked up with mighty little trouble" (ch. 4). There was room for both men in the Victorian legal world, with its different levels of work.

The higher level was the bar, which combined a gentlemanly ideal of service with a bourgeois philosophy of individualism. As advocates in the higher courts, barristers were the legal elite, from whose membership appointments to the judicial bench were made. Although Frank Buxton does not intend to practice, his legal training will give him knowledge necessary for the management of his estates, and will also stand him in good stead if, as his father hopes, he goes into Parliament. Typically, an aspiring barrister would be educated at a leading public school and at Oxford or Cambridge (where he would not study law); he would then undertake five years' apprenticeship at one of the Inns of Court, after which time he would be "called to the bar" and allowed to practice. This expensive ten-year education would have provided him with minimal legal training: in 1846 a parliamentary investigation reported that England had no legal education worthy of the name, and while the Inns of Court appointed Readers in 1847, and a Council of Legal Education in 1852, there were no compulsory bar examinations until 1872. The first law school was established at University College, London in 1826, nine years after Harvard Law School, but (unlike Harvard's) it failed to flourish. The legal profession in England had grown up outside the universities and, in keeping with its general resistance to formal legal education, resented their intrusion. Late in the century legal education became a serious enterprise in English universities, but the profession remained skeptical.

There was money to be made at the bar, particularly after the railway boom of the 1840s, and again after the joint-stock company boom 20 years later. Fitzroy Kelly was reported to have earned £25,000 in 1859, and estimates of the earnings of Charles Austin in the year 1857 alone vary from £40,000 to £100,000. In the 1880s Charles

Russell (who had successfully defended Parnell) charged £500 to accept a brief, and £100 per day thereafter. But these were established men, and a career at the bar took time to build. Fitzjames Stephen began work at the bar in 1854, and four years later was making only £50 a year. He reckoned that the turning point in his career came in 1861, when he made £100 on circuit. In the 1850s Charles Rann Kennedy earned a steady £800–900 per year from his provincial practice in the lower courts, which was a reasonable median income for a barrister. To put these figures in perspective: the prime minister's annual salary was £5,000, and annual judicial salaries in the higher courts ranged from £5,000–£8,000.

In Gaskell's tale, Edward Browne enters the lower level of the legal profession as represented by solicitors and attorneys (this term was abolished in 1875). As an articled clerk he would have been paid a modest annual salary (£200 maximum) and after five years would have been qualified to practice independently. The distinction between the levels of the profession was a matter of class and money; for whereas a barrister needed private means and had to be a gentleman, an attorney, who could earn his qualification, might only aspire to gentility, and when visiting a barrister's residence he would be expected to use the tradesman's entrance (Cornish and Clark 1989: 51). In *Orley Farm* Samuel Dockwrath, an attorney of questionable character, variously describes himself as "a commercial gentleman," "a professional gentleman," and "a commercial lawyer," a complex of terms which suggest his uncertain sense of his own social standing. Attempting to establish its credibility, the lower branch took the lead in both professional organization and legal education. The Law Society was established in 1825, the Bar Council not until 1893; and the Law Society provided lectures in the 1830s for entrants to the profession, and instituted examinations in the 1850s. Solicitors made less money than barristers – Kirk (1976) estimates that £500 was a reasonable annual income for a solicitor in private practice – but a town clerk in local government (usually a solicitor) might earn twice this amount, and proctors (the equivalent of solicitors in the civil law jurisdictions of Doctors' Commons) might earn up to £3,000. The respectable family solicitor – Tulkinghorn in *Bleak House* or Matthew Bruff in *The Moonstone* – was well paid for his confidential services. While pleading in the higher courts was the monopoly of the bar, the lower branch of the profession had its own monopoly on conveyancing (preparation of legal documents necessary to the transference of property). Attorneys were as eager to distinguish themselves from tradesmen as barristers were to distinguish themselves from the commercial classes, but each branch of the profession buttered its own bread through restrictive practices worthy of any trade union.

A suggestive indication of the difference in social and economic status between the levels of the profession is the fact that the electioneering agent, whose stock-in-trade is bribery and corruption, and who is invariably a solicitor, is as prominent a stock character in Victorian fiction as the briefless barrister, the privileged young man who is not obliged to work. However, the most significant fact about the levels of the profession is that their order was inverted by codes of professional etiquette. The bar was dependent for its business, and ultimately its payment, on the lower branch of the profession, so that such social superiority as barristers enjoyed over attorneys was in tension with their professional dependence on them. Barristers were employed by attorneys on behalf of the clients for whom they acted, and with whom barristers had no contractual relationship. While this absolved a barrister from incompetence, it also deprived him of the power to recover payment. In 1862 Charles Rann Kennedy sued Charles Broune and his wife (for whom he had acted exclusively for some years before the marriage) for £20,000 for professional services. A jury verdict in Kennedy's favour was overturned on appeal, on the grounds that a barrister could not sue for his fees; and Kennedy was a ruined man.

The complexities of professional hierarchy were compounded in other institutional structures of the law. When Victoria ascended the throne in 1837, the English judicial system consisted of an overlapping jumble of civil, ecclesiastical, and common law courts, with frequently confused jurisdictions. One case concerning Church rates wove its way through eight courts, from an ecclesiastical court of first instance to the House of Lords, over a period of 16 years (1837–53). It went through five levels of the legal hierarchy, and involved a total of 38 judge sittings (Waddams 1992: 259). In 1858 William Yelverton was charged with bigamy by Theresa Longworth before the English Divorce Court, which disclaimed jurisdiction in Scotland and Ireland where the events occurred. The case went slowly through the Scottish and Irish courts to the House of Lords, whose decision did not address the need for greater judicial coordination.

And the empire took problems of jurisdiction beyond the British Isles. A struggle between Canada and the United States over the extradition of a fugitive slave, John Anderson, was complicated when the English Court of Queen's Bench presumed to exercise jurisdiction in Canada by issuing a writ of habeas corpus, and the substantive issues of extradition and natural justice were overshadowed by the related questions of imperial authority and colonial independence. Indeed, English legal culture was most rigorously tested in imperial jurisdictions. Fitzjames Stephen, the legal member of the Viceroy's Council in India from 1869 to 1872, saw himself as a legal missionary, spreading "the Gospel of the English," which was its law. This gospel was challenged on a number of fronts: by Kipling, who suggested that the imposition of Empire was fraught with moral hazards for the empire-builders; by Stevenson, in whose Pacific tales the English legal system is brought into contact with native systems of justice, and found wanting; and by Housman, whose *A Shropshire Lad* (1896) offers a sardonic account of the empire – "Soldiers marching, all to die" (poem 35) – as a jurisdiction of injustice.

Although problems in legal education and uncoordinated jurisdictions were slow to resolve, substantive legal reform was more extensive in the Victorian period than at any time in English history since the revolutionary era following the Civil War. The effects were several. First, the power of positive law was increased and consolidated: "The whole of England is now policed and patrolled," it was said at the end of the century (Odgers 1901: 130). Second, a legislative network of basic public education (1870, 1876), health services (1848, 1875), and a carefully tiered system of local government (1888, 1894) characterized a general shift from a social discourse of character to a discourse of welfare (Wiener 1990). Third, the gradual movement towards democracy in the Representation of the People Acts – the Reform Bills – of 1832, 1867, and 1884, brought with it the legalization of trade unions (1871) and significant changes to employment law – reflected in the change of terminology from "master and servant" to "employer and workman" – culminating in the no-fault Workmen's Compensation Acts of 1897 and 1900.

The increasing power of the state represented by such reforms reflects the growing secularization of society, and the great marker of secular trends was a changing attitude to capital punishment, which in 1861 was effectively limited to the crimes of murder and treason. This legislation was coincident with the *Essays and Reviews* case (1860–2), in which legal action for heresy was taken against some clergymen contributors to a volume of theological essays. The ecclesiastical courts (in 1861–2) and then the Privy Council (in 1864) adjudicated on the legal status of the sacred language of the scriptures and of the Thirty-nine Articles. The Privy Council's judgment for the dissident writers, it was later said, "had dismissed hell with costs, and taken away from orthodox members of the Church of England their last hope of everlasting damnation" (Waddams 1992: 331). Law and theology met for a defining moment, as a declining belief in the eternal punishment of hell underwrote the declining moral credibility of the capital sentence.

Reform brought the two branches of the profession closer, and the solicitor rose in status as the century progressed; in Gissing's *The Nether World* (1889) Scawthorne moves from the nether world to the upper by becoming a solicitor. The reforms also made the legal profession less exclusively metropolitan. Provincial bars were established at such major centres as Birmingham and Manchester, and while London remained the hub of the legal system, the provincial administration of justice in Assizes and Quarter Sessions was supplemented, in 1846, by the establishment of County Courts. This devolution of legal authority represented an intensification of legal culture within provincial life. As the law entered the lives of more people, lawyers made other people's lives their business. In Victorian fiction solicitors and barristers do more detective-work than the police, and are key brokers in a growing "culture of information" in which secrets are up for bargaining (Welsh 1985). The sensation novel exploited such anxiety about secrets, suggesting to Henry James that "Society is a vast magazine of crime and suffering, of enormities, mysteries, and miseries of every description" (*Nation*, 1865). A series of poisoning cases in the 1850s and 1860s, and a subsequent increase in the commercial crimes of fraud and embezzlement, confirmed that the "society" about which James had been talking, long before Jekyll and Hyde, was the "respectable" middle class.

The outstanding procedural reform of the Victorian judicial system was embodied in the Judicature Acts of 1873 and 1875, which combined the common law courts (Queen's Bench, Exchequer, Common Pleas) with the equity court of Chancery and the civil courts (Ecclesiastical, Admiralty, Probate) into a single High Court of three divisions. The most controversial aspect of the reform was the merging of common law and equity. Chancery had, by the Victorian period, become bogged in its own procedures, the need to remedy which was both a major motive for the reform of the judiciary, and the inspiration for *Bleak House* (1853). But concern was expressed by equity lawyers for the principles of their jurisdiction: had these principles been lost in the reform of procedure? In *Bleak House* the language and principles of equity are constantly invoked with reference to the central equitable institution of the trust. Right of way – about which Boythorn and Sir Leicester are locked in litigation – was originally a form of trust. The sinister power of Tulkinghorn, who keeps the family secrets in trust for the perpetuation of aristocratic institutions, is countered by the partnership of Allan Woodcourt and Esther Summerson who, united by the creative secrecy of mutual fiduciary obligation, become common trustees of Richard in a model of responsible social relationship (chs 45, 51).

Esther Summerson functions throughout *Bleak House* as a figure of equity, and as the exemplification of Matthew Bagnet's belief that "the noun-substantive, Goodness, [is] of the feminine gender" (ch. 49). The common-law world was distinctly of the masculine gender, however, identified by such qualities as "that peculiar combination of mental and moral force which reveals itself in masculine common sense" (Stephen 1895: 131). Throughout Victorian literature, the relationship of women to legal institutions is analogous to the supplemental relationship of equity to the common law. Neither branch of the legal profession was open to women – who could find only the lowliest employment in the legal hierarchy, at the Law Copying Office in the Strand, and even this was felt by the profession to be a threat to its law-writers (Cocks 1983: 92) – and their exclusion is translated, in literature, into critical positions from which their interrogative voices can promote alternative systems of value. The prototype here is Portia in *The Merchant of Venice*, and her main Victorian descendants are Esther in *Bleak House* and Pompilia in *The Ring and the Book*, which can be read as an attempt to turn a victim of patriarchy into a counter-legal voice. In *The Moorland Cottage*, Maggie Browne's moral language similarly subverts the oppressive legal language of the men (ch. 9); while, at the trial of Felix Holt, Esther Lyons's extralegal defence of Felix uncovers matters which law has failed to disclose (ch. 46). While it is in writings by women that female figures most powerfully employ a language of their own to define themselves against the law, male writers also explore legal institutions, and legally instituted masculine modes of thought, in the light of equitable principles. The gendered complexity of Arthur's problematic role in *Idylls of the King* (1859–85) is illuminated by his status as a figure of equity, for "Arthurian society in Tennyson's poem is based on the radical, original meaning of Equity in England as the conscience of the King" (Petch 1997: 133). And Trollope distinguishes between masculine and feminine perceptions of legal issues in his treatment of the relationship between Lady Mason and Mrs Orme. "A Woman's Idea of Friendship" (*Orley Farm*, ch. 46) is not the same as a man's, and her sense of justice is based on sympathy rather than property (which she could not own).

"The criminal law stands to the passion of revenge in much the same relation as marriage to the sexual appetite" (Stephen 1863: 99). Principles that should here be identifiable by analogical reasoning are disturbingly swamped by the power of sex and gender. Throughout the masculinist legal discourse of Victorian England, language is inflected with the gender it was trying so hard to suppress. Thus, Hardy's invocations of natural law are imbricated with questions of gender in his obsessive writing on "the sexual relation." And "rights" and "duties," the terms which Maine borrowed from substantive law to illustrate his theory of contract, were themselves gendered terms, for as Mill demonstrated in *The Subjection of Women* (1869), women had no legal rights; and the duty of which Esther Summerson constantly reminds herself is exposed, in Gissing's *The Odd Women* (1893), as a dreary obligation imposed on women. In *Our Mutual Friend* a glimpse into a police station reveals a night inspector doing his clerical work, and studiously ignoring "a howling fury of a drunken woman . . . banging herself against a cell-door" (book 1, ch. 3) – an image which, read against Dickens's point (police efficiency), becomes a powerful emblem of the legal standing of women in Victorian England, and a subversion of the legal fiction spawned by Blackstone that woman was the favorite of the laws of England. The presence of a female monarch who was also a wife complicated assumptions about gender roles, as can be seen from a seriously comic conversation in *Mary Barton* (1848) between Mrs Wilson and Aunt Alice about the domestic difficulties for married women working in factories (ch. 10). The discussion fuses the constitutional question of who makes the laws – is it the queen? – with the domestic question of whether or not she obeys Prince Albert: the demands of these conflicting authorities are not resolved.

When Vholes, the respectable legal vampire of *Bleak House*, says, "I both have, and am, a father", he speaks from the very nub of the legal system, the point at which paternalism becomes continuous with patriarchy (ch. 39). In comparing the English bar to "a great public school" (Stephen 1895: 139), Fitzjames Stephen (who had been very unhappy at Eton) both cracked its social code and suggested its underlying anxieties. The gendered nature of legal authority is interrogated in Victorian literature through subtle exploration of the domestic contexts of legal professionalism. "The society of girls is a very delightful thing," says Tommy Traddles to David Copperfield. "It's not professional, but it's very delightful" (ch. 59). Traddles's own professional life is continuous with his domestic life, for his wife lives with him in his chambers – a domestication of his legal abode, but also a ratification of his professional authority as a barrister by his legal authority as a husband. In *Our Mutual Friend* the analysis of professional and gender ideologies is focused on Eugene Wrayburn, the self-styled "idlest and least of lawyers," who builds a kitchen into the chambers he shares with Mortimer Lightwood in an attempt to incorporate the feminine into his professional world (book 2, ch. 6). Failure of legal etiquette leads to a loss of domestic authority in *Orley Farm*. Furnival, a barrister infatuated with his client Lady Mason, does nothing illegal in allowing her to discuss her circumstances with him directly. But, as his jealous wife is quick to point out, his behavior runs against professional codes of conduct: "Ladies don't go to barristers' chambers about law business. All that is done by attorneys. I've heard you say scores of times that you never would see people themselves, and yet you see her" (ch. 49). Furnival's behavior undermines his authority as a husband, for "the wife, bound though she be by an oath of obedience, will not obey him" (ch. 21). Masculine professional and gender anxieties are most comfortably resolved in *Lady Audley's Secret* (1862), the subtext of which is the professional life of Robert Audley. The language of circumstantial evidence provides him with an institutional discourse with which to unlock the secret of Lady Audley's past; and as he acquires professional identity he also becomes a potential husband.

In contrast to Robert Audley, Rex Gascoigne in *Daniel Deronda* devotes himself solely to the pursuit of professional identity. Disillusioned by his experience with Gwendolen, and looking forward to ending his life as a judge and codifier, Rex justifies the profession in which he is yet to make his way with a fine balance between ambition and detachment, and he deserves the last word here:

> I don't see that law-rubbish is worse than any other sort. It is not so bad as the rubbishy literature that people choke their minds with. . . . Any orderly way of looking at things as cases and evidence seems to me better than a perpetual wash of odds and ends bearing on nothing in particular. And then, from a higher point of view, the foundations and the growth of law make the most interesting aspects of philosophy and history. (ibid.: ch. 58)

The Victorian jurists discussed at the beginning of this chapter would have agreed with his every word.

See also 1870; CLERICAL, MEDICAL; FICTION; SKINS

REFERENCES

Austin, J. (1885) *Lectures on Jurisprudence; or, The Philosophy of Positive Law*, 2 vols, 5th edn, rev. and ed. Robert Campbell. London: John Murray.

——(1954) [1863] *The Province of Jurisprudence Determined, and The Uses of the Study of Jurisprudence*. London: Weidenfeld & Nicolson.

Cocks, R. (1983) *Foundations of the Modern Bar*. London: Sweet & Maxwell.

Cornish, W. R. and Clark, G. de N. (1989) *Law and Society in England 1750–1950*. London: Sweet & Maxwell.

Dicey, A. V. (1905) *Lectures on the Relation between Law and Public Opinion in England during the Nineteenth Century*. London: Macmillan.

Kirk, H. (1976) *Portrait of a Profession: A History of the Solicitor's Profession, 1100 to the Present Day*. London: Oyez Publishing.

Maine, H. S. (1986) [1861] *Ancient Law: Its Connec-tion with the Early History of Society and its Relation to Modern Ideas*. New York: Dorset Press.

Odgers, W. B. (ed.) (1901) *A Century of Law Reform: Twelve Lectures on the Changes in the Law of England during the Nineteenth Century*. London: Macmillan.

Petch, S. (1997) "Law, Equity, and Conscience in Victorian England." *Victorian Literature and Culture*, 25/1, 123–39.

Stephen, J. F. (1863) *A General View of the Criminal Law of England*. London: Macmillan.

Stephen, L. (1895) *The Life of Sir James Fitzjames Stephen*. London: Smith, Elder.

——(1900) *The English Utilitarians*, 3 vols. London: Duckworth.

Stone, M. (1985) "Dickens, Bentham, and the Fictions of the Law: A Victorian Controversy and its Consequences." *Victorian Studies*, 29/1, 125–54.

Waddams, S. M. (1992) *Law, Politics, and the Church of England: The Career of Stephen Lushington 1782–1873*. Cambridge: Cambridge University Press.

Welsh, A. (1985) *George Eliot and Blackmail*. Cambridge, MA: Harvard University Press.

Wiener, M. J. (1990) *Reconstructing the Criminal: Culture, Law, and Policy in England, 1830–1914*. Cambridge: Cambridge University Press.

FURTHER READING

Baker, J. H. (1990) *An Introduction to English Legal History*, 3rd edn. London: Butterworths.

Cocks, R. (1988) *Sir Henry Maine: A Study in Victorian Jurisprudence*. Cambridge: Cambridge University Press.

Collins, P. (1964) *Dickens and Crime*, 2nd edn. London: Macmillan.

Dolin, K. (1998) *Fiction and the Law: Legal Discourse in Victorian and Modernist Literature*. Cambridge: Cambridge University Press.

Duman, D. (1982) *The Judicial Bench in England 1727–1875: The Reshaping of a Professional Elite*. London: Royal Historical Society.

——(1983) *The English and Colonial Bars in the Nineteenth Century*. London: Croom Helm.

Lansbury, C. (1981) *The Reasonable Man: Trollope's Legal Fiction*. Princeton: Princeton University Press.

McMaster, R. D. (1988) *Trollope and the Law*. London: Macmillan.

Miller, D. A. (1988) *The Novel and the Police*. Berkeley: University of California Press.

Pollock, F. (1882) *Essays in Jurisprudence and Ethics*. London: Macmillan.

Shanley, M. L. (1989) *Feminism, Marriage, and the Law in Victorian England*. Princeton: Princeton University Press.

Smith, K. J. M. (1988) *James Fitzjames Stephen: Portrait of a Victorian Rationalist*. Cambridge: Cambridge University Press.

Smith, R. (1981) *Trial by Medicine: Insanity and Responsibility in Victorian Trials*. Edinburgh: Edinburgh University Press.

Welsh, A. (1992) *Strong Representations: Narrative and Circumstantial Evidence in England*. Baltimore: Johns Hopkins University Press.

12
Medical

Lawrence Rothfield

As the young Pip is being brought upstairs to visit Miss Havisham, in chapter 11 of Dickens's *Great Expectations* (1861), he meets "a gentleman groping his way down" who turns the boy to the light to examine his face, questions him briefly, advises him with a frown, "You behave yourself!", and then releases him and continues downstairs. It is not until years later that Pip comes to know this man with the "disagreeably sharp and suspicious eyes" as Jaggers, the lawyer. Jaggers's legalistic view of humanity as guilt-ridden – "I have a pretty large experience of boys, and you're a bad set of fellows" – dominates the novel, not just because Jaggers sits in the center of the web of non-relations linking Miss Havisham's upstairs world of great expectations to Magwitch's downstairs world of crime, but also because the kind of power Jaggers exercises over Pip is only the most potent version of the punitive impulse we see at work throughout: in Pumblechook's browbeating, Mrs Joe's "tickling," and Pip's own internalized "oppressed conscience."

Yet even as Dickens registers this disagreeable dominance, he hints at another perspective Jaggers might have represented in a different world:

> With these words he released me – which I was glad of, for his hand smelt of scented soap – and went his way downstairs. I wondered whether he could be a doctor; but no, I thought; he couldn't be a doctor, or he would have a quieter and more persuasive manner.

As Pip's momentary interpretative puzzlement shows, doctors and lawyers in the mid-Victorian period occupy roughly similar positions within the cultural imagination. Both attend to individuals in need, both make house calls, and both wash their hands after seeing their clients; both have aptitudes for diagnosis based on physical observation, "large experience," and questioning. But such similarities only heighten the differences between the two sorts of professional. Jaggers discharges his duties by executing the intentions of Miss Havisham rather than tending to her infirmities, and when he washes his hands it symbolizes his disavowal of responsibility rather than self-consciousness about the medical benefits of cleanliness. His "manner" is accusatory, repellent and guilt-inducing, not the "quiet and more persuasive" manner of a physician, whose ideal type Dickens portrays in *Little Dorrit* (1857) as imbued with 'an equality of compassion no more disturbed than the Divine Master's of all healing was" (ch. 25).

"Manner" here stands, as it does everywhere in Victorian culture, not just for politeness but for something deeper: a way of exercising power and manifesting authority. And for Dickens, at least, the physician's power seems remarkably exempt from the critique leveled against lawyers and the policing of the liberal individual subject they help enforce. Yet the obliqueness of Dickens's positive allusion to medical power here is perhaps as relevant as anything the passage above implies about Victorian attitudes toward medicine itself. It is as if medicine's exemption from criticism were purchased at the cost of near-invisibility. Not only in Dickens, but in Victorian literature more generally, one finds a conspicuous absence of medical themes – of stories centrally *about* doctors interacting with patients, struggling against diseases, illness, or injury – at least until the 1870s. While there are a few attempts to depict medical men, most notably in Thackeray's *Pendennis* (1850) and Trollope's *Barchester Towers* (1857) and *Doctor Thorne* (1858), such depictions tend to focus only on the social and cultural standing of the apothecary or physician rather than showing doctors at work or in love. Even here, however, there is surprisingly little in Victorian literature, compared to the number of works that feature lawyers or churchmen.

One explanation for this may be that these latter professionals also qualified as "gentlemen" for those in higher society, with all the doors this opened not just literally but imaginatively for novelists, while most doctors could only aspire to such status, as one of Trollope's snobs in *The Vicar of Bullhampton* (1870) makes clear: "She would not absolutely say that a physician was not a gentleman, or even a surgeon; but she would not allow to physic the same absolute privilege which, in her eyes, belonged to the law and the church" (ch. 9). Lawyers or churchmen could be imagined as suitable romantic interlocutors in a way that medical men, for the most part, could not. Moreover, medical careers lacked the dramatic possibilities for cross-class mobility and conflict inherent in the lives of orphans, governesses, and industrial entrepreneurs, without offering writers the imaginative compensation of a well-established intra-professional code of manners that could enable a novelist like Trollope or Eliot to take clerical life as a synecdoche for the broader culture. There was, of course, a story to be told about the emergence of the modern medical profession from the ancient corporate hierarchy of physicians, surgeons, and apothecaries (each with its own privileges, coat of arms, ceremonies, dress, and rituals) into the structural form we are familiar with today: the division between general practitioners and consultants or specialists affiliated with hospitals. But while a few Victorians – Thomas Wakley, founder in 1823 of *The Lancet*, or Florence Nightingale – stood out as heroic figures battling for the medical good, the history of Victorian medicine lacked the kind of sharp break with corporate structures that would enable novelists to depict physicians as romantic world-historical individuals or even careerist wannabes.

Indeed, given the motley arrangement of colleges and societies, the ad hoc, apprentice-like nature of medical training, and the relatively low prestige, pay, and possibilities for advancement associated with work that involved manual labor, medicine hardly qualified as a career until well into the latter part of the century. Unlike lawyers or clerics, who could imagine themselves climbing a career ladder that could in principle extend into the stratosphere of politics or the higher echelons of the Church, aspiring physicians, surgeons, and apothecaries of the early Victorian era faced a slowly crumbling but still discouraging array of intellectual, social, and jurisdictional restraints on ambition. The typical student either apprenticed directly, or spent four years or so desultorily reading, attending lectures in private medical schools, and ward-walking before being crammed for an examination in which, an irate writer to *The Lancet* (1848) complained, "Scanty physiology and pathology, decked out in respectable Latin, will stand higher than mere professional excellence, marred by a false concord, or a fault of prosody." Those with family connections then made their way through nepotism into the London elite or settled for a quiet life in towns and villages outside the fifteen-mile limit that legally defined the privileged zone of London practitioners licensed by the Royal College of Physicians or the College of Surgeons. As London itself ballooned into a megalopolis, increasing numbers of underemployed medics began to develop a "general" practice within the city limits, taking second licenses to be able to practice surgery as a physician or give medical advice as an apothecary; but despite the efforts of Wakley and others to tear down all the institutional walls, the GP remained more or less an underling with dim prospects.

After the passage of the Medical Registration Act of 1858, which abolished regional licensing and formally installed the hospital as the seat of medical instruction, the lot of the average physician improved somewhat. At the very least, it was now possible to imagine a great career beginning in a provincial medical school and ending in a London hospital at the pinnacle of what was now a unified profession. Those in this new order who made it to the top as consulting physicians could imagine that there were no limits to medical power; hence the flowering, in the late Victorian period, of larger-than-life representations of physicians as both godlike and demonic. But even – indeed, especially – after the passage of the Medical Act, licensing was by no means rigorously enforced, leaving the average practitioner in an ongoing struggle for authority against folk healers, midwives, and other traditional providers of medical aid, as well as a slew of quacks and charlatans who now poured into the medical marketplace. Promising electric cures for nonexistent diseases, competing fiercely for medical trade by unabashedly advertising or even luring unsuspecting patients into "museums" of anatomical curiosities connected directly to examining rooms, these medical entrepreneurs made life miserable for the rank and file practitioner. Unable to perform medical miracles that might clear a career path in this crowded field, the average doctor was doomed to a life of accommodation and ingratiation, bone-setting and pill-prescribing, with at best the hope of respectability, at worst the specter of penury. In short, medicine was not the stuff of which dreams or plots of great expectations are made.

If the average medical career did not lend itself easily to thematization, however, changes in medicine's social structure nonetheless did make themselves felt culturally in a variety of ways. Woodcourt in Dickens's *Bleak House* (1853) and Tom Thurnall in Kingsley's *Two Years Ago* (1857) embodied Wakley's reforming impulse (though not particularly memorably), and Nightingale provided the template for a number of vocationally hungering heroines of the 1860s and 1870s, including Dorothea Brooke in Eliot's *Middlemarch* (1872). *Middlemarch* also stands out, of course, as the only Victorian novel to provide a fully realized characterization of a physician caught up in the murky professional politics of the period. Yet even Eliot found it necessary to deviate from the average in order to make a medical life narratable. Her Tertius Lydgate is an odd bird in the English context, trained not in London but in Paris and Edinburgh, where medical visionaries made it possible to conceive of medicine as a heroic undertaking which could lead to an epic life or tragic failure; even so, Eliot ultimately feels compelled to apologize to her readers in the book's "Finale" for defining as a tragic figure one who ends as "what is called a successful man."

But the relative paucity of explicit literary representations of physicians does not mean that medicine is marginal to Victorian culture. On the contrary, as Pip's comment indicates, medicine's quietness of manner indicates its very persuasiveness. Indeed, Victorian medicine has been so persuasive that we tend to overlook the astonishing changes it imposed on British culture, changes quite as profound as those associated with the Industrial Revolution, changes which run so deep that we no longer can recognize their revolutionary character. In the course of Victoria's lifetime (1819–1901), smallpox vaccination was made compulsory; the postmortem autopsy became routine; anatomy and pathology were established as standard elements of a medical school education; inhalation anesthesia was introduced; physicians discovered that at least some diseases were transmitted not by atmosphere-corrupting poison seeping from decomposing organic matter but by germs; antiseptic surgery began to be practiced; preventive and occupational medicine as well as public health and sanitary medicine were founded. The general practitioner appeared, along with the professional nurse and a range of specialists in fields such as psychiatry, neurology, sexology, and obstetrics. New kinds of disease and patient identities came into being: possession was redefined as hysteria, sodomy as homosexuality, hypochondria as neurasthenia, pregnancy as a medical condition. The hypodermic needle was perfected, along with injectable drugs like cocaine, supplementing the use of opium, morphine and other pain-killing medications and helping consolidate and complicate the concept of addiction and the figure of the addict. Artificial insemination was invented by the Victorians, as was vivisection. There also emerged a slew of medical ideas and practices which mercifully have not survived, or have survived as jokes: now-vanished disease entities such as spermatorrhea, masturbatory insanity, monomania, hysteria, fever; bizarre or kooky practices such as clitoridectomy, wet dressing, the cold-water bath, electric medicine, mesmerism, and phrenology.

These various technological, conceptual, and professional innovations each had an impact on Victorian culture. Taken together, they amount to a vast extension of the powers and capabilities of medicine. Doctors by the end of the nineteenth century were simply able to do more to, with, and for their patients – not only because they had a much wider array of diagnostic and therapeutic techniques available to them, nor because some of these techniques actually eased suffering or even in rare cases cured or prevented disease, but because the domain of medicine expanded dramatically. In what can only be called a massive medicalization of Victorian life, aspects of existence and forms of behavior that formerly had been either not problematized at all or thought of in nonmedical terms came to be understood as matters in which health and disease were at stake.

Describing medicalization in this way makes it seem a rather sinister event, a sort of power grab, and indeed in some manifestations Victorian medicine did involve a seizing upon groups – women, the poor, those with distinctive sexual habits or emotional makeups or cognitive capacities – whose difference could be defined as pathology in need of monitoring, therapy, regulation: in need, in short, of discipline.

The most egregiously coercive of these disciplinary medical practices were those connected to social medicine and the public health movements, which took shape in the early Victorian period through what social historian Frank Mort has called a "medico-moral" political alliance between medics and moral reformers. Spurred by the cholera epidemic of 1831, doctors, clerics, and local officials who had earlier collaborated only when dealing with prisoners or lock-hospital patients began focusing on the urban poor, whose immoral lifestyle was thought to make them agents of contagion. This new focus is reflected in literature in the subgenre of industrial fiction that flourished during the 1840s, when Elizabeth Gaskell and other reform-minded novelists led readers into dank Manchester basements where sewage seeped up from the earth floors and drunkenness, licentiousness, and class resentment festered. Correlating working-class unrest with unsanitary conditions on one hand and lax morality on the other, such novels helped the Victorian bourgeoisie symbolically to transform a political crisis into a social problem by locating the roots of conflict in conditions at once pathological and vicious.

Concern about political unrest from below, and efforts to repress the unruly poor or send in clerics to help relieve their suffering and counsel submission, were of course nothing new. What *was* novel in the Victorian period was the involvement of medicine in such policing, and – particularly important for students of Victorian literature and culture – the concurrent effort to justify such policing by defining the body politic in specifically medical terms. Earlier eras had defined state power by appeals to a metaphysical notion of the body politic (a notion allegorized in the conception of the king's two bodies); more recently, Robert Malthus had redefined the body politic in the nightmarishly materialist terms of political economy, as a mathematically predictable entity – population – defined by its natural tendency to reproduce until checked by the laws of nature, laws enforced by diseases (among other agencies). As Mary Poovey (1988) has pointed out, the Victorians built on Malthus's foundation of a body subject to disease while rejecting its law-bound determinism for a more therapeutically optimistic vision of the population, which they renamed "the social body."

Fusing (or rather confusing) medical and ethical norms, the metaphor of the social body was at once more flexible and more far-reaching than the older metaphors of the body politic or population had been. A body defined in medical terms necessarily would exhibit disorder not simply as outbreaks of political violence or the dismal inevitability of sexual reproduction, but in subtle processes occurring in the hidden depths whence diseases emerge. Thus, for example, James Kay, one of the leading figures in the early public health movement (and a man who began his medical career publishing papers on brain and circulatory diseases), could speak of "the moral leprosy of vice" as "capable of corrupting the whole body of society, like an insidious disease." Leprosy was an ancient trope for moral disfigurement, of course; what was new was the medical twist Kay gave to it by emphasizing its gradualness as a pathological process. In doing so, he was simply extending to the social body the logic of medical research that Eliot's Lydgate expressed more nobly as aimed at piercing "the obscurity of those minute processes which prepare human misery and joy, those invisible thoroughfares which are the first lurking-places of anguish, mania, and crime, that delicate poise and transition which determine the growth of happy or unhappy consciousness" (ch. 16).

Lydgate, however, represented a very different brand of physician from Kay, a clinician rather than a public health official, and the reference to "minute processes" for a clinician would have meant something very different from what it meant for a practitioner of social medicine. Even within social medicine itself, the social body went through several different incarnations over the course of the century. It is important, therefore, to look more closely at the rhetorics of pathology that came into play, because different theories of disease causation gave rise to quite distinct sorts of "therapeutic" interventions and literary practices.

Social medicine relied on the miasmatic theory of disease causation, which held that epidemic influences in the atmosphere become malignant when combined with the poisonous effluvia arising out of decomposing organic matter. Scientifically reasonable in its materialism, easily graspable and illustratable – think of the fever-bearing fog that seeps through Dickens's London – and yet also traceable to human agents, miasma theory allowed early sanitary reformers to argue that bad personal habits could engender disease as well as moral decay, and lent scientific legitimacy to the call to empower public health officers not just to isolate and quarantine those found to be already infected, but to enter into households and "improve" living conditions to prevent disease.

By the 1860s, however, the miasmatic theory had been largely discredited, after epidemiologists discovered that death rates from cholera correlated directly with the pumps and cisterns of specific London water companies, leading to the conclusion that the disease was transmitted by bad water rather than bad air. Social medicine then turned to a different rhetoric of pathology that helped shift the focus of medico-moral power and redistribute authority within the sanitary movement. Doctors specializing in venereal diseases, the most notorious of whom was William Acton, called for health officers to turn their attention away from diseases transmitted by miasma in order to focus instead on the danger to the social body posed by syphilis and gonorrhea, and on the need to monitor the agents of these contagious diseases. In principle, such an appeal was neutral with regard to who the agents might be; in calling for the state to take over the administration of public health, doctors set themselves up as objective scientific reformers opposed to the inept moralistic meddling of philanthropic amateurs. In practice, however, the public health measures enacted in the 1860s – most notably the Contagious Diseases Act of 1864 – proved to be, if anything, more biased than earlier policies. Only the target had changed, from class to gender. The new public health initiatives identified prostitutes rather than the working poor as agents of infection, giving wide latitude to local physicians and police in identifying suspected carriers. As a result, women found that their mere presence on the streets had been redefined as a medical danger; indeed, within the medically dubious physiology of sex purveyed by Acton and his followers, female sexuality was defined as both dangerous to others and pathological per se, as opposed to male sexuality, which Acton argued was uncontrollable by nature and therefore both unregulable by law and a feature of health in men.

While the Contagious Diseases Act was repealed within a few decades, it portended a much more long-lasting and frightening development within medico-moral policing: the medicalizing not only of sexuality but of other categories of deviance as well. Seen as an event within the history of Victorian medicine, sexual policing appears as part of a broader development of medical surveillance. Beginning in the 1860s, psychiatrists began to discriminate between a number of different sorts of "partial" or "latent" insanity, replacing the earlier catchall legal defense of monomania with a spectrum of neurasthenias; Victorian psychologists began to distinguish among cognitive disabilities (retardation, imbecility, cretinism, etc.); and sexologists created what Foucault has called "a mosaic of perversions" that medicalized behaviors such as fetishism, sodomy, and even masturbation. Such efforts came to a head in the late 1880s and early 1890s, when Richard von Krafft-Ebing, Professor of Psychiatry at Vienna, published *Psychopathia Sexualis*. Confusing as Krafft-Ebing's logic was (he waffled on whether the pathologies he was describing were congenital or the effects of degeneration), his book was incredibly influential in establishing in the public mind the conviction that figures such as the "lust-murderer" and the "invert" were not just criminals but pathological types. Max Nordau's equally popular *Degeneration* (first translated in 1895) simply extended Krafft-Ebing's medical argument from individuals to intellectual groups of "sick" artists.

Whether they supported medical policing or were themselves the target of it, Victorian writers were caught up in this movement. Inevitably its fantasies of sensationally lost self-control, pursuit by normalizing authorities, radically alterable sensibility, and degenerative morbidity found cultural expression. From Mary Elizabeth Braddon's Lady Audley – confined for life in an asylum because a physician is willing to declare that "there is latent insanity! . . . She has the cunning of madness, with the prudence of intelligence. . . . She is dangerous!" (ch. 37) – to Browning's Porphyria's lover to Stevenson's Mr Hyde and Wilde's Dorian Gray, late Victorian literature is replete with hounded, haunted figures who represent the dangerously pathological.

Looking back on these fictions and the medical ideas underlying them today, it is difficult to understand how anyone could have taken them seriously. They seem to show that when the social body is taken as a real thing, the metaphor opens the door for mischief, enabling bad medicine and tendentious social policy to masquerade as real, disinterested science, and giving rise to grotesque fictions. In clinical medicine, on the other hand, where doctors focus on anatomies rather than behavior, individuals rather than groups, one might expect to find a more even-handed application of medical practices across classes and genders. Yet even here, notoriously, a double-standard prevailed for the bodies of the poor and women. In the Anatomy Act of 1832, for example, as Ruth Richardson (1988) has brilliantly shown, the need for cadavers in medical research led to passage – in the face of widespread political opposition and even rioting – of a measure that singled out the destitute for dissection. (As late as 1864, in the figure of Betty Higden in *Our Mutual Friend*, Dickens could still movingly evoke the terror this Act generated in elderly poor facing the possibility of dying in the workhouse without money to pay for burial.) And the anatomical conceptualizing of the body as an economy of vital forces connected by a network of tissues did not prevent physicians from claiming that the female body was both more sensitive physiologically and distinctly organized with the uterus as the center of its anatomical web; the result was an array of horrendous medical interventions directed at women (ovariotomy, clitoridectomy, the rest cure).

Given that all these coercive horrors were legally sanctioned, it is difficult not to take the opposition we began with, between Jaggers's lawyerly bullying and the quietly persuasive manner of a doctor, as an ideological ruse masking a fundamental equivalence or at least strategic alliance between legal and medical power. This jaundiced view of Victorian medicine, developed in the earlier work of Foucault and his followers, stresses the essential continuity between the overtly punitive and repressive power of the police and the softer but perhaps more constraining power exercised by agencies like medicine. The police force us to behave; the doctor orders us, but we usually follow these orders consensually. As a result, as D. A. Miller (1988) puts it, the disciplinary force inherent in medicalization "never passes for such." In Miller's brilliant reading of the Victorian novel, novelists themselves participate in this disciplinary project – not by representing triumphant doctors and compliant patients, but by "putting in place a perceptual grid in which a division between the normal and the deviant inherently imposes itself" (ibid.: 18).

The Foucauldian approach to medicalization brings into high relief a crucial tendency within Victorian culture. But it does so at the cost of giving a slanted and partial account of what was in reality an extremely complex and uneven development. Medical power picked out women, the poor, and deviants for special scrutiny, it is true, but focusing exclusively on double standards misses the more fundamental point that Victorian medicine aimed at subjecting *all* bodies to its gaze. The Anatomy Act itself, for example, began as an effort to persuade all citizens that it was their duty to donate their bodies to science (as Bentham did his), not as the punitive measure addressed only to paupers that it ultimately became. Similarly, women were thought to be more susceptible by nature to hysteria, given their higher general level of sensibility and anatomical organization, but since the fundamentals of physiology applied to both sexes, men could and did suffer from hysteria too.

Moreover, medicine's relation to juridical and moral practices was not always collaborative. In some cases one might even argue that doctors were downright progressive. For example, sexologists – including Krafft-Ebing himself – stood in the vanguard of those calling for decriminalizing same-sex sodomy, and they did so on the basis of biological and medical arguments. And as A. J. Youngson (1979) and Mary Poovey (1988) have shown in very different ways, the mid-century battle over the introduction of chloroform anesthesia into midwifery pitted doctors against clerics who maintained that the pangs of labor resulted from God's curse on the daughters of Eve. This is not to say, to be sure, that submitting to chloroform anesthesia was an unalloyed good, only that in assessing the effect of this sort of medicalizing it is important to take account of the context in which doctors were operating.

The negative view of medicalization obscures these struggles for power in Victorian culture, since it defines all forms of power as equally bad and equivalent in operation. It also fails to distinguish between different *kinds* of concern. If, for example, doctors worried about sexual matters, they did not all worry for the same reasons. Acton and the sexologists may have focused on sexual diseases, but they were considered oddballs by the vast majority of clinical practitioners, most of whom treated sexual matters as impinging on health only where they affected basic physiological functions such as digestion, respiration, secretion, sensation, or reproduction. Masturbation was a worry because it overstimulated the bodily economy, but so did overwork, overeating, and speculating; as an irritant, masturbation could be the cause of a nonsexual disease such as epilepsy, and could be prevented, according to an 1834 *Lancet* article, by "counter-irritation to the part affected" (ouch!) or by a diet of fish and grains. The interchange-ability of masturbation with overeating and the weirdness of the prescription points up the fact that sexual matters were not for the most part pathologized in themselves.

Finally, viewing medicine through the lens of policing power reduces what medicine did to a single effect, that of subduing the untamed, unregulated social or sexual body to docility. Victorian medicine did foster a vision of the patient as compliant, as what one guide to aspiring practitioners calls "clinical material" to be fingered. This was, after all, the era that developed a set of distinctions – between voluntary and involuntary physiological functions, between controlled actions and reflex actions, between sensibility and sensation, between the signs reported by the patient and the symptoms revealed by physical examination, between individual reports and statistical evidence – which peeled the life of the body off from that of the self who inhabited it. The Victorians also were the first to realize this ideal by developing first mesmerism and then effective anesthetics like ether and chloroform as well as painkilling drugs such as morphine and cocaine.

But dissociating the self from the body – whether by defining what is happening to the body as a case, reducing patients to statistics, numbing the body or rendering the self insensible – does not mean that the self is destroyed or rendered simply docile. The aim of social medicine, after all, was not just preventive, but hygienic: as William Farr, inventor of what came to be known as "vital statistics," put it in an article on hygiene in *The Lancet*, social medicine sought "to increase the *sum of vitality* by extending individual life to its full term (averting death); by obviating sickness; and by increasing the energy of all the vital forces, whether nutritive, formative, locomotive, or sensitive and intellectual." More generally, as Bruce Haley (1978) has shown, Victorian culture envisioned such vitality not as an absence of disease, but in positive terms that made the quest for health a privileged form of self-development. A case, in other words, can be interesting, and not just for the doctor: as Henry James's Milly Theale puts it, her own illness can assume "the beauty of the idea of a great adventure, a big dim experiment or struggle in which she might more responsibly than ever before take a hand" (*The Wings of the Dove* [1902], ch. 13). Less romantically but more daringly, the participation of many late-Victorian intellectuals in what we call, after all, a drug *culture* shows that they were well aware that anesthetics could be used for exploring new kinds of aesthetic experience. Aestheticism itself derived much of its force from the daring claim to be turning the analysis of the experience of beauty into a kind of vivisection of oneself (as Oscar Wilde's Lord Henry puts it) that located the origins of strange maladies in "some pearly cell in the brain, or some white nerve in the body" or "some strange poisonous germ" (*The Picture of Dorian Gray* [1891], ch. 11). The darker side of this experimentation was brought out in science fiction depicting chemical and vivisectional exploration run amok, as in Robert Louis Stevenson's 1886 *Dr Jekyll and Mr Hyde* (Jekyll buys his house once belonging to a "celebrated surgeon" and, "his own tastes being rather chemical than anatomical" [ch. 5], turns the former dissecting rooms into a laboratory for self-experimentation) and H. G. Wells's *The Island of Dr Moreau* (1896).

It is important to note that such fictions, relying as they did on the assumption that physiology and pathology were essentially matters not just of the body but of cells, and taking an experimental attitude toward the body, could only emerge (in England, at least) relatively late in the century. Here we must emphasize one last kind of uneven development in Victorian medicine: an unevenness of scientific knowledge within medical practice. Celebrants of progress like Macaulay may have included "the science of healing" among the many things the Victorians had "carried to a perfection which our ancestors would have thought magical," but the reality was that English medicine lagged behind its counterparts on the Continent. The scientific knowledge was there: by the 1840s, chemists had shown that one could identify albumen in urine, making it possible to diagnose granular kidney disease at an earlier stage; tumors and nervous physiology were being investigated at the cellular level in the 1830s by German physiologists. In England itself, the 1832 Anatomy Act made it increasingly evident that doctors needed to "open up a few corpses," in the famous words of the father of pathological anatomy, Xavier Bichat, in order to be properly educated. Yet as continental medicine was moving into cellular pathology and microscopy, English medical education still did not include formal training in pathological anatomy. As a result, even the gains made in the early nineteenth century by French medicine – most

fundamentally, the conceptual linking of physiology or normal vital functions (digestion, respiration, secretion, sensation) with pathology or abnormal functions, and the
localizing of these functions in tissues rather than in organs or humors – were only
gradually absorbed into English medical practice. Doctors trained in Bichatian medicine could distinguish pericarditis from myocarditis or endocarditis, where their
English counterparts continued to speak of "inflammation of the heart" (Bynum 32),
unless trained in Paris or Edinburgh. Eliot highlights precisely this unevenness by
having the French-trained Lydgate diagnose what the other Middlemarch physicians
call Casaubon's "fit" as "fatty degeneration of the heart" using Laennec's recently
introduced stethoscope.

Pre-cellular but tissular physiology may have been avant-garde to many doctors,
but it provided metaphors and analogies that had a powerful impact upon Victorian
society, in large part because they differed from the dominant medical metaphors of
the body. While proponents of social medicine relied on an essentially eighteenth-
century medical epistemology of what Poovey (1995) calls "anatomical realism,"
radical critics of modernization used the more up-to-date language of pathological
anatomy to redefine the problems suffered by the social body. Thomas Carlyle, for
example, argued in "Characteristics" (1831) that the social body, like the individual
body, consisted of a "vital articulation," and in *Sartor Resartus* (1833) he defined this
articulation as a forming of "organic filaments" into "Pericardial Nervous Tissue (as we
named it) of Religion." The force of the analogy lay in the diagnosis it enabled Carlyle
to make, as well as in the therapeutics he could then reject or embrace: just as the vital
forces inherent in living tissue were distinct from the forces inherent in inorganic
nature ("what the Physiologists call *irritability*" being considered irreducible to either
chemical processes or galvanic reflexes), so, Carlyle declared, vital social forces were
distinct from the "spasmodic, galvanic sprawlings" of merely reflexive religious practices or the mechanistic relations of the cash nexus. A few decades later, from the left,
Marx would ridicule the political economists (whose fears had paradoxically helped
spawn the social body metaphor in the first place) for not looking deeply enough into
society to recognize that the social body was an evolving organism.

If the organic and tissular metaphors for the social body opened up the possibility
for radical critique of a new kind, they also opened up the more general possibility for
a kind of social thought. What we now call sociology was founded by the Victorians
out of the sense that society needed to be analyzed not as a set of rules or laws – as was
the case for economics and political economy – but as a complex system of organic
functions that define norms and demand adjustments. Nowhere is this assumption
more densely elaborated than in the work of the founder of the discipline, Herbert
Spencer. Spencer borrowed from the latest medical physiology the structure for his
theory that social organisms, like plants and animals, develop from homogeneity to
heterogeneity, and combined it with Darwinian elements to produce a kind of sociological fantasia of progressively differentiated interdependency and diffuse causality of
"insensible gradations." Ultimately Spencer's vision would inform not only sociology
but also the novel, providing the metaphorical underpinning for Thomas Hardy's and

George Eliot's realism, with its reiterated reference to social relations as weblike, variegated, complexly determined, and involved in gradual, almost imperceptible change.

Eliot's fiction, as Henry James observed, marks a limit to the development of the English novel; as I have argued elsewhere, the emergence of cell theory and evolutionary biology called into question the physiological perspective that grounded her analyses of social life. Within a few decades of her death Victorian medicine would itself be reorganized almost beyond recognition both epistemologically and institutionally, as the Pasteurian focus on germs gave rise to Lister's antiseptic surgery, as scientifically centered medical education became the norm, and the National Health Service bureaucratized the medical profession while massifying the social body.

Even as it was passing away, however, Victorian medicine spawned one last great cultural work: Conan Doyle's detective fiction. Trained as a doctor at the very moment when the new science was displacing the old, Conan Doyle was somehow able to apotheosize nearly all the culturally significant features of Victorian medicine – its affiliation with social policing (Holmes's "deductions" are modeled on the diagnostic technique displayed by Conan Doyle's medical school professor, Dr Joseph Bell, but he uses this technique to help identify socially dangerous individuals rather than "those minute organisms that disseminate cholera and fever, tubercle and anthrax" as Bell [1893] does); its unevenness as a science and as a procedure (inscribed in the hierarchical difference between Holmes's scientifically specialized way of seeing and the simpler yet more human viewpoint of the general practitioner Watson); its uneven application across genders (as in "A Scandal in Bohemia," where the double standard is both exhibited and exposed); and its capacity to define cases in a way that at once reduces persons to diagnosed, detected individuals and makes them interesting as cases. If we can still feel the pleasures and anxieties of reading *The Adventures*, it is at least in part because, in spite of Freud on the one hand and the technologizing and bureaucratizing of medicine on the other, we can still identify with both doctor and patient as the Victorians created them. In that sense, we remain – in spirit at least – other Victorians.

See also GROWING OLD, PASSING ON, SEXUALITIES; SKINS, PARAPETS

REFERENCES

Bell, Joseph (1893) "Introduction" to A. C. Doyle, *A Study in Scarlet*. London: Ward, Lock & Bowden.

Bynum, William F. (1994) *Science and the Practice of Medicine in the Nineteenth Century*. Cambridge: Cambridge University Press.

Farr, William (1835–6) "Lecture on the History of Hygiene." *The Lancet* 1, 773–6.

Foucault, Michel (1978) *The History of Sexuality*, *Volume I: An Introduction*, trans. Robert Hurley. New York: Random House.

Haley, Bruce (1978) *The Healthy Body and Victorian Culture*. Cambridge, MA and London: Harvard University Press.

Kay, James Philips (1832) *The Moral and Physical Condition of the Working Classes Employed in the Cotton Manufacture in Manchester*. London: James Ridgway.

Kraff-Ebing, Richard von (1908) *Psychopathia Sexualis, with Especial Reference to Contrary Sexual Instinct*, trans. Gilbert Chaddock. Philadelphia: F. A. Davis.

Macaulay, Thomas Babington (1835) "Sir James Mackintosh." In *Critical, Historical, and Miscellaneous Essays and Poems*. London and New York: Chesterfield Society.

Miller, D. A. (1988) *The Novel and the Police*. Berkeley: University of California Press.

Mort, Frank (1987) *Dangerous Sexualities: Medico-Moral Politics in England Since 1830*. London and New York: Routledge and Kegan Paul.

Nordau, Max (1895) *Degeneration*. New York: D. Appleton.

Poovey, Mary (1988) *Uneven Developments: The Ideological Work of Gender in Mid-Victorian England*. Chicago: University of Chicago Press.

——(1995) *Making a Social Body: British Cultural Formation, 1830–1864*. Chicago and London: University of Chicago Press.

Richardson, Ruth (1988) *Death, Dissection, and the Destitute*. London: Penguin Books.

Spencer, Herbert (1868) *Essays Scientific, Political, and Speculative*. London: Williams and Norgate.

Youngson, A. J. (1979) *The Scientific Revolution in Victorian Medicine*. New York: Holmes & Meier.

FURTHER READING

During, Simon (1988) "The Strange Case of Monomania: Patriarchy in Literature, Murder in *Middlemarch*, Drowning in *Daniel Deronda*." *Representations* 23, 86–104.

Foucault, Michel (1975) *The Birth of the Clinic: An Archaeology of Medical Perception*, trans. A. M. Sheridan Smith. New York: Random House.

Gallagher, Catherine (1986) "The Body versus the Social Body in the Works of Thomas Malthus and Henry Mayhew." *Representations* 14, 191–209.

Gilman, Sander L. (1985) *Difference and Pathology: Stereotypes of Sexuality, Race, and Madness*. Ithaca, NY: Cornell University Press.

Jacobus, Mary, Fox Keller, Evelyn, and Shuttleworth, Sally (eds) (1990) *Body/Politics: Women and the Discourses of Science*. New York: Routledge.

Jordanova, Ludmilla (1989) *Sexual Visions: Images of Gender in Science and Medicine Between the Eighteenth and Twentieth Centuries*. Madison: University of Wisconsin Press.

Laqueur, Thomas (1990) *Making Sex: Body and Gender from the Greeks to Freud*. Cambridge, MA and London: Harvard University Press.

Oppenheim, Janet (1991) *'Shattered Nerves': Doc-tors, Patients, and Depression in Victorian England*. New York: Oxford University Press.

Peterson, M. Jeanne (1978) *The Medical Profession in Mid-Victorian London*. Berkeley: University of California Press.

Rothfield, Lawrence (1992) *Vital Signs: Medical Realism in Nineteenth-Century Fiction*. Princeton: Princeton University Press.

Russett, Cynthia Eagle (1989) *Sexual Science: The Victorian Construction of Womanhood*. Cambridge, MA: Harvard University Press.

Showalter, Elaine (1986) "Syphilis, Sexuality, and the Fiction of the Fin de Siècle." In R. B. Yeazell (ed.) *Sex, Politics, and Science in the Nineteenth-Century Novel: Selected Papers from the English Institute, 1983–1984*. Baltimore: Johns Hopkins University Press.

Sontag, Susan (1979) *Illness as Metaphor*. New York: Vintage Books.

Spear, Jeffrey L. (1985) "Filaments, Females, Families and Social Fabric: Carlyle's Extension of a Biological Analogy." In James Paradis and Thomas Postlewait (eds) *Victorian Science and Victorian Values: Literary Perspectives*. New Brunswick, NJ: Rutgers University Press.

13

Military

John R. Reed

The first thing to understand about the armed services of nineteenth-century Britain is that they were entirely determined by class difference. The commissioned officers were understood to be gentlemen, the noncommissioned and warrant officers might possibly have gentlemen among them, but the common soldiers and sailors were, for most of the century, seen as a separate and grossly inferior breed. It is necessary, then, to regard members of the services in distinct categories, since conditions in the service were different for masters and men.

The Commissioned Officers

The army and the navy provided thoroughly desirable professional opportunities for men in nineteenth-century Britain, but there were complicating features in both services that made them unpopular choices for a large part of the population. Some of these were peculiar to one service, but others were common to both. There was, to begin with, the question of class already mentioned. Officers were gentlemen and therefore professionals. Officers for both services were recruited from the aristocracy, the gentry, and the middle classes. An officer, as a professional man, found himself having to deal with men who could seldom be considered fit companions for him. In the navy this meant that officers consorted with one another and, on shipboard, formed an elite that constantly had to reinforce its elitist qualifications. In the army the officers, with greater freedom of movement, nonetheless kept mainly to themselves, though obliged to supervise men generally less amenable to discipline than sailors. A military officer would thus constantly be obliged to prove himself worthy of his position and his authority and be prepared to risk his life in circumstances that included combat, inclement weather, and disease, all in the company of men he generally was taught to regard as inferiors. For many young men considering career options, these features of military life alone would make it unattractive. Dickens, however, was more sympathetic to the men in the ranks than to officers. He mocked blustering officers in *The Pickwick Papers* (1837) and pilloried Major Joey Bagstock in *Dombey and Son* (1848). By contrast, in *Bleak House* (1853) he rendered favorable portraits of ex-trooper George Rouncewell and ex-artilleryman Matthew Bagnet. Army officers in fiction and on the stage were often associated with sexuality, both as objects of desire and as seducers. Captain Hawdon is an example in *Bleak House*, but perhaps the most notable instance in Victorian fiction is Sergeant Troy in Hardy's *Far from The Madding Crowd* (1874).

The general perception through much of the nineteenth century was that sons of the aristocracy and gentry were the best source for army officers because of their familiarity with horsemanship, the use of weapons for hunting, and their habit of directing the activities of inferiors. Although a large number of army officers were from such families, as the century continued more and more officers tended to come from the middle classes. Thackeray, an astute observer of army types, recognized this trend in his fiction. In *Vanity Fair* Rawdon Crawley is the son of a baronet, but George Osborne and his friend Dobbin are sons of men made well-to-do by trade. In *The Newcomes* Jack Belsize is from a titled family, but Colonel Newcome is from the established middle class.

The navy presented a slightly different situation. There tradition held that the humblest person could rise to the highest rank on merit alone, something utterly impossible in the army. Horatio Nelson was held up as an example of such progress. But although Nelson had been born into a modest family (his father was a minister of the Church of England), he was scarcely of humble origins. He began under good auspices and benefited much from the interest of his friends, including an uncle who was a captain in the navy and subsequently became its Comptroller. In any case, by the beginning of the nineteenth century the rough professional from humble life had effectively disappeared. Nonetheless, although the rags-to-riches pattern was highly unlikely in the navy, opportunities for cross-class movement existed there to some degree, as they did not in the army. The tendency to admit potential officers into ships at a very young age, often as young as 13, meant that much of their training occurred on the job, though after achieving midshipman status a young man would still have to pass appropriate examinations to gain his lieutenancy. Then through service, merit, and "interest" (the common term for patronage), he would rise to commander (with command of a relatively insignificant vessel), captain, and finally post captain, which meant that he was put in command of a substantial ship, such as a frigate. From this point onward, his promotion was by seniority. A naval officer who did not disgrace himself could not be removed from the active list. In effect, he held tenure, though this did not guarantee him service in a ship or on land; when not on active service he was entitled to half pay. As the nineteenth century progressed, the Lords of the Admiralty paid greater attention to the formal education of potential officers at their own schools and on training ships, and changes were gradually made in the half-pay system. In the 1870s new examinations affected the military as they did the civil service. Most significantly, the purchase system was abolished.

The purchase system allowed for the official sale of military commissions below the rank of general. Military service tended to run in families, with sons following their relatives into navy or army. The famous Lord Cochrane, later tenth Earl of Dundonald, began his military career along with his brother in His Majesty's 104th Regiment of the Horse Guards, but Thomas quickly changed to the navy in his uncle's frigate the *Hind* (Lloyd 1947: 7–8). Sometimes this tradition was followed out of family honor or patriotic feeling, but in many families the military was seen as a likely source of income, especially for a younger son. This was often the case in Ireland, where social rank was not always accompanied by a commensurate income. Whatever the reason for established families' sending their sons to be officers in the navy or army, there was always some room for newcomers. Lord Malmesbury asserted in 1855 that military patronage was not dominated by interests of the younger sons of the landed classes, and subsequent research supports this claim. Half the army officer corps at mid-century was middle class, and the nonaristocratic and nonlanded character of the Indian army was even more marked (Bourne 1986: 87).

If class was important, so were income and interest. Army commissions could be bought and sold until roughly the third quarter of the century. Although this practice was theoretically controlled, with established prices for the various officer ranks, in practice there was a good deal of "illegal" negotiation. These purchases were over-whelmingly at the junior ranks, where young men were beginning their careers. The highest ranks were not open to purchase. Certain regiments were more prestigious than others. The most desirable were the cavalry and infantry Guards regiments, which served the Royal Household. Their uniforms were appropriately elegant, and they had the advantage of largely ornamental service in the London area. In the period 1834–8, for example, 76 percent of promotions to lieutenant were purchased, as were 80 percent to captain, and 72 percent to major, with only 58 percent to lieutenant-colonel (Harries-Jenkins 1977: 73). This system of purchase did not obtain in the Royal Navy, where all patronage was in the gift of the Lords of the Admiralty; nonetheless, interest here (the lobbying of relatives, members of Parliament, and other influential people) played a significant part. In both services promotion was possible through merit during combat or accomplishments over time. In the navy promotion beyond the rank of captain went entirely by seniority. In the army seniority was important, but there were many exceptions. In the letters and memoirs written by military men during the nineteenth century, promotion is a frequent subject.

But even if promotion was possible for young men without powerful interest, not everyone could afford to become or remain an officer. Military pay was notoriously inadequate for the expenses incurred by officers, who had to pay for their own uniforms, weapons, and other paraphernalia and who had to live in a manner worthy of a gentleman. An officer's pay in the navy was equated not with his rank or seniority, but with the post that he occupied. *Rank* (first lieutenant, captain, admiral, etc.)

qualified an officer for certain assignments, but the assignment (in a frigate or man-of-war, in a battle zone or on peacetime patrol) or *posting* determined reward. Most young officers required money supplements, either from their own resources or from their families. In 1867 a lieutenant might earn £118 12s 6d and have interest and expenses of £53 19s 5d, leaving an annual remainder of £64 13s 1d. For a major, with greater obligations, the amounts would be £292, £249 10s 4d, and £42 9s 8d (ibid.: 87). To contemplate a career as a military officer, then, was to anticipate a long period of economic dependence, and it is largely for this reason that families with comfortable incomes were the likeliest to place their sons as navy and army officers.

As we have seen, a principal attraction for becoming an officer in the navy or army was that it brought with it the recognition of gentlemanly status. But there was an added allure for the higher-ranking officers. Unlike some other professionals, especially early in the century, officers were admitted to good society and to elite clubs. The daughters of officers of higher rank were entitled to presentation at court. When John Ruskin listed what he called the five great intellectual professions, he placed the Soldier first. All of these professions required self-sacrifice, but the soldier's (and implicitly the sailor's) was the most obvious. Ruskin said the reason the world "honours the soldier is, because he holds his life at the service of the State" (*Unto this Last* [1860], Essay I). Many honors and rewards were available to officers. For outstanding service in action they might receive special honors, such as the Order of the Bath, or even be knighted. With continued excellent service they might rise in the ranks of the aristocracy. Wellington, for his great service, rose all the way to a dukedom. Such forms of recognition usually were accompanied by substantial financial rewards. Naval officers had special opportunities for additional sources of income. During wartime captured enemy ships could be adjudged prizes and the value of the prize distributed among those associated with the action, according to a regular scale by which those concerned – from the admiral of the fleet down to the common sailor – received their share. For the senior officers these rewards could be substantial, running into thousands of pounds. Another source of income was the transporting of treasure, known in the navy as freight. Here the rewards could be enormous. Captain Frederick Chamier, who went on to become a novelist, brings his autobiography to a close with his return from the West Indies in command of a ship with a freight worth upward of 700,000 dollars; for this assignment he anticipated a very comfortable reward.

Chamier was one of a group of novelists who wrote in a Victorian subgenre most often associated with Captain Frederick Marryat, the naval novel. These were rousing tales usually involving young men rising into the officer ranks. Marryat's *Peter Simple* (1834) and *Jacob Faithful* (1834) are perennial favorites, enjoyable as adult or juvenile fiction. The army had its subgenre too, most notably represented by the novels of Charles Lever, such as *The Confessions of Harry Lorrequer* (1839) and *Charles O'Malley* (1841). Lever has survived best among the military novelists, though others, like William Hamilton Maxwell and Captain Michael Rafter, had respectable reputations in their day.

Gentlemanly status, honor, and opportunities for social and financial reward all made the role of naval or military officer attractive, but the advancements, recognitions, and awards were not distributed with an impartial hand. We have already noted how those with wealth could afford to purchase choice commissions in the army and those with personal influence could see to it that early promotions and attractive assignments went to their friends and family. Officer positions continued to appeal to young gentlemen and their families because the navy's reputation was high after the Napoleonic Wars and remained extremely high throughout the nineteenth century. The army's reputation was less secure, but on the whole it fared well in public opinion, generally improving as the century continued. But the realities of naval and military life through most of Victoria's reign were not as glorious as they might appear.

In the navy there was a large surplus of officers, many of whom remained on half-pay almost their entire careers. Here again interest was important, for the person with influential friends would find himself with a ship to command while others cooled their heels at the Admiralty offices hoping for any assignment. Captain Frederick Marryat made a good income from his popular novels, but while he was ashore writing them, he was still hoping for active service. The peculiarity of the naval service was that, although promotion was by seniority after the attainment of a captaincy, there was no obligation on the Admiralty to appoint any officer to an active assignment by reason of seniority. Because for most of the century there was a redundancy of naval officers, a young man's prospects without financial and political resources were not especially good. Moreover, the opportunities for service were not the best. One might command a prison ship going to Australia. There was still the slave trade, which remained a viable possibility until the 1880s, and there were surveying and exploratory ventures. Closer to home there was coast guard duty, an important assignment in the earlier part of the century. If the end of war eliminated most possibilities for prize money, the slave trade still offered such opportunities both on the west and east coasts of Africa; but this service was offensive in many ways, not the least being the danger of disease and the risky method of using ships' boats for most of the cruising activity on the east coast of Africa. Substantial rewards were also possible for coast guard officers who managed to catch smugglers; such officers were selected for their rectitude and capacity to resist temptations to illicit activities themselves, although vigorous smuggling diminished as the century wore on.

Some officers left British naval service either entirely or for a time to serve other nations. Lord Cochran commanded the Peruvian and later the Greek navy, but the huge rewards he was promised did not materialize. Lieutenant Lloyd Matthews left the service to lead an Arab sultan's army at Zanzibar. Generally speaking, however, these adventurers were the rare exception. Captain Alexander Maconochie made a reputation in the convict colony at New South Wales as an innovative penologist, and brought his system home to England, where he became a much-appreciated reformer. A navy officer, by virtue of his position, surely had the respect and admiration of the general population. But unless he had the good fortune to be already well placed in the social hierarchy, he had to be largely content with that respect and admiration.

The half-pay officer of either service was so familiar a figure in Victorian society that he appeared regularly in the literature of the time, frequently as the genteel but impoverished father of a novel's heroine. One of the best-known half-pay officers in Victorian fiction is the retired army officer Captain Brown in Elizabeth Gaskell's *Cranford* (1853), who is described as follows: "He was a half-pay Captain, and had obtained some situation on a neighbouring railroad, which had been vehemently petitioned against by the little town; and if, in addition to his masculine gender, and his connection with the obnoxious railroad, he was so brazen as to talk of being poor – why, then, indeed, he must be sent to Coventry" (ch. 1). Instead, however, his kindliness and disciplined habits make him a favorite in the town.

The situation was different for the army. There was always sufficient occupation for the officers of this branch of the service because the empire made enormous demands on Britain's armed forces, especially the land forces. There was India to be subdued and policed. Here an officer could manage, one way and another, to acquire a considerable fortune. Many became senior administrators in India, especially after the East India Company ceded control to the government. There were two important outbreaks of war in the middle of the century – the Crimean War (1854–6) and the Indian Mutiny (1857). The former called forth from Tennyson "The Charge of the Light Brigade," "The Charge of the Heavy Brigade," and *Maud*. There was much popular poetry on this subject, but also some worthwhile, if more obscure, recognition of the fighting man, as with Sir Francis H. Doyle's "The Return of the Guards, 9th July 1856." The Crimean War turns up in contemporary fiction as well, for example in Charles Lever's *Davenport Dunn* (1859). Tennyson responded to the Indian Mutiny with "The Defense of Lucknow," and there was an outpouring of literary treatments of this event (Brantlinger 1988). The army was involved in many lesser but nonetheless important struggles during the later part of the century, such as the Afghan Wars (1839–42, 1878, 1880), the wars against Ashantis and Zulus (1873–4 and 1879), conflicts with the Boers (1880 and 1899–1902) and the Egyptian campaigns (1882–4). Although high honors were rarer during most of the century than they had been during the Napoleonic Wars, knighthoods, baronies, and higher stations were still possible for outstanding military service. Sir Garnet Wolseley achieved a Viscountcy through distinguished service in Burma, the Crimea, India, China, Canada, and Africa, crowned by the relief of Khartoum. Most officers had to content themselves with lesser positions if they chose to leave the service and accept them. Those who did became minor administrators, prison wardens, railway officials, and the like. Well-known officers were occasionally asked to serve on important boards. Some military figures were elected to Parliament. The Scottish aristocrat Lord Cochran was a Radical MP for Westminster while still on active naval service, and General Sir Edward Bruce Hamley was elected Conservative member for Birkenhead when his military career was drawing to a close. The hero of George Meredith's *Beauchamp's Career* (1875) is a naval officer who is unsuccessful in his campaign for a seat in

Parliament as a radical. Meredith had assisted his friend Frederick Augustus Maxse in a similar but successful campaign.

Uncommissioned Officers

Beneath the captain and lieutenants in the navy was a second elite group comprised of marine officers, the ship's master, surgeon, purser, and chaplain. These men were frequently gentlemen or of gentlemanly bearing. For the surgeon and chaplain, practice aboard ship was inferior to decent positions ashore. The master (responsible for navigation), surgeon, purser (in charge of the ship's stores), and chaplain were warrant officers, petty officers who received their warrants from the Navy Board rather than commissions from the Admiralty, as other officers did. There were, in a large ship, several other warrant officers, chief among them the gunner, boatswain, and carpenter. These three generally remained with the same ship and therefore had a degree of career stability unavailable to those above and below them in the ship's hierarchy, but they were not classed with the gentlemen.

In the army, there was nothing quite comparable to the navy structure beneath the commissioned officers' ranks, but there were the quartermaster, responsible for food, clothing, and equipment, and sergeants responsible for various duties, such as the paymaster sergeant, the hospital sergeant, and so forth. Then there were drummers, and corporals, the latter the lowest rank that could in any way be regarded as an officer's rank. Captains in the army were equivalent to lieutenants and warrant officers in the navy, lieutenants to mates, and ensigns to midshipmen. Men from the ranks could rise to sergeant and upon occasion quartermaster.

The Men

Conditions for ordinary sailors and soldiers improved markedly during the nineteenth century. At the beginning of the century sailors had to endure cramped and unhealthy quarters and long voyages, fed on miserable fare. Scurvy and dysentery were still significant health hazards along with accidents of various kinds, many associated with severe weather. Ordinary seamen in the navy had ratings or ranks, but these were not so distinct as the ranks of officers. Still, a sailor could move from seaman to able-bodied seaman on up to boatswain or even master, by gradual steps. The overwhelming majority remained ordinary seamen. They signed on to a ship – or, early in the century, were impressed for service against their will – for the term of a ship's commission, generally a three-year assignment. At the end of that time the ship might receive a new commission, be put up for repairs, or be retired. If the ship was going out of commission the ship's company was paid off and the hands sought new berths or retired from the service. During the Napoleonic Wars there was a chronic shortage of seamen, many dying from combat and disease, and others deserting in large numbers. After the wars a smaller navy and improving conditions for seamen made it generally easier to man the navy, and a sailor with a good reputation could always find some berth.

A sailor's pay was minimal and paid out at widely separated intervals; there were some arrangements for directing money to families, but often a sailor's dependents had to wait a considerable time for assistance. It was difficult for seamen to marry, partly because of the difficulty of financial arrangements and partly because the men were away for long periods of time. But many did get married, often to women with employment of their own on shore. Seamen did not, however, lack female companionship. When ships were in port, women flocked to them by the hundreds and sometimes were illegally concealed on the ship and sailed with the men, even assisting, at times, during sea battles. By mid-century this practice was extinct.

Discipline was severe and usually immediate. Captains had great authority and often exercised it sternly, considering obedience and attention to duty crucial to the welfare of the ship. The most common form of corporal punishment was flogging. During the first half of the century there were many debates about the value of flogging, which gradually gave way to other means of discouraging bad behavior and encouraging good. During the Napoleonic years sailors often remained on board ship for many months, even years at a time, not having shore leave because captains feared they would desert, as they often did when they had an opportunity. Many British deserters took service with American vessels. The conditions established during the Napoleonic years set the pattern for many years to follow and reforms in the navy and the army were allowed only grudgingly. Most practices died away, in fact, mainly with the gradual disappearance of the generation that had experienced the Napoleonic Wars. One of the chief improvements in the ordinary seaman's lot during the nineteenth century was, along with more comfortable and more sanitary conditions aboard ship, the institution of long-term service, which made the navy sailor's career more secure. For the first half of the century sailors bore the reputation of being good-naturedly rough when sober and disgustingly brutish and dissolute when drunk. This image improved with time until, near the end of the century, the "bluecoat" was viewed with pride and respect.

The soldiers of Wellington's army were regarded as the nation's trash. Although preferred recruits were men from the militia, many joined up to avoid obligations and penalties of various kinds – from criminal prosecution and sexual liability to financial debt or simple poverty. Army pay was bad and often intermittent, and, during wartime, conditions were dreadful. Medical assistance was crude and inadequate, an issue that received dramatic attention during the scandals associated with the Crimean War, made prominent by the new immediacy of war reporting in the press and by the improvements instituted by Florence Nightingale, which made her a popular heroine. Punishment for offenses was harsh, ranging from flogging to hanging. There were few established barracks for soldiers at the beginning of the century, so that they were often billeted upon the citizenry, a policy that did not improve public attitudes toward them. But regular garrisons were established as the century progressed. One positive feature in the soldier's life was his uniform: many memoirs of enlisted men indicate that the right to wear a uniform influenced their decision to enlist. A soldier's pride in his uniform might extend to national patriotic feelings, but it was characteristically limited chiefly to his regiment. Through the Victorian period, however, with its increasing sense of imperial power, the association of uniform with national identity increased. During the Napoleonic War a soldier's daily food ration was supposed to be a pound of meat, one and a half pounds of bread or biscuit and a third-pint of rum or a pint of wine, but even these amounts were often not forthcoming in the field. Improvements in the commissariat were slow but steady during the century, though the blunders of the Crimean War proved that they were still inadequate at mid-century.

At the beginning of the century enlistment was for 20 years, effectively the active period of a man's life at a time when men were considered old at 50. There were few provisions for retirement, except for some few wounded in battle. Soldiers could marry, but only six wives per company were allowed to travel on service. Earlier, camp-followers were commonplace with the army, but well before mid-century women were prohibited from accompanying either service. Most army service was abroad, in India, the West Indies, Canada, and elsewhere as needed. Regiments were not supposed to enjoy more than five years at home to every ten abroad.

Apart from the prestigious Household regiments, whose troops ordinarily remained in England, the cavalry was the premier service for enlisted men, though the artillery and engineer corps were also desirable. During the nineteenth century artillery gradually became more important, whereas the significance of the cavalry waned. Improvements in weaponry kept the ordinary infantryman essential. The military strategists were slow to change battle tactics, and as late as the Egyptian campaigns of the 1880s soldiers were still forming battle squares as they did in the Napoleonic days. But much of the fighting required of soldiers during the Victorian period involved skirmishing and irregular methods. Precise, long-distance repeating rifles and Gatling guns changed the dynamics of battle, but the infantry was still required for final assaults upon fortifications and for the routing of enemy troops in the field. From the 1830s onward, reforms improved housing, sanitary, and dietary conditions, reduced the severity of punishments, especially flogging, and instituted positive inducements such as good conduct medals. Short-term, renewable enlistment improved the quality of recruits, and better educational and training programs ensured a more professional rank and file.

Nineteenth-century Britain saw a steady but ultimately dramatic transformation of its armed services. Each became more technical and more humane; each changed from an aristocratic and loosely organized structure to a democratized and precise system. Navy and army officers remained prominent professionals, but whereas the navy retained its lustre, the army senior officer corps was badly tainted by the disasters of the Crimean War. A series of reforms gradually established in both services better basic educational preparation, better professional training, and finally, with the reforms of 1870, open examinations for commissions and the abolition of patronage and purchase as modes of promotion. The armed services were now becoming not only a profession, but professional as well. The fervor for empire during the last quarter of the nineteenth century enhanced the honor of the military officer once more, elevating figures like Gordon and Kitchener to national heroic status. The shock of the Boer War failures aside, Great Britain approached World War I with a growing sense of modern naval and military competence. The greatest improvements were those affecting the enlisted men, who moved from barbarous conditions to relative comfort. By the end of the century the navy and the army, both officers and men, had the respect of the civilian population.

At the beginning of the nineteenth century popular culture offered stereotypes of the drunken but carefree sailor, and the riotous and low-bred soldier, along with the bluff but honest navy captain and the sexually seductive army officer, most likely from a regiment of dragoons. These stereotypes persisted in popular songs, theatrical performances, and conventional fictional narratives of the time. But growing up alongside these stereotypes were different, more individualized images of the men of the armed services. We have already noted Dickens's tendency to offer a more positive view of the enlisted man. In *North and South* (1854–5) Mrs Gaskell complicates Margaret Hale's problems by involving them with her brother's naval delinquencies. Charlotte Yonge makes the two principal male protagonists in *The Clever Woman of the Family* (1865) military officers. Both have been wounded in the service of their country during the period of the Indian Mutiny; both are morally upright and dependable, their military self-discipline and capacity for self-sacrifice being stressed as the basis of their trustworthiness. By the end of the century the aura of Empire had conferred on both army and navy a heroic character. This is evident not only in the balance of applause with scrutiny that Rudyard Kipling's works provide, but also in the uncritical championing of military power in the large body of writing for young boys represented in the writings of authors such as Mayne Reid and G. A. Henty. When Queen Victoria died in 1901, the army and navy, as complete institutions, were enjoying a level of prestige that they had scarcely experienced before.

See also 1870; SKINS, SHORES

REFERENCES

Bourne, J. M. (1986) *Patronage and Society in Nineteenth-Century England*. London: Edward Arnold.

Brantlinger, Patrick (1988) *Rule of Darkness*. Ithaca, NY: Cornell University Press.

Gaskell, Elizabeth (1895) *Cranford*, preface by Anne Thackeray Ritchie, illustrated by Hugh Thomson. London: Macmillan.

Harries-Jenkins, Gwyn (1977) *The Army in Victorian Society*. London: Routledge and Kegan Paul.

Lloyd, Christopher (1947) *Lord Cochrane: Seaman–Radical–Liberator: A Life of Thomas, Lord Cochrane 10th Earl of Dundonald*. London: Longmans, Green.

FURTHER READING

Ballard, Admiral G. A. (1934) "The Navy." In *Early Victorian England 1830–65*, 2 vols, ed. G. M. Young. London: Oxford University Press.

Barnett, Correlli (1970) *Britain and Her Army 1509–1970: A Military, Political and Social Survey*. New York: William Morrow.

Baynham, Henry (1969) *From the Lower Deck: The Royal Navy 1780–1840*. London: Hutchinson.

——(1971) *Before the Mast: Naval Ratings of the Nineteenth Century*. London: Hutchinson.

Fortescue, John (1934) "The Army." In *Early Victorian England 1830–65*, 2 vols, ed. G. M. Young. London: Oxford University Press.

Harries-Jenkins (1977) *The Army in Victorian Society*. Toronto: University of Toronto Press.

Lewis, Michael (1948) *England's Sea Officers: The Story of the Naval Profession*. London: G. Allen and Unwin.

——(1965) *The Navy in Transition 1814–1864: A Social History*. London: Hodder and Stoughton.

Skelley, A. R. (1977) *The Victorian Army at Home: The Recruitment and Terms and Conditions of the British Regular, 1859–1899*. London: Croom Helm.

Spiers, Edward M. (1980) *The Army and Society, 1815–1914*. London: Longman.

Strachan, Hew (1984) *Wellington's Legacy: The Reform of the British Army, 1830–54*. Manchester: Manchester University Press.

——(1985) *From Waterloo to Balaclava: Tactics, Technology, and the British Army, 1815–54*. Cambridge: Cambridge University Press.

14
Educational
Thomas William Heyck

Education in nineteenth-century England and Wales produced a number of very different experiences and career patterns for teachers. (The educational systems of Scotland and Ireland were so different that this chapter will deal with England and Wales only.) These experiences and patterns were profoundly affected by a set of common social and cultural factors: the rapid expansion of demand for education for all levels of society and at all levels of learning; the formation of class divisions in the social structure; the secularization of both thought and institutions; and rigidity in assumptions about gender differences. Schooling at all stages of education, from universities down to elementary schools, expanded during the Victorian period, as England for the first time became a "schooled society." This expansion greatly increased the number of teachers and made them more important to society. Moreover, all levels of Victorian educational institutions became secularized – that is, they shifted from the orbit of the Christian churches to that of secular authorities. At the beginning of the century most teachers were clergymen and almost all were under the supervision of Christian churches or agencies; at the end of the century few were clergy and many worked outside the influence of any denomination. Together, the expansion and secularization of education encouraged teachers in England to take significant steps towards professional autonomy and status; yet the complications of class and gender made for very different aspirations, standards of living, and careers.

Class and gender constituted the main divisions in Victorian society. The sense that Britain in the course of industrialization and urbanization had become divided into three broad layers – the landed, middle, and working classes – and that these classes competed over the distribution of wealth and power, significantly shaped politics, identity, and social relations. The vocabulary of class dominated assumptions about both a person's place in the social structure and the proper function of social institutions. Education did not escape class thinking; thus the Victorians generally assumed that there should be different kinds and levels of schools, with different educational objectives, for each social class. At the same time the conviction that men and women differed not only biologically but also in intellect, psychology, and emotions, sup-ported a belief in the "separate spheres" – the public for men and the private for women. This strong sense of different gender roles contributed powerfully to both the evolution of Victorian educational institutions and the careers of women teachers. For all these reasons, whether in terms of the quantity or of the quality of life, it made all the difference whether a teacher in, say, the 1820s was a woman trying to scratch out a living as mistress of a "dame school," or a man serving as headmaster of an elite public school; or whether a teacher in the 1890s was a male fellow at reformed Oxford or Cambridge, or a female teacher in a state elementary school.

The University Teachers

As Jude Fawley, the idealistic but poor stonemason in Thomas Hardy's novel *Jude the Obscure* (1895), discovers to his own bitter disappointment, university education in early Victorian England was open strictly to upper-class males; consequently, univer-sity teachers themselves were men almost exclusively from landed and professional families. Until the 1830s there were only two universities in England and Wales – the ancient universities of Oxford and Cambridge – and despite the later foundation of additional universities, Oxford and Cambridge remained much the wealthiest and most prestigious. The two old English universities in the first decades of the century were extremely small, with no more than 1,500 students between them. Moreover, they remained what they had been since the Reformation of the sixteenth century, quasi-seminaries of the Church of England. They had essentially religious functions: the training of the clergy of the established Church and the education of the nation's social elite in Christian morality. Given these functions, "Oxbridge" emphasized not research but what was taken in the day to be a liberal education – classics at Oxford and mathematics at Cambridge – because these subjects were thought to give unique mental and moral discipline. Further, the two universities were organized on the collegiate model, which meant that they were federations of relatively autonomous colleges in which the teachers and students lived and worked. Though a small number of chaired professors delivered lectures, the great majority of instruction was done by the college tutors, who taught on the tutorial or "catechetical" method, which they regarded as the best method for moral training.

This situation meant that there were few careers in university teaching in early nineteenth-century England. The tutors were drawn from the ranks of the fellows of the colleges, of whom there were only about 540 at Oxford and 350 at Cambridge. All of the fellows had to be graduates of one of the two universities, but only about 20 percent of the fellows actually taught; the others enjoyed the income of their fellow-ships while they prepared for the bar or studied for ordination. As for the tutors, the only requirements for their posts other than a degree were that they had to take holy orders in the Church of England, usually within seven years of winning their fellow-ships, and that they had to remain unmarried. Underlying these requirements was the assumption that a celibate clerical teaching staff was best for the essentially moral and religious educational objectives of the universities. But these requirements dictated that for the great majority of tutors the main career pattern led *out* of the universities, into parish appointments, rather than *up* within the universities. If a college tutor did not want to become ordained or wished to marry, he would have to leave the university. In Anthony Trollope's novel *Barchester Towers* (1857), for example, the clergyman Mr Arabin becomes a tutor while he waits for a parish living to open up. Those who remained enjoyed lifetime appointments in the often luxurious surroundings of their colleges, where they lived isolated from the world yet with no prospects for promotion inside the university. Inevitably, the lack of careers in education elicited from many tutors uninspired teaching, and this tendency was reinforced by the centrality of the honours exams, which were crucial for all serious students. The tutors had to teach strictly for the exams, which turned them into crammers of routinized information and examination skills.

By mid-century, however, both the universities themselves and the careers of the professors and tutors had been transformed by a powerful reform movement. The campaign to reform the English universities derived from a number of different sources, all drawing on the Victorian belief in progress. One was natural science, which traditionally played only a minor role in Oxford and Cambridge. By mid-century, status-hungry natural scientists were claiming positions in the universities commensurate with science's growing research achievements, not least in evolutionary biology and geology. English natural scientists wanted to improve their own professional standing and cultural authority by dislodging the clergy from their monopoly over the universities' endowments, and to have the universities conform to the scientific ideals of research and specialization. Another force for reform was utilitarianism, which sought to make the ancient universities more useful to the activities and values of the middle class – to business and industry, but also to political and social progress generally. To the utilitarians it seemed inefficient that Anglican clergymen taught secular subjects, in which they were unlikely to be specialists. A third impulse towards university reform came from the English Nonconformists (i.e. non-Anglican Protestants). The Nonconformists felt that they comprised the central corps of England's rapidly growing commercial and industrial class, and they resented their exclusion from the faculty and student body of the universities by the religious tests. These three broad forces resulted in the foundation in 1828 of University College, London, which joined the Anglican King's College, London in 1836 to form the University of London; and from the 1850s they brought about the establishment of provincial universities in England's largest industrial cities.

Meanwhile, the reform movement found support among the dons (faculty members) within Oxford and Cambridge. Some of the internal reformers shared the values and goals of the scientists, utilitarians, and Nonconformists. Others were motivated by evangelicalism and romanticism to reinvigorate the old universities so as to produce a morally and spiritually elevated cultural elite, who in turn might restore the cohesiveness of English society. But the most important element among the internal reformers were the tutors who wanted to establish genuine careers in university teaching. They were responding in part to the increasing seriousness of their students and their parents, who were themselves much influenced by evangelicalism. Such people wanted the tutors to provide better teaching and a more intense work ethic. And many tutors were frustrated by the demand that they teach the same subjects and texts repeatedly, regardless of their own special interests and abilities, in order to cram students for the examinations. They wanted to become masters of their special subjects, to require that a much larger proportion of fellows share the teaching, to open the fellowships to competition, and to erect a career hierarchy *within* the universities for professional teachers. To establish a structure for professional careers, they wanted to abolish the requirements for holy orders and celibacy, and to designate the professorships as the top rungs on their academic career ladder.

As a result, Oxford and Cambridge became much more "professional" institutions in the 1850s and 1860s, and this change profoundly affected the lives of the dons. Royal Commissions on Oxford and Cambridge led to legislation for the two ancient universities in 1854 and 1856; and the tutors themselves adopted higher standards of teaching as well as certain practices that encouraged specialization. Both universities were opened to Nonconformist students by the abolition of the requirement of subscription to the Anglican Thirty-nine Articles; and in 1871 subscription by the fellows was also abolished. New courses of study in natural science, law, modern history, and moral science were adopted. The tutors at both universities began to divide up the broadened curriculum in order to specialize in teaching. Most fellowships were opened to competition by examination, and a much larger number of them were devoted to teaching. The requirement that fellows remain unmarried was gradually abolished by the 1880s, and as a result an increasing number of tutors no longer actually resided in their colleges. The professoriate was established as the top rung on a career ladder to which the tutors might aspire. Many earnest tutors, hopeful of instilling in their students an ethic of Christian morality and public service, sought to "reach" the students through athletics and close friendship. The character of John Hardy, an idealized tutor in Thomas Hughes's novel *Tom Brown at Oxford* (1858), epitomized the new professional don: Hardy not only makes reforms in his college in order to keep undergraduates out of trouble, he also encourages serious reading by students and takes a very active role in collegiate and university rowing. Hardy is a professional teacher, deeply learned in his special subject and a conscientious tutor. Oxford and Cambridge colleges were full of real-life Hardys from the 1850s on; and, as the character of Henry Grey in Mrs Humphrey Ward's *Robert Elsmere* (1888) shows, the ideal don was alive and well three decades after *Tom Brown at Oxford*.

In the last 30 years of the century, however, the academic profession in England began to change again. For one thing, provincial university colleges at Manchester, Birmingham, Leeds, and Liverpool reached autonomous university status, and they added an element to the university system that was devoted not only to research and to "modern" subjects but also to the German-style "professorial" lecturing, as opposed to the tutorial method of teaching. The teaching staff at these "red brick" universities, arranged in a hierarchy of lecturer, reader, and professor, clearly had professional career structures organized around research as well as teaching. Some of the professors, like the chemist Henry Enfield Roscoe of Manchester, established close connections with local industries.

Nevertheless, Oxford and Cambridge remained by far the wealthiest and most prestigious institutions of higher education in England, and their graduates tended to monopolize the highest posts at the red bricks. Within the ancient universities themselves, the tutors continued to define their work as educating the nation's political and social elite, but they found that scholarship and research had become much more important in their careers. One reason for that development was the increasing value assigned by English society in general to professional expertise: professionals were increasingly seen as the "new gentry" of Britain, and professionalism required specialized knowledge. But another reason was that the placing of the professors at the top of the academic career ladder had the unanticipated consequence of valuing "learning" (research) over teaching. In their reform campaign the tutors at Oxbridge had sought to retain control over teaching; hence they had identified the professoriate with learning rather than teaching. Research scholarship thereby gradually became a qualification for a professorship. By the end of the century research had been widely accepted alongside teaching as one of the essential functions of Oxford and Cambridge; thus not only were the professors supposedly distinguished by their contributions to scholarly knowledge, but also the tutors had become harder-working, specialized, and laicized professionals who sought to combine research with teaching.

It was also the case by the end of the century that not all university teachers were men. Women had been excluded from the universities by the Victorian assumptions that women were not suited by temperament or intellect either for the clergy or for public life, and that they were not capable of the sustained, rigorous work required by the university studies. Moreover, through the first half of the century, not even middle- and upper-class women could obtain a strong secondary education, still less the training in Latin and Greek that was the prerequisite for matriculation at either university. And many proper Victorians, men and women alike, felt that advanced education would spoil women's cherished innocence and nurturing instincts. During the course of the century increasing numbers of women, and a few male advocates like John Stuart Mill, argued that women were in fact as intelligent and as capable of higher education as men; but proposals that women be admitted to Oxbridge roused reactions of either shocked indignation or raucous laughter. One clerical opponent of admission of women to Oxford declared in a sermon in 1884: "Inferior to us [men] God made you [women], and inferior to the end of time you will remain" (Brittain 1960: 69). The persistent and touchy defensiveness of the Victorian establishment to the prospect of women's university education found early expression in Tennyson's *The Princess* (1847), a work whose ideological evasiveness earned it a second lease of life as light operetta in Gilbert and Sullivan's *Princess Ida* (1884).

Despite such opposition heavy and light, women reformers and their male allies worked persistently in the 1850s and 1860s for coeducation at Oxbridge. Their efforts formed one aspect of a broad-ranging feminist movement that sought to open public life and the professions to women, and to end what Mill in 1869 called "the subjection of women" to males. Emily Davies, for instance, having failed to get the University of London opened to women, sought to establish a college for women in Cambridge. Similar efforts were made at Oxford. By the end of the 1870s two women's colleges had been founded at Cambridge (Girton and Newnham) and two at Oxford (Sommerville and Lady Margaret Hall). The universities would not allow the young women of these colleges to take their degrees until the twentieth century, but step by step in the late-Victorian decades women won the right to take the regular university examinations, to attend lectures offered by the tutors and professors of the men's colleges, and in general to enjoy official recognition of their presence. At the same time, the women's colleges, which from the outset had female heads, began to appoint women as their own teaching staff. By 1900 the four colleges employed more than 50 women tutors and lecturers, whose career aspirations copied those of their male counterparts in combining research scholarship and teaching. They worked in close, high-minded association with their students, for the women's colleges emphasized both ladylike decorum and a family atmosphere as well as high intellectual ideals. Meanwhile, the provincial universities and university colleges abandoned their barriers to women students, and by the 1890s most had small but growing numbers of women lecturers, mainly in French, music, and English literature. These pioneer women teachers produced increasing numbers of women graduates, many of whom would go on to staff secondary schools for women, and thus generate more women applicants to the universities.

The Public School Teachers

Until fairly late in the century secondary education in Victorian England was available only in the old endowed grammar schools and the even more prestigious "public" schools. The public schools had been founded in the sixteenth century to train young men for the Church and public service, and by the nineteenth century were not "public" in any real sense at all, save that they were not owned by any one individual and not conducted mainly for private profit. Most public schools were actually private, boarding schools offering training in the classics to sons of the well-to-do, and all had close ties to the Church of England. At the beginning of the century there were only nine of these institutions in England (Eton, Harrow, Rugby, Winchester, Westminster, Shrewsbury, Merchant Taylors', St Paul's, and Charterhouse), but the number grew, especially after 1850, as the public school system expanded to meet the demand generated by the expanding middle class. The public schools supplied most of the students to Oxbridge; but the social prestige of the public schools was enormous in its own right. In a time when a university degree was not always the necessary qualification for ruling-class employment, the schools gave a boy the deportment, accent, habit of authority, and connections ("the old school tie") that opened to him a myriad of positions in Church and State. To send a son to a public school marked social and financial "arrival" for middle-class families. The Victorian public schools transmitted aristocratic attitudes and ideals to middle-class boys; thus, though they reflected anti-utilitarian and anti-industrial values, the public schools were among the most important of all English social institutions.

However, the public schools at the beginning of the nineteenth century had fallen into disorder, disrepute, and financial trouble. Although the headmasters and staff were Anglican clergymen, their treatment of the boys combined permissiveness and brutality. The teachers were poorly paid and of a lower social status than many of their students, who held their teachers in sovereign contempt. The teaching staff were remote from the students and allowed them outside of class to behave as they pleased. In class, on the other hand, the headmasters and assistant masters enforced discipline and diligent memorization of the lessons by constant flogging with birch and ash rods. Hostility between teachers and students was the typical result, and outright student rebellions, which sometimes had to be put down by armed force, were not uncommon. At the same time, uncontrolled bullying of the younger boys by the older was universal, as was the practice of "fagging," whereby senior boys demanded personal services from the juniors. Enrollments fell in all the schools; Charterhouse, for example, had 489 students in 1825 but only 137 in 1832.

Conditions in the public schools began to improve in the latter 1820s, when they entered a period of reform and expansion that was to last several decades. The leading reformer was Thomas Arnold, who became headmaster of Rugby in 1828 and transformed it into an immensely influential model school. He was celebrated in the most famous public-school novel, Thomas Hughes's *Tom Brown's Schooldays* (1857). But Arnold did not bring about the alteration of the public schools single-handedly, for there were other reforming schoolmasters; and all were responding to criticism from a growing number of politicians as well as to the impulses of evangelical religion and the demands of the middle class. Arnold was typical in that he saw the public schools as essentially religious. To him, life was a struggle between good and evil, and in school, outside of the control of their families, boys needed firm guidance to avoid evil. Arnold wrote: "It is *not* necessary that this school be a school of 300 or 100 or fifty boys; but it *is* necessary that it be a school of Christian gentlemen" (Gathorne-Hardy 1977: 72). Thus, he set out not only to improve the teaching at Rugby but also to shape the character of the boys. As he said many times, "What we must look for here is, 1st, religious and moral principles; 2ndly, gentlemanly conduct; 3rdly, intellectual ability" (Stanley 1846: 95). To these ends, Arnold raised the status and pay of his assistant masters, moved the boys from independent "dames' houses" in the town to houses in the school headed by carefully recruited housemasters, enlisted the senior boys (the sixth form) as prefects to enforce discipline, and took over teaching the sixth form himself, as well as the office of chaplain and chief preacher. Arnold retained corporal punishment and did little to change the Rugby curriculum, but his kind of reforms spread among the other public schools (18 Rugby boys went on to serve as headmasters of public schools). Victorian public schools became morally serious, intensely religious institutions that consciously engaged in "character-building," preparing an expanding ruling class for their duties as governors of the nation and empire.

The reformed public schools proved to be immensely attractive to the richer elements in the middle class who wished to have elite status. Enrollments in all the schools recovered by about mid-century, and from the 1850s new public schools were founded and old grammar schools were converted into full-fledged public schools. Although it is not easy to distinguish the public schools from all the other 500 or so private schools that sprang up to educate middle-class British boys in the nineteenth century, a good estimate is that in the 1890s there were between 64 and 104 public schools in Britain as a whole, with many more claiming that exalted status. The public schools served only a tiny proportion of the age group (they had only about 7,500 students in 1865 and 20,000 in 1890), but their graduates dominated admission to Oxbridge, ordination to the clergy, entry into the professions, officerships in the army, posts in politics, and appointments in the imperial and domestic civil services. As one Victorian expert on the public schools declared, "The great Endowed Schools are less to be considered as educational agencies, in the intellectual sense, than as social agencies" (Staunton 1865: xxix–xxi).

In the late-Victorian period the public schools changed somewhat from the Arnoldian pattern, becoming in the process more in-turned, regimented, and above all devoted to athletics. Headmasters of Arnold's generation did not emphasize sports and games; to them, as to Arnold, the cherished "manliness" of character meant Christian religiosity, independence, and a mature sense of personal responsibility. But in the second half of the century "manliness" came to connote loyalty, physical courage, endurance, and discipline, as well as Christian morality. The schools became institutions inculcating "muscular Christianity," the cult of athleticism, and patriotism, which together encouraged a distinct anti-intellectualism. Clearly, there was a strong resonance between the imperialism and militarism of the late nineteenth century and the cultivation of sports in public schools. It was in the late-Victorian period that the saying "Waterloo was won on the playing fields of Eton" was concocted and attributed to the Duke of Wellington. But compulsory sports, like the simultaneous regimentation of the students' lives, were also responses to problems that were internal to the public schools – namely, the perpetual problem of disciplining the students and the perceived need to distract them from the sexual impulses of adolescence. A boy who had been trained to severe self-discipline and tired out by daily sports was thought less likely to engage either in rebellious behavior or in the sexual activities inherent in an all-male environment.

The careers of the headmasters and their assistant masters reflected the centrality of the public schools to upper-class Victorian life. Headmasters from the time of Arnold through the end of the century enjoyed not only dictatorial power over their schools but also the prestige and pay of eminent professional men. Because of the religious function of the schools, the headmasters all were clergymen (the overwhelming majority of them Anglican priests, though a few Catholic and Nonconformist schools were established), the first lay headmaster of Rugby winning appointment only in

1903. Most were of relatively high status before becoming headmasters, being off-spring of professional families and graduates of either Oxford or Cambridge. Their pay put them well up in the ranks of well-to-do professional men: in the 1860s the headmaster of Rugby made £3,000 a year, those of Eton and Harrow even more. Since their work was regarded as essentially religious, successful headmasters could expect to be promoted into important posts in the Church of England. A common career pattern would begin with a boy going to a public school, then to Oxford or Cambridge; after taking his BA he would have a college fellowship, followed by a period of teaching at a public school, a headmastership, and then a cathedral deanship or a bishopric. Six of the eight Archbishops of Canterbury appointed between 1860 and 1960 had been public school headmasters. But the headmasters carried heavy loads: they stood *in loco parentis* to the boys; they were expected to be both good teachers and inspirational preachers; and they had to worry about keeping the numbers of students at their schools up and, as Oxford and Cambridge increasingly valued merit by examination, about the success of their boys in university academic competition.

One of Thomas Arnold's most important reforms was to raise the status and quality of his assistant masters. So widespread were the effects of this reform that appointment as an assistant master in a public school became a very desirable position for a young graduate of one of the ancient universities. Indeed, fellows of Oxbridge colleges wishing to get married often went into schoolteaching. Moreover, since the assistant masters for the first two-thirds of the century were almost always ordained, they found that college fellowships, parish livings, and assistant masterships were largely inter-changeable. There was much traffic of clergymen among the three types of post. The pay of assistant masters put them solidly among the middle class, though young teachers often had to delay marriage until they had been promoted. In the 1870s, for instance, when the standard salary for a college fellow was £200, the average salary of assistant masters at the bigger public schools was £250, clearly a middle-class income but not enough for a gentleman to support a home, family, and the requisite three or four domestic servants. A few – most of them classics teachers – made much more: the average pay and perquisites of Rugby's 13 classics assistant masters in 1861 was £966, which placed them among the Victorian upper middle class. In some cases, in order to retain excellent teachers, the headmasters appointed them as housemasters, because housemasters enjoyed the board-and-room payments of their students and thus could make as much as £1,500 a year (Honey 1977: ch. 5; Gathorne-Hardy 1977: 106–9).

During the course of the century public schoolmastering took the first halting steps towards becoming a profession in itself. After the reforms of the Arnoldian period, most assistant masters took their teaching seriously, and their promotion in terms of salary and posts depended largely upon merit. They did not, however, take much interest in teacher training, because both they and their headmasters believed that the main requirement of a public school teacher was simply to be a gentleman. In the late-Victorian period, headmasters increasingly valued athletic prowess and coaching ability among their assistant masters. Teaching in a public school became a profession in the senses that the schoolmasters eventually separated from holy orders and thought of their careers as confined to the schools themselves. The Victorian public school teachers gradually became laicized: as late as 1870, for instance, a majority of teachers at ten leading public schools were ordained, but in 1889 only 28.7 percent were, and in 1906 only 13.3 percent. Yet the lay schoolmasters, whose career hopes now focused on promotion to a headmastership and not to ecclesiastical preferment, faced a problem in the fact that, until the end of the century, the headmasterships all required ordination. The teachers' resentment was one of the early signs of the same kind of emerging professional consciousness seen in the universities; other indicators in the late-Victorian period included a desire among assistant masters to have pension funds for their retirement years and security of tenure against the traditional power of the headmasters. But the prevailing tradition of the "gentleman amateur" and the culture of passionate loyalty to one's own school prevented the assistant masters from going very far along the road to professionalization during the nineteenth century.

After mid-century, public schools for girls began to be built, and these institutions provided a growing number of secondary teaching posts for women. The public schools for girls were the result of dissatisfaction in middle-class families with the educational opportunities for their daughters. At the beginning of the century families of gentle status (aristocracy, gentry, and middle class) educated their daughters either by hiring governesses or by sending them to private schools operated by gentlewomen who were down on their luck and in need of income. Neither type of schooling provided adequate education for the girls or decent careers for the female teachers. To be a governess was among the least happy walks of life for a Victorian lady, and a woman of good family – say, the daughter of a poor clergyman – would resort to it only because she needed income and had few other choices for "respectable" work. The pay was very poor – in the first half of the century less than £50 a year plus board and room. Nevertheless, by the 1850s there were more than 21,000 governesses in Britain. Governesses rarely had much education themselves and even less frequently any training in teaching. For the most part, governesses taught the "accomplishments" – subjects regarded as useful to middle- and upper-class girls, such as music, French, drawing, and needlework – but often they had to teach subjects – geography, arithmetic, history – about which they knew little themselves. Moreover, families hired them because of their gentle status but then often treated them with contempt. Charlotte Brontë, who worked for a time as a governess, wrote in 1839: "I can now see more clearly than I have ever done before that a private governess has no existence, is not considered as a living and rational being, except as connected with the wearisome duties she has to fulfill" (Renton 1991: 74–5). She was to depict the position of governess in even more depressing terms in *Jane Eyre* (1847). Mistresses of private schools for girls fared little better. They, too, banked on their status as ladies to attract students, usually no more than ten or twenty in number, to their little boarding schools. Schoolmistresses rarely made more than £300 a year, from which the expenses of the school had to be paid. Moreover, because they taught ladies' accomplishments rather than academic subjects to girls whose sole goal in life was marriage to a gentleman, schoolmistresses could never develop any consciousness as professional teachers, as opposed to exemplars of ladylike behavior.

By mid-century, however, the desire among feminists and some middle-class families for better education for young women began to produce better secondary schools for girls. The prestige of the boys' public schools insured that the new schools for girls would be private boarding schools. The most influential were Cheltenham Ladies' College, founded in 1854 and led from 1858 by Dorothea Beale, and Roedean, founded in the 1880s by the Lawrence sisters, Dorothy, Penelope, and Millicent. By the 1890s there were more than 200 private schools for girls, of which more than 20 were regarded as full-fledged public schools. The majority of all these schools adopted the same emphasis on religion, moral training, and sports as the boys' schools.

The public schools for girls created professional teaching careers for women in their posts of headmistresses and assistant mistresses. In their quest for professional standing, these women had to distinguish themselves from both the ladylike private schoolmistresses and the working-class women who taught in the nation's elementary schools. One headmistress wrote: "Parents will have to realise that the teacher is an expert professional and is entitled therefore to the deference shown to the skilled professional opinion of the doctor, lawyer, or architect" (Pedersen 1991: 46). But it was difficult at first for women to obtain the requisite professional education. Some received advanced education at Queen's College and Bedford College (London), which had been established in the 1840s to give better training to governesses but which developed into university-level institutions. As London and the provincial universities gradually opened themselves to women, aspiring public schoolmistresses in the late-Victorian period could earn degrees from them. Increasingly, however, education in one of the women's colleges at Oxford and Cambridge became the prerequisite for a post at one of the public schools for girls. By the same token, the relatively high status of these positions and the idealism of the schools attracted more than half of all the women who had studied at Oxford and Cambridge. The subjects they taught were confined neither to the accomplishments of the lady schoolmistresses nor the classics of male public schoolteachers. English and foreign literatures predominated, but women teachers also offered mathematics and sciences. Since the career opportunities for public schoolmistresses were so limited, the schools had little turnover and both excellent and poor teachers could be frozen in place for decades. Nevertheless, by the last 20 years of the century public headmistresses were not only preparing their students for roles in the public sphere, but also themselves achieving distinction as experts in scholarship, local government, and civic affairs.

The Elementary School Teachers

The so-called "elementary" schools of Victorian England were for the working class. However, for the first three-quarters of the century many members of the working class had no access to schooling at all, for there was no state school system until 1870. The prevailing assumption held that the state ought to interfere as little as possible in the workings of the economy and society. Education was a matter for religion: as one Bishop of London put it, "The church is the authorised and recognised organ and instrument of national education" (Midwinter 1970: 37). Further, working-class boys and girls were supposed to go to work before they were ten years old and to work full-time after they were eleven. For those that had the time and money, early- and mid-Victorian England had only a patchwork quilt of different types of private or "voluntary" schools. For example, there were thousands of Sunday schools, first established by the various Christian denominations in the latter part of the eighteenth century. The Sunday schools became an important social institution in urban working-class communities, but they could not offer any education beyond the most basic. Their teaching staff were volunteers, devoted to teaching the rudiments of reading and religion. There were some small "charity" schools for the poor that had been set up in the eighteenth century by philanthropists for religious purposes. A few model schools like the utilitarian knowledge factory run by Mr M'Choakumchild in Dickens's *Hard Times* (1854) were established by Victorian middle-class progressives to advance what they called "the march of mind." Other private schools, usually very cheap (charging as little as nine pence a week, or a little more than £1 a year), were set up by men or women, often unsuccessful tradesmen or shopkeepers, who were simply trying to make a living. Pip attends one of these in Dickens's *Great Expectations* (1861). These schoolmasters and schoolmistresses were usually unqualified, and most of the schools were very small and disappeared when the founder–teacher failed, moved on, or died.

But the most important types of school before 1870 were established by two religious foundations – the (Anglican) National Society and the (Nonconformist) British and Foreign School Society. Even they fell far short of reaching the entire working-class population. The National Society and the British and Foreign School Society became semi-official in the 1830s, when they received recognition by the state in the form of an annual grant for the construction of additional schools. However, the continuing inadequacy of the school "system" as a whole is shown by the illiteracy rate: by a conservative estimate, one-third of all men and half of all women in England and Wales in the 1850s were illiterate by even minimum standards. Perhaps a quarter of all parishes in England and Wales had no school at all. Some middle- and upper-class Victorians regarded this situation as dangerous to religion and public order; but more conservative people felt that education of the working class would itself be politically dangerous and destructive of the deference properly demanded from working people.

Teaching as a walk of life in the elementary schools was profoundly shaped by these conditions. The managers of both the charity schools and those run by the two denominational societies took cheapness as their key consideration. An adult teacher might make as much as £60 a year, which was only the equivalent of the wages of a semi-skilled worker but enough to discourage a philanthropic organization from hiring more than one per school. In order to serve more students both of the denominational societies adopted the "monitorial" system that had been invented in the last years of the eighteenth century, whereby a single adult teacher, training older children as monitors to teach the younger, might supervise the teaching of up to 500 students. Since the monitors, rarely more than 12 or 13 years old and barely educated themselves, received only a few weeks' training as teachers, the monitorial system provided instruction by rote memorization at best. Their skill level allowed them only to drill their students in the most basic three Rs according to rigidly planned lessons. Teachers in the monitorial system assumed that the students were passive recipients of information as well as stained by original sin and inclined to wicked behavior. Teaching therefore had to be a process of forcing students to memorize factual information while applying corporal punishment for discipline. The teachers themselves were regarded by the middle and landed classes as nothing more than tradesmen; indeed, the upper classes thought it important to recruit adult elementary teachers from the working and lower-middle classes so that the teachers would not rise socially "above" their pupils. The teachers were not treated as professionals and thus were of distinctly lower status than the public schoolmasters and schoolmistresses. Obviously, the monitorial system bore an analogy to the factory system in industry; and the monitorial system combined with the mechanical mode of teaching – memorably depicted in Dickens's *Hard Times* – to keep the role and status of the teacher comparable to that of a factory worker.

In an effort to improve elementary education, James Kay-Shuttleworth, secretary to the Education Committee of the Privy Council, inaugurated the "pupil–teacher" system in 1846. Kay-Shuttleworth meant to work major changes in the training and provision of teachers, but his pupil–teacher plan can be seen as an outgrowth of the monitorial system. By it, boys and girls between 13 and 18 years of age could be given apprenticeships in teaching. For a small salary these pupil–teachers both taught classes and received training in teaching each week. After completing an apprenticeship a pupil–teacher could apply for a scholarship to one of the teacher-training colleges (which were in fact secondary schools) that had been established in the 1830s and 1840s. Whether attending a teacher-training college or not, a pupil–teacher could obtain certification of teaching competence after government examination. Finally, Kay-Shuttleworth's scheme provided small augmentations to the teacher's salary for mentoring pupil–teachers. By 1861 there were 14,000 pupil–teachers and 35 teacher-training colleges – 17 for men, 14 for women, and four co-educational.

The pupil–teacher system of 1846 had a significant positive effect on the elementary school teachers' competence and status. It gave them higher incomes, a system for certification of skills, and a quasi-civil service standing. A Royal Commission in 1861 found that the average pay for certified schoolmasters was £94 3s 7d, which was the equivalent of the pay of a skilled artisan, and some schoolmasters were also given housing. Certified women teachers earned less for the same work: in 1861 certified women teachers made an average of £62 4s 10d, which was about the same as an *uncertified* male teacher (Newcastle Commission 1861: 63–7). Most teachers still worked alone in their schools, save for their pupil–teacher apprentices; but many had good relations with the local Anglican clergyman, who often was the chief figure in the local school council.

Kay-Shuttleworth had never intended to make professionals of the elementary teachers: "We hoped to inspire them with a large sympathy for their own class. To implant in their minds the thought that their chief honour would be to aid in rescuing that class from the misery of ignorance and its attendant vices" (Tropp 1957: 14). Nevertheless, many teachers, who by the 1850s felt that they stood in an anomalous position – above the workers by their own estimation but not regarded as equals by middle-class and professional people – believed that their social rank ought to be higher than merely working class. *The School and the Teacher*, a schoolteachers' journal, declared in 1855: "It is no strange thing that men who in education, tastes and habits, have all the qualifications of 'gentlemen', should regard themselves as worthy of something very much higher than the treatment of a servant, and the wages of a mechanic. . . . What in short the teacher desires is, that his 'calling' shall rank as a 'profession'" (Tropp 1957: 26). Of particular annoyance to the teachers was the government's policy of excluding them from serving as Her Majesty's Inspectors of the schools; these well-paid posts were reserved strictly for university graduates (the most famous being Matthew Arnold), none of whom had any training or experience as elementary school teachers.

The higher pay, improved training, and consequent status restlessness of the elementary teachers eventually generated a reaction among influential middle- and upper-class people who felt that elementary teachers were seeking to rise above their proper station. One school manager in Wales accused teachers of extravagance "in their houses, mahogany furniture, sofas, etc., when painted deal would do" (ibid.: 20). Another critic of the teachers, an Anglican clergyman, said that the claims of the teachers were pretentious, and that until the teachers "are taken from the same rank of society and have undergone the intellectual training and the social discipline which is absolutely necessary to the doctor, the lawyer and the clergyman . . . I must confess myself to be one of those . . . who cannot accede to the national schoolmaster a rank on the level with the learned professions" (ibid.: 37). The Newcastle Commission, which reported in 1861, heard much testimony along these lines and concluded that a large portion of students were not well taught, in part because the best-trained teachers found it hard to do the drudgery of teaching. Hence, the Commissioners recommended ending the pupil–teacher system of 1846 in favor of "payment by results" – paying teachers according to the results earned by their students in national examinations. Robert Lowe, the Palmerston administration's chief educational official, issued in 1862 a Revised Code establishing a new set of rules for elementary schooling based largely on the findings of the Newcastle Commission and his own commitment to the doctrines of Political Economy. Payment by results became the main educational principle of the day: teachers would be paid according to attendance records and the performance of the students on examinations administered by the Inspectors. Pay for pupil–teachers and their mentors was abolished.

The elementary school teachers found the revised code disastrous to education and a blow to their own professional aspirations. The number of pupil–teachers and applicants to the training colleges declined rapidly. At the same time as university tutors were developing careers as professional teachers and research scholars, elementary teachers had to teach strictly to the exams, and thus to drill their students incessantly to give memorized answers to the texts and problems that they would face. The exams themselves became artificial performances by students for the Inspectors, with anxious teachers standing by nervously. Matthew Arnold, perhaps the most thoughtful of all the Inspectors, regretted that the Revised Code made it impossible for the Inspectors to explore "the intellectual life of the school" as a whole, for the Inspectors had no time for anything except examining each student. Moreover, he stated in 1867, "The work of teaching in school is less interesting and more purely mechanical than it used to be." Under the 1846 system, he wrote, the teacher had felt he was "a fellow-worker with the national government"; but now "he is told that he has greatly overrated his importance and that of his function" (Arnold 1889: 112–14).

Not surprisingly, the teachers suffered a blow to their morale and to their fledgling attempts to form professional associations. These efforts had begun as early as the 1830s but had yielded national associations (one for Anglican and one for Nonconformist elementary teachers) only in the 1850s. In the latter 1860s the teachers' morale began to recover, and their associations began to apply political pressure on Parliament to raise teachers' status. Their renewed efforts were made more urgent by passage of the Reform Act of 1867, which extended the vote to most urban working-class males. As Robert Lowe himself told Parliament, "I believe it will be absolutely necessary that you should prevail upon our future masters to learn their letters" (*Hansard* 1867: 1549). Elementary education for the working class seemed more important than ever before, not least to the teachers. In 1870 teachers of all denominations, after many years of dispute over religious issues, reached agreement endorsing religious education (Bible study for all in national schools, plus a "conscience clause" that would excuse those whose families objected). They formed the National Union of Elementary Teachers, which set out to elevate the status of the teachers by securing appointment of teachers to the Inspectorate, tenure against clergy interference, adequate salaries, retirement pensions, exclusion of unqualified people from teaching, and control over the examinations admitting teachers to the profession. In the last 30 years of the century they made significant progress on all of these items, except for the professional monopoly implied by the last two.

Meanwhile, the Gladstone government passed the vitally important Education Act of 1870, which established the first state school system in Britain. The Act was extremely controversial because it incorporated all the voluntary denominational schools into the system and thus established new, nondenominational schools and school boards only in localities where the denominational schools were inadequate or nonexistent. As late as 1900 a majority of elementary schools in England and Wales remained denominational. Moreover, payment by results continued to prevail until 1895 and thus to dominate teaching. And schoolteachers, especially in the villages, often had to do extra duties as required by the local clergyman, such as playing the organ and training the church choir, even though the NUET won agreement to the principle of letters of appointment that specified the teacher's duties. But whatever

the controversial aspects of the 1870 Act, it radically expanded the school system —
and the number of teachers. In 1870 there were 12,467 certified teachers (about evenly
divided between men and women); in 1895 there were 52,941 teachers (two-thirds
women), relatively few of whom had been trained in teacher-training colleges. The
number of pupil–teachers also grew, from more than 14,000 in 1870 to more than
29,000 in 1895 (almost 80 percent of whom were women). But the teachers had not
won the right to exclude uncertified and poorly paid teachers, and by 1895 there had
been a twenty-four-fold increase of uncertified teachers (Tropp 1957: 114).

By the end of the century the elementary school teaching force in England and
Wales was composed of a relatively small core of trained and certified teachers working
amidst a very large number of untrained and uncertified teachers and pupil–teachers.
To be sure, teachers' pay had improved: in 1895 the average salary of certified male
teachers stood at £123 a year and that of a female certified teacher £80. But these
wages were still little better than those of a skilled artisan or barely educated clerk.
Most teachers continued to be recruited from the working class. They still felt socially
anomalous, isolated from the working class by their superior education but not
accepted as equals by the clergy or other professionals. Moreover, their relative social
mobility concerned many middle-class people, who resented the teachers' claims to
middle-class or professional standing. The teachers' unsettled position in society was
reflected in their thinking about their national association (renamed the National
Union of Teachers in 1883). Was it a trade union or a professional association? Like a
union, the NUT did try to influence Parliament and the government; but otherwise it
did not behave like a union. Instead, it devoted itself to improving the status of the
teachers, on grounds that raising their social position would improve education and
therefore English society generally. But if the teachers were as yet socially neither fish
nor fowl, contemporary social observers like C. F. G. Masterman forecast a promising
future for them in a society that increasingly demanded an educated population.
Masterman wrote in his famous *The Condition of England* (1909) of "the new type of
teacher":

> [The teachers] are not only doing their work efficiently, but are everywhere taking the
> lead in public and *quasi*-public activities. They appear as the mainstay of the political
> machine in suburban districts, serving upon the municipal bodies, in work, clear-headed
> and efficient; the leaders in the churches and chapels, and their various social organiza-
> tions. They are taking up the position in the urban districts which for many generations
> was occupied by the country clergy. (Ibid.: 67)

At the end of the nineteenth century, to conclude, teaching in England remained
divided into three very different walks of life. The university dons and the public
school teachers retained their traditional elite connections and relatively high social
status as educators of the ruling class. To be sure, there were distinct differences in
quality of life between the Oxbridge dons and the teachers at the provincial universities, for the professors and fellows at Oxford and Cambridge enjoyed an elegance in

their surroundings, as well as contact with the top levels of society, that were unavailable to most red brick teachers. But all university faculty members were well along the way to careers as specialized and professional teacher–scholars, and the professors clearly held prestigious positions as "scientific" research scholars. Women in increasing numbers were winning their way into university teaching, though not even in the twentieth century have they achieved anything like equal numbers to men. Like the university teachers, public school teachers (except for the headmasters) had become laicized by 1900, and they thought of their careers as moving within the circle of public schools themselves. The rapid increase in the number of public schools gave them a much expanded range of opportunities. But instead of moving towards professional training as teachers or research scholarship, public school teachers had been caught up in the cult of the amateur who must reach his students through patriotism, school loyalty, and organized sports.

   The number of elementary school teachers had increased rapidly after passage of the Education Act of 1870, and by 1900 these teachers showed clear signs of consciousness of themselves as professional teachers. Women constituted the fastest-growing group among the elementary school teachers, even though the social assumptions of the day allowed them to be paid less than men. Overall, the importance of the teachers to English society had risen as the English political public realized that education of the working class had become essential for the nation's political and economic strength. By 1900 the state had taken responsibility from the churches for elementary education, and there was a growing sense that secondary education for the masses would also have to be provided. The teachers in 1900, as in the 15 years after 1846, worked as quasi-civil servants. Yet the teachers' pay had not risen much faster than the overall cost of living. Moreover, they were still recruited largely from the working class and, despite their generally improved training, they still found that middle- and upper-class people did not accord them the status as professionals that they claimed. In the early twentieth century schoolteaching would provide a way out of traditional working-class occupations for young people like D. H. Lawrence, but teachers had a long way to go before acquiring professional, or even middle-class, standing.

See also 1870; GROWING UP, MOVING OUT; CLERICAL, MEDICAL; LITERARY CRITICISM; SKINS

REFERENCES

Arnold, Matthew (1889) *Reports on Elementary Schools, 1852–1882*. London: Macmillan and Sons.

Brittain, Vera (1960) *The Women at Oxford*. London: George G. Harrap.

Gathorne-Hardy, Jonathan (1977) *The Old School Tie: The Phenomenon of the English Public School*. New York: Viking Press.

Hansard's Parliamentary Debates (1867) Third series, vol. CLXXXVIII. London: Cornelius Buck for Hansard's Parliamentary Debates.

Honey, J. R. de S. (1977) *Tom Brown's Universe: The Development of the Victorian Public School*. London: Millington.

Masterman, C. F. G. (1960) [1909] *The Condition of England*. London: Methuen.

Midwinter, Eric (1970) *Nineteenth Century Education*. London: Longman.

Newcastle Commission (1861) Report of the Commissioners appointed to inquire into the state of Popular Education in England. *British Parliamentary Papers* (1861), XXI, Part I. London: HMSO.

Pedersen, Joyce Senders (1991) "Schoolmistresses and Headmistresses: Elites and Education in Nineteenth-century England." In Alison Prentice and Marjorie R. Theobald (eds) *Women Who Taught*. Toronto: University of Toronto Press.

Renton, Alice (1991) *Tyrant or Victim? A History of the British Governess*. London: Weidenfeld & Nicolson.

Stanley, A. P. (1846) *The Life and Correspondence of Thomas Arnold*, 6th edn. London: B. Fellowes.

Staunton, Howard (1865) *The Great Schools of England*. London: S. Low, Son, and Marston.

Tropp, Asher (1957) *The School Teachers: The Growth of the Teaching Profession in England and Wales to the Present Day*. London: Heinemann.

FURTHER READING

Armytage. W. H. G. (1955) *Civic Universities: Aspects of a British Tradition*. London: Benn.

Bamford, T. W. (1960) *Thomas Arnold*. London: Cresset Press.

——— (1967) *The Rise of the Public Schools*. London: Nelson.

Bill, E. G. W. (1973) *University Reform in Nineteenth-Century Oxford: A Study of Henry Halford Vaughan*. Oxford: Clarendon Press.

Engel, Arthur (1983) *From Clergyman to Don: The Rise of the Academic Profession in Nineteenth-Century Oxford*. New York: Oxford University Press.

Fletcher, Laadan (1978) *The Teachers' Press in Britain, 1802–1880*. Leeds: University of Leeds Press.

Garland, Martha M. (1981) *Cambridge Before Darwin*. Cambridge: Cambridge University Press.

Heyck, Thomas William (1982) *The Transformation of Intellectual Life in Victorian England*. London. Croom Helm.

McWilliams-Tullberg, Rita (1977) "Women and Degrees at Cambridge University, 1862–1897." In Martha Vicinus (ed.) *A Widening Sphere: Changing Roles of Victorian Women*. Bloomington: Indiana University Press.

Mangan, J. A. (1981) *Athleticism in the Victorian and Edwardian Public School*. Cambridge: Cambridge University Press.

Newsome, David (1961) *Godliness and Good Learning*. London: John Murray.

Rich, R. W. (1933) *The Training of Teachers in England and Wales during the Nineteenth Century*. Cambridge: Cambridge University Press.

Rothblatt, Sheldon (1968) *The Revolution of the Dons: Cambridge and Society in Victorian England*. London: Faber.

Simon, Brian and Bradley, Ian (eds) (1975) *The Victorian Public School*. Dublin: Gill and Macmillan.

Smelser, Neil J. (1991) *Social Paralysis and Social Change: British Working-Class Education in the Nineteenth Century*. Berkeley: University of California Press.

Sparrow, John (1967) *Mark Pattison and the Idea of a University*. Cambridge: Cambridge University Press.

Wardle, David (1976) *English Popular Education, 1780–1975*. Cambridge: Cambridge University Press.

15
Administrative
Robert Newsom

Hard though it may be to believe, "Administration" was positively an exciting topic for many Victorians. This was not because they were so very easily excited, nor because, being "Victorians," they denied themselves excitements in many other areas opened up to pleasure in the twentieth century. It was because, rather, thinking about administration was relatively a new thing and a thing that therefore held out tantalizing hopes. It was felt to be a marvelous new technology, an essential part of the great tale called "Progress." The thought of what might be done with a new department could make a Victorian's heart race as surely as the thought of what might be done with a really powerful new personal computer does yours or mine. The Victorians had not accumulated sufficient experience of really large bureaucracies, that is to say, to confront the possibilities that some administrative problems might be simply insoluble or that in time administration itself might prove monstrous.

Not that administration *per se* was new, of course. The word was already available in English by the end of the fourteenth century, and there had been plenty of things to administer long before that. The ancient Romans were necessarily sophisticated administrators in order to manage their enormous empire, and the Roman Catholic Church naturally copied many of its features. But much useful administrative lore was lost in the Middle Ages as the need for administration declined with the diminishing reach of imperial and kingly powers. What was relatively new, towards the end of the eighteenth century, was the idea that administration was something that could and should be theorized and professionalized, that it was more than a matter of merely following old practices or common sense, and that it could itself become the subject of a science.

Partly that new idea came about through necessity. As had been true for the Romans, the pressure to build large administrative structures was inevitably felt with the growth of empire, especially the growth of empire throughout the distant vastness of India. And partly, too, the new idea came about under the pressure of the Enlightenment enthusiasm for subjecting all human activity to reason and regulation. But there was an equally important third ingredient as well – the fact that such administration as there was tended to be inefficient and corrupt, bound by ancient practices, class prejudice, and patronage. Thus, administration among the Victorians tended almost automatically to be identified with administrative reform and the larger tide that has led some historians to characterize the period generally as the Age of Reform.

But before thinking too grandly about our subject, we need to overcome some obstacles to understanding just what Victorian "administration" was like, for the word is liable to conjure up images on some far larger scale than the reality merits. It is difficult for us not to associate administration with bureaucracy and the technologies of power – impersonal and forbidding offices, endless rows of desks, every official a perfect robot. In fact, the world of Victorian administration, even on the national scale, was by our standards tiny. Instead of imagining the Pentagon or the array of buildings surrounding the Washington Mall when trying to conceive of something as grand as the Colonial Office, for example, one needs to think about something on the order of the local English Department. In the very middle of the century the entire permanent staff of the Colonial Office numbered about 30. The whole of English centralized government would have fit quite comfortably within a university today.

Perhaps even more surprising to modern imaginations would have been the complete lack of a division of labor between what we think of as administrative functions and the most menial clerical tasks. A typical department consisted of a secretary (a cabinet minister), perhaps an under-secretary or two (usually MPs) and then its real body, the "permanent staff," which consisted of the clerks. Much of their daily business was simply the copying by hand of correspondence and documents, though their senior members might be entrusted too with interpreting and recommending policy through the drafting of correspondence, complex memoranda, and other instruments that could have far-reaching consequences. This was a world not only without a trace of modern office technology, that is to say, but also virtually without what today we think of as staff: no secretaries or clerks in the modern senses, no receptionists, no managers – just the men who made up the ranks of the various grades of clerk, from the beginners in their teens or twenties through the senior clerks, who might be in their fifties, sixties, or even seventies, and a small number of servants to look after their comforts and empty the chamber pots.

It is important to note too that, until the last quarter of the century, civil servants were exclusively male and almost exclusively gentlemen (or able to pass for such), and that the atmosphere in most offices was nearly club-like, though the quality of that atmosphere might range from the almost magnificent, at the Treasury, to the relatively shabby, at the Post Office. Office hours were as a rule ten to four, and even so there was in many departments plenty of time for reading and card-playing.

The smallness of the world of the civil service reflected not just the smallness of government generally, but also the smallness of the society of the educated Victorians, from whose ranks the clerks were drawn. (We are dealing in the middle of the period with a country of roughly 15 million people, of whom about half were literate; of the literate half, only a very small fraction went into what we would consider secondary education, and the number – until late in the period almost entirely men – who attended the handful of universities was tinier still.) The complaint frequently heard around the mid-century that the civil service was a haven for the younger sons of families with good political connections was often valid, but, so long as civil servants were drawn from among the ranks of gentlemen, the situation could hardly have been otherwise. This was a world in which everybody not only knew everybody but was everybody's cousin.

The corresponding inbreeding of the world of the Victorian intelligentsia is well known, but it looks much less like the indulgence of a taste for incest when one ponders the numbers. Just as the whole of the central government could have fit into one of our universities, so all the male intelligentsia could have fit into a single club. In fact, they almost all did. There may be no better way to gauge just how small the world of the Victorian was than to review the list of members of one actual club. The Athenaeum counted among its literary members Thomas Carlyle, John Stuart Mill, John Ruskin, Matthew Arnold, Thomas Babington Macaulay, Charles Dickens, William Makepeace Thackeray, Anthony Trollope, Robert Browning, and Edward Bulwer Lytton. The scientific side was represented by Charles Darwin, Michael Faraday, James Mill, Joseph Lister, Richard Owen, Thomas Henry Huxley, and Herbert Spencer.

One may ask if there is not a significant slippage in moving from the world of civil servants to that of the Victorian intelligentsia, but, again, the smallness of the educated Victorian world as a whole is evident in the degree of real overlap in its various subworlds. Among those members of the Athenaeum listed above, several were actually civil servants in addition to being major writers: both the Mills (at the East India Company), Macaulay (most notably as a member of the Supreme Council of India), Trollope (at the Post Office), and Arnold (as Inspector of Schools). And one – Dickens – by virtue of his active philanthropic interests, frequently acted in close concert with civil servants even as he was outspoken in his calls for administrative reform.

It is a nice question, moreover, whether the world of the civil service or of a club like the Athenaeum was more notable for its exclusivity or its inclusivity. For while it comprised a numerically tiny male elite, it was also remarkable in having embraced virtually the whole of the Victorian male intelligentsia, including men of very different ideas and disposition, though that group was itself not only intellectually but socially quite diverse. There was a large proportion of Scots, for example, and many members were either of poor (if genteel) or decidedly plebeian origins. Dickens's father had been imprisoned for debt, Faraday's father was a blacksmith; Carlyle's father was a mason.

The civil service was correspondingly disparate. While clerks in the civil service were expected to be drawn from the class of "gentlemen," that term of course admitted of varying meanings. Many clerks were in terrible financial distress before being appointed, and many were unmistakably middle class. If the civil service was characterized by patronage, it was in many instances patronage of a remarkably charitable kind. It is therefore quite difficult in fact to make large generalizations about the clerks as a group. This was as true of their talents as of their social position. While clerks were supposedly well-educated, and some had university degrees or had at least spent time at university, the schooling of many was sporadic. And variations among the clerks reflected comparable variations within departments of the civil service. There is perhaps no better account of this variety than the opening chapters of Trollope's early novel *The Three Clerks* (1858), which is a closely autobiographical record of his own early days as a civil servant. Trollope's particular brand of realism both makes for a highly detailed and accurate portrait of life in the civil service and challenges the kind of simplification that both reformers and supporters of the status quo were apt to fall into when the call for administrative reform became popular at mid-century. In short, an office of the Victorian civil service might be a very dreary place indeed, with little or no useful work being done by ill-schooled and ill-mannered clerks. Or it might be a model of intelligence and industry, staffed by verily the best and the brightest, men who would be remembered a hundred years hence as leading lights of their age.

Although administration and its reform turn up virtually everywhere in Victorian life, they everywhere bear the trace of one thinker above all others – Jeremy Bentham, who had died (at the age of 84) five years before Victoria came to the throne. As one historian of the Home Office puts it, "The name of Jeremy Bentham is a leitmotiv in any study of nineteenth-century government or public administration"; for it was Bentham who more than anyone theorized administration. His influence was felt primarily through a group of admirers that spread his ideas through both intellectual and political circles and that included such major figures as James and John Stuart Mill, the economist David Ricardo, the historian George Grote and the politician and Lord Chancellor Henry, Lord Brougham, as well as a train of private secretaries, several of whom subsequently achieved eminence, like Edwin Chadwick. Chadwick became England's most hated civil servant as the chief designer of the New Poor Law of 1834 – satirized memorably in *Oliver Twist* (1838) – and then in the next decade became one of England's most respected civil servants as the guiding force behind sanitary reform. Although Bentham still figures today importantly among the philosophers, he was to the Victorians the legal and administrative reformer *par excellence*, a man who had first set his sights on English law and the English constitution, then gradually extended them to every imaginable institution: prisons, schools, factories, workhouses, and the workings of government generally.

Bentham embodied, moreover, many of the age's characteristic conflicts. Obsessively rational, he was also a lively eccentric who gave possessions pet names ("Dapple" for a walking stick, "Dick" for a teapot), had his secretaries read him to sleep each evening to ward off a lifelong fear of ghosts, and directed that his skeleton be stuffed and mounted (wearing his customary dress) after his body was publicly dissected. Brought up a Tory and patronized by a powerful Lord for much of his early career, he became identified with Radical politics and headed the group known as the Utilitarians or Philosophical Radicals. An ardent feminist and defender of homosexuality and what we would today call animal rights, he actually disbelieved in rights of any kind, subordinating all such abstract principles, which he dismissed as "vague generalities," to the sole good of pleasure and the sole evil of pain. Ethics he summed up in the famous Greatest Happiness Principle, which asserts that it is the single obligation of individuals and legislators to "maximize" (a word of Bentham's coinage) the happiness of the greatest number of beings whose interest is in question. If it happens that the question is about a given nation, then it is all the inhabitants of the nation whose pleasures must be considered; if the scope of the question is "international" (another word of Bentham's coinage), then the pleasures of everyone in the nations under consideration must be consulted. Always eager to follow a thought out to a logical conclusion, Bentham readily extended his ethical horizons to include the pleasures and pains of "all sentient beings." The Greatest Happiness Principle had already been expressed by others in almost the same terms, but Bentham was uniquely rigorous in maintaining it as the fundamental ethical principle and in following out its logical implications.

One characteristic Victorian tension that escapes mere "administration" is apparent already in the Greatest Happiness Principle, the tension between the individual and the collective. For on the one hand the principle locates the good solely in pleasure as actually experienced by individuals, while on the other it refuses to value any one individual's pleasure over another's. It is no wonder then that Bentham has been hailed both as the champion of radical individualism and the champion of the state. And, given his influence, it is no wonder either that Victorian thinking about administration – and government more generally – betrays this same split, laying down a tradition of laissez-faire with one hand, while the other invents the welfare state and the bureaucracy of regulatory government.

Some of the complexity of this situation is apparent if we look at Bentham's relations with administrative reform and juxtapose those with probably the most famous literary accounts of maladministration of the period, Dickens's accounts of Chancery in *Bleak House* (1853) and the Circumlocution Office in *Little Dorrit* (1857). Bentham relates that he found his calling as a mere 11-year-old, when he happened to read the sensational memoirs of a famous prostitute whose one episode of respectability – her attempt to marry a solid member of the middle class – landed her in the middle of a tortuous Chancery suit. (The memoirs came to be written, indeed, in an attempt to pay off her £20,000 legal bill.) "While reading and musing" over the horrors of the suit, Bentham writes, "the Daemon of Chicane appeared in all his hideousness. What followed? I abjured his empire. I vowed war against him." Legal reform and administrative reform are of course two different things, but they tended to coalesce in Bentham's mind (as in Dickens's) insofar as they raised questions about corruption and inefficiency, and insofar as Bentham recognized that the one reinforces the other: a procedural maze conveniently masks corrupt aims, and corrupt aims of course divert institutional energies from their legitimate functions. But the greatest evil for him always is waste of energy. While somebody's pockets are filled and there is the appearance at least of gainful employment, nothing needful is done.

If Chancery provided the inspiration for Bentham's vocation as a reformer, subsequent encounters with the civil service proper kept that zeal alive and well. His most famous project, perhaps, was the Panopticon, a model plan for any institution in which monitoring is desirable – prison, school, hospital, factory – characterized by a radial design with a central watchtower from which a figure in authority could look into any room or cell without itself being seen. Bentham worked obsessively for several years trying to get the government to approve and build a prison according to his model, without success (though various Panopticon-like prisons and institutions were eventually built abroad), and the process of working with departments like the Treasury could bring him to actual tears. The design for the Panopticon derived from Bentham's brother Sam, an inventor, on whose behalf Bentham experienced further frustrations. The most notable of these involved a design for an improved bilge-pump which the brothers submitted to the Navy Board, who rejected it on the grounds that it was so good that Captains wouldn't put to sea without the improved pumps on board, which would occasion all sorts of trouble. Not satisfied with this patently absurd reasoning, the brothers persisted and at last discovered the deeper reason for the design's rejection: the Board had at the same time before them an inferior design, but one that happened to have been submitted by a navy captain who was a near relation of a duke. After more such frustrations, the disappointed Sam went off to Russia, where his talents were quickly recognized and rewarded.

This story – even down to the retreat abroad – bears an uncanny likeness to the experience of the inventor Doyce in *Little Dorrit*, whose frustrations with the Circumlocution Office bring him to the attention of Arthur Clennam, who becomes his partner and takes up his cause along with that of the Dorrits. Like Bentham, Dickens was peculiarly enraged by any combination of inefficiency and corruption, and, like Bentham, he found as fertile a ground for his anger in the civil service as he had a half decade or so before in Chancery. His satire was widely noticed and brought the term "Circumlocution Office" into currency. (Trollope used it the very next year in *The Three Clerks*.) Like Bentham, too, Dickens shows himself to be seriously divided on the question of the individual versus the collective. He looks to individuals both to blame and to provide the real basis for reform, and he decries the excuses of individuals who seek protection under the umbrella of "the system." (A rejected title for *Little Dorrit* was "Nobody's Fault," an ironic comment on the tendency to let institutional responsibility hide that of individuals.) But as much as he distrusted politics and government, he also recognized that good-hearted individuals could not by themselves bring about the kind of fundamental change that was needed, and so he joined and spoke on behalf of the privately organized Administrative Reform Association upon its founding in 1855. In good Victorian fashion his fierce interest and faith in the individual was balanced by an authoritarian strain that admired the police and institutions that seemed able to act powerfully and decisively (able to act themselves, that is, rather like individuals). Much of his frustration with officialdom, in other words, was precisely that, as often as not, it did *not* govern.

There are here again peculiar obstacles to understanding the Victorian perspective on administration, and Dickens himself may oddly be among these. We who have seen the evolution of bureaucracy in the twentieth century easily think of Kafka when we read *Bleak House* or *Little Dorrit*, and we may think of those novels as striking at something peculiarly modern. Dickens certainly was prescient in imagining in Chancery a great, pervasive, and monstrously evil institution populated mostly by rather ordinary people; and the Circumlocution Office, with its perfection of the principle of How not to do it, also seems immediate and recognizable. But Dickens would have been horrified to think he was pointing towards the future or that things could possibly get worse. Chancery is a medieval institution, literally and figuratively; it is appropriately central in a world that seems on every level incapable of escaping its own past. The Circumlocution Office is likewise meant to portray something musty and antique, precisely the sort of labyrinth of outmoded and irrational practices that "reform" of a Benthamite stamp was intended to sweep away, not through sheer destruction, but by replacing it with something very possibly bigger and better, something altogether efficient and modern.

The debates generated by Dickens's attacks are instructive. His contemporaries in the law and the civil service sometimes complained that he took the objects of his satire from the newspapers and targeted abuses that had already been identified and largely remedied. They also complained that he did not know enough about the institutions he satirized to make useful criticisms and that he overlooked the real achievements especially of the civil service. There was some truth to these charges. Chancery had been the subject of a series of leaders in *The Times* just before the writing of *Bleak House*, and administrative reform had been the subject in 1854 of a famous "blue book" (as parliamentary and royal-command papers were called, after the color of their covers), a report by Sir Charles Trevelyan and Sir Stafford Northcote – politicians and civil servants both – and shortly thereafter mismanagement in the army became the object of intense public interest when, during the Crimean War, inadequate preparations for winter warfare led to many thousands of deaths among British soldiers from disease and exposure. But neither Chancery nor the civil service would see fundamental reform within Dickens's lifetime. One of the Chancery suits that had inspired the central lawsuit in *Bleak House*, and which had begun in the eighteenth century, did not exhaust itself until the twentieth. The system of open competitive examinations for entrance to the civil service, the cornerstone of the Northcote–Trevelyan recommendations, was not fully inaugurated until 1870.

The most strident of Dickens's critics was James Fitzjames Stephen – critic and lawyer, son of a distinguished civil servant (and barrister in Chancery), and older brother of Leslie Stephen (father to Virginia Woolf) – who took Dickens to task for his account of the Circumlocution Office in at least two anonymous articles, one for the *Saturday Review* and one for the *Edinburgh Review*. Stephen apparently believed that it was his own family that was being satirized as the Barnacle clan in *Little Dorrit*, and his reviews were accordingly savage. While much of his criticism (of the kind detailed above) was arguably valid, he made a serious mistake in referring in his latter piece to Rowland Hill, the originator of the Penny Post: "Did the Circumlocution Office neglect him," Stephen asked sarcastically, "traduce him, break his heart and ruin his fortune? They adopted his scheme, and gave him the leading share in carrying it out." Stephen pretended that Hill's had been a story of bureaucratic success. But Hill initially had been strongly rebuffed, and it had taken a parliamentary committee and three years of maneuvering to gain his plan's adoption. Even then he was hardly given "the leading share" in carrying it out, for it was another six years before he was given a place in the Post Office, and that position was initially a specially created one of doubtful power. Ever quick to defend himself, Dickens wrote for *Household Words* a gleefully furious reply in which he detailed Hill's woes in gaining acceptance for his plan for a Penny Post and many subsequent postal reforms. At least some of Hill's problems were owing to his very disagreeable personality (discussed by Trollope in *An Autobiography* [1883]), but the record of his rebuff was clear, and Dickens at least on this score was decidedly the winner.

It is not at all clear that Dickens was aiming consciously at Stephen's father in portraying Mr Tite Barnacle, nor certain even that he knew that Fitzjames Stephen, then a mere 28, was the author of the *Saturday Review* and *Edinburgh Review* attacks, but there are a number of ironies in this clash between Stephen and Dickens notwithstanding. For one thing, Stephen's own program was decidedly reformist and Benthamite, and there was much more accord on matters of substance between the two men than the ferocity of their encounter would suggest. The Stephen clan, far from epitomizing the jobbery and patronage of the unreformed civil service, were typical of the first wave of highly able and earnest upper-middle-class professionals and intellectuals who came into their own with the passage of the First Reform Bill.

The expert insider, who understood perfectly well the history of the civil service and why things had therefore come to be done (or not done) in such and such a way, and the concerned outsider, who could see only injustices, irrational procedures, and absurd inefficiencies, were bound to clash. But the animus shown by both sides in this exchange was intensified by frictions about class, and here too the issues are not without some irony relevant to Victorian administration.

Stephen charged Dickens with not just technical ignorance of the government and the civil service, but with ignorance of the upper classes and a corresponding lack of gentlemanliness that, he strongly implied, was the result of a lack of breeding. He portrayed Dickens as unmanly, moreover, possessed of "a feminine, irritable, noisy mind." And he portrayed him as a cynical manipulator of vulgar opinion who would do real damage for the sake of a passing popular entertainment. Not content with setting the record straight as to the fate of Rowland Hill, Dickens returned charges of ungentlemanliness and unmanliness of his own ("even party occupation, the Reviewer's license, or the editorial plural," he railed, "does not absolve a gentleman from a gentleman's duty, a gentleman's restraint and a gentleman's generosity").

The issues here were partly public and partly personal. The public issues turned on the question whether civil servants needed to be gentlemen. This may seem a ridiculous consideration, like the restriction of the ballot to males who owned property of a certain value. But it looked very serious indeed to a society that had not as yet tested the proposition and that was sensitive to questions of interest. Just as you might not want to put control of the country into the hands of people with no real interest – that is, stake – in it (the vast majority: non-property-owning males and females whose interests were for the most part legally subsumed under those of their husbands and fathers), you might want, by the same token, to put its administrative affairs into the hands of people who were presumed to be disinterested by virtue of their absolutely secure social standing. The problem was complicated, however, by the difficulty in knowing exactly what a Victorian gentleman was. Was gentlemanliness a matter of "breeding" (itself a highly ambiguous word referring both to actual birth and to education), or of some innate merit not tied to family, such as an aptitude for sheer hard work that might lead to a significant rise in station? Anthony Trollope argues in *An Autobiography* that civil servants ought to be gentlemen, but recognizes the difficulty in defining the term and also plainly includes in its compass a much wider circle than that of men so secure in their rank as to be above self-interest.

Dickens very clearly did not believe that civil servants needed to be gentlemen except, perhaps, "in the sense in which the degree may be obtained by any man" – to quote Mr Twemlow in *Our Mutual Friend* (1865). Stephen very likely did. And here the personal histories of the adversaries become relevant.

The Stephens were Calvinistic Scots who had succeeded in farming, trade and the professions – respectable and, many of them, very well educated, but not genteel, and, indeed, suspicious of gentility. In the latter eighteenth century, and after settling in England, they followed a not unusual route into evangelicalism (and were central figures in the politically and intellectually influential Clapham Sect). Dickens's parents both had origins among the upper reaches of the servant classes; one grandparent was steward in a great aristocratic house, anther was housekeeper. Their religion was Church of England, though of the most relaxed kind, and they adopted an air of gentility, even though at the time of Dickens's birth his father had risen only so far as to become a clerk in the Navy Pay Office at Portsmouth. The Stephens had meanwhile attained real eminence and moved among the top rungs of the professions and government. Fitzjames, like his brother Leslie and their father, was educated at Cambridge and undeniably a gentleman, though his temperament and background ensured that he would be repelled by any scent of the merely refined.

These family histories would naturally have produced anxieties about class, especially in their more successful members, at a time when financial or professional or academic or artistic distinction might enable one to move even in aristocratic circles, and yet the finest of class distinctions continued to be noticed and therefore to make a difference. Dickens was sensitive about his class origins and concerned to cover them up (he went to some trouble to lay claim to a coat of arms) at the same time that he waged vigorous battle on behalf of a brand of professionalism that put one's achievements before considerations of birth, education, or money. The Stephens were no less committed to professionalism, but, having achieved the level at which a university education became a matter of course for their brighter sons, education seemed to them a natural prerequisite to professional distinction. Thus, Stephen's attack on Dickens was perhaps especially hurtful in coming from someone only a rung above on the social ladder who by virtue of his own origins and ideology ought to have been an ally under the banners of reform and professionalism, but who nevertheless delighted in pointing out what he took to be the older man's vulgarity.

The extent to which considerations of class in fact dominated debates about administrative reform (in spite of Bentham's much more modern brand of thought) is apparent also when one looks at the controversy inspired by the Northcote-Trevelyan report about making entrance into the civil service a matter of open competitive examinations and investigates the actual subject matter of those examinations. For even that most progressive document assumed that the examination would be in large part a "literary" one, which in the Victorian context would have naturally implied the classics. ("The knowledge of Latin and Greek," Benjamin Jowett wrote in a letter accompanying the report, "is, perhaps, upon the whole, the best test of regular previous education"; his choice of words is telling, echoing as it does the "regulation" we associate with administration.) Though the report called for civil service examinations to be "open to all persons" (meaning males), and though it also very reasonably called for rigorous examination in technical areas of knowledge related to particular departments, the sort of education to be tested would, practically speaking, have continued to limit the pool of applicants to a very small population indeed. Perhaps expectedly, Fitzjames Stephen's father was among those who dissented from Northcote-Trevelyan's "progressive" call; but perhaps unexpectedly, his grounds were not the openness of the examinations, but rather precisely their "literary" character. The qualities that the proposed examinations favored, Sir James believed, would lead to a generation of civil servants who were, as he put it in a now-famous phrase, really "statesmen in disguise" rather than the "intelligent, steady, methodical men of business" that the public service actually required. It is another nice question who was on this point the real progressive and who the conservative.

We may note (among other reasons so as not to be completely insular) that the kinds of complications we have been exploring – as between the individual and the collective, or between classes, or between progressives and conservatives – were peculiarly evident in English administration. While the history of administration on the Continent during our period parallels England's in many respects – for example, as to the smallness of the civil service relative to today's – there were significant differences too. Prussia and France were notably in advance of England when it came to the coherence and centralization of public administration. In large part this was because their respective state governments were much more highly centralized and authoritarian. They also were much more progressive in their entrance criteria and examinations; Prussia, for example, had a "merit system" in place by 1794. But just because of this greater coherence, perhaps, the civil service in Prussia and France also embodied to a lesser degree ambivalence about class or the tension between the individual and the collective so characteristic of Victorian administration. The continental experience may explain why Max Weber's famous distinction between "bureaucracy" and "charisma" as competing social and political forces – bureaucracies are characterized by regimentation and seek to perpetuate themselves and thus the status quo; the charismatic individual leader provides a natural countervailing force and society's real hope for change – does not map so neatly onto English experience, where bureaucracies have proven more tolerant of the charismatic (or merely eccentric).

If we look to Bentham for the excitement of the newly discovered thought that administration is something that can be theorized or made scientific, to Trollope for a realistic portrayal of what being a Victorian administrator was often actually like, to Dickens and Stephen for furious polemics pro and con, then we may – by way of a bit of final complication – round out the picture by considering briefly another major writer who also was a dutiful Victorian civil servant of long standing.

Like Trollope, Matthew Arnold became a civil servant for reasons chiefly financial. He was socially far better connected than Trollope, however, and came to his appointment as one of Her Majesty's Inspectors of Schools with help from his mother (widow of the celebrated headmaster of Rugby) and Henry Petty-Fitzmaurice, third Marquess of Lansdowne, who was head of the cabinet's Education Council and had recently employed Arnold as his private secretary (a post requiring little work, but also providing insufficient income to support a family). Although he came to his post by way of classic patronage, he filled it with care. This is complication number one. For 35 years, during all the years of his rise to eminence as one of England's finest poets and its finest critic, an international celebrity who lectured at home and abroad, Arnold worked earnestly at this terribly demanding job, much of it consisting of long railway trips across England and Wales (and eventually France, Italy, Germany, and Switzerland) to report in the most minute detail on hundreds of schools, hundreds of teachers and pupil–teachers whom he was required to examine individually (according to his best biographer, Arnold once orally examined 307 pupil–teachers in a single day), and thousands of students, whose examination papers he likewise read individually.

The experience deeply impressed him. In a famous passage from his 1866 essay "My Countrymen," Arnold writes:

> Your middle class man thinks it the highest pitch of development and civilisation when his letters are carried twelve times a day from Islington to Camberwell, and from Camberwell to Islington, and if railway-trains run to and fro between them every quarter of an hour. He thinks it is nothing that the trains only carry him from an illiberal, dismal life at Islington to an illiberal, dismal life at Camberwell; and the letters only tell him that such is life there.

This is the first-hand experience of someone who had actually spent hours and hours in railway carriages and who had plumbed the mind of the middle class through spending even more hours observing its schools and teachers. But what is evident here, too, in Arnold is another characteristically Victorian tension or ambivalence – complication number two – which characteristically appears whenever matters administrative are in question. On the one hand, Arnold is a dutiful laborer in the Benthamite mold (and a denizen of the small civil service world: Arnold's patron Lord Lansdowne was the son of Bentham's patron). To a very considerable degree, Arnold believes in the state and he believes in authority and conformity, reason and efficiency. He believes, necessarily and professionally, in "Inspection." But, as the quotation from "My Countrymen" makes plain, he is on the other hand far from prepared to make a fetish of such merely mechanical goods as reason or efficiency. The complaint about the emptiness of a life that is in a merely mechanical sense comfortable and well-managed is scarcely original; it carries on a theme first sounded among the Victorians by Carlyle. But its significance here is in coming from a person so centrally and officially placed. Not, again, that Arnold is in this unique. John Stuart Mill provides a very similar example. He was literally brought up at Bentham's knee, came to his post in the East India Company through family connection, served it dutifully for many years, but likewise chafed against the administrative ideal of the merely efficient and rational and in *On Liberty* (1859) championed the spontaneous and individual in almost Arnoldian terms.

Have we in our own century like instances of culture heroes among the bureaucrats? It surely tells us a great deal about the Victorians and Victorian administration that so many of their finest writers and minds were either civil servants or closely engaged with public administration – and deeply critical of administration as such. It surely tells us a great deal about ourselves and the relative place of administration and intellect in our culture, moreover, that a comparable overlap is nowadays quite unimaginable.

See also 1832, 1848; EDUCATIONAL; SAGE WRITING

REFERENCES

Finer, S. E. (1952) *The Life and Times of Sir Edwin Chadwick*. London: Methuen.

Harrison, Ross (1983) *Bentham*. London: Routledge and Kegan Paul.

HMSO (1855) *Papers on the Re-Organisation of the Civil Service*. London: Her Majesty's Stationery Office.

Honan, Park (1983) *Matthew Arnold: A Life*. Cambridge, MA: Harvard University Press.

Mack, M. P. (1963) *Jeremy Bentham: An Odyssey of Ideas*. London: Heinemann.

Pellew, Jill (1982) *The Home Office 1848–1914: From Clerks to Bureaucrats*. London: Heinemann.

Snow, C. P. (1970) "Dickens and the Public Service." In M. Slater (ed.) *Dickens 1970*. London: Chapman & Hall.

Weber, Max (1958) "Bureaucracy: The Sociology of Charismatic Authority." In H. H. Gerth and C. Wright Mills (eds) *From Max Weber: Essays in Sociology*. New York: Oxford University Press.

FURTHER READING

Annan, Noel (1955) "The Intellectual Aristocracy." In J. H. Plumb (ed.) *Studies in Social History: A Tribute to G. M. Trevelyan*. London: Longmans.

Childers, Joseph (1995) *Novel Possibilities: Fiction and the Formation of Early Victorian Culture.* Philadelphia: University of Pennsylvania Press.

Collini, Stefan (1991) *Public Moralists: Political Thought and Intellectual Life in Great Britain 1850–1930.* Oxford: Clarendon Press.

Finer, S. E. (1972) "The Transmission of Benthamite Ideas 1820–50." In G. Sutherland (ed.) *Studies in the Growth of Nineteenth-Century Government.* Totowa: Rowman and Littlefield.

Foucault, Michel (1979) *Discipline and Punish: The Birth of the Prison*, trans. Alan Sheridan. New York: Vintage Books.

Hume, L. J. (1981) *Bentham and Bureaucracy.* Cambridge: Cambridge University Press.

Mill, John Stuart (1969) *Autobiography*, ed. J. Stillinger. Boston: Houghton Mifflin.

Poovey, Mary (1995) *Making a Social Body: British Cultural Formation, 1830–1864.* Chicago: University of Chicago Press.

Roberts, David (1960) *Victorian Origins of the British Welfare State.* New Haven, CT: Yale University Press.

Stansky, Peter (ed.) (1973) *Government and Society in Victoria's Britain.* New York: New Viewpoints.

Taylor, Henry (1885) *The Autobiography of Henry Taylor.* London: Longmans.

16

Financial

Christina Crosby

Anthony Trollope, the eminent Victorian novelist, advances in his *Autobiography* (1883) his "theory," as he calls it, that

> the love of money is so distinctive a characteristic of humanity that . . . sermons [preached against it] are mere platitudes called for by customary but unintelligent piety. All material progress has come from man's desire to do the best he can for himself and those about him, and civilization and Christianity itself have been made possible by such progress. Though we do not all of us argue this matter out within our breasts, we do all feel it; and we know that the more a man earns the more useful he is to his fellow men. (Ibid.: ch. 6)

For all its bluff assertion of common sense, there *is* a distinctly theoretical element to this statement, and if Trollope here appears to be the crassest of materialists, one must acknowledge a certain idealism in his praise of the love of money. For money, after all, is the universally equivalent form of value, the form of value universally acceptable; and it is this fact that gives money its charm. "The enjoyment of money ownership undoubtedly contains an idealist element," Georg Simmel writes several decades after Trollope.

> To stress this element appears paradoxical only because, on the one hand, the means of making money usually lacks this element, and on the other, the person who utters the joy usually does so in a form altogether different from the idealistic one. This should not disguise the fact that the pleasure of money ownership as such is one of the most abstract enjoyments and is most remote from sensual immediacy since it is exclusively experienced through a process of thought and fantasy. It resembles the joy of victory which is so strong in some people that they do not even ask what they gain by such a victory. (Simmel 1978: 329)

The pleasures of literature, too, are abstract, experienced through thought and fantasy – however sensual – and this point of intersection may be the place to begin thinking about the relation of money to literature, or, more specifically, the relation of money in nineteenth-century Britain to Victorian novels. To note that money looms large in Victorian fiction is to observe the obvious, but it is worth our while to consider the matter more closely. Certainly the love of money starts, sustains, and resolves plots, establishes character, and makes a whole rhetoric of value available to Victorian writers who represent money as the condition of possibility for all good things even as they excoriate money-getting as a sign of moral decline. Moreover, the relations of capital shaped literary production, influencing both the content and the form of nineteenth-century novels: the triple-decker, for instance, is specific to developments in the Victorian publishing industry (Feltes 1986: 24–7). One could develop this argument further, following Jameson's reading of the relations of form to content: "form is . . . the final articulation of the deeper logic of the content itself," and in this sense money informs Victorian literature in the strongest sense – gives it the form its content requires (Jameson 1971: 329).

Yet in observing that Victorian novels are often "about" money, or analyzing the complex ways in which the economic shapes the literary, we are encouraged to overlook the "idealist element" of money ownership and the importance of the fact that money is a *form* of value. Economic value can assume many forms, of course, including the form of commodities, but money is sovereign over all; money is the shape all commodities must assume, ideally in their prices, and actually in the process of exchange when money changes hands. Both the pleasures of money ownership and the pain of being without money are determined by the particular logic of this form of value, and its peculiarities are crucial to thinking further about what literature might have to do with problems specific to economic life. I will argue that literature helps to render intelligible the abstractions and contradictions of money as money becomes a more and more imposing and insistent part of life in nineteenth-century Britain. Literature actively accommodates Victorians to the imaginary relations money effects, even as literary texts are riven by the contradictions inherent in money. Several questions follow: How does literature contribute to making intelligible the money form of value? How might literature make pleasurable the derealizations of the money-form and the distance from sensual immediacy it requires? How do Victorian texts make it possible for the Victorians to think money? And what follows from the observation that both money and literature are representations?

To approach these questions I will turn at the end of this essay first to melodrama, "the most important theatrical and literary form of the nineteenth century," according to one historian of the period (Walkowitz 1992: 86). Beginning with Dickens's melodramatic novel *Our Mutual Friend* (1865), and then referring briefly to Ruskin's essays on political economy, I will argue that melodrama stages the contradictions of the money form of value and in so doing urges through its pleasures an embrace of the abstracting logic of money. As we will see, *Our Mutual Friend*, like melodrama more generally, is a fictional world replete with material things that are charged with significance. In this novel, a huge fortune made from garbage is at the center of the several plots, and we find ourselves in a London everywhere decaying and corrupting as characters go about the business of getting and spending. On the one hand, the things Dickens represents militate against the abstraction from sensual immediacy required by money; on the other, everything in the novel, from the mounds of dust that loom so large in the story to the heavy silver plate which overwhelms dinner guests in the Podsnap establishment, is invested with moral significance. The insistent materiality of the text is thus contradictory, both an assertion of the immediacy and weight of an embodied life tending towards death and yet also nothing but the incarnation of immaterial moral concepts. Melodrama, which is as pervasive in Victorian culture as banking is in Victorian society, serves in this way to accommodate readers to the abstractions of equivalence (this is equal to that; this means that) which are the sine qua non of an economy driven by production for the market.

By way of contrast, I end with a consideration of Trollope's *Autobiography* and the claims he makes there for realistic representation. Refusing the pathos and sensationalism of melodrama, Trollope advances a theory of novel-writing that is deeply indebted to quantity and depends on the production of a certain number of words in a set period of time. The particular pleasures Trollope's novels afford are effects of his mode of producing them, and suggest how literary representation can accustom readers to wanting more, and more of the same. In this Trollopian realism makes the demands of quantification rewarding, and the credibility of realist representation underwrites the extension in the nineteenth century of financial credit. Realism, no less than melodrama, demonstrates the intimacy of the literary with the economic.

Banking: The Mobilization of Money Power

Students of nineteenth-century Britain know that the three great facts of that time and place are capitalization, industrialization, and urbanization, the transformation of local and agrarian economies and ways of life into the modern world of steam and iron, metropolitan centers and worldwide interdependencies. Britain under the queen sees the triumph of capital and the consequent unrelenting drive for innovation and expansion; as Hobsbawm notes of the nineteenth century, "revolutionary change became the norm" (Hobsbawm 16). By mid century business cycles of prosperity and recession spread across national economies (ibid.: 32), and by the 1880s the world is united by international markets and the consolidation of colonial ventures into empire. This "take-off into sustained growth," as the economists call it, could not have happened without the concomitant development of systems of finance to fund new enterprises, from the manufacture of the most familiar consumer goods (cotton cloth, most notably, but also all sorts of household items) to the development of hundreds of miles of railroads and the building of huge public works projects like docks or sewers. As one historian of banking in England has noted, "Funds had to be always easily accessible; the money power had to be mobilized; immobilized capital in such a dynamic age was a serious impediment to economic progress" (Richards 1929: 202).

Banking is thus necessary to revolutionary changes which began long before the nineteenth century and then developed exponentially from 1800 on. The Bank of England, founded to finance the government of William of Orange in the late seventeenth century – and to provide a steady stream of interest income from the national debt for the stockholders in the bank – retained its monopoly on joint-stock banking until 1818: before that date banks within 65 miles of London were prohibited from having more than six partners. The Bank of England became by virtue of necessity the bank of last resort and the first institution to try directly to control the economy through raising or lowering the interest (or "discount") rate charged for lending money. Yet its early monopoly and its incipient role as a central bank also encouraged the establishment of hundreds of private banks both in the country and in London: 940 country banks were operating by 1814 (King 1936: 9), often from a first-floor room in the substantial house otherwise occupied by the banker and his family (Davidoff and Hall 1987: 245). These banks often developed out of other commercial activities and were part of what Peter Mathias characterizes as "a face-to-face society of friends, cousins, and business associates," and bankers flourished to the degree that they were seen as men of unimpeachable credit, able to display wealth and status. Yet provincial banks were also part of the increasingly specialized business of supplying loanable capital to increasingly distant and even unknown debtors (Mathias 1983: 135). Indeed, banking helps to create and then must confront and manage the ever-more complex circuits of capital; bankers had to make up (in concert with industrialists, the government, and merchants) the various financial instruments which enabled business to be conducted over time and space. No longer face-to-face, money and commodity transactions depended on credit in the form of bills of exchange, accommodation bills, promissory notes, Treasury bills, Exchequer bills, bills of lading, bills of sale, drafts, cheques, stocks and bonds, and, of course, bank notes (see the Appendix to this chapter).

Crisis and Credit

These forms of transaction are different from, yet related to, the personal faith in the local bankers called for in this 1816 letter to the *Newcastle Courant*:

> That we may receive credit *from* [the bankers] let us give credit *to* them, and then mutual confidence will once more be reestablished. . . . These remarks are for the public good and the result of a strong conviction that this *running* and *hunting* down the credit of our banks is a *chase* in which no wise man ought to join. It may be "sport" to some now, but if persevered in it will be death hereafter. (Phillips 1894: 79)

Not just the Bank of England but provincial banks issued their own notes: promises to pay on demand a certain quantity of specie (or Bank of England notes understood to be always convertible into gold). A banker, however, has been defined as "one who does not seek to match every liability with an equivalent asset" (Pressnell 1956: 41), and the danger was always that there would be a run on the bank that would force the banker to stop payment if he could not quickly realize his investments. But in a crisis no one is a buyer and everyone (including the banker) is trying to sell to raise money to meet the bills (or bank notes) presented for payment. Commodities, whether goods in a warehouse or the assets a bank holds in the form of debts (bills, stocks, bonds, and so on), languish on the market. In a monetary crisis, then, the contradictions of money loom large: because it is useful not in itself but as the universally equivalent form of value, its usefulness can be realized only in exchange. Furthermore, useful things, the whole various world of goods and services, are worthless unless exchanged for money. To "give credit" to the bankers was thus to believe in them and in their notes, to credit that those notes *were* money in order to avoid the economic death consequent on a failure of circulation.

That such credit was tenuous is evident in the ongoing debate in the nineteenth century over how much money should be held in reserve (wealth withdrawn from the economy, making no money) proportionately to notes in circulation. Adam Smith said a quarter to a fifth, Alexander Baring said a third, but the cash ratios actually maintained by bankers were much smaller, a tenth to a twentieth (ibid.: 196). Moreover, a run on one bank would destabilize others as well, for, as Phillips (1894) puts it, "each holder of 'rag' [paper] money being anxious to have it changed into gold," the bank notes would come flooding back to the issuing banks. Country bankers in such a crisis would turn to London and borrow money to meet the demand, as happened in 1825, the first major crash of the nineteenth century. When the firm of Pole, Thornton, and Co. threatened to break (which it eventually did, involving 44 other, smaller country banks in its collapse), the young Henry Thornton went with John Smith, an older and well-established banker from another firm in Clapham, to meet the Directors of the Bank of England. His sister reports on this meeting in a letter to a family friend:

> John Smith began by saying that the failure of this House would occasion so much ruin that he should really regard it as a national misfortune, and also that what he had seen of the conduct of one of the Partners at a crisis of extreme peril, had convinced him that, could it be saved for the moment, it might be well managed in future, he then turned to Henry and said, "I think you give your word the House is solvent?" Henry said he could. "Then," says John Smith to the Directors, "your money is safe." . . . "Well then," said the Governor and Deputy Governor of the Bank, "you shall have four hundred thousand pounds by eight tomorrow morning, which will I think float you." (Shannon 101)

As the economic crisis deepened, however, Pole, Thornton, and Co. continued to be drawn upon by smaller country banks desperate for cash, and not even the £400,000 could save them. Yet the credit of Henry Thornton emerged from the crisis unimpeached, and within weeks he was a partner in the banking house of Williams and Co., as his sister reports:

A happier person I have seldom seen than Henry, after fourteen hours of intense work, but so pleasant he says, people pouring in with all their congratulations and their accounts – so that in spite of the numbers, who having wanted to pay their Christmas bills drew out of the House small sums – the number of new friends who paid in left them with a much larger sum than they had in the morning when they opened. (Ibid.: 108)

The bankruptcy of Pole, Thornton, and Co. was occasioned by unsuccessful speculations by one of the partners, which undermined the bank's assets, and by the fact that the fortune of another partner was much in land and thus impossible to realize quickly in cash. Despite the personal connections and good name of Henry Thornton, the firm was forced first to stop payment, then into bankruptcy. The failure of convertibility prompted outcries of "'Away with Old Rags. Gold for ever!'" (Phillips 1894: 2), but by the 1820s money was by no means gold alone, and the long process of the dematerialization of money (which in the late twentieth century is largely made up of electronic impulses) was well under way.

The monetary form of value thus steadily erodes the significance of face-to-face, interpersonal credibility, and the pleasantness of Henry's receiving both congratulations and cash because people believed in him was clearly a local phenomenon, soon overtaken by impersonal exchanges over greater and greater distances. Yet the waning significance of individual credibility and the steadily increasing abstraction of credit should not obscure the fundamental fact that banks no less than individuals depend on the public's belief in their worth and stability, and public trust in the value of their bank notes. The monetary crises which repeatedly wracked the nineteenth century, ruining widows and orphans, throwing men and women out of work, bankrupting large firms and small, were understood to be crises of confidence – of belief, faith, and credit. The fact that economic crises are the consequence of interrelated forces, far too contradictory to be solved by monetary policy (though economists have long hoped differently), in no way obviates the need for public trust in money and confidence in the financial and governmental institutions understood to secure its value.

Certainly the crisis of 1825, "one of the most violent of the century," demonstrates both the increasingly complex and impersonal relations of the early nineteenth-century economy, and the very local and devastating effects of a general collapse of the economic system. This crisis, which was the first but by no means the last to shatter fortunes and ruin firms, followed on a boom fueled by the floating of bonds for South American republics and South American mining projects; the Bank of England simultaneously was expanding credit to the government and to the East India Company; plentiful credit led to the buying of commodities and securities with borrowed money in order to sell again at a profit; an excess of imports led to a drain of gold (used for international payments) abroad. When the South American mining projects collapsed, the bank restricted credit to build up its reserve of gold; confidence in convertibility was shaken, and owners of paper money wished to realize it in cash (this is the point at which Pole, Thornton, and Co. broke, taking with it those country banks whose assets they held). Finally, the panic spread beyond financial institutions, as merchants and manufacturers, unable to borrow and desperate for money to pay bills coming due, dumped their commodities on the slumping market. As one historian writes, "In the winter of 1825–26 [the country] was within twenty-four hours of barter" (Chambers 1968: 105). When the crisis had intensified to the point of threatening the convertibility even of Bank of England notes, the bank again freely made loans, thus restoring confidence – and the recovery was encouraged with the discovery in the bank of a cache of bank notes of a small denomination that could serve as ready money (Collins 1988: 17; Chambers 1968: 105).

This crisis and the others which followed at about ten-year intervals (1837, 1847, 1857, 1866, 1878, and 1890 (Collins 1988: 630)), led repeatedly to cries of "gold for ever!" But an economy driven to expand cannot return either to gold or to barter. Indeed, despite controversies about the relation of paper money to gold which continued for the whole of the nineteenth century, various forms of "nominal money" (Goux 1988: 19) continued to be developed and refined, to the point where Walter Bagehot could declare in 1873 that the London money market is "by far the greatest combination of economical power and economical delicacy that the world has ever seen. . . . Concentration of money in banks, though not the sole cause, is the principal cause which has made the Money Market of England so exceedingly rich, so much beyond that of other countries." Great industrial projects (ship-building is one of Bagehot's examples) and worldwide trade both are predicated on the ready availability of that concentrated money. As Bagehot puts it, "English trade is become essentially a trade on borrowed capital, and . . . it is only by this refinement of our banking system that we are able to do the sort of trade we do, or to get through the quantity of it" (Bagehot 1873: 15, 17).

Debt (which is to say credit) is the condition of wealth and economic expansion, for borrowed capital is needed to finance industry and commerce on such a scale; and capital lent returns to the banks in the form of deposits which are lent out again. These successive transactions actually increase the supply of money: "One of the most confusing things for the beginner is to learn that under modern conditions the principal kinds of money – which we have defined as anything widely accepted in settlement of debts – themselves consist of debts or acknowledgment of debt" (Dacey 1951. 13). Anthony Brewer explains further, "Money deposited with the bank is re-lent (normally, in [the nineteenth century] by discounting bills) and the money thus lent out may be redeposited and lent out again. A multiple superstructure of credit can be built up on a limited basis of actual cash" (Brewer 1984: 162). Banks thus create money in the form of multiple deposits and bank notes, and, conversely, decrease money when they fail (Galbraith 1975: 19–20).

Money Making Money

As economic relations became more complex, distant, and anonymous, the personal credit a banker like Thornton could draw upon mattered less and other forms of credit mattered more. As early as 1802, in "An Inquiry into the Nature and Effects of the

Paper Credit of Great Britain," Henry Thornton's father traced the circulation of a £10 bill of exchange: drawn first by a farmer on a corn factor (meaning that the factor agreed to pay at a certain specified date in the future for corn delivered to him by the farmer), the bill passed from the farmer to a grocer (at a "discount," meaning that the farmer discharged a debt of less than £10, gaining in the moment the effect of ready money, losing some of the value of the bill for the advantage of immediacy), from the grocer to a sugar baker, from the sugar baker to a West India merchant, from the merchant to a country banker (who would redeem the bill from the corn factor at the full value of £10 when it came due; the banker thus gains from having bought the bill at a discount from the merchant who needed ready money). "The bill, in this case, will have effected five payments," Thornton writes, "exactly as if it was a £10 note payable on demand to bearer. It will, however, have circulated chiefly in consequence of the confidence placed by each receiver of it in the last endorser, his own correspondent in trade" (King 1936: 33). This face-to-face confidence, which closely associates trade "correspondence" with personal "responsibilities," and the ethical–affective register of "credit" with the economic form of the bill of exchange, could not continue to sustain the economy, however, for as the demand for capital increased in the industrializing north, country bankers turned increasingly to the growing market in bills not only as an investment, a way to put their assets to work, but also as a way to borrow even more assets (ibid.: 27).

By conflating a bill of exchange with a bank note, Thornton in 1802 ignores the signal fact of discount, the fact that money could make money. As W. T. C. King observes in his *History of the London Discount Market* (we would now call it the money market),

> Financial dealings in bills arise when they are viewed, not merely as acknowledgments of indebtedness or for payments to trade creditors, but as a means of raising money by the sale of the bills (and the debts they represent) to third party financiers . . . although the tangible commodity in the Discount Market is the bill of exchange, the commodity in which the market *deals* is not bills but the loans made by the purchase of bills. (Ibid.: xvii)

A banker is a dealer in debts, and, indeed, the assets that a bank holds are, precisely, debts that when discharged will bring in more money than the bank paid to buy them. As the economy expanded with this exponential abstraction of exchange value, finance became increasingly specialized, and with the development of a market in bills came bill brokers who served as intermediaries between buyers and sellers. Finance also became increasingly anonymous and speculative.

In his 1834 book on banking, J. W. Gilbert notes unhappily the intimacy between banking and speculation:

> It is the object of banking to give facilities to trade, and whatever gives facilities to trade gives facilities to speculation. Trade and speculation are in some cases so nearly allied

that it is impossible to say at what precise point trade ends and speculation begins. . . . Wherever there are banks, capital is more readily obtained, and at a cheaper rate. The cheapness of capital gives facilities to speculation, just in the same way the cheapness of beef and beer gives facilities to gluttony and drunkenness. (Gilbert 1834: 137, 139; quoted in Marx 1977: v. III, 406)

This impossibility of distinguishing with certainty between legitimate trade (in which wealth is derived from the making and exchange of useful goods) and the vice of speculation (devoted to nothing but money) haunted nineteenth-century writers, especially after the Joint Stock Companies Act of 1856. Before that date, any share-holder in a firm was liable, should the firm fail, "to the last shilling and acre" of his property no matter how small his investment. Unlimited liability effectively pre-vented the sale of stocks of small denomination and severely restricted opportunities for investment; after 1856, any seven or more persons could register a "memorandum of association" and create a corporation with limited liability (thus the familiar "Inc." and "Ltd." following the names of certain firms since mid-century). As one economic historian notes, "General limited liability had come, and with it the era of modern investment" (Shannon 1953: 378). Indeed, the value of quoted securities – the written proofs of ownership of stocks, thus negotiable instruments – traded on the Stock Exchange increased nearly twenty-fold over the course of the century, from £600 million in 1802 to over £11,000 million in 1913 (Morgan 1965: 139), an enormous quantitative increase that intensified worries of moral decline.

In 1876, shortly after the publication of Bagehot's book on the money market, an article on "Stockbroking and the Stock Exchange" appeared in *Fraser's Magazine*. Beginning with the requisite wonder at how the national debt, not only of Britain but of governments around the world, has "swollen prodigiously," the author observes that

for the purposes of the stockbroker it is much the same whether the "securities" he deals in are based in industrial undertakings or commerce, or are mere loans necessitated by a national bankruptcy or an ambitious war. His business is to buy and sell and get gain out of these bits of paper; and it is of the essence of that business that quantity should have weight with him, not quality, and of quantity it cannot be denied that the modern stockbroker has enough. (Anonymous 1876: 85)

As "bits of paper" the stocks are rhetorically depreciated, just as the security offered by "securities" is ironically undercut by the quotation marks. If the quantity of these stocks is assured (though one might wonder whether it is possible ever to have "enough" of pure quantity), it is equally evident that their quality is questionable, as is that of the men who deal in them:

For [stock exchange members] the market value of a given stock is never gauged by its intrinsic worth so much as by the speculative furor of the moment. . . . It is this that explains the marvelous effect of lies in the course of any one day's dealing. . . . It is business founded on opinion and on the chance of the moment. A thousand temporary

influences are at work appealing to the passions of the hour with ten-fold the force of the
permanent conditions or surroundings of the stock. (Ibid.: 91)

Ruled by their passions, the stockbrokers work in "an elaborately organized gambling
hell" and "the most upright men in it do things themselves, and are familiar with
doings in others, such as anyone with sound moral vision would shrink from and
shudder at" (ibid.: 93). The metaphors of vice and contagion (gluttony and drunkenness, a prodigiously swollen debt, speculative furor, the passions of the hour) accord
well with other nineteenth-century characterizations of financial dealings as a fever, or
frenzy, or mania, or panic – all excessive, all overwhelming.

Quantity versus Quality

The problem, then, is posed as one of quantity versus quality; market value versus
intrinsic worth; speculation versus business; vice against virtue. Value has a double
valence, both moral and financial, here separated only to be reunited at the close of the
Fraser's article in an illogical if bracing appeal to "open competition": "Mere rules and
regulations will do nothing; publicity and the risks and moral safeguards of open
competition are what is wanted to clear the air of this important centre of business
from its moral miasma" (ibid.: 102). The author is thus as troubled in his way by the
contradictions of finance as was Gilbert four decades earlier, for neither can say at what
precise point virtuous business ends and vicious speculation begins. An important
center of business is an elaborately organized gambling hell, and securities are but bits
of paper: this dilemma is produced by the logic of money and the necessity, in an
economy organized by production for the market, of turning money into capital:
money and commodities making more money and commodities, or, in the case of
finance capital, money making money. As *Fraser's* says of the stockbroker, "His
business is to buy and sell and get gain out of these bits of paper; and it is of the essence
of that business that quantity should have weight with him, not quality." Quantity –
that is, market value – is measured in money (thus, we calculate the value of quoted
securities in millions of pounds) and money itself is purely quantitative, abstracted
from any particular good or service. The *intrinsic value* of the stock, the actual railroad
or mine or national debt in which it confers a share, does not appear in the *quoted value*
of the stock, which is but so many pounds, shillings, and pence.

Just as the enjoyment of money is "remote from sensual immediacy," so is money
itself. Yet money is absolutely necessary whether to realize a business venture or to
experience a sensual enjoyment; one must have money to exchange for commodities.
This is the contradiction of money: it is the most desirable of things yet has no use
except when it passes from one's hands; it is purely quantitative yet, as Simmel
observes, "has the very positive quality that is designated by the negative concept of
lack of character" (Simmel 1978: 215). *Pecunia non olet*; money has no odor, as the
Roman emperor Vespasian observed to his son of the revenues he derived from taxing

public toilets. In the money-form, value bears no trace of its origin or destiny. It is precisely this positive quality of a lack of character which Victorian writers elaborate as the opposition of quantity to quality, market value to intrinsic worth, in an effort to solve the contradictions of the money-form of value. Yet the contradictions were not to be thought away. "Bits of paper" and "old rags" continued to be the form wealth assumed in Victorian Britain: "The biggest British fortunes were made in commerce and finance, not in industry, and by the late nineteenth century there were more millionaires among merchants, bankers, and ship owners than among landowners" (Cassis 1992: 2). Indeed, Simmel observes that those who own money profit from economic crises like those which recurred throughout the nineteenth century: "However many bankruptcies and business failures result from price slumps or from commodity market booms, experience has shown that the big bankers usually make a steady profit out of these dangers. . . . The services of money, as the neutral tool of economic processes, have to be paid for regardless of the direction or pace of these processes" (Simmel 1978: 215).

Finance capitalists actually found it easier to move into aristocratic circles than did industrialists, and were better able to maintain upper-class status while carrying on business; further, they had more access than industrialists to political power (Cassis 2). This makes sense in that money is odor-free, without the smell of the factory or mine, yet the fact that the only positive quality of money is a negative troubles Victorian writers, who repeatedly and emphatically link this negativity to the absence of moral qualities. Much of Victorian fiction is sustained by the contrast between material wealth and moral worth, and bankers and financiers are more often villainous than virtuous in the pages of novels. In Eliot's *Middlemarch* (1872) the cowardly Bulstrode, who controls the fortunes of the town as the local banker, contrasts poorly with the florid and philistine, but generous, manufacturer Vincy and even more with the idealized Caleb Garth, who reverences the "business" of surveying and building. Dickens's representation of the hypocritical banker Bounderby in *Hard Times* (1854) is as grotesque in its way as his characterization in *Little Dorrit* (1857) of the aptly named financier Merdle (whose name recalls the French *merde*). Even the quiet world of Mrs Gaskell's *Cranford* (1853) is deeply disturbed when the country bank in which meek and saintly Miss Matty's money is invested fails, leaving her destitute.

These specific representations of bankers and banking are motivated by the opposition of quantity and quality, but novels which have nothing to say about banking are also organized by the contrast between economic value and intangible but weighty moral worth: carriages, heavy plate, and large accounts at the bankers often belong to morally bankrupt characters; and if the good characters are well off in the end, as is often the case, the good things of the world are valorized by being in their possession, not the other way around. Wealth troubles nineteenth-century texts, as is evident in Dickens's vision of money as corrupting and corroding matter in *Our Mutual Friend* (1865). Even Trollope, who forthrightly declares his faith in "the love of money" as the basis of civilization and Christianity, is sure to punish those in his novels who love only money. Whatever sympathy he has for the great financier

Melmotte, that character comes to a horrible end in *The Way We Live Now* (1875), and
the value of landed property is confirmed even as credit, and fortunes made of credit-
money (stocks, mortgages, notes), vanish into thin air. In these texts, then, and many
others as well, money is valued according to a moral calculus; the literary, whether
Dickens's grotesque melodrama or Trollope's doggedly realistic representation, evidently endorses values which cannot be weighed and measured by the banker's scale or
entered into his accounts.

Melodrama and the Money Form of Value

We need also to consider the representational problematic in which both economic
value and literature are inscribed. Because money is the universally equivalent form of
value, a commodity must assume the form of money to realize its value – it must be
sold. Things in themselves are useful, but their value is given in a purely quantitative
and abstract measure. Money is thus a representation in which what economists call
use-value (the specific material quality of a thing which makes it of use – as flour is of
use in making bread to eat) disappears into exchange-value (a quantity measured in
money – the price of the loaf). Of course, material goods do not in fact disappear, nor
does use-value; but they assume what Marx calls in *Capital* a "phantom-like objectivity," present, but at a spectral remove mediated by their equivalence to money, which
must stand in for commodities if they are ever to be, in fact, used (Marx 1977: v. I,
128).

In *Our Mutual Friend* Dickens's tropes, from the most local metaphor to the most
encompassing figuration of the text, offer an experience of a representational process
common to both melodrama and money. That is, the melodramatic form of the novel
stages the money-form of value even as Dickens insists that money is lethal, a corrupt
and corrupting thing. The text is replete with figures of equivalence which obsessively
transform objects into animated entities, and people into lifeless objects; further, it is
dominated by a register of filth and decay which creates the novel's organizing
metaphor: money is death. But even while making a spectacle of money that reveals it
to be a baleful influence on human life, the text helps to accustom readers to the
contradictions, dematerializations and rematerializations, displacements and ghostly
embodiments of the money-form of value, and does so by the very form of its
melodramatic revelations. For in melodrama, too, the material world has but a
"phantom-like objectivity," and the things of this world are meaningful only relative
to the occult realm of good and evil which is the real stuff of melodrama. The presence
of this "moral occult" (Brooks 1976: 199) is what makes melodrama so moving: one
sees virtue misrecognized and endangered by vice; one longs to save the threatened
heroine or child who is alone in a fallen world and unloved; one gladly suffers this
pathos in the hope of reunion with a lost unconditional love (often imagined as
maternal and domestic); and one experiences the melodramatic world as everywhere
invested with moral significance.

Our Mutual Friend opens with a classically melodramatic tableau. There we see Gaffer and his lovely, motherless daughter Lizzie at his scavenging work on the Thames, he scanning the water intently, she rowing the boat which has "something" in tow. This "something," never named by the narrator, turns out to be a drowned and decaying body. Gaffer trades on death, for the bodies he finds in the river yield an inquest fee when he turns them over to the coroner; more immediately, their pockets yield up money which he robs, coins filthy from the rotting body and filthy river, but good money nonetheless.

Lizzie regards this business with a "look of dread or horror," shrinks from her father and turns away when he stretches over the stern of the boat to rifle the pockets of the corpse. Alone on the river, they form a tableau, Gaffer leaning towards money and death, Lizzie leaning away and drawing her shawl over her head. Their physical attitudes not only express their attitudes towards money, but also show how money separates father and child: the further Gaffer reaches for money, the further he is from Lizzie and the closer to death; and his own end, when he overreaches, falls into the river, is caught by his rope and drowned, is forecast here. Moreover, the setting makes concrete the moral of the scene, for the slime and ooze of the river, the mud and grime and polluted water, the body itself, which has "been a knocking about with a pretty many tides" and is rotting away, all establish material corruption and decay as inseparable from the getting of money.

From the first, then, the story is explicitly about money, which Dickens represents as something which fastens on living life and corrupts and kills; he figures money as fatal to the quality of life and even to life itself. In *Our Mutual Friend* not only do rotting corpses in the polluted Thames yield money to the waterman Gaffer and his like, but we discover in a parallel plot that waste is a valuable commodity. The mounds of dust (everything from ashes and broken crockery to dead cats) are the goods which have funded the substantial fortune that weighs so heavily on the lives of the protagonists. The odor of rot and decay thus pervades the book as Dickens confounds the maxim that money never stinks.

Yet in the novel everybody wants money because everything can be changed into money – indeed, the heaps of dust have almost all been sold, transformed into the fortune of £100,000 deposited in the Bank of England – and money can buy anything. Dickens insists on the alienating power of money by subjecting all the things in the novel (and the people are among the things) to a melodramatic logic which spectacularly displays money as corrupting and deadly. The London of *Our Mutual Friend* is polluted and polluting, corrupted and corrupting; the registers of filth and waste are not confined to the river or the dust mounds, but metaphorically extend to high society and to the Bank of England itself.

By the end of the novel the money which has been so insistently figured as stinking and deadly is nonetheless redeemed, and the hero and heroine are rewarded with a huge fortune that has been made from garbage. That money can be converted from an economic to a moral standard, from quantity (£100,000 on deposit) to quality (the reward of moral integrity), is consequent on the logic of Dickens's melodramatic rhetoric. From the very beginning, the text has determined that material things (whether corpses and garbage or the highly varnished furniture of the *arriviste* Veneerings) are but the bearers of immaterial moral concepts. The text thus makes qualitative distinctness disappear while retaining the semblance of material plenitude. That is, all the stuff which fills the pages of *Our Mutual Friend* – and Dickens's writing richly details the material world – has value insofar as it is equivalent to something else, the immaterial realm of virtue and vice, moral damnation or salvation.

Melodrama thus enacts in language the derealization necessary to the money-form of value; further, it redeems the violence of this abstraction and makes it pleasurable. This mode of representation, so widely generalized in Victorian Britain, thus spectacularly displays the dichotomous separation of ideal and real, immaterial and material. Dickens's text produces this separation only to give more force to the union of immaterial signification and insistently concrete material reality, a union in which the material world exists to realize the ideal. The popularity of theatrical melodrama in the nineteenth century, and Dickens's own prominence, suggest that the pleasures of the mode were much appreciated – a conclusion which seems reasonable given the relation between melodrama and the money-form of value. For money, too, is predicated on the dichotomy of the concept and the thing, the ideal and the real, and in Victorian Britain money changes everything. The revolutionary fact of production for the market ensures that money is the beginning and end of economic life – not only money, but most importantly capital, money which appears to be self-valorizing – and economic life revolutionizes all other ways of life over the course of the century. Money is nothing in itself, yet one can have nothing without it: all the things of the world are subject to it. Dickens makes this alienating and objectifying logic entertaining and uplifting, even comic.

If Dickensian melodrama is a comforting representation of the abstractions attendant on exchange and the universal equivalent, John Ruskin's later writings on political economy show a darker, indeed desperate, side of the effort to think the violence of abstraction and the logic of money. The desperation comes from his acute sense of the presence of the embodied world and his attention to sensual life – his early writings were devoted to aesthetics, after all – yet for Ruskin as for Dickens the ruin of the phenomenal world betokens a graver and more profound death of the spirit. In a private letter he reports his state of mind subsequent to writing *Unto this Last*, essays on political economy first published in 1861: "I am still very unwell, and tormented between the longing for rest and lovely life, and the sense of this terrific call of human crime for resistance and of human misery for help, though it seems to me as the voice of a river of blood which can but sweep me down in the midst of its black clots, helpless" (Ruskin 1909: viii). Unwell, he figures his torment in the same terms that he uses to represent economic circulation in his essay "The Veins of Wealth":

> The circulation of wealth in a nation resembles that of the blood in the natural body. There is one quickness of the current which comes of cheerful emotion or wholesome exercise; and another which comes of shame or fever. There is a flush of the body which is full of warmth and life; and another which will pass into putrefaction.

The analogy will hold, down even to minute particulars. For as diseased local determination of the blood involves depression of the general health of the system, all morbid local action of riches will be found ultimately to involve a weakening of the resources of the body politic. (Ibid.: 137).

Indeed, by the conclusion of the essay this is no longer an analogy, but a fully realized truth: "the true veins of wealth are purple – and not in Rock, but in Flesh" (ibid.: 143).

Flesh, however, is but the embodiment of spirit, for ultimately Ruskin wishes his readers to ponder "whether, among national manufacturers, that of Souls of a good quality may not at last turn out a quite leadingly lucrative one" (ibid.: 144). Ruskin, like Dickens, writes of bodies and things temporal to address things spiritual. One consequence of his faith in moral quality is his readiness to abandon the gold standard for what we might call the "good standard." Thus, for Ruskin, all money is, finally, fiduciary, a matter of belief alone, and not a value materialized in gold or any other commodity:

> The intricacy of the question [of the real nature of money] has been much increased by the (hitherto necessary) use of marketable commodities, such as gold, silver, shells, &c., to give intrinsic value or security to currency; but the final and best definition of money is that it is a documentary promise ratified and guaranteed by the nation to give or find a certain quantity of labour on demand. (Ibid.: 138)

Money, then, is textual and immaterial, though legally guaranteed in "civilized nations" to have material effects.

Similarly, for Ruskin the "moral or pathetic attributes of riches" which make some treasures "heavy with human tears" are "literally and sternly, material attributes of riches" (ibid.: 141). The material condition of England, with its deadened, desperate workers living in squalor and its rich, grasping merchants living in luxury, is the emanation of broken faith. This representation of the world is congruent with Dickens's, and that Ruskin cites Dickens approvingly in *Unto this Last* is not surprising. "He is entirely right in his main drift and purpose in every book he has written," Ruskin declares, "and all of them , , , should be studied with close attention and earnest care by persons interested in social questions" (ibid.. 121). Ruskin may take issue with the "brilliant exaggeration" of Dickens's "manner of telling" his truths, and regret that he chooses to speak on serious subjects from within "a circle of stage fire," yet Ruskin is every bit as indebted to the logic of melodrama as the novelist he admires, and his writing as evocative of the moral occult.

Realistic Representation and Credit

The double discourse of value which melodrama exploits is also at work in the writing of an author who sets himself resolutely against the pathos and popularity of melodrama, Anthony Trollope. To Trollope, the "loudness and extravagance of [the] lamentations" of a writer like Ruskin are objectionable because unreal: he simply cannot credit writing which asserts itself so insistently – such writing is faithless to the world it purports to represent (ch. 20). "I am realistic," he writes in his *Autobiography*, which is to say he declares himself to be "anti-sensational" (ch. 12). We have already seen his realistic appraisal of the love of money and the desire to own it; the *Autobiography* details how he developed a routine of work that enabled him to produce enough books, and to sell them for enough money, to announce himself the most prolific, if not the greatest, author in the English language. Yet this boast as to quantity is not really a disclaimer as to quality, for by a favored figure, that of litotes (understated affirmation by negation of the contrary), Trollope valorizes not only his mode of production but his product as the best on the market.

Indeed, in his *Autobiography* Trollope produces a carefully elaborated theory of writing, despite his repeated insistence that he thinks of writing as a trade or a craft, as untheoretical and down-to-earth as shoe-making. According to that theory, realistic writing is the best writing, writing which disappears as such, leaving the reader with the impression of a world unmediated by language. Such writing is produced by writing in the best way, which is to say according to the demands of a rigorous schedule. To be precise (which Trollope always is), the best writing is done under the "hot pressure" of the requirement to produce 250 words every quarter hour. With his watch set before him on the desk as he wrote, counting the words as he went, day after day and year after year, Trollope gave himself over to a reality which he imagines as fully calculable and measurable: so many minutes, so many words = so much reality represented. The public rewarded him with a substantial income from his novels, travel books, and stories, money which is detailed down to the last pence in a tally at the end of his account of his writing life.

Trollope is above all credible. That the peculiar credibility of his writing should be an effect of his submitting to the illimitable demands of quantity suggests that reading his novels is an education in the senses – not in any lushly sensual way, but in developing a taste for more; in coming to expect that more will be forthcoming, in renewing one's interest. As the Victorian critic E. S. Dallas writes of Trollope in 1859, "He writes faster than we can read, and the more the pensive public reads the more does it desire to read" (Smalley 1969: 103). As Dallas's irony suggests, there is no time to be pensive when reading a Trollope novel, no time to be lost in thought any more for the reader than for the writer. A Trollope novel gives immediate and absorbing pleasure, but when one is finished reading, the pleasure, which is in the immediacy of the reading, and not in reflection, fades. To renew it, one must read another, and another, and another. This desire for more of the same suggests that Trollope's realistic representation serves to accommodate readers not only to the pleasures of equivalence and quantity, but to the need to renew that pleasure. If melodrama naturalizes the money-form of value, Trollopian realist writing celebrates consuming on credit.

While melodrama as a literary mode has its own temporality and history, it relates to the nineteenth-century capitalist mode of production in its formal logic, and that relation is one element in the complex process whereby the structures and consequences of capitalist production and exchange became imaginable and livable. So, too, Trollope's theory and practice of novel-writing help to create a "pensive public" which derives pleasure from the repeated renewal of credible representations. Victorian literary modes as apparently antithetical as realism and melodrama thus both suggest the interrelation of the literary and the economic, and show how literary form makes the strangely dematerializing effects of money, credit, and capital familiar and even enjoyable, though the joy be so strong that one may not ask what is gained in such a pleasure, and what lost.

Appendix: Financial Instruments

Bank notes   Paper money issued by private banks, convertible to gold money (or Bank of England notes) on demand. Bank of England notes were declared legal tender in 1833, and the Bank Act of 1844 decreed that the Bank of England was to be the only bank of issue; all other notes were to be withdrawn from circulation (Collins 1988: 169).

Bill of exchange and accommodation bill   "Originally used only by merchants, [a bill of exchange] was not unlike a check. Merchant A out in the country instructed Merchant B in London to whom he had sent goods to pay C an amount equal to the value of the goods on such and such a date. B agreed by writing 'accepted' across this written instruction from Merchant A; the result was a bill of exchange. From being a technique used by merchants, however, the use of bills broadened into a way for private individuals short of cash to raise money. Either you wrote the bill out instructing yourself to pay or, if your credit was lousy, you wrote out instructions to a friend with *good* credit to play the part of Merchant B and pay C to whom you owed money or from whom you were borrowing. This second arrangement was called an 'accommodation bill'." (Pool 1993: 270)

Bill of lading   A document detailing the cargo in a shipment; it could be assigned as security for a loan.

Bill of sale   "A document giving rights in household furniture and other similar personal property. It worked like a mortgage; one gave a bill of sale on one's household goods to the person from whom one borrowed cash and if one didn't repay him in time he took the goods." (Pool 1993: 271)

Bonds   "Loans that investors make to corporations and governments. . . . [Bonds] pay a set amount of interest on a regular basis . . . and the issuer promises to repay the loan in full and on time." (Morris and Siegel 1992: 82)

Drafts and cheques   Documents drawing on an account on deposit at a bank, made out to bearer.

Promissory note   "A form of personal debt. . . . This transaction represented a loan of money upon the debtor's promise to pay the amount plus the interest, which was usually quite steep, by the end of a specified period. The loan might be extended or a new loan made at the end of the period, a process called 'renewing.' Promissory notes had to be drawn up in a prescribed form, bearing an official stamp; the stamp itself was sometimes used as a reference to such loans. . . . The original moneylender, the holder of the note, might sell the bill to someone else if he chose for a price less than the total amount of the loan plus the interest when the note became due. . . . Such negotiations were called 'discounting' bills, and a series of discounting transactions might take place before the bill actually fell due; the demand for payment might be made by a person whom neither the debtor nor the original creditor had ever seen before. . . . To 'accept' a note for a friend is to countersign it, indicating that one accepts the responsibility of repaying the note should the original debtor, one's friend, fail to do so." (McMurty 1979: 49)

Stocks   "Ownership shares in a corporation. They are sold initially by the corporation and then traded among investors. Investors who buy them expect to earn dividends as their part of the profit." (Morris and Siegel 1992: 34)

Treasury bill and Exchequer bill   Bills issued by the government; they were redeemable with interest at the end of a set period, and could be bought and sold on the market. These are distinct from the "funds," government securities in the form of annuities which paid an invariant rate of interest, 5 percent. The "Consols" were nine different annuities that were consolidated into one; these annuities paid 3 percent a year, and could be bought and sold, but not redeemed (Pool 1993: 290).

See also COMMERCIAL; POETRY, FICTION

REFERENCES

Anonymous (1876) "Stockbroking and the Stock Exchange." *Fraser's Magazine*, new series, v. 14, 84–103.

Ashton, T. S. and Sayers, R. S. (eds) (1953) *Papers in English Monetary History*. Oxford: Oxford University Press.

Bagehot, Walter (1873) *Lombard Street: A Description of the Money Market*. New York: Scribner, Armstrong.

Brewer, Anthony (1984) *A Guide to Marx's Capital*. Cambridge: Cambridge University Press.

Brooks, Peter (1976) *The Melodramatic Imagination: Balzac, Henry James, Melodrama, and the Mode of Excess*. New Haven, CT: Yale University Press.

Cassis, Youssef (ed.) (1992) *Finance and Financiers in European History 1880–1960*. Cambridge: Cambridge University Press.

Chambers, J. D. (1968) *The Workshop of the World: British Economic History from 1820 to 1880*, 2nd edn. London: Oxford University Press.

Collins, Michael (1988) *Money and Banking in the UK: A History*. London: Croom Helm.

Dacey, W. Manning (1951) *The British Banking Mechanism*. London: Hutchison's University Library.

Davidoff, Lenore and Hall, Catherine (1987) *Family Fortunes: Men and Women of the English Middle Class, 1780–1850*. Chicago: University of Chicago Press.

Feltes, N. N. (1993) *Literary Capital and the Late Victorian Novel*. Madison: University of Wisconsin Press.

——(1986) *Modes of Production of Victorian Novels*. Chicago: University of Chicago Press.

Galbraith, John Kenneth (1975) *Money: Whence it Came, Where It Went*. Boston: Houghton Mifflin.

Gilbert, G. W. (1834) *The History and Principles of Banking*. London. Quoted in Karl Marx, *Capital*, v. III (p. 406).

Goux, Jean-Joseph (1988) "Banking on Signs." *Diacritics*, 18, 2, 15–25.

Hobsbawm, E. J. (1964) *The Age of Revolution: 1789–1848*. New York: New American Library.

Jameson, Fredric (1971) *Marxism and Form: Twentieth-Century Dialectical Theories of Literature*. Princeton: Princeton University Press.

King, W. T. C. (1936) *History of the London Discount Market*. London: George Routledge and Sons.

McMurty, Jo (1979) *Victorian Life and Victorian Fiction: A Companion for the American Reader*. Hamden: Archon Books.

Marx, Karl (1967) [1894] *Capital*, v. III, ed. Frederick Engels. New York: International Publishers.

——(1977) [1867] *Capital*, v. I, trans. Ben Fowkes. New York: Vintage Books.

Mathias, Peter (1983) *The First Industrial Nation: An Economic History of Britain 1700–1914*, 2nd edn. London: Methuen.

Morgan, E. Victor (1965) *A History of Money*. Baltimore: Penguin Books.

Morris, Kenneth M. and Siegel, Alan M. (1992) *The Wall Street Journal Guide to Understanding Money and Investing*. New York: Lightbulb Press.

Phillips, Maberly (1894) *A History of Banks, Bankers, and Banking in Northumberland, Durham, and North Yorkshire, Illustrating the Commercial Development of the North of England from 1755 to 1894*. London: Effingham, Wilson and Co.

Pool, Daniel (1993) *What Jane Austen Ate and Charles Dickens Knew*. New York: Simon and Schuster.

Pressnell, L. S. (1956) *Country Banking in the Industrial Revolution*. London: Oxford University Press.

Richards, R. D. (1929) *The Early History of Banking in England*. London: P. S. King and Son.

Ruskin, John (1909) *Unto this Last and Other Essays on Art and Political Economy*. London: Dent.

Shannon, H. A. (1953) "The Coming of General Limited Liability." In E. M. Carus-Wilson (ed.) *Essays in Economic History*. London: Edward Arnold.

Simmel, Georg (1978) [1900] *The Philosophy of Money*, trans. Tom Bottomore and David Frisby. London: Routledge and Kegan Paul.

Smalley, Donald (ed.) (1969) *Trollope: The Critical Heritage*. London: Routledge and Kegan Paul.

Walkowitz, Judith (1992) *City of Dreadful Delight: Narratives of Sexual Danger in Late-Victorian London*. Chicago: University of Chicago Press.

FURTHER READING

Shell, Marc (1978) *The Economy of Literature*. Baltimore: Johns Hopkins University Press.

——(1982) *Money, Language, and Thought: Literary and Philosophic Economies from the Medieval to the Modern Era*. Baltimore: Johns Hopkins University Press.

17

Industrial

Herbert Sussman

Early Industrial England

Like Charles Dickens, Benjamin Disraeli, and even Friedrich Engels, Thomas Carlyle felt impelled to see for himself the most significant phenomenon of his time, "a system of life constructed on a new principle" (Briggs 1993: 12), a wholly unprecedented marvel, the new industrial cities of the English midlands. Of Birmingham in 1824 Carlyle wrote:

> Torrents of thick smoke, with ever and anon a burst of dingy flame, are issuing from a thousand funnels. . . . You hear the clank of innumerable steam-engines, the rumbling of cars and vans, and the hum of men interrupted by the sharper rattle of some canal-boat loading or disloading. . . . I have looked into their iron works where 150,000 men are smelting the metal in a district a few miles to the north; . . . their tubs and vats, as large as country churches, full of copperas and aqua fortis and oil of vitriol; and the whole is not without its attractions, as well as repulsions. (Froude 1882 I: 232)

Carlyle's rhetoric of awe exemplifies the wonder of his age at the transformation in the 1820s, 1830s, and 1840s of Birmingham, of Bradford and Leeds, Manchester and Sheffield, from small villages to smoky cities. But what appeared as miraculously sudden to Carlyle and his age was, in hindsight, the coming together of changes dating from at least the later eighteenth century, a confluence of existing technologies and new inventions within a particular economic system. The mule and spinning jenny invented in the eighteenth century for mechanizing the weaving process required increased power; mills shifted from the power of the waterwheel to the power of the steam engine, already in use in coal mines; the steam engines turning the shafts and belts of the mill needed coal; transport of coal from these mines brought the steam engine on wheels, the railway. And the seemingly unlimited production of woven cloth needed swift and economical transport by railway and steamships from the industrial city to consumers both domestic and global.

Driving this process was the desire to replace hand-labor by the machine. Weavers working in their own cottages in the Yorkshire countryside became obsolete; these destitute hand-loom operators lingered at the edge of industrialism and in its literature as real casualties and imaginative symbols of those whose craft and livelihood were destroyed by mechanization. For industrialism demanded centralization, the concentration of operatives in the new spaces of mills that housed the mechanized looms. A large population of skilled and often unemployed workers attracted new factories. Operatives must be within walking distance of the factory; a supporting population must be in place to feed and clothe these workers. And, in an economic system driven by entrepreneurial zeal and quick profit, and as yet unhampered by government regulation of such matters as air quality and sewage disposal, the industrial city expanded without constraint. Between 1821 and 1831 the population of Manchester increased by 45 percent.

For these industrial cities men and women left the drudgery of agricultural life in England, and sailed from impoverished Ireland, in search of a new way of life. To the mill-owners they were "operatives" or "hands"; Engels and Marx invented the name "urban proletariat." A preferable name now for this way of life that had never before existed is "industrial workers" or simply "workers," following Williams's (1983) brilliant account of the transformation in the meaning of "work" and "worker" during the early industrial period:

> The specialization of *work* to paid employment is the result of the development of capitalist productive relations. To be *in work* or *out of work* was to be in a definite relationship with some other who had control of the means of productive effort. . . . Time other than that spent in paid employment is significantly described as "your own time", "free time", or as "holiday" . . . or as "leisure time." (Ibid.: 335–6)

This division of time into only two categories, "work" and "leisure," is dramatized by the internal conflict of Tennyson's "Lotos-Eaters" and encapsulated in the singular paradox of Miss Havisham employing Pip to "play, play, play!" (*Great Expectations*, ch. 8).

In leaving the agricultural village the workers were themselves transformed. Left behind were the rhythms of the natural world; mechanization took command (Giedeon 1948). They no longer rose to cock's crow or ceased work at sunset. Rather, with their fellow operatives they rose for their shift to the mechanical time of the clock, the standardization of time being at the heart of the industrial system. Gas-lighting allowed work after dark; the working mill illuminated in the night became an icon of the unnaturalness of the age.

As a space and an institution, the factory was at once continuous with earlier disciplinary institutions such as the school and the army, and yet totally unprecedented. Under the division of labor, the central principle of efficiency within industrialism, a worker repetitively re-produces a single part or engages in an unchanging function. In such labor the worker is removed or alienated from the making of the total product as well as from the surplus value that accrues by the product in excess of the cost of his own labor. The working body is assigned a position in space, must bend to the regular rhythm of the steam engine, of the belts, pulleys, and spinning machines, must work at a specified speed defined by mechanical operations. Under constant visual surveillance, set to a specific unchanging task, like the prisoner, the soldier, or the student, the factory worker exists as a body within a complex system of "bio-power" (Foucault 1977). In contrast to the farm and field, a way of life within living memory, in the factory there was no time for talk or joking, only the adapting of emotional rhythms to the methodic rhythms of the machine.

In the early decades of industrialism the factories and textile mills were busy with men and women, and also with children. At the early industrial moment children were crucial to the enterprise, since their small bodies and tiny fingers were of particular value in tying threads amid the clashing machinery. Only in 1833 did Parliament pass regulations to exclude children under nine from factories and limit those under thirteen to forty-eight hours a week.

It is estimated that half the workers in the mills were female. These included young unmarried women often fresh from the countryside, as well as women married and unmarried who had lived their entire lives within the industrial society. Removed from the social supervision of family and of a traditional society, working alongside men, subject to the sexual power of supervisors, and often independent of spirit, the mill girls acquired a reputation for sexual looseness or, depending on one's perspective, sexual freedom. But it was expected by factory girls and by working-class society that they would eventually marry and take responsibility for home and children, with the husband supporting the family with his wages.

These new gender roles – husband as breadwinner, wife as childcare giver, unmarried son or daughter as factory worker – are generated from one of the most significant shifts created by industrialism, the separation of the workplace from the home. In agricultural society, labor and family life, workplace and domestic space exist within the single space of the farm. Husbands and wives, sons and daughters all participate according to gender roles in planting, in feeding the animals, in the harvest, in performing the endless tasks of farm life. But with the centralization of factory labor the husband, and unmarried sons and daughters as well, had to leave the home each day to earn their daily wage, while the wife stayed behind to care for the young children. From these material circumstances there developed the powerful nineteenth-century ideology of two separate spheres, the masculine public sphere of work, the private female sphere of domesticity, the competitive realm of business, the moralized space of the home. Of course, the boundaries of male and female spheres were highly permeable, especially for the working class. Given the vagaries of employment in industrial capitalism, married women often had to work, leaving the children without adequate care. And the muscular labor in mill and coal mine belied the supposed physical weakness of females.

Nor did the home life of the workers necessarily fit middle-class ideals of domesticity. The houses were "one or two-storied cottages in long rows, perhaps with cellars used as dwellings. . . . These houses of three and four rooms and a kitchen" were "badly ventilated, damp, and unwholesome . . . [and] at least one family sleeps in each room" (Engels 1845: 60, 106). Given the need that workers' homes lie within a short walk of the factory or mill, the working-class district of once red, soon sooty brick was packed tightly near the equally sooty mill or factory at the center of the industrial city. The result was a rigorous segregation of the industrial town by social class.

Within these working-class districts there existed a range of status and of economic well-being – from the skilled artisan and mechanic, to the unskilled laborer, to the Irish, who were seen as a distinct species. Furthermore, in spite of the middle-class tendency to see workers as an aggregate, they presented, as any large group will, a spectrum from the dissolute to the disciplined, from the enthusiastic Methodist to the distinctly irreligious. Still, for all these differences, there emerged a cohesive working-class consciousness (Thompson 1966), about which it is possible to generalize. In contrast to the individualist competitiveness of the middle class, there flourished a general sense of cooperation, of mutuality, seen for example in the Friendly Societies for mutual benefit and care. Workers identified themselves as members of a group or a class defined by difference from the masters or owners, held together by a powerful and always at least potentially radical political culture grounded in opposition to those with economic power.

There was also a distinct working-class intellectual and artistic culture. Although no public schooling was available for workers before 1870, two out of three industrial workers in the 1840s and 1850s were literate, with near universal literacy achieved by the end of the century. Through widespread individual reading and the growth of educational initiatives for the workers such as the Mechanics' Institutes, the working-class intellectual became a common figure, exemplified by Saunders Mackaye in Charles Kingsley's *Alton Locke* (1850) and in real life by the education reformer William Lovett. Academic canonization of the middle-class poetry and fiction of the period has obscured the oral and the print culture of the Victorian workers, which is now being recuperated. There were working-class newspapers, literary periodicals for factory girls, politically radical fiction, a theater, poetry often in the form of broadsides and ballads (Vicinus 1974), and, at the close of the century, a wealth of working-class autobiographies (Gagnier 1991).

The workers comprised, to use a favorite Victorian figure, a single nation, a class defined against another equally unprecedented social class, the owners of the mills and factories. Here again, a new way of life demanded a new name. To the Victorians these men were "masters"; to Carlyle they were "Captains of Industry"; to Marx and Engels "capitalists." We might call them industrialists or, more simply, owners.

In their entrepreneurial zest and instinct for technological innovation, the first industrialists the world had ever seen – for England was the first industrial country – seemed to act out the script of the "self-made man" promulgated by Samuel Smiles in *Self-Help* (1859), and widely accepted as Victorian gospel. That their power derived from wealth rather than from aristocratic birth, from the building of factories rather than the inheritance of land, created an entirely unprecedented form of power that challenged the traditional, hierarchical society into which most of them had been born. Furthermore, this acquisition of power and wealth was deeply individualistic, for in the early industrial period, from the 1820s through the 1860s, before limited liability laws and corporate ownership, the owner himself was fully at risk, his personal fortune tied up with the fortune of the mill, his personal credit and reputation fused with the credit of the factory. For good or for ill, this engagement with the enterprise based on private ownership grounds the intense identification of self with mill in such industrialists as Thornton of Gaskell's *North and South* (1855) or Robert Moore of Brontë's *Shirley* (1849).

Unlike the workers, the owner was not bound by the inflexible sound of the opening bell. He chose to live in the outlying area, the newly invented suburbs removed from his factory in the central city. The constructed space of the new industrial city quite effectively separated the classes, concealing the actual living conditions of the workers from the sensibilities of the bourgeoisie. Beyond the working class quarters

> lives the upper and middle bourgeoisie, the middle bourgeoisie in regularly laid out streets in the vicinity of the working quarters . . . the upper bourgeoisie in remoter villas with gardens . . . or on the breezy heights of Cheetham Hill, Broughton, and Pendleton, in free, wholesome country air, in fine, comfortable homes, passed once every half or quarter hour by omnibuses going into the city. And the finest part of the arrangement is this, that the members of this money aristocracy can take the shortest road through the middle of all the labouring districts to their places of business, without ever seeing that they are in the midst of the grimy misery that lurks to the right and the left. (Engels 1845: 79)

Here, in the suburban homes of the middle class, appeared most vividly the effect of separating home from workplace – the creation of the male and female, public and private spheres. The breadwinner took the omnibus to the mill; his wife and daughters remained at home, supposedly engaged in domestic activity. But in the homes of the middle class unmarried and married women had no real activity, although the "management" of a large staff of female servants was often seen as the analogue of male management of industrial workers. The drudgery of female servants carrying coal upstairs, scrubbing floors, and cooking was never recognized as contradicting the mistress's internalized middle-class belief in the mental and physical frailty of woman.

From the need of the bourgeoisie to comprehend and mitigate industrialism, or – from a more critical perspective – to control the workers and justify their own power, there emerged from this early industrial moment a new literary form, the industrial novel. Industrial novels by middle-class authors for middle-class readers include Frances Trollope's *The Life and Adventures of Michael Armstrong, the Factory Boy* (1840); Benjamin Disraeli's *Coningsby* (1844) and *Sybil, or The Two Nations* (1846); Elizabeth Gaskell's *Mary Barton* (1848) and *North and South* (1855); Charlotte Brontë's *Shirley* (1849); Charles Kingsley's *Alton Locke* (1850); and Charles Dickens's *Hard Times* (1854).

Whether written by Gaskell, the wife of a Manchester clergyman, or Dickens, a casual visitor to the midlands from London, the shape of the industrial novel replicates the shape of the industrial city. For the middle-class writer, representing working-class life necessarily involved a journey, socially between classes, geographically between districts, imaginatively between cultures – a journey analogous to colonial exploration. Henry Mayhew records his own travels into the unknown country of the poor in *London Labour and the London Poor* (1851). Dickens's *Bleak House* (1853) is structured around such expeditions to the sites of poverty, as are the philanthropic activities in George Eliot's novel of provincial life, *Middlemarch* (1872). As middle-class scout, the novelist returns with word of this unknown territory, but in doing so maintains and even strengthens the bourgeois perception of the workers as Other, reinforces as inevitable the distance and the difference between the two classes, the two nations.

For the middle-class novelists, for the middle class, and of course for the workers, the great question of the day was the relation between the classes, between workers and owners. Since in these decades the relation between capital and labor was a problem without precedent, a variety of models emerged. A communal or socialist pattern is exemplified by Robert Owen, who at New Lanark provided as early as the opening decade of the century housing and childhood primary education, sharing control with his workers in a community that became in the 1820s and 1830s a model for utopian settlements in America as well as for labor unionism and the cooperative movement. Some industrialists shaped their way of life, as Carlyle urged them to do in *Past and Present* (1843), on the style of the preindustrial rural gentry, as a paternalism with reciprocal responsibilities. An aristocratic or even feudal structuring of industrialism had a strong appeal, as in Disraeli's novelistic vision of industry as controlled and ameliorated by the noblesse oblige of an aristocracy of birth.

But the dominant model for the relation between owners and workers became not community but competition. Industrial capitalism admits no ties of responsibility, but only the nexus of contract, "cash-payment" in Carlyle's term (*Past and Present* book 3, ch. 10), and is grounded on the equation of the laws of the market with the laws of nature. The law of gravity cannot be repealed; the law of supply and demand cannot be abrogated. Industrialists opposed parliamentary regulations that would compel children to attend school no less than two hours per day and compel owners to fence machinery so that working children would not be mangled in the gears and pulleys. The reasons provided were that such external government interference would disrupt the "natural" functioning of the free market. In many ways, the contradiction between such assumed economic determinism and moral choice structures the industrial novel (Gallagher 1985).

According to the ideology of laissez-faire the capitalist purchases labor from another individual, the worker, who sells his or her labor in competition with other workers. The natural law of supply and demand then regulates wages; the "iron law of wages" arranges that wages never drop below subsistence, since if they did so the operatives needed to run the mill would starve to death, posing a distinct problem for the owners.

Within laissez-faire economics, then, each person becomes an isolated unit acting in the marketplace. Industrialism is not so much a walk of life as it is a continuous scrimmage. Atomistic competitiveness transforms all everyday behavior into self-interest:

> They crowd by one another as though they had nothing in common, nothing to do with one another, and their only agreement is the tacit one, that each keep to his own side of the pavement, so as not to delay the opposing streams of the crowd, while it occurs to no man to honour another with so much as a glance. The brutal indifference, the unfeeling isolation of each in his private interest becomes the more repellent and offensive, the more these individuals are crowded together, within a limited space. (Engels 1845: 58)

The workers, however, did not see the bond of cash payment as inviolable natural law. Instead, they considered their own rights as "free-born Englishmen" to be inalienable (Thompson 1966) and, denied the vote, looked to collective moral protest to obtain these rights. The largest workers' political protest of the early industrial period was Chartism, named for the "People's Charter" of 1,200,000 signatures calling for such reforms as universal male suffrage, the removal of property qualifications for election to Parliament, and the secret ballot. The Charter was presented to Parliament on several occasions in London during the 1830s and 1840s; each time Parliament overwhelmingly refused to consider it.

From the bourgeois political standpoint, workers who rejected atomistic competitiveness to join in collective, albeit peaceful, political action, such as Chartism, became dangerous. In the industrial cities the sheer number of people confined to a small space and no longer regulated by the hierarchical structures of the village seemed a source of potential revolution. As an aggregate, workers were figured in a politically charged vocabulary as a mass (as in the phrase "mass society"), the crowd (with implications of the loss of control), or the mob (sub- or nonhuman force beyond reason). Carlyle's favored tropes for the preindustrial lower orders in *The French Revolution* (1837) were the volcanic eruption, the tempest, and the ocean deeps; and Gaskell epitomizes the metaphoric transfer to factory conditions when she has Margaret Hale see "the slow-surging wave of the dark crowd come, with its threatening crest, tumble over, and retreat" (*North and South* ch. 21).

The contradiction between workers in groups as a threatening mob and individual workers as sympathetic British subjects structures the middle-class imagination. The industrial novel turns on members of the middle class forming affective relations with individual workers, such as the working-class autodidact, thus presenting workers as human beings with a subjective life (Poovey 1995). For Gaskell, the individual workers are noble, but only inasmuch as they resist absorption into the crowd. Dickens represents the workers of Coketown as machine-like, undifferentiated, "people equally like one another, who all went in and out at the same hours, with the same sound upon the same pavements, to do the same work" (*Hard Times* book 1, ch. 5); and yet the plot turns on the virtue of the individualized working man, such as Stephen Blackpool, a virtue measured by his tormented resistance to the temptation of joining a union.

This fear of the crowd or mob does much to explain the intense government repression in the early nineteenth century of what the age called "combination," the organization of working men into what we would call unions. In working-class political culture principles of association, community, and mutuality were, as Chartism demonstrates, valued as means of asserting political and economic power. This collective consciousness remained strong, as shown by the continuing growth of unions in nineteenth-century England. But to the owners and the government the association of working men into unions with strong leadership posed a clear and present danger to the dominant power structure. This fear of workers' becoming organized is registered in the bourgeois industrial novels' representation of union organizers and all leaders of the working class as deceptive, bloodthirsty villains: witness *Hard Times*, *Shirley*, and *Sybil*.

With the failure of paternalism or mutuality and in spite of continuing episodes of violent class warfare – the Luddite frame-breaking in Yorkshire in the 1810s depicted in *Shirley*, Peterloo (1819), Bloody Sunday (1877) – the dominant form of struggle between capital and labor became economic. The industrial strike became the central agon of the early industrial age and the dramatic center of the industrial novel. Dickens journeyed from London to Preston to observe a strike that he made the focus of *Hard Times*. A walkout is the plot crux of *North and South*.

And yet, although class conflict occupies the center of the industrial novel, incidents of violence and industrial disputes are regularly subsumed within an overarching courtship plot. If industrialism had separated the middle-class woman from the activity of industrialism, the process also generated by reaction a desire among women somehow to influence the public sphere from which they had been excluded. The movement of Margaret Thornton (*North and South*) or Shirley Keeldar (*Shirley*) between the male and female sphere, between factory and home, can be read as a protofeminism suggesting that women be given agency within the public sphere of industrialism. But the closure in marriage between the hard industrialist and the soft female also clinches the ideological work of the industrial novel. This bourgeois literary form represents – and indeed seeks to effect imaginatively – a mediation whereby laissez-faire industrialism grounded on economic law may be moralized and feminized, so as to enable the system to endure, but remain under bourgeois control.

Time/Space/Consciousness/Culture

For the industrial worker walking on cobbled streets amid brick houses, fields and woods that lingered in memory had disappeared from daily view, as had sun and sky now obscured by what John Ruskin called the pestilential "Storm-Cloud of the Nineteenth Century" (1884). Even the vestiges of the natural in the urban landscape, particularly the rivers on which all industrial cities had been founded in the days of water power – the "slime pools" of Manchester's Irk "from the depths of which bubbles of miasmatic gas constantly arise" (Engels 1845: 83), Coketown's "river that ran purple with ill-smelling dye" (*Hard Times* book 1, ch. 5) – signaled the fouling of the natural world by industrial and human waste.

But the transformation of William Blake's "green & pleasant Land" into an England of "dark Satanic Mills" (*Milton*) should not be overstated. Industrial development was confined to a range of cities in the midlands; the cherished countryside of village and field largely remained unchanged. Early Victorian England had become, in Gaskell's terms, an industrial north and an agricultural south. Even in the manufacturing districts, in the days before urban sprawl a clear boundary marked the edge of the industrial city and the preindustrial country; in coal districts sheep grazed in the next field from the pit heads. Workers could easily take expeditions to a rural world that started at the edge of town. As recorded in the literature of industrialism, the easy physical movement from central city to sheep fields and country inns, from industrial north to rural south not only registers the varied landscape of the period, but also enables a complex genre of industrial pastoral, a physical and also a psychological journey into the rural world that remained a vivid memory for the first industrial generation.

The city/country opposition that industrialism strengthened was also paradoxically reduced by industrialism, and particularly by the railway. Indeed, it was the introduction and rapid spread of railways in the 1830s that most radically altered the Victorian categories of space and time. Space may be described as the distance between two points on the map, but in experiential terms this physical distance is measured not only in miles, but also in the time taken to traverse this space; a place may be described as "two hours" away. For those living in the 1830s and 1840s who still recalled travel on stage coach over muddy roads, space seemed to collapse with the coming of "railroad speed." To the first railway generation the space-time between city and country, between the metropolis and the rural home, between industrial towns, had virtually been eliminated. And since the government had demanded that railways provide special low fares, a Victorian of any class using the Bradshaw railway guide could move with heretofore unimaginable swiftness. Magic and fantasy provided the only rhetoric, as shown in Carlyle's letter of 1839 describing his first experience of railway travel:

> Out of one vehicle into another, snorting, roaring we flew: the likest thing to a Faust's flight on the Devil's mantle; or as if some huge steam night-bird had flung you on its back, and was sweeping through unknown space with you. (Froude 1884 I: 144)

For travelers, railway speed provided an entirely new form of visual perception, the world seen from the window of a speeding train. Objects in the background remained relatively stable while the foreground virtually dematerialized as the eye/brain registered streaking impressions rather than the solid physicality of the material object (Schivelbusch 1986). Some writers attempted to register this new mode of experience. Elizabeth Barrett Browning's "The Cry of the Children" (1844), Tennyson's "Locksley Hall" (1842) and *Maud* (1855), Dickens's vigorous prose in *Dombey and Son* (1848, ch.

20) are exemplary. In J. M. W. Turner's painting *Rain, Steam and Speed: The Great Western Railway* (1844) the hard outlines of the iron locomotive dissolve, fuse with the storm to offer pure energy, the speed of industrialism itself.

But most Victorian writers and artists joined in a counter-revolution, repudiating the industrialization of space, time, and perception by valorizing alternate forms of cognition and the art of the preindustrial times. The railway lurks as an absent presence, whose rejection shapes Victorian aesthetics and art. Ruskin, the most influential art writer of the age, is exemplary. His descriptions of Venetian architecture in *The Stones of Venice* (1851–3), for example, assume a virtually motionless viewer occupied intensely with the foregrounded detail of a sculpted capital as the implicit antithesis of the railway traveler glimpsing a distant cathedral from a moving train. Similarly, the Pre-Raphaelite artist's equally obsessive detailing of a foreground pond or wall necessitated spending days and even freezing nights in immobile observation (Schivelbusch 1986).

The railway expanded mechanization of time beyond the space of factory and mill. In the preindustrial world the time rung by the church clock varied slightly from village to village. Such local times posed no particular problem for an agricultural society, but running trains on the different times of different localities would mean shattered metal on the track. Thus, what we now call "standard" time was set for the entire country by the railway and sustained by the telegraph. The entire population now moved in a mechanical synchrony. Time, no longer grounded in the revolution of the planet or the rising of the sun, became an artifice, a human construct to which all events referred. Quite appropriately, if quite foolishly, the anarchists in Conrad's *The Secret Agent* (1907) seek to blow up the Greenwich Observatory and thus Greenwich Mean Time.

Again, although literature in some few instances registers this mechanical time, notably in the opening of the aptly titled *Hard Times*, the imposition of a mechanical time on the entire population generated a literary and artistic counter-revolution, a valorization of an oppositional, pre- or anti-industrial time. George Eliot endows Adam Bede with a sense that his carpentry work is regulated only by inward satisfaction: "I can't abide to see men throw away their tools in that way, the minute the clock begins to strike, as if they took no pleasure i' their work" (*Adam Bede* book 1, ch. 1). By the end of the century writers became increasingly occupied with time as measured by feeling or mood, not by a clock outside the self. This occupation with irregular rhythms of the psyche, with duration, with the inner flow of natural feeling is exemplified in the impressionism of Walter Pater's "Conclusion" to *The Renaissance* (1873): "For art comes to you proposing frankly to give nothing but the highest quality to your moments as they pass, and simply for those moments' sake."

The way industrialization thus generated aesthetic counter-formations took material form in the shape of the industrial city. At the center of Manchester the Manchester Art Museum was built in Gothic style, its colored patterned brick and hand-carved ornament challenging the severe functional style of the surrounding factories. At the center of industrial Birmingham the city fathers built an art museum in classical style, its white stone, severe columns, and carved pediment presenting a similar contrast to the urban environment. Arriving at a Victorian railway station, the traveler passed from the street through a medieval, classical, or Egyptian facade, then entered the train shed, a vast hall of prefabricated iron columns supporting a roof of standardized glass panes, ingenious products of industrialism, in which the smoking locomotive waited.

Establishing a preserve of space sacred to art at the center of the city or covering the fact of the train with a facade from times gone by exemplifies the ambivalence of an industrialized society toward the new way of British life that was producing great wealth, and great poverty. In creating an astonishing material culture and technology, industrial capitalism generated its antithesis. As much as industrialism invented the railway and the textile mill, industrial capitalism also invented "culture," music, literature, painting, sculpture, and architecture valued as activities that "attack what was seen as the 'MECHANICAL' character of the new civilization then emerging: both for its abstract rationalism and for the 'inhumanity' of current industrial development" (Williams 1985: 89).

A like ambivalence was lived out by the industrialists themselves, who resided outside the manufacturing city, often married into the landed gentry, bought ancient country houses, and took pride in acquiring Italian Renaissance paintings as well as richly colored Pre-Raphaelite art, rather than representations of gritty industrial England. This opposition of culture and industry is inscribed and mediated within the industrial novel. In *North and South* an Oxbridge man teaches Greek to a captain of industry. In *Hard Times* the factory and the circus are opposed.

But Dickens wrote only one industrial novel, as did Charlotte Brontë. Working within the discourse of "culture," Victorian writers and artists chiefly turned away from their own industrial age, refused to attach any aesthetic or imaginative value to the technological wonders of their time. Emily Brontë wrote of a primal world isolated from the weavers of Yorkshire, George Eliot in *Middlemarch* and *Adam Bede* of society on the brink of industrialization. Tennyson wrote of a lady weaving not in a mill but in a tower on the road to Camelot, Robert Browning of Renaissance artists rather than textile designers, Arnold of an ancient Greek philosopher rather than a contemporary inventor. Industrial workers appear only indirectly, coded in legendary terms as Tennyson's overworked, leisure-besotted Lotos Eaters. The industrial landscape appears as a dream landscape in "Childe Roland to the Dark Tower Came." As an exception, like the female writers of industrial novels, Victorian women poets such as Elizabeth Barrett Browning, Caroline Norton, and Eliza Cook bring reformist sympathy into poems criticizing the factory system.

Because our twentieth-century perception of the early industrial age has been filtered through this Victorian tradition of culture that privileges art over industry, the justifiable pride of workers, technologists, engineers and just plain citizens in their very great, very human accomplishments has been denigrated, or written out of memory. Victorians by the tens of thousands flocked to the Great Exhibition of "The Industry of All Nations" in 1851. Within this technological tradition, the industrial machine becomes a prosthesis, an enhancement of human capacity. An extant photo of

Isambard Kingdom Brunel before huge metal links of anchor chain bespeaks his vast pride, and that of his society, in the creation of iron-hulled steamships to carry Victorians swiftly across the Atlantic.

From the factory, specifically from the textile mills, also emerged the dominant apparatus of the late twentieth century, the intelligent machine. In the Jacquard loom, patterns punched into paper cards ran the complex weaving operations. On the model of this loom, Charles Babbage conceived of his never completed "Analytical Engine," the first modern computer, a universal machine that could be programmed to perform different functions. This blurring of the boundary between the category of the human and the mechanical remains one of the most lasting legacies of the first industrial age.

The New Industrial Age

By the 1860s the structure of industrialism had changed. Workers continued to toil in factory and mill, but under new limited liability laws ownership of a factory and mill by a single master gave way to ownership by a corporation. The entrepreneurial vigor of the independent capitalist whose fortune was one with his firm disappeared; his place was taken by a new figure, corporate or managerial man, divorced from contact with the worker, separate from the activity of production. The white-collar worker, the clerk, and the accountant employed in a large office and preoccupied with job security, promotion, and pension, each a prop of the lower-middle-class status he was desperately concerned to maintain, became the central figure in the new landscape of corporate industry. So, too, the landscape of the industrial city shifted. The population at the center of industrial cities declined as the outer ring filled with respectable suburban terraces from which clerks commuted by tram and railway to their offices in the central city.

Working-class women, primarily unmarried women, of course continued to work. The entry of middle-class women into the work force in the later nineteenth century was an overdetermined development, but one enabling factor was the creation of respectable female employment in the managerial domain that stood at one remove from the factory floor. Starting in the 1880s the job of office assistant or secretary gradually shifted from a male to a female activity. The literature of the later decades of the century engaging the condition of women turns not on how females might moralize the male sphere of industry, but rather on how they might learn new technologies and participate in the managerial sphere. The association of the female with the newly invented typewriter is represented in works as diverse as *Dracula* (1897) and George Gissing's *The Odd Women* (1893).

During the later nineteenth century class conflict was not resolved, but it assumed a different shape. Against the fierce arguments of the early industrialists, by mid-century the principle of government regulation of working hours and factory safety had been established. The work day for the textile mills had been set at ten and a half hours, the work week at sixty hours, and the worst abuses of child labor had been eradicated. By the late 1860s large trade unions, unions organized along craft or occupational lines, had become legal. With some exceptions, such as Bloody Sunday of 1877 when police violently broke up a socialist meeting in Trafalgar Square, class conflict had been absorbed into the political process. By the end of the century the Labour Party had become a powerful force.

By the 1860s workers in England still toiled in factories and in mills, railways still ran, industrial cities still bellowed smoke into the air, but industrial novels had ceased to be written. We can only speculate as to the reasons for the strange death of this genre. Perhaps there was no longer the shock of the new, as the industrial world of the midlands was absorbed into common consciousness, unremarkable as a tree or a flock of sheep to a countryman. Perhaps, too, the salary man puttering in the small garden of his respectable semi-detached house did not offer the heroic possibilities of a captain of industry such as John Thornton or the broad comic possibilities of a Bounderby. Unlike their contemporaries Frank Norris in America and Emile Zola in France, bourgeois English writers turned from the ongoing oppression and struggle of the working class.

The turn of late-Victorian high literature and art from the practice of realism and the subject of industrialism marks the triumph of the domain of "culture" (Gallagher 1985; Poovey 1995). Asserting the autonomy and the identity of the aesthetic and the psychological continued the project of "culture" begun with the coming of industrialism, constructing an alternative realm to the industrial. Henry James's valorization of psychological complexity, Pater's locating the "real" in the flux of inward sensation, Whistler's transformation of London warehouses to bits of color in his Nocturnes all manifest the desire for a counter-world of pure immaterial feeling, eradicating from art the material forms, working people, and energy of the industrial.

At the end of the nineteenth century the saga of industrialism found a new hero, the imperialist. However multiform the reasons for the intense expansion of British and European colonialism in the 1880s, certainly one major impulse was that the limitless productivity built into industrial capitalism demanded global markets, particularly with saturation of the domestic market. Whatever role the imperialist actor took – explorer of lands unmapped by Europeans, officer or soldier in an imperial army conquering and controlling indigenous peoples, colonial administrator, colonial merchant – his way of life maintained industrialism by guaranteeing consumers abroad for the patterned cloth and the metal knives that continued to pour from the mills and factories of Manchester and Birmingham.

See also 1848; Moving Out, Sexualities; Commercial; Fiction; Parapets

References

Briggs, Asa (1993) *Victorian Cities*. Berkeley: University of California Press.

Engels, Frederick [1845] (1984) *The Condition* *of the Working Class in England, From Personal Observation and Authentic Sources*. Chicago: Academy.

Foucault, Michel (1977) *Discipline and Punish: The Birth of the Prison*, trans. Alan Sheridan. New York: Pantheon.

Froude, James Anthony (1882) *Thomas Carlyle: A History of the First Forty Years of His Life, 1795–1835*, 2 vols. London: Longmans, Green.

——(1884) *Thomas Carlyle: A History of His Life in London, 1834–81*, 2 vols. London: Longmans, Green.

Gagnier, Regenia (1991) *Subjectivities: A History of Self-Representation in Britain, 1832–1920*. Oxford: Oxford University Press.

Gallagher, Catherine (1985) *The Industrial Reformation of English Fiction: Social Discourse and Narrative Form, 1832–67*. Chicago: University of Chicago Press.

Giedion, Siegfried (1948) *Mechanization Takes Command: A Contribution to Anonymous History*. New York: Norton.

Poovey, Mary (1995) *Making a Social Body: British Cultural Formation, 1830–64*. Chicago: University of Chicago Press.

Schivelbusch, Wolfgang (1986) *The Railway Journey: The Industrialization of Time and Space in the 19th Century*. Berkeley: University of California Press.

Thompson, E. P. (1966) *The Making of the English Working Class*. New York: Vintage.

Vicinus, Martha (1974) *The Industrial Muse: A Study of Nineteenth Century British Working Class Poetry*. New York: Barnes and Noble.

Williams, Raymond (1966) *Culture and Society, 1780–1950*. New York: Harper & Row.

——(1983) *Keywords: A Vocabulary of Culture and Society, Revised Edition*. New York: Oxford University Press.

FURTHER READING

Bodenheimer, Rosemarie (1988) *The Politics of Story in Victorian Social Fiction*. Ithaca, NY: Cornell University Press.

Certeau, Michel de (1984) "Railway Navigation and Incarceration." In *The Practice of Everyday Life*. Berkeley: University California Press.

Hobsbawm, E. J. (1989) *The Age of Empire, 1875–1914*. New York: Vintage.

Rabinbach, Anson (1992) *The Human Motor: Energy, Fatigue, and the Origins of Modernity*. Berkeley: University of California Press.

Seltzer, Mark (1992) *Bodies and Machines*. New York: Routledge.

Serres, Michel (1992) *Hermes: Literature, Science,*

Philosophy, ed. Josué V. Harari and David F. Bell. Baltimore: Johns Hopkins University Press.

Sussman, Herbert L. (1968) *Victorians and the Machine: The Literary Response to Technology*. Cambridge, MA: Harvard University Press.

Ure, Andrew (1835) *The Philosophy of Manufactures: An Exposition of the Scientific, Moral, and Commercial Economy of the Factory System of Great Britain*. London: Charles Knight.

Ward, J. T. (1962) *The Factory Movement: 1830–55*. London: Macmillan.

Woodward, Llewellyn (1962) *The Age of Reform, 1815–70*. Oxford: Oxford University Press

18

Commercial

Jennifer Wicke

The Uncommercial Traveller (first edition, 1861), Charles Dickens's extraordinary collection of sketches of British life, begins with what its first-person narrator, a traveling writer not to be confused with Dickens himself, calls a "negative introduction": by presenting his "brief credentials" as the opposite of those held by a commercial traveler, in short, by listing what the uncommercial traveler is *not*, Dickens's disingenuous stand-in outlines the terrain of Victorian commerce:

> No landlord is my friend and brother, no chambermaid loves me, no waiter worships me, no boots admires and envies me. No round of beef or tongue or ham is expressly cooked for me, no pigeon-pie is expressly made for me, no hotel-advertisement is personally addressed to me, no hotel-room tapestried with greatcoats and railways wrappers is set apart for me, no house of public entertainment in the United Kingdom greatly cares for my opinion of its brandy or sherry. When I go upon my journeys, I am not usually rated at a low figure in the bill; when I come home from my journeys, I never get any commission. I know nothing about prices, and should have no idea, if I were put to it, how to wheedle a man into ordering something he doesn't want. As a town traveller, I am never to be seen driving a vehicle externally like a young and volatile pianoforte van, and internally like an oven in which a number of flat boxes are baking in layers. As a country traveller, I am rarely to be found in a gig, and am never to be encountered by a pleasure train, waiting on the platform of a branch station, quite a Druid in the midst of a light Stonehenge of samples.

If we reverse the negatives in this paragraph, a panoramic visual catalogue of the contours of commercial life at mid-century magically appears, the trick revealing the rabbit of commerce hidden within the twists and turns of the passage. Dickens's narrator professes to travel not on business per se, but for "the great house of Human Interest Brothers," and to "have rather a large connection in the fancy goods way." The book as a whole is an ethnography of Victorian commerce, with the narrator a type of travel-writer *manqué*, who is also free to indulge in fictionalization. The metaphor of the writer as traveling salesman, who brokers human interest and who delivers the language of fiction as fancy goods, already establishes the pervasiveness of commerce in the period, the dissemination of its special vocabulary, and the mediating nature of literature as a fancy goods business in its own right.

To discuss "commerce" in Victorian literature and culture is a tricky negotiation, almost seeming to call for the same device of negative definition deployed by Dickens. The challenge for this chapter is to extricate commerce from its companion terms and practices. It is easier to say what commerce is not, than what it is: we can perhaps agree that commerce is business, although immediately the latter word requires more specificity, since commerce is not restricted to industry, despite industrialization's role as the driving engine of modern commerce. On the other side of the coin, literally, commerce cannot be confused, although it always threatens to be, with the circulation of money, or with money in the abstract, since commerce is not restricted to finance, albeit intimately connected with wealth in all its forms. Dickens's homegrown if negative descriptions of a traveler immersed in the warm bath of commerce can helpfully delineate the outlines of commercial culture for us: commerce might truthfully be said to be all that is not uncommercial – and that turns out to be a remarkably small set of activities, in Victorian Britain as elsewhere.

More than this, the word "commerce" is a cultural coinage, a discursive entity as much as a "real" state of affairs. The discourse of commerce reflects upon itself across the Victorian century, in the form of philosophical and political critiques, in literary works of poetry and prose, in the guise of economic history and flamboyant rhetoric alike. "Commerce" permits a huge volume of cultural work to be done, and unlike the realms of capitalist industry or capitalist high finance, whose discourses were largely reserved for experts, Victorian commerce has a discourse which cuts across boundaries of class and education, political persuasion and profession, ranging from the popular to the rarefied: everyone talks about commerce in Victorian Britain, everyone employs its vocabulary, and almost anyone can buff or tarnish its discursive surface. Commerce as a word or category has this nebulous, fantasmatic side to it: it is brought into being, or recognized, in and through a special and specific language, nominally a culture-wide possession, but often as not through the back-door of what it is *not*.

After all, following out the arc of Dickens's antinarrative, commerce is embedded in or exemplified by the menu at a restaurant, a glass of sherry, railway schedules, paved roads, tourist outings, magazine advertisements, shoe polishing and sales techniques. Commerce covers virtually all of the exchanges between and among human beings in daily life, from the most humble and limited personal errands, to shop-going, businesses of commissions and sales, international trade, and imperial commerce. Our category for commerce has to be broad enough to admit the pies sold by the village baker, the large commercial firm of the sort depicted in *Dombey and Son* (1848), the funeral home business and Covent Garden marketplace, the manufacture and distribution of books by publishers such as Chapman and Hall, who put out *The Uncommercial Traveller*, and the public lecture-tour manager: the agent, say, who brought such profit to Dickens through commercializing his readings that the great uncommercial traveler himself died from exhaustion. This handful of examples should be enough to indicate the wide parameters of commerce, and also to indicate its long past, which stretches back to prehistoric societies.

As the Victorian theorist of political economy Karl Marx was to demonstrate in *Capital* (1867), the fruit of years of research and writing from his carrel in the British Museum's Reading Room, capitalism was a relatively modern phenomenon in history, originating in Renaissance Europe and only culminating in the later eighteenth century as a decisive rival capable of superseding – and overthrowing – the agricultural *ancien régime*. By mid-century, as Marx began his seminal work and Queen Victoria had settled into her long reign, capitalism had become the most descriptive single word for the British economic system. Commerce now emerged under the general heading of capitalism, the latter word being indeed a synonym for organized commerce. It is a synonym which cannot be allowed to slip into tautology, however – even in Victorian Britain, as in Europe and the United States, capitalism did not encompass all of commerce. Marx's genius, in following his great Victorian mentor Charles Darwin (without the latter's knowledge, of course), was to discern the forest of capitalism out of the discrete trees of commerce, to deduce what he thought of as the natural laws governing that forest of human making, and to chart its historical evolution over time, even as Darwin's *The Origin of Species* (1859) formulated the evolutionary laws governing the natural world.

One way of locating Victorian commerce would be to trace the capitalization of its commerce, staying alert to those commercial practices or forms that persist as vestiges of ages-old commercial behavior outside, or in relation to, the capitalist concentration of the market. One small literary example of the persistence of older modes of commerce within capitalist commerce is the portrait of the hand laundry run by Old Betty in Dickens's *Bleak House* (1853). Her laundry, whose mangle is famously turned by the lost boy Jo, is a manifestation of noncapitalist commerce, a cottage industry as it were, except that Betty is only able to launder for enough money to buy those few manufactured staples she and everyone else rely upon for food, clothing, and shelter – her commerce takes place in a shadowy corner of the ever-expanding house of capitalist commercialization. Eventually, poverty forces the elderly Betty to try to elude the workhouse by traveling the roads until her death, an uncommercial traveler of another kind. Victorian literature is a privileged site for witnessing the collisions of earlier with later modes of commerce, not all of them so catastrophic as Betty's, some even more so. As a heuristic tool for interpretation or a lens with which to view Victorian culture, commerce enables a more internally differentiated, dare one say heteroglossic glimpse of socioeconomics than an analysis of capital tends to do; theories of capital perhaps necessarily elide the coexistence of commercial forms, and again perhaps necessarily occult the creativity, as well as the destructiveness, of commercial behavior. Betty's fate, like Jo's and any number of other Victorian literary characters', is a synecdoche for the immiseration of millions of actual people; at the same time, even Marx observed the powerful benefits of capitalist commerce, and acerbically noted their absence in "backward" Asian societies under "Oriental despotism" (ch. 12).

Coming at commerce from the other direction, that is, by way of money and finance instead of capitalist industrialization, leads to some of the same ironies and complexities. Commerce did not and does not always involve money, as there can be trades for goods or services which bypass the money form. Commerce in the sense of human commercial exchange is self-evidently ancient, and includes the practices of barter, the public market or bazaar, trade, and even slavery. Some of these types of commerce survive well into the Victorian era, coexisting with financial activities in many cases. The literary staging of this overlap between nonmonetary commerce and financial commerce – i.e. nonmarket and market commerce – occurs repeatedly in the work of Thomas Hardy. His pseudo-imaginary county of Wessex is largely rural and agricultural but contains several market towns, and many of his works feature the surviving rural tradition of the market fair as a pivot of their action. These traveling market fairs were held at regular intervals in the larger towns – thus their name – and drew people from far-flung villages to join in trading their wares or foodstuffs, at the same time as they enjoyed entertainments like music, dancing, games, and festivals. Hardy depicts startling customs still obtaining at the market fair, such as the public auction or sale of wives, along with less disturbing medieval remnants like puppet shows or contests of skill. *Tess of the D'Urbervilles* (1884) is only one of several books which represent the vigorous market fair tradition gradually being eroded or invaded by what Carlyle first called "the cash nexus," and we may call the modern market – invisible, anonymous, abstract. Tess Durbeyfield, oldest daughter of a poverty-stricken family of small farmers, sets out early in the tale for the market fair, loaded with the jars of honey her mother hopes to have her exchange there, for other food items and for a chance to hear the newest songs. By the novel's end, Tess has been imprisoned for murder, and is hung from the prison gallows on the hillside, while below in the town the market fair commences again. Before this fatal crux is met, Tess travels restlessly throughout her small pocket of Wessex, which increasingly becomes inhospitable to barter or exchange. Eventually, driven by poverty and eviction, she hires on as a farm laborer working for wages, side by side with a menacing threshing machine, harvesting grain to be sold at markets outside the county, and even outside the country, far from the music of any market fair. The selling of the grain novelistically threshed by the character Tess, and even the selling of "grain futures" in the financial markets, based on predicted rates of production, are both indubitably "commerce." So, however, is the business transacted in the pub secreted behind closed curtains in a village neighbor's living room, and the purchase of the ordinary jar of marmalade which Tess uses emptied as a marker for her dead child's grave. Commerce in Hardy's market fair persists in an intermediate state, where money is only part of the commercial equation.

"Commerce," then, is a ductile word, capable of many meanings, but perhaps best captured by the sense of trading hands, whether exchange passes literally from hand to hand or takes place on a more systemic plane – the "macrolevel" of commerce, where trade is king. The denigrating sense of the phrase "to be in trade" persists as a sneer and a smear to this very day in Britain. Even commerce that produces staggering wealth carries a whiff of the hand-to-hand materiality of "trade," and it is correspond-ingly disdained – only high finance or land-based wealth can purify commerce of its lower-class vestiges – and a title, as many a Victorian gentleman came to recognize, didn't hurt either. In *A History of Commerce* (1907), the major text of its period, the economist Dr Clive Day of Yale declares emphatically that in "the study of the development of commerce in different countries we shall take up first the country which at the beginning of the nineteenth century, and at its end as well, held the leading position, England" (Day 1907: 344). Victorian Britain was the unequivocal leader of the entire world, because it was the world leader in trade. In addition to the careful historical and statistical researches which describe this preeminence, Day's analysis includes an account of the politics of trade that allowed for Britain's su-premacy. In the modern world as in the ancient, trade is carried out between countries or nations. The importance of this for an understanding of Victorian commerce cannot be underestimated, since it was through exports and imports that Britain became a commercial powerhouse. Even in 1907 economic historians could see the significance of three major developments of the latter half of the nineteenth century:

> (1) The English people were the most advanced, in industrial and mercantile ability, of any people in the world. . . . (2) The geographical situation of England, and the physical resources of the country, especially its coal, made the English superior to most peoples and equal to any, in this age of transportation and manufacture by steam. (3) The commercial policy of the government allowed the people to make the most of their advantages. (Ibid.: 367)

What Day meant by the last of these three reasons, although hardly the least, was the huge political upheaval that brought about free trade in Victorian England.

The critical political maneuvers which changed commercial policy were effected by parliamentarian Sir Robert Peel's bills of 1842, which secured the reduction of crippling tax duties on 750 items, and of 1845, which abolished 430 out of 813 import duties. Until the reform movement began in the 1820s, Britain had languished under restrictive taxes which hindered trade at every turn, and which forbade "free" trade in every instance. Customs tariffs on imports were astronomical, and duties on exports equally prohibitive. So paralyzing were these taxes that smuggling was actu-ally a regulated profession, with a tariff modeled on, but of course lower than, the regular tariff. Smuggled goods, such as silk handkerchiefs, were openly brandished – Day recounts that a member of the House of Commons whipped his out of his pocket and said, "Here is a foreign ware that is totally prohibited. Nearly every one of you has a similar illicit article in his pocket. So much for your prohibition" (ibid.: 355). Such a pocket handkerchief veto was augmented intellectually when London merchants with a vested interest in the free swish of silken scarves urged a return to the principles of free trade outlined by Adam Smith in his *Wealth of Nations* (1776). The restrictions imposed by the government even extended to a ban on the emigration of skilled workmen, who were seen as an "export" the government refused to allow. The reform movement eased emigration procedures, so that the free trade in goods was accompanied by a freer trade in human skills across national boundaries. The irony of this facet of reform in light of the international slave trade – an embedded feature of Victorian global commerce despite the national Abolition Act of 1833 – cannot be overlooked.

William Gladstone's bills of 1853 and 1860 capped a free-trade campaign whose most visible struggle had involved repeal of the corn laws. Importation of grain was prevented by the high custom duties which the landed classes, and their aristocratic representatives in Parliament, had demanded; while Britain in the nineteenth century was decisively becoming a manufacturing, not an agricultural, economy, the aristocracy still held sway in government. The Anti-Corn Law League movement began outside Parliament, with a mercantile group who insisted that the high price of basic foodstuffs brought on by the protection of British grain, when it was produced so much more cheaply elsewhere, was a life-or-death question for commerce and thus for the body politic. Laborers could not afford to buy bread on their wages; the crop failures of 1841, and the Great Hunger in Ireland of 1845 and after, indicated clearly that Britain could no longer afford to produce its own food, let alone export it. The repeal of the corn laws in 1846 was "a momentous act in English history. It marks the formal and final recognition that England had grown from an agricultural to an industrial and commercial state" (Day 1907: 387). Any number of Victorian literary works illuminate the ostensibly dry debates over commerce in corn, wheat, and barley, casting into sharp relief their human ramifications. An extremely poignant charting of these ramifications occurs across the oeuvre of Charles Lever, an Anglo-Irish novelist whose effervescent Irish sporting-life novels give way over time, and in the aftermath of the famine, to an engagement with political and economic forces which together have conspired to obliterate so many Irish lives, through death or forced emigration. Ireland was perforce an agricultural colony, not allowed to develop commercially outside of British control, and the devastation wreaked there by the failure of the potato crop was due in part to the refusal either to import foodstuffs or to set aside its own harvest, earmarked for exportation to England, for the feeding of the starving Irish populace. Writing in Britain, and as a member of the Anglo-Irish ascendancy, Lever nonetheless conveys the agony of these commercial machinations as they filter down to real people. His final work, *Lord Kilgobben* (1872), is set squarely on a desolate bog, whose boundaries are so inhospitable to commerce that they form a no-man's land.

England's emergence as a commercial colossus gave growing power to the middle classes in Parliament and in civil society, even as it shifted the tenor of world relations. Victorian Britain's imports exceeded even her massive exports by century's end. The table of commercial trade levels for 1880 is eye-opening; imports amounted to $1,720,000,000; exports to $1,700,000,000. The imbalance may strike a reader as belying the nation's commercial strength. Far from it – what this statistic reveals about Victorian commerce in Britain is the liminal quality of its importations. The ship-owning nature of British commerce meant that Britain was carrying goods and passengers all over the world – a form of profitable export hidden within the import column. England received huge commissions on facilitating trade between other countries, another export masquerading as an import. Finally, the British empire entailed capital investment around the globe; Britain's many imports from its own colonies were further exports disguised as investment dividends and stock options. While two-fifths of British trade was with all the combined countries of Europe, another one-fourth was with its colonies, especially British India, of which Victoria had been named Empress; in the third place at century's end was trade with a single country, the United States. The special trading relationship between Victorian England and the US has implications of a postcolonial kind, which reverberate in such major events as the US Civil War. Dickens's *Martin Chuzzlewit* (1844) gives a jaundiced version of this active commercial alliance, wherein a morally bankrupt and corrupt United States tricks innocent Britishers into immigration by proffering a vision of paradise that turns out to be a fraudulent land deal.

Free trade is a misnomer in the most egalitarian of times; when imperialism reached its height by the 1880s, the phrase became more than a misnomer – it was a scandal. There is nothing "free" about trade in a colonial or imperial relationship, and as Britain commanded the largest world empire since ancient Rome, its commercial trade increasingly took place under the sign of empire. Possibly the greatest late Victorian political economist was J. A. Hobson, the man who explained British imperialism, and argued against it, or at least certain forms of it, at the historical zenith of British commerce. Hobson's *On Imperialism* (1897) examined the transmutation of commerce into the differing forms of imperialism, which each had their own mode of commercial production, whether the extraction of raw materials was paramount, or the creation of new consumer markets in the case of settled colonies, or the extension of financial markets, as in the stock speculation on far-away imperial ventures in mining or railroad construction. He joined another unlikely Victorian, the Polish Joseph Conrad, in protesting the most virulently exploitative forms of imperialism, such as the genocidal imperialism of the Belgian Congo: King Leopold's atrocities there served as the basis for *Heart of Darkness* (1899), for Hobson's own critique, and for the concerted efforts of the anti-Leopold league they both belonged to. In another register, more analytic than ethical, Hobson pointed out the tension between the economic interests of empire and nation – he saw that imperial commerce would negatively affect everything from prices to employment levels back at "home." This commercial split between global, imperial markets and homegrown, national activity, which Hobson had the prescience to see, shows once again what we glimpsed above in Hardy's fiction: that Victorian commerce, for all its might, was less univocal and less monolithic than we might think. To be sure, the goals of commerce are not altruistic – the profit motive is forever at the fore. Still, there is commerce, and then there is commerce. In those kindly merchants the Cheeryble brothers (*Nicholas Nickleby*, 1839) Dickens depicts – not without special pleading and sentimentality, to be sure – the flip side of Mrs Jellyby in *Bleak House*: the brothers preside like Santa

Claus twins over a firm run for the benefit of its British workers. The Quaker brothers in Mrs Gaskell's *Sylvia's Lovers* (1863) offer another portrait of commerce as the milk of human kindness. For these Victorian writers the civilizing mission of commerce begins, and belongs, at home.

One remarkable apologist for commerce as the quintessence of civilization, where fraud and exploitation are exceptions to a spendid rule, was the Victorian economic historian/ideologue H. Gordon Selfridge, who waxes poetic in his opening peroration to *The Romance of Commerce*, a 1902 book whose title surely says it all: "To write on the subject of Commerce or Trade and do the subject justice would require more volumes than any library could hold, and involve more detail than any mind could grasp. It would be a history *in extenso* of the world's people from the beginning of time" (Selfridge 1902: 1). Selfridge properly widens his canvas of commerce to include all of time and human history, but then zeroes in nonetheless on the glories of English merchants and traders. Rather endearingly, he proposes that the most salient human talents are commercial, so much so that any worthwhile human endeavor is mercantile. Selfridge anoints all people ("except the idlers") as merchants, his highest accolade, and credits their efforts as commercial in essence. "We give this title exclusively to the man who buys and sells merchandise, but the artist sells the work of his brush, and in this he is a merchant. The writer sells to any who will buy, let his ideas be what they will. The teacher sells his knowledge of books – often in too low a market – to those who would have this knowledge passed on to the young . . ." And so on *ad infinitum*, with the doctor, the lawyer, the statesman, the preacher, the actor, the farmer, the employee: "all have something to dispose of at a profit to themselves, and the dignity of the business is decided by the manner in which they conduct the sale" (ibid.: 2–3). Selfridge's bestowal of his mark of favor upon so many professions, endeavors, and ways of life, is actually an incisive move: it has taken nearly a century to acknowledge without a knee-jerk recoil that commercial practices enmesh literature, art, education, religion, science. Selfridge embraces this fact a little too ardently and uncritically, but his apotheosis of commerce is nonetheless a helpful corrective to the entirely minatory view of commerce as an interloper and a threat. For every merchant prince or capitalist owner, there is also an equivalent to Mr Venus, the eccentric shopkeeper of Dickens's *Our Mutual Friend* (1865), who plies his trade as the articulator of skeletons and bizarre taxidermist, selling moribund, fantastical marvels of a necrophiliac's dream. There is a market, it would seem, for anything.

The "wild romance and adventure," the "fantasies of commerce" Selfridge wishes to wring from his account of commerce, have affinities with art-making; he wants to invest the domain of commerce with the aura of art, and vice versa. In another uncanny and surely unwitting imitation of Marxist analysis the book argues for the totality of commerce in human life:

> Just as in a beautiful tapestry there must be the groundwork, the foundation upon which the design is woven, so has Commerce acted as the underlying warp and woof in the development of civilization. . . . Or to change the simile, Commerce is the foundation

upon which nations are built; but it is also the superstructure, and provides the bands of steel which support every part of the national edifice. (Selfridge 1902: 348)

Granted, this is over the top rhetorically, but the echoes of "base" and "superstructure," the emphasis on interwoven indistinguishability, pose a problem for those who would see the paragraph as pure ideology. If it is nothing but that, how then does it anticipate the very terms used to critique what has come to be called the ideology of capitalism? Selfridge's paean to commerce wonderfully typifies the positive Victorian outlook on commerce, yet its rhetorical fabric reveals once again the puzzling, elusive nature of commerce as a discourse: commerce is groundwork, but also foreground, base but also superstructure; it is the tensile strength of the threads that make up the cloth of society, while it is also the evanescent sheen of color and the shimmering design inscribed in that tapestry. There is an echo here of the indeterminacy found in Conrad's famous description of narrativity in chapter one of *Heart of Darkness*, where the narrator Marlow says that in contrast to the seaman's tale, which wraps a nutshell around a kernel of meaning inside, his story unfolds only "as a glow brings out a haze." The "spectral illumination of moonshine," suggesting a meaning so lambent and diffuse that it cannot really be located, exists in tandem in the book with Marlow's (and presumably Conrad's) Victorian paean to work – "work has a kind of truth to it" – and with the ambivalence each brings to the commercial work of empire. Selfridge, too, exalts work (commerce in its active form) with such effusions as "work may be full of excitement, of satisfaction, of joy and happiness" if accompanied by "the springs of imagination," in the "alchemy" that is Commerce (Selfridge 1902: 358). He is unexpectedly Conradian in seeing commerce as both stalwart and gossamer, a haze around a glow around a nut with kernel intact: in other words, an essentially imaginative affair.

There is a canker in the romantic rose of commerce, however, and that canker is advertising. Selfridge will not award advertisement any commercial laurels; for him, it is a parasitic worm on commerce's body. Advertising inevitably lies, according to him, and "we need a new philosophy here" (ibid.: 424). Selfridge turns out to be wrong; as historical hindsight lets us see, advertising *was* the new philosophy, and Victorian commerce is unthinkable without it. A thread of argument across this chapter involves the mediated nature of Victorian commerce: commerce does not go unaccompanied, as Selfridge might have it, into its multifarious transactions. Commerce in the Victorian period and afterwards required a mediating nimbus, usually conferred by advertising. Of course, advertising taken separately is also commerce, and the establishment of advertising agencies in 1845 in Britain, and in 1865 in the United States, marked the beginning of a unique commercial history, as advertising became a business, and its agencies "shops." Commercial exchanges of all sorts, from the local to the global, from the Victorian era forward needed the conduit of an advertising message to funnel goods, to announce their availability, to explain their superiority, to blazon their identities. The goods of commerce were invisible, as H. G. Wells may have surmised, without their advertising cloaks. Not all of Victorian culture is as resistant to advertisement as Selfridge appears to be, and Victorian literature especially is replete with references to, and adjudications of, this new commercial philosophy.

Anthony Trollope's novel *The Struggles of Brown, Jones, and Robinson* (1862) is a storehouse of commercial references; its first sentence invokes the commercial aspects of reading in the Victorian age, when its narrator, one George Robinson, modestly demurs at having his name on the title page of what he insists is a memoir. "It will be observed by the literary and commercial witnesses" (i.e. readers) to this "transaction" (i.e. the book), he says, that he had no wish to court a "lawsuit" from the firm of Brown, Jones, and Robinson by having his "name advertised as the author of this account." What follows is a satirical send-up of a legal disclaimer-cum-advertisement for the book the reader currently holds in hand, as Robinson traces his conversations with the other members of the firm on the issue of authorship. It quickly becomes apparent that the firm these three contentious partners belong to is an advertising firm. Robinson's narrative is a doubled one – as he scores points off his "vain" and "old-fashioned" partners he simultaneously gives us a rhapsodic business lesson: "Advertise, advertise, advertise. And I say it again – advertise, advertise, advertise! It should be the motto of British commerce." Robinson clues us in to the new demands of commerce:

> It won't suffice now-a-days to stick up on a blank wall a simple placard to say that you have forty thousand best hose just arrived. Any wooden-headed fellow can do as much as that. That might have served in the olden time that we hear of twenty years since; but the game to be successful in these days must be played in another sort of fashion. There must be some finish about your advertisements, something new in your style, something that will startle in your manner. If a man can make himself a real master of this art, we may say that he has learnt his trade, whatever that trade may be. Let him know how to advertise, and the rest will follow.

Robinson's clarion call sets the tone of a work that wittily professes to recount "the commercial, not the domestic histories" of the firm of Brown, Jones, and Robinson, as it sticks to the last of advertisement. Chapter two is ushered in on a reverent note of worship: "O Commerce, how wonderful are thy ways, how vast thy power, how invisible thy dominion!" Despite the palpable irony hovering over Trollope's deadpan treatment of this discourse, his book beautifully displays the invasion of advertisement into all styles of writing, including the literary, and exposes by default the invisible omnipotence of the commerce it accompanies.

Buried in the Victorian triple-decker *No Name* (1862) is a veritable dissertation on advertising philosophy. Wilkie Collins's novel is chock-full of commercial nuggets of the greatest interest, but to touch only on advertising is to hit a mother lode. Without sketching the action of this complex book, it suffices to know that Magdalen Vanstone, the No Name of the title, who has been stripped of her surname and inheritance by a latter-day revelation of illegitimacy, is living incognito as a traveling actress. She is attended in her exile by the Wragges, a dubious couple consisting of the acute and devious Captain Wragge, and his slow-witted but deeply good and probably battered wife. The trio are staying in the neighborhood of Vauxhall Gardens, the fabled public amusement park, now defunct: "where the beauty and fashion of London feasted and danced through the summer seasons of a century – spreads, at this day, an awful wilderness of mud and rubbish; the deserted dead body of Vauxhall Gardens mouldering in the open air." On the "site where thousands of lights [once] twinkled" now "Commerce is not turbulent, nor is the public consumer besieged by loud invitations to 'buy'." The dead body of commerce is a forlorn, even a tragic spectacle; and the silencing of voices exhorting customers to buy, however hectoring to the ear, is evidently a loss, a kind of death. Collins situates a major section of the narrative at the crossroads of older commerce – the once-magical Vauxhall Gardens – with newer possibilities, provided by advertising, department stores, and theater, and largely imaginary in kind.

> Mrs. Wragge was seated at the table, absorbed in the arrangement of a series of smart circulars and tempting price-lists, issued by advertising trades-people, and flung in at the cab-windows as they left the London terminus. "I've often heard tell of light reading," said Mrs. Wragge, restlessly shifting the position of the circulars, ". . . here's light reading, printed out in pretty colors. Here's all the Things I'm going to buy when I'm out shopping tomorrow. Lend us a pencil, please – you won't be angry, will you? – I do so want to mark 'em off." She looked up at Magdalen, chuckled joyfully over her own altered circumstances, and beat her great hands on the table in irrepressible delight. . . . Her hands began to drum on the table louder than ever, until Magdalen quieted them by presenting her with a pencil. Mrs. Wragge instantly recovered her dignity, squared her elbows on the table, and plunged into imaginary shopping for the rest of the evening.

Mrs Wragge's childlike delight in her imaginary shopping is more than slightly pathetic, but bathos aside, her pleasure in conjuring a shopping world out of light reading is portrayed as a redemptive respite from her travails at home. The ads on pretty paper are accepted as fiction, rather than reviled as lies, and Mrs Wragge's mental shopping exercises her imagination as few things can in the "wilderness" of her uncommercial, unhappy surroundings. She catalogues her potential purchases with the exacting precision of a crazed accountant:

> "Give us the pencil," said Mrs. Wragge, shuffling the circulars in a violent hurry. "I can't go to bed yet – I haven't half done marking down the things I want. Let's see, where did I leave off? *Try Finch's feeding-bottle for infants.* No! There's a cross against that: the cross means I don't want it . . . *Elegant cashmere robes; strictly oriental, very grand; reduced to one pound, nineteen, and sixpence. Be in time. Only three left.* Only three! Oh, do lend us the money and let's go and get one!" (Third Scene, ch. 1)

Mrs Wragge does get her strictly oriental robe later in the book, as a commercial consummation devoutly to be wished by the reader; Magdalen Vanstone, through other means than shopping, i.e. via the chicanery of a sham marriage, gets her name back. The posters advertising her performances under an assumed name have made her a household word, a desirable commodity, and thus commerce has given her leverage in the marriage market. Both transactions are commercial, and nominative, and they are so in reciprocally determinative ways. Advertising, on the positive side of its ledger, does provide a name and thus a habitation for desire, and Collins's novel reveals the unsettling limbo of modern commerce, where nothing can have no name.

Inability to fix the parameters of commerce, and susceptibility to its glamour, in contradistinction to its grubby practicalities, affects most of the key Victorian critics of commerce. Although Selfridge begins his book with an epigraph from John Ruskin, wherein Ruskin declares there to be "five great intellectual professions existing in every civilized nation," with Merchants (ranked number two) figuring among Soldiers, Pastors, Physicians, and Lawyers in their unique duty "to provide for" the nation, Selfridge was in fact Ruskin's opponent in the Victorian debate about commerce. Ruskin, along with other Victorian social prophets like Thomas Carlyle and William Morris, was obsessed with commerce and its depradations, and in his massive works dealing with commerce single-handedly established a large corner of the market on discourse about commerce, as distinct from commercial discourse. In a centenary volume of 1912 celebrating Ruskin's birth, the late-Victorian economist Hobson meticulously delineates Ruskin's abiding importance. Hobson acidly refers to the contempt excited in the business mind by Ruskin's claim to be "a teacher of the science and the art of political economy." Seeing him as an interloper in the field, Ruskin's critics asked, "But what could an art critic, a literary dilettante, know about the business world? To the academic, as to the business man, it never seems to have occurred that wealth is primarily a quality, not a quantity, and that the understanding or appreciation of that quality demanded qualifications which Ruskin had, and they had not." This fascinating declaration of the qualitative dimension of commerce or business, of its inherent aesthetic and Ruskin's concomitant skills in teasing out those qualities, accompanies Hobson's critique of political economy after Adam Smith, and explains his preference for Ruskin over John Stuart Mill and other experts. Smith's liberal vision of the discipline was supplanted by a "degrading process," in Hobson's words, where political economy became the "bondslave of the rising manufacturing and trading classes, who needed it to work their intellectual mill." Ruskin's knowledge of both work and consumption, and his "subtle mastery of words," allowed him a wider purview than the hired guns of economic thought could command. "Everywhere the loose materialism of commerce has obscured the human significance of industrial terminology as of industrial processes themselves." The very words of commerce – value, profit, consumption – have an extraordinary significance, for which Ruskin may be the best guide. How one chooses to gloss these words changes what they mean, and what constitutes commerce (Hobson 1920: 83–4).

Hobson is as acutely aware of Ruskin's blindnesses as of his insights. Ruskin valorized the landed gentry, possibly thanks to his enjoyable carriage rides in the country as a small child, and he ultimately idealized the upper classes as "composed of the best bred, the most energetic and most thoughtful of the population." These blind spots aside, however, what Ruskin's treatment of commerce provided was a shift from a quantitative economy to a qualitative economy, based on "vital satisfaction" rather than pecuniary value. Hobson, who should know, goes so far as to call this teaching "genuinely revolutionary," for its insistence upon consumption and not production as the final goal of economic activity. Consumption, Ruskin saw, entailed the resolution of commercial into human values, for value could be measured only in the form of the "vital use" people can enjoy from what they consume – whether wholesome food or beautiful art. Ruskin states it thus: "A horse is no wealth to us if we cannot ride, nor a picture if we cannot see, nor any noble thing be wealth except to a noble person" ("The Political Economy of Art," 1857). By putting the end-value of consumption before the fore-value of production, Ruskin vigorously transformed the configuration of commerce at the intellectual level, as his admonitions about the conditions of work and the division of wealth did on the social. Ruskin founded the Guild of St George in 1871 on the principle that "the highest wisdom and the highest treasure need not be costly or exclusive." The seeming gulf between Ruskin's nuanced version of commerce and Selfridge's encomia to it is bridged by Hobson's choice of adjectives to describe the greater theorist of commerce: the "pure romance" trailing all of Ruskin's thought, which "belongs to the literature of power."

The svelte epilogue to Ruskin's massive oeuvre on commerce could be Oscar Wilde's chic essay, "The Soul of Man under Socialism" (1891). A savagely anti-Victorian Victorian, Wilde offered a take on commerce surprisingly akin to Ruskin's aristocratic socialism, in its emphasis on the human benefits of wealth and prosperity. Any number of important Victorian cultural movements, from the Pre-Raphaelite circle of artists and poets to the decadent movement of which Wilde was a leader, participate in an oppositional commercial discourse. Oppositional, yet often reliant on commercial prosperity or even commercial technique. For Wilde, wealth and commerce should not be shunned, because it is they that provide the means for the flowering of individual talents and tastes. That Wildean flowering would depart from Ruskin's moralized ideals, perhaps, but Wilde concentrates just as Ruskin does on the consumption end of commerce, the "vital use" to which goods can be put, in order to make a case for idyllic self-actualization. Where they part company is over the issue of modernity. Wilde embraces contemporary commerce, with its machines and tools for living, and excoriates the nostalgic yearning of Ruskin and Morris for feudal, preindustrial England. One can perhaps credit Wilde's Irishness with his ability to see the contradictions implied in William Morris's vaunted return to artisanal handwork. The handmade objects Morris favored and produced, whether fabrics or pottery or wallpapers or the gorgeous publications of his Kelmscott Press – were incredibly expensive, out of the reach of ordinary people; it was their machine-made knock-offs that made huge commercial profits for Morris and his Firm. A commercial spade should be called a spade; the plantation system of land usurpation in Ireland during Morris's and Wilde's lifetime sufficed to quench the glow from that picture of precapitalist England. Art, including the aesthetics of identity, depends on commerce for Wilde, and there can be no escape into the past from the mechanisms of modern commerce. Nor does there need to be: commerce will free people to be artists. The irritating grain of contradiction hidden in the Wildean artistic pearl is crystallized in the essay's harping on middle-class tastes (very bad) and middle-class culture (worse). For an artist who was veritably a creature of commercialization – in the multiplication of his image in advertising, popular music, lecture performances, gossip columns and public spectacles, and the international popularity of his work – Wilde protests a bit too much. He draws the line where commerce encroaches too far on art, and labels it Philistinism. That high culture high-water mark defies the deeper message of his own work, and his life, which makes clear how hard it is to separate the bathwater of commerce, publicity, and popularity from the baby of art, autonomy, and self-fashioning.

The apotheosis of commerce in Victorian times is encapsulated in its chief invention, the department store. Other than the book, to which we shortly turn, there is no Victorian site so apropos for the consideration of commerce. What the book and the department store have in common derives from their being repositories of commercial transaction, mediated by language in the case of the book, and by spectacle in the case of the store. To trot out that pesky but useful Victorian eyewitness Selfridge again: he closes his romantic book on commerce with a chapter on what he calls "The Great Distributing House," his name for the department store. An extraordinary – and no doubt extraordinarily expensive – foldout is included in the leaves of this chapter. When unfolded to its full and stunning length, it is a schematic rendering in red ink of the distributional calculus of the store, from its "flower mounting" and "baby linen" stock to its "aero firm alarm system," its "mess hall attendants," "glove repair" section, staff magazine, sewage maintenance operations, purchasing department and foreign offices. The vast web of interrelated commercial activities centrifugally spun by the department store is the nexus of commerce inscribed in one place. Some of the visionary impetus of the department store as Commerce centralized and fantasized arose from Prince Albert and his plans for the Crystal Palace at the world-famous Exhibition. That expanse of soaring glass, giving architectural support to the anthology of British commerce housed within, translated within a few decades into the structure of the department store, which was at once an exhibition hall, a palace of dreams, and a bureaucratic hub.

Victorian literature is littered with department stores, or their avatars, the gleaming shop windows before which so many characters stand transfixed. While Michel Foucault's notion of nineteenth-century power as a panoptical regime of the eye has become a staple of theoretical approaches to Victorian culture, it might be wise to stop short of the surveillance paradigm and to give proper attention as well to the magical properties of the commercial palace. Edmund Gosse's exceptional memoir *Father and Son* (1907), a painful account of the inevitable estrangement of a nineteenth-century Calvinist father from his *fin de siècle* secular son, movingly describes the latter's childhood escape from the austerities of Christian fundamentalism by way of the enchantments of the store, the shop window, and advertisement. He was never allowed to buy anything on these forays, yet received a vicarious baptism in commerce, as it were, when the family's serving-maid went down the street to make a purchase for herself, and "if I did not hold the rose of merchandise, I was very near it" (ch. 5). Echoing both Romantic and spiritual language, Gosse's "rose of merchandise" may appear oxymoronic or appalling, but he touches on what many late Victorians recognized for themselves as consumers: the transfiguring romance that was commerce made of its venue the department store an everyday sacrament.

If commerce is a discourse as well as a set of economic practices within Victorian culture, as I have been arguing, then the metalevel of the discourse of commerce involves the book trade. Books are commercial commodities of exchange, and no arena of commerce saw a greater change during the Victorian period than the book market. In the Victorian period the decisive switch to modern forms of the production, distribution, and consumption of the book (and magazine and newspaper) took place. Terry Lovell's *Consuming Fictions* (1992) explores this Victorian territory: the best medium for circulating the discourse about commerce – the novel, newspaper editorials, magazine articles, political cartoons, pamphlets, and ads, etc. – was created by commercial means.

The ultimate cautionary tale for the commercialization of the book trade, and thus the commercialization of literature and domesticity, must be George Gissing's *New Grub Street* (1891). Written near the end of the century which had wrought such major changes in literary production, Gissing's book is a *cri de coeur* for the author dispossessed by the grubby new traffic in books. The novel is a veritable archeology of the *fin de siècle* book trade. Its characters include a thinly veiled autobiographical portrait of a serious novelist who is impaled on the cusp of the transition from the Victorian triple-decker, a man of letters whose literary reviews and essays come to depend on the sheer exploitation of his daughter's research for him at the British Museum Reading Room, a male author in search of an old-style patron, a female author who leaves him in the commercial dust by playing the market for all it is worth. *New Grub Street* ends tragically and hyperbolically, with suicide, blindness, starvation, and the immolation of a precious manuscript in a fire, a twilight of the gods of "pure" literature on the bonfire of trade.

There was another, and less morbid, side of the commercial story to tell. Just as Mrs Wragge got a reprieve from her violent homelife in the fantasies of shopping granted her by advertising's light reading, so the cadre of women writers in the Victorian period found a (partial) haven from gender discrimination in the very commercialism which was anathema to writers like Gissing. The brisk trade in books, centralized around publishers and increasingly independent of either elite patronage or university ties, made it possible for women to enter literature and its precincts in great numbers. The spectrum ranges from the greatest of Victorian literary writers, like Charlotte Brontë and George Eliot, who had masculine *noms de plume* but were widely celebrated, and others like Elizabeth Gaskell who wrote under their own names and were enormously popular. Writing was indeed one of the few professions women could hold in

Victorian society, even pseudonymously, and women's writing of the period is as imbricated by and in commerce as male writing – and perhaps more so.

George Eliot's masterpiece *Middlemarch* (1872) enacts the paradoxes of commercialism for the Victorian world of literature and for the female gender within the world of Victorian culture alike. Predicated on the historical anonymity of its main protagonist, Dorothea Brooke Casaubon Ladislaw, who unlike her prototype St Theresa, who founded a reforming order of nuns, cannot become a famous reformer, but is destined for the "hidden life" of marriage and motherhood, *Middlemarch* is heady with the details of commerce – wealth, property, trade, debt, business, profession, credit. This is a novel which can date the action of a chapter by a commercial and political allusion – "It was just after the Lords had thrown out the Reform Bill" is the sentence which opens chapter 84's intense, if oblique, reflection on the trade reforms earlier mentioned in this essay. The pure-spirited Dorothea brokers the commercial failures and successes of her many acquaintances, thanks to her inherited fortune; the novel dwells on commercial debt and professional exigencies with a fierce business acumen. As a Victorian woman, and not a heroic nun, Dorothea is prohibited from a public career herself – she can only mediate the careers of men like Dr Lydgate, whom she offers to rescue financially.

> "It would be quite worth my while," said Dorothea simply. "Only think. I am very uncomfortable with my money, because they tell me I have too little for any great scheme of the sort I like best, and yet I have too much. I don't know what to do. I have seven hundred a year of my own fortune, and nineteen hundred a year that Mr. Casaubon left me, and between those three and four thousand of ready money in the bank. I wished to raise money and pay it off gradually out of my income which I don't want, to buy land with and found a village which should be a school of industry. . . . So you see that what I should most rejoice at would be to do something good with my money." (ch. 76)

Dorothea is forced into philanthropy because she cannot exercise her own money commercially. Her "scheme" (as it is called throughout the novel) is dedicated toward the public good, of course, and not to commercial profit, but there is nothing commercially innocent about either Dorothea or George Eliot for that matter. While Dorothea ultimately gives up her fortune to marry a reforming member of the House of Commons, in defiance of her landed-class origins, one could construct a gendered commercial allegory out of Eliot's narrative to set beside the story of the triumph of the bourgeoisie others have noted within it. Unlike Dorothea, George Eliot, albeit not as Mary Ann Evans, *is* able to enter public life, through the door of commerce represented by the book. *Pace* Gissing, she thereby recognizes that, tainted as commerce may be in contrast to the worlds of art and philosophy, all human exchanges however aesthetic or intellectual will include commerce, and will take place in some sort of market. The pure "marketplace of ideas" does not exist. Moreover, Eliot's work suggests that in any event such a marketplace would only be a utopia for a few – who, under Victorian conditions, would inevitably be wealthy men. Commerce is ineluctable, Eliot sees, and to shun it or demonize it entirely is to live blind to one's own conditions. For certain groups, and women of all classes would surely be included here, to say nothing of female intellectuals, commerce can paradoxically offer an arena less beset by exclusion, prohibition, or tradition.

Dorothea Brooke's story, set within the context of George Eliot's novel and then within the large context of Victorian culture, is an allegory of the mediating powers of commerce, to harm and blight as well as to enable, and of commerce's own abiding need for the mediation of creative artistry and agency. Dorothea's fictive tomb may well lie unvisited, but Eliot's Victorian masterpiece is not now and never went unread. The commercial traffic around her book, and every other Victorian book one could cite, is messy, often crude, sometimes vulgar and always arbitrary. If it had not been marketed, circulated, advertised, and promoted, *Middlemarch* could never have reached anyone's attention, could never have entered into the melee of commercial exchanges which constitute the literary market, and might have gone as unremarked as Dorothea's gravesite. Commerce is fierce, unjust, and unequal, but it can resurrect books, ideas, and even people in the afterlife of its market. The skeins and the schemes of commerce, in their resemblance to literature's skeins of language and narrative schemes, can sometimes intertwine to result in surprisingly creative, transformational energies. Improbable though it may seem, in this George Eliot is commerce's prophet.

See also 1870, 1897; FINANCIAL, INDUSTRIAL, SPECTACLE, PUBLISHING; FICTION, SAGE WRITING

REFERENCES

Day, Clive (1907) *A History of Commerce.* New York: Longmans, Green.

Hobson, J. A. (1897) *On Imperialism.* London: Chapman & Hall.

——(1920) "Ruskin as Political Economist." In *Ruskin as Prophet: A Centenary Study,* ed. J. Howard Whitehouse. New York: E. P. Dutton.

Lever, Charles (1872) *Lord Kilgobben.* London: Harmsworth Press.

Lovell, Terry (1992) *Consuming Fictions.* London: Verso.

Selfridge, Hugh Gordon (1902) *The Romance of Commerce.* London: William Bredon & Sons.

FURTHER READING

Altick, Richard D. (1957) *The English Common Reader: A Social History of the Mass Reading Public 1800–1900.* Chicago: University of Chicago Press.

Baudrillard, Jean (1975) *The Mirror of Production.* St Louis: Telos Press.

Bowlby, Rachel (1985) *Just Looking: Consumer Culture in Dreiser, Gissing and Zola.* New York: Methuen.

Brewer, John and Porter, Roy (eds) (1992) *Consumption and the World of Goods.* London: Routledge.

Freedman, Jonathan (1990) *Professions of Taste: Henry James, British Aestheticism and*

Commodity Culture. Stanford: Stanford University Press.

Gagnier, Regenia (1986) *Idylls of the Marketplace: Oscar Wilde and the Victorian Public*. Stanford: Stanford University Press.

Hendrickson, Robert (1970) *The Grand Emporiums*. New York: Stein and Day.

Hobsbawm, E. J. (1987) *The Age of Empire*. Cambridge: Cambridge University Press.

Nunokawa, Jeff (1994) *The Afterlife of Property: Domestic Security and the Victorian Novel*. Princeton: Princeton University Press.

Poovey, Mary (1988) *Uneven Developments: The Ideological Work of Gender in Mid-Victorian England*. Chicago: University of Chicago Press.

Richards, Thomas (1990) *The Commodity Culture of Victorian England*. Stanford: Stanford University Press.

Said, Edward (1993) *Culture and Imperialism*. New York: Alfred A. Knopf.

Wicke, Jennifer (1988) *Advertising Fictions: Literature, Advertisement, and Social Reading*. New York: Columbia University Press.

19
Spectacle
Joss Marsh

Victoria's reign was the era not only, as educational catchphrase had it, of "learning by looking," but also of *living* through looking. The nineteenth century saw an explosion in visual technologies: the kaleidoscope (1815), the daguerreotype and the photograph (1826/1835), the stereoscope (1849), the cinema (1895), besides the optical toys and physiological experiments that preceded it (like the thaumatrope, zoetrope, and "wheel of life"), the long-familiar magic lantern, and the techniques of photomechanical reproduction that saturated the world in images from the 1880s. And that explosion was underpinned by what Jonathan Crary has called the philosophical "reorganization" of human vision between about 1810 and 1840. The nineteenth-century break with classical models – Renaissance perspective, "objective" geometrical optics – signaled the birth of a new type of "subjective observer," enmeshed in a visual environment that became more and more abstract as the century lengthened. As such, he was "both a product of and at the same time constitutive of modernity in the nineteenth century" (Crary 1990: 9).

The "reorganization" Crary charts found persistent expression in the new language and imagery of literature, a trait especially remarkable in the works of Dickens, but noticeable even in run-of-the-mill publications like an 1871 shilling guide to *The Educational Places of Amusement in London*. Here, we read, Covent Garden market must be viewed "very early on Saturday morning" to be seen "as a *spectacle*" (p. xii); the British Library is a "phantasmagoria of the human mind" (p. 22); the South Kensington Museum is "a beautiful kaleidoscope" (p. 26); the Crystal Palace at Sydenham offers not only (courtesy of casts and reproductions) the greatest collections of Art, Nature, and Science but "fairy scene[s]" in the shrubberies (p. 93) and an unrivaled "panorama" from the upper terrace (p. 89); while London demands at all times of all visitors that they keep open their "greedy eyes" (p. 44). Light, vision, movement, and virtuality were as much keynotes of Victorian spectacle and exhibition as were the profit motive of capitalistic enterprise and the educative impulse of expanding democracy. Their history is also a history of the present, and the Victorian observer-spectator is the grandfather of today's online, TV-watching consumer.

Victorian "show business" centered firmly in London, feeding the expanding appetite of an urban population that swelled from one to three million between 1801 and 1861. "Exhibitions then," Richard Altick records in his indispensable *Shows of London*, "were as much of an institution as the theater" (Altick 1978: 221); in any "moderate" year, metropolitan sightseers alone spent £4 million annually (ibid.: 420). Even the Duke of Wellington was an inveterate showgoer, who enjoyed reenactments of the Battle of Waterloo in 1827 and 1849, and left orders with Madame Tussaud's in 1835 to update him on new additions to her famed waxwork Chamber of Horrors. The eight railway lines opened between 1836 and 1848 made it possible for foreigners and country visitors, too, to "see the lions" – not just the ancient menagerie at the Tower of London, as originally meant, but all the sights of the town. (The animals moved to Regent's Park Zoo in 1834.) *En route*, from the train windows, the new visitors enjoyed nineteenth-century observers' first experience of moving pictures.

In the year Victoria came to the throne, until some time after the Great Exhibition of 1851, the bulk of London's attractions were the same that had charmed pennies from pockets for centuries. Freaks, fat boys, bearded and fireproof ladies, dwarves (live and embalmed), "learned" pigs, and exotic creatures: early Victorians suffered like their fairgoing ancestors from what *Punch* caricatured as "Deformito-mania" (September 4, 1847: 90). They wondered at the same clockwork inventions, though by the 1840s these included a speaking automaton – imaginatively recalled by Charlotte Brontë in *Jane Eyre* (1847: chs 19, 23) and George Eliot in *Middlemarch* (1872: ch. 32) – and the "Eureka" machine, which could turn out sixty Latin hexameters an hour. Doing the rounds of sights with his old nurse Pegotty in Dickens's novel of 1849–50 (ch. 33), David Copperfield visits some long-gone "perspiring Wax-work, in Fleet Street"; "Miss Linwood's Exhibition" at Leicester Square, a "Mausoleum" of needlework copies of Old Master paintings "favorable to repentance," which drew disconsolate crowds for nearly forty years to 1846; the Norman Tower, which housed the royal armory (hence Wellington's fiat that no more than a hundred visitors be allowed in at any one time); and St Paul's Cathedral, reduced to a "two-penny show" by the notorious functionaries who controlled admission and – as at Westminster Abbey – charged extra fees for tombs, side-chapels, Nelson's remains, and all other exploitable features (the total could easily reach to five shillings).

Dickens's earliest work, *Sketches by "Boz"* (1836), added to the list of attractions such pleasure-grounds as venerable Vauxhall Gardens, London's premier *al fresco* entertainment, though distinctly flyblown in daylight. It was here that balloons were spectacularly launched in the 1830s, and that Wellington relived his Waterloo triumph. Surrey Gardens, which had a lake, specialized in the reconstruction of naval battles and "Pictorial Typoramas" – enormous modeled canvas "views" – of Vesuvius (1837–8), the Great Fire of London (1844), etc., accompanied by fireworks at 9:30 p.m. sharp. In the later 1840s, concerts by Jullien's "monster" orchestra brought Surrey its greatest fame. Cremorne Gardens, to the north, were a favorite spot for dancing and assignations. Thomas Carlyle was one of the near Chelsea neighbors who complained about the noise. They were satisfied when Cremorne finally closed in 1878, twenty years after Vauxhall was sold for building lots. The age of the pleasure-ground was over: respectable public parks, like the Embankment Gardens (laid out in the 1850s), were the new order of the day.

For sheer staying power, the most successful of London's show-places throughout the century was Egyptian Hall, Piccadilly, an exotic architectural fantasy adorned with fake hieroglyphics. Here, from 1812, were miscellaneously shown the Natural History collection of its founder, William Bullock (1812), the first in England displayed in realistic postures and "habitat groups"; two ground-breaking exhibitions of ancient Egyptian and Mexican artifacts (1821 and 1824); colossal canvases by romantic artist Benjamin Haydon (1820 and 1846); an artfully enlarged mastodon skeleton billed as the "Missouri Leviathan" (1839); George Catlin's paintings of Native American life, which cashed in on a vogue for travel writing in 1840, and were re-exhibited with a troupe of "Ojibbeway" Indians hijacked from Manchester in 1843, the year the Ethnological Society was founded; various electro-biological displays; Barnum's famed midget, Tom Thumb (1844–6); and a group of South African Bushmen, who performed "the very kind of routine that monkeys sometimes were taught" in 1845 (Altick 1978: 280), with other "Kaffir," "Aztec," and aboriginal manifestations of the anxious interest in the human family that ushered in Darwin's evolutionary revelations.

Higher-class premises, like the Cosmorama Rooms in Regent Street, typified early Victorian practice by alternating between sacred and profane subject matter, and between the exhibition of single rare objects and discrete collections: Charlemagne's so-called manuscript Bible, shown in 1836, for example, or a display of disguises, manacles, and other criminal bric-a-brac timed to publicize the 1845 publication of his memoirs by the real-life model for the all-seeing hero of nineteenth-century detective fiction, the former chief of the French Sureté, François-Eugène Vidocq. Complex models of foreign cities were popular through the century: Jude Fawley leans deep in study over a miniature Jerusalem in Hardy's last novel, *Jude the Obscure* (1895), exactly as pious showgoers examined Brunetti's 100-square-foot model of the Holy City in 1847.

Near the bottom end of the social scale were shabby wonder-houses like Pollard's Museum in lower-class Lambeth. Beneath were the pavement exhibitors who showed Punch and Judy, peepshows, trained animals, telescopes, and mechanical figures, of whom Henry Mayhew's *London Labour and the London Poor* (1861–2) preserves intimate record. One clockwork puppet exhibit brought together a fiend in a den, Daniel and the lion of Bible story, Queen Victoria (holding a sword), Nebuchadnezzar (eating grass), Napoleon, and the Indian prince Tippoo Sahib – a "raree show" indeed, model for the miscellanies offered up to children by cheap publishers like Thomas Tegg, who tried to hire Dickens to write one in 1836.

Spectacle both moved off the streets and took to the road under Victoria. In London, as the law-and-order lobby gained ground, "rude and demoralizing amusements" and the "brutal exhibitions of cock-fights and bull-baiting" were forced to give place (*Educational Places*, p. 32). Bartholomew Fair, where Wombwell's Menagerie and Richardson's Theater once ruled the roost over giants, jugglers, fire-eaters, games of chance, infant prodigies, beer shops, and penny shows, was put down in 1840; Dickens's wonder-packed *Old Curiosity Shop* (1841) implicitly laments its passing. There was compensation, of course: London's resplendent shop and (later) department store windows – plate-glassed from the 1870s – were a world-famous show, though they could only be considered "free" – like city markets, sandwich men, billboards, or omnibus advertisements – if one discounted the hidden costs of capitalist spectacle. "Puffery" was standard practice: the seven-foot-high, perambulating Hat by which the London Hatter of Carlyle's *Past and Present* (1843) hopes commercially to be "saved" was its "topmost point as yet" (book 3, ch. 1); while the exhibits at mid-Victorian shows were often either ticketed for sale or displayed with an eye to attracting support for business or missionary ventures.

Astley's pioneer circus company stayed put in its London "Amphitheater of the Equestrian Arts" through the century. But elsewhere the first great mass entertainment to which it gave birth in the 1770s packed its Big Top and spangled "properties" into wagons to tour the provinces. Eight well-known troupes were on the road in the 1830s; the thirty years from 1870 to the end of the century were the traveling circus's golden era. It was "wonder" that made circus "wander," suggests a linguistic slippage in Dickens's 1854 *Hard Times* (ch. 8), a novel that pits its spontaneous and "fanciful" joy against the mechanized grind of industrial "Coketown"; the self-styled "King" of the tenting circus, "Lord" George Sanger, called his Ring a "magic circle." But the "open road" was often "strewn with thorns" (Sanger 1926: 1). When his infant son dropped dead of convulsions, in the winter before Dickens wrote, Sanger had to parade through Stamford, Lincolnshire, smiling, with the corpse in the back of a van, to drum up the money to bury him. Such private hardships, like the crippling dangers of high wire, trapeze, and (in late century, when circus was mechanized) man-hurling cannon were no less a fact of its life than the invisible labor that enabled the circus illusion of effortless play to which hard-working Victorians responded rapturously.

The circus was unusual among Victorian spectacles in *really* delivering wonder. Others presented a simulacrum. In 1794 a strange new building had risen above Leicester Square. Entering from the street after paying a shilling, spectators moved through a darkened passage to the center of the huge circular edifice, ninety feet in diameter. Inside, they emerged on a platform thirty feet wide, surrounded on all sides by a breathtaking view: London seen from the superb vantage point of Albion's Mills, on the south side of the river. The experience was no trick of mesmerism or magic carpet, but the effect of the first "panorama," a giant painted representation painstakingly constructed in superb detail, that lived up to its ancient Greek name of an "all-embracing," 360-degree view. The brainchild of an Edinburgh portraitist called Robert Barker, the panorama was a logical fulfillment of *trompe l'oeil* traditions extending back to Roman times: pictures of bowers on villa walls, false perspectives or "prospects" in pleasure-grounds, theatrical scenery. What convinced the eye that what it gazed on was real was Barker's realization that, to offset the effects of circularity, what appears straight in nature must be curved in panoramic reproduction, and the spectator kept at a strict optimum distance from the image. Precluded by barriers and enclosures from seeing above, behind, or around the canvas, unaware (by design) even of the light-source that illuminated it, the spectator did not merely look at but stood within the illusion.

Handed down from Barker to his son and their partner Robert Burford, London's first panorama flourished until mid-century, giving character to the sometimes seedy Square as London's show business center, where also were displayed "anatomical" waxworks and near-nude female *poses plastiques* in supposed imitation of classical art, a far cry from the decorously suggestive tableaux which Brontë's governess watches performed in *Jane Eyre*. The panorama lasted until 1863. Pendennis takes in the view, in Thackeray's novel of 1848–50, without seeing his way any clearer to romance; David Copperfield is shown its splendor by Steerforth in Dickens's competing text of 1849–50, without seeing through his false friend, as if to extend the visual pun. The panorama was *the* early Victorian London show, a quintessentially urban art. Before cheap trams, the Underground, and workmen's railway fares brought green space and the grand amenities of suburban pleasure-sites within reach of city crowds in the second half of the century, the panorama offered virtual escape into a lost world of space, long vistas, and clear air. Uplifted by its bird's-eye view, like Dickens suspended above the city in the basket of a balloon in George Cruikshank's frontispiece to *Sketches by "Boz"*, spectators gained temporary visual power over the enveloping brick-and-mortar labyrinth in which they spent their lives.

That sense of vicarious experience was exaggerated by the Leicester Square panorama's greatest rival, the Colosseum near Regent's Park, erected in 1824. In the huge rotunda, 112 feet high, was installed the fruit of several years' recording of the burgeoning metropolis from atop St Paul's dome, 2,000 meticulous sketches by a Yorkshire land surveyor called Thomas Hornor. Transferred to canvas by a painter with an equal head for heights, Hornor's project offered a facsimile experience of the view without climbing hundreds of stairs or finding it obliterated by smog. To complete the illusion, visitors even stood on a replica of the cathedral's real viewing platform, reached by the first passenger elevator in London, and looked out at the spectacle through a three-dimensional mock-up of the scaffolding in place while Hornor had sketched. Instinctively, they drew back from the edge; some claimed they saw figures move across the canvas, or heard ghostly sounds of life ascending from the painted streets.

The Colosseum management invested (necessarily, given the cost) in very few standing shows, and ultimately were bankrupted. But as the great building's fortunes declined, a new attraction sprang up beside it in 1848, the Cyclorama, where four times a day customers could experience the sensational sights *and* sounds of the Lisbon earthquake of 1755: "Never," said one Victorian man-about-town, "was better value in fright given for the money" (Edmund Yates, in Altick 1978: 158). Meanwhile, since the anxious days of the Napoleonic Wars, which made bodily touristic travel impossible, the original panorama and its other rivals had varied the scenes to which they transported spectators in illusive "reality": Dublin, Paris, Berlin, Rome, and (three times at Leicester Square) Constantinople, each city more glamorized by distance than the last. Before the railway brought Mont Blanc and other sublimities within reach, the panorama offered ordinary people a virtual "grand tour." "Moving panoramas," first introduced on the pantomime stage in the 1810s, took the illusion still further. In the 1830s vertical ones even made vicarious balloon flight possible. In 1848 the most popular show in town was New Yorker John Banvard's "monster" three-mile narrated excursion up the Mississippi, during which bluffs, prairies, cabins, wigwams, plantations, levees, and steamboats scrolled past the astonished spectators. Opening at Easter 1850, "The Overland Route to India" was seen by a quarter of a million people.

Serious Victorians took the panorama seriously, buying sixpenny guides to individual shows, and flocking in the 1840s to representations of the Holy Land: here was a spectacle that Evangelical scruple allowed one to view. At their best, wrote John Ruskin, panoramic shows had "an attention to truth and a splendour and care in the execution" which made them "very truly a school both in physical geography and art" (quoted in Altick 1978: 174). The images' size played to what scholars call nineteenth-century art's "cult of immensity"; their superabundant detail may have helped create later taste for the photographic meticulousness and bold coloration of Pre-Raphaelite painting. Moreover, like the historical paintings of the period – Sir George Hayter's 170-square-foot picture of the House of Commons, for example (exhibited 1843) – the panoramas were intended to picture history as it was made. The Punjab War Battle of Sobraon was depicted with the aid of military dispatches in 1846; rebellious Delhi and Lucknow were spectacularized for patriotic view in 1857–8. However, just as their topographical function declined with developments in transportation, so the panoramas' topical role was eroded in mid-century by the technology that made possible pictorial papers like the *Illustrated London News* (founded 1842), though their sheer size still spoke to the nation's sense of imperial grandeur, and stylish comic commentary made a hit of Albert Smith's *The Ascent of Mont Blanc*, shown 2,000 times between 1852 and 1858.

Since panoramas depended for illumination on sunlight from concealed skylights, their hours of operation were limited to daytime, and strictly curtailed in foggy winters. Light was the greater problem and desideratum of nineteenth-century representation as showmen conceived it. From the 1850s panoramic spectacle lost its status as the apogee of realism to the photograph or "sun picture," in which – as if by autogenesis – the world traced its own physical image by that very medium of light alone. Exploiting first the single-plate process patented by the Frenchman Daguerre, then the negative–positive technique discovered by England's Fox Talbot in 1835, photographic studios proliferated across London; the number of professional photographers in England grew from 51 in 1851 to 2,534 in 1861 (Green-Lewis 1996: 52). From today's perspective, Roger Fenton's much-praised 1855 exhibition of sanitized Crimean War photographs provides a crucial foundational instance of how Victorian exhibition practices, like the photograph itself, could claim to offer wholly naturalized expressions of the world, not images mediated by human agency (ibid.: 120). And that same promise of the real was the key to the final "domestication" of panoramic impulse by the portable home stereoscope of the 1860s (Altick 1978: 233). Simultaneously viewed, its left- and right-eye photographic images produced a compelling illusion of three-dimensionality.

Earlier Victorians paid to stare at a different spectacle that Daguerre sent to London in 1823: the diorama, a screen-like picture on canvas or lawn, painted in a combination of opaque and translucent paints, roughly 70 by 45 feet, granted dynamic brilliance and the dramatic illusion of depth by the influx of sunlight controlled through a series of skylights and windows in a specially designed and darkened auditorium. The interior of a cathedral was thus seen alternately bathed in light and shadowed by clouds; a storm brewed above the Swiss Alps. In the 1830s novel "transformation" effects – achieved by painting both sides of the screen, as in late eighteenth-century pantomime design – allowed views before and after an avalanche, or before and after the 1823 fire at Rome's St Paul basilica (a show revived in 1837, 1838, and 1843). As Altick remarks, it is hard to judge how far the diorama's play of light may have impacted the practice of painting, like Turner's revolutionary handling of light (ibid.: 195). For writers it seemed to promise the redemption of history and a key to memory. "Lo, the past is hurled / In twain," declares the experimental poet of Browning's *Sordello* (1840), "a darkness rears / Its outline, kindles at the core, appears / Verona," with "many a lighted face" of its long-dead inhabitants (book 1, 11. 73–7, 45); while "the memory," Eliot notes in *Middlemarch*, "shifts its scenery like a diorama" (book 5, ch. 53): elsewhere, photography, prisms, the panorama, and lantern "images" all further her investigation of consciousness, psychology, and desire.

The diorama's appeal faded in mid-century, when Daguerre's building was put up for auction, but the essential principle survived. The magic lantern, first commercially exploited at the turn of the nineteenth century as the spectral phantasmagoria, and newly powered by oxyhydrogen "limelight" (first used in lighthouses from 1826), which made possible brighter and smoother "dissolving views," now enjoyed a nation-wide Victorian renaissance; portable models with cheap photographic glass "sliders" found their way into middle-class homes (including Dickens's) from the 1860s. Finally, in 1896, the "kinematograph" opened in London, fulfilling the showman's promise of nearly two hundred years before to present "moving" (that is, mechanical) or even "animated" (i.e. revivified) pictures, the ultimate light show and illusion of life.

Light, perspective, and optical pleasure were keynotes of the greatest exhibition of the nineteenth century, symbolically dividing the age of show and spectacles from the age of exhibition and public museums. The Great Exhibition of the Works of Industry of All Nations was held in London's central Hyde Park from May 1 to October 11, 1851. It had had a long genesis. Exhibitions of "arts and manufactures" had been held in Leeds, Sheffield, and Liverpool in the late 1830s and early 1840s, inspired by

Mechanics Institutes and artisans' schools of design (whose booklets on how to attend exhibitions advised patrons to change from grubby work-clothes into "[your] Saturday night suit" [Bennett 1995: 73]). Abroad, the earliest industrial exhibition was held in a revolutionary "Temple of Industry" at the Paris Louvre in 1798. At home, Prince Albert and Henry Cole laid the last groundwork for a *popular* as well as *international* Exhibition with an Exhibition of Ancient and Medieval Art in 1850. The Great Exhibition these two brought to fruition took in machinery and scientific instruments; raw and processed minerals and materials (including a huge lump of coal carved in the shape of a Greek temple); architectural and engineering models; sculpture, mosaic, and musical instruments; "Indian curiosities" and other imperial products. Thirty-four nations participated, grouped together in the East Wing, while Britain alone dominated the West.

The Exhibition was the machine as wonder: a "stupendous Locomotive Engine," for example, "capable of driving a train of 120 tons gross at an average speed of 60 miles an hour (the flight of a pigeon)" (Timbs 1851: 125). It was the product as power fantasy: "Not only has the surface of the earth been made to minister to the wants . . . of man," especially Englishman, rhapsodized the *Illustrated Exhibitor*, "but the solid contents of the globe itself have been formed into one vast laboratory, wherein the Great Master Mind has prepared ready to the hands of his pupils, the materials of dominion." The Exhibition defined and celebrated the triumph of "mass production, prefabrication, mass communications, and urbanization" (Greenhalgh 1988: 142). It was "the most lavish of shows, the apotheosis of the lofty ideal of 'rational entertainment'" (Altick 1978: 456), taking to utopian heights the idea of the "object lesson," by which (wrote George Ricks in a textbook of that name) the child at school was "assisted" and "guided" to "discover the properties of things . . . for himself," rather than having information "poured . . . into his mind like wheat into a sack" (quoted in Davison 1988: 159). It whetted public appetite for systematic collection and national display. It had numerous offspring, in the great expositions and World's Fairs of the century across Europe, America, and the colonies. (Later London exhibitions were marred by commercialism and took up overtly national themes, like "Greater Britain" in 1899.)

But more – despite contrary claims (by Dickens, for example) – the Exhibition did not simply sate public desire for mechanical spectacle and leave the imagination untouched. Its great success depended on the extraordinary design of the great greenhouse-like iron-and-glass building in which it was housed, erected in only four months by an army of London workmen, and inspired by study of the ribbed leaf formations of the giant African *Victoria regia* lily. Cruciform like a church in design, but three times as long as St Paul's Cathedral, covering fully nineteen acres of ground, Joseph Paxton's "Crystal Palace" brought all classes together in an elevating environment of space and light. The Exhibition it housed became a "Diorama of the Peaceful Arts," declared Charles Babbage, inventor of the calculating machine (Altick 1978: 457); here, against the "distant background" of glass and blue-painted girder, "all materiality" seemed "blended into the atmosphere" (L. Bucher, quoted in Gideon 1962: 251). The Palace's visual impact was celebrated in illustration and caricature by the *Illustrated London News*, Cruikshank, and numerous others.

"The glass," however, as Wellington warned, "[was] very thin" (Altick 1978: 457). London's chief commissioner got a thousand extra men to police the crystal walls, while public figures like Dickens, Thackeray, Mill, and Forster, editor of the liberal *Examiner*, joined a Central Working Classes Committee to consider how to control attendance. Others (Prince Albert complained) feared catastrophic accidents, disease, and famine brought on by crowds; a few thought the Palace a second Tower of Babel (Allwood 1977: 18). But all precautions were proved unnecessary. In the six months it stood open, over six million people crowded into the Exhibition, over two-thirds of them from the provinces, and a huge number on cheap shilling days, without a single serious incident. The bogey of the insurgent crowd that had haunted the Victorian imagination – so that guns were handed out to British Museum employees when Chartist marchers converged on London in 1848 – was finally laid to rest; the "Workers" to whom the Exhibition was formally dedicated had shown themselves fit inhabitants of "the World's Hive."

The Exhibition of 1851 triggered a Victorian museum explosion. It had been a long time coming. Sir Hans Sloane willed his extensive collections, the core of the British Museum, to the nation in 1752, not only that they might foster "the use and improvement of physic and other arts and sciences," but as "tending" to "the glory of God" (Altick 1978: 229). But access to this treasure-house was thwarted by dilapidated premises, incrementally rebuilt 1823–52 and (until 1997) half-devoted to library purposes. There were no scientists on the board of trustees, although the museum housed the nation's greatest natural history collections as well as antiquities (until mid-century, almost exclusively Greek and Roman remains). In the library there was no up-to-date catalogue, and overcrowded reading rooms brought on "museum headache" and "museum fever."

From the public's point of view, however, the worst problem was the museum's peremptory elitist policies. It took commoner William Hone, later editor of the famous *Every-Day Book*, eighteen months to obtain access to the manuscripts on which he founded his pioneer study of medieval mystery plays. "Do you not think that one object of the Museum is to improve the vulgar class?" director Sir Henry Ellis was asked during a public inquiry in 1835. "I think the mere gazing at our curiosities is not one of the greatest objects of the Museum," he replied. Besides: "People of a higher grade would hardly wish to come to the Museum at the same time with sailors from the dock-yards and girls whom they might bring with them" (Altick 1978: 444–5). And if the library were open in the evening, it would attract "lawyers' clerks, and persons who would read voyages and travels, novels, and light literature" (Miller 1973: 140).

Yet – again – when the museum was first opened during a public holiday, on Easter Monday 1837, and packed with 23,000 persons, not one breach of its peace occurred. Attendance leapt from 81,228 in 1827–8 to 897,985 twenty years later.

More enlightened leadership and better funding expanded book collections from 150,000 volumes in 1827 to 520,000 in 1856 and over a million by 1871; the number of readers leaped to 188,266 by 1857; electric lights saved their eyes after 1878. Belatedly, the state had entered into competition with commercial show-business for the "leisure-time custom of the multitude" (Altick 1978: 454), recognizing the truism expounded by *Blackwood's Magazine* that museums "make the libraries of those who have no money to expend on books, and are the travels of those that have no time to bestow on travel," instilling knowledge "drop by drop, through the eye into the mind" (April 1842: 419).

Early Victorian museums were hybrid operations: spectacular, commercial, and educational. They recalled the extraordinary "jumble" Tennyson describes in the opening lines of *The Princess* (1847): costly curios, fossil ammonites, and Gothic fragments in the hall, model steamers and telegraphs in the yard, while above the "strange" spectacle a "maiden Aunt" takes it for "text," to "preach . . . / An universal culture for the crowd" (11. 17, 107–9). Astronomical lecture-demonstrations for the Lenten season, an inheritance from the eighteenth century, were a London fixture until mid-century: comets, tides, gravity, and eclipses were explained by means of huge transparencies or (later) lantern slides. At the Royal Institution, from 1801 through the 1880s, the inventor–educators Humphry Davy, Michael Faraday, and John Tyndall demonstrated their skills as popular showmen as well as advocates for science to society's upper 10,000. Other profit-minded or altruistic public men made the benefits of science visibly tangible for the masses. As much as *Chamber's Edinburgh Journal* or the utilitarian *Penny Magazine* (one of numerous periodical publications to take title and terms of reference from commercial spectacular culture: "repository," "bazaar," "magazine"), the Polytechnic Institution on Regent's Street, founded in 1838, typified the popular "March of Mind." Here, lectures explained the "atmospheric" or vacuum-driven railway, gun-cotton (cellulose nitrate) used for blasting, thunderstorms, and the potato blight that reduced Ireland to famine in 1845. A pneumatic telegraph, models of the ear and eye, brick- and pin-making machines, a "hydrostatic" bed, steam-engine designs, and two astronomical clocks were exhibited and demonstrated. From 1841, on the roof, as at the rival Adelaide Gallery (founded 1832), was a photographic studio. But the most famous attraction was a three-ton cast-iron diving bell in a deep-water tank, in which (for an extra shilling) visitors could be submerged. This topped even the Adelaide's steam-powered machine gun, discharged every hour, and its oxyhydrogen microscope displays of the thousands of microbes infesting a single drop of Thames water – the unsuspected cause of London's repeated typhoid and cholera outbreaks.

The Crystal Palace, moved to the suburb of Sydenham, enlarged, and re-erected in 1854, partook of the general hybridity. Ten of its "courts" offered the history of architectural styles, from Egypt to the Middle Ages, while others housed machinery in motion, a picture gallery, and scientific collections. In the grounds a fake Ichthyosaur disported with a fake Megalosaurus, next to "the largest geological model in the world," of which the author of *The Educational Places of Amusement in London* had "no hesitation in saying that the inquiring visitor may learn more about the earth's crust in an hour than he could by the aid of books in a month" (p. 85). But hybridity declined all too easily into mere novelty: the Palace became a stage to the tightrope-walker Blondin in the sensation-seeking 1860s, dwindling eventually into a giant hall of variety entertainment, while the Polytechnic stooped to mounting "spectral optical illusions" by "Professor Pepper," and another rival, the Royal Panopticon, closed its doors on Science and Art in only two years, to reopen as the sinful Alhambra Music Hall in 1858.

The greatest legacy of the Great Exhibition thus eventually proved not the physical building, but its clear profit of £186,000. This was the seed from which grew the great cluster of public museums that is modern-day South Kensington: the Museum of Practical Geology, opened two evenings a week from its commencement in 1851, and free on Saturdays, by order of its first director, Prince Albert's co-projector Henry Cole; the later Natural History Museum, to which the British Museum's ill-kept and jumbled collections moved in 1881; and the South Kensington Museum, specializing in the ornamental and fine arts, first opened in 1852 as the "Museum of Manufactures," relocated to a much-ridiculed temporary home (the iron "Brompton Boilers") in 1857, and later rebuilt as the Victoria and Albert Museum (begun 1899, opened 1908). The original institutions were radical, utilitarian, and populist, children of the same political imperative that passed Forster's universal Education Act of 1870. Food exhibits gave workers practical lessons in health and housekeeping; new internal designs moved them through the halls in a linear fashion, as if to reinforce the institutions' belief in historical and evolutionary progress (Bennett 1995: 181), while the perusal of new rows of transparent cases also encouraged them to overlook each other's behavior as well as the objects displayed (ibid.: 53–5); the museum became self-teaching, open to all. Between 1857 and 1883 the "Boilers" accommodated over 15 million visitors, 6.5 million of them during generous evening opening hours. The South Kensington institutions concluded, however – like the Great Exhibition itself – in putting Britain's power and riches on display, and advertising the nation's intellectual and actual control of other cultures; their first projectors, like Cole, resented their gathering emphasis on fine art and expensive purchase. Inexorably, though slowly, other collections scattered across the capital were consolidated: the Royal United Service Institution's, for example, was eventually absorbed into the Imperial War Museum. The laying out of the Kensington complex spurred expansion, too, of museums for the provinces, where legislation of 1845, 1850, and 1855 already set aside a small tax for the purpose. In 1860 there were 50 significant provincial museums; in 1900 there were 200.

In the matter of art exhibition, however, Manchester had set an example, mounting the nation's first wide-ranging loan exhibition in 1857. Public taste for art was both untutored and unsatisfied in the earlier years of Victoria's reign: London was the last great European capital, trailing Paris by thirty years, to build a national collection, funded by government and directed to public use. In the home, its citizenry slaked their thirst on engraved reproductions of inaccessible masterworks; in town, they patronized grotesqueries like an exhibition of "flowers" made entirely from fishbones. After forty-two years attempting to "elevate" their taste in works like *The Raising of Lazarus* and *The Burning of Rome*, as he announced in an extraordinary *Times* advertisement of 1846, the painter Haydon shot himself when Tom Thumb outsold him at Egyptian Hall by £600 to £5 13s 6d (Altick 1978: 414).

Like museums, early Victorian galleries were exclusive institutions. A very few noblemen's private collections were thrown open on select days, though never at times when working people could get to see them. Sabbatarianism kept both museums and galleries holy until 1896; Sunday opening was rejected by 376 votes to 48 in the House of Commons in 1856. In between, Sunday opening hours for public houses were extended to 1–3 p.m. and 5–11 p.m., giving fuel to the fears of institutions like the Royal Academy that cultural enfranchisement would irrevocably breach that "propriety" ensured by its one-shilling entrance fee. The National Gallery (opened 1824) did away with the fee, but repeatedly outgrew its premises until it was relocated at Trafalgar Square in 1839, and secured in full control of its purpose-built buildings some time later. Attendance quadrupled from 127,000 in the 1820s to half a million in 1840, though some of the attendees may well have used the gallery as an indoor picnic spot and refuge from rain. By mid-century, public access to aesthetic experience finally answered to the democratization of subject matter exemplified by the crowded and spectacular genre paintings of W. P. Frith, like *Derby Day* (1858) and *The Railway Station* (1862), and presaged in the street scenes of eighteenth-century artists like Hogarth, whose bequest of paintings formed a core part of the Academy's collection.

Thus – like antiquities, like scientific wonder – even art, it was finally found, could serve to quiet a working population that resented its lack of access to power from the Great Reform Act of 1832 through the Third Reform Act of 1884: this was the "modern museum idea" (George Brown Goode, quoted in Bennett 1995: 20). Paintings, concluded the author of *The Educational Places of Amusement in London* in 1871, were "silent monitors" of those who beheld them (p. 37). *Silent monitors*: the phrase is a summary of the relationship Crary argues between the "panoptical" Benthamite surveillance that redesigned the nineteenth-century workshop, asylum, and prison as places where one was controlled by one's own visibility, and the spectacle of streets, shops, railways, parks and gardens, museums and show-places. "Looking" was not to be divorced from "being looked at," and both contributed to the "disciplining" of the Victorian subject (Crary 1990: 18, citing Foucault). But while, in the long view of political history, uplifting the people might also have meant keeping them down, on the day-to-day level of lived experience it also brought millions aesthetic pleasure, empowering knowledge, temporary release from toil, and the vision of worlds unseen.

The author gratefully acknowledges the material assistance of Richard Menke and Lisa Jenkins in completing this essay.

See also COMMERCIAL; DRAMA; PARAPETS; SHORE

REFERENCES

Allwood, John (1977) *The Great Exhibitions.* London: Studio Vista.

Altick, Richard (1978) *The Shows of London.* Cambridge, MA: Harvard University Press.

Bennett, Tony (1995) *The Birth of the Museum: History, Theory, Politics.* London and New York: Routledge.

Crary, Jonathan (1990) *Techniques of the Observer: On Vision and Modernity in the Nineteenth Century.* Cambridge, MA: MIT Press.

Davison, Graeme (1988) "Festivals of Nationhood: The International Exhibitions." In S. L. Goldberg and F. B. Smith (eds) *Australian Cultural History.* Cambridge: Cambridge University Press.

The Educational Places of Amusement in London (1871) London: James Hogg.

Gideon, S. (1962) *Space, Time and Architecture.* Oxford: Oxford University Press.

Greenhalgh, Paul (1988) *Ephemeral Vistas: The Expositions Universelles, Great Exhibitions and World's Fairs, 1851–1939.* Manchester: Manchester University Press.

Green-Lewis, Jennifer (1996) *Framing the Victorians: Photography and the Culture of Realism.* Ithaca, NY: Cornell University Press.

Miller, Edward (1973) *That Noble Cabinet: A History of the British Museum.* London: Deutsch.

Sanger, "Lord" George (1926) *Seventy Years a Showman.* New York: Dutton.

Timbs, John (1851) *The Year-Book of Facts in the Great Exhibition of 1851.* London: David Bogue.

A Tribute to the World's Industrial Jubilee (1851) Special issue of *The Illustrated Exhibitor.*

FURTHER READING

Bailey, Peter (1978) *Leisure and Class in Victorian England: Rational Recreation and the Contest for Control, 1830–1885.* London: Routledge and Kegan Paul.

Beard, Mayall, et al. (1852) *Tallis's History and Description of the Crystal Palace, and the Exhibition of the World's Industry in 1851.* London: Tallis.

Bowlby, Rachel (1985) *Just Looking: Consumer Culture in Dreiser, Gissing, and Zola.* New York: Methuen.

Chadwick, George F. (1966) *The Park and the Town: Public Landscape in the Nineteenth and Twentieth Centuries.* New York: Praeger.

Cocks, Anna Somers (1980) *The Victoria and Albert Museum: The Making of the Collection.* London: Windward.

Croft-Cooke, Rupert and Coates, Peter (1977) *Circus: A World History.* New York: Macmillan.

Fay, Charles Ryle (1951) *Palace of Industry, 1851: A Study of the Great Exhibition and its Fruits.* Cambridge: Cambridge University Press.

Gernsheim, Helmut and Gernsheim, Alison (1968) *L. J. M. Daguerre: The History of the Diorama and the Daguerreotype.* New York: Dover.

Mayhew, Henry and Cruikshank, George (1851) *The World's Show, 1851: Or, The Adventures of Mr. and Mrs. Sandboys.* London: David Bogue; New York: Stringer and Townsend.

Physick, John (1982) *The Victoria and Albert Museum: The History of Its Building.* Oxford: Phaidon-Christie's.

Ritchie, J. Ewing (1858) *The Night Side of London,* 2nd edn, revd. London: William Tweedie.

Sala, George Augustus (1971) [1858] *Twice Round the Clock, Or, the Hours of the Day and Night in London.* Leicester: University of Leicester Press.

Schivelbusch, Wolfgang (1979) *The Railway Journey: Trains and Travel in the Nineteenth Century,* trans. Anselm Hollo. New York: Urizen.

20

Publishing

Richard D. Altick

Victorian publishers were the means by which two of the period's most powerful forces, entrepreneurial capitalism and technological advances, left their imprint on the form and often the content of literature. They were, as their predecessors the book-seller–printers had been, the indispensable middlemen between authors and readers. But in the Victorian years the familiar three-party relationship, scarcely changed since Elizabethan times, grew more complicated and the cash–payment nexus, as Carlyle called it, was more crucial in determining the quantity and quality of what the printer, another essential partner in the transaction, converted from manuscript into print. The printed word was, more than ever, a commodity, in its raw (manuscript) state to be priced, bargained for, and bought; and then processed, again priced, distributed, sold, consumed, and then, unlike other commodities that ended with consumption, stored away for further use. Near the end of the century, in George Gissing's novel *New Grub Street* (1891), the leading male characters – three men seeking, with various degrees of desperation, to make a living by their pens – repeatedly spoke of markets and trade: "Literature nowadays is a trade. Putting aside men of genius, who may succeed by mere cosmic force, your successful man of letters is your skilful tradesman" who turns out "marketable stuff" (ch. 1).

In effect, the book trade financed contemporary literature on behalf of an audience whose size, purchasing power, and diversified interests were only beginning to be realized at the start of the era. The delay was due in part to publishers' general lack of interest in popular culture as a potential source of profit, their inability to conceive that "the million," as they called the lower-middle and working classes, were capable of forming a mass market for the printed word. The meager desires of such an audience, supposedly only for broadside ballads, easy-to-read chapbooks, and other street literature, were, they thought, adequately met by slum printers like John Pitts and James Catnach. But in 1858, writing in Dickens's *Household Words* for August 21, Wilkie Collins announced, almost as if it were a previously unknown planet, the existence of an "unknown public" whose members, he predicted, "will be the readers who give the widest reputations, who return the richest rewards, and who will, therefore, command the service of the best writers of their time. . . . When that public shall discover its need of a great writer, the great writer will have such an audience as has never yet been known."

This enormously enlarged readership, as it had become by the end of the century, was partly the result of the spread of literacy in a population that had itself grown at an unprecedented rate. The ability to read, though not necessarily with ease and comprehension, was more widely shared than ever before, and the expanding middle class and to some degree the working class enjoyed an increased amount of disposable income they could spend for nonessential purposes such as books and periodicals.

As the urban population grew it offered a more concentrated market for those commodities, one which became more easily reached as the old skeletal distribution system, consisting of booksellers in a few towns and hawkers in the country lanes, was replaced by a network of bookshops and newsagents in every sizable population center. These were supplied by the railways, which brought a daily flow of stock from the publishing houses in London and Edinburgh. New marketing techniques supplemented the staid announcements, no bigger than classified ads, that were a staple of book-trade print advertising throughout the era. No firm, to be sure, went to the excesses practiced in the 1820s by Henry Colburn, the brash, unscrupulous maverick who hyped his line of "silver fork" fiction, first by planting in newspapers scandal-tinged stories purporting to identify the blue-blooded originals of characters in a forthcoming novel, and then by inserting enthusiastic reviews in the periodical he owned. But when Dickens launched his weekly *All the Year Round*, in 1859, a saturation publicity campaign called not only for posters on London buses but for a quarter-million handbills to be passed out in the streets. A few years later, Matthew Arnold's wife found herself walking down Regent Street behind a sandwich man advertising her husband's essay on Marcus Aurelius in the latest number of *Victoria Magazine*. In the century's last decades even the most sedate firms helped make celebrities out of their most popular authors by placing innocuous news items about them in the daily papers and arranging for home interviews, a new journalistic device, fiercely resisted by some as unbefitting the dignity of the literary profession, in middlebrow magazines.

As railways added mobility to everyday life, use of them entailed hours of tedium which books and papers were admirably suited to relieve (no record seems to exist of anyone reading with any comfort inside a jolting over-the-road coach). At home, improved lighting — the transition from candles to oil lamps to gas — meant that reading, despite the small type in which newspapers and some magazines were printed, became more pervasive as a leisure-time activity.

To meet and exploit this growing demand, publishing, heretofore a cottage industry which had always been situated on the fringe of the nation's economy, developed into a major industry with an annual turnover of several million pounds. As social and cultural interests multiplied in this increasingly complex society, new firms sprang up to cater to these sub-audiences, and old mainstream houses adopted specialties alongside their general lists. John Murray's already venerable firm was known for its guidebooks and travel narratives, the even older house of Longman for its textbooks, Cassell's for education-at-home titles in response to the self-help movement sparked by the well-publicized Society for the Diffusion of Useful Knowledge, Routledge for cheap reprints, Moxon for poetry, Bentley, Tinsley, and Macmillan (in addition to its highly regarded "serious" list) for fiction.

Innovating publishers also brought old genres to new stages of development and invented new ones. The mid- and late-Victorian years, for instance, are looked back upon as the golden age of children's books and magazines, engagingly designed and produced, not least with an eye toward nurturing future generations of adult book buyers. Other money makers, devised specifically for the Christmas trade, were short fictions packaged as gift books – Dickens's *A Christmas Carol* (1843) and *The Chimes* (1844), and Thackeray's *The Kickleburys on the Rhine* (1850) and *The Rose and the Ring* (1855) – and lavishly illustrated holiday numbers of family periodicals. These in particular reflected publishers' growing awareness of the power of physical appeal to sell books, which encouraged the invention of state-of-the-art mechanical modes of illustration, printing, and binding. Books formerly were sold in sheets and bound to the order of individual purchasers; now cheap binding cloth and machinery to apply it to the folded sheets, and equipment to stamp lettering and designs on it, made "publishers' bindings" standard throughout the trade. These came in several qualities and degrees of decoration, so that some houses advertised whole hierarchies of editions of a standard work or author, their formats ranging from the luxurious and costly to the cheaply ornate.

This was the more energetic aspect of an industry otherwise noted at the time – the older houses more than the less tradition-bound newcomers, such as Heinemann at the end of the era – for its financial conservatism. All Victorian firms were organized as family concerns or partnerships; none were companies owned by shareholders. Having no easy means of raising additional capital at times when the ledgers were being written up in red ink, they were unusually dependent on cash flow, which required quick returns on investments, which in turn required that the product for sale find an immediate market (and that booksellers pay their bills promptly). Thus, they were at the mercy of public taste. Vogues in books, especially fiction, came and went. The silver fork novel and the Newgate (criminal) novel of the pre-Victorian decades were succeeded by the Irish novel in the forties, the sensation novel in the sixties, and the "New Woman" novel in the nineties. Other special-interest genres, such as religious and sporting novels, had substantially longer lives. In a competitive trade affected, more than most merchandisers, by the popular appetite for novelty and by the quickening pace of everyday life, solvency, not to say healthy profit, was contingent on an astute sense of what the public wanted at the moment. "I hope it's not historical, Mr Trollope?" an employee of one house famously asked that novelist when he brought in the manuscript of *The Three Clerks*. "Whatever you do, don't be historical; your historical novel is not worth a damn."

The word "bestseller" was not invented until the 1890s, but the idea it represented was current much earlier. It always was a relative concept, meaning a book that sells in decidedly larger quantities than the common run of titles in its class, either in the short term — a year or two — or the long (a decade, a generation; thus a fortunate publisher's money cow, as Dickens's novels were at Chapman & Hall for many years, even after the copyrights expired). Early in the century, when an ordinary "serious" title such as a biography or a history was printed in an edition of 750 copies and the customary print run for a novel was no more than 1,000 or at most 1,250 copies, Scott's successive volumes of poetry were clear record-breakers: *The Lay of the Last Minstrel* (1805) sold 15,000 copies in five years, *Marmion* (1808) 13,000 in the first six months and six editions by the end of the year, and *The Lady of the Lake* (1810) 30,000 or more in the first year. So Scott's Midas touch was already operative when he turned to writing romances. The first printings of *Rob Roy* (1818) and *Ivanhoe* (1820) ran to 10,000 each; of *The Fortunes of Nigel* (1822) 7,000 copies were sold in London alone on the morning of publication day.

Such sales, previously unimaginable, were harbingers of far greater successes in the Victorian years. Short-term bestseller figures, the actual numbers of copies sold, as opposed to numbers of "editions" of undivulged size, are hard to come by, but these reported sales are representative: the first monthly numbers of *Nicholas Nickleby* (1838–9) and *The Mystery of Edwin Drood* (1870), 50,000 each; John Richard Green's *Short History of the English People* (1874), 35,000 in the first year; H. Rider Haggard's *King Solomon's Mines* (1885), 31,000 in the first fifteen months; Robert Louis Stevenson's *The Strange Case of Dr Jekyll and Mr Hyde* (1886), 40,000 in six months. These short-term sales may be compared with the steady sales of other titles over a period of years, usually in cheap reprints: Richard Harris Barham's three series of *Ingoldsby Legends* (1840/47–63), 52,000; Coventry Patmore's *The Angel in the House* (1854/62–96), between 200,000 and 250,000; Charles Reade's *It Is Never Too Late To Mend* (1856–63), 65,000; *Alice in Wonderland* (1865–98), 180,000.

Such quantities were made possible by several technological breakthroughs that revolutionized the printing industry, all but one of which were in place as the era began. The exception affected the first process in the production sequence, the setting of type, which continued to be done by hand until the very last of the Victorian years, when the Monotype and Linotype machines were introduced from the United States. But the lack of mechanization in the composing room was no bar to swift production; authors could begin to receive proofs within weeks of turning in their manuscripts, a celerity that dwellers in today's technological utopia can only regard with impotent envy. Only six weeks elapsed between the publisher George Smith's acceptance of the manuscript of *Jane Eyre* (1847) and the appearance of the finished book in the shops, and this was not an extraordinary event.

The next step, the actual printing, saw the hand-operated press, which had remained essentially unaltered since Caxton's time, replaced by steam-driven "printing machines," first used by newspapers but widely adopted for book work by the 1840s. These, at the very least, doubled or tripled the rate of production, and, with the introduction of another American invention, the high-speed, web-fed Hoe rotary press, in the sixties, printers were able to meet almost any demand time-pressed publishers laid upon them.

Equally important, by the 1840s the stereotyping process came into its own in the manufacture of books. This meant that, instead of tying up quantities of expensive, hand-set type for reprints that might never be called for, a printer could make a metal (later papier mâché) impression of the pages for later use, thus freeing the type for other jobs and at the same time preserving the pages for future printings as needed. It was this money-saving capability that made it possible for a publisher to build up a profitable backlist, rendering him less vulnerable to shifts in taste. Thanks to stereotypes, initially successful titles could be kept in print indefinitely, as in the instances just mentioned. Stereotyping also enabled publishers to undertake collected reissues of the works of living and still productive authors such as Dickens and Bulwer-Lytton. Sometimes these progressively cheaper editions came from the original publisher or by arrangements with him, but as copyrights expired, other houses brought out their own editions. By the end of the century cheese-paring paperback reprints might cost as little as sixpence. One effect of this practice, though certainly not with Scott (whose oeuvre was the first to be reprinted on a grand scale, beginning with the Author's Edition in 1829) and certainly not with Dickens, either, was to prolong an author's reputation beyond its natural life. Because they were cheap and kept in print, the books continued to be bought even when their author was no longer popular.

This was one respect in which technological improvements actually reduced the price of books, even despite the printers' heavy investment in the machinery that made cheap books possible. It was, in fact, an anomalous situation: while the average price of most nonfiction eventually declined, in part because the quarto format gave way to the cheaper (because smaller) octavo, the inflated price of original fiction was artificially maintained for most of the century. Although some one- or two-volume novels continued to appear, from Scott's *Kenilworth* (1821) onward the standard format of fiction was three volumes (hence the term "three-decker") costing 31s 6d, or a guinea and a half, therefore 10s 6d per volume. This was a price beyond the means of all but the wealthiest patrons of bookshops. But the publishers counted on selling most of the press run to the circulating libraries, which were given bulk-rate discounts as deep as 50 or 60 percent of the bookshop price. It was a cozy arrangement for all concerned, except the reader who wanted to own the books he or she read. The publishers were saved the expense of marketing the product at retail, and the libraries put Benthamite economics to profitable use by multiplying the number of readers a single copy would serve. Readers who subscribed a guinea a year to Mudie's Select Library, which became the mogul of the trade soon after it was established in 1842, were entitled to take out a volume at a time; another guinea allowed them to borrow as many volumes as they wished.

This was a form of snobbery easily purchased (note the "elite" connotation of the word "Select"): as mentions in many novels attest, the conspicuous presence of "books from Mudie's" in a home was a token of genteel social standing, if not necessarily of discriminating taste. In retrospect, one disadvantage of the system was that it empowered Mudie to wield what amounted to a veto power over the production of fiction. Publishers obtained their sense of public taste and tolerance second-hand, not through retail sales but through Mudie's conviction that he knew what his subscribers wanted to read, or, more precisely, what he, as a fervent, hymn-writing evangelical moralist, wanted them to read – or be protected from. The publishers' (and authors') primary market, so to speak, was not people but a faceless commercial institution that could make or break them. And the fact that in his own advertising, supplementing the publishers', Mudie announced how many copies of a given title he stocked was, in itself, the best publicity a book could have, irrespective of its literary quality.

This near-monopoly on the distribution of original fiction – it might today be called a conspiracy in restraint of trade – was sustained by publishers and circulating libraries at a time when common sense, as well as the ascendancy of free trade as economic orthodoxy, held that a cheapening of the manufacturing process should be reflected in cost to the consumer. Year in and year out, for eight decades, the guinea-and-a-half price was sacrosanct, despite repeated protests from free-trade politicians and from authors who wanted a wider, uncontrolled market for their wares. Only in 1894 did the rickety old vessel finally founder, a landmark book-trade event celebrated by Kipling in a ballad titled "The Three-Decker." Ostensibly a lament over maritime obsolescence, like Turner's painting of *The Fighting "Temeraire" Tugged to her Last Berth to be Broken Up*, its true subject was made clear by its epigraph: "The three-decker novel is extinct."

This matter, however, should be kept in perspective. Since Mudie's is always written about in connection with its pernicious effect on the fiction of its time, it must be remembered that novels were not the only kind of books it stocked in large quantities. Of the five million volumes it circulated between 1842 and 1888 only a third were fiction, and of the 960,000 it bought between 1853 and 1862 only about half were novels, as against 215,000 volumes of history and biography and 125,000 of travel and adventure. Mudie, it is true, bought 2,000 copies of *The Mill on the Floss* in 1860, but five years earlier he had bought 2,400 of the third and fourth volumes of Macaulay's *History of England* and had to set aside a special room to check them out to importunate borrowers.

Meanwhile, beginning in the 1830s with the short-lived firm of Colburn & Bentley (the perpetually feuding former partners later were caricatured as Bungay and Bacon, respectively, in Thackeray's *History of Pendennis* [1850]), the hunger of readers with only modest incomes was somewhat appeased by the introduction of five- or six-shilling one-volume reprints, appearing after the market for the expensive library edition was exhausted. It was in this series of "standard novels," as the firm called them, that six of Jane Austen's novels were first reprinted (1833).

The next step in this cheapening process occurred at mid-century, when long lists of reprinted titles, "railway novels" priced at one shilling in colorful, eye-catching pictorial board covers ("yellowbacks"), were prominently displayed at the bookstalls the firm of W. H. Smith & Son occupied, from 1848 on, at every railway station of any size in the country. But the major houses' policy, in respect to established authors, was to reprint in the "standard novel" format, reduced in the 1870s to 3s 6d. The interval after initial publication varied with the author: a year or two in the case of Eliot and Trollope, three to five in that of Thackeray, and substantially longer in that of Dickens.

One momentous development at the very beginning of the Victorian era provided the common reader, unserved by the libraries, with an opportunity to read fiction hot from the writer's pen. This was serialization, a practice often employed in the eighteenth century for certain kinds of titles, and now revived and adapted to the changing market. Serialization took two forms, both of which had the advantage to the reader of spreading the cost of a full-length work over many months. One was publication in magazines, which had often been used for printing minor fiction on the installment plan. The other was the part, or number, issue, which burst into view when it was employed for *Pickwick Papers* in 1836–7. Priced at an affordable shilling and sold over the counter like conventional periodicals, these monthly (less often, weekly), illustrated, thirty-two-page paperbound "parts" reached a large public that seldom if ever ventured inside a bookshop. It was in this form that Dickens was catapulted to early fame, with the fifteenth number of *Pickwick* selling the then unearthly total of 40,000 copies. In the next two decades several other novelists, including Thackeray with *Vanity Fair* (1848), *Pendennis*, and *The Newcomes* (1855), published their new novels in parts. In the fifties and sixties the part issue was gradually superseded by shilling monthly magazines specializing in fiction along with a variety of other material, but several of Trollope's novels appeared in numbers and Dickens clung to the practice to the very end of his life.

These innovations – the three-decker novel and the newly adapted two forms of serialization – presented authors with a mixture of opportunity and constraint, of flexibility and pressure. Gissing described his author-character Edwin Reardon as being both restive and cynical under the "astonishing system" imposed on workaday novelists by the tyranny of the guinea-and-a-half novel, which was described in a practical guide to authorship (1829) as a work consisting of three volumes containing from 300 to 324 pages each, each page having twenty-two lines to the page and eight words in each line. This fossilized and procrustean format, including large type, wide spacing, and as many blank pages as possible – the printers' way of coping with the problem of making more out of less obviously called for an intolerable amount of literary padding to swell into the obligatory three volumes. Reardon, as he said, "kept as much as possible to dialogue; space is filled so much more quickly, and at a pinch one can make people talk about the paltriest incidents of life" as makeweight. At the same time, novelists had to stretch their plots and complicate matters with subplots and to indulge in "lengthy description of locality" and "deliberate analysis of character and motive," which, in terms of sheer craftsmanship, may or may not have been bad (ch. 9). Certainly, the exigencies of three-decker publication and serialization were largely responsible for what some modern readers consider the verbosity, inordinate length, qualitative unevenness, and sometimes the sheer formlessness of much Victorian fiction.

The celebrated formula attributed to Wilkie Collins, "Make 'em cry, make 'em laugh, make 'em wait," summarized the most obvious requirements imposed by serialization. Besides one or more dramatic episodes relevant to the ongoing narrative, each installment should contain a judicious balance of sentiment and humor, and above all, it should end with a suspenseful situation that would ensure a healthy sale of the next number, which would reveal "what happened next." Recent scholarship, carefully examining the overall structure of the parts, has shown that it was not all that simple, but the general principle still obtained. Novelists had to fashion a product that was both complete (i.e. contained a good shilling's worth of mixed obligatory ingredients) and left readers impatient to get on with the story – next month.

Writers of serialized fiction, therefore, as Dickens's surviving working papers ("mems") richly testify, confronted problems of structure, arrangement, pace, and emphasis that had to be solved as they proceeded, within the strictly ordained physical limits of each installment, under the inexorable pressure of deadlines, and without a chance to review and revise what they had written before it went to the printer, whose errand boy was often at the door, awaiting new copy. Some adjustments could be made in proof, but only hurriedly and still within the unbreachable confines of the number. Only a major emergency, such as Dickens's prostration following the death of Mary Hogarth while he was writing *Pickwick Papers* and *Oliver Twist* simultaneously, and Thackeray's serious illness in the midst of *Pendennis*, could be allowed to interrupt the steady rhythm of production.

Unlike most early three-volume novels, serialized fiction was regularly illustrated, each number containing one or more engravings by popular artists like George Cruikshank and "Phiz" (Hablot K. Browne). Authors came to realize that illustrations, prepared under their supervision and integrated with the text, helped readers visualize the characters and scenes, and so, after the middle of the century, fiction in volume form also came to include pictures. John Everett Millais, for example, drew some 100 illustrations for four of Trollope's novels.

Serialization brought novelists closer to their audiences and made them more responsive to their expectations than ever before. Dickens and Thackeray cultivated a familiar style suitable to monthly vicarious visits to their readers' firesides, reducing the subtle psychological barrier of print that ordinarily kept writer and reader at a distance. Month-by-month sales figures, moreover, supplied an instantaneous measure of buyers' satisfaction, a grassroots expression of "reader response" which antedated by more than a century the department of literary theory known by that name. Reacting to this early warning system, novelists could change course while there was still time, a benefit not available to those whose books came before the public in finished form. When in 1843 the monthly sales of *Martin Chuzzlewit* fell alarmingly below the level set by Dickens's previous novels, he took the drastic step of moving his characters to America, a land of immediately topical – satirical – interest. Serialization also enabled writers to receive feedback directly from readers and, if they found it persuasive, to act upon it. Dickens, learning that his depiction of Miss Mowcher in *David Copperfield* (1850) offended some Jewish readers, made rather awkward amends in a later number.

Thackeray, hearing a fellow diner make a casual remark about closing a puppet box, promptly adopted it as the closing metaphor in *Vanity Fair*. Trollope, overhearing a clergyman at his club complaining to another that he was bored by Mrs Proudie, then appearing in *The Last Chronicle of Barset*'s weekly numbers (1866–7), went home and killed her off.

Samuel Johnson is often said to have been the first important literary figure to have lived exclusively by the pen. This is not quite accurate, but it does provide background for the fact that by the early nineteenth century the profession of letters, in the sense of a full-time occupation, was still sparsely populated and socially stigmatized, as the pejorative ring of the eighteenth-century phrase "writing for the booksellers" suggests. But the new economics of publishing as influenced by the technological revolution, the growing visibility and acceptance of the products of the press in the ordinary byways of life, and dawning consciousness of a vast, previously unnoticed and potentially lucrative market, went some way toward gentrifying Grub Street, even though, as Gissing's title implies, it was far from being razed. Full-time authorship, especially novel-writing, appeared to be a viable (and, to the inexperienced, easy) way to make a good living. There was a great deal more money in the literary pot and increasing numbers of authors competing to share it. As early as 1843, in a now totally forgotten novel, *Joseph Jenkins*, the hack journalist James Grant said, on unspecified authority, that "in London alone, the number of persons who have adopted authorship as a profession, and who have no other means of subsistence, is from 3,000 to 4,000. To these are to be added the thousands who have commenced a literary career with a view to following it as a profession." The writer went on to say that the total number of those who were either living as best they could by some form of writing, or who had tried and quit within the past twenty years, was "about 10,000." It followed that only a minuscule portion of would-be professional authors succeeded in making a "permanent and ample living" at their desks (3: 169–70). In 1888 Walter Besant, himself a bestselling novelist (*All Sorts and Conditions of Men*, serialized in *Belgravia Magazine*, 1882) and founder of the professional guild called the Society of Authors, estimated that there were then in London alone "fourteen thousand men and women who live by writing," of whom all but a thousand were "in some way connected with journalism" (*Fifty Years Ago*, new edn, 1892, pp. 176–7).

Not wholly incidentally, it may well have been realization of the power of the audience's purse that led to a heightened sensitivity on the part of authors to their standing with that audience and the general problem of fame: witness Browning's poem "Popularity" (1855) and his more personal, wry address near the end of *The Ring and the Book* (1868–9) to the "British public" who "may like me yet," as if they had some distance to go. (He was right: the first 3,000-copy edition of volumes 1 and 2 was to last twelve years.)

One effect of this conception of literature as a dependable generator of income was to demystify the art as romanticized by Shelley and Carlyle: the hieratic coarsened into the crassly materialistic. Aspirants to the profession of letters came to define their hoped-for success as much in terms of pounds sterling as in gratifying but not necessarily remunerative popular acclaim. The profession was all the more alluring because it was open to all talents, the first respectable Victorian occupation to be an equal opportunity, affirmative action employer. It required no capital or equipment beyond one's active mind, an inkwell, pens, a quire of paper, and postage. Social rank was not a consideration, since manuscripts could be submitted by mail, with only a signature, or a pseudonym, to indicate the author. Nor was gender, as is attested by the number of women who entered the field. Of the 878 novelists listed in John Sutherland's *Stanford Companion to Victorian Fiction*, 312 were women. And that does not take account of the many women who wrote nonfiction of various kinds. Other things being equal, a reasonably talented women with a profligate father or husband to support had as much chance of success as a harried father of a large young family.

The methods of payment underwent a revision that occupied most of the century. The old subscription system, by which friends and patrons of an author in effect underwrote the printing of his work by promising to buy one or more copies, had virtually disappeared in favor of two widely employed practices. One was the outright sale of a work's copyright, the author receiving a lump sum from the publisher, after sometimes strenuous bargaining. This meant that he or she totally surrendered the property to the publisher, and if the publisher subsequently made a handsome profit from it, so much the worse for the author. In a variation of this arrangement, the publisher leased the copyright for a stated period, after which it reverted to the author, who was then free to offer it elsewhere. The much-used alternative was publication on a profit-sharing basis, in which author and publisher split the proceeds, if any, half and half or in some other proportion, but only after the publisher had recovered his costs. As a regrettable number of unwary writers learned the hard way, this was a common means of defrauding writers. More than a few sharks lurked in the depths of Victorian publishing, as was demonstrated by the experience of both Emily Brontë and Trollope, whose debuts were grievously mismanaged by one T. C. Newby, who in the course of his career ran up a record of misdeeds as long as a Victorian sermon. Such occurrences were not uncommon in those years, and they ultimately contributed to the adoption, by the end of the century, of the more straightforward and easily policed royalty system.

A few writers did find Golconda. Smith, Elder lured George Eliot away from Blackwood by offering £10,000 for *Romola* (1863); she settled for what she regarded as an even better deal, £7,000 for the copyright, with the proviso that it would revert to her after six years. Longman credited Macaulay with £20,000 on the third and fourth volumes of his *History of England* (1855), and had enough left over to pay the prime minister, Disraeli, £10,000 for his last novel, *Endymion* (1880). At the height of Trollope's popularity in the sixties his income from writing averaged a very comfortable £4,500 a year, two or three thousand per novel. But the two preeminent money makers among the Victorians were the monarchs of their respective realms. The size of the estates Dickens and Tennyson, men especially gifted with business acumen, left behind, translated into late twentieth-century terms, clearly placed them among the millionaires of their day. It was a sign of the times that a new fictional embodiment of worldly success was the hero who made good as a writer, notably David Copperfield and Arthur Pendennis.

Since money was at the root of the transactions between publishers and authors, their relations were normally, one might say almost congenitally, adversarial. Carlyle made no bones about his detestation of publishers. Authors suspected that publishers were out to cheat them and complained, like Swinburne and any number of modern authors, that they did not spend enough on advertising. Publishers, for their part, were convinced that authors did not understand how business operated or the extent to which publishers', and for that matter authors', profits were hostage to the caprices of popular taste. Trollope, himself a shrewd and tough bargainer, dealt with sixteen different publishers during his busy career but made close friends with none of them. One wonders which provided the model for Lady Carbury's publisher, the senior partner in the descriptively named firm of Leadham & Loiter, in *The Way We Live Now* (1875).

There were, however, memorable instances of business relations ripening into personal cordiality, even apart from publishers' recognition that self-interest required them to cultivate the money-spinning writers on their lists, to be sure they did not stray to another house. Some successful publishers and their star authors belonged to the same London clubs. Tennyson and Edward Moxon, "the publisher of poets," had a friendship that ended only with Moxon's death. Later, Tennyson was on equally warm terms with Alexander Macmillan, who was also Matthew Arnold's friend. Charles Kingsley was godfather to Macmillan's children. George Smith, one of the most sympathetic and open-handed of publishers, was a close friend of Thackeray, the Brontë sisters, Browning, and Ruskin, among others. From the literary standpoint, perhaps the most fruitful of these half-professional, half-personal friendships was that between George Eliot (and George Henry Lewes) and John Blackwood. Their voluminous correspondence is replete with discussions of production and sales, of authorial problems on her side and suggestions on such matters as style and characterization on his.

In this latter regard, Blackwood performed the function served in other firms by the "literary adviser" or in-house reader, a type of professional employee who seems to have come into being some time in the 1830s. This person, usually university-trained and an established author in his own right, became indispensable when heads of firms had to devote themselves to management, with less time to spare for the editorial side of the business than in more spacious days. He (or she, in the case of the Carlyles' feminist friend Geraldine Jewsbury, who worked for Richard Bentley for fifteen years) was paid to deal, in the first instance, with what twentieth-century publishers would come to call the slush pile of unsolicited manuscripts as well as submissions of new work by writers already published by the firm, and then give the head of the house advice on the ones that survived the first go-through. Advisers also might be charged with bringing promising new authors to the firm, as Smith, Elder's W. S. Williams did, thus acting in the capacity of a modern acquisitions editor. The lawyer and editor John Forster worked both sides of the street, as Chapman & Hall's longtime literary adviser and the friend and sometimes the agent of Dickens, Leigh Hunt, Carlyle, Bulwer-Lytton, and Walter Savage Landor. His successor at the firm, George Meredith, is enduringly remembered as the seer with the clouded crystal ball who rejected such eventual bestsellers, in the hands of more perceptive publishers, as Mrs Henry Wood's sensational novel *East Lynne* (1861) and some of the novels of "Ouida" (Marie Louise de la Ramée), a queen of the circulating libraries. He also turned thumbs down on Samuel Butler's *Erewhon* (1872) and early productions of George Bernard Shaw, but on the other hand he was an early champion of Gissing, among others. Edward Garnett, who worked for several firms, cultivated and advised a number of important late Victorian and Edwardian writers, especially Joseph Conrad, whose early career he carefully nurtured. The history of Thomas Hardy's attempt to become a novelist is largely that of his struggles with publishers and editors and their advisers, including a sympathetic Meredith, to conquer their nervousness over his use of realistic detail.

Manuscript readers acted as surrogates not only for their employers but, in respect to fiction, for their employers' de facto employer, Mudie's library. Not merely surrogates but censors, they were charged in effect with enforcing the strict code of evangelical morality that was Mudie's criterion of acceptability. Ever fearful of losing library business, publishers had an ineradicable phobia against even the faintest suggestion of realism. Decorum had to be maintained, at whatever expense of candor. There was appreciable irony in the fact that Meredith, for many years Chapman & Hall's faithful watchdog, saw his own *Ordeal of Richard Feverel* (1859) banned from Mudie's shelves.

Poetry, traditionally the supreme literary genre, was little affected by Mudie's domination of the original-edition market. While it is true that the first nineteenth-century bestsellers were not novels but expensive editions of poetry (*Marmion*, 31s 6d; *The Lady of the Lake*, two guineas), original editions subsequently were priced to sell to what publishers evidently considered to be a small market of poetry lovers, Tennyson's multitudes of admirers aside. Tennyson's and Browning's successive volumes cost six or seven shillings each, significantly less than the per-volume cost of a three-decker. Even after Browning's reputation was belatedly established, his publishers ordered initial print runs of only 2,000 copies. Occasionally publishers sought to apply to volumes of poems the same formats they used so successfully with novels, hoping for the same results, but to no avail. Earlier (1841–6), Moxon had experimented with part-issue, then the latest thing in aggressive publishing, by bringing out Browning's *Bells and Pomegranates* at irregular intervals, in eight booklets priced from 6d to 2s 6d. This brought no profit to either publisher or author, nor did Moxon's later Illustrated Edition of Tennyson for the carriage trade (1858), a lavish production in the format and at the price of a guinea-and-a-half novel, but containing in its single volume only the contents of the poet's 1842 collection. Ten thousand copies were printed but they encountered massive price resistance, and in the end half of the edition was ignominiously remaindered. Still, this was only a momentary stumble in Tennyson's triumphant progress toward bestsellerdom. The next year, the first books of *Idylls of the King* sold 10,000 out of a first printing of 40,000 in the first week; in the first few weeks after publication in 1864 *Enoch Arden and Other Poems* sold 40,000, including 2,500 bought by Mudie, and 20,000 copies of *Demeter and Other Poems* (1889) were snapped up in the first week. No other Victorian poet of lasting stature even approached such figures.

Apart from being chiefly responsible for the triumph of fiction as the most popular literary genre, displacing religious books in the rankings by the 1870s, publishers' greatest contribution to Victorian middle-class culture was their sponsorship of a wide field of periodicals which, among other things, ended the domination of the longwinded and expensive (six shillings) highbrow quarterlies, the *Quarterly*, the *Edinburgh*, and the *Westminster*. Alongside these had appeared, early on, such ground-breaking general-interest magazines as *Blackwood's* (1824) and three founded in the immediate pre-Victorian years, *Fraser's* (1830), *Tait's Edinburgh Magazine* (1832), and *Bentley's Miscellany* (1837). All four of these half-crown magazines, it will be noted, had the effect of keeping their respective publishers' names before the book-buying public, as a kind of house advertisement.

The same promotional purpose was behind the naming (*Macmillan's*, *Longman's*, *Tinsley's*, *Cassell's*) of several of the score or more of periodicals established after the explosive success in 1860 of Smith, Elder's *Cornhill Magazine*, edited by Thackeray and paying some of the highest fees in the business. Typically priced at a shilling, these magazines and reviews supplied publishers with a regularly renewed showcase for their house authors as well as for promising young talent who might, in the future, provide them with book-length manuscripts. They bought the work of, all told, thousands of authors, a versatile army (see the roll call in the fifth volume of the *Wellesley Index to Victorian Periodicals*) whose aggregate production embraced not only serialized and short fiction but seemingly every topic of possible interest to middle-class readers.

At one end of the spectrum were magazines that went in for light fiction and popularized knowledge, among them *Longman's*, *Tinsley's*, and *Temple Bar*, plus Dickens's two mass-circulation weeklies, *Household Words* and *All the Year Round*. Somewhere in the middle lay the *Cornhill* and *Macmillan's*, which also printed fiction but balanced it with more substantial factual fare. At the heavy end, most directly displacing the old magisterial quarterlies, were the *Saturday Review*, *Nineteenth Century*, and *Fortnightly*, addressed to the educated elite: "journals of opinion" that as a group fulfilled John Stuart Mill's ideal of a supermarketplace of ideas, political, social, religious, economic – whatever subjects engaged the public mind at the moment. It was in these latter periodicals that the so-called higher journalism flourished, a peculiarly Victorian institution that enlisted the minds and pens of many if not most of the leading exponents and arbiters of contemporary thought.

If the intellectual history of the Victorian era is a record of constant ferment and debate, the entrepreneurial, competitive spirit of publishing can be thanked. Some of the seminal works of Victorian literature originated as informal series of articles known to later generations in their collected form: Arnold's *Essays in Criticism* and *Culture and Anarchy*, Ruskin's *Unto This Last*, Pater's *Studies in the History of the Renaissance.* . . . The distinctive forms such prose of exposition and controversy acquired, and the styles their authors adopted, were due in no small degree to the matrix in which they first appeared. Consciously or not, contributors were affected by the qualities of the periodical they had in view – not only the level and ideology of its readership, but its tone and its editorial policy, which might involve commitment to certain principles or, on the other hand, might be, as Trollope said of the *Fortnightly*, "neither conservative nor liberal, neither religious nor free-thinking, neither popular nor exclusive" (*Autobiography*, ch. 10).

All these developments occurred on the socially superior level of the middle-class audience, effectively separate from Collins's "unknown public," which, from the time he wrote (1858) onward, was increasingly spoken of as a "mass" readership. Like "bestseller," the concept the adjective represented was indeterminate, as it remains today, its magnitude and demographic spread depending on the immediate context. In its most restricted Victorian sense, it referred to the large, but still circumscribed, lower-middle-class market that lay outside Mudie's "select" clientele. Most broadly, it represented the totality of men, women, and children who were at least able to read simple texts and possessed at least a penny or two at a time to spend for some sort of agreeable printed matter.

It was to this latter extensive audience, nebulously conceived at the outset, that two publishers – exceptions to the general indifference mentioned at the beginning of this chapter – had addressed themselves in the 1820s. Scott's publisher, Archibald Constable, confided to his bestseller author his dream of supplying the mass market (as he did not call it) with cheap books selling "not by thousands or tens of thousands, but by hundreds of thousands – ay, by millions!" He went bankrupt shortly afterward, so that his projected saturation of the market did not have a fair trial. But at the same time (1826) the newly formed Society for the Diffusion of Useful Knowledge was launching two "libraries" (series) of "useful" (scientific and utilitarian) and "entertaining" (somewhat less heavy) volumes, sold in sixpenny fortnightly parts. These had the implicit purpose of weaning their intended working-class readers from the cheap radical publications whose easy availability and inflammatory messages seemed to threaten the nation's stability. But their popularity was short-lived if not wholly illusory, and the initially large circulation of the society's *Penny Magazine*, somewhere between 100,000 and 200,000, and of its commercial rival, *Chambers's Edinburgh Journal* (both 1832) was not long sustained, although the latter, which printed crowd-pleasing fiction as the *Penny Magazine* did not, lasted well into the twentieth century.

These and other experiments in the first half of the Victorian period taught commercial publishers valuable lessons, however costly some of them may have been. Their idealism (naiveté?), when applied to their sense of an immense, largely untapped market "out there," had led them to misjudge popular taste. Apart from a strong interest in religious publications, which in any case was more typical of the lower middle class than of the working class, what the mass – poorest, least educated – public wanted, they discovered, was not so much uplifting books and periodicals on "useful" subjects as the red meat of their demonstrably favorite reading fare, the weekly papers that served up ample portions of sensation, salacity, sex (in high places), crime, and radical politics – in all but the last respect, the direct forebears of today's London tabloids.

Such lessons eventually proved to have been well learned. By the closing decades of the century publishers' command of the mass audience, attended by cut-throat competition on the part of the downmarket firms, was all but complete. Certain pieces of legislation helped. The abolition of the newspaper tax in 1855 opened the way for cheapened daily papers: the *Daily Telegraph* went down to a penny in 1856 and other London papers followed suit, and dailies sprang up for the first time in provincial cities. Newspaper reading for the first time became as much a habit of day laborers as of gentlemen in clubs, and the profit and power accruing from catering to it bred a new kind of plutocrat, the so-called press baron. Forster's Education Act (1870), which made elementary education universally available, produced a whole new generation of literates. New technology also helped. Printing presses with ever-greater capacity and the adoption of chemically treated wood pulp as the main ingredient in machine-made paper cheapened the product. It was no accident that the very word "pulp" came to designate magazines containing, as the *Concise Oxford Dictionary* puts it, "sensational or poor-quality writing." Indeed, a momentous but still little-studied effect of mass-market publishing was its encouragement of a simplified prose style, suited to the limited comprehension of many readers, which, inverting a law of cultural gravity, had a trickle-upward impact on the style of the higher journalism and literary writing in general.

In this outpouring of books and magazines, justifiably advertised as "miracles of cheapness!", there was plenty to satisfy every taste. "Shilling shockers" issued in weekly parts and "penny dreadfuls" complete in thirty-two pages continued the robust tradition of thrillers stemming from the Gothic romances of a century earlier. And for those who preferred canonical authors, there were, for example, a shilling edition of Shakespeare's complete works, purchasable in penny numbers; Waverley novels at 3d; a 473-page illustrated Byron at 7d; and a sixpenny *Sartor Resartus*, which sold 70,000 copies in 1882. All these products of price-cutting wars were paperbacks, and they were textually as well as physically shoddy, with strenuously small type often printed in double columns. But it was doubtless inevitable that literary quality and the visual appeal of format should both have been sacrificed when print culture enveloped all of English society.

Amidst all the vicissitudes, frustrations, frictions, bad guesses, lucky accidents, triumphs, and defeats that were inevitable when two disparate and vigorous social entities, commerce and culture, were brought into uneasy partnership, Victorian publishing was, in the long run, genuinely "creative." It made readers of millions of people who would not otherwise have exercised their semi-literacy beyond reading labels on merchandise and posters on walls and buses; for better or worse, it revolutionized literary culture by making Britain into what no country had ever been before, a nation of avid novel readers; under its patronage, the clerisy – the intellectual elite – increased in number, prospered, and had a decisive influence on the acts and opinions of the age. In fact, the form and content of Victorian literature, and by reflection the characteristic tone of society at large, would have been very different had it been generated and made available under another set of circumstances.

See also 1897; COMMERCIAL; POETRY, FICTION, SAGE WRITING, LITERARY CRITICISM

REFERENCES

Altick, Richard D. (1957) *The English Common Reader: A Social History of the Mass Reading Public, 1800–1900.* Chicago: University of Chicago Press.

Anderson, Patricia J. and Rose, Jonathan (1991) *British Literary Publishing Houses, 1820–1880.* Dictionary of Literary Biography 106. Detroit: Gale Research.

——(1991) *British Literary Publishing Houses, 1881–1965.* Dictionary of Literary Biography 112. Detroit: Gale Research.

Buckler, William E. (1958) *Matthew Arnold's Books: Toward a Publishing Diary.* Geneva: Librairie E. Droz.

Dooley, Allan C. (1992) *Author and Printer in Victorian England.* Charlottesville: University Press of Virginia.

Erickson, Lee (1996) *The Economy of Literary Form: English Literature and the Industrialization of Publishing, 1800–1850.* Baltimore: Johns Hopkins University Press.

Feltes, N. N. (1986) *Modes of Production of Victorian Novels.* Chicago: University of Chicago Press.

Gatrell, Simon (1988) *Hardy the Creator: A Textual Biography.* Oxford: Clarendon Press.

Gettmann, Royal A. (1960) *A Victorian Publisher: A Study of the Bentley Papers.* Cambridge: Cambridge University Press.

Griest, Guinevere L. (1970) *Mudie's Circulating Library and the Victorian Novel.* Bloomington: Indiana University Press.

Hagen, June Steffensen (1979) *Tennyson and His Publishers.* University Park: Pennsylvania State University Press.

Hamer, Mary (1987) *Writing by Numbers: Trollope's Serial Fiction.* Cambridge: Cambridge University Press.

Hughes, Linda K. and Lund, Michael (1991) *The Victorian Serial.* Charlottesville: University Press of Virginia.

Jordan, John O. and Pattern, Robert L. (eds) (1995) *Literature in the Market Place: Nineteenth-Century British Publishing and Reading Practices.* Cambridge: Cambridge University Press.

Kent, Christopher (1969) "Higher Journalism and the Mid-Victorian Clerisy." *Victorian Studies*, 13, 181–98.

Myers, Robin (1973) *The British Book Trade from Caxton to the Present Day: A Bibliographical Guide.* London: André Deutsch.

Patten, Robert L. (1978) *Charles Dickens and His Publishers.* Oxford: Clarendon Press.

Plant, Marjorie (1939) *The English Book Trade: An Economic History of the Making and Sale of Books.* London: Allen & Unwin.

Shillingsburg, Peter (1992) *Pegasus in Harness: Victorian Publishing and W. M. Thackeray.* Charlottesville: University Press of Virginia.

Stone, Harry (ed.) (1987) *Dickens' Working Notes for His Novels.* Chicago: University of Chicago Press.

Sutherland, J. A. (1976) *Victorian Novelists and Publishers.* Chicago: University of Chicago Press.

——(1995) *Writers, Publishers, Readers.* New York: St Martin's Press.

Webb, Robert K. (1955) *The British Working Class Reader, 1790–1848: Literacy and Social Tension.* London: Allen & Unwin.

PART FOUR
Kinds of Writing

21

Poetry

E. Warwick Slinn

I

In 1853 Matthew Arnold enacted a defining event in Victorian poetry: he withdrew from publication *Empedocles on Etna*, the title poem of his previous volume (1852). Poetry should "inspirit and rejoice," he wrote in his famous 1853 Preface, but *Empedocles on Etna*, he said, did neither. In portraying the sustained agonizing of a philosopher–poet, whose suffering found no release in action other than a leap to his death in the crater of Mount Etna, this poem failed to "charm" or "delight."

Because Arnold's aesthetic values were inherited from antiquity – from Sophocles who "saw life steadily and saw it whole" – and from Romanticism – which emphasized the virtues of homogeneity (in consciousness) and cohesion (in form) – he was determined to argue, in spite of his own poem's potential subversiveness, that poetry's "eternal objects" are those "elementary feelings which subsist permanently in the race, and which are independent of time." Thus, he hoisted his aesthetic flag to the masthead of humanist essentialism, influencing whole generations of subsequent readers to the extent even of minimizing features of his own poetry. While that poetry is still admired for its plangent and elegiac lyricism, Arnold's continuing struggle to relieve fellow sufferers from the "strange disease of modern life" ("The Scholar-Gipsy," 1853, 1. 203) tends to be accompanied by a sense of division and irresolution rather than deliverance. His claim in the essay on Maurice de Guérin (1862), for instance, that poetry may reconcile self and world is hardly enacted in poems where speakers are fenced in cloistral rounds, separated from buried lives or trapped on darkling plains. So it makes sense to read Arnold's poetry in terms of Romantic irony rather than Romantic metaphysics (Ryals 1990), and to attend to the repressed poem, *Empedocles*, with its problematic explorations of what can be known, felt, and understood, as more indicative of the radical features of Victorian verse than even Arnold cared to admit.

Arnold's seminal declaration that *Empedocles* embodied a growing cultural emphasis on "the dialogue of the mind with itself" (Preface 1853) points to its concern with self-consciousness and the conditions of subjectivity. Indeed, "mind" suggests that separation of self from world so famously promulgated by Cartesian idealism, the dualistic consequences of the formulaic *cogito ergo sum* ("I think, therefore I am"), where the thinking mind turns in upon itself. Internal dialogue, no matter how divided, would sustain that dualism and its accompanying illusion of a separate, essential self. But the poem is about more than internalized division. It is also about the representations of mind: about not just the conditions of subjectivity, but the means of representing it, about its relationship with language therefore, and about whether indeed subjectivity may be separated from the constructive processes of those very representations. Hence the protagonist himself fears that consciousness may be lost or obliterated in language, "overlaid . . . with words" (II. i. 29–30), or that he may be imprisoned forever in the very forms, modes, and "stifling veils" of mind and thought (II. i. 354).

In these fears Empedocles demonstrates the humanist and idealist desire for a transcendent ego, for that power of origination which was so seductive a feature of Romantic idealism, where the speaker may author herself without falling prey to the modes of otherness. Yet Empedocles is a poet and physician who doubts the value of representation, rejecting the functions of art and action. He presents the dilemma of a person who is no longer able to make meaningful contact with the world through language: the fragments and parables which represent beliefs about the world are regarded by Empedocles as but fragments and parables, linguistic fabrications. In him there is a loss of faith, therefore, not only in providence, but in the creative and communicative possibilities of art.

Although once a youthful idealist and poet like Callicles, whose songs attempt to woo him away from his climb up the crater, he no longer trusts the forms of his earlier trade. To that extent the possibilities for redemption and cohesion through language remain but the trappings of Callicles's hopeful lyricism. By the end of the poem, Empedocles's only alternative is to submit to the materiality of death, to enact meaning by refusing the difference between sign and referent, refusing representation in order to embrace, indeed become, the thing itself. His suicide is hardly a grand action embodying the transcendent joy of a teleologically defined universe, but it is nevertheless conceived by Empedocles in triumphant terms. What is crucial to his perception of this final act, therefore, is its testimony to his own role as agent, its function as the enactment of a freely choosing and independent mind. Consciousness, representation, language, and agency: these are the issues which dominate Arnold's repressed poem and which persist elsewhere in Victorian poetry. The action of *Empedocles on Etna*, combined with Arnold's act of suppression, focuses a defining historical moment because it combines the poetic portrayal of the rupture of humanist idealism with the simultaneous and self-conscious attempt to hide that rupture, to sustain in its place the creative and restorative possibilities of poetic language.

II

While it has been common enough to observe the way Victorian poetry evinces contemporary qualities of introspection, questioning, and perplexity, the example of *Empedocles on Etna* teaches that it is not sufficient to observe these themes without also recognizing that their representation in poetry renders them different from the univocal, polemical writings of the period. Victorian poetry is quite simply more sophisticated, more politically, intellectually, and emotionally complex, than has been credited. It is increasingly being analyzed as a poetry of multiple action which enacts discursive conflict, ideological struggles for the sign, dialectically founded sites for contested meaning. Such discursive process, figuratively and formally constituted as both affirmation and critique, relates in more subtly various ways than are suggested by the singular and passive metaphor of "reflection" to the cultural debates and structures of its time. Victorian poets continued the Romantic rejection of neo-classical decorum (with its hierarchical list of genres from trivial lyric to serious epic); but through the innovations of the dramatic monologue and through an experimental variety of longer forms, they also developed a sense of dynamic heterogeneity which questioned the assumptions of Romantic lyricism, their main and dominating inheritance.

Scholars increasingly emphasize the disruptive counter-side of Romantic writing itself, its disjunctions and mixed genres, the struggles of the speaking subject to establish authenticity. Yet the phenomenological inheritance of the Romantic odal hymn ("Ode: Intimations of Immortality," 1807; "Ode to the West Wind," 1820) bequeathed to Victorian poets a lyric voice which presented itself as autonomous, self-conscious, atemporal, and male, and an aesthetic which promoted the possibilities of transcendence, of attaining through metaphor a universality not bound by time, class, or gender. Several of the Victorian male poets appear to have realized all too quickly the contingency of this practice, and the women poets were faced with a choice about gender conformity – a choice between being written and thereby appropriated by a patriarchal poetics, or opposing that structure and being banished to its margins. Whether gendered through or against the hegemony, however, from the 1830s and 1840s the cultural value of the lyrical voice was in trouble. Its assumed singularity and transparency proved multivalent and mediated. Its expressiveness, its metaphorically flaunted ideality, its atemporal formalism, were increasingly to be recognized as contingent, discourse-based, and ideologically colonized.

Some poets continued writing conventional lyricism, affirming the values of personal feeling, whether as women's celebration of community (identifying consciousness with unmediated inwardness) or as men's celebration of women (identifying consciousness with externalized desire). But others were more questioning. They conducted various experiments in poetic dramatization, whether Elizabeth Barrett Browning's attempt to represent an assertive independence for female speakers,

Christina Rossetti's daring exploration of erotic sublimation, or the ironies of consciousness proposed by Robert Browning, Tennyson, Clough, and Meredith. The attempts to structure feeling in terms of aesthetic stability and universality fell afoul of language which slipped from control. Consequently, readings of Victorian poetry now emphasize its fractured and ambivalent status, whether in terms of the deconstruction of lyrical homogeneity, the ironies of subjective production, or the feminism of patriarchal subversion. What was once represented as a poetry of sentiment and thoughtlessness, or "rumination," which related uneasily to the Romantic requirements of organic unity or mellifluous splendor, becomes now read as problematic structuring, process, and contestation.

Our current understanding of poetry is characterized by recognition of what ought to be obvious in poetic forms: the way poetic language draws attention to itself as language, to its status as sign. So students of Victorian poetry have become attuned to the implications of idealist language (Armstrong 1982), the allegorical (Rowlinson 1994), and linguistic moments where the sign floats free of its referent (Miller 1985), where the requirements of rationality or truth no longer control meaning or cultural signification. Current criticism also proposes the importance of social and ideological contexts (Sinfield 1986; Armstrong 1993), dialectical process (Slinn 1991), Romantic irony (Ryals 1990), intertextuality (Harrison 1990), psychoanalysis (Rowlinson 1994), gender construction (Leighton 1996), and a "cultural neoformalism" which aligns poetic affectiveness with historical specificity (Tucker 1993). The sign, then, the poetic word, as self-consciously displayed and deployed in Victorian verse, is now being read less as the focus for private expressiveness and more as the point where self and world are constructed – the focus for relationships, structured through the intersections of radical otherness and internalized desire; and the locus where subject production, gender difference, and secular power coalesce in moments of conflicting, excessive, frequently confounded utterance.

III

Working within the combined hegemony of utilitarianism and political economy, Victorian poets, with their interest in more symbolic means of signifying, sought to enforce values other than those provided by the capitalist market. Utilitarianism of course also provided them with considerable political and ethical impetus. While they opposed its materialist principles, that opposition nevertheless provided cultural definition, and the writings of William James Fox and Jeremy Bentham offered to early Victorian poets a democratic politics and a theory of fictions (Armstrong 1993). Unfortunately, utilitarianism in its more homogenized and economic form left poets few choices: relegation (poetry is culturally trivial), incorporation (poetry celebrates the delights of commodification), or marginalization (poetry portrays an area of special experience, but remains politically unimportant). The more mythic–symbolic poets who followed Coleridgean idealism – Tennyson, Barrett Browning, Arnold, Christina

Rossetti, Swinburne, Michael Field – generally affirmed areas of special, usually spiritual or metaphorically personal, experience. But whereas Shelley's political poetry, Friedrich Engels reported, was read and understood by the working class, these idealist poets tended towards an ultimately middle-class aestheticism and liberalism. Although the claim of special experience sustained a place in which to assert their ethical and aesthetic values, it inevitably facilitated their incorporation into hegemonic aims. In accepting marginalization they sustained and were structured by the very system they sought to challenge (Sinfield 1986: 17–21).

Yet to the extent that poetic language, more intensively figured than other forms of writing, draws attention to its condition as text, the poetry itself may display a covert radicalism, through representing the means of representing, the means by which hegemonic belief structures were sustained. As suggested by Arnold's *Empedocles*, Victorian poetry frequently enacts a form of expressiveness which in the very act of producing itself as commodity, as material sign, simultaneously provokes a deep sense of resistance to that commodification, whether as an aspect of psychology (Robert Browning's "Pictor Ignotus," 1845), form (*Aurora Leigh*, 1857), temporal presence (Tennyson's "Tithonus," 1860), or theme ("Goblin Market," 1862). In this, it is radically (in the root sense of that term) and inquisitively political, even if, as some cultural theorists would argue, that resistance emerges from the economic institutions of capitalism itself.

Within Victorian poetry, then, commodification functions covertly as the economic and material other to aesthetic and moral value. This dialectical relationship means that the marginalized area of poetic experience, the figuration of feeling and the figuration of figuration, leads back to the materialist center, the figure as itself material. Hence, the poem indicates its own modes of production, both as a physical object and as an instrument in the making of cultural value. Moments of deep poetic crisis therefore tend to incorporate moments of semiotic self-awareness, as, for example, in the climactic episode of Tennyson's *In Memoriam*.

Published at mid-point in the century (1850) and quickly requiring several editions, *In Memoriam* emerged privately from Tennyson's grief at the death of Arthur Hallam, his close friend at Cambridge, and publicly from the widespread religious doubt which accompanied the early nineteenth century increase in new scientific knowledges and questioning of established biblical and political authorities. It focuses therefore an array of cultural issues. The poem fully acknowledges the potential incoherence of a universe without a controlling deity; yet it also forges a brilliant poetic fusion of apocalyptic and scientific discourses. Affirming finally a teleological goal, Tennyson offers, at least momentarily, a reassuring fiction of closure. "Next to the Bible," Queen Victoria is reported to have told him, "*In Memoriam* is my comfort" (Sinfield 1986: 1). But this is not just a poem portraying historical agonizing over faith and doubt. Tennyson also pushes the language of representation to its extremes, relocating the boundaries of conventional thought as he registers, for instance, two crucial shifts in cultural perception. Through a revisionary image of nature ("red in tooth and claw," sec. 56), he replaces the benevolent, feminized nature of pastoral

Romanticism, signaling a move from Romantic valorization of the natural object to Victorian poetic use of nature as an imagistic resource field; and through metaphors of material dissolution ("The hills are shadows, and they flow," sec. 123) he marks the expanded historical consciousness emerging from the new geological time scales. Further, and remarkably, he tests the boundaries of poetic construction. When relating the mystical experience of renewed contact with the dead Hallam (sec. 95) he cleverly deploys the language of paradox ("silent-speaking words" and "love's dumb cry") to diffuse the boundaries between literal and figurative, and thus to initiate the climactic moment when the dead man's "touch" is indeterminately literal and/or figurative in an ecstatic release from the binary structures of spirit and matter: "all at once it seem'd at last / The living soul was flash'd on mine." The sentence threatens to lose coherence: "The steps of Time – the shocks of Chance – / The blows of Death." At which point the poet struggles with the stylistic necessity of structuring the perception in conventional speech: what "matter-moulded forms" are appropriate, or even possible? Herein lies the focus of radical doubt – that uncertainty which observes not only the vicissitudes of faith or the consequences of new knowledge, but also, with Arnold's Empedocles, the problematic of representing the ineffable, of thinking and perceiving outside the requirements of language.

This moment of intensely private experience also acknowledges the role of public and symbolic value in the construction of poetic language. Insofar as doubt focuses on spiritual values, it focuses also on the symbolic constitution of (cultural) wealth, so that while *In Memoriam* overtly deals with the abstractions of faith, those abstractions are rooted in the materiality of loss, the loss, for instance, of Hallam's "touch." The climax of the poem therefore is a moment when touch, both literally and figuratively, is restored. Such moments are to do with formalizing, finding "form," which for Victorian poets means physical manifestation, "meaning" incarnate, poetic creativity linked homologously to spiritual incarnation. The biblical Word made flesh parallels symbolic meaning in the poetic and material word, which in turn necessitates the commodified word, Tennyson's "truths" which are made "current coin" (sec. 36). Much of the Victorian poetry of spiritual crisis similarly explores these boundaries and homologies, probing lines of division, suggesting an interpenetration of flesh and spirit, or conversely positing belief as the mere reflexiveness of metaphoric thinking: Arnold through his devastating image of cultural and spiritual displacement, "Wandering between two worlds, one dead, / The other powerless to be born" ("Stanzas from the Grande Chartreuse," 1855, ll. 85–6); Robert Browning through the dialectical coils of sceptical bishops and sensual monks (1855), or the ironic reflexivity of Caliban's natural theology (1864); Barrett Browning through the possibilities of a New Jerusalem in *Aurora Leigh*; Clough through his doubly dividing and divisible "Dipsychus" (1850–69); Christina Rossetti through the liminality of convent thresholds (1858); and Hopkins unceasingly, whether through a divinely inspired and poetically realized "shipwrack" ("The Wreck of the *Deutschland*," 1875, l. 248) or the sacral interconnectedness of "Brute beauty" ("The Windhover," 1877, l. 9).

During the century the intensively physical aspect of the intermingling of symbol and material becomes increasingly apparent. In Augusta Webster's "A Castaway" (1870), for example, Tennyson's "coin" of spiritual truth becomes the explicitly economic "coin" of a courtesan's life (l. 555). Again the image is both literal (the woman's body as an object of exchange) and figurative (her life is defined, culturally and morally, by how it is "spent"), thus constituting the meeting point of political economy and female worth, and dramatizing in the process the means by which women are ideologically commodified. In such a moment the poet's interest in symbolic value coincides with the economy's focus on market value, both sets of value being focused through the single material image. Again, poetic focus on symbolic meaning enacts a relationship between idealist value and commercial product. That relationship was consummated by Dante Gabriel Rossetti and William Morris when they engaged directly in the physical production of their writing. As Morris well knew, the making of art always confronts the resistances of the material: language incarnate means not just themes and images but papers, bindings, and markets.

IV

The possibility for figurative language to enact its own self-referentiality, effectively allegorizing its moments of self-production (Rowlinson 1994), is one key to what is radical in Victorian poetry. Furthermore, as suggested for *In Memoriam*, it is a reflexiveness which incorporates historical and political contexts. In *Maud* (1855), for instance, the condition of England and the condition of the deranged hero are represented "as utterly congruent and as reciprocally determined" (Tucker 1988: 407). Crucially, however, linguistic self-reference or self-enactment, simultaneously formal and thematic, is a feature of what has become recognized as the main Victorian contribution to poetic form, the dramatic monologue. Conventionally associated with Robert Browning (though his own term was "dramatic lyric" or "dramatic romance"), it was nevertheless invented contemporaneously by Tennyson, and dramatic poems (employing speakers other than the poet) by Felicia Hemans and Letitia Landon predate the early monologues of both Tennyson and Browning.

In many respects the dramatic monologue was an unprecedented poetic phenomenon. From its inception in the 1830s and 1840s, its use spread rapidly, flooding the literary market and requiring puzzled reviewers to learn to describe its idiosyncrasies and implications. It appeared in numerous variants and was employed by an incredible array of poets, both men from Tennyson to Swinburne, and women from Hemans to Webster. As a literary form it was utterly immersed in the cultural conditions of its time – philosophical, aesthetic, political, and especially psychological.

In the first half of the century the concept of psychology was shifting from an earlier focus on the human soul or mind, as distinct from the body, to embrace both mind and body through mental pathology – aberrations and diseases. Central to this movement was a changing definition of insanity, and it is that which most relates to the advent of dramatic-psychological poetry. The understanding of madness broadened from loss or impairment of reason, through deluded imagination, to what the French called "rational lunacy" (*folie raisonnante*) or the British "moral insanity." After J. C. Prichard's *Treatise on Insanity* (1835), insanity became widely known in England as a quasi-moral condition: a "morbid perversion of the feelings, affections, and active powers," often coexisting with "an apparently unimpaired state of the intellectual faculties" (Prichard, cited in Faas 1988: 45). The boundaries between the mad and the sane were thus being blurred, and this possibility of a rational yet morbidly, even comically, excessive mind clearly fascinated Tennyson ("St Simeon Stylites," 1842; *Maud*) and Robert Browning ("Porphyria's Lover," 1836; "Too Late," 1864). At the same time, moral insanity also rendered intense passion somewhat precarious. Any hint of excess could suggest mental imbalance: merely "moral delinquency," for instance, or when a "modest female" acts in a "bold" and "indecent manner" (Faas 1988: 45). Poets exploited all of these aspects. By choosing aberrant or excessive speakers, they kept poetry as a genre for passion, though no longer in the discredited terms of Romantic lyricism; they also encouraged the reader to become an active participant and to contemplate the political as well as the psychological significance of the passion indulged: "I am not mad: I am black," asserts Barrett Browning's infanticidal slave mother ("The Runaway Slave at Pilgrim's Point" 1848, l. 218).

Accompanying the professional psychological development was an even broader tradition of introspection, which emerged from the growing desire to define the nature of selfhood in the late eighteenth and early nineteenth century. Self-analysis had been established by figures such as Locke, Hume, Hartley, Reid, and Priestley as a primary prerequisite to study of the mind, and this, combined with an equally strong Romantic aesthetic emphasis on expressiveness fueled by philosophical idealism, meant that by the early Victorian age there was a widespread obsession with self-scrutiny (Shaw 1987: 47–74). It was also claimed by some psychologists that the only way to understand the insane was to identify with their plight, to imagine what it must be like to see with their eyes. These are also the techniques of the Romantic poet, the powers of sympathetic identification, what Arthur Hallam praised as the young Tennyson's "power of embodying himself in ideal characters" (Armstrong 1993: 340), or what Fox equally admired in Tennyson as "the secret of the transmigration of the soul" (Faas 1988: 61).

Philosophically, the dramatic monologue can be read as a response to Romantic idealism and the crisis of dualism (body and soul, material and ideal, public and private, culture and nature) inherited from Western metaphysics and the Cartesian *cogito*. The form challenges dualism through representing the self not as a separate unit, but as tied to linear history and an open cultural system. It also represents the contradictions and differences of the self in language, continually enacting the doubled subject as both homogeneous "true person" and heterogeneous, disappearing moment of speech or signification (Martin 1985: 28–31). Foregrounding textual difference and its constitutive processes (Slinn 1991: 33–7), the monologue form thus shifts aesthetic ideologies from homogeneity and wholeness to continuity and incompletion. Combining lyric with narrative and dramatic elements, it disrupts atemporal universality, introduces mimetic particularity, and emphasizes the dialogical nature of language, challenging as it does so idealist notions of the essential and single self.

The political implications of the form emerge from Robert Browning's responses during the 1830s to the contemporary theories of John Stuart Mill, which led him to realize how it might be possible to stage a cultural critique through the structuring processes of a poetic monologue. Mill's famous account of poetry as the expression of "overheard" feeling was parodied in Browning's early monologues, "Porphyria's Lover" and "Johannes Agricola" (1836; later called "Madhouse Cells," 1842), showing how the solipsism of isolated personal feeling leads to delusion and visions of omnipotence. Mill's distinction between poetry and rhetoric effectively produced what Isobel Armstrong calls a "poetics of exclusion" (Armstrong 1993: 137), denying to poetry externality, agency, or the validity of public knowledge. Browning circumvented Mill's lyrical cul-de-sac, Armstrong argues, through ideas derived from the liberal milieu both he and Mill shared. W. J. Fox's theories, for example, drawing on features of drama (dialogue, relationship, objectification), allowed for cultural criticism, showing how psychological conditions are grounded in history. These theories did not, however, allow for the function of constitutive fictions (crucial to an art-form based on dramatic illusion), and for that Browning turned to the godfather of utilitarianism, Jeremy Bentham. For Bentham, fictional constructs are potentially iniquitous, yet culturally indispensable; essential to language and conceptualizing, they intervene substantively in the world, effecting choices and actions. By combining these dramatic and fictive theories Browning thus constructed a poetic which is both culturally interventionist and an escape from solipsism (Armstrong 1993: 148–51).

One consequence of the claim for intervention is a recurring play with the possibilities for agency: the dramatic monologue offers a tacit paradigm for the exigencies of subjective and subjected action. It displays, for instance, an array of acts which play upon the meaning of assertiveness. Such acts exhibit an enormous emotional and psychological diversity, ranging (to take the political just in terms of the female other) from the tyranny of negation ("Porphyria's Lover") and ideological construction (D. G. Rossetti's "Jenny," 1870), to the rebellion of the woman *as* other (Barrett Browning's "Runaway Slave") and the self-appraisal of political economy by one of its products (Webster's "A Castaway").

As the form is developed it becomes fundamentally dynamic. The substantial monologues of Robert Browning's maturity, for example, display an endlessly dynamic process of subjectivity in discourse. Numerous borders are approached or transgressed as speakers proffer various versions of "the dangerous edge of things" ("Blougram," l. 395), that liminality where our fascination follows not simply ambivalence (Blougram's "tender murderer" is too static a nomination for Browning), but interplay, a discursive restlessness which readers and critics have yet fully to identify or understand. Speakers become linguistically bacchanalian, energetically excessive, representing in order to re-present, as if living in a textualized culture means, as in the world of commodities, an unceasing proliferation of signs. Such proliferation induces psychological uneasiness, disease, and a consequential search for the conclusive, concluding word which never arrives because words are discursive, achieving signification only through their movement and mobility as signifiers. The dramatic monologue is characterized by this restless dynamic, although there is a difference between monologues which dramatize the dilemma of speakers sympathetically, in effect soliloquies, and those which suggest ironic discrepancies within the speakers' representations: their ludic excess ("St Simeon Stylites"), solipsistic omnipotence ("My Last Duchess," 1842), subtlety of revenge (Barrett Browning's "Bertha in the Lane," 1844), enabling blindness ("Andrea del Sarto," 1855), or eroticized spirituality (Christina Rossetti's "The Convent Threshold," 1858). Robert Langbaum's (1957) emphasis on the tension between sympathy *and* judgment induced by the "full" dramatic monologue remains a useful criterion. At the same time, the widespread Victorian production of poems which exhibit varieties of contestation, where expressiveness is placed in a context which objectifies its process (Arnold's "Grande Chartreuse"), or where a speaker objectifies herself for self-scrutiny (Webster's "By the Looking-Glass," 1866, or "Faded," 1870), marks a cultural phenomenon of monologues which are "dramatic." Through such monologues the politics of textual and cultural construction are held up for scrutiny, and the ideological assumptions of the classic "overheard" lyric are analyzed and rewritten.

V

Ideological formations in Victorian England as in all societies engendered certain patterns and conformities for gender and class relationships. Within the predominant bourgeois, patriarchal, capitalist formations, gendered positions in particular were assumed to be essential (fundamentally true) and were inhibiting as well as empowering for all classes and sexes. Yet various poetic representations of the way men read and write women, or how women might read and write themselves, began to question this essentialism. There was both the "Woman Question" and what could be called a "Condition of Manliness Question" (Sussman 1995); and both questions for poets related inevitably to creativity as well as sexuality. Lyric poetry, for instance, as a genre associated with feeling, was culturally feminized and subject thereby to both formalist and psychological control. The idealist-based, expressive poetics which generally prevailed during the century enjoined all poets to develop a "healthy" release of emotions: that meant insanity, for both men and women, was the threatened price for either repressed or excessive passion. This injunction included working-class poets who were exhorted to write inspirationally, that they might model for others a balanced expression of feelings which could otherwise turn morbid (or sociopathic).

Women in this context faced the difficult – because naturalized – barrier of gender prejudice. If women poets transgressed the feminine requirements of the demure and sympathetically sentimental, they were deemed "coarse," unnatural; if they conformed to the ideological feminine, they were deemed merely women and thereby muted. In *Aurora Leigh*, for example, Romney tells Aurora what to expect from male readers: they will judge not what is "mere work" but "mere woman's work," producing certainly "the comparative respect", but that means "the absolute scorn" (II. 232–6). Even for women to have their poems read within established circles entailed overcoming male attitudes which regarded women themselves as the poem, not their writing. Again Romney, famously, states the case: women "give us doting mothers, and perfect wives, / Sublime Madonnas, and enduring saints," but they provide "no Christ," and therefore no "poet" (II. 220–5). While self-sacrificing purity was expected of women, the ideological and scriptural authority of masculine redemption and creation was not. Christina Rossetti challenges this expectation through Lizzie's role in "Goblin Market," and *Aurora Leigh* tells the story of Aurora's persistence with poetry and her eventual integration of both love and work, both sexual and poetic identities.

In the poetry of high culture the inscription of woman as textual object, as in herself a poem to be read, is also sustained by the literary conventions of courtly love, where the woman is passive, inaccessible, idealized, and silent. The complaining poet, frustrated by the unavailability of remote and enduring charms, is by definition male. The point of writing the poem is not to seek sexual consummation, but to sustain the structural relationship between desiring male subject and desirable female object, a structure which constitutes the poet as active agent. For as long as the poet speaks, he maintains his sexual identity as acting, expressive male.

When, conveniently, the desired object is silent, it may be more easily interpreted, rendered mysterious, or endowed with cosmic significance. Hence, in D. G. Rossetti's sonnet sequence *The House of Life* (the paradigm of Victorian courtly idealism; 1870/1881), a woman is that strange code, the "meaning of all things that are" ("Heart's Compass," l. 2), and Rossetti's liberal male speaker in "Jenny" enacts the classic bourgeois reduction of woman to sign, textualizing the female body within male discourse: "The woman almost fades from view," and what is left is "A cipher . . . A riddle" (ll. 277–80). Clearly, lurking in the courtly tradition is a politics of appropriation, which Robert Browning exposes ironically in poems where men declare eternal love for women who never knew they existed: "Cristina" (1842), "Evelyn Hope" (1855), "Too Late." These men introspectively and passively reenact courtly fantasies, but psychic appropriation may also be dangerous if the figurative power of the poet is enacted literally. In D. G. Rossetti's "True Woman: Her Love" (1881) the celebration of reciprocal love rests upon the unquestioned assumption that the woman's passion is "a glass" (l. 3) which mirrors the man's desire. But that same assumption allows Porphyria's lover to strangle her in accordance with what he believes her "darling one wish" (l. 57).

Women poets, then, if they would write of love, confronted a tradition which required their silence, idealizing the feminine only to disempower it. So they sought strategies for intervention. Barrett Browning employs parody in "Lady Geraldine's

Courtship" (1844), while in *Sonnets from the Portuguese* (1850) her method is more elaborate, writing as both poet–lover and beloved in a reflexive relationship with a beloved who is also poet–lover. A complex of roles and reversals empowers the speaker to write and speak for herself, and the sequence ends in an acclaimed interdependence. Christina Rossetti took an opposite strategy in *Monna Innominata* (1881), a sonnet sequence conceived as something of a reply to *Sonnets from the Portuguese*, where she writes as one of the unnamed, silent women. Whereas Barrett Browning sought a place for the woman poet within and through received discourses, Christina Rossetti attempts to act outside them, speaking for the women whom they marginalize and repudiating their worldly assumptions by having her speaker surrender instead to divine love. While Rossetti may shift the terms of the amatory relationship, the radical structural element remains: when her persona speaks of spiritual love, she speaks as a desiring poet of a remote beloved, God. A logocentrically grounded structure of desire which engages unequal agents remains, then, difficult to elude, although in the brief lyric "Day-Dreams" (1857) Rossetti employs another, more subtle strategy. Here she explores the structural ambiguities of courtly relationships through a speaker of undefined gender, who observes and interprets the beloved who "doth not answer" (l. 26). Read in terms of the full possibilities provided by this gender uncertainty, the poem suggests the complex female identity, simultaneously passive and active, which is denied by an appropriating, distinctively male (poet's) gaze; here courtly structures themselves are used to expose and diffuse their assumptions.

Another dominant gender influence on poetry was the doctrine of separate spheres, the bourgeois domestic ideology which immured women in the home while men could wander free. In Robert Browning's "Meeting at Night" and "Parting at Morning" (1845), the contrasting moments of an unnamed speaker who enters the world of private sexual fulfillment at night, only to return to the public world of commercial "gold" the next day, would be gendered male (Sussman 1995: 104–6). An accompanying moral double standard which required women to emulate the impossible ideal of the virgin mother while men were encouraged to sow their seed variously, and to the homosocial approval of their peers, produced many poems about mothers and the requirements of self-effacement (treated ironically in "Bertha in the Lane"), and about prostitution. Women poets from Barrett Browning to Adelaide Procter and Webster resist the denigration of prostitutes, and several poems by men portray the self-justifying casuistry of male complicity ("Jenny," Robert Browning's *Fifine at the Fair*, 1872). In "Lord Walter's Wife" (1862) Barrett Browning brilliantly attacks men's evasions of their own ambivalence and the hypocrisy which transfers moral responsibility to women.

The increasing complexity of nineteenth-century sexuality and the proliferation of its coded performances makes it another area where poetry is generically suited to explore the problematics of discursive representation. Certainly poems display an array of gender-related issues, dramatizing uncertainties, blurring boundaries, exposing the textual artifice of differences: male femininity in *The Princess* (1847) and *In Memoriam*, or the speaker's cry for a new masculinity in *Maud*; redefined roles for women in *Aurora*

Leigh; Robert Browning's representations of homosocial rivalry and the undercurrents to heterosexual success; sisterhood in "Goblin Market"; Clough's and Patmore's explorations of the factitiousness in sexual and religious thinking; Swinburne's combination of dissidence and innocence; the lesbian poems of Michael Field. Many women wrote to affirm the feminine, though few eluded being structured through reference to bourgeois categories (Armstrong 1993: 323). They commonly wrote, for example, about "home, the market, mothers and muses" (Leighton 1996: x), and attempts such as that by Michael Field to construct a separate aesthetic realm through a muse which fuses Sappho, Virgin and Tiresias (White, in Leighton 1996) rest upon categories of established metaphysics. But that is not to militate against their role and influence within contemporary culture. A poem such as *Aurora Leigh*, while it now provokes reservations in some readers about its feminism, quickly became cited within debates about the Woman Question.

If women wrote in relationship to bourgeois culture, so too did working-class poets. The forms and sentiments of their expression, for instance, are frequently the forms and sentiments of middle-class culture. The Parnassians among them, so labeled by Brian Maidment (1987) as those who sought recognition for their cultural achievement, frequently combined neo-classical forms with Romantic natural imagery. Employing Spenserian stanzas (Charles Swain's *The Mind*, 1832; Thomas Cooper's *The Purgatory of Suicides*, 1845), sonnet stanzas (John Rogerson's "Manchester," 1844), couplets (John Prince's "The Death of the Factory Child," 1841; Thomas Cleaver's "Night," 1848), and a form of truncated rime royale (Ebenezer Elliott's well-known "Steam at Sheffield," 1840), they wrote repeatedly with moral indignation, pathos, and pastoral idealism, traditional sentiments to which their traditional stanzaic forms represented a social–historical hearkening back. Prince's "Factory Child," for example, conducts an outraged lament for the death of a boy factory worker exhausted by his labors. The child dies heroically after a sequence in which his mother's memories of his naturalized childhood, when like a young Wordsworth he "knew each sylvan and sequester'd nook" (l. 79), contrast savagely with the industrially wasted body. Tone and imagery are melodramatic, although the outrage maintains the dignity of clearly focused anger.

The mixed elements of this poem indicate the larger dilemma of the working-class poet. There are confused aims and methods, for instance, as Prince mixes elegiac pathos with the hyperbole of political protest, and the "kind philanthropists" who are called on "to emancipate the British slave" (ll. 129–32) remain idealistically classless and so effectively powerless. Prince's use of conservative sentiment rather than political analysis is basically an appeal to moral justice and common humanity, which may be easily read as the dissemination of middle-class British liberalism; yet what better way of appealing to the sympathies of those with political influence? Unfortunately, the middle-class readers who did read this poetry tended to focus precisely on its literary weaknesses as a way of deferring its political challenge. The more aggressive language of the Chartist poets, for instance (Elliott, Gerald Massey, or W. J. Linton, whose doggerel epic *Bob Thin – or, The Poorhouse Fugitive*, 1845, tied weaver Bob's life to the history of British capitalism), was described as an "unpoetic" linguistic violence which threatened poetry itself (Maidment 1987: 288). The conservative, even at times anachronistic, literary ideology of these self-taught poets is no doubt a mimicry which performs their colonized condition, but their energetic and moralizing presence nevertheless became an acknowledged part of the Victorian literary scene. As their work became noticed by middle-class readers like Carlyle and Kingsley, aspects of artisan history and conditions "were made relevant to early Victorian industrial culture" (ibid.: 100).

VI

Finally, a brief polemic: in an age which produced huge works, the poem which stands as the colossus astride Victorian verse is *The Ring and the Book* (1868–9). There are strong competitors in *Aurora Leigh* (1857) and Tennyson's *Idylls of the King* (1859–85), both of which present complex narratives of social and political significance, and both of which incorporate a variety of genres – autobiography, satire, treatise, lyrical prophecy in *Aurora Leigh*; lyric, tragedy, romance, epic in *Idylls of the King*. The *Idylls* stood for a long time as the monumental achievement of Victorian indirection, constructing from the medieval materials of Arthurian legend an epic vision of Britain's imperial splendor and internal decline. As Arthur's impossible morality fails to sustain the Round Table, the poem transforms Tennyson's repeated theme of loss into a symbolic mythos of changing order. Here, as in Arnold's *Empedocles*, is recognition that the inherited values of humanism and patriarchal instruction will no longer suffice.

Aurora Leigh offers a now canonical Victorian statement of women's claims to social and artistic equality. Through its challenge to the conventional feminine, it makes a radical break with its age, although it also enjoyed immense popularity. It flaunts "the woman's figures," exposes debilitating discrepancies between the idealized "natural" and the actual, describes slum dwellings and the working-class poor, represents male brutality and the humiliation of rape victims, displays the competitiveness between women provoked by patriarchal commodification, approaches the potential for same-sex relations between women, and above all dramatizes the experience of a female poet in a bourgeois society. In short, it combines the classic feminist themes of the age: education, love, marriage, creativity, sexual politics.

The Ring and the Book, however, produces a level of formal experimentation and ironizing self-reference that adds an epistemological cutting-edge not found in the other two works. The thematic exploration of truth, through a maze of public opinion, legal fictions, and church structures, combined with a methodological awareness which examines creativity and cultural construction, places the poem at the heart of Western history and metaphysics, and thus at the heart of what was most innovative in Victorian poetry and poetics. It is at once the apotheosis and the critique of the influential Western traditions of idealism and humanist essentialism.

Its demands on readers are legendary. Twice the length of *Paradise Lost*, its sheer size and sustained textual intensity make reading a daunting task. The poem recounts a Roman murder story three times in book I and then through ten discrepant variations from the three protagonists (young wife, aged husband, idealistic priest), members of the populace, lawyers, the Pope, and through further reports in the final book, where there would be an end "had anything an end" (XII.1). But plot is hardly the point. The poem is intent upon problematizing representation. Its concerns lie with evidence, eyewitness accounts, hearsay, history, narrative, imagination, institutional patterning. What happens, the poem asks, to morality, belief, and identity in a culture where signs and discourses multiply and defer, yet where we cannot know otherwise than through "worth of word" (I. 837)? The poem disperses all centers, confusing readers from Henry James onwards who have sought to restore some locus for belief and meaning, a center of consciousness. In all this *The Ring and the Book* culminates those repetitive obsessions of Victorian poetry nominated by Arnold's *Empedocles* – consciousness, representation, language, and agency. It also enacts an evanescent historical margin between Romantic phenomenology and a postmodernist culture of endless differentiation, proliferating simulacra, textualizing representations without closure.

See also 1897; SEXUALITIES; MEDICAL, FINANCIAL, INDUSTRIAL, PUBLISHING; LITERARY CRITICISM

REFERENCES

Armstrong, I. (1982) *Language as Living Form in Nineteenth-Century Poetry*. Brighton: Harvester.
——(1993) *Victorian Poetry: Poetry, Poetics and Politics*. London: Routledge.

Faas, E. (1988) *Retreat into the Mind: Victorian Poetry and the Rise of Psychiatry*. Princeton: Princeton University Press.

Harrison, A. H. (1990) *Victorian Poets and Romantic Poems. Intertextuality and Ideology*. Charlottesville: University Press of Virginia.

Langbaum, R. (1957) *The Poetry of Experience: The Dramatic Monologue in Modern Literary Tradition*. New York: Random House.

Leighton, A. (ed.) (1996) *Victorian Women Poets: A Critical Reader*. Oxford: Blackwell Publishers.

Maidment, B. (ed.) (1987) *The Poorhouse Fugitives: Self-Taught Poets and Poetry in Victorian Britain*. Manchester: Carcanet.

Martin, L. D. (1985) *Browning's Dramatic Monologues and the Post-Romantic Subject*. Baltimore: Johns Hopkins University Press.

Miller, J. H. (1985) *The Linguistic Moment: From Wordsworth to Stevens*. Princeton: Princeton University Press.

Rowlinson, M. (1994) *Tennyson's Fixations: Psychoanalysis and the Topics of the Early Poetry*. Charlottesville: University Press of Virginia.

Ryals, C. de L. (1990) *A World of Possibilities: Romantic Irony in Victorian Literature*. Columbus: Ohio State University Press.

Shaw, W. D. (1987) *The Lucid Veil: Poetic Truth in the Victorian Age*. London: Athlone.

Sinfield, A. (1986) *Alfred Tennyson*. Oxford: Blackwell Publishers.

Slinn, E. W. (1991) *The Discourse of Self in Victorian Poetry*. London: Macmillan; Charlottesville: University Press of Virginia.

Sussman, H. (1995) *Victorian Masculinities: Manhood and Masculine Poetics in Early Victorian Literature and Art*. Cambridge: Cambridge University Press.

Tucker, H. F. (1988) *Tennyson and the Doom of Romanticism*. Cambridge, MA: Harvard University Press.

——(ed.) (1993) *Critical Essays on Alfred Lord Tennyson*. New York: G. K. Hall.

FURTHER READING

Christ, C. T. (1984) *Victorian and Modern Poetics*. Chicago: University of Chicago Press.

Gibson, M. E. (ed.) (1992) *Critical Essays on Robert Browning*. New York: G. K. Hall.

Leighton, A. (1992) *Victorian Women Poets: Writing Against the Heart*. London: Harvester Wheatsheaf; Charlottesville: University Press of Virginia.

Maynard, J. (1993) *Victorian Discourses on Sexuality and Religion*. Cambridge: Cambridge University Press.

Mermin, D. (1989) *Elizabeth Barrett Browning: The Origins of a New Poetry*. Chicago: University of Chicago Press.

Tucker, H. F. (1980) *Browning's Beginnings: The Art of Disclosure*. Minneapolis: University of Minnesota Press.

22

Fiction

Hilary Schor

There would seem to be two reasons not to read another critical essay about the Victorian novel. The first is, quite simply, that everyone already knows enough about the novel. Even the most rapid survey course in English literature will pause at *Hard Times* or *Jude the Obscure*; film and television versions of Henry James and George Eliot continue, startling as it might seem, to win audiences; the annual parade of *Christmas Carol*s and the spectacle of bright-backed Penguin paperbacks in airports would argue that the Victorian novel has won its place at the heart of our culture.

That very cordial relation between Victorian culture and our own might suggest the *other* reason we do not want to think further about Victorian fiction: some of the best recent criticism of the novel has suggested that it is not only overly familiar, but downright bad for us. Novels, it has been variously argued, are an integral part of a system of individual discipline and social formation that took its current, powerful form in the mid-nineteenth century, and has been shaping (and mis-shaping) individual readers and the culture in which they read ever since. In their very form, their forward-moving and morally progressive plots, their emphasis on individual solutions, their mirroring of a diverse but finally all-inclusive social sphere, they inscribe their readers more comfortably, and therefore more insidiously, within a master-plot of cultural control. As D. A. Miller (1987) argues, the very way novelists contrast our unbounded subjectivity to the various boxes, cells, and coffins their novels contain seems to argue ourselves "open" or uncontained – the most dangerous and containing fiction of all. And as Lennard Davis (1987) asks, in a simpler and equally compelling critique of our eagerness to abandon ourselves to "novel" beings: Isn't there something very odd about the spectacle of an airport full of readers poring over novels, and not even moving their lips?

This essay will not begin by disrupting either of these notions. Certainly, something we recognize as the Victorian novel did win a certain amount of cultural authority and has continued not only to be a popular form, but to stand in for "culture" for many readers, both amateur and professional. The Victorian novel is, for many of us, still the most accessible and most beloved form of "masterpiece," with or without television costume dramas. And certainly with that cultural power come other forms of power – though I would hope to complicate a little the chicken-and-egg question of how literature comes to matter to people, and what difference literature makes in the "real world." This essay can perhaps best begin by complicating two ideas on which both the easier assumptions rest: the first, that there is some "natural" relationship between the real world and its fictional representation; and the second, that the Victorian novel had a comfortable relationship to representing that world. But let me begin by raising some questions about what we mean by the "Victorian novel," and whether we are all sure we know what we are reading when we carry these novelistic packages around.

When an undergraduate begins her Victorian novel survey, she is likely to confront a row of orange- or black-backed paperbacks, all with the comfortable apparatus of an introduction, footnotes, and a dim black-and-white apparition of an author on the inside cover. The book is invariably fronted either by a crowd scene, depicting Victorian England as a fairground or railway station, a bazaar of commodity culture, or by a single, solemn-faced, Whistleresque heroine, staring earnestly back at her reader, promising the moral revolutions of the inner life. Victorian novels come to us, that is, poised between questions of outer and inner, public and private life; they tend to contrast and finally to oppose the individual to cultural forces.

They also come to us as a result of a certain lineage, or at least to assume their place in a literary curriculum in such a guise. To return to the literature survey, in most courses (including my own) the Victorian novel comes "after the Romantics," which usually means the Romantic poets. It is a rare student (at the undergraduate or graduate level) who comes to the novel from the essays of Thomas De Quincey or Charles Lamb, or even from the *Sketches* of Boz. The Victorian novel, once approached in survey form, may be even further sealed off from extra-novelistic contamination: even in a course focusing on Victorian literature, the novel is most often opposed to "poetry," usually the intensely psychological monologues of Tennyson and Browning, and to "nonfiction prose," usually the social rantings of Carlyle, Ruskin, and Arnold. The novel, that is, again seems to occupy some uneasy ground between the individual and the collective; and yet its very form, the central plot moving individual from childhood to moral revelation, would seem to focus readers not only on individual stories and individual resolutions, but on the univocal power of plot and personality.

For many first-time readers of Victorian fiction, it may be enough to point out that *all* nineteenth-century novels did not appear in the first instance with orange and black backs. While many contemporary editions attempt to recreate some conditions of Victorian reading – including serial publication, three-volume publication, illustrations, and bindings – it is difficult to disrupt the homogeneity of late-twentieth-century publishing practices. It is even more difficult to disrupt the homogeneity of literary inheritance and pedigree with which we approach the Victorian novel, one of the central factors convincing us (wrongly, I would argue) that we understand what we are holding in our hands.

A different account of the rise of the Victorian novel might offer a more complicated response to my initial claims, that we know all too well what the Victorian novel is, and that it is not terribly good for us. That other version might suggest that the Victorian novel has a more disruptive history than both novel-lovers and critics propose, and poses more difficult problems of form and meaning; that it contains within it a less simplistic (and less socially complicit) account of individualism, society, and representation.

The Victorian novel seems to most critics to have emerged with the spontaneity of its most famous early incarnation: like gravity, when a single apple fell from Newton's sky, the novel began with a single inspiration, the young Boz sitting down to write and "thinking of Mr Pickwick." From there, and from the emergence of *The Pickwick Papers* (1837) from Pierce Egan's flash tales of the London adventurers Tom and Jerry and the sketchy pages of Robert Surtees's *Jorrock's Jaunts* (1838) and other tales of sporting life, came a novel that "placed before the reader a constant succession of characters and incidents," "painted in vivid colours" and "rendered . . . life-like and amusing." I am quoting from Charles Dickens's later preface to the novel, but the coincidence of Dickens's avowedly "realist" definition of his enterprise, its astonishing and culture-wide success, and its publication in the years surrounding Victoria's ascension, make *Pickwick* and its publication-mate *Oliver Twist* (1838) easy markers for the Victorian novel.

But this straightforward birth-narrative needs some roughing-up, or at least some hint of digression. *Pickwick* owes much more to the sketch tradition from which it emerges, and indeed the novels Dickens wrote in those early years bear much less resemblance to the more coherent later cultural productions of the late 1840s, the 1850s, and 1860s. It is worth asking what else was going on in the years of *Pickwick* to make it possible. Against what was Dickens writing, and what earlier strains of nineteenth-century fiction, in particular the novels of the 1830s, was he echoing and amplifying?

The literary forms of the 1830s, like the culture itself, are incredibly diverse, and largely lost to literary history. In contrast to the novels of the earlier Romantic period (Walter Scott and Jane Austen, in particular) the novel moved in the 1830s back into London — and into particular neighborhoods. The novels of the period are highly marked by social indicators: the novel of high society, or "silver fork" novel; the novels of lower-class and criminal life, or "Newgate" novel; the budding social-realist novel, focusing on factory and industrial–urban life; the novels of middle-class or "domestic" realism. Like the details rendered in these novels, their readers are imagined in highly particular ways: as male or female; as themselves living in particular neighborhoods or following specific social practices; as having certain relationships to reading, whether sentimental or cynical, tremulous or aggressive. These novels have failed to retain any readership, in part because they are not very well written by modern standards, by which I mean that they fail to present smooth, seamless prose offering a coherent narrative point of view from which to observe a variety of characters possessing coherent (and sense-making) selves. That is to say, they lack what the Victorians made inevitable, omniscience in the external and internal world, and a cohesion of social and individual perception. (When these do not cohere in Victorian and post-Victorian fictions, we know we are in the presence of madmen and postmodernists.) The earlier novels are also difficult to read because they contain clunky, ill-fitting, and digressive novelist apparatuses: glossaries; footnotes; chunks of text in foreign languages and technical argot. (This is again to say, they are mad and more than a little postmodernist.) These apparatuses are linked, however, to my point about their different relationship to individual and social narratives. The novel does not assume that all readers move easily in all worlds: the world of Edward Bulwer Lytton's Pompeii, in *The Last Days of Pompeii* (1834), is hardly more foreign then either the dandiacal high society of his silver-fork novel *Pelham* (1828), which earned Thomas Carlyle's rage in *Sartor Resartus* (1834), or the thieves' dens he depicts in his Newgate novel *Paul Clifford* (1830). In both novels, Bulwer's habit of introducing untranslated passages of Latin, painstakingly detailed elaborations of dress and social manner, local custom and map-making, and "dropping" into poetry, make England as alien as Pompeii – and as "novelistic." The play of genres we instantly identify in the 1830s is indicative of a deeper play of social identity and anxiety over social representation.

The two figures who make it easier to discuss these issues, and to locate the "rise" of the Victorian novel from this multiplicity of forms and imagined readers, are Thomas Carlyle and Charles Dickens. Carlyle was the most influential reader of novels of the early Victorian period, and no one is more striking in his response to that prickly Victorian sage than his unwished-for disciple, Dickens. Again, the tyranny of survey syllabi has exiled Carlyle to the "social critics" roster, but it is useful to remember that Carlyle attempted to write an historical novel before he turned to the essay (Oscar Wilde called Carlyle's 1837 *French Revolution* the greatest novel of the nineteenth century), and more importantly, that his insanely didactic *Sartor Resartus* contains within its fragments of social vision and prophecy a *bildungsroman*, the story of young Diogenes Teufelsdröckh, who moves from loss to gain, from doubt to certainty, from a love story to a prophetic vision, in true novelistic fashion. Critics often take Teufelsdröckh's admonition to "close thy Byron, open thy Goethe" (return to the world of natural wonder, not artificial, "literary" sensation) as a directive to turn from fiction to fact, but fail to note the highly fictional nature of Diogenes's wanderings or his metaphoric perorations. Similarly, readers take seriously Carlyle's inveighing against the novel in essays like "Biography" (1832) without weighing equally his concession that even "the stupidest" novel written can contain something of value, some insight into the world of mystery and wonder around us, the mystery and wonder in each human soul.

For the young Dickens, turning from the sketchy pages of Boz and his *Pickwick Papers* to the writing of serious fiction (which for Dickens, as for his contemporaries, meant the novels of Scott), the Carlylean imperative to turn to the wider social world, to place individual consciousness within the progress of history, was a weighty one indeed. But along with the charge to a wider vision came a different attention to individual consciousness, but an individual consciousness being now imagined (like the readerly consciousness) as more uniform, and more homogeneous. This move is made clear by the physical appearance of *Oliver Twist*, the "parish boy's progress" which owes much of its energy and melodramatic passion to its roots in the Newgate novel, and spends as much of its energy in denying this inheritance. This novel, unlike other contemporary novels of thieves, prostitutes, and street-Jews, has no glossary or footnotes explaining its slang; it buries its geography, so that readers are only occasionally aware of famous London landmarks or the changes in neighborhood (Nancy remarks in passing to Bill Sikes that they are near a prison near a slaughterhouse – almost literally burying the reference to Newgate prison); its workhouse-born hero and gutter-raised heroine both speak perfect English; and (despite its frequent shifts from broad comedy to horrifying pathos) it contains a denunciation of the "streaky bacon" of novels that blend theatrical melodrama and hardened realism. The author's preface contains a lengthy attack on the Newgate novels of Bulwer Lytton, Harrison Ainsworth, and Thackeray, and turns back to Hogarth for its defense of its vicious criminals and modest maidens. The novel all but wears a sandwich-board proclaiming its high literary calling, and one would hardly know from its pages that its young author was simultaneously completing the romps of Pickwick – unless one remembered, of course, that Pickwick himself spends several late numbers of the *Papers* in prison for debt, and listens to one gothic tale of criminal nightmare and masochistic love after another, in the interpolated tales that impede that portly pilgrim's progress.

Critics have written persuasively of the investment Dickens made in creating himself as a serious novelist in the 1840s, and have argued (perhaps unintentionally) that the novel grew up alongside him. But a specter haunts that progress as well – the edgy and less complacently "fictional" novels of the 1830s, with their different claims to realism. The glossary and footnote, awkward as they seem, point to a realization that readers do not all speak a uniform English, or populate an easily navigable urban landscape, or recognize the same forms of social interaction or party-going manners. All this anxiety over social representation continues strong in the early Victorian novel and its social whirl, as in the beginning of Elizabeth Gaskell's *Mary Barton* (1848) where "a Manchester tea-party" must be explained in careful terms. Readers know, by the end of the first chapter, how many tea-cups a family would have, and where they would be kept, and from whom others would be borrowed, and with what toast (and what ill-promising social results!) the tea would be consumed. When the narrator of Gaskell's *Cranford* (1853) asks her readers, "Do you ever see cows dressed in grey flannel in London?", she is harking back to some of these earlier anxieties about how socially placed readers read – and yet, with considerably less doubt that readers are comfortably placed somewhere in an urban, cosmopolitan world, in which they expect different experiences to be served up with a minimum of fuss for well-developed novel-readers. The coherence of the Victorian novel as well as its social success – indeed, its status as a *guarantor* of social cohesion – is well underway.

But let us return briefly to *Oliver Twist* to note again the transformations that made the invention of Victorian fiction (and the fiction of that fiction) possible. I have said that *Oliver* dispenses with the technical aids of earlier novels: glossaries, footnotes, maps. How can it do this, and still "translate" a strange world to readers who might otherwise be lost in the alleys of St Giles or the mazes of Newgate? Most simply, by introducing Oliver himself, the "boy," a character who is, in the novel's terms, "green." By having a central character who is foreign to the novel's world, and watching him translate, learn the lingo, master the map, the novel can help us translate as well. Oliver is, in a sense, the novel's interpretive device, the space of the dictionary or wall-map – and since he rarely understands what is said to him or knows where he is, he performs this plot-function (and narratorial function) admirably. This is not to say that the narrator of *Oliver Twist* is smooth or invisible – like the clunkiest of Newgate or silver-fork narrators, he is jokey and intrusive and mock-ironic and mock-heroic by turns; and yet he need not do much of the work of interpretation which readers can now convince themselves they are doing on their own. The *process* of social movement has been made invisible; tiny novelist touches that used to signal "the new" have been rendered unnecessary, and difficult to retrieve.

Why does the disappearance of these signposts matter to the history of the novel – or to the reader of, say, *Middlemarch* (1872), a signal achievement of high Victorian realism? Am I arguing that it is *Oliver Twist* that makes *Masterpiece Theatre* possible? In part, I am. After the move from *Pickwick* to *Oliver Twist* and on to *Nicholas Nickleby* (1839), *Barnaby Rudge* (1841), and *Martin Chuzzlewit* (1844), Dickens was committed to novels of increasingly complicated form, thematic development, and social vision – the commitment most critics see fulfilled in *Dombey and Son* (1848), the first of the "planned" novels and the first to begin with a thematic, formal, and narratorial scheme: the depiction of Dombey's "pride," and his reformation at the hands of his loving daughter. As the character of the loving daughter develops, in fact, it becomes the site of greatest fictional experimentation for Dickens, in Esther Summerson's shared narration of the divided novel *Bleak House* (1853), as well as in Amy Dorrit's letters, fairy tales, and moral force that provide an internal commentary on the problem of "nobody's fault" in *Little Dorrit* (1857). One can argue that, both in the problems of documentary social realism Dickens engages during the 1850s and 1860s, and in his experiments with point-of-view and narrative uncertainty, the narrator of Dickens's novels is often, as *Dombey* would have it, "a daughter after all" (chs 16, 59).

There is much more to say about the way the novel achieves coherence around the story of female redemption, the way the daughter's moral inheritance plots the culture's story of social reconciliation; but let us stay briefly with the relationship between the individual story (think of Carlyle's Teufelsdröckh, and the heroic

progresses of Nicholas Nickleby and young Chuzzlewit) and the novelistic representation of the social (Nicholas's peregrinations across England with the pathetic
Smike; Martin's travels to America). Carlyle's jeremiad called out for a cleansing
of the world, the transformation of the "actual" into the ideal, but it began with the
world of the actual – and so, in turn, did the novels of the 1840s. If the power of the
novels of the 1830s lay in taking seriously Romantic claims that the child is father of
the man, and *society* the most important father of that child (a lesson most of the
novelists seem to have learned as much from William Godwin as from William
Wordsworth), then the fiction of the 1840s moves from the particular social novels of
the earlier decade (Frances Trollope's *Michael Armstrong, Factory Boy* [1840]) to that
wider blend of individual and world-historical: *Sybil, or the Two Nations* (1846) and
Mary Barton: A Tale of Manchester Life (1848). Suddenly, all of England is present in
the novel – and all of England is expected to *read* the novels, precisely to learn what
Carlyle called in his "Biography" essay the grand secret: "the significance of Man's
Life."

It is difficult to recapture just how much novels meant at the time. While contemporary readers of novels have returned to an earlier trivialization of fiction as "light
reading" or to an even earlier notion of the novel as "just a good story," for better or
worse, to Victorian critics the novel meant more. To read well was to imagine a world
worth living in, and a self fully capable of acting morally in that world. As James
Fitzjames Stephen notes in 1855, "Novels, in the proper sense of the word, are used
for a greater number of purposes than any other species of literature" ("The Relation
of Novels to Life," in Eigner 1985: 97). The cultural power awarded novels is
suggested best by the range and violence of opposition they earned: "That fiction,
except in the form of apologue or allegory, should have ever become an instrument to
illustrate or enforce moral order or religious truths, or even practical lessons in the life
it professes to delineate, is incomprehensible" ("Fiction in the Cheap Periodicals"; in
British Quarterly Review, 1859). But, in fact, it had become such an instrument, and
David Masson, always an astute reader of novels, suggests the conflation of reasons
why:

> There are no symptoms yet that the Novel is about to lose its popularity as a form of
> literature. On the contrary, there is every symptom, that in one shape or another it will
> continue to be popular for a long time, and that more and more of talent will flow into
> it. . . . The Novel, we have found, has been becoming more real and determinate, in so
> far as it can convey matter of fact, more earnest, in so far as it can be made a vehicle for
> matter of speculation, and more conscious, at the same time, of its ability in all matter
> of phantasy. (Masson 1859; in Eigner 1985: 152)

This blend of "fact," "speculation," and "phantasy" was a terrifically potent one, and
suggested that Carlylean mixture of physical reality and spiritual allegory which was
(as Dickens himself suggested, in the language of "vivid colours" and "life-like and
amusing" incidents) at once *of* this world and *heightening* it.

But the note which Masson seems to be adding is not of the "real" so much as of the "earnest," and this is the note of Victorian fiction most prominent in the minds of readers today. Indeed, if we trace the evolution of the novels of the 1830s into the novels published in 1859, the year of Masson's review essay, we find ourselves at the publication of *Adam Bede*, George Eliot's first novel, one that follows the sketchier *Scenes of Clerical Life* (1858), and that announces itself aggressively as offering a new version of both what is real and determinate ("matter of fact") and what is a "matter of speculation" – and which, indeed, heralds a new "consciousness" of fiction, and the role of "phantasy" within it.

What is missing from this developmental history is not only the powerful new example of the great novels of the 1840s, to which I turn now, but the question which haunts my history, what happened to those more varied and differently conscious novels of the 1830s? One way to answer this question (and to continue to develop the changing relationship between the representations of the individual and of the social) is to read the novels of the 1840s *through* the genres of the 1830s. I have suggested already the ways the "Condition of England novels," the major industrial novels of the period, push at the more specific and localized versions of industrial fiction in the 1830s. It is much harder to consider a novel like *Dombey and Son* or even *Hard Times* (1854) "industrial fiction," despite their attention to changing conditions of "masters and men"; and the task of locating the specifics of social discourse and historical change becomes even more difficult with a novel like *Felix Holt the Radical* (1866), which almost explicitly disavows the social realm in favor of more "speculative" questions. If the criminal fictions of *Paul Clifford* and *Eugene Aram* (1832) were already in part silenced (like the forbidden name Newgate) in *Oliver Twist*, how much more deracinated is the discussion of prison life in *David Copperfield* (1850), where the embezzling swindler Uriah Heep is imprisoned as much for his working-class ambitions as for his crimes, or in *Little Dorrit*, where the murderer Blandois is among the characters who spends the *least* amount of time in prison, and is finally imprisoned not by the turnkeys but by the novelist, who buries him under a falling house. The only prison in *Little Dorrit* is the Marshalsea, the debtors' prison, already long since destroyed when the novel was published in the 1850s.

This is not to say that the social, political, trivial, fashionable, *local* interests of the novel of the 1830s are banished by the late 1840s, but only to say that many of the concerns explicitly addressed in these novels – and often explicitly addressed *to the readers*, in the form of narratorial direct address and readerly apparatus – have been submerged into more general and generalizing narrative strategies that we now take for granted. For the seamlessness of omniscience and the perfect wisdom of narrators have become the stuff of fiction to us, completely naturalized as "the fictional." Narrators who single out male and female readers; parodies and pastiches of other literary genres; chunks of undigested poetry; old ballads and newspapers; addresses to readers in their homes, their clubs, their ballrooms or their beds – where are they in *Jane Eyre, David Copperfield, Dombey and Son* or *Mary Barton*?

There is one place in the 1840s where such things have gone, and it is into a novel that seems today even more of an aberration in literary history than it did in 1848; that novel is *Vanity Fair*. The original subtitle of the novel, "Pen and Pencil Sketches of English Society," accentuates one part of its relationship to its literary forebears; "A Novel without a Hero," its original title and the subtitle under which it was published, suggests the ways in which it continually violates the rules of its contemporaries. Indeed, that subversive, decentralizing energy is part of what still engages even the most novice readers: from the moment when Becky Sharp hurls Johnson's *Dictionary* at Miss Pinkerton, crying out "Vive Bonaparte," the novel seems to offer a consistent critique of both heroes and hero-worship. Precisely that refusal to concede to anyone a higher ground, no matter how much it might cheer readers who sense the moral certitude of George Eliot looming around the historical corner, turns *Vanity Fair* into an increasingly unstable ground for readers as well as heroes – or heroines. This novel, however in touch it might be with "phantasy," is committed to a world of sobering fact, and deeply anxious about the grounds of "speculation."

In fact, "speculation" (of moral, economic, and philosophical varieties) is at the heart of *Vanity Fair*'s enterprise, in ways that look both forward and backward in the novel's history. On one hand, its "sketchiness" reminds one of the clumsier qualities of the novels of the 1830s, even if its play with genres is both more deliberate and more critical. One of the most brilliant moments in *Vanity Fair* is the scene at the beginning of chapter 6, when Amelia Sedley comes downstairs to welcome George Osborne, and the narrator imagines her descent in the voice of a Newgate narrator, a silver-fork narrator, and *The Mysteries of Paris* (Eugène Sue's bestseller, tr. 1845). As Thackeray revised the novel between its first and second editions, the parodies got shorter and shorter, until only a ghost of the past narrators remains; but his parodic and pastiching instincts, the instincts of a cultural *bricoleur* as much as a *raconteur*, still pervade the novel.

On the other hand, though Thackeray seems at times as interested in style as he is in the substance, the "stuff," of fiction, he is intensely interested in the problem of telling stories, of who is telling what to whom, in ways the novelists of the earlier period cannot match, and in ways that will make the more complicated (and in some ways more sophisticated) narratorial experiments of George Eliot and Henry James possible. What Thackeray seemed to sense in the various genres of the 1830s was the possibility of different relationships not just between characters and narrators, but between narrators and readers. The sense of local plots, of the need for highly specific versions of narratorial intrusion, is among the most notable things in *Vanity Fair*, as the narrator addresses "Jones at his club" or the women readers who will scorn the meek Amelia Sedley. But the narrator will also thank his local informant, Tom Eaves, and (most startling of all) will remark on his own witnessing of his other characters' behavior at the German resort of Pumpernickel, and remark on the parts of the story he has heard from William Dobbin himself. It is almost impossible to reconcile the versions of story and storytelling the novel puts forward with any account of realism, but this poses problems not only of literary form but of *social* reality. How are individuals, whether narrators or not, to judge, or even to tell, stories? Can the novel actually occupy the space of the "life-like" and the "colourful" at the same time – and what life (or is it "whose"?) is it to represent?

On the wrapper of the original monthly numbers of *Vanity Fair* appears a moralist preaching to his congregation while wearing donkey-ears – ears also worn by his congregants. The illustration echoes a famous passage in Carlyle's essay "Biography," in which the "distressed Novelwright" asks the critics how he knows "that this my Long-ear of a Fictitious Biography shall not find one and the other, into whose still longer ears it may be the means, under Providence, of instilling somewhat?" The essayist answers that "None knows," and therefore he should "write on, worthy Brother, even as thou canst, even as it has been given thee." This passage is quoted at the beginning of Gaskell's *Mary Barton*, published at roughly the same time, and it raises again questions about the status of fiction, about biography ("the significance of Man's life") and about the relationship of the novel to the larger society, even as it suggests some of the difficulties the novel experienced in *claiming* Carlyle's larger social project, "under Providence, of instilling somewhat." Thackeray could be as scathing as any about the cultural project of fiction-making: in his brilliant series of parodies *Novels by Eminent Hands* (1847) he imagines "A Plan for a Prize Novel," which is to write an advertisement novel.

> Look over the *Times* or the "Directory," walk down Regent Street or Fleet Street any day – see what houses advertise most, and put yourself into communication with their proprietors. . . . Walk into the shops, I say, ask for the principal, and introduce yourself, saying, "I am the great Snooks; I am the author of 'the Mysteries of Mayfair'; my weekly sale is 281,000; I am about to produce a new work called 'The Palaces of Pimlico, or the Curse of the Court,' describing and lashing fearlessly the vices of the aristocracy: this book will have a sale of at least 530,000; it will be on every table – in the boudoir of the pampered duke, as in the chamber of the honest artisan. . . . So, Mr Taylor, or Mr Haberdasher, or Mr Jeweller, how much will you stand if I recommend you in my forthcoming novel? You may make a noble income in this way, Snooks.
>
> For instance suppose it is an upholsterer. What more easy, what more delightful, than the description of upholstery? As thus: –
>
> "Lady Emily was reclining on one of Down and Eider's voluptuous ottomans, the only couch on which Belgravian beauty now reposes, when Lord Bathershins entered, stepping noiselessly over one of Tomkin's elastic Axminster carpets. 'Good heavens, my Lord!' she said – and the lovely creature fainted." (6: 536)

This parody is only a step away from the society novels of the 1830s and earlier 1840s, and a rare parody by Dickens in *Nicholas Nickleby* offers some of the same critique of the fiction of commodities; but Thackeray's more thorough-going critique suggests some of the doubt he carried over from the earlier genres – precisely the doubt that the novel would have any existence *apart* from commodity culture, any place "outside" the world from which to criticize it. When Becky Sharp thinks, later in *Vanity Fair*, "It isn't difficult to be a country gentleman's wife . . . I think I could be a good woman if I had five thousand a year," she is both commenting on the price the world places on virtue (only those who have money can afford to rise above it) and revealing more than she thinks about her own complicity with the world she in some ways sees so clearly. The novel is performing some of the same double-cross: it is both commenting on the socially determined nature of personality (and morality), and laughing at its own place in social (moral) negotiations. This novel may not have a hero, but it offers a version of hero-worship to the goddess of seeing-through-everything, at the same time that it offers itself as a version of the ultimate commodity or status-object, the perfect piece of self-conscious self-representation.

The more conventional novels of the 1840s share some of this ambivalence about their own status both as "fictions" and as "social representations." The scandal Charlotte Brontë unwittingly provoked by dedicating a second edition of *Jane Eyre* to William Thackeray, who had his own insane wife in custodial care, suggests some of the dangers of novels that were too "realistic," at the same time that the more extreme responses to Brontë's novel and its heroine's violent imagination suggested that its power of "phantasy" (to return to David Masson's word) was an even more dangerous social instrument. Similarly, where *Mary Barton*'s effort to represent the "dangerous classes" to middle-class readers won it the praise of Carlyle himself for its message of fear and hope, the very detail that seemed to promise true connection between workers and masters also won it the vilification of factory owners, who indeed felt misrepresented by its sympathetic realism. While the extravagant parody and self-critique that make up *Vanity Fair*'s speculations may seem beyond anything in the period (and indeed, as I am suggesting, seem to look backwards in political force and fictional play), these speculations have much in common with the other novels of the 1840s, and raise some of the same anxieties of fiction-making that will haunt the fictions of George Eliot and others in the next decades.

Eliot's novels, from *Adam Bede* on through *Felix Holt, Middlemarch*, and *Daniel Deronda* (1876), are hardly "novels without a hero," though it is interesting to reflect on the ways in which they may be even more novels with heroines. Or rather, one can see them as posing in considerably less ironic form the problems Becky Sharp herself raised: what we might call the Napoleon question, or how one is to reconcile individual stories to world-historic events; and what we might call the cash-nexus of morality question, of how historic events or social structures make *possible* as well as militate against individual moral action. When Eliot asks in *Daniel Deronda* what is the relationship of Gwendolen Harleth's puny moral life to large historical change – or even why this small consciousness matters at all in light of large social events – she is raising a question that, as we have seen, is central to the history of the novel, and raises serious questions about the status of fiction itself. But the answer she gives is that it is, in some sense, women who will wage the real battle of consciousness, the struggle of individuals anywhere to achieve a consciousness of and beyond themselves.

In some ways it might seem that we have returned to the insights not so much of the Victorian survey course as of the book jackets it has produced: that wistful Whistler heroine, trapped by her own plot but craving a larger consciousness – as if, indeed, she wanted to be reading the book with all the people on the cover. When George Eliot asks, in *Middlemarch*, "why always Dorothea?", perhaps she is anticipating just such a dilemma – although the novel's full title (*Middlemarch: A Study in Provincial Life*) forces us to draw the two plots together, and reminds us that the original novel "Miss Brooke" is only one part of the very complicated whole that is *Middlemarch*, for long sections of which Dorothea disappears. But for Eliot, Dorothea's struggle to consciousness is not only part of the social struggle for reform in the 1830s, but the sign of a significant social failure: the failure to educate women for lives of moral usefulness and "speculative" genius. Dorothea's struggle, like that of many who struggle under "prosaic conditions" and "rest in unvisited tombs," will have largely been in vain – which is also to say, it will have been "fictional."

But the novel's setting in the time of the first Reform Bill might lead us somewhere other than into the social debates of the 1860s when the novel was written – the debates over the second Reform Bill that led Matthew Arnold to write *Culture and Anarchy* (1869) and Thomas Carlyle to write *Shooting Niagara* (1867), neither work terribly optimistic about the possibility of social transformation, and Arnold hopeful only about the possibilities of self-culture. While it will not lead us back into the generic complexity and formal incoherence of the novels of the 1830s, it might lead us back to their insight that characters, readers, and narrators are all placed in various ways in their societies, and in their reading practices – which for George Eliot means their practices of sympathy, and their habits of moral imagination. It is that rushing of sympathy, that effort of imagination, which marks Dorothea Brooke as a sympathetic reader of her fellow Middlemarchians – which causes her to turn to sympathize with Tertius Lydgate and his wife Rosamond, and prompts Rosamond's sudden and unexpectedly generous renunciation of the love of Will Ladislaw, and her assurance to Dorothea that it is she whom Will loves – "you are thinking," she says, "what is not true." It is a similar effort – to think things that are true – that Eliot hopes we will make, when we turn to the unattractive Edward Casaubon or the hypocritical Nicholas Bulstrode, but even more so when we recognize that Dorothea's failure to achieve success is a socially determined failure. Even if *Middlemarch* does not expect that we will all read as women read, it expects us to recognize that women still read differently, and that, to be successful readers of novels *and* of our culture, we might learn to carry out at least the outlines of that reading.

I have been arguing two slightly different things about Victorian fiction. The first is that something valuable was learned from the novel of the 1830s, something that was subsequently lost, although Thackeray's novels carried on the experiment after many of his fellow wearers of motley abandoned it. That experiment, that lesson in fiction, had to do not only with the play of genre that marked the earlier novels, but with some of the roughness and the interventionist tactics of their narratorial strategies. These novels are marked as *strategic*, and some of the coherence the novel acquired along the way (most strikingly in the hands of Dickens) meant that both the strategies and the self-awareness (of the novel, of narrators, of readers) were lost. But the second thing I am arguing is that one enduring lesson from that period of experimentation was that gender marks a crucial difference not only in the reception of fictions, but in the nature of stories told, and that this lesson lives on not only in the first-person experiments of Esther Summerson in *Bleak House* or Amy Dorrit in *Little Dorrit*, but in the much more seamless and less visibly experimental exercises in consciousness George Eliot carried out in *Felix Holt, Middlemarch*, and *Daniel Deronda* with heroines who attempt to see wider truths. The form these exercises take, and the ways they put front-and-center the problems of individual subjectivity and social represen-tation, made the Victorian novel the particularly successful production it was, but also raised questions about the nature of fiction, and its balancing of individuals and larger forces, which continue to intrigue us today. The Victorian novel "packaged" subjectivity in culturally appealing ways, but also continued to question its forms of containment.

By the time of *Middlemarch*, or even *Felix Holt*, readerly practices had shifted again: the serial publication of *Our Mutual Friend* was an anachronism; the three-volume novel had gained a certain ascendancy, and publication in more magisterial journals like *The Cornhill Review* offered more variety of length and seriousness. The obsessive quarreling with three-volume form that marks George Gissing's brilliant social novels of the 1890s, like the equally obsessive quarreling between Thomas Hardy and the editors of literary journals in the same decade, suggests that some of the cultural authority the novel held in the period of "high" Victorian fiction was a more precarious thing than it looked. We might indeed question if novels were still "used for a greater number of purposes" than other forms of literature. The authority of the individual consciousness can be seen as giving way in similar fashion: the literary impressionism of Henry James, Joseph Conrad, and Virginia Woolf can be seen as continuing the experiments in realism Dickens undertook when bringing the "colouring" of imagina-tion to the life-like events of his characters, but in ways perhaps less "vivid." Rudyard Kipling would seem to be one of the lone purveyors of anything like Victorian realism at the end of the century, and even his expansive accounts of the "great road" and the small consciousness that was the boy Kim do not seem to sustain the remarkable reach and variety the Victorian novel offered at its height.

But it seems to me of limited interest to follow the well-trodden path from High Victorianism to High Modernism. Instead, and in keeping with the spirit of generic crisis I have been attempting to invoke (or is it revive?), perhaps we might take a much further leap forward. While a series of great modernist novels invoke the Victorians – James Joyce's *Ulysses* as sentimental source and other; Virginia Woolf's *The Years* as historical archive and prison; Doris Lessing's *The Golden Notebook* as moral exemplum – I am more interested in the postmodernist versions of Victorian fiction that suddenly seem to be everywhere. Not only the costume-dramas of large and small screens, but Victorian pastiches seem to be "at home and receiving." A. S. Byatt's *Angels and Insects* and *Possession* and Andrea Barrett's *Ship Fever* have joined John Fowles's *The French Lieutenant's Woman*; Kazuo Ishiguro's brilliant *Remains of the Day* seems to offer a subtle revision of Dickens's *Great Expectations*, and Salman Rushdie's *Midnight's Children* of absolutely everything else. It is unlikely that people will ever stop adapting Dickens (who was nowhere near so adaptable in his lifetime, of course), but I am considerably more intrigued by the return of the Victorian debates over the nature of fiction itself, and the multi-volume form these debates have taken. Like Byatt's *Angels and Insects*, which is obsessed with the problem of material reality and the status of "material" fictions, Margaret Drabble's recent trilogy *The Radiant Way*, *A Natural Curiosity*, and *The Gates of Ivory* seems to interrogate the nature of human and natural relationships in the greater sweep of history. But Drabble has not returned to period-dress or attempted historical ventriloquizing: the three heroines she follows in these novels of middle-age are English, contemporary, inquisitive, and readers of other centuries as well as their own. But in the final volume of the trilogy, Drabble not only reinvents characters of her previous fictions (several characters from *The Needle's Eye* and *The Middle Ground* reappear, as do others from earlier novels) but she moves her central heroine to the war-torn fields of Cambodia, in search of a lost friend. It is truly as if the Victorian novel had encountered the killing fields – and as if those fields were not so unfamiliar after all.

I am calling Victorian the multiplot and the multivolume novel; but I am also identifying as Victorian that effort at enlisting larger sympathies, expanding the sweep of human history, and putting the individual consciousness back into the arena of world-historical events. Earlier in this essay I somewhat jokingly identified the confusions of the early Victorian novel as postmodernist, and it is perhaps not so startling that those displacements, as well as the greater effort at connection the later Victorian novels evinced, continue to shadow the progress of the novel. But this suggests a slightly different response to my initial question: Why return to Victorian fiction at all? It is less easy to identify the Victorian novel as so snugly a part of the effort at cultural discipline when one sees the genre as itself more ragged than it might initially appear; it is of profound importance to me that novelists writing at the end of the twentieth century and attempting to document the barbarism as well as the triumphs of the individual *and the social* consciousness are returning to the Victorian experiments in consciousness and "phantasy."

Perhaps what this essay has most attempted to prove is that we do not know everything we think we know about the Victorian novel – and much of what we hold most certain (the coherencies of our ideas about the coherencies of Victorian fiction) is least certain after all. The fact that the forms of the Victorian novel can still be used to *displace* what passes for knowledge about the world is what I continue to value about it – and my attempt to defamiliarize the novel is my own tribute to its ability to make us less complacent about the world. The novel is, to use a favorite Victorian word, a very "curious" genre, one that both contains its own mysteries and refuses to conform to anyone's ideas about it – certainly not my own. If novelists, readers, and scholars continue to return to the novel, perhaps it is with the sense that the novel itself is always moving on, and (although it evinces perhaps an unnatural rather than a natural curiosity) that it remains one of the most fascinating ways in which to represent the world – and through which to engage with it. Our world, ourselves as readers, and our most profound ideas about the novel itself, are little more, still, than other forms of "Victorian fiction."

See also 1832, 1848; GROWING UP, PASSING ON; FINANCIAL, INDUSTRIAL, COMMERCIAL, PUBLISHING; LIFE WRITING, SAGE WRITING, LITERARY CRITICISM; SHORE

REFERENCES

"Cheap Literature" (1859) In *The British Quarterly Review*. Reprinted in Ira Bruce Nadel (ed.) (1986) *Victorian Fiction: A Collection of Essays from the Period*. New York and London: Garland Publishing.

Davis, Lennard (1987) *Resisting Novels: Ideology and Fiction*. New York and London: Methuen.

Masson, David (1859) "British Novelists Since Scott." In Edwin M. Eigner and George J. Worth (eds) (1985) *Victorian Criticism of the Novel*. Cambridge: Cambridge University Press.

Miller, D. A. (1987) *The Novel and the Police*. Berkeley: University of California Press.

Stephen, James Fitzjames (1855) "The Relation of Novels to Life." Reprinted in Edwin M. Eigner and George J. Worth (eds) (1985) *Victorian Criticism of the Novel*. Cambridge: Cambridge University Press.

FURTHER READING

Barthes, Roland (1974) *S/Z: An Essay*. New York: Hill and Wang.

Beer, Gillian (1983) *Darwin's Plots: Evolutionary Narrative in Darwin, George Eliot and Nineteenth-Century Fiction*. London: Routledge and Kegan Paul.

Bersani, Leo (1984) *A Future for Astyanax: Character and Desire in Literature*. New York: Columbia University Press.

Bodenheimer, Rosemarie (1988) *The Politics of Story in Victorian Social Fiction*. Ithaca, NY: Cornell University Press.

Brooks, Peter (1976) *The Melodramatic Imagination: Balzac, Henry James, Melodrama and the Mode of Excess*. New York: Columbia University Press.

——(1984) *Reading for the Plot: Design and Intention in Narrative*. New York: Knopf.

Chittick, Kathryn (1990) *Dickens and the 1830s*. Cambridge: Cambridge University Press.

Duncan, Ian (1992) *Modern Romance and Transformations of the Novel: The Gothic, Scott, Dickens*. Cambridge: Cambridge University Press.

Eigner, Edwin M. (1978) *The Metaphysical Novel in England and America: Dickens, Bulwer, Melville and Hawthorne*. Berkeley: University of California Press.

Ermarth, Elizabeth Deeds (1983) *Realism and Consensus in the English Novel*. Princeton: Princeton University Press.

Gallagher, Catherine (1985) *The Industrial Reformation of English Fiction, 1832–1867*. Chicago: University of Chicago Press.

Jaffe, Audrey (1991) *Vanishing Points: Dickens, Narrative and the Subject of Omniscience*. Berkeley: University of California Press.

Levine, George (1968) *The Boundaries of Fiction: Carlyle, Macaulay, Newman*. Princeton: Princeton University Press.

——(1981) *The Realistic Imagination: English Fiction from Frankenstein to Lady Chatterley*. Chicago: University of Chicago Press.

Marcus, Steven (1965) *Dickens from Pickwick to Dombey*. New York: Basic Books.

Miller, D. A. (1981) *Narrative and its Discontents: Problems of Closure in the Traditional Novel*. Princeton: Princeton University Press.

Newsom, Robert (1988) *A Likely Story: Probability and Play in Fiction*. New Brunswick and London: Rutgers University Press.

Sutherland, John (1976) *Victorian Novelists and Publishers*. Chicago: University of Chicago Press.

Tillotson, Kathleen (1956) *Novels of the Eighteen-Forties*. Oxford: Oxford University Press.

Welsh, Alexander (1981) *The City of Dickens*. Oxford: Clarendon Press.

23
Drama
Alan Fischler

Contexts

"The most striking thing to a foreigner in English theatres is the unheard-of coarseness and brutality of the audiences," wrote Prince Hermann Pückler-Muskau after his 1826 visit to London. Shouted vulgarities regularly drowned out the performers, he said, and fragments of orange peel and other foodstuffs were showered by the denizens of the gallery upon the more expensive seats below. "The consequence of this is that the higher and more civilized classes go only to the Italian Opera, and very rarely visit their national theatre" (Pückler-Muskau 1833: 51).

As the qualifier "rarely" suggests, it is an oversimplification to say that the early Victorian bourgeoisie boycotted the theaters – exceptions might be made when Covent Garden and Drury Lane produced either original plays with literary pretensions or Shakespeare under such high-toned managers as William Charles Macready – but it is also substantially true. And the effects of their absence were ruinous for the West End playhouses presumed to be the preservers of English drama. To be sure, entertainment flourished elsewhere in England: in the provinces, where resident "stock" companies played their repertory in the Theatres Royal found in most major towns, and in the capital itself, where saloon theaters and music halls packed in the working classes of the East End, and where the King's Theatre (later Her Majesty's) served up opera to aristocrats. But in mainstream theaters, where only the cheap seats were consistently filled, where even the prices on these had periodically to be lowered from 1815 to 1860, and where the sole sources of financial relief – aristocratic patronage and state subsidies – belonged respectively to the past and the future, the cultivation of the drama was not a profitable venture. Little wonder that, in 1847, Covent Garden abandoned plays and reconstituted itself the Royal Italian Opera House.

By the early years of Victoria's reign there was marginal improvement upon the Regency situation: at least the prostitutes whom Pückler-Muskau had seen soliciting in the foyers were expelled by Macready from Drury Lane in 1842. But worse remained. Through the first half of the century, a typical evening of theater began at 6:30 and ended in early morning, with half-price admission available between 8:00 and 9:00. This bargain was a boon to poorer patrons, who might miss the short comedy that opened the evening, but could still catch most of the featured melodrama, as well as the farce or pantomime that followed. But those who took advantage of this arrangement had often spent the preceding hours at the pub, and were drunk and dangerous by the time they arrived. Nor was the behavior described by Pückler-Muskau their worst. In 1809, when John Philip Kemble had attempted to raise prices at Covent Garden and add more seating for the gentry, the result was the "O. P." (Old Price) Riots, which lasted for 67 nights until Kemble caved in and apologized; as late as 1880, when Squire and Marie Bancroft reopened the Haymarket after upgrading some of the cheap seats, they were met with a similar outburst on the first night.

As the bourgeoisie were thus being warned against trespassing upon territory that the working class regarded as its own, they were also being admonished that attendance at plays constituted a trespass of another sort. In 1832 Charles Kemble complained to a parliamentary committee that "religious prejudice is very much increased," so as to "take away a great number of persons from the theatre who formerly used to frequent it" (Booth 1991: 22), and, indeed, the chorus of voices preaching against the theater ran up the scale from Low Church evangelicals to Cardinal Manning. Many in the middle class developed an almost superstitious fear of entering any establishment with "Theatre" in its name; thus, when Priscilla and Thomas German Reed opened for business in 1856, they were careful to call their hall a "Gallery," which presented "illustrations" instead of "plays." But the problem lay deeper than nomenclature. The values espoused by the Victorian middle class (in public, at least) revolved around devotion to duty, which meant submission of the individual will to the direction of some higher authority, be it father, husband, God, law, or the unwritten code of morality that trumped all else. But the values of the dominant genres of drama, as practiced in the early nineteenth century, were quite otherwise: melodrama moralized on the unjust restraints of law upon the poor, farce was preoccupied with avoiding or disentangling the bonds of matrimony, the climax of pantomime featured a magical transformation to a state of anarchy in which the protagonists could now wage nonstop comic warfare against the authority figures who had formerly balked them, and comedy continued to work variations on the basic plot handed down from the Romans, in which obedience to parents is set at naught if it conflicts with the fulfillment of erotic desires. And the essence of drama is that, unlike most other forms of literature, it is consumed in public. Under the eyes of the very neighbors whom the newly arrived bourgeoisie were so anxious to impress with their respectability, entering a playhouse, especially when it purveyed such politically incorrect fare, was simply out of the question.

So it was for the very best authors. When Victoria became queen, the number of buyers to whom they might sell plays without music totaled two. Such had been the case since 1660, when Drury Lane and Covent Garden were granted a monopoly (shared in summer by the Haymarket) on the presentation of spoken drama. These were the "major" theaters which, because of their special legal rights, were said to produce "legitimate" drama; all other playhouses were therefore "minors" and their plays, perforce, "illegitimate." The majors were also major in size – with the population of London almost tripling in the first half of the century, Covent Garden and Drury Lane expanded accordingly, to capacities of 3,000 and 3,600 respectively – but certain minor houses, such as the Britannia and Astley's, held even more. In such huge theaters, conducted mainly for uneducated audiences who, like the groundlings scorned by Hamlet, were "for the most part . . . capable of noting but inexplicable dumb shows and noise," spectacle reigned supreme. In 1823 William Moncrieff's *The Cataract of the Ganges* was produced at Drury Lane with an actual cataract on stage, while the mandatory "sensation scenes" of later melodramas featured simulated ship-wrecks, avalanches, boat races, and volcanic eruptions; in 1835, Edward Fitzball's *Paul Clifford* put on the Covent Garden stage a coach and six horses – hardly competition for Astley's, where plays were produced in a circus ring custom-built for equestrian drama. Moreover, the vast distance to the gallery required nothing short of bellowing on the stage, so that actors became strangers to subtlety who would not only "tear a passion to tatters" but do the same to the meaning of the text. Authors had small literary incentive to contribute to theaters in which their carefully wrought words would be bleated, unheard, or upstaged by an elephant.

Nor did they have much financial incentive. Managers purchased pieces outright from dramatists, and there was no additional remuneration if a play turned out to be a hit: thus, Douglas Jerrold received £60 for *Black-Ey'd Susan* (1829), even thought it made £5,000 for the manager of the Surrey and eventually yielded £60,000 to T. P. Cooke, who played the sailor-hero William throughout his career. As late as the fifties, authors typically earned a maximum of £50 per act. To make a living at such meager wages required prodigious productivity: Dion Boucicault, for instance, claimed to have written 250 plays (though "only" 141 of these can be verified), J. R. Planché produced 176, and "Fitzball's efforts seem almost incalculable" (Nicoll 1930 1: 76). Under these circumstances, originality, let alone quality, became an unaffordable luxury, and dramatists regularly resorted to adaptations of popular novels, or to outright translations. Managers had occasional pangs of conscience about promoting such practices: in 1843 the Haymarket offered a £500 prize for the best original comedy on British manners, but *Quid Pro Quo*, by Catherine Gore, did not exactly furnish the foundation of a new national school, as it disappeared after five weeks. In 1859 Fitzball had to acknowledge that contemporary English drama was still "almost all composed of translations" (ibid.).

Nonetheless, the dominant presence on the early Victorian stage was a native author: Shakespeare. In 1843, when the Theatre Regulation Act finally did away with the monopoly, the way was cleared for his works to be played in formerly "illegiti-mate" houses. Thus began the distinguished series of productions, covering 31 of Shakespeare's plays, which Samuel Phelps mounted at Sadler's Wells from 1844 to

1862; thus, too, was enabled Charles Kean's traversal of much the same territory at the Princess's from 1850 to 1859. Like other managers, Kean exploited the opportunities for spectacle in Shakespeare, yet his was spectacle with a difference: following the archeological fashion that Planché had begun in 1823, Kean not only consulted scholarly sources on the trappings appropriate to the period of each play but flaunted them on his playbills, with essays attesting to the historicity of his costumes and sets. With his Eton education and antiquarian authorities, Kean made his Shakespearean productions respectable – and he did the same for melodrama, acting both the title twins in Boucicault's *The Corsican Brothers* (1852) in a restrained and gentlemanly style that deliberately departed from the rant and bluster characteristic of this genre. The difference was not lost on Queen Victoria, who came five times to see this piece; though she was criticized for doing so, her attendance was the thin end of the wedge, and the emboldened middle class soon followed her through the ever-widening opening.

Meanwhile, eight years after providing Kean with the perfect vehicle, Boucicault effected another change of more lasting importance to the history of drama. Having proven the popularity of *The Colleen Bawn* in New York, Boucicault proposed to Ben Webster a novel financial arrangement for its run at the Adelphi, whereby, once house expenses were cleared, he and the manager would share the nightly profits. In 1841 Boucicault had sold *London Assurance*, his first hit, for £300; now, in the first year of its London run, *The Colleen Bawn* brought him £10,000. Later in the sixties, the Bancrofts began to pay Tom Robertson a set fee for each performance of his plays; though these "royalties" amounted to less than Boucicault got from profit-sharing, they too signaled the demise of the impoverishing system of outright purchase. With relief from the pressure of constant productivity, originality became an option, attracting more and better dramatists to the profession. It has been estimated that about 700 authors wrote for the English stage between 1800 and 1850; in the next 50 years, their numbers soared to beyond 3,000.

As playwrights rushed in where their predecessors had feared to tread, there were also more playhouses to employ them. With the theater gaining both respectability and accessibility (the latter thanks to new railways from the middle-class suburbs), and with the population of London doubling to six million in the second half of the century, conditions were prime for a building boom. In 1851 there were 19 theaters devoted to English plays in London; in 1899 there were 61. The boom also extended to music halls, which began to draw the working class from the playhouses into a more comfortable environment where they could enjoy a varied evening of entertainment while smoking and drinking; this class migration further promoted the gentrification of the theaters. The new theaters were mostly smaller, permitting playwrights now to make their points not through spectacle but dialogue, which inevitably became more literate as it became more audible; meanwhile, managers liberated from the need to fill thousands of seats each night by means of heterogeneous and ever-changing programs now gravitated toward more specialized repertory. One result was the paring of the playbill: Kean had dispensed with the afterpiece during his tenure at the Princess's, but the Bancrofts went even farther at the Prince of Wales's, eliminating the curtain raiser and limiting the evening to a single play. Moreover, the single play that remained was now allowed to run night after night. Kean led the way, staging 102 consecutive performances of *The Winter's Tale* in 1856; seven years later, Tom Taylor's *The Ticket-of-Leave Man* began a streak of 407 performances.

Not surprisingly, the chief beneficiaries of these changes were dramatists willing to suit the tastes of the newly available, temptingly lucrative, middle-class audiences. Preeminent among them was Tom Robertson. In the fifties he had been prompter for Madame Vestris, a premature pioneer who, as early as 1831, was providing other producers with a model of refinement and meticulous attention to detail; in the sixties he applied her lessons to recreating on the stage of the Prince of Wales's a cozy and carefully correct middle-class milieu that made the Bancrofts' bourgeois audiences feel at home. Even the hut in the last act of *Ours* (1866), supposedly situated in a military camp in the Crimea, was equipped with all the domestic props necessary to turn the final scene into a roly-poly-pudding-making party. In 1898 Arthur Wing Pinero affectionately memorialized the creator of these "cup and saucer comedies" in *Trelawny of the "Wells"*, where the playwright Tom Wrench (a thinly disguised Robertson) declares "I won't have doors stuck here, there, and everywhere; no, nor windows in all sorts of impossible places" but rather "Just where they should be, architecturally. And locks on the doors, *real* locks, to work" (Act 2). Indeed, Robertson's production methods, complemented by the refreshingly uninflated rhetoric of his dialogue, associate his mid-century plays with the movement toward realism then sweeping the arts in Europe.

Conversely, the major works of Robertson's protégé, W. S. Gilbert, constituted a retreat from realism: the libretti he wrote for Arthur Sullivan, like most of his other plays, are generally set in remote eras or locales – sometimes as far as Fairyland. But in such settings, Gilbert undertook the very practical task of catering to the post-Darwinian prejudices of his middle-class patrons. He developed a new approach to comedy, where duty and human law replace Providence as the source of the happy ending, and the authority of parents and magistrates is neither denied nor deflated. The most solid sign of his success was the Savoy Theatre, which Richard D'Oyly Carte built in 1881 expressly to house the Gilbert and Sullivan operas, and the loyal patronage of this house by prosperous burghers enabled such pieces as *The Mikado* (1885) and *The Gondoliers* (1889) to achieve runs of 672 and 554 performances respectively. By 1883 Henry Arthur Jones was complaining that "Victorian drama reeks of the spirit of successful tradesmen" (Booth 1969 2: 10), but managers smelled money in this trend and continued to adapt their operations accordingly. To accommodate the dinner hour of polite society, curtain times were pushed back as late as 8:30; to tap into the growing market of those at leisure during the day, matinees were introduced by the Bancrofts – experimentally during the run of Robertson's *School* (1869), then regularly in 1878 – and soon became established throughout the West End.

To a great extent, matinees were both for and about women, who made up a major part of the audience; and questions about the code governing their social – and, especially, sexual – conduct became increasingly prominent in the plays they saw

presented. Daytime became the domain of avant-garde drama, as rising native playwrights might hire theaters in daytime as their only means of getting such pieces
performed. By far the most famous (or notorious) matinees were those devoted to the
works of Henrik Ibsen, which furnished the theatrical battleground of the nineties. At
the head of Ibsen's supporters was the critic William Archer, who published translations of Ibsen's plays in 1889–90; first among his lieutenants was the then unknown
George Bernard Shaw, whose screed entitled *The Quintessence of Ibsenism* was as much an
attack on prevailing bourgeois attitudes toward home, family, and women as it was a
defense of the Norwegian master. Shaw's work appeared in 1891, the same year in
which J. T. Grein initiated the Independent Theatre with *Ghosts*, a play that touches
on both incest and syphilis. Though not the first production of Ibsen's work in London
(*Pillars of Society* had appeared as long ago as 1880) it was the one with the greatest
impact. *Punch* responded with a regular feature devoted to "Ibsenity," while Clement
Scot, long-time drama critic for the *Daily Telegraph* and senior spokesman for the
conservative bourgeois perspective, declared *Ghosts* "an open drain," "a loathsome sore
unbandaged," "a dirty act done publicly" (Rowell 1978: 129).

The hysteria of Scott's response suggests a desperate man who fears his side is losing
– and so it was. The rebellion against the demand for moralism in the arts, which
began with Pater and the aesthetic movement of the seventies and eighties, now
escalated into outright rejection of the righteous code of respectability supposed to
govern society. The essential agenda of Ibsen's plays was exposure of the rot beneath
such hypocritical righteousness; in English drama of the nineties the particular focus
became the sexual double standard and its persecution of "the fallen woman." Some
playwrights, like Jones and Oscar Wilde, merely raised questions about the status quo,
while others, like Pinero and Shaw, mounted full-scale attacks on it. But the very fact
that such themes were being addressed meant that the English stage had again become
a forum for serious consideration of ideas, for the first time since the early seventeenth
century: witness Jones's 1895 book entitled *The Renascence of English Drama*. Yet the
irony was that this rebirth only brought drama back to what it had been at the start
of Victoria's reign: a critique of mainstream middle-class values.

Drama and Melodrama

Melodrama, quite simply, means drama plus melody; its initial attraction was that it
let minor theaters dodge the monopoly that restricted productions of plays unaccompanied by music. One enterprising manager got away with presenting *Othello* by
having a musician at the pianoforte strike a chord every five minutes during the
performance, thus making it a melodrama. Underscoring of dialogue remained
a prominent feature of the genre throughout the century, but it soon evolved
other distinctive characteristics: liberal doses of pathos, clear-cut characterization in
which the hard-working poor imbued with virtue (always rewarded) are sharply
distinguished from the rich and powerful infected with vice, sensation scenes with

spectacular – sometimes supernatural – special effects, and happy endings (often involving last-minute rescues) wrought by the hand of Providence. The preoccupations of melodrama varied – the prevailing fashion was first Gothic, then nautical, and finally domestic – as did its theatrical venues.

This "illegitimate" dramatic form was distinctly antilegal in its prejudices, which held the possessors of power to be the enemy. The popularity of brigand-heroes is exemplified by the appeal of Walter Scott's *Rob Roy*, which appeared in at least ten stage versions between 1818 and 1828. Peasants were also prime protagonists: the title character of J. B. Buckstone's *Luke the Labourer* (1826) is actually portrayed as a villain, but he has watched his wife starve to death in the wake of an employer's callousness and now does his vindictive deeds as henchman for an evil squire. Melodrama is more often unambiguous in its affirmation of the underclass: Jerrold's *The Mutiny at the Nore* (1830) shows the justice of the sailors' grievances, while John Walker's powerful *The Factory Lad* (1832) endorses the righteous rage of industrial workers displaced by machines. *Black-Ey'd Susan* paints law and authority figures in the blackest of colors: the title character's persecutors include a landlord, a bailiff, and her husband's captain, who attempts to rape her. William is condemned to hang for striking the drunken captain, but is saved at the curtain from the sentence of "His Beelzebub's ship, the Law" (Act II, scene i).

Though all these pieces played at minor houses, melodrama ironically became a staple event at the only two theaters with no need to circumvent the monopoly. Isaac Pocock's two most popular takes on romantic brigands, *The Miller and His Men* (1813) and *The Robber's Bride* (1829), were both produced at Covent Garden, which so coveted *Black-Ey'd Susan* that Cooke, in costume, migrated nightly over the Thames to play William again in an afterpiece. Jerrold's *The Factory Girl* (1832), with its protests against child labor and industrial working conditions, proved too strong for the nonproletarian elements in the Drury Lane audience, but *The Rent Day* was a hit for him in the same theater and year: its attack on the abuses allowed by an absentee landlord was perhaps made palatable by a dash of spectacle, as the first two acts began with tableaux vivants duplicating well-known paintings by Sir David Wilkie. The verse in which Edward Bulwer-Lytton decked much of *The Lady of Lyons* (1838) may have elicited from Covent Garden audiences the respect due to "literature," but the radical politics of the piece were essentially those of melodrama: Claude Melnotte, as the prime repository of virtue in the play, is necessarily a peasant, which earns him the scorn of the aristocratic Pauline but in no way hinders his meteoric rise through the ranks of the revolutionary Napoleonic army, where plain merit is evidently rewarded.

The popularity of melodrama at the major houses may be accounted for by the simple fact that, with their high proportion of working-class patrons, it sold. So did Shakespeare, but the spectacle expected at productions of his work could easily empty pocketbooks: "Shakespeare spells ruin" became a maxim among managers. Far less popular, but often as expensive, were those contemporary dramas of "literary merit" that the legitimate theaters valiantly tried to cultivate and abysmally failed to harvest.

The problem with both the poets and poetasters who wrote for the stage was their fascination with rhetoric, psychology, and philosophical abstraction – which did not offer much to early Victorian actors and audiences, for whom the essence of theater was sensational action. Joanna Baillie, for instance, published three series of *Plays on the Passions*, with each drama dedicated to exploring a different emotion; mercifully, only five of her twenty-six efforts actually reached the stage. *Virginius* (1820) by Sheridan Knowles reeked with historical grandeur, but its most appealing feature proved to be the melodramatic pathos of the father–daughter relationship: as Richard Hengist Horne complained, "We have Roman tunics, but a modern English heart; the scene is the Forum, but the sentiments those of the Bedford Arms" (Booth 1969 1: 76–7). The cold neo-classicism of Thomas Noon Talfourd would have better belonged in an eighteenth-century playhouse; both his *Ion* (1839) and Knowles's *Virginius* were hits mostly because each provided a meaty part for Macready. More worthy in its ambitions was Westland Marston's *The Patrician's Daughter* (1842), an attempt to breathe life into poetic drama by treating a contemporary political theme; though critics con-sidered the archaisms and blank verse inappropriate, Marston repeated the experiment in *Anne Black* (1852). The poetry of Horne's work was admired by such as Poe, Carlyle, and Elizabeth Barrett Browning, but theatrical managers smelled disaster in his heavy historical dramas, and not one was produced. The cultivated classicism with which Arnold imbued *Empedocles on Etna* (1852) and Swinburne *Atalanta in Calydon* (1865) would surely have made them caviar to the general; happily, neither had any apparent aspirations toward staging these static works. Robert Browning's plays may as well have remained unproduced: *Strafford* (1837), a treatment of the prelude to the Civil War which Charles I himself could not have followed without footnotes, lasted four nights at Covent Garden, and *A Blot in the 'Scutcheon* (1843) ran for three at Drury Lane. Browning's crabbed, elliptical syntax was simply inimical to the instantaneous communication which has to happen in a theater. The verse of Tennyson would seem more suitable, but even at the crest of bourgeois patronage it was not much more successful: *Queen Mary* (1876) disappeared after 23 performances, while the premiere of *The Promise of May* (1882) was hooted from start to finish. In 1879 Henry Irving refused the honor of producing *Becket* at the Lyceum because, as he frankly told Tennyson's son, he did not think it would make any money; when he finally did bring it out in 1893, the year after the poet's death, he had the good sense to adapt it first.

Meanwhile, at mid-century, respectable Victorians in search of serious theater were left to choose between melodramas they could not attend and poetic dramas they could not stand – until Boucicault, then writing for Kean, stepped forth with a third alternative: "gentlemanly" melodrama. Meaning to market his product to polite audiences, Boucicault did not draw the hero of *The Corsican Brothers* from the lower classes or imply that virtue was theirs only. More strikingly original was his portrayal of Château-Renaud, not as the standard snarling villain but as a well-mannered, credible aristocrat. In the sixties, when he began to write melodramas on his native

Ireland and to produce them on both sides of the Atlantic, he took an apparently more dangerous tack, yet even this was calculated to permit maximum popularity. It is true that the hero of *The Colleen Bawn* (1860) is an all-purpose outlaw, while those of *Arrah-na-Pogue* (1864) and *The Shaughraun* (1874) are active in the Fenian cause, but it is also true that the villains are not the consistently benign English authorities but rather Irishmen who skulk for protection under English coattails. Boucicault was also closely associated with the trend toward urban realism, which began in the forties with such plays as Moncrieff's *The Scamps of London* (1843), billed as "A National, Local, Characteristic, Metropolitan, Melodramatic Drama of the Day." In Boucicault's hands, such local color became a cottage industry in a mobile home: *The Poor of New York*, produced there in 1857, was transformed for each city it toured, becoming successively *The Poor of Leeds, Manchester*, and *Liverpool*, and *The Streets of Islington, London, Dublin*, and *Philadelphia*.

More important plays on the underside of urban life were Taylor's *The Ticket-of-Leave Man* (1863) and *The Silver King* (1882), by Jones and Henry Herman. As in earlier melodrama, men who have lived outside the law are the heroes of these pieces; however, for the benefit of the upstanding middle classes who had now returned to the theaters, there is a crucial revision of values. Law is no longer the enemy of the virtuous; rather, the former criminal associates of Bob Brierly and Wilfred Denver dog the attempts of the former to lead a respectable life and persecute the family of the latter, while police detectives become instrumental to their salvation. Nor does law prosecute the burgomaster Mathias in Leopold Lewis's *The Bells* (1871); it was more gratifying for bourgeois audiences to see one of their own punished for his crime by his own properly guilty conscience.

Meanwhile, the black-and-white morality of melodrama remained much as it had been: a title like *The Lancashire Lass; or, Tempted, Tried and True* (1867) by H. J. Byron, speaks for itself. But the specific vices now on view were those that preoccupied the new middle-class audiences, so that the crimes condemned by melodrama became mostly marital and domestic, such as the bigamy of the title character in *Lady Audley's Secret* (1863), and the conduct of Lady Isabel, who not only elopes with a lover but abandons her children in *East Lynne* (of which the most enduring version appeared in 1874). Providence still intervened to punish the wicked: Boucicault's *The Octoroon* (1861) is resolved by a *deus ex* (a literal) *machina*: an unattended camera decisively records the guilt of the murderer, who is told, "The eye of the Eternal was on you — the blessed sun in heaven that, looking down, struck upon this plate the image of the deed" (Act 4). But this was two years after *The Origin of Species*, and the subsequent progress of Darwinism made such stuff ever harder to swallow; thus, in the last decades of the nineteenth century and even into the twentieth, traditional melodrama retained its popularity primarily among less intellectually sophisticated working-class and provincial audiences. Meanwhile, the beleaguered clergy began to realize that the lessons of faith and morality so widely preached from the stage actually served to second their own sermons, and a new attitude toward theater emerged. The year 1879 saw the founding of the Church and Stage Guild; by the nineties, the Lyceum – especially respectable under the management of Irving – was said to be a favorite haunt of clergymen. And devout dramas on explicitly religious subjects, such as Wilson Barrett's *The Sign of the Cross* (1896) and Hall Caine's *The Christian* (1899), gained acceptance for the first time in the century.

In the midst of – indeed, because of – this flood of righteous piety, the "problem play" began its perilous voyage, with sexual morality its chief concern. Far too early an essay was Gilbert's *Charity* (1874), with its uncomfortably positive picture of Mrs Van Brugh, who has given her life to good works but is nonetheless ostracized when her bourgeois neighbors learn of her "past"; damned for sympathizing with "the fallen woman," the play closed after 80 performances. Likewise premature was Pinero's *Mayfair* (1885), condemned for its depiction of a woman who is tempted to pay back her husband's infidelity in kind. But the tide had evidently turned by 1892 when Wilde, working also at the St James's, scored a hit with *Lady Windermere's Fan*, which is plotted along strikingly parallel lines. *Lady Windermere*, like *A Woman of No Importance* (1893) and *An Ideal Husband* (1895), is melodramatic at its core: beneath the glossy veneer of the famous epigrammatic wit, the plots of all three are driven by a shameful secret from someone's past. Yet Wilde was no rebel, arranging instead to avoid the implications of his themes: Lady Windermere stops on the brink of adultery, and Sir Robert Chiltern never actually has to take the consequences of defying his blackmailer, so that the essential moral questions – about the price of sin in the one case and of rectitude in the other – remain unanswered. And the answers proferred in the problem plays of Jones were ultimately reactionary. Declaring himself "still in favour of what is called bourgeois morality" (Nicoll 1946 1: 169), he made mouth-pieces of older, wiser males who, in both *The Case of Rebellious Susan* (1894) and *The Liars* (1897), dissuade young wives from answering their husbands' brutal insensitiv-ity with infidelity; in *Mrs. Dane's Defence* (1900), the equivalent character heroically prevents a woman who was not wise in time from reentering respectable society.

But other dramatists dissented. In *The Second Mrs. Tanqueray* (1893), Pinero set his sights on the sacred double standard: when Aubrey sees his "poor wretched wife" tortured by the pressure of her past, he cries out against her former lover:

> Yes, I do curse him – him and his class! . . . He has only led "a man's life" – just as I, how many of us, have done! The misery he has brought on me and mine it's likely enough we, in our time, have helped to bring on others by this leading "a man's life"! (Act 4)

Paula's suicide follows moments later, making the point still sharper. Archer justly called the play "epoch-making" (Nicoll 1946 1: 181) and it was also profitable: that Pinero made £30,000 on *Mrs. Tanqueray* did much to establish the theatrical viability of such pieces. There followed *The Notorious Mrs. Ebbsmith* (1895), his semi-sympathetic treatment of a feminist; a more interesting play about a woman with a will of her own was Harley Granville-Barker's *The Marrying of Ann Leete* (1899), in which Ann seems a sort of early Lady Chatterley when she rejects the effete aristocrat intended for her and chooses instead the apparently more virile gardener. More frankly sexual was *Alan's Wife* (1893), an Independent Theatre piece by Florence Bell and Elizabeth Robins, in which the title character declares her reason for having refused the local minister: "We can't all marry scholars, Mother dear – some of us prefer marrying men instead" (scene 1).

Shaw's comedies of the nineties dealt also with sexual politics, but his more "serious" plays of the period – *Widowers' Houses* (1892) and *Mrs. Warren's Profession* (1898) – put a socialist twist on the Ibsenite attack against bourgeois respectability by exposing the sources of the wealth that funds it: slum tenements in the one case, and prostitution in the other. Still, Shaw was not beyond taking a respectful backward glance at the plays that he and his fellow "new" dramatists had displaced: *The Devil's Disciple* (1897) was billed as "A Melodrama," and the interrogation scene at its core is clearly modeled upon the trial of Shaun the Post in *Arrah-na-Pogue*.

Comedy

In its attitude toward law and authority, early nineteenth-century pantomime was the comedic mirror to melodrama. Its parts were a short "opening," in which (most often) the heroine's father refused the hero her hand, and a much longer "harlequinade," which followed a magical "transformation scene" where the characters assumed identities derived from Renaissance *commedia dell'arte*: the hero became Harlequin, the heroine Columbine, her father Pantaloon, and his servant Clown. The harlequinade was a virtually nonstop chase, featuring abundant action but little or no dialogue; with its mischief, murder, and mayhem – much of it directed by Harlequin and Clown against Pantaloon and policemen – it was a holiday from normal restraints on behavior. Appropriately, pantomime was generally given at holiday time, especially Christmas and Easter, but even at such seasons its insurrectionary values were hardly in harmony with those of law abiding burghers.

This problem was clear to Planché who, in his attempt to second Vestris's too early efforts to attract the patronage of polite society, created a new genre, for which he adopted the name "extravaganza." Structurally, extravaganza was pantomime minus the offensive harlequinade; the transformation scene now became the grand finale, and the insatiable Victorian appetite for spectacle caused it to become continually more elaborate. Scenic designers such as William Beverley greatly enhanced the appeal of extravaganza, but it was the gentleness and gentility of Planché's writing that decisively distinguished it from pantomime: for all the puns and topical references, the dialogue has grace, and the airy magic of the fairy tales he adapted is allowed to emerge. Moreover, these tales have morals: Emeralda in *Riquet with the Tuft* (1836) and Laidronetta in *The Island of Jewels* (1849) each are heroines whose selflessness is rewarded when her beloved is transformed into a handsome prince.

As the middle classes returned to the theaters, pantomime attempted to woo them by moving closer to extravaganza. After the retirement of Joseph Grimaldi, who reigned supreme as Clown from 1806 to 1823, the harlequinade had started to become shorter. By mid-century it was roughly equal in length to the opening and eventually became a vestigial tail irrelevant to the preceding plot. The script for *The Sleeping Beauty and the Beast* (1900), by J. Hickory Wood and Arthur Collins, calls for only a two-scene harlequinade and does not bother to specify the action of either; by contrast, that of *Harlequin Harper* (1813), by Thomas Dibdin, has 12 such scenes and gives blow-by-blow stage directions for the action of each. *Sleeping Beauty* was produced at Drury Lane, as were most of the works of E. L. Blanchard, who dominated the genre between 1852 and 1888; indeed, pantomime enjoyed a renaissance there under the management of Augustus Harris (1879–96), who lavished care on every aspect of his productions, spending as much as £20,000 on each.

Alongside pantomime and extravaganza there flourished burlesque, which was often confused with the latter. But there was a difference, as Planché asserted when *The Sleeping Beauty in the Wood* (1840) was "announced as an extravaganza, distinguishing the whimsical treatment of a poetic subject from the broad caricature of a tragedy or a serious opera, which was correctly termed a 'Burlesque'" (Rowell 1978: 70). An essentially parasitic form, Victorian burlesque also drew sustenance from Shakespeare, history, and contemporary melodrama, Planché himself resorted frequently to the subject matter of classical mythology; indeed, Vestris began her managerial career with *Olympic Revels; or, Prometheus and Pandora* (1831), which he and Charles Dance named for her theater. A century later, Granville-Barker still found this piece praise-worthy for its "simplicity, delicacy," "taste and tact"; Planché, he said, "knows when to stop" (Granville-Barker 1932: 109). But the same could not be said for his successors. Burlesque soon degenerated into a riot of execrable puns, with little other point. The titles of such pieces as *Faust and Loose* (1886) by F. C. Burnand, and *The Corsican "Bothers"; or, The Troublesome Twins* (1869) by H. J. Byron, adequately indicate the content and character of the work of the two leading writers in this genre. Sharing pride of place with puns was transvestism, which allowed women in male roles to display their legs in tights. When John Hollingshead took it upon himself to see that "the sacred lamp was kept burning" in the seventies and eighties (Rowell 1978: 143), and made his Gaiety Girls an increasingly prominent part of his productions, the seeds were sown for the twentieth-century transformation of burlesque into striptease.

Farce, too, had its different phases. Throughout the era its stock-in-trade was a quick-paced series of complications and misunderstandings, the accumulating pressure of which was typically brought to bear upon a single frenzied protagonist. Until the seventies, characters and settings were generally as proletarian as the audience: *The Area Belle* (1864), by William Brough and Andrew Halliday, shows the housemaid Penelope receiving her suitors, including a policeman and a milkman, in the kitchen, while the title characters of *Box and Cox* (1847), by John Maddison Morton, are respectively a printer and a hatter who work different shifts and are unknowingly sharing the same room in a lodging house. And since both working-class prudery and official censorship proscribed sexual content, the energy thus repressed burst forth in the form of scurrying, screaming, and violence: Jerrold's *Mr. Paul Pry* (1826) has a red-hot poker thrust against him and a box of fireworks in which he is hiding ignited, while the title of Morton's *Slasher and Crasher* (1848) pretty well describes the behavior of its characters. As in melodrama, the enemy is law, particularly the legal bonds of matrimony. Escape from present chains is the object in Joseph Stirling Coyne's *Did You Ever Send Your Wife to Camberwell?* (1846); avoidance of prospective fetters preoccupies the heroes of Coyne's *How to Settle Accounts With Your Laundress* (1847) and *The Mudborough Election* (1865), by Brough and Halliday, in which Widgetts and Veskit, having each promised marriage to a woman as a way of wiggling out of a debt, now attempt to wiggle out of the marriage. Similar is *Box and Cox*, in which Box has pretended to be deceased for the last three years in order to escape his engagement, and where he and Cox – who is, of course, now betrothed to the same woman – toss coins and throw dice in hopes of losing Penelope Ann to the other.

As farce adapted to bourgeois audiences in the seventies, the characters became more socially elevated but their concerns remained the same. Gilbert's *The Realm of Joy* (1873), Boucicault's *Forbidden Fruit* (1876), and James Albery's *Pink Dominos* (1877) all deal with attempts at infidelity; though the authors substantially sanitized the French originals they adapted, and the adulterous intentions of the characters remain unconsummated, such mildly naughty fare was still too highly spiced for the upright bourgeoisie. Pinero, however, found the right recipe with a variation on holiday comedy, which involves a temporary departure from social norms but no full-fledged defiance of them. Thus, the title characters of both *The Magistrate* (1885) and *The Schoolmistress* (1886), and the clergyman Dr Jedd in *Dandy Dick* (1887), are all ultimately – and quite willingly – returned to respectability after their various lurches into lunacy. Nor is law malign: indeed, the plot of *The Magistrate* is disentangled only when a brother magistrate takes the situation in hand. By the end of the era the farcical ruse perpetrated by Jack and Charley in Brandon Thomas's *Charley's Aunt* (1892) is aimed not at avoiding but at achieving marriage with Kitty and Amy; that the play registered the longest run of the century (1,466 performances) signifies its success in appealing to all classes of society.

Meanwhile, in the first half of the century, the attempts of the major houses to produce "pure" comedy – unmixed with magic, mayhem, or men in skirts – yielded only occasionally better results than their efforts to mount poetic drama as an alternative to melodrama. Shakespeare, again, set the standard, but also lured authors into slavish imitation: Knowles's three comedies were bogged down in Elizabethan settings and self-consciously archaic language. Boucicault was more successful, but only a bit more contemporary, with *London Assurance* (1841), which affects not only the aristocratic manner but also the amorality of Restoration comedy in depicting a son's triumph over his father in a fully mercenary love competition. Bulwer-Lytton's *Money* (1840) is even less sympathetic to the sensibilities of the bourgeoisie: the title indicates its concern with the very basis of their social status, but it shows the pursuit of money to be the root of fraud and feigning. If middle-class patronage contributed to the popularity of either of these pieces, it was probably because of the intelligent productions and star performances that Vestris bestowed on the former and Macready on the latter.

In the fifties, however, just when Boucicault and Kean were remaking melodrama in an image acceptable to bourgeois audiences, Taylor began to do the same for comedy. In both *Still Waters Run Deep* (1855) and *Victims* (1857) a susceptible wife falls under the spell of a man after her money, but ultimately comes to appreciate the quietly heroic virtues of her husband, a retired businessman in the former piece and a stockbroker in the latter. *Our American Cousin* (1858) is today remembered for its unfortunate association with the assassination of Abraham Lincoln; in Taylor's time it was famous for E. A. Sothern's performance as the foppish Lord Dundreary, whose aristocratic idiocy provided a pleasing butt for bourgeois laughter. And in *New Men and Old Acres* (1869), written with Augustus Dubourg, Taylor arrives at the apotheosis of the British businessman: Brown is described as "one of England's merchant princes – one of the class which has made of this tiny island an empire on which the sun never sets" (Act 1), and his chivalrous behavior becomes the salvation of an otherwise helpless noble family. Thus, when Byron brought forth *Our Boys* in 1874, the way into the hearts of the middle class had been prepared for him. According to the critics, its sentimental portrait of the retired butterman Middlewick, who tries to play the heavy father but melts into kindness when he later finds his boy in straitened circumstances, was the prime cause of its phenomenal success: a run of 1,362 performances spanning three and a half years.

Byron, in turn, had already prepared the way for a better playwright by introducing his friend Robertson to Marie Wilton, who opened the renovated Prince of Wales's with *Society* (1865). Robertson's plays came to be identified with this theater, though a variety of venues housed the premieres of such works as *Progress* (1869), *Birth* (1870), and *War* (1871). These aggressive, one-word titles might make him seem a social critic, but he was not. To be sure, the anti-aristocratic prejudices of the melodramas from which Robertson learned his craft persist in his plays – the priggish pride of Lady Ptarmigant in *Society* and the Marquise de St Maur in *Caste* (1867) represents the chief problem for the young lovers of each play – but he stopped short of egalitarianism, which would not have pleased his nouveau-bourgeois patrons who were still relishing their rise in society. "Caste's all right," declares George in the play of that name:

> Caste is a good thing if it's not carried too far. It shuts the door on the pretentious and vulgar; but it should open the door very wide for exceptional merit. Let brains break through its barriers, and what brains can break through, love may leap over. (Act 3)

In other words, love levels all ranks, but it does not therefore follow that ranks ought altogether to be leveled.

The most immediate heir to Robertson's gentle comedic style was Albery, whose *Two Roses* (1870) was a hybrid: new in its portrait of a lawyer of incorruptible integrity, and old in the manner of its resolution which – with its revelation of an old, dark secret and its explicit acknowledgment that Providence has wrought all – hearkens back to melodrama. But such, claimed Boucicault, was the kind of play the public preferred: "The public pretend they want pure comedy; that is not so. What they want is domestic drama, treated with broad comedy character" (Sawyer 1931: 74). Likewise, the most important comedies of the era's most successful playwright, W. S. Gilbert, were mixed up with both burlesque and music: the former is in the mockery of melodrama so integral to *H. M. S. Pinafore* (1878) and *Ruddigore* (1887), while the latter derived from Arthur Sullivan's original scores – an element unknown in burlesque, where lyrics were written to fit existing music.

Equally original was Gilbert's crafting of comedy to fit the prejudices of the bourgeoisie – but this was a skill that he had to learn the hard way. In 1877 he brought out *Engaged*, possibly the best comedy of the nineteenth century but hardly the best received. Every character in the play speaks in the rhetoric of idealized love, and acts quite otherwise: Belinda, for instance, professes to love Belvawney "with an imperishable ardour which mocks the power of words" but will not marry him without "a little definite information about the settlements" (Act 1), while the Scots peasant Angus weeps sentimental tears in wooing Maggie, then sells her to Cheviot for two pounds. The critics raged: "From beginning to end of this nauseous play," fumed the *Figaro*, "not one of the characters ever . . . does a single action that is not inseparable from the lowest moral degradation" (Booth 1969 3: 391). Gilbert did not make the same mistake in his subsequent libretti for Sullivan. His characters there are brazenly benevolent – most notably the parents, who are almost never obstacles to the romantic aims of their offspring, and the magistrates, many of whom cheerfully patter about their own incompetence in the autobiographical songs Gilbert made famous, thus making themselves immune to exposure and humiliation. Middle-class audiences must have been relieved by this affirmative approach to characterization, so different from that of traditional comedy, and gratified to see law become a savior: while some rigid rule or code of conduct may create the initial problem in *Patience* (1881), *Iolanthe* (1882), *The Mikado*, and *Ruddigore*, it also produces their happy endings.

Other authors carried Gilbert's practices into the next decade. In *A Pair of Spectacles* (1890) Sydney Grundy gilds Goldfinch, who is both landlord and parent, with the utmost goodness. Basil Hood, who also worked with Sullivan, brought many of the features of the Gilbertian light opera libretto into the next century, collaborating with Edward German on the popular *Merrie England* (1902). But Gilbert's own penultimate piece for Sullivan, *Utopia (Limited)* (1893), was not a brilliant success, and *The Grand Duke* (1896) was an outright failure. As the fashionable arts distanced themselves from bourgeois values, Gilbert's work went out of favor – but the new style proved ironically similar to that which he had been forced to abandon in the seventies. Just as sympathetic plays about fallen women now flourished, too late for *Charity*, so Wilde now picked up the pieces of *Engaged* to fabricate the greatest comedy of the nineties: *The Importance of Being Earnest* (1895). *Earnest* was indebted to *Engaged* not only for a number of situations but also for its overall approach to middle-class sentimentality: its high-sounding speeches are transparent coverings for actions that evince the vanity of Gwendolen and Cecily, the self-regarding snobbery of Lady Bracknell, the callous lust of Algernon, and the two-faced hypocrisy of Jack. If Wilde's play was not better than Gilbert's, yet the time was ripe for it, and it was enthusiastically received. Wilde's works were, however, distinctly superior to those of Pearl Craigie, such as *The Ambassador* (1898) and *The Wisdom of the Wise* (1900); though she thought herself his equal in wit, she actually rivaled him only in cynicism.

Cynicism was an unsuitable stance for the essentially idealistic Shaw, but he was nonetheless an iconoclast even when dealing with iconoclasm: in *Candida* (1895), for instance, he reverses the polarities of Ibsen's *A Doll's House* as a means of asserting that the dynamics of marriage are more likely to depend upon a strong woman who allows her husband to remain a child. *Arms and the Man* (1894) and *Caesar and Cleopatra* (1899) deromanticize war and history respectively – perhaps in reaction against the pomp and pageantry then puffing up the period pieces that Irving was producing at the Lyceum and Herbert Beerbohm Tree at Her Majesty's. Shaw even deromanticizes romance, mixing it with Darwinism in *You Never Can Tell* (1898), which reads like an early draft of *Man and Superman* (1903): both plays feature a male who fancies himself the pursuer but is actually the prey of a woman who embodies the Life Force that advances the species. And it was Shaw, of course, who embodied the advance of English drama as it crossed the threshold marking the end of the Victorian era and the start of a new century.

See also LEGAL, SPECTACLE; FICTION; PARAPETS

REFERENCES

Booth, Michael R. (ed.) (1969) *English Plays of the Nineteenth Century*, 5 vols. Oxford: Clarendon Press.

——(1991) *Theatre in the Victorian Age.* Cambridge: Cambridge University Press.

Granville-Barker, Harley (1932) "Exit Planché – Enter Gilbert." In John Drinkwater (ed.) *The Eighteen-Sixties: Essays by Fellows of the Royal Society of Literature.* Cambridge: Cambridge University Press.

Nicoll, Allardyce (1930) *A History of Early Nineteenth Century Drama, 1800–1850,* 2 vols. Cambridge: Cambridge University Press.

——(1946) *A History of Late Nineteenth Century Drama, 1850–1900,* 2 vols. Cambridge: Cambridge University Press.

Pückler-Muskau, Hermann (1833) *Tour in England, Ireland, and France, in the Years 1826, 1827, 1828, and 1829.* Philadelphia: Carey, Lea, and Blanchard.

Rowell, George (1978) *The Victorian Theatre, 1792–1914,* 2nd edn. Cambridge: Cambridge University Press.

Sawyer, Newell W. (1931) *The Comedy of Manners from Sheridan to Maugham.* Philadelphia: University of Pennsylvania Press.

FURTHER READING

Adams, W. Davenport (1891) *A Book of Burlesque.* London: Henry & Company.

Archer, William (1882) *English Dramatists of To-*

Day. London: Sampson, Low, Marston & Company.

Bailey, J. O. (ed.) (1966) *British Plays of*

the Nineteenth Century. New York: Odyssey Press.

Broadbent, R. J. (1901) *A History of Pantomime*. London: Simpkin, Marshall, Hamilton, Kent & Company.

Davies, Robertson (1983) *The Mirror of Nature*. Toronto: University of Toronto Press.

Disher, Maurice Willson (1949) *Blood and Thunder: Mid-Victorian Melodrama and Its Origins*. London: Frederick Muller.

Emeljanow, Victor (1987) *Victorian Popular Dramatists*. Boston: Twayne.

Fawkes, Richard (1979) *Dion Boucicault: A Biography*. London: Quarter Books.

Fischler, Alan (1991) *Modified Rapture: Comedy in W. S. Gilbert's Savoy Operas*. Charlottesville: University Press of Virginia.

Gardner, Vivien and Rutherford, Susan (eds) (1992) *The New Woman and Her Sister: Feminism and Theatre, 1850–1914*. Ann Arbor: University of Michigan Press.

Huberman, Jeffry H. (1986) *Late Victorian Farce*. Ann Arbor: UMI Research Press.

Jenkins, Anthony (1991) *The Making of Victorian Drama*. Cambridge: Cambridge University Press.

Meisel, Martin (1963) *Shaw and the Nineteenth-Century Theater*. Princeton: Princeton University Press.

Planché, J. R. (1872) *The Recollections and Reflections of J. R. Planché: A Professional Autobiography*, 2 vols. London: Tinsley Brothers.

Powell, Kerry (1990) *Oscar Wilde and the Theatre of the 1890s*. Cambridge: Cambridge University Press.

Savin, Maynard (1950) *Thomas William Robertson: His Plays and Stagecraft*. Providence: Brown University Press.

Scott, Clement (1899) *The Drama of Yesterday and To-Day*, 2 vols. London: Macmillan.

Scullion, Adrienne (ed.) (1996) *Female Playwrights of the Nineteenth Century*. London: J. M. Dent.

Shaw, George Bernard (1932) *Our Theatres in the Nineties*, 3 vols. London: Constable.

Stephens, John Russell (1992) *The Profession of the Playwright: British Theatre, 1800–1900*. Cambridge: Cambridge University Press.

Tolles, Winton (1940) *Tom Taylor and the Victorian Drama*. New York: Columbia University Press.

Watson, Ernest Bradlee (1926) *Sheridan to Robertson: A Study of the Nineteenth-Century London Stage*. Cambridge: Harvard University Press.

24
Life Writing
Timothy Peltason

It is difficult to define, but impossible to ignore, the category of "Life Writing" in Victorian literature, a category that includes not only the many thousands of auto-biographies and memoirs that were produced in the period, but the hundreds of biographies as well, and the many novels and poems that borrow the form or share the motives of biography or autobiography. "From my youth upwards," wrote Harriet Martineau in 1855, "I have felt that it was one of the duties of my life to write my autobiography" (Martineau 1877). She was not alone, and unprecedented numbers of Victorians, impelled variously by duty or by inclination, by the desire to offer instruction, to bear witness, to give pleasure to themselves or others, left behind some written record of their lives. Many of these records were brief and artless, the only written work of persons little known in their time and forgotten in ours. Others were written by persons of considerable contemporary reputation like Martineau, a distinguished novelist, journalist, historian, and political economist. These works continue to be valued for reasons as various as their authors – because they offer irreplaceable information about important social struggles; because they satisfy our curiosity about the lives of remarkable people; because some of them are among the great and compelling books of the century.

It tells us something about the age – that is, it connects in revelatory ways with other features of Victorian life and literature – that these autobiographies and memoirs were written at all. First, and most obviously, the Victorian taste for the writing and reading of autobiography connects with the allied, though distinct, taste for the writing and reading of biography. We look to the eighteenth century for the greatest biography in English, Boswell's *Life of Samuel Johnson*, but to the Victorians for a pronounced and culturally significant increase in the production of biography. One of the monuments of late Victorian scholarship is the *Dictionary of National Biography*, commissioned by the publisher and entrepreneur George Smith in 1882, largely executed by its first editor, Leslie Stephen, and published over 15 years (1885–1900) in 63 volumes, containing 29,120 lives. An equally impressive and quite different scholarly accomplishment is Henry Mayhew's four-volume work *London Labour and the London Poor* (1849–62), an investigation of the types and conditions of lower-class London street life, for which Mayhew interviewed hundreds of individuals who told him their stories. For Mayhew, as for so many of his contemporaries, the natural unit of investigation and exposition was the character sketch or brief life. Although many biographies of the period study the great figures of British and world history, the distinctive Victorian Lives were lives not just by, but of Victorians. Froude's greatest work was his multi-volumed biography of Carlyle, who was one of the most deeply and widely influential persons of the age; and Carlyle's great work, among many, was the peculiar biography of himself – a self displaced, transformed, made mythic – that he produced in *Sartor Resartus* (1834). The writing of biography was one of the chief means by which the Victorians presented their accomplishments and their ideals – the complex image both of what they were and what they aspired to be – to themselves.

To the extent that biographical subjects were taken as ideals, the taste for biography is connected also to the taste – indeed, the hunger – for heroes, a hunger that is connected in its turn to the central spiritual crises of the age. Another of Carlyle's books was entitled *On Heroes, Hero-Worship, and the Heroic in History* (1841), a book that proclaims as its theme that "The History of the World is but the Biography of Great Men." John Stuart Mill was a great reformer, writer, and activist, a leading figure in the administration of British affairs in India as well as in the history of philosophy and of political theory. Although he and Carlyle were radically, almost comically, different in temperament, they were early associates, and they had in common this reverence for heroic lives and for their place in the formation of character. "Long before I had enlarged in any considerable degree, the basis of my intellectual creed," Mill wrote in his *Autobiography* (written 1853–4; published 1873), "I had obtained in the natural course of my mental progress, poetic culture of the most valuable kind, by means of reverential admiration for the lives and characters of heroic persons" (ch. 4).

If only the rarest and least guarded of autobiographers would put him- or herself forward as heroic, there were many who presented themselves confidently – not to say immodestly – as exemplary persons from whose experiences much could be learned. And these autobiographers recognized that the best way to teach their lessons was not by the making of an argument, but by the telling of a life story. A widespread belief in the special powers of narrative, of story, is another of the larger cultural facts with which the vogue for biography and autobiography is connected. Mill is particularly interesting and explicit on this point, because he not only offers himself as an example, but conducts a book-long argument about the indispensability, indeed the inevitability, of teaching by example. In his case, the powerful teacher and example was his father, James Mill: "Though direct moral teaching does much, indirect does more; and the effect my father produced on my character, did not depend solely on what he said or did with that direct object, but also, and still more, on what manner of man he was" (ch. 2). Under his father's stern and systematic tuition, John Mill attained to an astonishing and costly precocity. He read Greek at three, taught Latin to his siblings at eight, and produced at fourteen an abstract of his father's lectures on political economy, which his father then used as notes in the writing of a major book on the subject. But he suffered, too, from his father's failure to recognize the emotional and practical needs that might have been met by a less extraordinary boyhood.

Starting in his later teens, Mill fell into recurrent depressions and breakdowns, the most serious of which forms the subject of the often-anthologized chapter, "A Crisis in my Mental History." Having trained all his childhood for a career as a reformer, the young adult Mill, suffering from lowness of spirits, asked himself whether even the fulfillment of his dreams of reform would make him happy and was crushed when "an irrepressible self-consciousness distinctly answered, 'No!'" Becalmed, depressed, Mill gradually felt his way forward into a better state, with the help of Wordsworth's poems – "They seemed to be the very culture of the feelings, which I was in quest of" – and with the new conviction of the importance of "the internal culture of the individual" (ch. 5). James Mill had neglected to teach his son that the social world he needed to live in, and that he was being trained to reform, was composed not of the abstraction "humanity," but of individual persons; it was a part of the healing and redirection of energies that brought Mill forward from his moment of crisis to recognize the animating effect of other people, and especially James Mill himself, on his own life. The relationship between intellectual positions is realized in Mill's *Autobiography* as a relationship between persons, and the son tells us what he has learned from his father – and how his learning has gone beyond that of his father – not just by describing the course of formal instruction but by evoking the human circumstances of the teacher and the learner both.

Harriet Martineau also knew the importance of teaching by examples, of embodying the abstract in the concrete. By an odd coincidence both she and Mill wrote their autobiographies in the 1850s under the mistaken impression that they were suffering from fatal diseases and must hurry to record their stories, but both then lived on for 20 more years. She narrates in *Harriet Martineau's Autobiography* (written 1855; published 1877) the great turning point of her life as a writer, when she hit upon the scheme for the *Illustrations of Political Economy* (1832–4). Unlikely as it may now seem, these stories, each written to illustrate a particular principle of the dismal science, were a great popular success, stretching eventually to nine volumes and earning Martineau her reputation and her modest fortune. She tells to great effect the story of her moment of inspiration, and the subsequent struggle to bring her inspiration to published life: "It struck me at once that the principles of the whole science [of Political Economy] might be advantageously conveyed . . . by being exhibited in their natural workings in selected passages of social life" (Martineau 1877 I: 138). The idea just comes to her – as such ideas do so often in these Victorian narratives, leaving no way to explain the event save to tell the story. Discouraged by everyone to whom she attempted to explain her idea – including James Mill, who told her publisher that her "method of exemplification" would never work (ibid.: 169) – Martineau persisted dauntlessly, as she relates in some of her most affecting pages. Equally affecting is the opening portion of her narrative, which describes the emotional pains and frustrations of her childhood. Although her family was reasonable, loving, and comfortably situated, she spent her early years feeling frightened and cut-off, unable to alleviate her fears and self-reproaches by confiding in anyone, a victim of the poor fit between her own temperament and the stern, but hardly brutal, childrearing practices of her family and of the time. She is a remarkable woman, curious, eager, energetic, easy to wound and often reproachful, but impossible to discourage and always fair-minded. Her book is crowded with sharp observations and with the evidences of a character at once typical and extraordinary.

Thomas Carlyle merits a special place in this chapter as both the author and subject of Victorian biography, and as a memoirist whose *Reminiscences* (1881) tells much about his own life in the course of offering biographical sketches of those closest to him, including his father and his wife, Jane Welsh Carlyle. But the most influential of his life writings is the hard-to-categorize *Sartor Resartus*, subtitled in the 1838 British edition "*The Life and Opinions of Herr Teufelsdröckh.*" The book offers itself as an account by an anonymous "Editor" of "a quite new branch of Philosophy," the "Philosophy of Clothes," and "what seemed scarcely less interesting, a quite new human Individuality, an almost unexampled personal Character, that, namely of Professor Teufelsdröckh the Discloser." Both the professor's subject and his name, which means "Devil's shit," mark him as an object of satire. But the Teufelsdröckh Clothes-Philosophy, for all its absurdity, becomes the agent of Carlyle's earnest and inspired criticism of his contemporaries, as well as of a full-dress Romantic metaphysic. And Teufelsdröckh himself lives out crucial episodes of Carlyle's own life, so much so that the book is conventionally – if somewhat dubiously – listed as a Victorian autobiography.

If not quite that, it is clearly what Froude calls it in his *Thomas Carlyle: A History of the First Forty Years of His Life* (1882), "a revelation of Carlyle's individuality" (vol. 2, ch. 6). The one episode that, according to Carlyle, "occurred quite literally to myself" (vol. 1, ch. 7) is the spiritual crisis described in book II, chapter 7, "The Everlasting No." In language wholly unlike Mill's, Carlyle describes a crisis of purpose kindred to Mill's, a conviction that all of his life-projects were meaningless and the universe a lifeless mechanism; and then a process of conversion, spiritual without being Christian, in which the worst is fronted and a sense of purpose is restored. For Carlyle, as for Mill, the path of healing is not a sequence of reasons, but a sequence of events to be narrated. "For it seems as if the demonstration lay much in the Author's individuality," as Carlyle says earlier of Teufelsdröckh, "as if it were not Argument that had taught him, but Experience" (book 1, ch. 8). When this is the case, nothing but a narrative record of experience will suffice.

John Henry, later Cardinal, Newman was another of the great figures of the age who discovered at a crisis that the only way to make his point effectively was to tell his story. The result is another of the century's great books, the *Apologia pro Vita Sua* (1864), literally "an explanation, or justification, of my life." After completing his studies at Oxford, Newman remained there as a fellow of Oriel College, a priest of the Church of

England, and, in his 30s and early 40s, one of the central and charismatic members of the Oxford Movement. For many of its members this movement led gradually, but inexorably, to Rome; Newman was converted to Roman Catholicism in 1845. Two decades later he wrote the *Apologia* in response to remarks by Charles Kingsley, a liberal clergyman who accused him of a sinuous and un-English dishonesty.

Newman wrote, then, with the particular focus and intention announced by his subtitle, "Being A History of his Religious Opinions." But what he wrote, though not the life-story that a biographer would have written for him, is nevertheless a narrative, a work of life writing rather than a religious treatise. In an earlier series of essays, collected as *The Tamworth Reading Room* (1841), Newman had written about the special power of human examples: "The heart is commonly reached, not through the reason, but through the imagination, by means of direct impressions, by the testimony of facts and events, by history, by description. Persons influence us, voices melt us, looks subdue us, deeds inflame us" (Letter 6). These sentences help to explain why Newman turned to autobiographical narrative to make his case; in addition they display the rhetorical power that helped him to make that case so effectively. Writing of the relationship between the established Roman Church and what he famously called "the wild living intellect of man" (*Apologia*, ch. 5), Newman both described and embodied the impressive human result of that shaping conflict and thus refuted, in his own person, Kingsley's claims that the Roman Church suppressed and distorted human nature. "The energy of the human intellect 'does from opposition grow;' it thrives and is joyous, with a tough elastic strength, under the terrible blows of the divinely-fashioned weapon, and is never so much itself as when it has lately been overthrown" (ch. 5).

One of the great sentence-writers of a great century of sentence-writers, Newman was judged the winner of his debate with Kingsley not because his judges – the English reading public – were converted to Catholicism, but because they found Newman's presentation of himself compelling and plausible. Newman persuades – if he does – by the vigor and particularity of his language, and what he persuades us of is not the truth of the Roman revelation, but the richness and plausibility of his experience of it. The argument from experience modulates into that distinct, but intimately related thing, the argument from personality, and Newman ends by producing what is more truly and completely a piece of life writing than he likely intended.

In section V of Alfred Lord Tennyson's *In Memoriam* (1850), a patterned sequence of lyrics that constitutes, among other things, one of the great Victorian narratives of crisis and recovery, the poet expresses an ambivalence about self-disclosure: "I sometimes hold it half a sin / To put in words the grief I feel; / For words, like Nature, half reveal / And half conceal the Soul within." Later in this lyric Tennyson's figures are more clearly borrowed from *Sartor Resartus* – "In words like weeds I'll wrap me o'er / Like coarsest clothes against the cold" – but the earlier image of a dialectical relationship between revelation and concealment is also indebted to Carlyle, whose strategies of indirection in life writing were a great imaginative and formal resource for Victorian poets and novelists.

Unlike William Wordsworth, whose autobiographical poem *The Prelude* (1850) is one of the great documents of nineteenth-century life writing, the major Victorian poets and novelists tended to make art of their experiences by reporting them obliquely. Both Tennyson and Robert Browning wrestle in their early poems with what Mill, in a note on Browning's first volume, referred to as "intense and morbid self-consciousness," and both needed to discover modes of writing in which they revealed themselves obliquely rather than directly. For Browning, this led to the dramatic monologue, a genre of which he became the master; his monologues, especially those of *Men and Women* (1855), offer some of the most remarkable character sketches in Victorian literature — chances for characters to step forward and tell their stories, to represent themselves in words. Tennyson's most successful early poems either avoided the first-person singular or attributed it to a fictional speaker. Even when the first-person makes its great, central appearance in *In Memoriam*, it is carefully placed by Tennyson: " 'I' is not always the author speaking of himself, but the voice of the human race speaking through him" (Tennyson 1897, I: 305). Not *always* the author speaking of himself, but often enough to be the form in which Tennyson could best represent his own grief and recovery after the death of his beloved friend, Arthur Hallam; speaking for the race as well, the poet of *In Memoriam* takes on the familiar autobiographer's duty to be at once a distinctive individual and an example.

Other poets wrote their lives in their lyrics, constructing larger narrative structures out of a sequence of lyric moments: George Meredith's *Modern Love* (1862), a loosely autobiographical account of marital crisis, is a notable example, as is Dante Gabriel Rossetti's sonnet sequence *The House of Life* (1870/1881). The most ambitious and full-dress instance of Victorian life writing in verse is Elizabeth Barrett Browning's *Aurora Leigh* (1857). This remarkable work is at once a novel in verse, a meditation on the condition of England and on the responsibility of artists and activists to remedy that condition, a faux-autobiography of its eponymous heroine, and an oblique and selective life history and self-portrait of its famous author. Reflecting on the need to embody the abstractions of social analysis in the concrete particulars of individual lives, and thus, by extension, on the need for poems like *Aurora Leigh* to be written, Aurora's cousin Romney says to her: "There's too much abstract willing, purposing, / In this poor world. We talk by aggregates, / And think by systems" (8: 800–2). Speaking clearly for her author, Aurora has proposed a remedy in lines that haunt Romney so effectively that he repeats them back to her many years and many lines later: "You will not compass your poor ends / Of barley-feeding and material ease, / Without a poet's individualism / To work your universal" (2: 475–8; 8: 427–30).

The great Victorian novelists also found ways of engaging in life writing by blending elements of both autobiography and biography into their fictions, notably into those novels that critics have called by the name *bildungsroman*. This German word – literally "the novel of formation" – names a loose and unofficial category which includes such classics of Victorian fiction as *David Copperfield* (1850) and *Great Expectations* (1861) by Dickens, *The Mill on the Floss* (1860) by George Eliot, *Jane Eyre* (1847) and *Villette* (1853) by Charlotte Brontë, and such less-read but still central achievements as Meredith's *The Ordeal of Richard Feverel* (1859), Thackeray's *The History of Pendennis* (1850), Kingsley's *Alton Locke* (1850), William Hale White's *The Autobiography of Mark Rutherford* (1881), and Samuel Butler's *The Way of All Flesh* (1903). In their varying ways these novels derive their structures from the unfolding shape of an individual life, offering their central figures as examples, if not of conduct, then of development. The two greatest novels of the period, Dickens's *Bleak House* (1853) and Eliot's *Middlemarch* (1872), also contain within their more panoramic plots a central story of growth and development: in *Bleak House*, the first-person narrative of Esther Summerson; in *Middlemarch*, the "home epic" of Dorothea Brooke. Most of these central characters share defining traits or life events with their authors; a few are virtual self-portraits.

Only Anthony Trollope, of the major Victorian novelists, wrote an undisguised autobiography (1883). Titled simply *An Autobiography*, it is a curious and attractive book best known for the disarming frankness with which Trollope discusses his workmanlike approach to authorship and the money he earned from it. Trollope furnishes few details about his personal life or about his long and happy marriage, but he does offer in the early chapters an unsparing account of childhood awkwardness and misery, a misery for which he consoled himself by the construction of long, imaginary narratives. In the next chapters of his life, the more moving for being so plainly told, Trollope tells a story not of crisis and conversion, but of steady and gratifying self-development: he works hard and steadily at his career in the Post Office and then in his spare time at establishing himself as a novelist, gradually emerging into a successful adulthood. In the course of this plain-spoken account, and of his protestations that he had no special gift but persistence, Trollope's special gifts are clearly on display.

Dickens did write, though he never published, an autobiographical fragment that is quoted extensively in the 1876 biography written by his friend John Forster. To compare the fragment with its fictional transmutation in *David Copperfield* is to discover yet again the uses of indirection in life writing. The single, searing episode that dominates Dickens's brief narrative and Forster's discussion is one in which the ten-year-old Dickens was sent to work by his parents in Warren's blacking factory, preparing and relabeling the bottles in which boot-polish would be sold. Although Dickens's life story is significantly different from that of David Copperfield, he shares with his hero defining attributes, ambitions, and childhood memories, chief among them this interlude of child labor. David is an orphan, sent to work by a cruel step-father, cleaning and relabeling the wine bottles at the warehouse of Murdstone and Grinby. But his feelings of desolation and abandonment are exactly those of the young Dickens, expressed in sentences that are taken directly from the autobiographical fragment. "No words can express the secret agony of my soul as I sunk into this companionship. . . . That I suffered in secret, and that I suffered exquisitely, no one ever knew but I. How much I suffered, it is, as I have said already, utterly beyond my power to tell." These sentences appear in both accounts. In the fragment, Dickens goes on to say that "No man's imagination can overstep the reality" of his sufferings, but this curiously flat and unconvincing sentence merely suggests that Dickens's own imagination could do justice to this episode only by displacing it into the experience of an alter ego and into a fictional context in which comic and dramatic invention lightens and animates these intensities of sympathy. The great strength of *David Copperfield*, the immediacy of feeling with which it renders David's childhood experience, is a weakness of the autobiographical fragment in which there is nothing to complicate or disguise the picture of a person whose urgent and unmastered sympathies are with himself.

The biographer, too, must balance sympathy and judgment, and in the best Victorian biographies, of which Forster's is one, the challenge is met by means that may be compared to those of the poet and novelist, or the autobiographer. J. A. Froude's biography of Carlyle was really two two-volume works of 1882 and 1884 respectively, *Thomas Carlyle: A History of the First Forty Years of His Life 1795–1835* and *Thomas Carlyle: A History of His Life in London 1834–1881*, surrounded and interrupted by six more volumes, edited by Froude, of letters and reminiscences by Carlyle and his wife. In the judgment of some late Victorian reviewers (the novelist Margaret Oliphant among them, whose autobiography we will consider soon), Froude failed in sympathy for Carlyle, and judged too harshly Carlyle's failure of others, notably of his wife. Late-twentieth-century readers are likelier to feel that Froude judged too leniently the intemperate and spiteful political judgments of some of Carlyle's later works. But they are also likely to recognize that Froude's discussion of marriage is deeply sympathetic to Carlyle, never more so than when registering the harshness with which Carlyle judged himself. The great subject of these fascinating volumes, as Christopher Ricks has shown, is the remorse that Carlyle experienced upon his discovery, after his wife's death, of the many unhappinesses she had suffered at his hands. Froude, and Carlyle – both in his own words and Froude's – touch upon the subject repeatedly and powerfully, as in this passage late in the second volume of *The First Forty Years*:

> There broke upon him in his late years, like a flash of lightning from heaven, the terrible revelation that he had sacrificed his wife's health and happiness in his absorption in his work; that he had been oblivious of his most obvious obligations, and had been negligent, inconsiderate, and selfish. The fault was grave and the remorse agonizing. For many years after she had left him, when we passed the spot in our walks where she was last seen alive, he would bare his gray head in the wind and rain – his features wrung with unavailing sorrow. (Ch. 18)

"Unavailing" makes a powerful and quiet comment. Reading back and forth between the Carlyles' own letters and memories and Froude's incorporation of those documents into a text he makes his own, the reader can gain a full sense not only of Froude's subjects, but of his method, the method by which the biographer is true both to his documents and to himself as their interpreter. Autobiographers are free to apportion their attentions unevenly; they owe a duty to memory that is real, but still quite distinct from the duty owed by biographers to the written record and to their subjects. Unsurprisingly, then, autobiographers are likely to write much more of childhood – where memories are plentiful and documents scarce – or to turn their autobiographies to a specific purpose, the vindication of a particular position, the explanation of a particular change of heart: or else to produce records that are frankly miscellaneous and impressionistic. However truncated or rearranged, the life account of the skilled autobiographer will inevitably offer a sense of his or her character. In order to achieve the same goal – to do some justice to the biographical subject – the biographer must attend carefully to documents. Hence arises that special Victorian creation, of which Froude offers one distinguished example, the "Life and Letters," a biography that includes wherever possible the words of its subject, and thus provides an occasion for reflection on the relationship between the words of the biographical subject, which are commentary already, and the biographer's commentary on them.

Another great example of the Victorian Life and Letters is Elizabeth Gaskell's *The Life of Charlotte Brontë* (1857), the account of one distinguished novelist by another. Referring at one juncture to "the conviction, which I have all along entertained, that where Charlotte Brontë's own words could be used, no others ought to take their place" (ch. 14), Gaskell quotes frequently and at length from Brontë's letters, but places herself in the narrative, too, as is justified both by her friendship with Brontë and by the resultant vividness, complexity, and inwardness of the narrative. Her opening description of Keighley, near the Brontës' Yorkshire home, aims at capturing what Gaskell calls "the smack and flavour of the place" (ch. 3). The higher, but congruent, ambition of the succeeding pages is to capture the special flavor of Charlotte Brontë herself: reserved, hard to approach, diffident; eager, loving, fearlessly sure and clear in judgment.

Gaskell is clear, but unblaming, and she makes clear, among other things, that the difficulties that Brontë may have presented were partly explained, and wholly dwarfed, by the difficulties that she had faced. The biographer's task, undertaken by Gaskell with moving success, was not only to construct a portrait of Charlotte Brontë, but to tell a tragic story of loss and early death – the deaths, first, of Brontë's mother and three siblings, and then her own. Still another task that confronts any biographer whose subject is also a (usually greater) writer is to clarify without oversimplifying the relationship between life and work. This Gaskell does, too, partly in documenting the relationship between experiences and their fictional transmutations in *Shirley* (1849), *Jane Eyre* (1847), and *Villette* (1853); partly by employing her own novelistic skills.

What pained the child Dickens most – and the adult Dickens, too, looking back on the child – was the sense of sinking, of being "cast away" (Forster 1966 I: 21) into hopelessness and irremediable ignorance, in short, into the working class. It won't do simply to scold Dickens for snobbery or to make light of the horror he felt at the prospect of his fall. His loss would truly have been grievous – and so would ours – had his education been stopped and a life of hard labor started when he was first sent to the blacking factory. In fact, he was rescued by a small reversal of family fortune and restored to a life, not of gentlemanly leisure, certainly, but of invention and aspiration and upward mobility. In this he resembled the other writers we have discussed, most of whom worked hard to support themselves, but none of whom was among the great majority of Victorian men and women who lived lives of constant hardship and meager expectations like the one that Dickens briefly and so traumatically fell into.

Although Dickens was surely right to suppose that his own prospects would have been badly damaged by such a fall, it is striking how many men and women of the working classes did manage to educate themselves in spite of their hardships, and, with or without benefit of formal instruction, to tell their stories forcefully and eloquently. The amplest Victorian collection of working-class stories is offered by Mayhew's *London Labour and the London Poor*. But many working-class men and women wrote their own stories, too, and several recent studies and anthologies have paid these stories new and well-deserved attention (Burnett 1974; Gagnier 1991; Vincent 1981). Many of these working-class texts are brief and fragmentary; predictably, they are dominated by different concerns and motivated by different needs from the autobiographies of Mill, Carlyle, Martineau, and Newman. But just as predictably, they share many of those authors' interests and concerns. Any of these texts gratifies our hunger for information and helps us begin to do justice to the variety, and often the terrible difficulty, of Victorian lives. Many of them offer other gratifications as well: the engagement of human stories compellingly and convincingly told; the surprise of unexpected affinities of feeling; a freshened and focused sense of the human realities that made – and that still make – political struggle so urgent and consequential.

Two of the more substantial and successful of these working-class autobiographies were the *Life and Struggles of William Lovett in His Pursuit of Bread, Knowledge and Freedom* (1876) and James Dawson Burn's *The Autobiography of a Beggar Boy* (1855). Lovett's is the more familiar and more satisfyingly shaped of the two, because he writes from a secure sense of himself and describes the growth of strong and clear, if also frustrated and conflicted, political commitments. Born in Penzance, at the extreme southwest corner of England, he tells a childhood story of daily struggles and pleasures, filled with anecdotes that convey a sense both of his own personality and of the difficulties of his historical and social position. Barred from a sailor's or fisherman's life by sea-sickness, Lovett apprenticed himself to a ropemaker, and then, finding no work in subsequent years, retrained himself as a cabinet-maker, working against both the hardships of the economy and the workingmen's rules that would bind him to a single trade. Finally establishing himself in London, Lovett describes the worldly frustrations and the new learning that together led to his political commitments. In the familiar language of autobiographical self-discovery, he finds himself "awakened to a new mental existence" by his reading on religious and political questions and, at several points, "forcibly struck" by the injustices of existing social and political arrangements. But if the language is familiar, the milieu is distinctive. When Lovett is kept from an important political meeting because he must finish and deliver a set of dining tables for a gentleman, the reader is reminded of the daily demands of a working life. When that meeting is brutally attacked by the police, and when one reasonable and modest demand after another is denied by the holders of power, the reader is likely to be forcibly struck, too, by the injustice of a hierarchical society and by the dignity and moral power of Lovett's character and position.

The Autobiography of a Beggar Boy is a fascinating, but far less heartening book. James Burn tells the story of an unsettled and brutalized boyhood, a story that *ought* to be heartening if only because of the resiliency and persistence that enabled its author to survive and write the book that we are reading. But Burn never quite emerges from his difficulties, either into material comfort or into a settled sense of his identity and the meaning of his own experiences. He closes his book with effortful optimism and with an improving moral – "The battle of my life is well calculated to prove to young men what energy and determination of character are able to accomplish when rightly directed" – but the reader learns rather different things from Burn's book, which makes vivid both the particular circumstances and hardships of a poor and wandering life and the human and psychic damage that such a life causes.

In one of the lighter and more engaging episodes of William Lovett's story, he describes the difficulties of his courtship, and how his future wife, a lady's maid, broke off their engagement when she could not satisfy herself that he had a right view of the Christian sacrament of holy communion. Too principled to dissemble, Lovett accepted the separation, though it felt to him "like the parting of the mental and bodily powers." After a year's separation and study, he and his beloved opened with one another "a kind of controversial correspondence on [religion] . . . the result of which was that our religious opinions became perfectly satisfactory to one another, and terminated by her coming over to England and accepting me as her husband, we being married on the 3rd of June, 1826." The story is a charming and revealing one – for what it tells us of Lovett's principled uprightness, and his wife's, and of the creaturely eagerness with which they accommodated their principles to their love for one another. But it reveals also how omnipresent the subject of religion was – not just to clergymen like Newman, and not just as the background and metaphor-provider for spiritual struggles like Mill's or Carlyle's, but as an instructive and obstructive fact of social and family life.

Two more of the notable life writings of the period focus in their quite different ways on religious differences in Victorian family life. In *The Way of All Flesh* Samuel Butler tells the story of Ernest Pontifex, the son of a mean-spirited and narrow-mindedly pious father like Butler's own. Anticipating the eponymous joke of Oscar Wilde's *The Importance of Being Earnest* (1895), Butler says that Ernest's father chose that name because "the word 'earnest' was just beginning to come into fashion, and he thought the possession of such a name might . . . have a permanent effect upon the boy's character" (ch. 18). Writing in the 1870s and 1880s (though the novel was not published until 1903, after Butler's death), Butler is bracingly astringent and un-Victorian, as so many Victorians were. "'I have been thinking,' [Ernest] said, 'that I may perhaps never recover from this illness, and in case I do not I should like you to know that there is only one thing which weighs upon me. I refer,' he continued after a slight pause, 'to my conduct towards my father and mother. I have been much too good to them'" (ch. 80). The relationship between the novel's narrator and its central character, both of whom seem to be Butler, is confusing – resulting not in an achieved strategy of indirection but just a wobbly point of view – and the novel loses its way at several points. But the story is an immensely appealing one even so, moving beyond its satiric inversions to endorse a humane and loose forgivingness of manner; an unsystematized following of impulse; a life writer's subordination of doctrines to persons: "Our most assured likings have for the most part been arrived at neither by introspection nor by any process of conscious reasoning, but by the bounding forth of the heart to welcome the gospel proclaimed to it by another" (ch. 64). "No man's opinions . . . can be worth holding unless he knows how to deny them easily and gracefully upon occasion in the cause of charity" (ch. 86). This is a limited point of view – you can't make a religious movement or a political revolution with it – but also an extremely attractive one.

Edmund Gosse's *Father and Son*, published in 1907, after the death of Queen Victoria, tells another representative and distinctive Victorian story of family struggle and the loss of faith. Unlike Butler, Gosse loves and respects the father from whom he must nevertheless separate himself. His story makes plausible and vivid both the religious urgencies of Philip Gosse – a scholar, a naturalist, and a deeply committed member of the Calvinist sect called the Plymouth Brethren – and Edmund Gosse's gathering sense that he was called away from his father by the world of humanistic understanding. It was the reading of fiction, for Edmund, that "did more than anything else . . . to give fortitude to my individuality." And when he tells the story of his public baptism at age ten, "the central event of my whole childhood," he does so with a novelist's eye for the complex human motivations and responses of all the actors involved – his father's pride and his own in such precocious piety; the doubtfulness of his spiritual examiners, vanquished by his fluency and by the impressive new furnishings of his family's drawing room. To see the event in such purely human terms, however, is next door to nonbelief, and Gosse leaves his father's world behind, impelled by the very tastes and attributes that make his book so successful.

Four more books, dramatically unlike one another in their construction of the autobiographer's task and unlike any others we have discussed, will complete our survey of Victorian life writing with a thesis-humbling reminder of how various the subject is. Oscar Wilde's *De Profundis* was written from prison in 1897, posthumously published in an abridged and altered version in 1905, the full text appearing only in 1962. Like so many life writings, *De Profundis* is generically hard to place, a long letter addressed to Wilde's estranged lover, Lord Alfred Douglas, detailing the troubled history of their relationship and of Wilde's own career, but also the story of Wilde's trial and imprisonment "for committing acts of gross indecency with another male person," a story that then modulates into a lengthy meditation on love, sorrow, society, and the figure of Christ. The result is a strange, manipulative blending of reproach and forgiveness, careful documentation and revisionist history, inimitable elegance of address and all-too-imitable self-dramatization. The dizzying changes that Wilde records and the instability of his tone as he records them seem a failure of will and control, rather than the controlled triumph of will over mere event that he celebrates in his most accomplished earlier works, "The Decay of Lying" (1889), "The Critic as Artist" (1890), and, preeminently, *The Importance of Being Earnest*. To say, as a more wholehearted admirer of *De Profundis* might wish to, that Wilde triumphed over circumstance, would be to deny the full horror and brutality of the punishment he received and to underestimate the power of a brute stupidity to have its way in the world. But to say simply that he was defeated would be to ignore the gallant serio-comic performance of his own nature that sustained him, in prison and afterwards, and that is at once a legacy to his readers and a gift from his art to his life.

Charles Darwin's *Autobiography*, written in spare afternoon hours during the summer of 1876, is a frankly miscellaneous account of the childhood and career of the scientist who wrote what might plausibly be called the most consequential book of the century, *The Origin of Species* (1859). Darwin writes to amuse himself, he announces, and because his narrative "might possibly interest my children or their children" (ch. 1). He is rightly aware that his life story possesses wider importance and interest not because of the dramatic power with which he invests it in the telling, but because of the momentousness of what he has done. He tells the stories accordingly of how he came to take the exploratory voyage of the *Beagle*, from which so much else followed; and he "can remember the very spot in the road, whilst in my carriage, when to my joy the solution occurred to me" (ch. 7) of a central problem in the theory of evolution. Our knowledge of the eventual significance of his discoveries does make these stories of interest; it adds force, too, to the appealingly deflationary sequence in which Darwin reports first his "glow of pride" when Sir James Mackintosh said of him, "There is something in that young man that interests me." And then comments: "This must have been chiefly due to his perceiving that I listened with much interest to everything which he said, for I was as ignorant as a pig about his subjects of history, politicks, and moral philosophy" (ch. 1). A nice piece of self-irony, made nicer by the fact that it is Charles Darwin who offers it. Professing to write "as if I were a dead man in another world looking back at my own life," Darwin offers a sequence of convincingly spontaneous recollections out of which emerge fascinating brief portraits of his father and others, and, with increasing definition throughout the book, a nuanced and believable portrait of himself.

John Ruskin's *Praeterita* (1885–9) is an ampler and greater work, as one might expect from the author who wrote 39 volumes of visionary commentary on art, architecture, literature, and society, in sentences rivaled in the nineteenth century only by those of Newman and Dickens for rhetorical power. Ruskin wrote *Praeterita*, he tells us, to give pleasure to himself and others and to pay homage to his parents, who were strict, demanding, loving, and indulgent in equal measures, and who loom large throughout the book, but especially in the opening chapters, which may be compared instructively with John Stuart Mill's account of his over-managed childhood. Writing for pleasure, Ruskin makes no mention of many painful episodes – his annulled marriage, the bouts of madness that interrupted his career and finally reduced him to silence. Although this last work is touched by both sorrow and anger, it has none of the inspired, but hectoring, fury of many of Ruskin's earlier works. It does offer a wonderful account of Ruskin's childhood, and appreciative and varied reports on the places and objects of beauty that formed his character and that were the subjects of such great earlier works as *Modern Painters* (1843–60) and *The Stones of Venice* (1851–3). Like so many autobiographers of the period, Ruskin tells of crisis and recovery, of the discovery of vocation, of the transmutation, rather than simply the loss or the restoration, of religious faith. But uniquely, and somewhat confusingly, Ruskin tells not one but many such stories; it is a distinguishing feature of both his writing and his character that though he speaks often of the beauties of simplicity and order, he does so lushly and digressively. The way to simple clarity is effortful and complex; *Praeterita* is melancholy as well as mellow, a record of sublime sightings, but also of losses. At its best, the book brings Ruskin and his reader together to such extraordinary moments as the closing evocation of the night-skies of Siena – "the fireflies everywhere in sky and cloud rising and falling, mixed with the lightning, and more intense than the stars" – in the last and perhaps the greatest paragraphs that Ruskin ever wrote.

To move next, and last, to the *Autobiography* (1899) of Margaret Oliphant (1828–97) will seem an anti-climax. This brief and broken narrative, strangely modest and even more strangely moving, was written in fits and starts by a prolific and successful writer of novels that are now mostly out of print. These novels repay attention, but the *Autobiography*, recently and authoritatively edited by Elisabeth Jay, is a good place for new readers to start and for this account to end. More than any other of the life writings here discussed, with the possible exception of *Sartor Resartus*, this is a book whose *tone* it is both difficult and crucial to determine. Oliphant is disingenuous at times, afflicted with a poor-me-ism, and an off-putting fondness for locutions like "my poor little unappreciated self". These are such evidently false modesties, however, and they are so quickly and unblinkingly noted as such by Oliphant herself, that they take their part in a complex and affecting self-portrait. Asserting her claims at one moment, denying or qualifying them at the next, Oliphant puts forth a steady, middle-voiced stream of shrewd, sharp, affectionate, ironic descriptions of both herself and others, especially of the succession of weak and erring men – husband, brother, sons – she had to support and direct. She tells a story of industry and self-sacrifice, of "a heart [that] contrived to rise whenever it had a chance," but that was cast down repeatedly by a series of crushing losses – a story interrupted by crisply phrased judgments that may strike the reader's ear as either bitter or brave, slyly aggressive or admirably undeluded. Finally, however, the book turns the tables and challenges that listening reader to imagine just what tone would be the right one in which to recount the deaths of Oliphant's mother, her two newborn sons, an infant daughter, her husband, her ten-year-old daughter, both her brothers – after years of total dependence upon her – and then, in their early 30s, her two, last, struggling sons. Looking back from the vantage point of all but the last of these deaths, she saw her life's happiness as embodied supremely in a moment "so curiously common and homely, with nothing in it . . . the moment after dinner when I used to run up-stairs to see that all was well in the nursery, and then to turn into my room on my way down again to wash my hands, as I had a way of doing before I took up my evening work . . . I can see it now, the glimmer of the outside lights, the room dark, the faint reflection in the glasses, and my heart full of joy and peace – for what? – for nothing – that there was no harm anywhere, the children well above stairs and their father below" (Oliphant 1990: 63–4). After the last death, and just a year before Oliphant's own, she ended her *Autobiography* differently, and starkly, with two one-sentence paragraphs:

> And now here I am all alone.
> I cannot write any more.

   Trying to decide what to think of these last sentences in Oliphant's book, whether to find in them the sought-after intensities of melodrama or the found poetry of authentic feeling, we do not cease being readers of literature, but we remember also that we are reading a true story. Nearly all of the valuable critical writing about autobiography over the last few decades has made the point, one way or another, that memoirs and autobiographies, like novels and poems, are the products of art and imagination and not just the documentary transcription of reality. But this important half-truth has surely had its day and needs correcting and completing. It is true that biographies and autobiographies, like fictions, must be constructed; it is equally true, and necessary to remind ourselves, that they must be constructed *unlike* fictions, too, according to other laws and contracts. The category of Victorian life writing includes by courtesy those novels and poems that pose as truthful documents or that are known to have borrowed much of their matter from the life stories of their authors. But it is defined and anchored by the avowedly biographical and autobiographical narratives that make distinctly different truth claims – for all the powers of imagination that were required in their construction – and that thus offer to the contemporary reader distinct pleasures in reading and distinct forms of access to that familiar and deeply entangled Victorian couple, Letters and Lives.

See also GROWING UP, MOVING OUT; FICTION, SAGE WRITING

REFERENCES

Burnett, John (ed.) (1974) *Annals of Labour: Autobiographies of British Working-Class People 1820–1920*. Bloomington: Indiana University Press. Also published as *Useful Toil: Autobiographies of Working People from the 1820s to the 1920s*.

——(ed.) (1982) *Destiny Obscure: Autobiographies of Childhood, Education and Family from the 1820s to the 1920s*. London: Allen Lane.

Forster, John (1966) [1872–4] *The Life of Charles Dickens*, 2 vols, ed. J. W. T. Ley, revd A. J. Hoppe. London: J. M. Dent.

Gagnier, Regenia (1991) *Subjectivities: A History of Self-Representation in Britain, 1832–1910*. New York: Oxford University Press.

Martineau, Harriet (1877) *Harriet Martineau's Autobiography*, 3 vols. London: Smith Elder.

Oliphant, Margaret (1990) *The Autobiography of Margaret Oliphant: The Complete Text*, ed. Elisabeth Jay. Oxford: Oxford University Press.

Ricks, Christopher (1996) "Victorian Lives." In *Essays in Appreciation*. Oxford: Oxford University Press. [On Gaskell's Brontë, Froude's Carlyle, and other Victorian biographies.]

Tennyson, Hallam (1897) *Alfred Lord Tennyson: A Memoir by His Son*, 2 vols. London: Macmillan.

Vincent, David (1981) *Bread, Knowledge and Freedom: A Study of Nineteenth-Century Working Class Autobiography*. New York and London: Methuen.

FURTHER READING

Amigoni, David (1993) *Victorian Biography: Intellectuals and the Ordering of Discourse*. New York and London: Harvester Wheatsheaf.

Arrowsmith, William (1982) "Ruskin's Fireflies." In John Dixon Hunt and Faith Holland (eds) *The Ruskin Polygon: Essays on the Imagination of John Ruskin*. Manchester: Manchester University Press.

Burnett, John, Vincent, David and Mayall, David (eds) (1984–9) *The Autobiography of the Working Class: An Annotated Critical Bibliography*, 3 vols. New York: New York University Press.

Cockshut, A. O. J. (1974) *Truth to Life: The Art of Biography in the Nineteenth Century*. New York. Harcourt, Brace. [Chapters on Froude and others.]

Corbett, Mary Jean (1992) *Representing Femininity: Middle-Class Subjectivity in Victorian and Edwardian Women's Autobiographies*. New York: Oxford University Press. [On Wordsworth, Carlyle, Martineau, Oliphant, and others.]

Danahay, Martin (1993) *A Community of One: Masculine Autobiography and Autonomy in Nineteenth-Century Britain*. Albany: State University of New York Press.

Davis, Philip (1983) *Memory and Writing from Wordsworth to Lawrence*. Liverpool: Liverpool University Press. [On Oliphant.]

Fleishman, Avrom (1983) *Figures of Autobiography: The Language of Self-Writing in Victorian and Modern England*. Berkeley and Los Angeles: University of California Press. [Chapters on Carlyle, Mill, Newman, Ruskin, Dickens, Butler, and others.]

Henderson, Heather (1989) *The Victorian Self: Autobiography and Biblical Narrative*. Ithaca, NY: Cornell University Press. [Chapters on Newman, Ruskin, Gosse, Dickens.]

Landow, George (ed.) (1979) *Approaches to Victorian Autobiography*. Athens, OH: Ohio University Press. [Essays on Ruskin, Newman, Oliphant, Dickens, Robert Browning, and on other themes and problems in Victorian autobiography.]

Machann, Clinton (1994) *The Genre of Autobiography in Victorian Literature*. Ann Arbor: University of Michigan Press. [Chapters on Newman, Mill, Martineau, Trollope, Ruskin, Darwin, Gosse, and others.]

Peltason, Timothy (1988) "Imagination and Learning in George Eliot, Mill, and Dickens." *Essays in Criticism*, 38: 1, 35–54.

——(1990) "Ruskin's Finale: Vision and Imagination in *Praeterita*." *ELH*, 57, 665–84.

Peterson, Linda (1986) *Victorian Autobiography*. New Haven, CT: Yale University Press. [Chapters on Carlyle, Ruskin, Newman, Martineau, Gosse.]

Reimer, Gail Twersky (1988) "Revisions of Labor in Margaret Oliphant's Autobiography." In Bella Brodzki and Celeste Schenck (eds) *Life/Lines: Theorizing Women's Autobiography*. Ithaca, NY: Cornell University Press.

Sanders, Valerie (1989) *The Private Lives of Victorian Women: Autobiography in Nineteenth-Century England*. New York: St Martin's Press. [On Oliphant, Martineau, and others.]

25

Sage Writing

Linda H. Peterson

On the Origins of Sage Writing in Early Victorian England

Sage writing emerged in the early Victorian period as a distinctive form of nonfictional prose – one that confronted the new and difficult problems posed by modern industrial, urban life and that proposed solutions to those problems, whether specific modes of action or more general philosophical principles. John Holloway, the literary historian who gave the name "sage writing" to this body of Victorian literature, included both essayists and novelists in his analysis; for Holloway, the defining attribute of sage writing was an "interest of a general or speculative kind in what the world is like, where man stands in it, and how he should live" (Holloway 1953: 1), not the literary genre *per se*. Given this broad definition we might conclude that virtually every historical epoch has had some version of sage writing, some prose form that has addressed social problems both speculatively and practically. Indeed, in our own era we have a similar kind of writing which we frequently call "cultural criticism" or "cultural critique" and which we identify with writers like Norman Mailer, Joan Didion, and Susan Sontag. Yet the Victorians are particularly noteworthy for their commitment to identifying and analyzing social, political, economic, religious, and philosophical problems; and Victorian sage writers are noteworthy, too, for their development of a prose form that provided not only a site of analysis but also the rhetorical tools for conducting such analysis.

Victorians faced a number of problems familiar to us but new to them as the first participants in a modern society: the development of industry with its sometimes detrimental environmental and economic effects; the growth of cities and the problems related to rapid urbanization; the new discoveries in science and the attendant challenge to religious authority; the expansion of democracy in a series of reform bills that gave the franchise to middle-class, then working-class citizens; the campaigns for women's rights, including changes in marriage laws, educational opportunities, and career possibilities. All of these changes – and others – became the subject matter of Victorian prose and provoked much thought and debate. But sage writing would not have emerged so distinctively as a form had it not been for other significant influences.

Recent scholarship in the history of the book, for example, has suggested that it was the dramatic increase in nineteenth-century periodicals and newspapers that gave sage writers a place to promulgate their ideas and reach increasingly diverse groups of readers. Between 1815 and 1835 periodicals like the *Edinburgh Review*, the *Quarterly Review*, the *New Monthly Magazine*, *The Literary Gazette*, *Fraser's Magazine*, *Blackwood's Magazine*, and the *Athenaeum* – to name only some of the most prominent – expanded rapidly, increasing their sales as well as their payments to authors. By 1818 the *Edinburgh Review* reached a circulation of 13,500; the *Quarterly Review*, 14,000. During the 1830s the circulation of the weekly *Athenaeum* rose from 3,000 to 18,000 readers (see Erickson 1996: 78–80). As circulations rose, freelance writers, as they came to be called, discovered that they could earn 20, 30, even more guineas per sheet for their literary contributions – thus making it possible to pursue authorship as something more than a sideline or avocation.

Related to the growth of periodicals, then, was the rise of the man (or woman) of letters, the professional writer who made a living by the pen. Thomas Carlyle, the preeminent sage writer of the early Victorian period, argued that it was "the wondrous art of *Writing*, or of Ready-writing which we call *Printing*" that made possible the new "Hero as Man of Letters" (*Heroes and Hero-Worship*, 1841). The critic G. H. Lewes noted at mid-century that "in the present state of things a man who has health, courage, and ability can earn by literature the income of a gentleman," i.e. approximately £300 a year (Lewes 1847). Of course, not all writers who placed their work in periodicals were "sages." Many were hacks, grinding out pages for quick (and sometimes not so quick) payment. But, as Lee Erickson has argued, the sheer number of outlets for writing "soon made professional journalism a respectable profession and also made it necessary for the weekly and monthly magazines to hire full-time editors, subeditors, and staff writers who were salaried and who wrote when no one else would" (Erickson 1996: 88). Carlyle started by writing for the *Edinburgh Review* and published his ground-breaking work *Sartor Resartus* (1833–4) in *Fraser's Magazine*. George Eliot began as a subeditor on the *Westminster Review*. Harriet Martineau started by contributing to a small but influential Unitarian journal, *The Monthly Repository*. Even John Henry Newman, not particularly identified with his periodical writing, was influenced by the literary reviews of the early nineteenth century; as a boy of 14 he imitated the rivalry of the *Edinburgh* and *Quarterly* by writing "two periodicals – that is, papers called the 'Spy' and 'Anti-Spy.' They were written against each other" (Erickson 1996: 89).

If the rise of periodicals made possible the rise of the man and woman of letters, recent scholarship on professional authorship has suggested yet another factor spurring the development of sage writing *per se*: the *anxieties* created by authorship as a profession. To avoid the charge of writing hackwork or piecework, authors needed to justify their "brain work" and offer their readers something more than the daily pap of newspaper reportage. James Eli Adams points out that Victorian writers were "explicitly concerned to legitimate vocations devoted to intellectual labor" because of the previously amateurish status of writing and because of "the perplexities that followed from the Victorian 'feminizing' of such labor" (Adams, 1995: 12). Carlyle assumed the role of the sage or prophet in part to justify his intellectual labor, in part to avoid the charge of dilettantism or dandyism, in part to set himself apart from ordinary, inferior writers. When as a young man he considered moving to London to pursue writing as a profession, he wrote (somewhat jocularly) to a Scottish friend: "If I break forth some day in Cockney-land, like some John the Baptist, girt about with a leathern girdle, proclaiming anew with fierce Annandale intonation: 'Repent ye, ye cursed scoundrels,' for &c &c you will not think it miraculous" (ibid.: 22–3). However ironic, the allusion to John the Baptist suggests that Carlyle intended to lift his writing to a higher, prophetic mode.

Of course, not all sage writers suffered the anxieties of Carlyle about their brain work. John Ruskin, the son of a wealthy importer of sherry and fine wines, had no need to earn money from his writing; Matthew Arnold, the son of an eminent Victorian educator, held a position as Inspector of Schools for most of his adult life, thus obviating the need to justify authorship as his profession; Walter Pater was, first and foremost, an Oxford don. Women writers like Harriet Martineau, George Eliot, and Frances Power Cobbe suffered anxieties about their professional writing – but of a different sort. For them, as for many women, the decision to enter a profession (and thus leave the domestic sphere) was the primary anxiety. Their need to demonstrate a capacity to do brain work, an activity many Victorians thought women incapable of, sometimes led them to produce sage writing self-consciously in the mode of their male counterparts, sometimes to experiment with forms of writing different from men's, as we shall see.

In any case, the Carlylean desire to make the writer a professional – more than that, to make the man of letters a modern hero – helped to formulate the concept of the "sage writer." In his essays and books Carlyle drew on the features of Old Testament prophecy (hence the sometimes interchangeable terminology of "sage" or "prophet"), as well as on traditions of eighteenth-century satire and nineteenth-century homiletics, to present his views. And in Carlyle's turn to biblical and sermonic modes we can trace a final influence on the development of sage writing: the substitution of the secular prophet or sage for the religious minister or priest. As Carlyle himself argued in his seminal essay "Characteristics" (1831), "Literature is but a branch of Religion, and always participates in its character." By the beginning of the Victorian age, however, the clergy had lost some of its prestige and power, and as the century progressed, Victorian religion was repeatedly challenged by evolutionary science and other emerging fields of specialized knowledge. Thus, in Carlyle's prophetic words, "the ancient 'ground-plan of All' belies itself when brought into contact with reality; Mother Church has, to the most, become a superannuated Stepmother, whose lessons go disregarded; or are spurned at, and scornfully gainsaid" ("Characteristics").

Sage writers offered an alternative to the Church as a source of wisdom – about the problems of life on earth, for the most part, but sometimes even in regard to the hereafter. In *Heroes and Hero-Worship* Carlyle argued that this development was logical, even necessary. After his discussion of "The Hero as Divinity" and "The Hero as Prophet," Carlyle turned – in what he viewed as a historical progression – to "The Hero as Poet" and then "The Hero as Man of Letters." "The hero as divinity, the hero as prophet, are productions of old ages; not to be repeated in the new," he asserted. The modern hero, embodied for Carlyle in men of letters like Samuel Johnson, Jean-Jacques Rousseau, and Robert Burns, carries on the work of these older heroes by "discharging a function for us which is ever honourable, ever the highest": "He is uttering-forth, in such a way as he has, the inspired soul of him." This uttering-forth – this speaking and writing of genuine, original, divinely given truth – became the defining mark of the sage.

The Rhetoric of Sage Writing: Some Characteristic Strategies

Carlyle's early *Edinburgh Review* essays, "Signs of the Times" (1829) and "Characteristics" (1831), mark the emergence of sage writing as a form and show several of its classic rhetorical strategies. With the title of the first, Carlyle alludes to Christ's words in Matthew 16:3, "O ye hypocrites, ye can discern the face of the sky; but can ye not discern the signs of the times?" – a biblical allusion that signals his intention to assume the prophetic mode, to read the signs of his own times, analyze their meaning, and offer his pronouncement on the spiritual inadequacies of his age. With the second title, "Characteristics," Carlyle adapts the German term *Charakteristik*, meaning a sketch or characterization, thus again signaling an intention to analyze the dominant features of his age – which for him was a "Mechanical" one – and to pronounce judgment on its mistakes and misunderstandings. In both essays Carlyle assumes the role of sage or prophet, demonstrating intellectual discernment in analyzing his society and spiritual integrity in calling for its reform.

Several features of Carlyle's essays became common in sage writing as other prose writers imitated him or developed features of his style – in addition to biblical allusion, the use of aphorism, metaphor, and a distinctive prophetic "voice." For example, Carlyle begins "Characteristics" with an aphorism or wise saying: "The healthy know not of their health, but only the sick: this is the Physician's Aphorism; and applicable in a far wider sense than he gives it." This aphorism may be Carlyle's original invention, perhaps an adaptation of Goethe's distinction between classicism as *gesund* and romanticism as *krank*, or perhaps a modern version of the well-known Bible verse, "They that be well need not a physician" (Matthew 9:12). Whether original or borrowed, the aphorism introduces in compact language the argument Carlyle intends to make throughout the essay: that a healthy society, like a healthy body, functions unself-consciously; that a sick society, like a sick body, is "too conscious of many things . . . oftenest the fierce jar of disruptions and convulsions." Carlyle applies the aphorism first to the individual body and soul, then to the social body and body politic, and finally to what he calls "the Condition of our own Era." By beginning with an aphorism, Carlyle suggests through his rhetorical form that his words convey important truth.

Victorian sage writing is replete with aphorisms, as other examples from Carlyle's works suggest: "Wonder is the basis of Worship" (*Sartor Resartus*); "The true University of these days is a Collection of Books" (*Heroes and Hero-Worship*); "Blessed is he who has found his work; let him ask no other blessedness" (*Past and Present*, 1843); or "Genius . . . is the transcendent capacity for taking trouble first of all" (*The Life of Frederick the Great*, 1858–65) – all of which have sufficiently entered our cultural vocabulary that they are today included in *Bartlett's Familiar Quotations*. Other sage writers were equally famous for their aphoristic style: John Ruskin, as in "Remember that the most beautiful things in the world are the most useless: peacocks and lilies for instance" (*The Stones of Venice*, 1851–3) or "All books are divisible into two classes: the books of the hour, and the books of all time" (*Sesame and Lilies*, 1865); Matthew Arnold, as in "Conduct is three-fourths of our life and its largest concern" (*Literature and Dogma*, 1873); and especially George Eliot, as in "We are all of us born in moral stupidity, taking the world as an udder to feed our supreme selves" (*Middlemarch*, 1872). Eliot's novel *Middlemarch* is a virtual treasure-trove of original aphorisms, which may explain why she, known primarily as a novelist, is also known as a sage writer.

Such aphorisms evoked the prestige of wisdom writing, as seminally found in the Book of Proverbs or Ecclesiastes; they gave sage writers a vehicle for clarifying and condensing thought and simultaneously challenged readers to ponder the multiple, profound ramifications of the sage's words. When, late in the century, aesthetes like Oscar Wilde wanted to parody the Victorian sage – and steal his thunder – they too used this characteristic aphoristic style. Wilde's preface to *The Picture of Dorian Gray* (1890), for instance, is simply a list of aphorisms about art beginning with "The artist is the creator of beautiful things" and ending with the now-famous line "All art is quite useless."

Another feature of sage writing, the use of metaphors, especially a dominant structural metaphor, complements the aphoristic style. Just as the aphorism condenses the sage writer's argument into a crystalline sentence, so the metaphor crystalizes into an object or word the ideas or arguments the writer amplifies throughout the essay. In "Signs of the Times," for instance, Carlyle calls his era "the Mechanical Age," and in example after example, he follows out the implications of this metaphor in British life – from the machinery that has transformed British industry or the steam railways and steamships that now transport British trade, to the mechanical approach that dominates the British philosophy to utilitarianism and the concept of the "Machine of Society" that motivates British politics. Carlyle's criticism focuses on what this "mechanical" view of things omits: the dynamic and organic forces that are truly important to our life and development. Despite the negativity of his critique, Carlyle's metaphor leads him to prophesy "that Mechanism is not always to be our hard taskmaster, but one day to be our pliant, all-ministering servant; that a new and brighter era is slowly evolving itself for all men." Even his prophecy involves a metaphor, that of a taskmaster becoming a servant.

Much of what we today retain from Victorian sage writing involves metaphor: Arnold's "sweetness and light" to characterize the Greek heritage in Western culture (*Culture and Anarchy*, 1869) or his "touchstones" to determine what ranks as great literature ("The Study of Poetry," 1880); Carlyle's "steamroller" of a universe, smashing the hopes and aspirations of every human being who comes in its way (*Sartor Resartus*); or Ruskin's "queens' gardens" to locate the feminine influence in English culture (*Sesame and Lilies*, 1865) or his "storm-cloud" to describe the environmental and moral degradation of his age and its apocalyptic effects ("The Storm-Cloud of the Nineteenth Century," 1884). Such metaphors help to crystalize and visualize thought. They are also, for some (but not all) sage writers, an alternative to traditional, logical forms of argumentation. For Carlyle in particular, the healthy understanding "is not the Logical, argumentative, but the Intuitive" ("Characteristics"). Thus, Carlyle tended to employ metaphor as a means of grasping what the logic of his contemporaries missed: "To figure Society as endowed with life," he argued in "Characteristics," "is scarcely a metaphor; but rather a statement of fact by such imperfect methods as language affords."

These features – the use of aphorisms, metaphors, and biblical allusions, the assumption of the role of social critic or latter-day prophet – produced in most sage writers a distinctive "voice." One early reviewer of Carlyle's work, John Sterling, noted that it "exhibits all the vehemence and self-reliance of a prophet" (Seigel 1971: 101) – and, indeed, *prophetic* is a term frequently used to describe the voices of Carlyle, Ruskin, and Arnold. (Arnold was called, by a disparaging reviewer, an "elegant Jeremiah," a phrase evoking the Old Testament prophet of doom and gloom but also acknowledging in a grudging way the cultured sophistication of Arnold's analyses.) According to George Landow, the prophetic voice of the Victorian sage derives from his peculiar stance:

> Whereas the pronouncements of traditional wisdom literature always take as their point of departure the assumption that they embody the accepted, received wisdom of an entire society, the pronouncements of the biblical prophet and Victorian sage begin with the assumption that, however traditional their messages may once have been, they are now forgotten or actively opposed by society. . . . The style, tone, and general presentation of the sage derive from the fact that his voice resides at the periphery; it is, to use a Ruskinian etymological reminder, an eccentric voice, one off center. (Landow 1986: 23)

By his eccentricity or marginality, the sage achieved a unique perspective on his society and set himself off from the mistaken masses.

In addition to "eccentric" we might offer the words "elevated" or "disinterested" to describe the sage's voice – the latter the preferred term of Matthew Arnold, suggestive less of an idiosyncratic stance than of a desire to remove the sage from the immediate political fray. In "The Function of Criticism at the Present Time" (1864) and again in *Culture and Anarchy* Arnold argued that what England most needed was not writers representing their own political points of view, as was usually the case in Victorian periodicals, but rather "critics" who were "disinterested" – that is, above party politics, inhabiting "the world of ideas, not the world of catchwords and party habits." Arnold's "critic" (his term for what we call "sage") less frequently occupies the eccentric position of a Ruskin, or the knowable political position of a Mill or Martineau, than he ideally strives to articulate "the best that has been thought and known in the world" ("Sweetness and Light"). The Arnoldian ideal of disinterestedness exerted a strong influence over later sages, most obviously Walter Pater, who removed sage writing entirely (or almost so) from the realm of politics into that of aesthetics and whose definition of the critic's task begins, citing Arnold, "To see the object as in itself it really is" (Preface to *The Renaissance*, 1873).

Whatever their rhetorical techniques or political commitments, sages were, above all else, cultural interpreters. Whether they chose to adopt the prophetic voice (as did Carlyle and Ruskin) or whether they instead modulated their voices within the bounds of traditional rhetoric (as did writers like Harriet Martineau and Frances Power Cobbe), sage writers interpreted the signs of their times. Thus, the premier technique of sage writing became the identification and interpretation of ordinary, even trivial phenomena as keys to cultural meaning. This technique was used with effect by virtually every Victorian sage and has been passed down to twentieth-century cultural critics such as Joan Didion, Tom Wolfe, and Hunter Thompson. Matthew Arnold used, for example, the murder of an illegitimate child by a woman named Wragg to critique the current state of British culture in "The Function of Criticism" (1864). In the *Latter-Day Pamphlets* (1850) Carlyle chose a statue erected in honor of George Hudson, the railway king, to reveal the low level to which English heroism and hero-worship had fallen. In "What Shall We Do with Our Old Maids?" (1862) Frances Power Cobbe began with a report from the Convocation of Canterbury to raise issues about women's education and employment. And John Ruskin, in a brilliant example of this technique in the essay "Traffic" (1862), focused on the architectural styles of the churches, schools, and houses of the industrial town of Bradford to interpret the current state of religion and commerce.

According to Ruskin, "All good architecture is the expression of national life and character; and it is produced by a prevalent and eager national taste" – an argument he had developed in *The Stones of Venice* and repeats at the beginning of "Traffic." Ruskin notes that the buildings in Bradford belong to two different architectural styles: churches and schools use the Gothic style, whereas mansions and mills "are never Gothic." What, Ruskin asks, does this peculiar phenomenon mean – given that, during the Middle Ages, all buildings were constructed in the same Gothic style, houses and churches alike? Ruskin interprets the modern division of architectural styles to mean that "at the root of the matter, it signifies neither more nor less than that you have separated your religion from your life." "Traffic" goes on to argue that the true religion of Bradford is commerce (*traffic*, in its nineteenth-century usage) rather than Christianity. The phenomena of everyday life become the occasion for – and evidence of – the sage's cultural analysis. Whatever the phenomena, the goal is critique and, ultimately, reform.

Women Writers as Cultural Sages

John Holloway's *The Victorian Sage: Studies in Argument* (1953) included only one woman author: George Eliot. Eliot's high seriousness, her sense of "the high responsibilities of literature that undertakes to represent life" (ibid.: 111), not to mention her brilliant use of metaphor, aphorism, and allusion, made her an undeniable candidate for sage status. Other women writers were omitted, however, and only in the past decade has there been intense discussion about women writers who belong in this category – thanks in large part to Thaïs Morgan's *Victorian Sages and Cultural Discourse: Renegotiating Gender and Power* (1990) and Andrea Broomfield and Sally Mitchell's *Prose by Victorian Women: An Anthology* (1996). The essays in Morgan's collection raise important critical issues about women writers taking on the role of sage; Broomfield and Mitchell's volume provides ready access to examples of women's nonfictional prose.

As several contributors to Morgan's collection point out, most notably Carol Christ and George Landow, Victorian women writers faced a number of cultural prejudices that turned them away from sage writing as a genre. Proper ladies were not supposed to speak out; they were not supposed to meddle in politics or other public issues; they were, at best, supposed to compose domestic treatises, devotional tracts, or sentimental poetry – literary genres beneath the designation "sage." Even professional women writers who resisted these prejudices tended to be associated not with sage writing but with the novel. Women's success in fiction was so noticeable that George Henry Lewes (George Eliot's partner) commented:

> Of all departments of literature, Fiction is the one to which, by nature and by circum-
> stance, women are best adapted. Exceptional women will of course be found competent
> to the highest success in other departments; but speaking generally, novels are their
> forte. The domestic experiences which form the bulk of women's knowledge find an
> appropriate form in novels; while the very nature of fiction calls for that predominance
> of Sentiment which we have already attributed to the feminine mind. (Christ 1990: 22)

Lewes's view coincides with twentieth-century statistics: of the 11 Victorian women listed in the *Wellesley Index to Victorian Periodicals* with more than 50 entries to their name, half are better known as novelists than as nonfiction writers (Christ 1990: 21–2).

Even so, a significant number of Victorian women writers donned the prophetic mantle and wrote in the mode of the sage. Their work – what they wrote about, what rhetorical techniques they adopted, how they resembled or differed from their male counterparts – broadens our sense of sage writing in the Victorian period. Indeed, it makes us rethink the contributions of other prose writers, men and women alike, who have not usually been called sages but who added their voices to debates about the pressing social and political issues of their day.

Most prominent as a female sage writer in the biblical mode was Christina Rossetti who, in prose commentaries such as *Seek and Find* (1879), *Called to Be Saints* (1881), and *Time Flies* (1885), used the liturgical calendar and traditional Anglo-Catholic devotional practices as the basis for a modern rearticulation of spiritual wisdom and practical piety. Most prominent in the classical prophetic mode was Florence Nightingale who, in *Cassandra* (written in 1852), spoke out against the social pressure to marry and the trivialization of the lives of women who didn't. "Why have women passion, intellect, moral activity," Nightingale asked, yet "a place in society where no one of the three can be exercised?" The title of Nightingale's prose piece – which names the visionary Trojan princess who prophesied truthfully but whose words were never believed – signals her own prophetic intentions. So, too, do Nightingale's adaptations of Old Testament prophetic strategies and her (mis)quotations of John the Baptist who, in the New Testament, is figured as the "voice of one crying in the wilderness" (Landow 1990: 42–4). For Nightingale, the modern prophetess cries "in the crowd, 'Prepare ye the way of the Lord,'" and what she prepares for is a female Christ and female followers who will truly live by Christ's sayings. The self-designation as Cassandra may, however, suggest that Nightingale feared her message would not be heard or even that she was ambivalent about assuming the prophetic role (a conclusion supported by her decision not to publish *Cassandra* but to circulate it privately among friends).

Other women writers were less ambivalent. Harriet Martineau, Frances Power Cobbe, and Eliza Lynn Linton also wrote as sages, though typically not in the prophetic vein of Carlyle or the classical, feminine mode of Nightingale. Martineau was proud of the fact that, as a child, she had attended a boy's grammar school and had mastered the traditionally masculine subjects of rhetoric and composition; Martineau, Cobbe, and Linton all pursued careers as journalists, Linton becoming the first salaried woman reporter (for the *Morning Chronicle*) and Cobbe noting with pride that she daily went to the office to do her work "like a man." When these women wrote about contemporary social problems, they wrote in what G. H. Lewes would have deemed a masculine style, utilizing the rhetorical tools of *logos* and eschewing *pathos*. Martineau's style emphasizes balance, and her prose often depends on the hypothetical syllogism (If x is true, then y is true; if y is not true, then x is not true) – as in her argument in *Household Education* (1849) about women's intellectual capacities: "If it is said that the female brain is incapable of studies of an abstract nature, – that is not true: for there are many instances of women who have been good mathematicians, and good classical scholars." Cobbe similarly emphasizes the logic of her approach, as in "The Rights of Man and the Claims of Brutes" (1863), where she begins, "Let us endeavour to arrive at a clear analysis," or in "Wife-Torture in England" (1878), where she explicitly states that she will "avoid making this paper more painful than can be helped" – tactics that stress her reliance on masculine logic and her avoidance of feminine emotion or sensationalism.

The rhetorical approaches of Martineau, Cobbe, and Linton remind us that not all sage writers distrusted logic as Carlyle did, nor did all sage writers explicitly invoke the biblical model of the prophet. Martineau, for example, employed a modern version of scientific prophecy that "predicted" the future by systematically studying the causes and influences of the past; according to Martineau's interpretation of Auguste Comte and his positivist philosophy, every present event can be understood as the result of antecedent causes, and by projecting antecedent causes forward, we can anticipate the future. Or, to cite the case of a male sage, Matthew Arnold may have been disparaged as an "elegant Jeremiah," but in his reliance on the tactics of classical rhetoric, his style is closer to Martineau's than to Carlyle's. Similarly, John Stuart Mill was committed to the uses of logic in essays like *On Liberty* (1859) and *On the Subjection of Women* (1869), even if he explored its limits in his *magnum opus*, *A System of Logic* (1843).

Among women writers, Eliza Lynn Linton was most like the prophetic Carlyle in her approach and style, sometimes echoing his key words or metaphors. In her now-infamous (because antifeminist) "Nearing the Rapids" (1894) Linton picks up on Carlyle's antidemocratic essay "Shooting Niagara: and After?" (1867), which protested the passing of the Second Reform Bill and the extension of the franchise to men he considered uneducated and ill-prepared to be voters. In "Nearing the Rapids" Linton similarly comments with disdain on the extension of the franchise to independent women who were heads of house. To her, this extension would include far too many women of dubious morality, poor education, or provincial interests – none of whom could possibly contribute to "the perfection of good government," which she holds out as the ideal goal of granting the vote. Her opening phrase – "Those rash pilots, the Women's Rights men and women, bent on shooting Niagara and wrecking the old-time womanly ideal" – reinvents Carlyle's metaphor of pursuing a dangerous course. In other essays, however, Linton invented her own key phrases – as in her famous essay, "The Girl of the Period" (1868), a critique of the fashion-conscious, money- and status-mad modern woman. "The Girl of the Period" became so standard a phrase that it gave to the Victorians their own meaning of the acronym "GOP."

Other Sage Writing: A Complementary Tradition

If the work of women writers expands our sense of the traditions and techniques of sage writing, it reminds us too that many Victorians who wrote about contemporary problems did not fall into the prophetic mode (even though they laid claim to wisdom) or deliberately assume an "eccentric" or "disinterested" perspective. We tend to distinguish between practical wisdom and special wisdom, the latter being the province of the sage writer. But many Victorian essayists preferred to write from the stance of the practical man or woman, emphasizing the commonsensical or even the mundane as their source of knowledge. Their writings, enormously popular and widely read in their day, are complements to the prose of a Carlyle, Ruskin, or Arnold and, in a different way, are "sage" as well.

In writing about the "State of the Country" in his *Rural Rides* (1830), for instance, William Cobbett literally became the man on horseback, riding through the English countryside via fields and back lanes, observing the state of agriculture and the lives of rural laborers, and assuming the professional writer's privilege of commenting on what he observed. But Cobbett's perspective is that of a practical man who understands agriculture, who has written books on *Cottage Economy* (1822) and *The Woodlands* (1825), and who can thus speak to the "signs of the times" as a man who has seen them close up. His perspective is not that of the Arnoldian "disinterested" critic but that of a politically committed radical.

In *Rural Rides* Cobbett criticizes a political system that has allowed the lives of rural workers to become wretched, a system that relies on statistics rather than direct observation to prove things are fine and that foolishly believes protective tariffs on English grain will solve whatever agricultural problems there may be. Cobbett's writing is "sage" in that it is knowledgeable, but he does not rely particularly on metaphor or aphorism or biblical allusion. If his is a distinctive voice, it is because it has the earthy, even racy quality of an outdoorsman or because it reproduces the strident, forthright harangue of a political orator. "Radical," Cobbett liked to explain, "means, *belonging to the root; going to the root*":

> Our system of husbandry is happily illustrative of our system of politics. Our lines of movement are fair and straightforward. We destroy all weeds, which, like taxeaters, do nothing but devour the sustenance that ought to feed the valuable plants. Our plants are all *well fed*; and our nations of Swedes and of cabbages present a happy uniformity of enjoyments and of bulk.

His agricultural allegory typifies his political beliefs, but in its literariness it is relatively atypical of Cobbett's commentary.

What Cobbett does employ, in common with other Victorian sages, is the telling anecdote, the revelatory phenomenon, the small detail that reveals the true state of things. As he rides through the fields around Cirencester, he observes that it is a "fine, clean, beautiful place" with laborers "pretty well as to dress and healthiness." How does he know? Because "the girls at work in the fields (always my standard) are not in rags, with bits of shoes tied on their feet and rags tied round their ankles, as they had in Wiltshire" (ibid. I: 24). If shoes tell a tale about rural fieldworkers, a donkey-cart tells a related tale about the gentry. In nearby Bollitree, Cobbett sees a "pleasant-looking lady" and "two beautiful children" riding "in a little sort of chaise-cart, drawn by an *ass*." This contrivance proves to Cobbett that the lady is an intelligent women ("a real *practical radical*") and her husband, a blessed man. Why? Because the donkey-cart avoids the expense of a carriage and pair of horses; it avoids "feeding those cormorants who gorge on the taxes" (ibid. I: 29–30) – and presumably it means that the man and his wife are reinvesting their wealth in the land. Such details are not disinterested in the Arnoldian sense, however; they reveal people's politics, whether the individuals know it or not.

Cobbett's practical and political writings about agricultural scenes represent a larger body of writing about rural England, the counterpart to Carlyle or Ruskin's commentary on urbanization and industrialization. If Carlyle drew his emblematic anecdotes from life in the city, Cobbett and his cohort – William Howitt, his wife Mary Howitt, and Mary Russell Mitford, to name only a few of these rural sages – found them in the country. If Carlyle in *Past and Present* or Ruskin in *The Stones of Venice* looked back to the Middle Ages for their ideal social order, these writers recalled a traditional agricultural society in which both laborers and landowners lived well in peace, plenty, and social harmony. If Carlyle brought to his readers' attention the "Condition of England," Cobbett showed them the "State of the Country."

Some of this rural sage writing is obviously nostalgic. When Mary Mitford wrote a series called "Our Village" in the 1820s and 1830s, the same period in which Carlyle published "Signs of the Times" and "Characteristics," the circulation of the magazine that carried her essays increased eightfold. London readers, as well as their country counterparts, wanted to read her sketches of life in a classic English village – the sort of village that industrialization and urbanization were destroying. Or, when William Howitt published his enormously popular *A Boy's Country Book* (1839), a series of tales based on his growing up in rural Derbyshire, London readers participated vicariously in rural pastimes and pursuits that were fast becoming extinct. On the face of it, Mitford's or Howitt's sketches of rural English life seem completely antithetical to Carlyle's analyses of modern urban existence: Mitford chronicles life in a small village, focusing on cottages and houses and the folks who live in them, taking her readers on a series of "walks in the country" to show them flowers, trees, and other country pleasures; whereas Carlyle discusses model prisons, new poorhouses, modern railways, and distressing features of urban life.

Yet these strains of writing, however different their authors' politics, are two pieces of the same prose puzzle – the one looking analytically at the modern scene, the other looking descriptively (and often nostalgically) at a lost Eden. The urban sage inveighs prophetically, critically, even angrily; the rural sage speaks practically, sensibly, sometimes lovingly and sadly. Victorian readers had both (in fact, multiple) points of view available to them: they could think analytically about urban problems or they could mentally escape to a peaceful country village; they could consider English culture "disinterestedly" or they could lament the state of English agriculture along with politicians.

Both strains of sage writing come together in the prose of George Eliot; indeed, Eliot makes a strong case for the importance of both perspectives in the work of the Victorian sage. When Eliot was primarily a book reviewer and translator – that is, before she embarked on her career as a novelist – she wrote an influential essay, "The Natural History of German Life" (1856), ostensibly a review of two German books by the author Wilhelm Heinrich von Riehl. This essay includes a discussion of the crucial role of community-building in the work of the modern sage and quickly becomes an argument for the necessity of a combined knowledge of rural and urban life as the basis for the sage's work.

Riehl had compiled a book about the "general characteristics of the German peasantry" and their variations from geographical region to region. Eliot believed that similar sociological studies needed to be done of English peasants and workers. Otherwise, true sage writing, true insight into and advice about modern existence, could not be had. According to Eliot, many Victorian writers on contemporary issues failed to offer sound advice, let alone genuine wisdom, because they lacked this basic sociological information:

> The tendency created by the splendid conquests of modern generalization, to believe that all social questions are merged in economical science, and that the relations of men to their neighbours may be settled by algebraic equations, – the dream that the uncultured classes are prepared for a condition which appeals principally to their moral sensibilities, – the aristocratic dilettanteism which attempts to restore the "good old times" by a sort of idyllic masquerading, and to grow feudal fidelity and veneration as we grow prize turnips, by an artificial system of culture, – none of these diverging mistakes can coexist with a real knowledge of the People, with a thorough study of their habits, their ideas, their motives.

If Eliot is here attacking certain strains of sage writing, the utilitarian as well as the nostalgic, she is also arguing for the importance of that complementary tradition of prose writing about rural life that is so often omitted from our modern discussions of the Victorian sage. We cannot understand Victorian nonfictional prose without both. We need to expand our definitions of the sage and his (and her) rhetorical stances and techniques. The rural rides of a Cobbett or the village rambles of a Mitford inform the political, social, and literary contexts in which – and about which – Carlyle, Ruskin, and Arnold wrote. Indeed, they are part of the context and part of the literary tradition, whether or not we choose to call them "sage."

Whatever the designation, this complementary tradition gives us a broader perspective on Victorian nonfictional prose and its interconnections. Cobbett's detailed observation of the "State of the Country" influenced, it could be argued, the subsequent strains of both urban and rural writing the urban in the rich, investigative sociologies of Edwin Chadwick (*Report on the Sanitary Condition of the Labouring Population of Great Britain*, 1842), Henry Mayhew (*London Labour and London Poor*, 1861–2), or William Booth (*In Darkest England*, 1890); the rural in the radical utopian visions of William Morris (*News from Nowhere*, 1890) or Samuel Butler (*Erewhon*, 1872). The influence may be more stylistic than ideological in some cases, more ideological than stylistic in others, but it is illuminating to read Mayhew's descriptions of mudlarks and scavengers while recalling Cobbett's accounts of rural fieldworkers. In future scholarship we might continue to explore such connections.

See also 1832; CLERICAL, ADMINISTRATIVE, PUBLISHING; LIFE WRITING

REFERENCES

Adams, James Eli (1995) *Dandies and Desert Saints: Styles of Victorian Masculinity*. Ithaca, NY and London: Cornell University Press.

Broomfield, Andrea and Mitchell, Sally (eds) (1996) *Prose by Victorian Women: An Anthology*. New York and London: Garland.

Christ, Carol T. (1990) "'The Hero as Man of Letters': Masculinity and Victorian Nonfiction Prose." In Thaïs E. Morgan (ed.) *Victorian Sages and Cultural Discourse*. New Brunswick and London: Rutgers University Press.

Cobbett, William (1908) *Rural Rides . . . During the Years 1821 to 1832; with Economical and Political Observations*, ed. Pitt Cobbett. London: Reeve and Turner.

Erickson, Lee (1996) *The Economy of Literary Form: English Literature and the Industrialization of Publishing, 1800–1850*. Baltimore, MD: Johns Hopkins University Press.

Holloway, John (1953) *The Victorian Sage: Studies in Argument*. London: Macmillan. Rpt. Hamden, CT: Archon Books, 1962.

Howitt, William (1839) *The Boy's Country-Book: Being the Real Life of a Country Boy, Written by Himself*. London: Longman, Brown, Green, and Longmans.

Landow, George P. (1986) *Elegant Jeremiahs: The Sage from Carlyle to Mailer*. Ithaca, NY and London: Cornell University Press.

——(1990) "Aggressive (Re)interpretations of the Female Sage: Florence Nightingale's *Cassandra*." In Thaïs E. Morgan (ed.) *Victorian Sages and Cultural Discourse*. New Brunswick and London: Rutgers University Press.

Lewes, G. H. (1847) "The Condition of Authors in England, Germany, and France." *Fraser's Magazine*, 35, 285–95.

Mitford, Mary Russell (1824) *Our Village: Sketches of Rural Character and Scenery*, 2nd edn. London: Geo. B. Whittaker. Rpt. London and Poole: Woodstock Books, 1996.

Morgan, Thaïs E. (ed.) (1990) *Victorian Sages and Cultural Discourse: Renegotiating Gender and Power*. New Brunswick and London: Rutgers University Press.

Seigel, Jules Paul (1971) *Thomas Carlyle: The Critical Heritage*. London: Routledge and Kegan Paul.

FURTHER READING

Altick, Richard D. (1962) "The Sociology of Authorship: The Social Origins, Education, and Occupations of 1,100 British Writers, 1800–1935." *Bulletin of the New York Public Library*, 66, 389–404.

Collini, Stefan (1991) *Public Moralists: Political Thought and Intellectual Life in Britain, 1850–1930*. Oxford: Clarendon Press.

Corbett, Mary Jean (1992) "My Authorship Self." In *Representing Femininity: Middle-Class Subjectivity in Victorian and Edwardian Women's Autobiography*. New York and Oxford: Oxford University Press.

Cross, Nigel (1985) *The English Common Writer: Life in Nineteenth-Century Grub Street*. Cambridge: Cambridge University Press.

David, Deirdre (1987) *Intellectual Women and Victorian Patriarchy*. Ithaca, NY: Cornell University Press.

Gross, John (1969) *The Rise and Fall of the Man of Letters*. New York and London: Macmillan.

Harrison, Antony H. (1990) "Christina Rossetti and the Sage Discourse of Feminist High Anglicanism." In Thaïs E. Morgan (ed.) *Victorian Sages and Cultural Discourse*. New Brunswick and London: Rutgers University Press.

Helsinger, Elizabeth K. (1997) *Rural Scenes and National Representation: Britain, 1815–1850*. Princeton: Princeton University Press.

Landow, George P. (1981) "Ruskin as Victorian Sage: The Example of 'Traffic.'" In Robert

Hewison (ed.) *New Approaches to Ruskin: Thirteen Essays*. London: Routledge.

——(1993) "How to Read Ruskin: The Art Critic as Victorian Sage." In Susan Phelps Gordon and Anthony Lacy Gully (eds) *John Ruskin and the Victorian Eye*. New York: Abrams.

Levine, George (1968) *The Boundaries of Fiction: Carlyle, Macaulay, Newman*. Princeton: Princeton University Press.

Levine, George and Madden, William (eds) (1968) *The Art of Victorian Prose*. New York: Oxford University Press.

Mermin, Dorothy (1993) *Godiva's Ride: Women of Letters in England, 1830–1880*. Bloomington and Indianapolis: Indiana University Press.

Peterson, Linda H. (1990) "Harriet Martineau: Masculine Discourse, Female Sage." In Thaïs E. Morgan (ed.) *Victorian Sages and Cultural Discourse*. New Brunswick and London: Rutgers University Press.

Poovey, Mary (1995) *Making a Social Body: British Cultural Formation, 1830–1864*. Chicago: University of Chicago Press.

Saunders, J. W. (1969) *The Profession of English Letters*. London: Routledge and Kegan Paul.

Williams, Raymond (1958) *Culture and Society, 1780–1950*. New York: Columbia University Press.

26

Literary Criticism

David E. Latané, Jr

In the twilight of Georgian England, Dr William Maginn sat down, still in the convivial company of brother scribblers for *Fraser's Magazine,* and wrote an unsigned review of Mr Grantley Berkeley's novel *Berkeley Castle,* which exposed the aristocratic pretensions of the author (a member of Parliament), and concluded, "*Berkeley Castle* in conception is the most impertinent, as in execution it is about the stupidest, it has ever been our misfortune to read. It is also quite decisive of the character of the author as a 'gentleman.'" Maginn's review, while accurate to a "T," was also clearly fueled by a stronger brew, as well as by the animosity he felt, being an inordinately learned but somewhat unfortunate Irishman afloat in London, at snubs inflicted by semi-literate English snobs. A duel ensued, in which both politician and critic missed their marks several times. It was in the next year, 1837, that Victoria came to the throne. By the time of her death, two long generations later, politics remained much the same; yet literary criticism had become more polite, as well as more scholarly, professional, and (metaphorically) on target. A. C. Bradley's *Shakespearean Criticism* (1904), a work that was hailed as a masterpiece of psychological analysis and which occasionally is cited without caveat by critics today, may be taken as an end point. Midway between these dates, Matthew Arnold in "The Function of Criticism at the Present Time" (1864) made a precise and famous definition of criticism as "*a disinterested endeavour to learn and propagate the best that is known and thought in the world.*" For him, one word summed up the rule that should govern the critic: *disinterestedness.*

For the student of criticism in the Victorian age, it might be safest to disrespect the *dis-,* for Arnold's dictum was born as a counterweight to the prevalence of criticism of the most crudely biased sort, in which gain for one's political party, religious sect, bank account, or ego ledger was transparently the motive. In 1802 the founding of the *Edinburgh Review* had opened a new era in periodical criticism, and the *Edinburgh,* its quarterly imitators, and new magazines like *Blackwood's* established a "damnatory style" of anonymous reviewing which continued well into the Victorian era (Coleridge, *Biographia,* ch. 21; see also Woolford 1982). Alongside outrageous condemnation went the art of "puffing," or broadsiding the reading public with favorable short notices (planted, for instance, in the new weekly *Athenaeum*'s "Our Weekly Gossip on Literature and Art") as well as through longer articles. The publisher Henry Colburn – the Rupert Murdoch of his day – was notorious for buying periodicals which then gave the novels he published very fine reviews indeed. Writers even on occasion abused anonymity by reviewing their own books – with only Walter Scott giving himself a lukewarm treatment. Carlyle showed at least one thinking writer's contempt for the state of criticism at the beginning of the reign when he republished his bad notices as a badge of honor in the 1838 edition of *Sartor Resartus*. By 1886, however, a leading critic such as Arthur Symons could proclaim, "I have ever held that the rod with which popular fancy invests criticism is properly the rod of divination: a hazel-switch for the discovery of buried treasure, not a birch-twig for the castigation of offenders" (Preface to *An Introduction to the Study of Browning*).

Our standard accounts of Victorian criticism have tended to take the high road, emphasizing the work done by poet–scholars and men (rarely women) of letters such as Arnold, Cardinal Newman, G. H. Lewes, Walter Bagehot, Leslie Stephen, Symons, and "Vernon Lee" (Violet Paget). Though we may occasionally be more amused by the style of "Walt Whitman is as unacquainted with art as a hog is with mathematics" (1856; quoted in Woolford 1982: 111), it is the more thoughtful work, where "the critic . . . before abandoning himself to the oratorical impulse [classifies] the phenomena with which he is dealing as calmly as if he were ticketing a fossil in a museum" (Leslie Stephen, *Cornhill*, 36 [1877], 723–37), which leads Harold Orel to remark that "We may legitimately wonder whether the techniques for analysing and evaluating literary texts used in our century are all that superior to those used by Victorian critics" (Orel 1984: 3). More recently, canvassing the widest range of cultural activity, we have begun to map the byways, as well as the bylines, of the lesser known or anonymous critics, to explore the "cultural work" or ideology of critics both mundane and outrageous (if not profound). Examining, for instance, the ways in which the shapings of literary criticism coincide with alterations in national identity or attitudes towards empire, we are quick to ask, for instance, what it means when Carlyle's "Editor" in *Sartor Resartus* (book II, ch. 1) says, "Tombuctoo [*sic*] itself is not safe from British Literature." We are also exploring our master tropes of gender, class, and race, and finally, though self-interestedly, we are uncovering the Victorian story of how literary criticism established itself in university literature departments.

Arnold is of course an exceptional figure, born onto the intellectual center-stage. His father Thomas was an historian, theologian, famous headmaster of Rugby School, and then Regius Professor of Modern History at Oxford; his godfather was the tractarian divine and poet John Keble; Wordsworth was a family friend. Educated at Winchester, Rugby, and Oxford, Arnold won prizes and scholarships, obtained in 1845 a Fellowship at Oriel College and was appointed to the largely ceremonial position of Oxford Professor of Poetry at age 34, although the income that allowed him to marry and start a family came from the more mundane job of government Inspector of Schools. From the point of view of the sociology of authorship, foregrounding a man like Arnold distorts one's view of the practicing literary critic in the Victorian era. More typical would be the unknown William Henry Smith (1808–72), a friend of Lewes who wrote books of poems, plays, and philosophical dialogues that are not without merit (though utterly without success). A failure at the law, he made his meager living penning over 130 articles, chiefly on literary subjects, for periodicals such as *Blackwood's* at ten guineas a sheet. Sometimes his perceptions were keen; he is always thoughtful rather than contemptuous or puffing.

Still, Arnold remains the place to start in considerations of Victorian literary criticism. This is because he is more a superb propagandist for criticism (social, of course, as well as literary) than a practicing literary critic. Wilde, whose witty inversions of Arnoldian precepts are well known, owes an ironic debt to Arnold for making it possible to view "The Critic as Artist" (an essay of 1881), one perhaps superior to his or her putative subject. Arnold's critical ideal, in the words of René Wellek, compassed "curiosity, flexibility, urbanity, a free articulation of ideas" (Wellek 1965, 4: 156). Why then is Arnold so widely viewed with suspicion, even dislike, at the close of the twentieth century?

Arnold's legacy has come under scrutiny in recent years as scholars have become increasingly suspicious of poses of objectivity that mask positions which advantage *sub rosa* particular groups or causes. Many currents in contemporary Anglo-American criticism and theory have become energized by a dislike of the Arnoldian stance; in an interview the cultural historian Raymond Williams, one of the first modern theorists to criticize Arnold severely, when asked to reconsider, replied *au contraire*, "I would have to be savage today, nothing less would do" (Williams 1979: 124). Terry Eagleton speaks for many when he remarks in his *Ideology: An Introduction*, "We are generally right to suspect that appeals to see the object as it really is can be decoded as invitations to see it as our rulers do" (1991: 166). Arnold is seen as a "worn out man of letters," "with a frippery of phrases about sweetness and light, seeing things as they really are, knowing the best that has been thought and said in the world, which never had very much solid meaning." But this last-quoted judgment is no modern assailant's but Arnold's own – a piece of self-mockery from "A Liverpool Address" of 1882 – and it should therefore give us pause. The more one actually reads Arnold, the more difficult it becomes to turn him into a straw man.

Arnold's earliest criticism appears in his letters of the 1840s, especially those to his friend, the poet and fellow Rugby student Arthur Hugh Clough. (Throughout the century some of the most acute practical criticism occurs in letters from one poet to another, the Brownings', for instance, or Hopkins's letters to Robert Bridges.) It was when he took the extraordinary step in his preface of censuring and excising some of his own poems from his collected volume of 1853 that Arnold's critical impulse first came to the public eye, as a champion of the classical mode against the prevailing, and by now seedy, Romanticism. His position was contested by G. H. Lewes in prose, and Elizabeth Barrett Browning in a modern epic poem, *Aurora Leigh* (1857), which advocates for narrative verse the appropriation of the contemporary subject matter of the novel. Arnold's greatest impact comes, however, in *Essays in Criticism* of 1865, a miscellaneous collection of his writing from the previous few years. The volume possesses, in the words of Stefan Collini, "a surprising unity and coherence" because of "the presence in each essay of the idea of criticism itself, embodied in that distinctive Arnoldian voice" (Collini 1988: 62). Arnold lays out the case for disinterestedness, flexibility, objectivity, and a wide range of sympathy as he examines a range of authors, chiefly French. His abhorrence of criticism as a practical or utilitarian tool in the service of some extra-literary agenda, combined with Newman's anti-utilitarian ideal of a liberal education as an end in itself (see his *The Idea of a University*, 1873), might be seen as the bedrock of the Anglo-American approach to academic literary criticism for the next hundred years. Arnold's later writing, much taken up with social and religious matters, adds little that is new to his critical position as such.

In some ways the critical activities for which many know Arnold best – his ranking, naming of "touchstones," and general fastidiousness – are least important. Arnold airs his blind spots (Chaucer was "not one of the great classics") where many others remain silent, or mouth pieties. As a practicing critic his range – compared for instance to G. H. Lewes's or others' who earned their living with the pen – is small, taking practically no notice of the novel, or American literature, or living poets. He wrote essays on minor French writers that interested him, and left us without his criticism on Dickens, or George Eliot. What he left us instead was the notion of criticism itself.

Criticism of the Literature of the Past

Arnold's first book-length critical study was *On Translating Homer* (1861), and, indeed, in the absence of an academic literary criticism, a characteristic feature of the times was a strong interest in the history of literature. *The Temple Bar*, for instance, was one of the early shilling magazines of the 1860s – a "London Magazine for Town and Country Readers." In its first year it published articles on Bacon, the *Kalewala* (Finnish epic), Herrick, "Ancient Classical Novelists," Rabelais, Herbert, Donne, Gray, and Shelley. While this historical criticism did not escape the vices that plagued the contemporary reviews, it did offer greater latitude for reflection, and it was accessible to a wider audience than discussions of the same topics generally are now.

Today, criticism primarily concerns the literature of the past; books such as this one introduce readers to topics, and send for further reading to professional journals and university press monographs. In their consideration of their literary heritage, as in everything, the Victorians were industrious, but nothing like our professional critical "industry" existed, and Ian Small is correct to caution that in our use of the phrase "literary criticism" to describe, for example, writings of both Ruskin and Roland Barthes, we "presuppose . . . that they are doing the same 'thing,'" – and perhaps they are not (Small 1991: 18). Universities were few in number, and the study of modern languages and literatures was not part of the traditional curriculum. Scholars of ancient languages rarely wrote what we would recognize as literary criticism; their increasingly specialized work took the form of philological research and textual editing. Much of the criticism of older literature was necessarily amateur in origin, or driven by journalistic necessity. The establishment of the first chair in English literature at the new University of London in 1828 may portend the prevalence of professional literary scholarship at century's end, though it is still something of a surprise to discover that "English" didn't fully arrive at Oxford and Cambridge until the turn of the twentieth century. Before that, publishers, meeting the needs of an enlarging reading public, as well as of colleges and schools with an English curriculum, began producing numerous editions requiring critical introductions in the modern style, as well as series such as *The English Men of Letters* (begun 1877). Series editor John Morley elicited many distinguished contributions: Trollope on Thackeray, J. A. Symonds on Shelley, Stephen on Swift, Chesterton on Browning, Huxley on Hume. Canonical poets and novelists now arrayed by scholarly monographs on their afterwakes in criticism had first to have their lives and works traced, and late Victorians rose to the call. The past lay all before them, and if by our lights their steps were wandering, they were seldom slow. Most modern critical histories begin with the Victorians. The career of Shakespeare critic A. C. Bradley (1851–1935) is paradigmatic for English studies, as he ascends from Professor of Modern Literature at Liverpool (1882–90), to Professor of English at Glasgow (1890–1900), and finally to Professor of Poetry at Oxford. The astonishing production of George Saintsbury (1845–1933), a journalist and then an Edinburgh professor, became possible in this climate. Unlike earlier Victorian critics, Bradley and Saintsbury did not write across a range of nonliterary subjects; they confined their efforts instead to what Leslie Stephen dubbed in 1876 "aesthetic criticism" (see his "Thoughts on Criticism, by a Critic"; also Brake 1986).

The ancient text that had the most thorough-going, professional cadre of critic-interpreters was the Bible, and from the perilous field of German biblical hermeneutics came many of the innovations in secular criticism, filtered through intermediaries such as Coleridge, Carlyle, and Julius Hare. Despite protracted resistance fed by English parochial suspicion – "the Critic leaves no air to poison; / Pumps out with ruthless ingenuity / Atom by atom, and leaves you – vacuity" (Robert Browning, "Christmas-Eve," 1850, ll. 899, 911–13) – criticism of the Bible and the Graeco-Roman classics often took the form of sophisticated textual and interpretive commentary that accompanied new editions, for instance Connop Thirlwall's of Schleiermacher's *St. Luke* (1825), or Sir Alexander Grant's Hegelian commentary on Aristotle's *Ethics* (1857–8). From examples such as these, more complex philosophical approaches spread into literary criticism proper, as for instance in the writings of Walter Pater. Mundane practices, too – the compiling of "canon" and the listing of commentary resulting in what Saintsbury called an "atlas of the actual facts" (quoted in Wellek 1965, 4: 422) – descend ultimately from treatments of the Bible.

Victorian responses to earlier British literature may be categorized by period. Romantic critics such as Coleridge, Lamb, and Hazlitt had opened up the Elizabethan period, not only in Shakespeare studies, but also in the recovery of many other dramatists and poets from previous centuries' neglect. Victorian scholars followed through with such monuments as the 11-volume Moxon edition of Beaumont and Fletcher (1843–6). Special note should be taken of the Victorian Shakespeare business; it comprises numerous elements, many of them subcritical – Dr Bowdler's *Family Shakespeare* for instance, or Landor's imaginary account of the deer-stealing episode, or Anon's 1862 *Shakespeare: Was He a Christian?* (others proved him atheist, puritan, and Catholic). The Victorian Shakespeare is above all a *national* poet, essential to English-ness. Carlyle's lecture in *Heroes and Hero-Worship* (1841) poses a hypothetical either/or: *Empire* or *Shakespeare?* "Indian Empire will go, at any rate, some day; but this Shakespeare does not go, he lasts forever with us; we cannot give-up our Shakespeare!" Bagehot's essay "Shakespeare – The Individual" (1853) mines the plays to prove the Bard a "no nonsense" optimistic fellow who became "a person of capital . . . a gentle-man to be respected" – in short, an honorary Victorian. The heroines are of particular interest; early in the era Maginn argues that Shakespeare's range compels him "to bring females prominently forward in every variety of circumstance," and that, with the slight exception of Lady Macbeth, these heroines are "pure, honourable, spotless, – ever ready to perform a kind action, – never shrinking from a heroic one" (*Bentley's Miscellany*, 2 (1837): 558; see also Anna Jameson's 1832 *Characteristics of Women*, and Lootens 1996: 77–115). These greatly imagined women then stepped out of the confines of the script, like 60 paragons in search of an author, and into such bestsellers as Mary Cowden Clarke's *The Girlhood of Shakespeare's Heroines* (1850). Shakespeare and his characters exhausted, William Black late in the century invents a sister in his bestselling novel of 1884, *Judith Shakespeare: A Romance*. (It was left to Virginia Woolf to demolish the subtitle.)

Much of the more respectable effort is antiquarian and biographical. The first Shakespeare Society was founded in 1840 with the scholar–editors Revd William Dyce, Charles Knight, John Payne Collier, and James Halliwell at its core. This generation made many remarkable discoveries among Renaissance manuscripts – too many, in fact, for Collier was also a dedicated forger, and the Society was dissolved in 1851, its legitimate work under a cloud. Halliwell did, however, produce the century's most substantial biography of the Bard. When the New Shakspere Society called its first meeting in 1874, it was at University College, with the cranky F. J. Furnivall, master of Victorian literary societies, in the chair. Much of the sound and fury that ensued concerned textual matters, as members labored over minute theories of style or prosody to prove that this or that play preceded or followed another. Otherwise, respectability was maintained. But what sort of Shakespeare criticism did the Victorians leave us that built upon the landmarks left by Johnson, Coleridge, and Hazlitt? While individual essays such as Pater's on *Measure for Measure* stand out, the stronger critical minds did not produce their best on Shakespeare.

The literature of the eighteenth century was sometimes treated by Victorian critics in a "yes, but" fashion. Critics dismayed with the poets of the Byronic era, beginning with Byron himself, preferred Pope. In fiction, eighteenth-century masters such as Fielding were used as a yardstick; the rich humor and variety of human life in *Tom Jones* was used to measure each successive wave of novels-of-the-day. As public literary life began to reflect a more narrow, middle-class sense of decency, however, squeamishness arose about writers such as Swift, Sterne, and Smollett, whose works sometimes treated frankly the indecency of the body and the realities of social relations. We are somewhat bemused, I think, by Thackeray on Sterne: "The foul Satyr's eyes leer out of the leaves constantly: the last words the famous author wrote were bad and wicked" ("Sterne and Goldsmith," in *English Humourists of the Eighteenth Century*, 1853). Sterne is contrasted with the "sweet and unsullied page" of Dickens (though one suspects that Thackeray understood the joke of having a boy with his hands in his pockets constantly referred to, in *Oliver Twist* [1838], as "Master Bates"). Criticism of this sort by poets and novelists is hardly disinterested; reproving a licentious eighteenth century was perhaps one way of keeping Mrs Grundy from complaining about contemporary novelists. The eighteenth century went on to become the focus of a wider debate. In an interesting "Dialogue on Poetic Morality" published in the *Contemporary Review* (1881), Vernon Lee writes:

> Our modern familiarity with the intellectual work of all times and races has made people perceive that in past days indecency was always a part and parcel of literature, and that to try and weed it out is to completely alter the character of at least a good half of the literature of the past. Hence, some of us moderns, shaken as we are in all our conventional ideas, have argued that this so-called indecency is a legitimate portion of all literature, and that the sooner it is re-introduced into that of the present the better, if our literature is to be really vital and honest. (p. 698; reprinted in Stasny 1986)

The endlessly debated question – should literature depict things as they ought to be (Romanticism) or as they have been and are now (Realism)? – is latent in all such discussions. What has become a *locus classicus*, that the novelist should "aspire to give no more than a faithful account of men and things as they have mirrored themselves" in the novelist's mind, is satisfyingly part of an historical novel set in the late eighteenth century (*Adam Bede* [1859], ch. 17).

Among the learned and thoughtful critics of the previous century's literature, one stands out above the others. The work of Leslie Stephen (1832–1904) survives as one of the most original treatments in English of the relationship among literature and culture and society. Stephen, who is famous for all sorts of things – being an open agnostic, editing the *Cornhill Magazine* (1871–82), selecting the novels for Macmillan, founding and then writing 378 articles for the *Dictionary of National Biography*, inspiring characters in two masterpieces (*The Egoist* and *To the Lighthouse*), climbing many an Alp, fathering Virginia Woolf – devoted enormous energies to studying eighteenth-century England. His method, in one sense, is amateur, in that he confesses, "I at any rate love a book pretty much in proportion as it makes me love the author" ("The Study of English Literature"), but his scholarship and intellectual honesty take him beyond "appreciations" and "impressions." His own critics have found him cool, anti-aesthetic, overly intellectual, moralistic, and utilitarian in orientation. These very characteristics, however, might make his stock rise at present, when a view of literature as "a particular function of the whole social organism" (*English Literature and Society in the Eighteenth Century*, 1904) has its appeal. Stephen's work "was not only a pioneering clearing-away of the rubble, enabling Victorians to see the full dimensions of what the preceding century had accomplished; it remains today the most readable and informative introduction" to the age (Orel 1984: 122). Stephen's common sense can be appreciated best, perhaps, by reading him in parallel with the belletristic descendents of Charles Lamb, such as Augustine Birrell, who were popular at the turn of the century.

Theories of Poetry and Fiction

Victorian criticism of and response to Romantic-era writers is rich, copious, and almost impossible to categorize. The Romantics, despite their famously early deaths, were very much a real presence, whether in the flesh (Wordsworth, Landor, Hunt, and Peacock) or in memory and memorabilia. One thing is certain: by 1893, with the publication of the Yeats/Ellis edition of Blake, Victorian taste-makers had prepared for delivery to the twentieth century the restricted, all-male canon of Blake, Wordsworth, Coleridge, Byron, Shelley, and Keats. One could assert that it was in the course of thinking through that quintessential Romantic question, "What is Poetry?" that this restriction came about. Bentham, when not comparing poetry to children's games, had given the pragmatic definition – poetry is writing that doesn't extend to the right margin of the page. Responses like those of Leigh Hunt in *Imagination and Fancy* (1844) – "poetry is imaginative passion" (Stasny 1986: 4) – go so far in the other direction as to be meaningless. John Stuart Mill's refinements in his essays of the 1830s are more precise, but take the same tack. Mill rejects the rhetorical, didactic, and intellectual aspects; poetry effects a sharing of emotions, and the best poetry appears to us as overheard song, rather than purposeful speech. The wide discussion of what is, after all, a purely theoretical question (everyone recognized poetry when they saw it) gave the Victorians a consensus opinion that "poetry" was immediate, passionate, imaginative, lyric. Ultimately this meant, despite famous attempts to thin the flock (e.g. Arnold's dubbing Shelley an "ineffectual angel, beating in the void his luminous wings in vain"), that the answer to the question "What is Poetry?" could be given as that roll call of six Romantic names.

Early Victorian critics – from Arthur Hallam's precocious analysis of Tennyson, to Mill's brief but influential excursion into poetic theory, to Keble's Oxford lectures – attempt to consolidate the innovations of the Romantics. (Shelley's "Defense," it might be mentioned, was also first published in 1840.) Faced with the phenomena of the time, theories of poetry and accounts of poetic practice veered towards taxonomy. Thus, we have Hallam's poets of "sensation" and "reflection," Browning's "objective" and "subjective" poets ("Essay on Shelley," 1852), Bagehot's "pure," "ornate," and "grotesque" (1864), Buxton Forman's "idyllic," "psychological," "preraphaelite," and "renaissance" groupings (*Our Living Poets*, 1871), and the very complex systems of E. S. Dallas in his *Poetics: An Essay on Poetry* (1852). Dallas was educated at Edinburgh, and had a strong grasp of the German and Scottish philosophical traditions. He represents the closest thing to a Victorian "theorist," and in *The Gay Science* (1866) he breaks with the association psychology generally used to explain literary effects, "to probe the breaks, rather than the links, in the chain of association – dreams, intuition, delirium, involuntary memory" (Hughes 1985: 1). For better examples of theoretically informed and imaginative criticism, one must go to the Continent, to Taine, Sainte-Beuve, Kierkegaard, or Nietzsche, whose *Gay Science* is with good reason better known.

The Romantic novel cast no such shadow over the Victorians; though Walter Scott was omnipresent, he was not oppressive. Victorian critics developed a theory of realism in part by demolishing the steady stream of unrealistic or silly novels that issued from the press. Comparisons were often made to painting (Hogarth and Wilkie, or the "Dutch School" George Eliot admires in *Adam Bede*) as well as to the new art of photography. In an omnibus look at novels by women, Lewes declares in 1852 "that only *that* literature is effective, and to be prized accordingly, which has *reality for its basis* (needless to say that emotion is as real as the Three per Cents.), *and effective in proportion to the depth and breadth of that basis*" (Olmsted 1979, 2: 40). This criterion, which valorizes both Austen and Brontë, appeared again a few years later when George Eliot attacked "mind-and-millinery" novels in which "a child of four and a half years old" talks in "Ossianic fashion" ("Silly Novels by Lady Novelists," Olmsted 1979, 2: 281). Countervailing the dominant theory of realism, however, was a principle of amusement, which licensed other modes, giving rise to the controversy over sensation fiction that began in the 1860s, and subsequently to a critical divide between the "art" of fiction, and more popular narrative modes. Olmsted remarks that the "period roughly 1880 to 1900 saw more writing directly concerned with the art of fiction than had appeared in the previous half-century" (ibid.: 3: xiv). Henry James in "The Art of Fiction" (*Longman's Magazine*, 1884; Olmsted 1979, 3: 287) observes that the English novel "had no air of having a theory, a conviction, a consciousness of itself behind it – of being the expression of an artistic faith, the result of choice and comparison." The belated Victorian theoretical effort gave rise to the art novel (Meredith through Joyce), and brought this subgenre closer to the status of poetry, in sophistication and prestige, as well as in profitability.

Gender, and the Woman Critic

Literary criticism and commentary were diffuse and unspecialized throughout the era, and our current cultural studies approach is allowing us to see more of this wide field. In addition to probing the 48 mainstream monthlies and quarterlies indexed in the Houghtons' *Wellesley Index to Victorian Periodicals, 1824–1900* (a key reference work which identifies authors for most anonymous articles), we are also recovering criticism from such unlikely places as Margaret and Beatrice De Coucy's *Ladies' Cabinet of Fashion, Music, and Romance* (1836–7), which includes, alongside colored fashion plates of morning visiting dresses, articles such as "Modern Swedish Literature," "Coleridge's Poems," and "Influence of Female Intellect upon Literature"; or from the Chartist *Northern Star*, where we find an interesting dialogue, "Critic and Poet," and an essay on "The Beauties of Byron" that emphasizes the poet's politics (see Murphy 1994). These investigations, carried out in large part by members of the Research Society for Victorian Periodicals, are changing the shape of critical history, giving us nonmale or nonbourgeois perspectives on established writers such as Dickens or Robert Browning, and sometimes pointing, though less often than one might hope, towards interesting writers submerged or marginalized in received literary history.

Cross (1985) estimates that of writers in general 20 percent were female, most of these novelists or authors of children's literature, and that women wrote a relatively small percentage of the published literary criticism. But we look at gender issues in the criticism from several perspectives, not just the sex of the critic. Reception historians have scrutinized in increasingly subtle ways the fate of women writers at the hands of the reviewers, and we are also studying how gendered figures of speech used early in the century produced more concrete, though still radically unstable, critical categories: "manly," "feminine," "womanly," "effeminate" (Ferris 1992). New scholarship based in "queer theory" reads subtexts more than contexts, exploring, for example, how criticism uses these terms to "participate in an aesthetic minoritizing discourse whose project is to construct an alternative masculinity" (Morgan 1993: 320). While we must be alert here to the orbit of the "hermeneutic circle" (Matt. 7: 7) there is ample evidence in Victorian criticism supporting such a rich subtextuality; in commenting on Tennyson's *The Princess*, Aubrey de Vere explores how Ida's "Amazonian philosophy" might "extirpate from the soul of man those feminine qualities which the masculine nature, if complete, must include. . . . We dare not, however, undertake the exposition of all Mr Tennyson's hidden meanings" (*Edinburgh Review*, 1849, in Stasny 1986: 210). Alongside these more theoretical approaches to gender, scholars are working to identify in the periodical archive significant female practitioners of the art.

There is no doubt that women authors were treated differently from men, both in the course of the immediate review-response, and in more retrospective estimations and attempts to define movements or the *Zeitgeist*. While attitudes change (for better and for worse) over the course of the century, one might begin with the notion of a double standard, based in part on the stereotypical shortcomings of the female intellect, coupled with the equally stereotypical superiorities of the female heart. This meant that critics were quite happy to judge women's writing favorably within a "separate sphere," but reluctant to rate it equitably when it was perceived to step outside that magic bubble. Thus, the women poets who came into prominence from 1820 to 1850 (Hemans, L. E. L., Barrett Browning) had to fulfill the generic saintliness of "woman," and at the same time match the ideal of the *sui generis* poet-genius. The ensuing dissonance meant that in poetry "nineteenth-century feminine literary canonization became a virtual recipe for critical disappearance" (Lootens 1996: 10). But because reviewers were anonymous, and many novelists were as well, some attempts at stereotyping went spectacularly awry. An *Athenaeum* reviewer, for instance, states definitively of one of Rhoda Broughton's novels, "the author is not a young woman, but a man, who, in the present story, shows himself destitute of refinement of thought or feeling, and ignorant of all that women either are or ought to be" (Casey 1996: 155); another reviewer believed that Tennyson's anonymous *In Memoriam* (1850) came from "the full heart of the widow of a military man."

We are just beginning to sort out the complexities of reviewing and reception in the nineteenth century. While egregious cases of gender bias are easy to locate, reviewers were powerless to banish women from the field of literature, unlike the law and other professions. Gaye Tuchman and Nina Fortin mount a complex argument in *Edging Women Out* (1989) to show that women's authorship declined over the course of the century, as men seized prose fiction, formerly marginalized and despised, and enforced their new preeminence through the control of reviews. Ellen Casey (1996), however, in her examination of over 11,000 anonymous reviews of fiction in the weekly *Athenaeum* finds scant evidence for an "edging out," and instead uncovers a record of amelioration towards the end of the century in the damage wrought by the double standard. Other feminist critics, focusing on the reception of the "new woman" novelists of the 1890s or on the diminution of the reputation of George Eliot after her death, support the view that embattled male critics mounted more focused gender-biased attacks, thus enabling the late-Victorian canonization of male novelists like Hardy and Conrad.

Hostile reviews of *Tess* (1891) and *Jude* (1895), we might remember, helped edge Hardy into poetry, which is the genre most paradoxically gendered. While some feminist critics view official poetic theory and practice as almost entirely phallocratic, poets were culturally seen as weak and effeminate throughout the period, from the Dickens sketch of the "Poetical Young Gentleman" (1838), to such caricatures of the aesthetes as Gilbert and Sullivan's "Bunthorne" or the Irish poet "Joyday Flowers" in Sarah Grand's *The Winged Victory* (1916). Even more than in prose fiction, however, gender was related to style, and male and female poets were expected to keep to their respective sides of the road. The brawny and bearded Tennyson, paradoxically, was attacked most frequently with gender-terms. Alfred Austin, in a sally so notorious it might have come from an alley rather than a respectable publisher, finds the laureate typical of the "feminine, narrow, domesticated, timorous Poetry of the Period," and goes on to fault a descriptive passage because "There is no dust, and clang, and hot blood in it . . . still life is not a masculine, but a feminine propensity" (Bristow 1987: 124–6). Tennyson's natural propensities, apparently, are insufficiently red in tooth and claw. From a different angle Swinburne sees Tennyson's pernicious influence in the "idyl" form: "It is naturally on a lower level than that of tragic or lyric verse. Its gentle and maidenly lips are somewhat narrow for the stream. . . . It is very fit for the sole diet of girls; not very fit for the sole sustenance of men." Swinburne's utopia of an art that is "noble and chaste in the wider masculine sense" was perhaps wider than others would allow (ibid.: 9–10).

Gender is also factored into reviews according to the presumed or implied audience. The prototypical novel reader was a young girl, with a "passive, languorous body displaying itself on a sofa and neglecting domestic duties as it 'devoured' the texts that fed its romantic and sexual fantasies" (Ferris 1992: 18). One major function of Victorian criticism was to censure such novels, and praise those which would be safe for the "young person," a phrase which like the prudish "Mrs Grundy" became a common figure of speech. In poetry, however, chaste verse suitable for girls was generally chastised. Bagehot, for instance, makes some brilliant comments about the austerity and tactility of Wordsworth, noting that his poetry had become "the Scriptures of the intellectual life"; he then adds, "And therefore he has had a whole host of sacred imitators. Mr Keble, for example, has translated him for women" ("Hartley Coleridge" [1852] in *Literary Studies*). This in fact may be true; a case could be made that the extraordinarily popular *Christian Year* found its audience among religious, primarily female readers, who responded to the way it bent the tones of Wordsworth's secular poems to the round of the ecclesiastical calendar. The intent of remarks like Bagehot's, however, is not to analyze but to sneer. Thus, G. K. Chesterton in 1913: "There is a moment when Carlyle turns suddenly from a high creative mystic to a commonplace Calvinist. There are moments when George Eliot turns from a prophetess into a governess. There are also moments when Ruskin turns into a governess, without even the excuse of sex" (*The Victorian Age*, 1966, p. 69).

Of the many women who wrote literary criticism, chiefly for periodicals, the best-known names earned their fame as poets or novelists. Elizabeth Barrett contributed critical essays to R. H. Horne's *A New Spirit of the Age*, an important volume of 1844; Mary Ann Evans (George Eliot) wrote extensively for the *Westminster Review*, Margaret Oliphant was a loyal *Blackwood's* writer, and Mary (Mrs Humphry) Ward reviewed for *The Times*. Oliphant, following in the footsteps of versatile earlier writers like Anna Jameson, is a particular force on the literary scene in the last 40 years of the century, generally (in line with *Blackwood's*) taking a conservative stance. Others we are just now disentangling from the archive, in effect creating them as "authors." One such is Edith Jemima Simcox, who wrote for *Saint Pauls*, *The Contemporary Review*, and *The Nineteenth Century* in the 1860s to 1880s, and there are many more. By the end of the century some women earned separate reputations as critics, notably Vernon Lee, whose work extends into the modern era. Because women critics, like their male counterparts, frequently wrote under the cover of anonymity, the extent to which gendered features can be discerned and elaborated into a separate aesthetic will be a source of debate among future Victorianists. Oliphant's and George Eliot's commentaries demonstrate that aesthetic solidarity along gender lines can be slight, and since periodicals had strong editors and overt political and ideological positions, one might expect to find conformity to such positions trumping the power of the sisterhood.

Aesthetic

René Wellek observes that 1850, the Victorian noon, could also be considered the midnight of English literary criticism; promising critics such as Mill and Carlyle had taken to "history and social pamphleteering," and poetic theory was "a remote derivative of popularized romanticism" (Wellek 1965, 4: 141). He goes on, however, to outline four strands that would give impetus to new critical modes, and provide the platform for twentieth-century criticism: a new historicism, a new classicism, a new realism, and a new aestheticism. The changes become most evident in the last decades, and are "related to changes in the nature of *intellectual* authority in all disciplines of knowledge, changes which coincided with the wholesale professionalization and institutionalization of knowledge" (Small 1991: vii). "Isms" and "izations" have been with us ever since. Of all of Wellek's strands, "aestheticism" most clearly illustrates the growing interdependence of criticism and literature, for it takes its departure from critical precepts rather than from the manifold interdependency, which had been paramount previously, between individual writer and reading (buying) public. The godfathers of Victorian aestheticism are found in a newly canonized Keats ("A thing of beauty is a joy forever"), whose letters were first published in 1848; in Pre-Raphaelitism and the exhortations of Ruskin and Morris; and in the discussion of mid-century French imports such as Gautier and Baudelaire. Swinburne's *William Blake: A Critical Essay* (1868) is an important marker – a young poet furthers his career with a book-length critical study of the unknown Blake, using the occasion to ridicule a "British brigade" of "Philistia" obsessed with "moral custom" (a nod to Arnold's recent attack on philistinism); to praise "a living critic of incomparably delicate insight" (Baudelaire); and above all to proclaim "Art for art's sake first of all, and afterwards we may suppose all the rest shall be added to her . . . but from the man who falls to artistic work with a moral purpose, shall be taken away even that which he has." The dual thrust of Swinburne's *Poems and Ballads* (1866) and his critical essays might for once justify that overused term, "an intervention." He provoked some of the last masterpieces of the condemnatory style, notably from John Morley and Robert Buchanan, whose "The Fleshly School of Poetry" (*Contemporary Review*, 1871), was a decisive attack on Swinburne's friend D. G. Rossetti as well. From the 1860s on, with varying levels of intensity, combat was waged over "art for art's sake."

Aesthetic criticism placed great emphasis on the subjective nature of our apprehension of the art object, and twentieth-century criticism that traces the phenomenology of the act of reading descends from Pater & Co. Like Leslie Stephen, but from the other side of the blanket, Pater has a filial relation to Arnold, and some have seen his work "as the apotheosis of the 'disinterested' critic; though his sort of disinterestedness undeniably leads to narcissism" (Parrinder 1991: 179). Though disparaged by modernists such as Eliot, Pater is the most clearly modern critic of his time; he develops his corollary to Arnold's dictum about seeing "the object as in itself it really is" – that one must first "know one's impression as it really is, to discriminate it, to realize it distinctly" (Preface to *The Renaissance*, 1873) in fairly systematic and interesting ways. (We would now rewrite Pater to say that one must first be aware of the ideological structures that condition one's impressions.) Small argues that this emphasis on the subjective impression represents "an attempt to reinstate the value of literature in order to protect its autonomy: to preserve it, as it were, from competing explanations of its value provided by the newly professionalized literary historians, philologists, and textual scholars" (Small 1991: 8); feminists might add that the emphasis on "pure art" tended to create a purely male avant-garde sphere, after the more popular genres had fallen to female practitioners. In Pater's case, however, criticism is a form of autobiography, and the "autonomy" of literature or art takes second place to the inevitable, quasi-tragic isolation of the perceiving mind. His quest is to bridge the chasm between subject and object through the appreciations of art, and in this he is the late-century heir to Romanticism, continental and insular. Ruskin's 1857 drawing manual notes how we must recapture "what may be called the *innocence of the eye*," so that we may deconstruct the world into "flat stains of colour" (*Elements of Drawing*, letter 1, note). Pater would like to train the mind to use the many-colored stain of the art object to reconstruct the world (as he would quickly add, "for me"). Pater's criticism is also notable for understanding what we would now call the "intertext": "Product of myriad various minds and contending tongues, compact of obscure and minute association, a language has its own abundant and often recondite laws" ("Style," *Appreciations*, 1889). Literary artists are thus by necessity "scholars" alive to the ways in which a living language leaves traces powerful enough to efface the intention of the "author." From the artist as scholar it is a short step to the "Critic as Artist," and thus to Pater's somewhat unwelcome disciple, Oscar Wilde.

Wilde's status as a critic is open to debate; he can be cast in the train of "dandies, scoffers and professional immoralists" (Warner and Hough 1983 2: 2) who took their cue from the conclusion to Pater's *Renaissance*. And the myth of his life can obliterate any sense of what he wrote, which can then be passed off as a witty, but unoriginal recycling of Ruskin, Pater, and Whistler. But beneath the integument of the aesthete, who glories in the notion that "All art is quite useless" (Preface to *Dorian Gray*, 1890), Wilde's critical stance bears close attention, as a conscious reaction against the authority of the academic or scholarly communities – as opposed to individual "sages" – that had usurped cultural authority by the 1880s. Wilde's cultivation of celebrity status, his demimonde friendships, and so forth, can thus be read as "a *strategic* reaction against this new equation which identified intellectual value with scholarly seriousness and with the restricted practices of academic institutions" (Small 1991: 113). Wilde's criticism is thus a kind of anticriticism, his "Mr W. H." a travesty of the Shakespeare business, his "The Critic as Artist" an apotheosis of flippancy, even when his perceptions are on target, as when he asks, "Who cares whether Mr Ruskin's views on Turner are sound or not?" since Ruskin's prose "is at least as great a work of art as any of those wonderful sunsets that bleach or rot on their corrupted canvases in England's Gallery; greater, indeed." Implicit in the inversion of Arnold ("the primary aim of the critic is to see the object as in itself it really is not") is the recognition that artists themselves work through such misprision, and Wilde here takes the final step from Pater's "for me" and into the abyss of the free play of signifiers explored by poststructuralist critics.

Conclusion

We read Victorian literary criticism for two reasons: to find out what was said about literary texts which we wish to understand and enjoy; and also to discover what the criticism reveals about the processes of reception and canonization, and thus about the ideological structures of Victorian literary culture in general. Scholars of Shakespeare or Austen, horrified at adding to the bulk of criticism with which they must wrestle, perhaps too easily consign Victorian criticism to the dustbin of "historical interest only." Much of contemporary criticism and theory – including the so-called postmodern – has its origins in the nineteenth century, particularly in the interrelations of practical criticism with philosophical theory in England and Germany during the first decades, and in the reactions to the mid-Victorian emphasis on utility and morality in art. And the academic scholarship that filled journals such as *Notes & Queries* (founded 1849), *PMLA* (1889), and the "proceedings" of various author societies has a direct, enumerated connection to our own practice. At the same time much has changed, and many critics now begin their activity without the *a priori* that literature has an aura, and can thus be differentiated in a meaningful way from other forms of writing. In Hegel's highly pertinent terms, fine art "can heal the breach" between the "merely external" world and the "spirit": "Art's peculiar feature, however, consists in its ability to represent in *sensuous form* even the highest ideas, bringing them nearer to the character of natural phenomena, to the senses, to feeling" (Preface to *The Philosophy of Art*). Browning's "Fra Lippo Lippi" (1855) somewhat inverts Hegel's emphasis, when he says that, because the artist allows us to see the sensuous phenomena ("The shapes of things, their colours, lights and shades" l. 284) in new light, "they are better, painted – better to us, / Which is the same thing" (ll. 303–4; Pater, take note). In such company Louis Althusser, an influential mid-twentieth-century theorist, can seem positively Victorian:

> Art (I mean authentic art, not works of average or mediocre level) does not give us knowledge in the strict sense. . . . What art makes us see, and therefore gives to us in the form of "seeing", "perceiving" and "feeling" (which is not the form of knowing) is the ideology from which it is born, in which it bathes, from which it detaches itself as art, and to which it alludes. (*Essays on Ideology*, 1984: 174)

The ideological critic here finds an ally, rather than a target, in the "authentic" work of art. Althusser has substituted "ideology" for the "ideal" that Victorians, following their Romantic predecessors, felt art might allow them to glimpse, but within his argument art actually occupies an extra-ideological perspective. So from Hegel to Althusser runs an aesthetic that, applied to literary criticism, incessantly grants rights and privileges to those poems and novels that are finally "Art." At the turn of the twenty-first century, by our own partial account we have completed the demystification of the aura of "Literature" and are now subjecting what's left to ideological critique. But probably the first thing to remember with regard to the Victorians' literary criticism is that for them, while the tide was out for faith, the sea of art was still at the full.

See also 1897; EDUCATIONAL, PUBLISHING; POETRY, FICTION

REFERENCES

Brake, L. (1986) "Literary Criticism and the Victorian Periodicals." *Yearbook of English Studies*, 16, 92–116.

Bristow, J. (ed.) (1987) *The Victorian Poet: Poetics and Persona*. London, New York and Sydney: Croom Helm.

Casey E. M. (1996) "Edging Women Out?: Reviews of Women Novelists in the *Athenaeum*, 1860–1900." *Victorian Studies*, 151–71.

Collini, S. (1988) *Matthew Arnold*. Oxford: Oxford University Press.

Cross, N. (1985) *The Common Writer: Life in Nineteenth-Century Grub Street*. Cambridge: Cambridge University Press.

Eagleton, T. (1991) *Ideology: An Introduction*. London and New York: Verso.

Ferris, I. (1992) "From Trope to Code: The Novel and the Rhetoric of Gender in Nineteenth-Century Critical Discourse." In L. M. Shires, *Rewriting the Victorians: Theory, History, and the Politics of Gender*. New York and London: Routledge.

Hughes, W. (1985) "E. S. Dallas: Victorian Poetics in Transition." *Victorian Poetry*, 23, 1–22.

Lootens, T. (1996) *Lost Saints: Silence, Gender, and Victorian Literary Canonization*. Charlottesville: University Press of Virginia.

Morgan, T. E. (1993) "Reimagining Masculinity in Victorian Criticism: Swinburne and Pater." *Victorian Studies*, 36, 315–31.

Murphy, P. T. (1994) *Toward a Working-Class Canon: Literary Criticism in British Working-Class Periodicals, 1816–1858*. Columbus: Ohio State University Press.

Olmsted, J. C. (ed.) (1979) *A Victorian Art of Fiction: Essays on the Novel in British Periodicals*, 3 vols. (vol. 1, 1830–1850; vol. 2, 1851–1869; vol. 3, 1870–1900). New York and London: Garland Publishing.

Orel, H. (1984) *Victorian Literary Critics: George Henry Lewes, Walter Bagehot, Richard Holt Hutton, Leslie Stephen, Andrew Lang, George Saintsbury and Edmund Gosse*. London: Macmillan.

Parrinder, P. (1991) *Authors and Authority: English and American Criticism 1750–1990*. Basingstoke: Macmillan.

Small, I. (1991) *Conditions for Criticism: Authority, Knowledge, and Literature in the Late Nineteenth Century*. Oxford: Clarendon Press.

Stang, R. (1959) *The Theory of the Novel in England, 1850–1870*. New York: Columbia University Press.

Stasny, J. (ed.) (1986) *Victorian Poetry: A Collection of Essays from the Period*. New York and London: Garland Publishing.

Tuchman, G. and Fortin, N. E. (1989) *Edging Women Out: Victorian Novelists, Publishers, and Social Change*. New Haven, CT: Yale University Press.

Warner, E. and Hough, G. (eds) (1983) *Strangeness and Beauty: An Anthology of Aesthetic Criticism, 1840–1910*, 2 vols. Cambridge: Cambridge University Press.

Wellek, R. (1965) *A History of Modern Criticism, 1750–1950*, vols 3–4. New Haven, CT: Yale University Press.

Williams, R. (1979) *Politics and Letters: Interviews with New Left Review*. London: New Left Books.

Woolford, John (1982) "Periodicals and the Practice of Literary Criticism, 1855–64." In J. Shattuck and M. Woolf (eds) *The Victorian Periodical Press: Samplings and Soundings*. Toronto: University of Toronto Press.

FURTHER READING

Armstrong, I. (1972) *Victorian Scrutinies: Reviews of Poetry, 1830–1870*. London: Athlone.

Bonnell, M. (1995) "Sarah Grand and the Critical Establishment: Art for [Wo]man's Sake." *Tulsa Studies in Women's Literature*, 14, 123–48.

Dale, P. A. (1977) *The Victorian Critic and the Idea of History: Carlyle, Arnold, Pater*. Cambridge, MA: Harvard University Press.

Goodheart, E. (1994) "Arnold, Critic of Ideology." *New Literary History*, 25, 415–28.

Graham, K. (1965) *English Criticism of the Novel, 1865–1900*. Oxford: Clarendon Press.

Robinson, S. C. (1996) "'Amazed at our Success': The Langham Place Editors and the Emergence of a Feminist Critical Tradition." *Victorian Periodicals Review*, 29, 159–72.

Schoenbaum, S. (1991) *Shakespeare's Lives*. Oxford: Clarendon Press.

Shaw, W. D. (1987) *The Lucid Veil: Poetic Truth in the Victorian Age*. London: Athlone Press.

Small, I. (ed.) (1979) *The Aesthetes: A Sourcebook*. London: Routledge and Kegan Paul.

Thompson, N. D. (1995) *Reviewing Sex: Gender and the Reception of Victorian Novels*. Basingstoke: Macmillan.

Tillotson, G. (1951) *Criticism and the Nineteenth Century*. London: Athlone Press.

Warren Jr, A. H. (1950) *English Poetic Theory, 1825–1865*. Princeton: Princeton University Press.

PART FIVE
Borders

27

Under Victorian Skins:
The Bodies Beneath

Helena Michie

Arnold J. Cooley's *The Toilet and Cosmetic Arts in Ancient and Modern Times* (1866) offers a characteristic mid-Victorian testimonial to the wonders of skin:

> [Skin] not merely acts as an organ of sense, and a protection to the surface of the body, but it clothes it, as it were, in a garment of the most delicate texture, and of the most surpassing loveliness. In perfect health it is gifted with exquisite sensibility, and while it possesses the softness of velvet and exhibits the delicate hues of the lily, the carnation, and the rose, it is nevertheless gifted with extraordinary strength and power of resisting injury, and is not only capable of repairing, but of actually renewing itself. (Ibid.: 197)

Cooley's paean to skin is typical of Victorian popular-science books in its rhapsodic tone. It is also characteristic of that genre that his admiration of skin is expressed in two different registers: the aesthetic and the scientific. Skin, with its "delicate hues" and "velvet" texture, is a sensuous as well as a sensual object. Even more wondrous, however, in an age newly preoccupied with science and particularly with microscopic discovery, is its anatomical function. If skin is, as the title of this section of our book suggests, a border, then Cooley speaks simultaneously of the inside and the outside. Skin's beauty and softness belie its strength, and its scientific properties are themselves beautiful. Cooley becomes even more rhapsodic when he turns more explicitly to what he sees as the functions of the skin:

> It is absolute perfection. It combines within itself the powers of an organ of sense, of excretion, secretion, respiration, and nutrition. The integrity of its function is not only highly conducive to health, but is absolutely essential to its perfect enjoyment, to both corporeal and mental vigour, and to beauty. (Ibid.: 201)

In this summary of skin's "powers" Cooley stresses the lexicon of science: words like "excretion," "secretion," "respiration," and "nutrition" point to mid-Victorian scientific models of the body as an intersection of various discrete "systems." Cooley moves from what would be read as scientific language to broader but still medicalized notions of health and, finally, in the last word of the passage, to, or back to, "beauty." Skin, then, exists on and marks the border of two worlds; it demonstrates the beauty of science and embodies what the Victorian calls the science of beauty.

We can see Cooley's discussion of skin as operating within the contours of yet another paradox: skin is infinitely permeable, allowing for the passage of air, food, and other substances into and out of the body, but it also, in Cooley's words, "clothes" the body and covers it up, "resists" injury, and makes of the body something separable from other bodies and from surrounding environments. Skin is, in this account, both the membrane through which the outside world enters the body and a barrier, a protection from the outside world – or, more accurately, from whatever is defined by the very existence of skin *as* outside the body.

Since skin was defined as simultaneously permeable and impermeable, and since skin in turn defined the contours of the body, it should not be surprising that permeability became a central issue in how Victorians imagined the body. When I speak of whether the Victorians imagined the body as "permeable," I mean to gesture not only toward whether they saw the body as susceptible to forces from outside, but also toward how they saw bodies in relation to others: whether, in the main, bodies were seen to be more like and connected to, or more unlike and distinct from, other bodies.

The question of the body's permeability has a long history in the West. Mikhail Bakhtin proposes that Western culture relies on a long-standing distinction between what he calls the "classical" or "aristocratic body" and the "grotesque body" of the populace or, later, the working class. The classical body, associated with high culture, is often literally represented as being on a pedestal: something to be gazed up at. More importantly for our purposes, the classical body has been historically represented as being impermeable, a body perfect and whole in itself, without orifices or openings. The grotesque body, on the other hand, is porous, its boundaries blurry: depictions of the grotesque body focus on its lower portions – on its buttocks and genitals – as well as on other orifices, typically, as cultural historians Peter Stallybrass and Allon White put it, on the "gaping mouth" (Stallybrass and White 1986: 22).

The "bourgeois body," the body of the middle-class subject or individual, is based on classical standards:

> The grotesque body stands in opposition to the bourgeois individualist conception of the body, which finds *its* image and legitimation in the classical. The grotesque body is emphasized as a mobile, split, multiple self . . . and it is never closed off from either its social or ecosystemic context. The classical body on the other hand keeps its distance. In a sense it is disembodied. (Ibid.)

The Victorians, then, inherited and, some would argue, perfected this notion of the bourgeois body with its roots in classical aesthetics. Their ideal of the bourgeois body was one that was, on many levels, closed off and separate from the bodies of others.

This ideal of the body, of course, owed much to contemporary ideals of individualism and expressed itself in a variety of contexts, from the increasingly privatized structure of middle-class housing to medical discourses about the need for each person, each body, to be surrounded by a certain number of cubits of fresh air at all times.

If the bourgeois body became the ideal for Victorian culture, Victorians were aware that not only their cities, in particular, but also the houses of the rural poor were inhabited by bodies far from ideal. Chapters 12, 17, and 28 of this book explore Victorian investments in the idea of sanitation: here I am interested in the consequences of sanitary ideals for ideas about bodies of different classes. The Victorians inherited and enlarged upon a tradition that took for granted that bodies belonging to people of different classes were in some essential ways different from one another, while at the same time their cultural investments in science were dictating a search for what George Eliot would have her fictional doctor, Tertius Lydgate of *Middlemarch* (1872), call a "primary tissue" linking all humans and perhaps even – here Darwin's discoveries of the late 1850s and early 1860s were important and disturbing – linking humans with other "lower" forms of life as well.

If, in the nineteenth century, lower- and middle-class bodies were represented in a variety of medical and popular discourses as being fundamentally different, the Victorian period was also a time of hyperbolic gender difference. Although differences between men and women have always to some extent been acknowledged, different cultures have emphasized or minimized those differences at different times. While, for example, medieval and early-Renaissance cultures organized men and women along a vertical axis according to their distance from God, the Victorians organized gender difference horizontally, where men and women were seen, not as part of a continuum, but as polar opposites where everything that was defined as not masculine was by definition feminine, and vice versa. Although the Victorian model was arguably more democratic than earlier accounts of gender, it was a model based on a historically unprecedented sense of the differences between the sexes that expressed itself, among other ways, in corporeal terms.

Thus, while during the nineteenth century scientists, doctors, philosophers, artists, and moralists sought universal laws that applied to all bodies, they also helped to construct a culture of separate corporeal realities where the bodies of men and women, the poor, the aristocracy, and the middle class were not only treated differently but were thought to have radically different needs and desires coming out of different bodily configurations. Sometimes this sense of difference was literal, as when some doctors thought that men and women had different internal temperatures and thus radically different sexual desires; sometimes those differences came out of a more diffuse sense of how bodies of different classes and genders should orient themselves to the world. This could lead, among other directions, to a widely divergent sense of what body parts were, in various classes or genders, important: worthy, for example, of repeated representation and discussion.

It is because different bodies were imagined differently that this essay will treat bodies of men and women in separate sections, and that, within each section, the ideal of the bourgeois body will be contrasted with ideas about the bodies of the working class and, in the case of the section on men, with ideas about what was often troped as the decaying body of the aristocracy. The final section, on sexuality, looks at how Victorians imagined male and female bodies coming together. Using the case study of the honeymoon, this section looks at the phenomenon I will be calling heterosexualization or reorientation, in which bodies kept literally and discursively apart were suddenly required by the institution of marriage to become, in the language of church and law, one flesh. The section chronicles some of the imperatives, difficulties, and joys of reorientation with particular attention to place – and to those boundaries, so significant in the honeymoon, between the domestic and the foreign, self and other, the old self and the new.

The Body at Home and the Body as Marketplace:
Women and Corporeality

If we imagine the body of the middle-class young lady as the fetishized body of Victorian culture – the body endlessly represented but always indicatively hidden from view – it is instructive to think about the sometimes startling assumptions about differences between middle- and working-class women. While middle-class women were imagined – at least ideally – to be delicate and refined, working-class women were traditionally seen as coarse and robust. Thus, conduct books could recommend "confining" middle-class women to their beds for weeks before and after childbirth, while working-class women would be expected by the same texts to return to work at a factory the day following delivery. While many conduct-book and popular medical writers imagined young ladies to be so modest that the use of a stethoscope could be perceived as a violation, working-class women's bodies were seen as places of public access, open not only to sexual advances by men but, for instance, under the auspices of the Contagious Diseases Acts of the 1860s, to inspections by public officials via the vaginal speculum.

Underlying these perceived differences were ideas of, on the one hand, circulation and exchange and, on the other, bodily integrity and impermeability. Working women were considered, above all, to be wandering out of the ideal feminine sphere of the home: relatively new ideas about the street as a marketplace suggested that women themselves were up for sale or exchange when they left the home. Thus, the prostitute, the monitory figure in Victorian culture for all women, was the "streetwalker," and the street a place of moral danger. In Anthony Trollope's *The Way We Live Now* (1875), paid work for women necessarily suggests a journey into the street and, by extension, the possibility of physical violation. The middle-aged Lady Carbury, who must turn to writing to support her family, allows, for strategic reasons, her editor to kiss her. Trollope dismisses this exchange, unthinkable for one of his notably pure younger heroines, as part of Lady Carbury's decision to work:

Of course when struggles have to be made and hard work done, there will be little accidents. The lady who uses a street cab must encounter mud and dirt which her richer neighbour, who has a private carriage, will escape. She would have preferred not to be kissed; but what did it matter. (ch. 1)

It is not too much to say that work has turned Lady Carbury, if not into a streetwalker, into a woman of the streets. Her work blurs the boundary between her body and others, undermining her bodily integrity and explicitly refusing her the right of shock and dismay when the editor exchanges a kiss for a positive review.

Work, then, makes the female body accessible both to the touch and to the eye. Advocates of certain kinds of work for ladies often couched their support in the defensive idiom of corporeal *in*visibility. Dinah Mulock Craik, for example, argues that working as an artist or writer is perfectly compatible with ideals of middle-class femininity. She defends these occupations by locating them, not only within the home and in the context of domestic duties, but, explicitly, away from the public gaze. Craik says of herself and her fellow artists and writers, "We may paint scores of pictures, write shelves full of books – the errant children of our brain may be familiar over half the known world, and yet we ourselves sit quietly by the chimney corner" (Craik 1858: 123). The books and pictures, those "children of our brain," may be errant (that is, *they* may err or wander from the home), but the artist, unlike her productions, must not be "known," must not err for fear of another – and linked – form of errancy. The body of the lady worker must remain aloof, protected both by those outer membranes, the walls of her home, and by the ideology of domesticity that turns a home into a moral fortress.

Other forms of circulation besides work were also suspect: in Charles Dickens's *Bleak House* (1853) Sir Leicester Dedlock objects to having even the portrait of his wife circulate in the form of engravings; when her secret sexual past is finally revealed, it becomes fitting that she dies in public, face downward on a London street. Similarly, the Duke in Robert Browning's "My Last Duchess" (1842) struggles for control over the circulation of his wife whom he accuses of smiling on everyone. His solution is to hide behind a curtain to which only he has access the portrait that captures her smiling glance. Novels and conduct books also suggest that a lady's name be prohibited from circulating, especially, but by no means only, in the form of sexual gossip.

While always in danger from without, the body of the young lady can also resist circulation and exchange. Anxiety about the vulnerability of the female body took many forms in the Victorian period, including a defensive insistence that the body in question was, finally, impervious to economic or social violation. This version of the Victorian cultural investment in the middle-class body often took the form, in novels, of the placement of a middle-class heroine in a position of danger by an initial act of class displacement: through no fault of her own a heroine might be forced out of her appropriate class circumstances. The task of the novel, then, would be to show the heroine as impervious to her degrading surroundings.

The most popular genre for this fantasy of class maintenance was the governess novel: the most important marker of the heroine's class integrity was her body. In the Countess of Blessington's *The Governess* (1839), for example, Clara, a young lady forced out of a traditional middle-class life by her family's financial troubles becomes a governess and thus enters a liminal social world in which she belongs neither to the servant class nor to the class of the family that employs her. What rescues the governess from her plight, however, is the almost parodic refinement of her bodily senses, which informs both characters in the novel and readers of it that she is "really," underneath the dowdy costume of the governess, a lady. Clara becomes physically sick when presented with "coarse" food; hers is a body that registers strong smells or tastes and loud voices or laughter as physical assaults. That her refinement inheres in her body is made clear by the novel's prose, with its continued recourse to anatomical constructions. When she goes downstairs to the dining room of her first employer, "the mingled odours of soup, fish, flesh, pineapple and melon struck most disagreeably on her olfactory nerves, as did the blaze of several lamps on her optic ones, as she entered the dining room" (Blessington 1839: 31). The clumsy parallel between "olfactory nerves" and "optic ones" is echoed, with slight modifications, in the depiction of Clara's entry into a busy street: "Her auricular faculties were stunned by the din of so many rough voices, and her olfactory ones no less disagreeably assailed by the mingled odours of spiritous liquors and tobacco" (ibid.: 20).

These characteristic encounters with unrefined characters and scenes are literally registered on Clara's body, whose delicate "olfactory nerves" become a sign of her true class status. The rendering of a body so sensitive to smell, sight, and sound gestures toward the paradox of the impermeable body: its integrity as a middle-class body, its very impermeability, depends on the fact of its sensitivity to being entered by stimuli from the outside world. This paradox is in part resolved by the very noticeable language of "nerves" and "faculties" instead of orifices. Clara does not register the world outside through her mouth, ears, or nostrils: her sense of what is outside her and different from her comes not through breaks in the skin but, more diffusely, through a network of nerves lying just below the skin's surface.

Muscularity and Middleness: Ideal Men and Others

While for the last 20 years scholars of Victorian culture have had much to say about how the female body was represented, only recently has the normative body of the middle-class Victorian man become a subject of much scholarly inquiry. Ed Cohen explains that this relative absence of attention "can be attributed to the fact that while women's bodies were often clearly marked as 'problematic' (for men?), thereby becoming the subjects of inquiries, observation, speculations, coercion, or violence, adult men's bodies were often taken to be the unmarked sites of political, economic, and sexual subjectivity" (Cohen 1993: 32). Invisible because of their presumed normativity, men's bodies were seen, by Victorians and Victorianists alike, as unremarkable.

Recent work in men's studies and in lesbian and gay studies has shown that the male body cannot be taken for granted as a steady baseline value against and in terms of which deviance – statistical, moral, psychological – can be calibrated. Instead, one must speak of plural and often contradictory "masculinities" and of changing masculine ideals. Masculinity, then, is subject to contradiction in two ways: first, because the meaning of masculinity is always contested, and second, because standards of ideal masculinity have changed over time. The Victorian period, many scholars argue, was pivotal in transforming ideals of masculinity. While at the end of the eighteenth century the ideal man was the landed and leisured aristocrat, with the emergence of middle-class culture came a new norm of masculinity explicitly defined against an aristocratic model that was seen as increasingly self-indulgent, immoral, and, indeed, effeminate. Thomas Carlyle's "Captains of Industry" was the most influential text to define the ideal man as a capitalist – and specifically someone who worked for a living.

We can find an early example of this change in the course of Jane Austen's novels: Fitzwilliam Darcy, the hero and desired love object of *Pride and Prejudice* (1813), while not an aristocrat, is granted by the author an estate worthy of, and probably modeled on that of, a duke. Darcy's work is the maintenance and the "improvement" of that estate; as an eldest son he has no need of a profession. The hero of Austen's last novel, *Persuasion* (1818), is a naval captain, Frederick Wentworth – indeed some people have claimed that the hero of *Persuasion* is the navy itself. At the very beginning of the latter novel, Sir Walter Elliot, self-appointed guardian of the aristocracy – and of its good looks – finally must leave his ancestral home, which he cannot afford to maintain because he has run up so many debts. His tenant is an admiral, brother-in-law to the hero. The novel begins, then, with the literal displacement of the financially irresponsible aristocrat at the hands of a member of the newly empowered professional class.

Austen carefully portrays this displacement in corporeal terms: one kind of male body replaces another as masculine power moves out of the aristocracy and into what will become, by the Victorian period, the middle classes. Sir Walter is still deeply attached to a masculine ideal of beauty that signifies aristocratic leisure. When he is initially informed that his prospective tenant is a naval man, he objects on two grounds: first, that the navy is "the means of bringing persons of obscure birth into undue distinction," and second, that, because naval men "are knocked about, and exposed to every climate," they run the risk of "becoming prematurely . . . object[s] of disgust" (ch. 3). Mrs Clay, a friend of Sir Walter's daughter, whose task within the family is to flatter Sir Walter at every turn, offers a taxonomy of the professions, according to the damage they do to the good looks of those who undertake them:

> The sea is no beautifier, certainly. . . . [B]ut then, is it not the same with many other
> professions, perhaps most others? Soldiers, in active service, are not at all better off: and
> even in the quieter professions, there is a toil and a labour of the mind, if not of the body,
> which seldom leaves a man's looks to the natural effect of time. The lawyer plods, quite

care-worn; the physician is up at all hours, and travelling in all weather; and . . . even the clergyman, you know, is obliged to go into infected rooms, and expose his health and looks to all the injury of a poisonous atmosphere. In fact, . . . though every profession is necessary and honourable in its turn, it is only the lot of those who are not obliged to follow any, who can live in a regular way, in the country, choosing their own hours, following their own pursuits, and living on their own property, . . . to hold the blessings of health and a good appearance to the utmost. (ch. 3)

Mrs Clay is speaking here for an ideal of a body unmarked by work; as Elaine Scarry (1983) notes in her discussion of rural labor, work was popularly supposed to leave its physical trace on the worker as though the worker's body were indeed defined by his job. The aristocratic male body is the unmarked body, impermeable to demands from the outside world. It is also, as we shall see later, a body that speaks of its own self-sufficiency in terms of ownership and property: it is men who live on their own property and own not only land but their own time who can remain unscathed.

By making the hero of *Persuasion* a bronzed (but still handsome) naval officer, Austen offers her reader a new kind of hero and a new kind of body as an object of desire. While Sir Walter would see Captain Wentworth's brown face as a sign of his distance from ideal masculine beauty, his daughter Anne, the heroine of the novel, translates it into a different idiom: time at sea has given the captain a "more glowing, manly, open look" (ch. 7). Both Sir Walter's Regency ideal and Anne's pre-Victorian one are articulated in terms of what is manly or masculine: it is only in hindsight and from the point of view of the newer ideal that Sir Walter seems, as he does to many twentieth-century readers, effeminate. The struggle over what constitutes manliness necessarily involves the feminization of earlier or opposed ideals.

If Austen's novels offer an early case study in the replacement of aristocratic men with professionals, Mrs Henry Wood ratifies this transition in her bestselling novel of the 1860s, *East Lynne*. This novel, too, begins with the takeover, in this case the purchase, of an aristocratic estate by a professional man: the impecunious debauchee Sir William Vane secretly sells the estate of the novel's title to the plainspoken lawyer Archibald Carlisle, who, not coincidentally, also marries Sir William's daughter, Isobel. Both Sir William and Isobel suffer from typically aristocratic weaknesses – and those weaknesses are visibly written on their bodies. Sir William suffers – and dies – from the gout, that illness associated in the Victorian imagination with aristocratic excess and, more specifically, with the consumption of rich food and drink. Isobel's less easily diagnosable delicate condition leads to problems in childbirth and to a more generalized inability to do useful work. It is also directly responsible for the jealous imaginings, conceived during a "child-bed fever," that her husband no longer loves her. This conviction dooms her to rehearse the fate of her mother, who fell in love with an unworthy man. In Isobel's case the man is her aristocratic cousin, whose characteristic gesture – flashing a diamond ring on a fine white hand – is linked to his identification as the novel's seducer figure and its social and political villain.

The change from aristocratic to middle-class ideals of manhood paralleled a shift in legal and social expectations of marriage and, more generally, in cultural expectations of the relations between men and women. Laws affecting the position of women – including those concerned with divorce, custody, battering, and rape – exhibit a trend, from the beginning to the end of the nineteenth century, away from the acceptance of physical violence in the conjugal relationship. Male power was being redefined, then, in relation to women's bodies as well as to men's. While at the beginning of the century physical cruelty was not a ground for a woman to pursue a divorce, by the very end of the Victorian period such cruelty was often taken into account in both divorce and custody cases.

The trend away from physical domination did not mean that Victorians – with some notable exceptions – saw men and women as equals. Instead, one can track a change in acceptable *forms* of male power over women and over other social subordinates. Anthony Trollope captures this change in the opening paragraph of his 1859 novel *The Bertrams*:

> This is undoubtably the age of humanity – as far, at least, as England is concerned. A man who beats his wife is shocking to us, and a colonel who cannot manage his soldiers without having them beaten is nearly equally so. We are not very fond of hanging; and some of us go so far as to recoil under any circumstances from taking the blood of life. We perform our operations under chloroform; and it has even been suggested that those schoolmasters who insist on adhering in some sort to the doctrines of Solomon should perform their operations in the same guarded manner. If disgrace be absolutely necessary, let it be inflicted; but not the bodily pain. (ch. 1)

Trollope here seems proleptically to flesh out the thesis of twentieth-century philosopher Michel Foucault in *Discipline and Punish* – that the site of punishment in the modern age moves from the body to the psyche, from what Trollope calls "bodily pain" to "disgrace." In joining a variety of historically painful sites – the bodies of soldiers, schoolboys, abused wives – Trollope identifies what he sees as a crucial shift in the deployment of bodies and punishment, a shift that he identifies as quite recent, and that he links to the increasing bureaucratization of society and in particular to one of his pet peeves, the institutionalization of competitive examinations like the Civil Service Exam. For Trollope, it seems, manhood was increasingly a matter of bureaucratic intervention; as manly success began to be defined in terms of standardized achievements, something of individual manhood was lost.

Trollope's discourse of individualism was by no means unique. Cohen (1993) argues that manhood came increasingly to be defined, not only in terms of the individual, but in terms of the individual body. Such "somatic individualism," as he calls it, stems from a Lockean ideal of the body as personal property and contributed to the Victorian insistence that the middle-class male body be kept separate from other bodies. The language of somatic individualism is also implicated in dominant Victorian ideas about cleanliness, contagion, and masturbation. Keeping the male body clean is a prominent focus of many of the popular nineteenth-century books on the new subject of "hygiene," in which self-sufficiency became allied with self-containment and self-containment with abstinence from sex of all kinds.

Another important site for debates about the male body was religion, in particular, in England, Christianity. Christianity, while often associated in the contemporary popular imagination with the mortification of the flesh and uneasiness about the body, has always featured two distinct strains marked by their differing accounts of the role of the body in religious life and thought. While in the Victorian period a variety of religious dominations and sects took up various positions on the importance of the body, perhaps the most public discussions of links between Christianity and the body were those associated with the "muscular Christianity" or "Christian manliness" movement in the 1850s and 1860s.

The movement's most famous proponent was the Reverend Charles Kingsley, whose personal struggles with sexual desire contributed to a reevaluation on his part of sexuality in general and, as he framed it, manliness in particular. Setting himself up against an earlier Victorian tradition that saw Christian life as a struggle to overcome the desires of the body, he popularized a counter-movement which emphasized the importance of the body to Christian life and, in particular, the corporeality and the "manliness" of Jesus. While his followers, like the novelist Thomas Hughes (*Tom Brown's Schooldays*, 1857), were less invested in the specifically sexual possibilities of religion, Kingsley and other proponents of muscular Christianity popularized the figures of Christ the fighter and Christians as soldiers in a religious war. This emphasis, partly because of *Tom Brown's Schooldays*, was particularly influential in educational circles and most especially in discussions of English public schools, where the role of the body and athletics in the education of middle-class and aristocratic boys had been hotly debated since the more ascetic doctrines of Thomas Arnold, headmaster of Rugby and father of the poet Matthew Arnold, had become dominant some 20 years earlier.

Kingsley's ideal of manly character owed much to the Platonic concept of *thumos* ("rage" or "pluck"), which Kingsley saw as a volcanic force fundamental to masculinity. This *thumos* was something to be respected and cultivated, indeed to be integrated with religious life and transformed into the basis of civic virtue. In the latter context Kingsley saw himself as building on the philosophy of Carlyle, whose influential *On Heroes, Hero-Worship, and the Heroic in History* (1841) was to define "manliness" as a quality central to leadership and leadership as the solution to what he saw as a rudderless age.

As Carlyle's title and Kingsley's use of Plato suggest, Victorians, in their attempts to construct a meaningful notion of masculinity, often looked to the past, to what they considered more heroic ages, for their models. While Kingsley looked to a warrior Christ, others looked to more ascetic traditions and, in particular, to communities of monks or other celibates for their ideals of masculinity.

Muscular Christianity (Kingsley was eventually to reject the phrase) was, predictably, the source of both enthusiasm and ridicule throughout the last half of the nineteenth century. Satires could be relatively gentle, as we see in Dickens's depiction of the "muscular" clergyman in *The Mystery of Edwin Drood* (1870):

> The Reverend Septimus Crisparkle (Septimus, because six little brother Crisparkles before him went out, one by one, as they were born, like six weak little rushlights, as they were lighted), having broken the thin morning ice near Cloisterham Weir with his amiable head, much to the invigoration of his frame, was now assisting his circulation by boxing at a looking-glass with great science and prowess. A fresh and healthy portrait the looking-glass presented of the Reverend Septimus, feinting and dodging with the utmost artfulness, and hitting out from the shoulder with utmost straightness, while his radiant features teemed with innocence, and soft-hearted benevolence beamed from his boxing-gloves. (ch. 6)

Despite Dickens's own benevolence here, we have elements of the standard parody of the muscular Christian: the opposition between the physical weakness of the six little brothers and powerful masculinity; the interest in the "science" of sport which echoes "natural laws" of gender difference; the penchant for cleanliness and boxing; and the narcissism of the muscular Christian as he watches himself in the mirror.

A more acerbic account of muscular Christianity is that of John Addington Symonds, one of the period's first self-identified homosexuals, who was himself very interested personally and theoretically in the definitions of masculinity. His description of Kingsley at a meeting of the Social Science Association, as "ranting and raging and foaming and swelling himself to twice his natural dimensions" (Symonds 1984: 158), suggests the violence that often undergirded muscular Christianity's masculine self-representations. Crisparkle's gentle narcissism is transformed into a spectacular and unappealing phallic pride.

It is clear, then, that at least by mid-century, masculinity was a contested term and that the masculine body itself, far from being taken for granted, was the site of much debate. If, in the middle years of the nineteenth century, this debate was primarily carried out in the entangled discourse of religion, nationalism, and athletics, by the end of the century the masculine body-in-question was that of the homosexual.

Foucault and others have argued that before the late nineteenth century, and perhaps before the coining of the term "homosexual" in German in the 1880s, sex between men was seen as a behavior, a series of acts, rather than as a defining or identity-conferring practice. In other words, despite the fact that men had been engaging in sexual acts with other men since the beginning of recorded history, these men did not think of themselves as homosexual or indeed define themselves, in whatever terms, according to the sexual act in which they participated. This shift from behavior to identity, from body to discourse, marks for Foucauldians the beginning of a specifically modern sexuality.

It is certainly true that many, although not all, Victorian men who were primarily attracted to other men did not, for a variety of reasons, place themselves in a separate category from those we would now think of as heterosexual. Many were married; some, like Symonds, had good if not completely satisfying relations with their wives. It is difficult to say whether many or most of these men would have continued their sexual ties to women in a culture more accommodating to homosexual identities. The Foucauldian thesis, however, does not take into account the overt struggles of many men for a term or terms denoting their feelings for other men and, more importantly for these purposes, denoting themselves as possessors of these feelings. Homophile men produced or appropriated from, for example, medical discourses a series of definitional terms for themselves and others they felt to be like them: "Uranians," "the third sex," "inverts," among others. Although the poet Alfred Tennyson never acknowledged a specifically sexual desire for other men, in his *In Memoriam*, an elegy for his friend Arthur Henry Hallam, Tennyson struggles to name his feelings for the young man who inspired the poem. At different points in *In Memoriam*, which took him many years to compose, Tennyson compares himself to a widower, a bride, and a mother. The repetitive quality of the poem as well as his restless substitution of one relational metaphor for another suggest an inability to find in language a name for his feelings for Hallam. Later in the century, Oscar Wilde was to find a term for homosexual love that ironically survived when others did not. He called it "the love that dared not speak its name."

If men who loved and had sex with other men were finding it difficult to name their feelings and experiences, the legal system was becoming increasingly adept at naming and punishing these same men. The Labouchere Amendment (Criminal Law Amendment Act) of 1885 made "the commission by any male person of any act of gross indecency with another male person" punishable by imprisonment of up to two years with or without hard labor. The most (in)famous legal case involving charges of homosexuality in the Victorian period, the trials of Oscar Wilde, revolved around accusations that he was a "sodomite." The first of the trials was actually initiated by Wilde himself as a libel suit against the Marquis of Queensberry, who, as the father of one of Wilde's lovers, had written a note accusing Wilde, strangely enough, of "posing as a somdomite." The misspelling of the word as well as the odd charge of "posing" suggest a deep discomfort at the level of naming, a discomfort the second trial of Wilde for gross indecency would all too easily assuage. While the first trial focused on character, the second put before the public the question of bodies and acts, found Wilde guilty of sodomy, and condemned him to two years of hard labor.

In the Wilde case, as in others brought under the amendment, it was not only the body of the sodomite that was put on trial – and on display. Wilde and his friends were repeatedly represented as aristocrats whose criminal acts were part of a spectrum of "decadent" behaviors associated with a decaying aristocracy. The class dynamics of the trial and of the cultural construction of homosexuality in general were complicated by the fact that many of Wilde's lovers were young working-class men whom he often paid for sexual services. Newspaper reports of the trial often relied on an idiom of protection, through which Wilde was presented as failing in his duties as a member of the upper class. Wilde's working-class lovers, no matter what their ages, were almost inevitably referred to as "boys," so that the rhetoric of class protection derived an additional emotional impact from an even more culturally evocative discourse of childlike innocence.

If dominant legal discourse used the body of the child as a central icon in denouncing homosexuality (the Criminal Law Amendment Act was actually an amendment to a bill raising the age of sexual consent in women), people within homophile communities were using examples from history and anthropology to celebrate sexual and affective bonds between older and younger men. Many relied on the topos of ancient Greece, while others looked to surviving "primitive" cultures where such bonds were culturally central. In the meantime, as commentary on the Wilde trials made clear, mainstream culture was intent on exiling homosexuality from England and from Englishness, associating it with the foreign and enshrining antihomosexual statutes at the moral center of English law.

Like the law, medicine was beginning to find words for male same-sex desire. And it was primarily medical texts that, by the century's end, resolved the identity/behavior debate in favor of identity and created the figure of the "homosexual." While many doctors were unsympathetic to homosexuality (Symonds was told by Acton to take a lotion for his inflamed eyes and to marry or take a mistress to cure him of his sexual proclivities), others, mostly from France and Germany, were beginning to see homosexuals as a "type" and "cure" as impossible. The taxonomy of inversion popularized by Havelock Ellis established homosexuality as part of character and not, for example, as a sin. Ellis and his followers, however, by identifying a homosexual or inverted type contributed to a disease model which was to dominate discourse about homosexuality for the next 30 years.

The history of male homosexuality in the Victorian period is one of complicated relations between bodily acts and public and private identities. Despite a shift to more identity-based paradigms, the body, as we have seen in the case of the Wilde trials, survived as an icon and, of course, as the site of punishment. Various male bodies, from the supposedly impenetrable body of the child to the decadent body of the aristocrat, were called into play. Caricatures of Wilde during the trials lingered on "characteristic" bodily elements: his nose, his posture, his clothing; at the same time these very bodily elements became, in the larger sense, *characteristics* of the homosexual, legible cultural signs of homosexuality. That legibility, of course, that taxonomy of telltale signs, was part of another linked tradition to be discussed in the next section. If the nineteenth century did indeed invent the homosexual, that invention was coupled, indeed yoked, to another ongoing process, the invention of what might seem at first to be only a defensive and derivative identity: that of the heterosexual.

Making One Flesh: The Two-Body Problem

In the twentieth century, sex is apt to be celebrated as a moment of union between two bodies and, in the rapt metonymy of much contemporary sexual discourse, between two souls or psyches. Certainly, this is part of a long historical tradition, religious and secular, from which the Victorians were by no means exempt. For the Victorians, however, "the" sexual act was also often perceived as a crisis in the integrity of the body, a moment, to shift valences from positive to negative, of breakdown as much as union. If both male and female middle-class bodies were ideally, in their different ways, to be impenetrable, what place did that leave for sexuality, especially for a phallically defined sexuality otherwise characteristic of Victorian thinking?

As James Eli Adams has argued in chapter 9 above, Victorian sexuality was a much more complex matter than recycled anecdotes about covered piano legs and sexual ignorance might seem to suggest. Still, for both men and women, the dominant narratives of Victorian sexual life were structured around the imperative of virginity before marriage: in other words, whatever the reality of individual experiences, ideas about sexuality and marriage were linked to a culturally powerful discourse of climactic transformation in which men, and especially women, were thought to become different people after the imagined sexual apotheosis accompanying marriage.

The middle-class woman became, in the cultural imagination, a different person after marriage; accompanying the indicative changes in name and legal status was a perceived bodily change, where boundaries between husband and wife and between wife and children were blurred. This sense of change could take the form of a legal injunction; as late-eighteenth-century legal commentator Sir William Blackstone put it in an elaboration of the doctrine of "coverture," after marriage husband and wife become one flesh, "and that flesh is the husband's."

The expectation of motherhood as a natural consequence of marriage, as well as an increasing sense throughout the Victorian period that pregnant women and mothers of infants could communicate thoughts, diseases, and even personal qualities to their children through gestation and nursing, also blurred the distinction between the mother and the child. The popular medical theory of maternal impressions, for example, held that what a mother saw or even thought about during conception and pregnancy would have an effect on the developing fetus. Under this dispensation, for example, a woman could be advised to hang pictures of beautiful children in her bedroom and to abstain from reading horror fiction or looking at ugly things in order to increase the odds that her own child, when born, would be attractive and free from deformity. Likewise, pregnant women were often advised that they could produce a child with a specific talent – say for music – by exposing the child, while still in their womb, to their own playing. Thus, the female body, once so carefully constructed as a separate entity, became, in the popular imagination, a body whose borders were defined, not by a liberal notion of the self, but by a more diffuse but equally rigid notion of the family. If marriage redefined the borders of the female body to include husband and children, it only made more impermeable the boundaries between home and the outside world.

Given the perception that marriage transformed the body, it might be particularly useful for scholars of Victorian sexuality to look closely at the moments of that imagined transformation and to linger on its rituals and locations. My own current work on Victorian honeymoons was inspired by what I saw as a need to chronicle this transformation in the absence of much primary information about actual sexual experience. Thus, I look at how the honeymoon, institutionalized as part of the landscape of upper-, middle-, and even upper-working-class marriage by the end of the century, allowed couples to articulate their sense of dislocation and even, at times, disorientation in geographical terms. The honeymoon posited, paradoxically, a highly visible and deeply private transformation, particularly on the part of the bride, whose changes of name and legal status were signified by and in turn signified a sexual change. The wedding journey represented for middle- and upper-class Victorian couples a geographical and psychological site for the transformation from single to married woman, a time and place for the shifting of bodily and geographical territories, for the checking of bodily coordinates against maps and expectations. For all of its enforced leisure, the honeymoon did – or was supposed to do – the difficult cultural work of reorientation: from a female body indicatively singular, virginal, and asexual to a body perhaps desiring and legibly sexual, and from a world essentially domestic and homosocial to a world defined around heterosexuality. It is perhaps not surprising that this undertaking so often, for those who could afford it, involved a journey away from familiar landscapes to a place that thematized otherness in its very terrain: upper-middle-class honeymoons, replete with their consuming rituals of tourism, sex, and shopping, produced, when successful, a different woman in a different body and different clothes, who answered with new knowledges to a new name.

I stress the expected transformations specifically for *women* here, because, although men too must have returned from their honeymoons with new ideas about themselves, their partners, and the sights of the Continent, their legal and sexual status remained unchanged. While before the period we are discussing men who married underwent a nominal if not legal change in status, achieving, in public usage, the title of "master" as opposed to "lad," in the nineteenth century women alone were renamed by marriage.

The nominal change undergone by women after marriage is a recurring theme in the diaries and letters of honeymooning women. In several cases the women noted the strangeness of the name orthographically by writing their new names in capital letters or italics beside the date of their wedding, or by practicing their new signatures in the margins of the text. The new names could appear abruptly in the body of the text interrupting the narrative flow of the entry. Accounts of nominal change in fiction and history make the connection between marital names and corporeal transformation; this could be figured as a rebirth or, with only a slight shift in valence, as a death. Victorian novels are filled with scenes like the one in Emma Guyton's *The Wife's Trials* (1858), where Lilian tells her sister Elizabeth, with a mixed sense of loss and pride, that upon her marriage she "will be Lilian Grey no longer!" Her sister's response, "You will be Lilian Hope, dearest!" suggests the powerful psychodynamics of a new beginning, a birth into a different identity. The process of transformation is less hopefully and more sinisterly rendered by George Eliot's lover, George Henry Lewes, as he orders Eliot's friend Barbara Bodichon not to call the woman he refers to as his "wife" by her maiden name again. Emphasizing the status of their union as a marriage, Lewes warns, "But, dear Barbara, you must not call her Marian Evans again: that individual is extinct, rolled up, mashed, absorbed in the Lewesian magnificence!" (Haight 1985: 281). Perhaps it is this "extinction" to which Alice Vavasour of Trollope's *Can You Forgive Her?* (1865) refers when she explains her novel-long premarital hesitation by telling her fiancé that in marriage, while he will "still be [his] own master," she "must change everything." "It will be to me," she says, "as though I were passing through a grave to a new world" (ch. 10).

The specifically sexual transformations of honeymoons, although harder to document, are often intimately linked to place. Some young women saw their honeymoons as the most delightful period in their lives and the locations of their honeymoons, whether cottages on the English shore or Alpine landscapes, as sites sacred to positive transformation. After a four-month honeymoon at the seaside, Martha Rolls memorializes her last day before returning to London: "Little Hampton – dear Little Hampton! where we have spent four as blessed months as mortals deserve, and sufficiently proved that we are all in all to each other and independent of the world." (And this after a honeymoon punctuated by Martha's frequent debilitating illnesses and crippling anxieties about not receiving letters from her mother and sister, as well as about the mysterious illness and recurrent depression of her husband, Edward.) Rolls explicitly sees her honeymoon as an identification with Edward across bodily boundaries, so much so that she experiences his facial aches and his depressions.

Other women found the site of their honeymoon contaminated by negative feelings about sexuality. Eliza Dickensen, despite claiming the utmost affection for her new husband, explained in her diary that she was glad to get away from the site of her honeymoon because, "though everything had been arranged for our comfort and it was the place I would rather have been at the last few days than anywhere else, yet it is associated with a period altogether I should think the most unpleasant in a girl's life [*sic*] one which I would not have recalled for all the world." Dickensen clearly feels that she is expressing not only her point of view but that of a generality of "girls" as they experience conjugal sex for the first time.

Whether the transformation was positive or negative, it was imagined to be a reorientation of corporeal reality. Symonds, whose description of his honeymoon and his later sexual life is one of the most explicit on record, notes the difficulty of that reorientation for some men and women. His honeymoon in Brighton remained one of his most humiliating memories. As he put it with his usual attention to place:

> It requires all the romance of a Romeo and Juliet to make a double bedroom in an English town hotel appear poetical. The first joys of nuptial intercourse ought not to be remembered in connection with places so common, so sordid, and so trivial. I shall not forget the repulsion stirred in me by that Brighton bedroom or the disillusion caused by my first night of marriage. (Symonds 1984: 158)

Symonds blames the horrors of that night, that "Brighton bedroom," on Victorian codes of propriety and on the imperative to ignorance he sees at work in the lives of men as well as women:

Truly we civilized people of the nineteenth century are more backward than the African savages in all that concerns this most important fact of human life. We allow young men and women to contract permanent relations involving sex, designed for procreation, without instructing them in the elementary science of sexual physiology. We do all that lies in us to keep them chaste, to develop and refine their sense of shame, while we leave them to imagine what they like about the nuptial connection. Then we fling them naked in bed together, modest, alike ignorant, mutually embarrassed by the awkward situation, trusting that they will blunder on the truth by instinct. We forget that this is a dangerous test of their affections and their self-respect; all the more dangerous in proportion as they are highly cultivated, refined and sensitive. (Ibid.)

Symonds is, of course, an example of what we might call failed reorientation; most contemporary critics see the problem as one of an avowedly homosexual man trying to conform to heterosexual norms. Symonds himself would tell a more complicated and conflicted story highlighting the difficulties of reorientation for most Victorians, as male and female bodies, imagined to be so distinct as to be virtual opposites, were compelled by marriage to become one flesh.

The issue of permeability with which we began, then, begins to take the shape and status of a paradox. Victorian discourses produced multiple bodies, divided by gender and class. They also produced powerful discourses of union, of which marriage is perhaps the most vexed example. These paradoxes in turn produced challenges – both for the Victorians and for us. If for Victorians an imaginative and moral challenge was to get under the skin of the other, to get under each other's skins, for Victorianists the challenge is to come to terms with the otherness of the Victorian period, with all of its contradictions, hypocrisies, and surprises. The Victorians, in other words, get under our skin.

See also MOVING OUT, GROWING OLD, SEXUALITIES; MEDICAL, INDUSTRIAL

REFERENCES

Bakhtin, Mikhail (1984) *Rabelais and His World*, trans. Helene Iswolsky. Bloomington: Indiana University Press.

Blessington, Marguerite (1839) *The Governess*. Philadelphia: Lea and Blanchard.

Cohen, Ed (1993) *Talk on the Wilde Side: Toward a Genealogy of a Discourse on Male Sexualities*. New York: Routledge.

Cooley, Arnold J. (1866) *The Toilet and Cosmetic Arts in Ancient and Modern Times*. London.

Craik, Dinah Mulock (1858) *A Woman's Thoughts about Women*. London: Hurst and Blackett.

Dickensen, Eliza (n.d.) *Diary*. Gloucester Records Office.

Foucault, Michel (1979) *Discipline and Punish: The Birth of the Prison*, trans. Alan Sheridan. New York: Vintage.

Guyton, Emma (1976) *The Wife's Trials*. New York: Garland.

Haight, Gordon (1985) *George Eliot: A Biography*. New York: Penguin Books.

Hall, Donald E. (ed.) (1994) *Muscular Christianity: Embodying the Victorian Age*. Cambridge: Cambridge University Press.

Rolls, Martha. *Diary for 1840*. Gwent Records Office, Rolls Family Papers.

Scarry, Elaine (1983) "Work and the Body in Hardy and Other Nineteeth-Century Novelists." *Representations* 3 (summer).

Stallybrass, Peter and White, Allon (1986) *The Politics and Poetics of Transgression*. Ithaca, NY: Cornell University Press.

Symonds, John Addington (1984) *Memoir*. Chicago: University of Chicago Press.

FURTHER READING

Gillis, John R. (1985) *For Better, For Worse: British Marriages, 1600 to the Present*. New York: Oxford University Press.

Hammerton, James A. (1992) *Cruelty and Companionship: Conflict in Nineteenth-Century Married Life*. New York: Routledge.

Kincaid, James R. (1992) *Child Loving*. New York: Routledge.

Marcus, Stephen (1964) *The Other Victorians: A Study of Sexuality and Pornography in Mid-Nineteenth-Century England*. New York: Basic Books.

Mason, Michael (1994) *The Making of Victorian Sexual Attitudes*. Oxford: Oxford University Press.

——(1995) *The Making of Victorian Sexuality*. Oxford: Oxford University Press.

Matus, Jill L. (1995) *Unstable Bodies: Victorian Representations of Sexuality and Maternity*. New York: Manchester University Press.

Michie, Helena (1987) *The Flesh Made Word: Female Figures, Women's Bodies*. New York: Oxford University Press.

Poovey, Mary (1995) *Making a Social Body: British Cultural Formation 1830–1864*. Chicago: University of Chicago Press.

Sedgwick, Eve Kosofsky (1993) "Jane Austen and the Masturbating Girl." *Tendencies*. Durham, NC: Duke University Press.

28

On the Parapets of Privacy

Karen Chase and Michael Levenson

I

In the final movements of *Our Mutual Friend* (1865), Dickens at last bestows his reward upon John and Bella Harmon. Accepting the rich inheritance of his cruel father, John carries his astonished wife out of their modest cottage in Blackheath and leads her north and west through London, until they enter the stately precincts of urban privilege, where they arrive at a large townhouse that the reader has known as the "eminently aristocratic family mansion." The building has most recently belonged to the Boffins, the old Harmon servants, who are deferentially prepared to surrender both it and its accompanying fortune, but it has entered the novel as the special claim of the corrupt street-vendor Silas Wegg. As Wegg sits at his stall on the public thorough-fare, he gazes possessively on the walls of the building he has never entered, "our house": "It was a great dingy house with a quantity of dim side window and blank back premises." Of its inhabitants we know nothing, confined as we are to Wegg's fantasies projected on the concealed domain and yielding a hypothetical family with "names of his own invention": Miss Elizabeth, Master George, Aunt Jane, Uncle Parker (book 1, ch. 5). In the punishing critique of Wegg the domestic fantasist, close cousin to Wegg the blackmailer, Dickens enforces the power of the wall to act as the shroud of privacy. Here is a barrier resistant to the intrusions of a cunning predator, a wall strong enough, blank enough, to condemn the enemy to harmless dreams of an unseen interior – and what kind of wall is that?

Identified as "a corner house not far from Cavendish Square," the house falls within London's great northwestern expanse of Georgian architecture, the stout, persistent legacy of a century whose values could be abandoned more quickly than its buildings. The square-edged townhouse, with its unrepentant uniformity, its brick in neutral tones of grey or brown, and its facade adorned by nothing more than the repetitive pattern of rectangular windows, was for Dickens, as for many of his contemporaries, an architectural vacancy signifying the death of sensibility. The dully staring house was the close counterpart of a dully staring bourgeois respectability. The Georgian brick front was the stolid face of a cold privilege.

When Bella Harmon (née Wilfer) finally crosses the threshold of the aristocratic mansion, the novel penetrates the dull wall to find a living core. What the street-seller could only desperately imagine is now rendered as a vivid domestic phantasmagoria, replete with ormolu clock, ivory casket, a nursery, and even an aviary with tropical birds flying above "gold and silver fish, and mosses, and water-lilies, and a fountain, and all manner of wonders" (book 4, ch. 12). This figure of the pleasure garden behind impassive walls stands as one luminous icon of mid-century domestic desire. By the time John Harmon is finished with refurbishment, the old dingy mansion has become a "dainty house," as if to enforce the essential topographical truth: that even the unprepossessing Georgian facade can be redeemed by a household visionary (book 4, ch. 14). The fish, the birds, and the fountain create the comic extravagance of a domestic carnival, but Dickens knows himself to be pursuing an excess resident within the emergent norm. That even grim walls can contain a dainty interior – this is the first principle of Victorian domestic ambition in a gray climate.

We begin, then, by fully acknowledging the social force of the wall that divides street and house, that conceals and inspires the invention of a household universe, and that stirs the fantasies of those locked outside in physical and social separation. The story of Victorian domestic discourse is to a considerable degree a tale of moving walls, but at its start there emanates the allure of the immovable barrier that separates privilege from dispossession, and privacy from public life. The Census of 1851 enunciates the norm (and ideal) of the bounded household, which achieves "the exclusive command of the entrance-hall and stairs – and the possession of the free space between the ground and sky" (p. xxxvii). The wall is what converts free space into a series of domestic parcels, and while it stands within a complex array of social meanings – legal, economic, symbolic – it also stands as a conspicuous physical object, which signifies only through its heavy materiality.

The brick simplicity of the Georgian facade encourages an image of a flat plane marking the barrier between two realms, a plane appearing both solid and eerily sheer. One instant you are in the social domain, theater of visibility; in the next, you turn a key, or the butler opens a latch, and you discover the blanket of intimacy. Indeed, it may well have been the sense of flush proximity between the Georgian house wall and the neighboring street that incited a more aggressive flourishing of the household edge. When John Nash undertook his triumphalist urban renovation for the Prince Regent, he lavished stucco on the palatial park terraces built for grandees. After the dull brick of the previous century, the creamy paste not only brightened the colors of the city, but it also invited a lordly elaboration of the forward wall of home. Given the infamous malleability of stucco, which could be smoothly molded atop a coarse underpinning, proud aristocrats, prosperous merchants, and successful professionals were able to adorn their homes with columns, pediments, and window treatments, converting the front of the townhouse into a commanding declaration of privilege.

The mid-Victorians would come to revile the "fakery" of the material, which concealed the "truth" of structure beneath the pretence of classical dignity. And yet there could be no turning back to the plainness of the Georgian surface. When the Queen Anne style emerged so successfully in the second half of the century, it replaced the creamy building paste with its own eager vision of a prosperous facade: red brick, sash windows, prominent gables, and high chimneys. For all their stylistic differences, what Queen Anne shared with Nash's stucco was an ambitious construal of household physiognomy, a refusal of gray brick blandness in favor of the assertions of an articulate wall. The color and the ornament were one indication of house pride, but the most conspicuous sign was the brazenly protruding doorway, extended through muscular columns or, as the century wore on, through elaborate glass awnings, stretching toward public space as if they were the advance guard of a militant domesticity. This elaboration of the house front, not only as a single proprietorial wall but as one in a commanding line along the street, represents the material precipitate of a social victory: the extension of privilege from aristocracy and gentry to the middle classes. In a district such as Cubitt's Belgravia, old and new types of family distinction met and mingled, and in the high-shouldered presentation of their robust facades they announced, even as they securely hid, the existence of pleasures out of sight.

II

Kept outside though he is, Dickens's Wegg manages to pitch his stall "over against" the wall of the town mansion, resembling "a leech on the house that had 'taken' wonderfully" (book 1, ch. 5). When the Harmons assume residence and when Wegg's schemes are fully exposed, he is told never to come outside the windows again – as if possession of the house brought control wherever the wall cast its shadow – and then in a last indignity he is flung into a scavenger's cart that happens to be standing on the corner. The novel conducts this entire sequence in vengeful tones representing the standpoint of the wealthy middle-class householder, and yet through all its harsh presentation of the rights of domestic privacy, it continually acknowledges the tumult just beyond the brick curtain. There are Wegg at his stall and the scavenger at his cart, two figures standing for the ceaseless parade through the public thoroughfare. "Up roar" is Dickens's chosen epithet, and as the work of Henry Mayhew had shown those who had been too blind to see, the streets outside the home were swarming with the poor, the plaintive, the insistent, the cagy. To cross the threshold and to enter the street was typically to meet not only the street-seller in a stall, but also the crossing-sweeper eager to clear the way of mud and horse droppings, the groom tending the carriage, and the inevitable mob of boys. "Leech" is the cruel name that nevertheless evokes the social life on the threshold between home and street, where privilege draws the veil, while dispossession wails and waits.

Even behind the stucco and the brick, the cozy home could not run on sensibility alone. Keeping the poorer classes outside the door was one consuming task in the ceaseless negotiation between private and public life, but another was the hiring of workers to enter the house and to maintain its composure and distinction. The realms of Home and Street must be seen as two great systems, linked topographically as well as socially, whose complexity lies not only in their opposition but in their mutual dependency – the anxiety of the well-to-do to repel the indigent but also to choose carefully among them, in order to assemble the corps of servants within, who will become allies against the petitioners seen through the window.

The question of walled protection changes its aspect when the question is no longer how to construct an imposing barrier against the roaring streets, but how to arrange a pattern of rooms, corridors, and staircases in order to manage those household workers, who confuse the boundary between inner and outer. To keep servants was the surest mark of ascendancy into the respectable orders, families being ranked according to the number they kept, but in the very act by which the newly genteel classes ratified their triumph in the social arena, they were obliged to puzzle deeply over how to maintain distance from those brought so close. The great discourse of domestic management was at its heart a discourse of suspicion. The hapless maid, the incompetent groom, and the feeble governess were all irresistible subjects in popular journals and household manuals, but the center of fascination and fear was the actively malignant servant, the one who exploited the chances of propinquity, waiting for the right moment to steal the plate or to betray the family secret. Even when no foul deed is committed, there remains a foulness in knowledge alone. "Remember this, husbands, and wives, fathers and sons, mothers and daughters, brothers and sisters," warns Mary Elizabeth Braddon,

> Nothing that is done in the parlour is lost upon these quiet, well-behaved watchers from the kitchen. They laugh at you; nay, worse, they pity you. They discuss your affairs, and make out your income, and settle what you can afford to do and what you can't afford to do; they prearrange the disposal of your wife's fortune, and look prophetically forward to the day when you will avail yourself of the advantages of the Bankruptcy Act. (Braddon 1863: 149)

In the bewildering choreography of inside and outside, the servants represent the intrusion of the street into the deep recesses of home privacy, and the family that has drawn sharp lines between the household interior and the turbulent world must now turn to defend itself from outsiders in its midst.

The spatial response to the social disturbance was to build a universe of interior walls, a matrix of divisions that would not only protect against the invasions of servants but would allow domestic life to become a strenuous exercise in the articulation of human experience. As the "respectable" household assimilated the contrivances of industrial modernity, it became a scale model of the Victorian economy, dividing between the producers and consumers of domestic pleasure. At the rear and down below, the servants operated the machinery of "convenience," while the family enjoyed the passive virtues of "comfort." The spirit of manufacture, from which the gentleman's house was to be a refuge, entered the house in a disciplined squad of modern domestics whose role was to protect home life from the very disruptions which they exemplified.

The success of this complex operation required a rigorous architectural logic. According to Robert Kerr's influential formulation of 1864: whatever the size of the house, "Let the family have free passageway without encountering the servants unexpectedly; and let the servants have access to all their duties without coming unexpectedly upon the family and visitors" (Kerr 1871: 68). The family must never catch sight of the scullery and the kitchen; the outer walks must be kept free from the servants' view. The starkness of this arrangement accords with the "foremost of all maxims," namely "that what passes on either side of the boundary shall be both invisible and inaudible on the other" (ibid.: 67). In the hands of a zealous architect and a wealthy client, walls could become the instruments of a radical differentiation within which forms of household pleasure and responsibility were framed in separate zones. Within grand Victorian architecture, "each territory was subdivided according to the activities that went on in it; this analysis of activities became more and more exact, and more and more activities were given a separate room" (Girouard 1979: 28). This describes the disposition of the country house, and nothing is plainer than that the general aspiration for the fully articulated house could only be fulfilled in the opulent houses of the wealthiest Britons. In the mid-sixties Kerr began designing Bear Wood for the owner of *The Times*, John Walter III. With its many scores of rooms (100 for the family, 97 for the servants) – including a gun-room, two beer-cellars, a school-room, an odd-room – it easily achieves that elaborate articulation of classes, sexes, generations, functions, and pleasures which is so widely accepted as a fundamental value, at once moral and architectural. A house such as Bear Wood is its own walled city, its own civil society.

At the end of his highly successful book *The English Gentleman's House*, which won him Walter's commission, Kerr includes a "table of accommodation," showing how walls and wealth moved in near-perfect synchrony. Forty thousand pounds will buy the discriminating topography of Bear Wood, but at ten thousand pounds one surrenders the gun-room; at five thousand pounds the billiard room vanishes; at twenty-five hundred, the morning room is relinquished; and at one thousand two hundred fifty pounds, the "very modest" bottom of Kerr's scale, both family and servants must make do with thirteen rooms each. At each lower rung in the ladder of gentility, the risk grows that children will be heard, servants will be seen, and privacy will be rudely assailed. The question, of course, is what will happen if one goes still further down Kerr's scale, if one carries through the logic of graphs and charts and diagrams, passing beneath the arbitrary limit of a thousand pounds to confront the hard-pressed circumstances in which most people lived? The book's silent and complacent assumption is that the downward movement of income will ultimately obliterate the articulation of household space, leaving a poor family to inhabit a home where walls disappear and distinctions perish.

Astonishingly, Kerr would soon go on to draw this brazen conclusion in public. During a series of meetings of the Royal Institute of British Architects (1866–7), he proposed what he called the "one-room solution." Given the dangerous housing crisis in the great cities, the only "unsentimental" and "professional" conclusion, he tells his colleagues, is to give the poor what they are willing to pay for and what speculative builders are willing to construct. He asserts that there are "degrees of delicacy" (Kerr 1866–7: 42), that the poor are not like the privileged, and the very poor are not like the poor. "Simple folk" require "simple dwellings," and to the charge that he advocates "pigging together in one room" (ibid.: 61–2), Kerr shruggingly replies that as professional men wanting to look reality in the face, they must accept "the expediency of keeping to the very lowest standard" (ibid.: 80).

A familiar distinction runs all through the conversation of these professional men at mid-century, the separation of the surging mass of the desperately poor from the "respectable" working classes, who keep their front doors closed, who keep their children off the street, and who live in whole floors rather than in single rooms. In fact, the more successful artisans now occupied individual terrace houses, modest versions of the middle-class norm, built along modest streets. The working-class ascent from room to floor to house seemed a validating arc of progress, the reassuring sign of assimilation to governing conventions of family privacy. But the success of an artisan elite only made the spectacle of mass failure more vivid.

III

Among those who held social power and the power of discourse, it was an article of complacent faith that the millions of poor who streamed through the cities had failed to comprehend the resources of the Wall. They were radically external creatures, whose exposure to open space, especially open urban space, deprived them of the indispensable pedagogy of home. In his exhaustive study of urban poverty, Henry Mayhew at once discovered a counter-world and confirmed a prejudice. The costermongers who hawked their wares in the street were "the Nomades of England, neither knowing nor caring for the enjoyments of home. The hearth, which is so sacred a symbol to all civilized races as being the spot where the virtues of each succeeding generation are taught and encouraged, has no charms to them" (Mayhew 1861: 43). The young girl who lives in the streets will resist the attempts to reclaim her; she suffers from a "muscular irritability" that "makes her unable to rest for any time in one place" (ibid.: 44). The poor appear as a great fluid or current, seeping past foundations and enclosures, enduring and then enjoying an escape from the boundedness so central to the prevailing definitions of home. As George Godwin tersely put it in *London Shadows*, "the health and morals of the people are regulated by their dwellings" (Godwin 1854: 10). The loss of the physical delimitations of the house incited a release of mobile appetite and rootless passion. Poverty was in its essence an anti-domesticity.

Nevertheless, there remains an undercurrent within the new ethnographic journalism that suggests another way of construing the unwalled poor. In Mayhew himself, for all the reiterated emphasis on the savage repudiation of home, one finds a fascinated attention to the persistence of family life. Under the most appalling conditions of deprivation, parents and children cling together as micro-economies, contrived to eke out subsistence. He notes that children "are sent out by their parents in the evening to sell nuts, oranges, &c" (Mayhew 1861: 24); he praises those loyal girls without whose help the family would be sent to the workhouse; and in a summative mood he notes, "When, as is the case with many of the costermongers, and with the Irish fruit-sellers, the parents and children follow the same calling, they form one household, and work, as it were, 'into one another's hands'" (ibid.: 479). Mayhew is silent on the apparent contradiction between the refusal of home and the persistence of these intimate ties, but his own evidence suggests the need for a sharp conceptual distinction between "domesticity" and "family." The poor may live on the streets without the protections and solicitations of the cozy middle-class fireside; they may prefer the beer-shop or the penny gaff, warmed by the presence of many other bodies, to the damp of a bare room. But it is clear that forms of familial webbing remain decisive for many of Mayhew's poor, who must be understood as anti-domestic families, families without walls.

If so many Victorian opinion-makers refused to see family life on the uproarious streets, this must surely be due to the unchallenged assumption that the definition of a family was architectural as well as biological. Thus, the Registrar General of the Census intones that "It is so much in the order of nature that a family should live in a separate house, that 'house' is often used for family in many languages; and this isolation of families, in separate houses, it has been asserted, is carried to a greater extent in England than it is elsewhere" (*Census*: xxxv). The very idea of a houseless family comes to appear a methodological anomaly and a national disgrace. If the poor move in hordes through the streets, it must be because the precious vessel has broken, spilling privacy into the public ways, where it can only wither and rot. The failure of the poor to enact the "isolation of families" is what brands them as savages.

But the challenge to walled isolation came not merely from the long day's swarming through the streets in search of a small sale, an odd job, or a wily cadging. The poor slept somewhere. At the point of exhaustion they too sought walls and a roof. Commonly, however, the architecture of poverty was not the self-contained house, but the corner of a room within a house in a court. Growing at such an extraordinary rate through the nineteenth century, the cities of Britain were ill-prepared to absorb their vast numbers. Old family houses were broken up into separate lodgings; new buildings crouched behind old buildings. The effect of the filling of rooms and the infilling of space was to create diverse systems of infamous courts, with hundreds of families squeezed together, facing one another across a narrow lane. "As by a fatal attraction," observes Thomas Beames, "opposite houses grow together at the top, seem to nod against one another, conspiring to shut out the little air which would pierce through for the relief of those beneath" (Beames 1852: 2–3). In Scotland and the north of England a familiar pattern was the arrangement of working-class housing into the notorious back-to-backs: two contiguous, parallel ranks sharing rear walls. Except at the end of rows each house would thus have common partitions with three others, leaving only the front exposed to any light and air; the walls were sometimes just a half-brick ($4^1/_2$ inches) thick; and to increase the density, the double rows would be matched with others, so that the one open side would face onto a narrow court (Burnett 1986: 67). In 1847 the *Quarterly Review* recounted the paradigmatic narrative of a young person arriving in London, who is directed to Duck Lane, St Giles's, Saffron Hill, Spitalfields, or Whitechapel, and then obliged to pass "through tight avenues of glittering fish and rotten vegetables, with doorways or alleys gaping on either side – which, if they be not choked with squalid garments or sickly children, lead the eye through an almost interminable vista of filth and distress." The rookeries of the major cities were the moral and social counterparts to the great country mansions; in their most sprawling and intricate arrangements, they became a monstrous inversion of the fortified castle.

Inside this new system of walls, then, is a second, more deeply disturbing, provocation of the poor. If on the one hand they affront the norms of enclosed domesticity by coursing so visibly through the streets or attaching themselves like leeches to the facades of respectable homes, they are all the more offensive when they recede from view behind walls of their own. Godwin remarks that "If there were no courts and blind alleys, there would be less immorality and physical suffering. The means of escaping from public view which they afford, generate evil habits" (Godwin 1854: 10). The relevant enclosure is not the individual household, providing that "exclusive command" of family space; it is rather the widely encompassing public barrier that surrounds the inhuman density of bodies and stirs images of a den, a nest, or a lair.

Within the pervasive decay of these wandering mazes there were special nodes of degradation, the lodging-houses of the great cities, temporary dwellings for masses of the poor, who would fall together in the ill-tended rooms, crowded, filthy, verminous. Mayhew made the lodging-houses a focus for his outrage and sorrow, and in parliamentary debates of 1851 Lord Ashley, soon to be the Earl of Shaftesbury, compelled the other honorable gentlemen in the room to listen to tales of horror. Ashley's premise was that "nothing produced so evil an effect upon the sanitary conditions of the population as overcrowding within limited spaces; and if people were in a low sanitary condition, it was absolutely impossible to raise them to a just moral elevation" (*Hansard*, cols 1259–60). From this high-minded principle he moved to chilling exposé, quoting the town clerk of Morpeth, who had described lodging-houses that have no beds

> but their occupiers are packed upon the floor, in rows, the head of one being close to the feet of another. Each body is placed so close to its neighbour as not to leave sufficient space upon which to set a foot. The occupants are entirely naked, except for rugs drawn up as far as the waist; and when to this is added that the doors and windows are carefully closed, and that there is not the least distinction of sex, but men, women, and children lie indiscriminately side by side, some faint idea may be formed of the state of these places, and their effect upon health, morals, and decency. (*Hansard*, col. 1263)

Such tales became almost routine at mid-century, leading to the passage of two Acts sponsored by Ashley in 1851 – the Common Lodging Houses Act and the Labouring Classes Lodging Houses Act – the first direct legislation on the problem of working-class housing.

According to the first of the two Acts, the Commissioner of Police must register lodging houses and must ensure the "well ordering" of the building and "the separation of the sexes therein." This requirement involved the ongoing inspection of the houses, an institutional resolve not fully appreciated by the targets of benevolence. For if, from the standpoint of privileged respectability, the courts and their lodging-houses were little more than "fever factories," from the perspective of inhabitants they were living communities vulnerable not only to fever but to the assaults of the authorities. Philanthropists who built model houses – cleaner, better equipped, fully supervised, and with higher rents – failed to grasp why their bounty was often refused, not recognizing that the greater cost was aggravated by the psychic burden of moral surveillance. Despite being a harsh critic of the moral degradation of court life, Mayhew discloses much evidence of the social formations created by these forcing-houses of collectivity. He records the case of a boy who had kicked at a policeman during a scuffle, noting that "The whole of the court where the lad resided, sympathized with the boy" (Mayhew 1861: 16). A young coster tells him that "all as lives in a court is neighbours" (ibid.: 40), and frequently one hears of the daily social ceremonies in the shared space between the clustered rooms: the gathering of men and women at the mouth of the alley, where they meet for a chat and a smoke. The physical arrangement of the court – the simple undifferentiated rooms so close beside one another, the narrow alley, and the common use of privies and water supply – brought about a "sharing of facilities in the private domain, a cellular quality of space in the public domain, and a threshold between public and private which was ambiguous and permeable" (Daunton 1990: 202). Within such a social topography the most decisive walls were the outer boundaries of the court, penetrated by a narrow entrance which opened into a world where meager accommodation (including the flimsy party walls) created a common life almost unimaginable to those of any substantial means.

IV

Indeed, insofar as respectable imagination gave itself to pictures of life behind the court walls, these were almost always pictures of foul blight, urgently demanding inspection if not eradication. In one of the most significant urban reconstructions of the first half of the century, the cutting of New Oxford Street broke up some of the most notorious rookeries of St Giles's. Hailed as a triumphant gesture of public hygiene, such engineering was also a defeat for social solidarity in hard-pressed conditions, for the effect of the sustained clearance was to redraw the relationship of private and public spheres, repudiating the rich ambiguity in favor of a stern differentiation between the determinate dwelling and the mere "connective tissue" of the street. The political result "was to 'open up' the city in order to make it visible for inspection" (ibid.: 204). In fact, all through the century the cutting of new streets was as much an exercise in social engineering as a development in the lines of transport. When John Nash undertook the massive renovation of London, he saw the course of the triumphal Regent's Street as an opportunity to divide luxury from need: "my purpose was, that the new street should cross the Eastern Entrance to all the streets occupied by the higher classes, and to leave out to the East all those bad streets" (Crook 1992: 90). As with other such projects through the century, the street was at once a thoroughfare and a wall, a means of facilitating movement along its length, but also obstructing once easy movement across its width.

Still, no matter how wide the boulevard, how imposing the stucco or brick facade, how well-managed the servants, there persisted conspicuous signs of anxiety that the fortress of home remained vulnerable. In the early 1860s a great furor erupted on the subject of street music. The Italian organ-grinder became a figure of violent loathing for a large section of the professional middle-class, which defined its seriousness and its status in opposition to the tumult outside the window. Spurred by the anger of such luminaries as Dickens, Tennyson, and Charles Babbage, the parliamentarian Michael Bass took up the cause. He edited a volume of documents called *Street Music in the Metropolis*, at the center of which were the splenetic outcries of a cultural elite that saw the constant distractions in the thoroughfare as dangerously corrosive, putting physical health and intellectual vocation at serious risk. Here is one sign of the pathos of the household wall: no matter how impenetrable to the petitioning "leeches," it would always be vulnerable to sound (Picker n.d.: 12). Ironically, the repeal of the window tax in 1851 had created a boom in the production of glass and had led to a brightening of the street wall with larger-paned windows, but this architectural improvement only exposed the home-dwellers more directly to the uproar on the street. The passage of Bass's Act made it easier to seek legal remedies from such noisemakers, but as long as the cities of Britain continued their steep growth in population and throbbed with the clamor of industry, no parliamentary act could ensure velvet domestic serenity.

Most frightening were the outbreaks of cholera in the middle decades of the century, especially the wave of illness in 1854, which in its attack on the parish of St James destroyed the comforting mythology of the immunities of wealth (Gilbert n.d.: 5). The growing public health movement, ratified by the example of Florence Nightingale, was able to compel recognition of environmental threats to the integrity of home. Attention to domestic hygiene cannot stop at the threshold, because toxic vapors and foul air respect no laws of property; the hazards of inadequate drainage, open sewers, and exposed dung heaps can creep beneath the thickest walls; and there can be no healthy house in a diseased neighborhood.

Was there to be no peace anywhere for the triumphant middle classes? The aristocrats, the great gentry, and the barons of industry could enjoy the sanctuary of their country houses, perfectly intact at the end of long rural roads. Tennyson's *The Princess*, in its rendering of the obedient multitudes permitted to spend a rare afternoon on the aristocratic green of Vivian-place, displays the easy governance of space enjoyed in the great country mansions. Their walls were as close to inviolable as the castles they imitated. But for the middle classes, who were growing in wealth and numbers – where might they hear the birds sing without the din of urbanism? The answer, of course, was in the suburbs. Beginning after the Napoleonic Wars and consolidating in the middle decades of the century, suburbanization offered a radical solution to the struggle between private and public domains. On the one hand, it allowed for the construction of a still more self-enclosed household space, either in the form of semi-detached or fully detached villas, which broke out of the linear patterns of urban terraced housing and offered the promise of walls surrounded on at least three sides by the pleasures of a garden. On the other hand, it secured a physical distance, becoming ever greater as railways confirmed the suburban boom, between the garden villa and urban pandemonium. In significant respects, the household wall was now stretched as wide as the train journey into the city.

V

Merely to watch the transformation of walls through the nineteenth century – the turn from Georgian gray and brown to creamy stucco and then Queen Anne's red brick, the internal partition into rooms and compartments, the infilling of urban space and the development of the maze of courts, the cutting of streets through that same offending maze, the march of walls into the green fields on the edge of town – is to follow a mobile topographical narrative, in which space is continually carved and molded, closed and opened. Then to restore people to the architectural scene is to recover a social drama of movement and barriers. In broad terms, the century of walls was a long disentangling of social mixtures. Architects devised ways to partition the house into male and female domains and to keep the family from its servants; city planners drove streets through the inner mysteries of poverty; building speculators developed suburban estates. As prosperous commercial magnates joined the world of the country house, many middle-class professionals rode the trains to the suburbs. The most fortunate of working-class families reached the dignity of terrace houses, but rising rents meant that the poorest were obliged to give up two or three rooms in order to test the awful efficacy of Robert Kerr's one-room solution.

From one perspective, then, the disposition of walls achieves the sharp clarity of articulated social space: the wealthy in the country, the middle classes in the suburbs, the artisans in their terraces, and the poor squeezed into their single rooms. But apart from those who enjoyed the astonishing privileges of the country house, the ordering of the social strata was an impure process, forever caught in forms of spatial snarl. The large urban centers continued to grow, and though many members of the middle class left on the suburban trains, others rose to take their place within the cities and found the same challenges to the life of household privacy. The movement of the laboring poor from courts and cellars into terraces was made unsteady by precarious economic conditions, so that any proudly rented house could break apart into the divisions of subletting: first a floor, then a room, then a corner of a room. Even for those seeking to make the suburbs their wall, history had ironies in store. What appeared in one decade as the safe distance from the vortex of the street was likely in the next to have been absorbed by the ooze of urbanism. Then, too, over-ambitious building specula-tors often had to lower the price on untenanted houses, giving the middle-class arrivals the surprise of working-class neighbors (Thompson 1993: 179).

The dream of impenetrable walls was the dream of an orderly society, tidily distributed according to function and fortune. No doubt for some – especially those wealthy few immured in rural settings – it must have seemed that the street was permanently distant and that the infolding of private virtue had been triumphantly achieved. And yet an abiding feature of the middle-class desire for enclosure, so widely embraced by other classes, is that after the scream of the railway, the spread of infectious disease, or the news of a violent crime, the act of self-containment must begin again. A house remains an object in social space, inevitably exposed to the winds of public life, and walls designed to keep inside and outside apart only sealed them in intimate antagonism.

See also 1848; GROWING UP, MOVING OUT, SEXUALITIES; MEDICAL, INDUSTRIAL

REFERENCES

Anon. (1847) "Lodging-Houses." *Quarterly Review*, vol. 82, December.

Bass, Michael (1864) *Street Music in the Metropolis*. London: John Murray.

Beames, Thomas (1852) *Rookeries of London: Past, Present, and Prospective*. London: T. Bosworth.

Braddon, Mary Elizabeth (1863) *Aurora Floyd*, 3 vols. London: Timbley Bros.

Burnett, John (1986) *A Social History of Housing, 1815–1985*, 2nd edn. London: Methuen.

Census of Great Britain, 1851 (1854) London: Longman, Brown, Green & Longmans.

Crook, J. Mordaunt (1992) "Metropolitan Im-provements: John Nash and the Picturesque." In Celina Fox (ed.) *London: World City, 1800–1840*. New Haven, CT: Yale University Press.

Daunton, Martin J. (1983) *House and Home in the Victorian City: Working-Class Housing 1850–1914*. London: Edward Arnold.

——(1990) "Housing." In F. M. L. Thompson (ed.) *The Cambridge Social History of Britain, 1750–1950*, vol. II. Cambridge: Cambridge University Press.

Dyos, H. J. and Wolff, Michael (eds) (1973) *The Victorian City: Images and Realities*, 2 vols. London: Routledge and Kegan Paul.

Gilbert, Pamela (n.d.) " 'Scarcely To be Described': Urban Extremes as Real Spaces and Mythic Places in the 1854 Cholera Epidemic." Unpub-lished paper.

Girouard, Mark (1979) *The Victorian Country House*. New Haven, CT: Yale University Press.

Godwin, George (1854) *London Shadows: A Glance at the "Homes" of the Thousands*. London: G. Routledge & Co.

Hansard Parliamentary Debates.

Kerr, Robert (1866–7) "On the Problem of Provid-ing Dwellings for the Poor." *RIBA Proceedings*.

——(1871) *The English Gentleman's House*, 3rd edn. London: John Murray.

Mayhew, Henry (1861) *London Labour and the Lon-don Poor*, vol. 1. London: Griffin, Bohn and Company.

Picker, John (n.d.) "Sound Proof: Victorian Profes-sionals Make the Case against Street Music." Unpublished paper.

Thompson, F. M. L. (1993) "The Rise of Suburbia." In R. J. Morris and Richard Rodger (eds) *The Victorian City: A Reader in British Urban History, 1820–1914*. London: Longman.

FURTHER READING

Cannadine, David, and Reeder, David (eds) (1982) *Exploring the Urban Past: Essays in Urban History*. Cambridge: Cambridge University Press.

Davidoff, Leonore and Hall, Catherine (1987) *Family Fortunes: Men and Women of the English Middle Class 1780–1850*. London: Hutchinson.

Jones, Gareth Stedman (1971) *Outcast London: A Study in the Relationship between Classes in Victorian Society*. Oxford: Clarendon Press.

Nord, Deborah (1995) *Walking the Victorian Streets: Women, Representation, and the City*. Ithaca, NY: Cornell University Press.

Olsen, Donald J. (1976) *The Growth of Victorian London*. London: B. T. Batsford.

——(1986) *The City as a Work of Art: London, Paris, Vienna*. New Haven, CT: Yale University Press.

Tarn, J. (1971) *Working-Class Housing in Nineteenth-Century Britain*. London: Lund Humphries for the Architectural Association.

——(1973) *Five Per Cent Philanthropy: An Account of Housing in Urban Areas Between 1840 and 1914*. London: Cambridge University Press.

Walkowitz, Judith R. (1992) *The City of Dreadful Delight: Narratives of Sexual Danger in Late-Victorian London*. London: Virago.

Williams, Raymond (1973) *The Country and the City*. London: Chatto & Windus.

29

"Then on the Shore of the Wide World": The Victorian Nation and its Others

James Buzard

As if Victorian Britain did indeed enjoy the divine favor often claimed for it, clouds gave way to sunshine on the morning of May 1, 1851, just in time for Prince Albert, husband of the queen, to open the Great Exhibition of the Works of Industry of All Nations at the so-called Crystal Palace in Hyde Park. Historians have tended to regard this event, as did mainstream organs of opinion at the time, not merely as the prince's greatest achievement (which it certainly was) but also as a summation or crystallization of the forces defining the Victorian age. All the peoples of the world – theoretically – were summoned to contribute their finest industrial and artistic products, their raw materials and crafted curiosities, to one grand display hosted by the indisputable leader in technological progress and commercial expansion, Great Britain. A spirit of peaceful competition was to prevail, implicitly marking the end of the turbulent 1840s, that decade during which economic crises and radical politics had rocked traditional regimes across Europe and, less dramatically but still disconcertingly, had called into question some certitudes of modern British society. One important aspect of the exhibition was its determined appeal to the British working classes to come to London (at specially reduced fares) to see for themselves the scope and grandeur of the industries in which they played their part. The vista was to instill in them a greater sense of identification with the firms employing them, as well as with the nation those firms "represented" at the exhibition. Proclaiming the troubled times of the "Hungry Forties" to be over, the exhibition also encouraged much grander imaginings, seeming to herald the end to all international bellicosity and bloodshed: a prospering British subject of 1851 might be excused for taking the attitude which one historian has labeled "Utopia Around the Corner" (Dodds 1952: 443–81). The transparency of the Crystal Palace itself – Joseph Paxton's overgrown greenhouse – seemed a metaphor for the obstructionless free trade that would guarantee this new era of peace.

The sociocultural ramifications of the Great Exhibition are rich and diverse indeed. Of greatest concern to the present discussion is the way the mid-Victorian extravaganza served as the vehicle for all sorts of questions, anxieties, and compensating ideas about the status and fate of the British nation. To judge by the promotional rhetoric, of course, there was little to question or be anxious about, and no need to compensate. The *Morning Chronicle* greeted the first of May by declaiming,

> Now, punctual to the month and the day, the vast work is complete in all its noble symmetry. It is probable that no other people in the world could have achieved such a marvel of constructive skill within so brief a period. It is to our wonderful industrial discipline – our consummately arranged organisation of toil, and our habit of division of labour – that we owe all the triumph. (ffrench 1950: 186)

In its enthusiasm the newspaper had forgotten what the Archbishop of Canterbury tried to introduce into his benediction on the event: that Britain reigned supreme "not because of works of righteousness which we have done" but because God had mercifully chosen it to lead the world toward the light of reason and the free market. Still, however much it recommended Christian humility, the archbishop's was plainly "the prayer of a successful people. A people who could remember no war on their own soil, no famine, no revolution, no social upheaval of any magnitude" (ibid.: 190), and who already held the largest empire in human history (shortly to grow even bigger).

What was there for such a people to be anxious about? Living up to its image, perhaps. In allotting display space to its guest-nations (and in reserving half of the space for itself), Britain tacitly claimed the right of the supreme industrial power to define each nation's place – in relation to its own – in the hierarchy of civilization. By "rhetorically positioning [itself] amidst the opposed examples furnished by rival countries," Britain aimed to produce an impression of "national regularity," of a collective mental orderliness and rationality not to be matched by other peoples (Miller 1995: 72). Contemporary reports often took the desired effect of the Great Exhibition for an achieved one, in arguing (as one of them did) that

> Britain stood out in bold relief the principal figure in the picture of the world, occupying and engrossing mainly the foreground, a rich and troubled sky above her, the principal light issuing from one cloudless spot, and of which she was the recipient, her surrounding grouped neighbours being but partially within its blaze, dimness and darkness increasing with the distance, till the horizon and sky blended, completing the picture. (Ibid.: 75)

Another source spoke of the "conscious greatness" implied in Britain's willingness to invite all nations of the world to its capital to display their finest products (ibid.: 76). But this national self-representation was rather a makeshift affair, requiring to be propped up and spared excessive scrutiny. The history of the exhibition's planning stages is one, not of confident mastery or "noble symmetry," but rather of energetic, often frantic improvisation and compromise. Confident British supremacy was undermined by the fact that the "philosophical" system for classifying entries needed seemingly endless tinkering, and never satisfied everybody. The very success of the exhibition planners in securing many kinds of materials from many (if not all) of the world's countries put a severe strain upon the image Britain projected to the world and to itself: if the "system" for arranging all these things looked less like a confident deductive embrace of variety than like a patched-together set of expedients for not drowning in multiplicity, what would become of the image of Britain as the world's preeminent seat of rationality and organization? And, as planners and watchers were fully aware, the influx of goods was to be followed by a tidal wave of visitors to London, from elsewhere in Britain and abroad (a total of about six million by the time the Crystal Palace closed on October 11): what was to be done with them all? Editorializing in print and image, some Britons worried that this triumphant testimony to British ingenuity and prowess would have the effect of swamping the capital city with foreigners. George Augustus Sala wrote of "The Foreign Invasion" in Charles Dickens's magazine *Household Words*. George Cruikshank's cartoon "All the World Going to See the Great Exhibition of 1851" shows the Crystal Palace perched atop a miniature globe which is covered by streams of people hurrying towards it, by ship, train, and caravan, from every point of the compass. In the image, Paxton's palace seems a vulnerable house of glass, and the confluence of visitors an advancing alliance of foes.

One convenient, and not too misleading, way of thinking of the British nineteenth century is as a period bracketed by powerful fears of invasion. After the defeat of Napoleon at Waterloo in 1815, the prospect of a foreign army actually penetrating British territory did not resurface in any serious form until the rather more fantastic fears of a German invasion started to circulate toward the end of the century, informing such popular literary sensations as Erskine Childers's *The Riddle of the Sands* (1903). Later still, of course, there were the fully justified anxieties about the possibility of a Nazi occupation during World War II. But if the long nineteenth century was an era free from actual threats from outside, it was also one for which the metaphor of invasion was remarkably and lastingly potent in mobilizing the desire for a national oneness. In certain novels written in the first decade of the twentieth century and presenting themselves as valedictories to the Victorian age – such as H. G. Wells's *Tono-Bungay* (1909) and E. M. Forster's *Howards End* (1910) – Britain appears menaced by alien forces, but these are not marauding armies; they are the less conveniently embodied, more insidious effects of trade (especially financial speculation) and empire. With particular reference to the Forster novel, Fredric Jameson has argued that it is when an imperial nation has come to feel its dependence upon that which lies outside it as the central fact of its social existence that such a nation fosters in art the compensating image of itself as "a self-subsisting totality . . . a utopian glimpse of an achieved community" (Jameson 1990: 58). I believe Jameson is wrong to locate such a dynamic as late as he does, and to associate it with modernism rather than nineteenth-century cultural developments: in their fictional recaps of the nineteenth century, Forster and Wells were reprising a romance gesture that their precursors had long been performing, even in the so-called "realist" novel and in professedly international efforts like the Great Exhibition. In a variety of forms, Victorian culture seems to have confronted the "offshore" basis of its national identity as something of an embarrassment and as a stimulus for the production of recuperative fictions of the nation's unity and self-reliance.

If the "global capitalism" we hear so much about nowadays was not born on May 1, 1851, it was consecrated on that day. Commodities were sacralized in the Crystal Palace, arrayed for admiration as if in the greatest imaginable emporium, yet lacking the sublunary element of price tags and so permitted to disclose their supposed "intrinsic" value. The building itself was like the cathedral of a catholic industrial capitalism: made out of mass-produced, interchangeable pieces of iron and glass, it was laid out on the cruciform plan of medieval cathedrals (it even contained, alongside its myriad novelties, the seemingly anomalous "Medieval Court"). And if Prince Albert had had his way, the whole affair would have epitomized global capitalism in an even more striking fashion, for he had wanted all the articles to be shown "without reference to their country of production" (ffrench 1950: 211). A member of that small international elite placed "above" the commoner's relationship to nationality, the philosophical German consort to the English queen had benignly intuited what late-twentieth-century observers have made a staple of comment on the spreading global market: that a truly free and international system of trade would render nations obsolete, sweeping them aside as capital sought opportunities wherever it could locate them, regardless of states and territories, of ethnic or religious ties. The fact that Paxton's structure was the least "site-specific" of buildings – made out of materials not bearing the signature of any particular terrain, capable of being taken down and reerected in other locations – perhaps unintentionally contributed to the delocalizing aura of a capitalism straining to be set free of conditions and barriers. On some level the energies behind the exhibition pointed toward a vision of the possible future that not even the staunchest British opponents of trade barriers were prepared to contemplate for long. There were logistical reasons for the commissioners to reject Albert's design, but some anxiety over the glimpse it afforded of a future without boundaries may also have played a part in insuring that the floor-plan would be laid out on national lines. When the exhibition opened, items were arranged "on a geographical basis," and nations competed for the number of medals they could amass for being the "homes" of praiseworthy goods (ibid.).

We are accustomed to thinking of nations as the positive expressions of particular peoples' desires for self-determination; we favor historical narratives about a people's emergence out of bondage into self-conscious nationhood. But the era that saw the rise of the nation-state as the predominant Western form of sociopolitical organization also provides ample evidence that, in the case of the West's dominant country, the category of the nation could function as a bulwark against implications of the very processes that had made it rich and powerful. Set entirely free, trade could dissolve the nation that promoted it; extended everywhere around the globe, empire could drain away or dilute the vital powers of the imperial center. Rather than something simply discovered by collective introspection, the identity of Britain throughout the nineteenth century was an ideal salvaged out of some prospect of danger or chaos which Britain itself had provoked. Rather than a goal attained once and for all, self-conscious British nationhood was "contingent and relational" (Sahlins 1989: 271), the product of "a protracted and uneven process," and "its maintenance [was] always precarious and imperfect" (Poovey 1995: 55).

The establishment of territorial and conceptual borders was quite messy and protracted in the case of many Continental European nations, but "British boundaries after 1707 seemed settled once and for all, marked out by the sea, clear, incontrovert-ible, apparently pre-ordained" (Colley 1992: 17). This was the year of the Act of Union joining Scotland to England (and Wales, which had been united to England in 1536). For one British island there was now one British people, led by one (English) Parlia-ment and, as had been the case since 1603, by one monarch. (The dominance of England within this new British union is the reason why, to the irritation of the Scots and Welsh, "England" and "Britain" continue to be equated with each other in loose common usage.) The sea that had long been an important natural defense for the inhabitants of the island now became, in the metaphor used by one proponent of the 1707 Act, a wall that "fenced in" the Britons, uniting them against outsiders (ibid.). However culturally diverse the Scots, Welsh, and English remained – to say nothing of narrower regional identities – their common interests seemed to be reinforced by events throughout the eighteenth and early nineteenth centuries. The British experi-ence provides persuasive evidence for the claim that "the process by which individuals or groups embrace the concept of the nation as the most meaningful context for self-definition necessarily involves temporarily marginalizing other categories that could also provide a sense of identity" (Poovey 1995: 55): this intermittent but recurrent marginalizing of their more local categories of identification was what Britain's various peoples learned to do.

The works of several early nineteenth-century authors aided them in this task. Publishing in the wake of the 1801 parliamentary Act which had formalized British control of Ireland (and created the new United Kingdom of Great Britain and Ireland), authors such as Maria Edgeworth and Sydney Owenson (Lady Morgan) wrote novels and tales that argued the common destiny of Britain and its much-maligned neighbor and dependent. Appropriating and adapting this model to the Scottish context, Walter Scott began producing the series known as the Waverley novels, perhaps the century's most acclaimed works of fiction, in 1814. It was Scott, above all others, who wrote the new British consciousness into existence. From his first novel he signaled his desire to balance the claims of allegiance to the power centralized in London (he was a close friend of the Hanoverian king) with a determination to preserve all those (cultural) features that "distinguish us as Scotsmen": *Waverley; or, 'Tis Sixty Years Since* is set in the time of the last Jacobite rebellion of 1745, and it manages to make repudiation of Bonny Prince Charlie's doomed campaign seem reconcilable with romanticization of it. Scott was the most famous representative of a vibrant intellec-tual culture based in Edinburgh which, since the late eighteenth century, had exer-cised a near-monopoly on the creation and institutionalization of British, and even English, identity. In *Ivanhoe* (1819) Scott gave memorable narrative shape to the originary myth of a hardy Saxon Britain straining to preserve itself under the "Norman yoke." The modern study of English and British history and literature, modern understandings of British imperialism, the "English" science of political economy, even the great *Encyclopedia Britannica*, were all begun by Scotsmen (see Morse 1993: ch. 2; Crawford 1992: chs 1, 2).

Chief among Britons' incentives to develop a working concept of British national identity was lasting conflict with Catholic France, which had sponsored that 1745 attempt to reinstate the Stuart line in Britain and which, more than any other country, served well into the nineteenth century as Britain's defining opposite. To a great extent, Britons' image of their nation as the preeminent defender of Protestantism – and its vaunted freedom of conscience and individual rights – had come to depend upon their conception of France as a priest-ridden, backward, and autocratic country all too eager to encroach upon British prosperity and territory. (Catholic Ireland after 1801 obviously had a different relation to the matter; only among the Protestant "Orangemen" of Ulster can there be said to have developed a United Kingdom identity comparable in rhetorical force to the British national identity attained by English, Scots, and Welsh.) Distrust of Catholicism, which Britons might regard as a rival empire to their own, afforded a dependable resource for mobilizing British nationalism. Guy Fawkes Day (November 5) was an annual reminder of the time (in 1605) when popish plotters "did contrive / To blow Old England up alive." The mob violence of 1780s anti-Catholic Gordon riots was not repeated in the next century, although reaction to the so-called "Papal Aggression" of 1850 suggests that violent feelings on the religious question could resurface at any time. What brought them up in 1850 was the pope's decision to reinstate the Catholic diocesan hierarchy in England for the first time since the Reformation. Patriotic Protestants might well have felt the establishment of Cardinal Wiseman and his cohorts a fitting insult to crown that dismal experiment, the Oxford (or Tractarian) Movement, which had aimed at revitalizing the Anglican Church but had wound up by making a papist of its most prominent advocate, John Henry Newman. The 1864 dispute between Newman and Charles Kingsley over the truthfulness of Catholic clergymen – Kingsley had begun it with a passing slur in the pages of *Macmillan's Magazine* – provided another opportunity for chauvinists to insist upon the equation of Britishness and Protestantism. All the while, British Protestant missionary activity had manifested exponential growth around the world: the 1911 *Encyclopedia Britannica* despaired of recounting the full history of "the hundred or more organized [missionary] societies of some size that have . . . come into being since the end of the eighteenth century, still less that of the three or four hundred smaller agencies" (vol. XVIII, p. 587). Missionaries served not only as the exporters of British ideas, but as the dispatchers of alien ideas back to Britain, where they could assist in the rhetorical labor of defining Britishness by opposition.

Animosity toward France had a long history before the nineteenth century, but it was galvanized as never before by the roughly 20 years of warfare with France stretching from the 1790s to 1815. Britons watched in horrified amazement as the radical democratic experiment of the French Revolution imploded in the Reign of Terror of 1793–4, then contorted itself into the aggressive empire of Napoleon Buonaparte. Until the victory over Napoleon at Waterloo in 1815, fears of a French invasion remained alive, permitting the British government to impose severe repressive measures against any activity smacking of pro-French (democratic) attitudes. Retaining the same enemy while altering the terms of opposition, British observers now began to highlight not their country's freedoms but the stability of its social structure, which they juxtaposed to the hubristic revolutionary gesture of rebuilding society from the ground up according to abstract ideas about "liberty, equality, and fraternity" or (in the words of Thomas Paine) "the Rights of Man." The radical freedom pursued by the French Jacobins was a chimera, warned Edmund Burke in his *Reflections on the Revolution in France* (1790): the abstraction "Man" did not exist; one could travel the world and never meet him, but only his localized, national avatars. Burke characterized those admirable English liberties which supposedly harked back to Magna Carta "as an entailed inheritance derived to us from our forefathers, and to be transmitted to our posterity; as an estate specially belonging to the people of this kingdom without any reference whatever to any other more general or prior right." What Burke favored was a "*social* freedom . . . that state of things in which Liberty is secured by the equality of restraint." It was a formula powerfully attractive to many later writers, riding out as they were the century-long process of political democratization taking place in Britain.

The travel writer Frances Trollope, to take one example, seemed to discover the truth of Burke's lesson on her many journeys abroad: as she wrote in *A Visit to Italy* (1842), she felt

> more and more, and more again, as I continue my rambles through the world, that the Constitution of ENGLAND when guarded with common prudence from the democratic innovations which have of late years buzzed about it . . . is the only one which appears to be formed in reasonable, honest, and holy conformity to the freedom of man as a human being, and to the necessary restraint inevitable upon his becoming one of a civilized, social compact. (Quoted in Buzard 1993: 100)

Walter Bagehot's *The English Constitution*, published in the year the great Second Reform Bill vastly increased the voting population (1867), expanded upon Burke's principle of cultural belonging as inheritance, describing a national collective mentality operating "instinctively, without argument, almost without consciousness" and centered on deference toward established hierarchies (see Herbert 1991: 128–49). Writing at the same time as Bagehot, Matthew Arnold repudiated the Jacobin fantasy of an abstract and universal rights-bearing humanity in favor of distinct, duty-bearing communities: he maintained in *Culture and Anarchy* that "the deeper I go in my own consciousness, the more simply I abandon myself to it, the more it seems to tell me that I have no rights at all, only duties; and that men get this notion of rights from a process of abstract reasoning, inferring that the obligations they are conscious of towards others, others must be conscious of towards them" (part 6, "Our Liberal Practitioners"). According to many voices besides these, the recommended English or British virtue was, as Thomas Carlyle had written in *Sartor Resartus* (during the ferment of the First Reform Bill, of 1832), "Do the duty which lies nearest thee" (book 2, ch. 9). The specification of that "nearest," the surveying of the territory to be covered by it, was the ideological work of many Victorian writers. In *Bleak House* (1853) Dickens defined a moral community based upon his heroine's model of the "circle of duty" that beings with people personally known and widens to include every unknown person belonging to the nation. The individual operating within this region is bound by the ethic summed up by Tennyson, in his famous "Charge of the Light Brigade," which celebrated the doomed cavalrymen at the battle of Balaclava with the words "Theirs not to reason why, / Theirs but to do and die."

The publication of Carlyle's massive study *The French Revolution* in the very first year of Victoria's reign helped guarantee that these older currents of British self-identification by differentiation would persist for decades into the new era. Although Edward Lytton Bulwer declared in his *England and the English* (1833) – which was addressed to the French diplomat Talleyrand – that "the English of the present day are not the English of twenty years ago" and that "*We no longer hate the French,*" Carlyle's portrayal of the French cataclysm encouraged Britons to continue regarding their cross-the-channel neighbors as the embodied potential for excesses of violence and vengefulness – and the periodic crises of French nineteenth-century politics (1830, 1848, 1870) seemed to confirm this view. Dickens cribbed from Carlyle extensively in his depiction of bloodthirsty Paris during the Terror, in *A Tale of Two Cities* (1859). The *eminence grise* of the murderous Jacobins in that novel is the silently knitting Mme Defarge, a combination of Frenchness and femaleness run amok. The more she knits at her list of "enemies of the people," the more she unravels the social fabric. How attracted Dickens was to this particular feminization of the foreign threat is suggested by the fact that he supplied a kind of trial run for Mme Defarge in the villainness Hortense of *Bleak House* (1853). In a novel determined to diagnose and cure Britain's ailing culture, Hortense – Frenchwoman, murderess, mouthpiece of underclass *ressentiment*, and possible lesbian – is the lone foreigner. She displays, as the novel's English heroine, Esther Summerson, sees it, "a lowering energy in her face . . . which seemed to bring visibly before me some woman from the streets of Paris in the reign of terror" (ch. 23). In both works Dickens poses British against French women, as if the former encapsulated all those virtues of their nation – reasonableness in the face of all-consuming wrath; openness in the face of secrecy and deceit; humility in the face of hubris – that must be defended against Gallic assault.

It is in fact striking that, in the era during which Britain attained unprecedented international clout – an era presided over by a queen who, in 1876, was officially declared an empress – Englishness or Britishness was so routinely allegorized not as some swaggering, militant character but as a vulnerable woman, who must either be defended by some father figure or defend herself by English pluck. In a list of idealized Victorian Englishwomen facing threats on English soil, Esther Summerson must be joined by other Dickensian creations, early and late, from the Nell of *The Old Curiosity Shop* (1841), to the title character of *Little Dorrit* (1857), to the patently allegorical Rosa Bud of *The Mystery of Edwin Drood* (1870). Dickens's works repeatedly plead for the proper exercise of a paternal authority – of a sort suggested perhaps by the rather chivalrous narrator's persona – that will nurture, contain, and protect the young Englishwoman who is so liable to be menaced by such monstrous, orientalized scoundrels as the Quilp of *The Old Curiosity Shop*, the Blandois of *Little Dorrit*, and the opium-crazed Jasper of *The Mystery of Edwin Drood*. All these villains function as human conduits for suspect influences from around the world. Quilp makes his living from "pursuits . . . diversified and numerous":

> He collected the rents of whole colonies of filthy streets and alleys by the waterside, advanced money to the seamen and petty officers of merchant vessels, had a share in the ventures of divers mates of East Indiamen, smoked his smuggled cigars under the very nose of the Custom House, and made appointments on 'Change with men in glazed hats and round jackets pretty well every day. (ch. 4)

The antagonist not only works in, but *is*, a port of entry, and his efforts to apprehend Nell are made on behalf of all those contaminating elements he invites into Britain. The novels by Dickens's friend Wilkie Collins – most notably *The Woman in White* (1860) and *The Moonstone* (1868) – also offer their own versions of British womanhood subject to the alien grasp.

If the national ideal depended to a great extent upon the threat of foreign influences, then it is not surprising that the motif of imperiled Englishness made itself felt with particular intensity in writings concerned with English people abroad. Commentators on the so-called Grand Tour had long debated whether a young Englishman's exposure to foreign customs would benefit or harm the country to which he returned. There was a certain amount of wishful thinking in Edward Gibbon's assertion that he had come back from his European tour "a better Englishman than when I went out" (Buzard 1993: 99); and for every Gibbon there was a dissenting voice – or more – to complain, as William Cowper did of the typical Grand Tourist,

> Returning he proclaims by many a grace,
> By shrugs and strange contortions of his face,
> How much a dunce, that has been sent to roam,
> Excels a dunce, that has been kept at home. (Ibid.)

The worry lest exposure to the outside world squander the potential of the young ruling-class Englishman, encouraging him to ape outlandish manners rather than perfect his own English ones, turned into a markedly more anxious concern when the traveler was female – as she was much more likely to be in the nineteenth century. A whole subset of travel literature originating in the immediate post-Napoleonic years consisted of fictions based on a "family abroad plot," which aired worries about national cultural security in stories about the misadventures of British families touring the Continent (Buzard 1993: 130–52). The engine of mischief in such fictions, usually the fashion-crazed and socially ambitious wife, is primed by the adolescent daughter, who attracts the suspect attentions of nefarious, penniless Continental noblemen and can be saved from marrying them only by the reassertion of paternal control. Failing that, the young Englishwoman loses her virginity, her happiness, and her identity to the lecherous adventurer. Some variety of authorial peroration typically ensues: in his early variant *The English in Italy* (1825) Lord Normanby says the fate of the once "petulant and vivacious" and now contrite Matilda should furnish

> a striking, and, it is to be hoped, not a useless example to the British fair, who learn, in the enthusiasm for foreign climes and habits, to contemn the domestic virtues of their country, – who mistake the mere charms of novelty for sources of lasting happiness, and who blush not to forfeit the name of English women, in yielding up their hearts and hands to the fickle keeping of a stranger. (Buzard 1993: 148)

Such unions were in fact rare – though Murray's 1858 *Handbook for Travellers in Southern Italy* took the prospect seriously enough to include a "Caution to English Ladies" which reminded them that "Englishwomen by marriage with a foreigner forfeit their nationality, and are precluded from seeking redress from British consuls or tribunals" (Buzard 1993: 148–9). In 1825 Normanby was responding with an exaggerated sense of peril common to the period during which Britons rushed abroad once again, after years of Continental wars had kept them pent up at home. The hunger for foreign experience, liable to carry scandalous sexual overtones when attached to a young Englishwoman, was seen as a dangerous proclivity toward cultural miscegenation. When Normanby's protagonist first sets foot on Continental soil, there is a dangerous, self-stimulating vibration in the words that pass through her overheated brain: "*Here I am*, was the extent of her reflections, but what a circle of delight stretched around that little centre!" (Buzard 1993: 147). In its treatment of two sisters, one easily swayed by foreign fashions, the other steadfastly English and humble, Dickens's *Little Dorrit* borrows from the pattern laid down by such early nineteenth-century works; it may be that the bad-marriage plots of George Eliot's *Middlemarch* (1872) and *Daniel Deronda* (1876) testify to the pattern by reversing it, since each involves the cruel wasting of an Englishwoman's youth and vitality at the hands of a morally compromised Englishman, and each holds out a young *foreigner*, met on the Continent, as a figure of redemption.

The ultimate target of the foreign suitor is, of course, the English real estate behind the traveling woman. The paterfamilias in one of these tales, learning that his daughter has fallen into the clutches of a dissolute French count, goes so far as to father an heir in order to safeguard that "inheritance derived to us from our forefathers, and to be transmitted to our posterity" of which Edmund Burke had spoken. "To think," this father tells a friend,

> that this fine estate would pass away at my death to a foreign swindler, was more than I could endure. The idea haunted me continually. By night I was tormented with dreams of executions in the house, and sales by auction of every familiar object; and by day, especially at twilight, all the family portraits seemed to look at me imploringly, as though they tried to speak, and beseech me to save them from coming degradation. Then, if I rode out, or took my gun, or strove in any way to amuse myself in the open air, it was all the same. The woods, the river, the very ground beneath appeared to reproach me, and I fancied that the fine old trees, as their branches waved aloft, cast a darker shade around, and groaned as though the axe were ready at work to hew them down to supply the wants of a gamester and a stranger. (Buzard 1993: 142).

Here the natural setting itself endorses the particular dynasty that occupies it: just as the soil of Ithaca nourishes the tree in which Odysseus carves his dynastic marriage bed, the English ground is full of spirits capable of sanctioning the uses to which it is put, and the users.

It is not accidental that the era that began with Britons' renewed access to the Continent, and that proceeded to make the Continent accessible to more and more segments of the population, should have fostered the rise of modern tourist institutions, which were seen as creating pockets of security around the British tourist – little seemingly inviolate "centers" of pleasure, like that surrounding Normanby's Matilda – as the tourist moved about in foreign fields. The first half of the nineteenth century saw the rise of Thomas Cook, that Emperor of Tourists, as well as of the systematic, endlessly helpful and protective guidebooks of Karl Baedeker and John Murray III – to say nothing of the improvements in transport, accommodation, and finance that facilitated freedom of movement and minimized entanglements with indigenous populations. In Cook's invention of the "package tour" is powerfully encoded the idea of a British collective body able to travel untouched and at will through alien territories. The Consular Act of 1825, which unified and professionalized the system of British consulates around the world, offered a similar guarantee. It was in these comparatively close-to-home developments that some of the foundations were laid for later imperial imaginings. Tourism was noted for having invented secure "little Englands" abroad well before the empire's hill stations, clubs, and cantonments gained the notice of a broad domestic public. Evident in those family abroad plots, and in much of modern tourism's planning, is a foreshadowing of empire's fixation upon the necessity of sequestering the British woman from the contaminating touch of the colonized man. British representations of empire often revolved around the dread of interracial rape, as if the vulnerable British woman might suffer a literal reversal of what Britons were metaphorically doing to the cultures they ruled; the expression of this dread reaches fever pitch in writings following the so-called "Indian Mutiny" of 1857, during which many such rapes were alleged to have occurred (Brantlinger

1988: ch. 7). The prospect of the white woman's violation exercised a lasting hold over the British literary imagination of empire: it forms the central element of Forster's *A Passage to India* (1924) and of Paul Scott's late novelistic meditation on race and empire, *The Raj Quartet* (1966–75).

It was after the great convulsion of 1857 that the British presence in India had once and for all to be formalized and the boundary between rulers and subjects clarified. Parliament dissolved the East India Company and assigned rule over India to a new secretary of state. A new phase of imperialism began, one aspect of which was the more determined solicitation of women to emigrate to the colonies, where with their soldier or administrator husbands they would form the nuclei of a hyperconscious, miniature British culture in foreign parts. In an earlier phase of colonialism, many unaccompanied European men had routinely taken mistresses and even wives from the local population; the arrival of missionaries after 1813 in the districts under East India Company control had cast a shadow on this practice. But after 1857 the planned presence of resident European wives was supposed to extirpate it altogether, since it was now increasingly regarded, for racialist reasons among others, as dangerous to the preservation of the British national character and its ruling temper. For these wives, "the tasks of homemaker and mother carried even greater implications for preserving 'civilization' when carried out in the outposts of the empire" than they would do at home (Strobel 1991: 17). With their children routinely sent back to England to be educated – which put a stop to excessive fraternization with "native" children and servants – imperial wives and mothers could devote themselves to their other function as gatekeepers of transplanted Britishness, and the society over which they presided "mirrored in more rigid form the practices found in Britain" itself (ibid.: 9). "Transported to distant parts of the empire," British home furnishings and art images (such as English landscapes) took on a new function as markers of a British social space that held other, "local constructions of place" at bay (Helsinger 1997: 13). Rudyard Kipling was the first writer to gain an audience in Britain for depicting this imperial hothouse culture, in stories of the 1880s such as those collected in *Plain Tales from the Hills* (1888).

The insistent identification and maintenance of Britishness that informed these garrison communities was also to be felt in the fictional model of the "Imperial Gothic," for which empire is "a barricade against a new barbarian invasion" – and an extremely porous barricade at that (Brantlinger 1988: 230). Concentrated in the last two decades of the century, but foreshadowed in earlier novels by Charlotte Brontë, Dickens, and Collins, among others, Imperial Gothic depicts a Britain alarmingly open to penetration by alien, even demonic forces that insinuate themselves into the fiber of British being. These are the nightmare products – in H. Rider Haggard's *She* (1887), in Bram Stoker's *Dracula* (1897), in Arthur Conan Doyle's Sherlock Holmes tales, and elsewhere – of that process known as "reverse colonization," by which people and cultural influences from colonized portions of the globe start to make themselves felt as unavoidable presences in the colonial metropolis itself (see Arata 1990; Duncan 1995). The secret addiction of the English cathedral choirmaster in *Edwin Drood* is the sinister byproduct of empire, the coming-home-to-roost of the Opium Wars that had "opened" China and gained Hong Kong for Britain. This novel entertains the possibility that not just the dismal East End dockland slums, but the quintessentially English cathedral town, could be the scene of that drug-induced madness and criminality to which, official opinion held, "primitive savages" were prone. In Haggard's sensational novel Ayesha, the dreaded "She-Who-Must-Be-Obeyed" who rules an unknown civilization in the African interior, has designs on the throne of her English counterpart: as the narrator puts it,

> the terrible *She* had determined to go to England, and it made me shudder to think what would be the result of her arrival. . . . In the end, I had little doubt, she would assume absolute rule over the British dominions, and probably over the whole earth, and though I was sure she would speedily make ours the most glorious and prosperous empire that the world has ever seen, it must be at the cost of a terrible sacrifice of life. (Ch. 22)

Somewhere midway through this passage the distorting mirror of Ayesha's possible empire becomes a clear one, for it was under Victoria that those events feared by Haggard's narrator did indeed happen. In another bizarre mimicry of Britain's own empire, the vampire Dracula is poised to establish in England "a new and ever widening circle of semi-demons to batten on the helpless" (Arata 1990: 629). Examples such as these suggest that, however much Victorians liked to consider their empire as "final and conclusive proof of Great Britain's providential destiny" (Colley 1992: 368), their "complacency" was shadowed by many expressions of anxiety about their nation's susceptibility to infiltration by the angry spirits empire had awakened half a world away.

Corresponding to the troubling suspicion that Britain's identity was something based offshore was the recognition that cohabitation within the physical territory of Great Britain failed to convey any meaningful sense of community, or even seemed a mockery of true community. The idea that Britain might lie open to all sorts of malignant infiltration from abroad was adapted to govern representations of the poor and working classes in Britain itself. These segments of the population were described as having been newly "discovered" by middle-class writers during the economic crises of the 1840s, and their haunts were regularly depicted as unknown or uncharted lands full of menacing savages. Investigators pondered what Carlyle called, in *Past and Present* (1843), the "Condition-of-England Question," and their findings were summarized most famously in a phrase appearing in Benjamin Disraeli's 1845 novel *Sibyl*: Britain was "[t]wo nations; between whom there is no intercourse and no sympathy; who are as ignorant of each other's habits, thoughts, and feelings, as if they were dwellers in different zones, or inhabitants of different planets; who are formed by a different breeding, are fed by different food, are ordered by different manners, and are not governed by the same laws" (book 2, ch. 5). This depressing prospect was given perhaps its most alarming expression in Henry Mayhew's monumental *London Labour and the London Poor* (1861–62), which proposed to consider the lower orders of British society as parasitic nomads both physiologically and morally distinct from the settled, privileged classes.

It was middle-class fear of "invasion" by this second, subordinate British nation – fear of class-leveling revolution, in other words – that gave rise to numerous compensatory ideas of the meaningful national whole that could reunite the polarized classes. Disraeli and his conservative "Young England" movement of the 1840s sought the "community of purpose that constitutes society," without which "men may be drawn into contiguity, but . . . still continue virtually isolated," in a romanticized vision of aristocratic charity and peasant deference; they were derided by reformers like Dickens for their pains. Elizabeth Gaskell, in novels of class conflict like *Mary Barton* (1848) and *North and South* (1855), campaigned for clear channels of communication between employers and employed, the establishment of which would enable all to see "that the interests of one were the interests of all" (*Mary Barton*, ch. 37). The fulcrum of arguments like Gaskell's was typically the necessity for British firms to fight foreign competition; workers were to accept reductions in wages, for example, because they recognized this necessity. Yet the moral rhetoric on which such writers relied was Christian-universal: British factory owners and hands were to acknowledge each other as brothers in Christ, but this was a category which, like unrestrained capitalism itself, really honored no national boundaries. Where was the Christian concern for the well-being of those German or Belgian brothers in Christ whose wages British competition drove down? Gaskell was a Unitarian – her husband was a well-known minister in Manchester – but the community she invoked was, implicitly at least, as specifically national as the one invoked by the national Anglican Church.

One of Gaskell's devices in *Mary Barton* for encouraging a single national consciousness is recurrent allusion to an English literary canon tacitly understood as the common inheritance of all classes. Motivated by a kind of ethnographic interest, the obviously middle-class narrator lards her text with "exotic" samples of Manchester workers' songs and speech, but she also consistently draws from a national literary culture (containing both elite and popular materials) from which certain autodidacts among her working-class characters draw as well. Similar pursuits of common linguistic, mythological, or racial legacies for England or Britain are to be found throughout Victorian culture. Widespread interest in English popular legends and songs dates from the publication of Bishop Percy's *Reliques of Ancient English Poetry* (1765), but it was mainly in the nineteenth century that the collection and study of materials that had come (in 1846) to be labeled "Folk-Lore" attained a quasi-scientific authority, under the auspices of the Folk-Lore Society (founded in 1878). Its members collaborated – and quarreled – with geographers and physical anthropologists in the massive and ultimately self-destructing project for an Ethnographic Survey of the United Kingdom, attempted by the British Association for the Advancement of Science between 1892–9. After a period of renewed political unrest and urban exposés in the 1880s and 1890s, this scientific grand illusion seems to have been motivated at least in part by the urge to reestablish British identity upon the bedrock of comprehensively understood British racial and cultural characteristics.

In the field of language, Richard Chevenix Trench invested the historical study of English with a religio-national significance in his influential lecture series *English Past and Present* (1855). "The love of our own language," Trench asked,

> what is it in fact, but the love of our country expressing itself in one particular direction? If the great acts of that nation to which we belong are precious to us, if we feel ourselves summoned to a nobler life by the nobleness of Englishmen who have already lived and died, and bequeathed to us a name which must not by us be made less, what exploits of theirs can well be nobler, what can more clearly point out their native land and ours as having fulfilled a glorious past, as being destined for a glorious future, than that they should have acquired for themselves and for those who come after them a clear, a strong, an harmonious, a noble language? (Lecture 1)

The care of the national language was a task made both more necessary and more inviting by the trials Britain was then undergoing in the international arena. Trench opened his lectures by alluding to the ongoing Crimean War, saying that

> it is one of the compensations, indeed the greatest of all, for the wastefulness, the woe, the cruel losses of war, that it causes a people to know itself a people; and leads one to esteem and prize most that which he has in common with his fellow countrymen, and not now any longer those things which separate and divide him from them. (Lecture 1)

Language was foremost among those common English possessions now worthy of new appreciation. Trench helped set in motion the campaign to produce a *New English Dictionary*, which began publication in 1884 and concluded (as the Oxford English Dictionary's first edition) in 1928.

Reflection on the Victorian definitions of nation and class show how partial was the reach of the Great Exhibition that opened its doors on May 1, 1851, how much it identified the interests of one rising class with those of the nation as a whole. What the exhibition represented was the ascendancy of a middle-class economic and cultural platform, masquerading as a great national expression, over the previously dominant "agricultural interest" of the landed classes. It took aim at, and was assailed by, the same protectionist forces that had been attacked since before Victoria's reign by the Anti-Corn Law League, a group devoted to the repeal of the system of tariffs designed to protect the landed interest by propping up the price of domestic wheat. The contest over these tariffs had been decided when, in 1846, Robert Peel, the Tory prime minister, switched from supporting protectionist measures to opposing them, mainly because the disastrous potato blight in Ireland had necessitated the importation of huge amounts of grain. Five years later, the mid-century festival in Hyde Park offered the panoramic vista of worldwide free trade – though, as we have seen, that vista itself remained protectively framed by the category of the nation.

Considering how much ink was spilt on the topic of what the exhibition would indicate about the condition of Britain, and what it would do in making the lower classes feel part of the national glory, it is interesting to note that the people interviewed in Mayhew's *London Labour* were evidently little touched by the exhibition mania. Conducting some of his survey in the period leading up to and during the exhibition, Mayhew repeatedly discovered how little purchase the whole affair had on the minds of his interlocutors, whom it is clear he regularly asked about it. Interviewees tended to say things like, "The Great Exhibition can't be any difference to me" (vol. 1, "Of the Experience of a Fried Fish-seller . . ."). Whatever recognition they accorded the event tended to be narrowly self-interested, as in the comment of a London milk-seller: "I don't understand about this Great Exhibition, but no doubt, more new milk will be sold when it's opened, and that's all I cares about" (vol. 1, "Of Milk Selling . . ."). With none of the appropriate reverence but with an economic practicality their social superiors ought to have admired them for, Mayhew's voices of labor and poverty debated only "whether the Great Exhibition would be 'any good' to them, or not" (vol. 1, "Of Street Piemen"). The happening that went by the grandiose official title of the Great Exhibition of the Works of Industry of All Nations (quite a mouthful in itself) was widely referred to by the "other Britons" – perhaps because it would temporarily fill their stomachs – by the terser label of "The Great Eggs-and-Bacon."

This is to say nothing of those far poorer, "forgotten" people Mayhew also studied, those desperate mendicants and river-scavenging "mudlarks" just emerging into official consciousness and still wholly outside the mainstream cultural order. It was, in great measure, on behalf of such people as these that Dickens began writing *Bleak House* in the fall of 1851, as if in answer to his own call (in *Household Words*) for a second exhibition "for the great display of England's sins and negligences, to be, by steady contemplation of all eyes, and steady union of all hearts, set right" (Dickens 1851: 338). The audacious and expansive masterpiece he produced turned away from the vaunted universalism of the exhibition in favor of a comprehensive indictment of contemporary Britain. It seemed determined to "depict England in terms almost exactly the opposite of those implicit in the idea of the Exhibition" (Page 1990: 27), to constitute itself an "anti-Exhibition" in novel form. In so doing, it may have illustrated in particularly bold relief a propensity of the Victorian novel generally. For this was the newly dominant literary genre in which Dickens, Thackeray, Trollope, Eliot, and others supplied "a slowly built up picture [of the world] with England – socially, politically, morally charted in immensely fine detail – at the center and a series of [unrepresented] overseas territories connected to it at the peripheries" (Said 1993: 74). Devoting the great preponderance of its attention to the unprecedentedly detailed portrait of English life and a small quantity of it to the colonies (which, wholly unrepresented, stood at the margins waiting to receive troublesome characters or resolve troublesome plots), the novel in effect aligned its formal boundaries with those of the imperial nation. This new orientation may have developed and been satisfying to its readers not because it expressed a swaggering confidence about Britain's ability to put the rest of the world in its place, but because it shored up or *reclaimed* the British nation (in fiction) from the worldwide network of dependencies in which that nation was (in fact) entangled.

See also 1832, 1848; SEXUALITIES; CLERICAL, LEGAL, MILITARY, SPECTACLE; FICTION

REFERENCES

Arata, Stephen (1990) "The Occidental Tourist: *Dracula* and the Anxiety of Reverse Colonization." *Victorian Studies*, 33/3, 621–45.

Brantlinger, Patrick (1988) *Rule of Darkness: British Literature and Imperialism, 1830–1914.* Ithaca, NY and London: Cornell University Press.

Bulwer, Edward Lytton (1970) [1830] *England and the English*, ed. Standish Meacham. Chicago and London: University of Chicago Press.

Buzard, James (1993) *The Beaten Track: European Tourism, Literature, and the Ways to "Culture," 1800–1918.* Oxford: Clarendon/Oxford University Press.

Colley, Linda (1992) *Britons: Forging the Nation, 1707–1837.* New Haven, CT and London: Yale University Press.

Crawford, Robert (1992) *Devolving English Literature.* Oxford: Clarendon Press.

Dickens, Charles (1851) "The Last Words of the Old Year." Household Words, 2/41 (Jan. 4), 337–9.

Dodds, John W. (1952) *The Age of Paradox: A Biography of England, 1841–1851.* New York and Toronto: Rinehart.

Duncan, Ian (1995) "*The Moonstone*, the Victorian Novel, and Imperialist Panic." *Modern Language Quarterly*, 55/3, 297–319.

Encyclopedia Britannica (1910–11) 11th edn. Cambridge: Cambridge University Press.

ffrench, Yvonne (1950) *The Great Exhibition: 1851.* London: Harvill.

Helsinger, Elizabeth K. (1997) *Rural Scenes and National Representation: Britain, 1815–1850.* Princeton: Princeton University Press.

Herbert, Christopher (1991) *Culture and Anomie: Ethnographic Imagination in the Nineteenth Century.* Chicago: University of Chicago Press.

Jameson, Fredric (1990) "Modernism and Imperialism." In Terry Eagleton, Fredric Jameson, and Edward W. Said, *Nationalism, Colonialism, and Literature.* Minneapolis: University of Minnesota Press.

Miller, Andrew H. (1995) *Novels Behind Glass: Commodity Culture and Victorian Narrative.* Cambridge: Cambridge University Press.

Morse, David (1993) *High Victorian Culture.* New York: New York University Press.

Page, Norman (1990) *Bleak House: A Novel of Connections.* Boston: Twayne.

Poovey, Mary (1995) *Making a Social Body: British Cultural Formation, 1830–1864.* Chicago and London: University of Chicago Press.

Sahlins, Peter (1989) *Boundaries: The Making of France and Spain in the Pyrenees.* Berkeley and Los Angeles: University of California Press.

Said, Edward W. (1993) *Culture and Imperialism.* New York: Knopf.

Strobel, Margaret (1991) *European Women and the Second British Empire.* Bloomington and Indianapolis: Indiana University Press.

FURTHER READING

Anderson, Benedict (1991) *Imagined Communities: Reflections on the Origin and Spread of Nationalism.* London: Verso.

Bhabha, Homi K (ed.) (1990) *Nation and Narration.* London: Routledge.

Bivona, Daniel (1990) *Desire and Contradiction: Imperial Visions and Domestic Debates in Victorian Literature.* Manchester: Manchester University Press.

Brantlinger, Patrick (1996) *Fictions of State: Culture and Credit in Britain, 1694–1994.* Ithaca, NY and London: Cornell University Press.

Hobsbawm, Eric (1990) *Nations and Nationalism Since 1780: Programme, Myth, Reality.* Cambridge: Cambridge University Press.

Ragussis, Michael (1995) *Figures of Conversion: "The Jewish Question" and English National Identity.* Durham, NC: Duke University Press.

Robbins, Keith (1988) *Nineteenth-Century Britain: Integration and Diversity*. Oxford: Oxford University Press.

Rose, Richard (1982) *Understanding the United Kingdom: The Territorial Dimension in Government*. London: Longman.

Trumpener, Katie (1997) *Bardic Nationalism: The Romantic Novel and the British Empire*. Princeton: Princeton University Press.

General Subject Index

Index of Victorian Works